PAUL FOWKES MBA
PARIS.

THE BUSINESS VALUE OF COMPUTERS

An Executive's Guide

PAUL A. STRASSMANN

THE INFORMATION ECONOMICS PRESS
NEW CANAAN, CONNECTICUT

Copyright © 1990 by Paul A. Strassmann

All rights reserved. No part of this book may be reproduced or transmitted in any form or by any means, electronic or mechanical, including photocopying, recording, or by any information storage and retrieval system, without permission in writing from the Publisher.

This publication is designed to provide authoritative information in regard to the subject matter covered. It is sold with the understanding that the publisher is not engaged in rendering a professional consulting service. If advice or other expert assistance is required, the services of a professional expert should be sought.

Graphics and Composition: Paul A. Strassmann using Macintosh Desktop Publishing

Editors: Vera Dolan, Annette Sherman, Prof. Herbert Spirer and Mona Strassmann.

Production Coordination and Design: Enoch Sherman, Renaissance Publishers, Wilton, CT.

Printing: R.R. Donnelley & Sons, Crawfordsville, Indiana

Printed in the United States of America
Revised text and improved graphics in second printing.
3 4 5 6 7 8 9 0

Library of Congress Cataloging in Publication Data
Strassmann, Paul A.
   The Business Value of Computers.
     1. Strategic Planning.   2. Information Technology
     3. Office Practice   I. Title
     1988   658.4
Library of Congress Catalog Card Number 88-80753
ISBN 0-9620413-2-7

Order Directly from Publisher:
THE INFORMATION ECONOMICS PRESS
POB 264
New Canaan, Connecticut 06840-0264
Telephone: 203-966-9495; Fax: 203-966-5506

To my children Vera, Andrew and Steven who are devoting their careers to extracting greater value from information technologies and to the memory of my son Eric whose software still lives in computers of students in many countries.

TABLE OF CONTENTS

Table of Contents v
List of Figures and Tables xi
The First Attempts..1
    Motivation Through Disaster 1
    Search For the Justification For Spending 4
    The Questionnaire 4
    Comparing Revenue-per-Employe 6
    Comparing Unit Costs per Invoice 8
    Comparing Information Technology-to-Revenue 10
Flexible Definitions..15
    You Can Get What You Asked For 16
    Shifting Data Input to Other Employees...................................18
    Shifting Data Input to Customers 19
    Shifting Programming Costs to Others 20
    Classification of Information Technology 24
Making Comparisons 31
    Controlling the Technical Means 32
    The Food Industry 33

Banking Industry Evaluations	35
Revenue-based Ratios and Business Structure	36
When IBM Speaks You Listen	38
The Most Effective Users of Information Systems	39
Ranking Excellence	50

Towards Experimentation 59
    Abandoning Revenue Ratios 60
    Testing Return-on-Equity 65
    Restating Accounting Information 66
    The PIMS 68

Return-on-Management 73
    About Measurement 73
    The Productivity of Information Systems 75
    Measuring Management Productivity 84
    Finding Management Value-added 86
    Management Productivity in the Public Sector 90
    Using the R-O-M Index to Evaluate Information Technology 91

Getting the Facts 99
    The PIMS Approach 101
    The Gaps in PIMS 103
    Defining Information Technology 105
    Data Collection 107
    The Data Form 111
    Who Uses Information Technology? 119

Research Findings 133
    Identifying Over- and Under-Achievers 133
    Comparing R-O-M with Other Measures 134
    Do Over-Achievers Spend More on Computers? 137
    Information Technology and Functional Spending 140
    Information Technology and Assets 144
    Information Technology and Organization Structure 145
    Changes During MPIT Study 148
    External Influences and Management Productivity 153

Strategic Investments 163
    Planning for Strategic Advantage 164
    Examples of Strategic Advantage 167
    Too Much of a Strategic Advantage? 179
    Computers and Small Company Opportunities 181

    Computers and Opportunities in Adult Education 183
    Managing Strategic Opportunities 184
Risk Analysis 195
    Current Approaches 197
    Payoff Computation Based on Vendor's Training Materials 199
    Payoff Computation Based on the Time Value of Money 200
    Payoff Computation with Time Value Plus Residual Value 201
    Payoff Computation With Explicit Risk Estimates 204
    Payoff From Vendor's Case – With Risk Analysis 209
Project Justification 227
    An Investment Case Study 227
    Employee Morale: The Ultimate Intangible 242
    Cashless Productivity Gains 245
    Who Justifies Computers? 248
    How Much to Spend on Project Justification 249
Cost Management 255
    Installation Costs 255
    Costs of Resource Sharing 256
    Cost Reduction 259
    Productivity Reporting for Computing Services 261
    Managing the Costs of Computing Services 263
    Competitive Simulation 270
Supporting Analyses 279
    Individual Productivity 280
    Measuring Quality 286
    Costs of customer Losses 288
    Capitalizing Computer Investments 290
    Software Valuation 290
People and Systems 295
    From "Supply" to "Demand" Orientation 295
    Systems Management is Everyone's Job 297
    The Chief Information Officer 299
    Staffing the Information Systems Function 303
    The Manager and the Technologist 306
    Adapting the Culture 307
    Computer Literacy 311
    Transfiguration of Organizations 311
    Counter-Productive Effects 312

    Spending on Ergonomics 315
    Spending on Training and Guidance 316
Learning from Mistakes...**323**
    Anticipate that all Cost Estimates will be Uncertain 324
    Never Install Software without Adequate Testing................325
    Make Sure the Competition Does not Wipe out Gains........327
    Make Only One Major Change at a Time.............................331
    Anticipate Changes..331
    Expect Operator Errors..333
    Expect Uncritical Acceptance of Computer Results 334
    Protect Against Computer-Controlled Damage...................335
    Do Not Count on Luck to Catch Your Mistakes....................335
    Make Sure That Testing Corresponds To The Risks 336
    Watch Out for Cost Over-runs and Unworkable Systems ...337
    Manage Your Risks...340
    Contracting Out Isn't a Substitute for Management............343
    Keep Away from Grand Designs 346
    Institutionalize Learning from Own Mistakes......................350
Computer-based Communication...**357**
    What is E-mail? 358
    The Opportunity Waiting for a Solution 359
    Electronic Conferences 361
    Electronic Mail as a Shared File System................................362
    From Individual to Group Productivity 365
    Representation of Knowledge...368
    Future Prospects 373
Opinions and Research..**383**
    Opinions..386
    Research 391
    Research Surveys 396
A Guide to Advice **401**
    Systems Assessment Indicators..401
    Sampling Of Customer Opinions 404
    Benefits Estimating Software..406
    "Blockbuster..407
    Faith and Visions 408
    Loss Avoidance Anecdotes...409
    The Group Estimating Method...414

Critical Success Factors	416
Classification Frameworks	417
Information Economics	422
Comprehensive Solutions	426
Computers and National Productivity	**435**
Productivity Computations	435
National Productivity Indicators	438
Productivity Comparisons of U.S. vs. Japanese Firms	444
Information Technology and U.S. Productivity	447
Computers and the Business Cycle	458
Financial Guidelines	**467**
Realizing Business Value	467
How to Manage Computer Opportunities	468
Planning and Budgeting for Computer Opportunities	480
Make vs. Buy Decisions	483
On Financial Justification	485
Controlling Systems Design	486
Executive Responsibilities	490
A Policy Checklist	**497**
Policy Formulation	498
Information Resources Management Organization	499
Information Systems Policy Guidance	503
Managing Projects	513
Information Technology Policy Guidance	515
Concluding Remarks	**519**
Index	**521**

LIST OF FIGURES AND TABLES

Figure 2.1: The Migration of Computer Costs from the Central Budget   16
Figure 2.2: Elements of a $23,500/year Workstation   17
Figure 3.1: Revenue per Employee in the Food Industry   34
Figure 3.4: I.T. Employee Ratio and Profitability   36
Table 3.1: Demonstration of Changed Ratios over Time   37
Table 3.2: Information Effectiveness Scoring Components   41
Figure 3.5: Service Company Profits vs. Effectiveness Scores   41
Figure 3.6: Manufacturing Company Profits vs. Effectiveness Scores   42
Figure 3.7: Service Company Profits vs. I.T. % of Revenue   43
Figure 3.8: Information Effectiveness and I.T. as % of Revenue   43
Figure 3.9: Information Systems Spending per Employee and Profits   44
Figure 3.10: The Penetration of Personal Computers vs. Profits   45
Figure 3.11: Information Systems Spending in the Services Sector   46
Figure 3.12: Classification of Service Firms According to Profitability   47
Table 3.3: Information Technology and Mean Measures of Performance   47
Figure 3.13: 1989 Effectiveness Scores and Profitability   49

Figure 3.14: Profitability and Information Effectiveness in Banking	50
Figure 3.15: Distribution of Companies by Profit/I.T. Expense Ratio	51
Figure 3.16: Excellence Rating and I.T. Spending	52
Figure 4.1: The Distribution of Food Companies' Revenues	61
Figure 4.2: Purchases as % of Revenues in Food Companies	62
Figure 4.3: Distribution of Food Companies by Assets	64
Figure 4.4: Actual vs. Calculated Return-on-Equity in Food Industry	66
Figure 4.5: Restating Accounting Information	67
Figure 4.6: Predicting ROE Across Industrial Sectors	69
Table 5.1: The Characteristics of Operations and Management	81
Figure 5.1: Vertical Integration Ratios for Manufacturing Companies	87
Figure 5.2: The Definition of Management Value-added	89
Figure 5.3: Classification of Public Sector Costs	90
Figure 6.1: The Definition of the "Served Market"	103
Table 6.1: Types of Information Technology Expenses	106
Table 6.2: Wage & Salary Costs Associated with Information Technology	107
Figure 6.2: Distribution of 1980 U.S. Spending on I.T.	108
Figure 6.3: The R-O-M Database, by Industry Classification	109
Figure 6.4: The R-O-M Database, by Geography	110
Figure 6.5: The R-O-M Database, by Employee Size	111
Table 6.3: Strategic Variables used in MPIT	112
Table 6.4: Organizational Information Used in MPIT	113
Figure 6.6: Measuring Organizational Complexity	113
Figure 6.7: Defining Operations and Management Information	115
Figure 6.8: Allocation of Information Technology and Labor Costs	117
Figure 6.9: Allocation of Materials and Services Costs	118
Table 6.5: Management and Operations Cost Categories	119
Figure 6.10: Information Technology Relative to Total Business Costs	119
Figure 6.11: Comparison Between Per Capita I.T. Costs	120
Figure 6.12: Comparison Between I.T./Salary Cost Ratios	121
Table 6.6: Importance of Information Technology Relative to Salaries	121
Table 6.7: Importance of Information Technology Relative to Assets	122
Table 6.8: Definitions of Operations and Management Costs	122
Figure 6.13: Migration of Computer Systems Missions	123
Figure 6.14: The Uses of the R-O-M Database	123
Figure 7.1: Classification of Company Groups by R-O-M	134
Figure 7.2: Profits, Management Costs and Management Productivity	135
Figure 7.3: Management Value-added, R-O-M and Productivity	135

Figure 7.4: Shareholder Value-added and Management Costs	136
Figure 7.5: Comparing Values of R-O-M, ROE and ROA	137
Figure 7.6: Information Technology Ratios and Productivity	138
Figure 7.7: Information Technology Spending,-per-Person	139
Figure 7.8: Information Technology Spending, per Wages & Salaries	139
Figure 7.9: The Deployment of I.T. And Productivity	140
Figure 7.10: Ratios of I.T. To Functional Wages & Salaries	141
Figure 7.11: Overhead and I.T. Ratios in Administration	141
Figure 7.12: Overhead and I.T. Ratios in Sales & Marketing	142
Figure 7.13: Deployment of Personnel and Productivity	143
Figure 7.14: I.T. Equipment to Total Plant & Equipment	144
Figure 7.15: Capital Intensity and Productivity	145
Figure 7.16: Organizational Complexity and Productivity	146
Figure 7.17: Support Ratios and Productivity	147
Figure 7.18: Knowledge Workers and Productivity	147
Figure 7.19: Compensation and Productivity	148
Figure 7.20: Changes in Financial Results and in Personnel	149
Figure 7.21: Changes in Employment	149
Figure 7.22: Growth in Revenue/Employee from Personnel Reductions	150
Figure 7.23: Changes in Purchasing Patterns	151
Figure 7.24: Changes in Employment and in Capital Structure	151
Figure 7.25: I.T. Expenses Grow Faster than Revenues	152
Figure 7.26: Information Technology Gains in Relative Importance	153
Figure 7.27: The Tax Rate and Productivity	154
Figure 7.28: Taxes as % of Business Value-added	154
Figure 7.29: Market Share, Quality and Productivity	155
Figure 7.30: Market Growth Does not Need Too Many New Products	156
Table 8.1: Speeding Responses to Customers	178
Figure 8.1: Diagnosis of Relative Market Share Position	186
Figure 8.2: Diagnosis of Administrative I.T. Intensity	187
Table 9.1: Financial Summary of a Computer Proposal	200
Table 9.2: The Benefit/Cost Ratio of a Computer Proposal	200
Table 9.3: A Conventional Benefit/Cost Ratio of a Computer Proposal	200
Table 9.4: Cash Flow Analysis for a Computer Proposal	201
Table 9.5: The Effect of Discounting on the Benefit/Cost Ratio ($000's)	201
Table 9.6: Cash Flow Analysis, with Residual	203
Table 9.7: Improving the Benefit/Cost Ratio with Residual Value ($000's)	203
Table 9.8: Risk-free Benefit/Cost Ratio, with Residual Value ($000's)	205

Table 9.9: Classification of Project Risks	207
Figure 9.1: Distribution of Project Costs for Class J Risks	208
Figure 9.2: The Distribution of Project Benefits for Class V Risks	209
Figure 9.3: The Distribution of the Expected Benefits	211
Figure 9.4: The Distribution of Expected Costs	212
Figure 9.5: Probabilities of Gain and Loss for Low Risk Alternative	212
Figure 9.6: Probabilities of Gain and Loss for Low Risk Alternative	214
Figure 9.7: Operating Risk, Low Risk Alternative	215
Figure 9.8: Benefit/Cost Ratio, Internal Development Alternative	216
Figure 9.9: Finding the Maximum Loss or Gain, Internal Development	217
Figure 10.1: Sequence for Analyzing Information Technology Invesments	229
Table 10.1: Proposed Increases in Information Technology Spending	233
Table 10.2: Business Effects of Plant Reorganization	234
Table 10.3: Cash Flow of Plant Reorganization Proposal	234
Table 10.4: The Value of the Information Technology Investment	235
Figure 10.2: The Risk Profile of Cumulative Cash for I.T.	236
Table 10.5: The Value of Restructuring the Factory	237
Figure 10.3: The Risk Profile of Cumulative Cash for Factory Project.	237
Table 10.6: Improving Shareholder Value through Better Systems	239
Table 10.7 Costs and Benefits for Plant Restructuring Case	240
Figure 11.1: Organization Costs are Larger than Technology Costs	256
Figure 11.2: Example of Per User Cost of Network Ownership	256
Figure 11.3: Economies in Airline Reservation Networks	257
Figure 11.4: Example of Activities for Setting Cost Reduction Targets	259
Table 11.1: Decline in the Market Price of IBM Computers	260
Table 11.2: Reporting Real Information Processing Productivity	262
Figure 11.5: Control over Computer Costs is Discretionary and Instant	269
Figure 11.6: Logic of Data Center Cost Simulation	271
Figure 11.7: Results of Data Center Cost Simulation	272
Figure 12.1: Percent of Directors' Time Using Computers	281
Figure 12.2: The Directors' Computer Activities: Communicating with Others	281
Figure 12.3: Computer Work Support - % of the Directors' Total Computer Time	282
Figure 12.4: Time on Computer and Time for Business Mission	283
Figure 12.5: Time on Computer and Time for Administration	283
Figure 12.6: Time on Computer and Time Working with Others	284
Table 12.1: Comparing Two Ways of Performing Identical Tasks	285
Figure 12.7: Different Rates of Customer Retention and Attrition	289
Figure 14.1: Development Costs for an Identical Application	324

Table 14.1: Estimates for IRS Laptop Project	339
Figure 14.2: A Motorcycle Designed by a Committee to Satisfy All Requests	345
Figure 15.1: Display Showing File Structure of a Tutorial	365
Figure 15.2 The Flow of Ideas in a Business Meeting	366
Figure 15.3 Filtering Ideas in a Business Meeting	367
Figure 15.4: Graphic Display of Context	369
Figure 15.5: Hypertext: Reader Examines Nodes and Links	370
Figure 15.6: Metatext - Reader Interacts with Nodes and Links	374
Figure 16.1: A Critical View of Computer Justification Methods	385
Figure 16.2: The Rapid Shifts in Top Systems Priorities	386
Figure 16.3: No Economies of Scale Among Insurance Companies	394
Table 17.1: Investment Returns for Superior Users of Computers	408
Figure 17.1: Profitability of After-the-fact Anecdotes	411
Table 17.2: Method for Computing Activity Savings	414
Figure 17.2: Savings Estimates for a Government Project Proposal	415
Figure 17.3: Example of a Descriptive Framework	418
Table 17.3: Assigning Score Values of Definitional Uncertainty	424
Table 17.4: Assessment Weights for P.B.T. Method Project Scores	425
Table 18.1: Comparing Productivity for Top Electronic Companies	446
Figure 18.1: Information Technology as % of Gross National Product	447
Figure 18.2: Information Technology and Productivity Gains	448
Figure 18.3: Importance of Information Technology Capital	449
Figure 18.4: Distribution of Capital in the Services Sector	450
Figure 19.1: The Difficulty and Time to Realize Benefits	469
Figure 19.2: How to Evaluate Indirect Benefits of Computers	473
Figure 19.3: The Variety of Planning Methods	479
Figure 19.4: Different Budgets to Match Different Planning Horizons	480
Figure 19.5: Budget Methods to Match Technological Lead Time	482
Figure 20.1: The Scope of Information Resources Management	498
Figure 20.2: The Organizational Units of Information Management	501
Figure 20.3: The Functions of Information Management	501
Figure 20.4: Comparing Cash Flows of Alternative Business Plans	504
Figure 20.5: Relating Information Technology to Business Planning	504
Figure 20.4: Information Management for Single Point Customer Support	506
Figure 20.7: Current Approach to Project Management	514
Figure 20.8: Recommended Approach to Program Management	515

INTRODUCTION

There is no relationship between expenses for computers and business profitability. This book will show why. You will find that similar computer technologies can lead either to monumental successes or to dismal failures.

My purpose is to shift your attention from information technology to the executives who manage it. The difficulty in discovering the business value of computers lies in their managerial applications. Computers on which you run information systems can deliver productivity gains. In isolation, they are just pieces of metal, plastic or glass. Therefore, my discussions will not deal with the worth of computers. Only *Management Value-added*, with or without computers, will tell you if computers produce a business payoff.

Measuring managerial productivity is the key to knowing how to invest in information technologies. Improve management before you systemize or automate. Make management more productive, by electronic means, if you know where, when and how. Automate success, not failure.

This book's theme has origins in my studies that examine why the relationships between profitability and computer spending appear to be random:

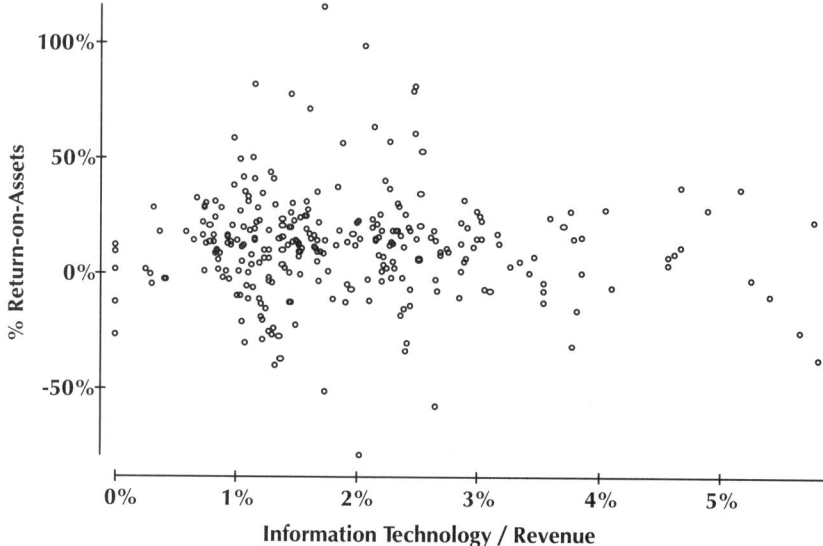

The lack of correlation between information technology spending and profitability is contrary to advertised claims. It defies the common belief that investing in electronic processing of information somehow leads to lower costs and results in competitive advantage.

Should these findings create doubt about the rapidly rising computer budgets of the last 20 years? Without good answers as to how to validate their gains, corporate executives kept voting with their checkbooks to automate the activities of their clerical and administrative employees. Computer budgets increased faster than purchases for any other class of equipment. Failing firms did not lag behind superior firms in the rush to install the best and latest computing equipment. There are unprofitable companies that spend more money on computers than similar firms that realize large profits. Does that signify that the decisions to purchase information technology is unrelated to results? My data suggest that corporate over-achievers differ from under-achievers. They also manage their computers differently.

Many have pointed out that investing in computers needs no justification if they serve managerial purposes. How do you compute investment returns from better management? Personally, such a question became more than a theoretical exercise. I had to find defensible explanations for the rapidly rising costs in the computer services Division I managed. Because I could not get the tools to prove the benefits of the computers I was buying, I resolved to search for better answers.

I shall share with you what I discovered. You will find that conventional financial ratios are unsatisfactory for measuring the benefits of management information systems. You also will learn that companies competing in equivalent markets, with a similar capital structure, with comparable production technologies and the same computer models can deliver remarkably different financial results.

My way to understand this diversity is to attribute business performance not to computers but to *Management Value-added*. Since the management of information is inseparable from management's general roles I view the processing of information by electronic circuitry as an extension of traditional management roles by other means.

This book speaks to those executives who are trying to extract value from their investments in computers. After reading it, you should have greater confidence in getting information technology to help your organization in achieving its goals.

New Canaan, Connecticut, October 1990
Revised and updated February 1991

1

THE FIRST ATTEMPTS

MOTIVATION THROUGH DISASTER

*Trying to supply computers without demand
is like pushing a rope to move it.*

The presentation to the Executive Committee was a disaster. Although I did not know it at the time, this meeting (fifteen years ago) took me on an exploration that has still not ended.

It happened on a Friday afternoon in April. It was my turn to review the status of information technology within the Xerox Corporation. The meeting was the key event of the annual long-term planning cycle. This began in October and ended in June with the company's five-year plan. My role was to present the consolidated global budget proposals for the information systems function. This was the first occasion that the information chief had the same time on the agenda as the manufacturing, marketing, research, engineering, finance and personnel functions.

The omens were not auspicious. That morning, Marketing delivered a gloomy assessment of our competitive situation. The day before,

Engineering announced its third delay in introducing a critically important new copier. Manufacturing had just projected increased costs that would place pressure on earnings. Research asked for an enormous budget increase. They had just finished the prototype of a computer workstation and were ready to launch it as a product.

Oblivious to the unhappy mood of my audience, I plunged into a 60-slide presentation. For the first time in five years since assuming the job as chief information executive of Xerox, I had my act together. Dozens of divisional Systems Review Boards labored for months to agree on project priorities. The data centers analyzed their operations and proposed much needed expansion in processing capacity to meet growing demands for computer time. Our plan called for installing 100 minicomputers and 20,000 terminals within the next four years. We would decentralize customer service to the sales districts and improve response time by 100%. We were launching a costly global standardization of materials databases to improve procurement. I had a good story, excellent slides (in color) and expected to walk away with a 28% budget increase to fund the customer-initiated projects.

Members of the Executive Committee did not wish to hear another hefty budget request. They never got beyond the first three slides. My financial summary showed a growth of computer expenses that was three times faster than the rate of revenue increase. The proposed 28% budget increase was a multiple of profit gains. These disparities created so much commotion that the entire allotted time was consumed in debating what was the business value of information technology. Our President sat through all this without a word. When my time was up, he suggested that the Company would be better off if M.I.S. concentrated on controlling costs instead of seeking new ways to increase its scope.

What went wrong?

When I took over as information chief early in 1969 the annual expenditure for information technologies was $39 million. Five years later, it was $145 million. I was projecting a quarter billion dollar systems budget for the early 1980's to an audience concerned with making the next year's profit target. It was the ratios that got me into trouble. In the early 1970's (and still today) it was fashionable to talk about systems as a percentage of company revenue. A company would be progressing through the commonly accepted "stages of growth" to greater systems maturity if that ratio grew. Despite this theory, growing computer expenses from 3.3% to 4.0% of revenue did not appeal to the Executive Committee. The chief financial executive noted that I was projecting systems costs near expected corporate profits. Unfortunately, I could not prove how information systems related to profits.

The agenda shifted from talking about systems plans and systems costs into an inquisition about computer payoffs. The executives were interested in finding out how much cash would come from productivity gains from present and future computer investments. I was surely not ready to deal with that. I also confessed that nobody knew how to come up with such explanations.

Years later, a wise friend observed that the Committee apparently trusted my views about technology. The Committee saw no need to spend time on that. Instead, they decided to elevate the context of the discussion to talk about *results*.

I spent my entire career trying to satisfy the explosively growing demands for computer services. We were approaching the limit on the share allocated to computers out of the total corporate expenses. It took even longer to find out how difficult it is to prove if computer expenses improved or detracted from business profit performance. In retrospect, I agree that the Xerox Executive Committee, like similar committees throughout the world, asked the right questions. They deserved good answers. The trouble was that I could not find a consultant or researcher who could offer a method for coming up with explanations that could withstand financial probing.

Without a cogent rationale about the relationship between computer expenses and company profits, the Committee decided that the next year's requested budget increase would be cut in half.[1] As an afterthought, the Committee requested that I report whether there was any relation between the profitability of operating divisions and their computer expenses. In that request is the origin of my research into characteristics that distinguish profitable users of information technology. After a 20-year career engaged in finding workable technical solutions, I was diverted from concerns about *costs* to issues related to *benefits* of information technology. My reorientation from the *supply-side* technology to the *demand-side* of computers began as I left the boardroom.

SEARCH FOR THE JUSTIFICATION FOR SPENDING

The same data can support different arguments.

If your management disapproves of your proposal, you can start accumulating different data to support your position. This is one corporate way in fighting for budget dollars.[2] Hiring consultants or quoting an academic authority[3] are other ways of repackaging lost causes. In my situation, 15 years ago, outsiders could not offer any help. We could not find any authority who could analytically prove the favorable relationship between computerization and profitability.

Following an across-the-board budget cut, corporate executives like to send their operations people back for more data instead of simply denying specific requests. It was not surprising that corporate finance[4] took a special delight in requesting whether Xerox operating Division profits related to their computer activities.

The Xerox way called for collecting exhaustive information as a prelude to re-submitting a long range plan. More facts were the only trustworthy approach to dealing with this situation as opposed to relying on another attractive presentation. The prevailing conditions called for presenting a completely different plan as a pre-requisite to a new hearing.

THE QUESTIONNAIRE

*If you ask too many questions you may find out
something you wish you did not know.*

With the prospect of a 50% cut in the proposed increase in information technology budgets, my Divisional M.I.S. counterparts consented to cooperate in filling out an elaborate questionnaire. As is usual in exploratory studies, we did not know exactly for what we were searching. It could be readily seen that reported profits and information technology budgets bore no relationship to each other. Everyone realized that finance sent us on a "wild goose chase." But, we could not deny the challenge of trying to prove that our work was somehow contributing to corporate profits. How would you feel if you were running a hospital and you could not prove that most people were better off with you than if they had stayed at home?[5]

We concocted a monster questionnaire. The originators of data-gathering forms have the advantage that they do not pay the costs in filling them out. Whoever composes a questionnaire has every incentive to ask as much as is tolerable. Besides, the Division staffs can always justify more people because Corporate staff keeps them busy.

Our list included everything: lines of code, machine running time, data center operating hours, equipment configurations, costs of supplies, programming maintenance by application and by function, data entry costs, number of communications lines, and so on. To explain over one hundred million dollars of expenses per year a survey can conceive of almost unlimited questions. If you do not know how you will use the data, you will ask for more and never for less.

Two staff-years of effort and six months later, we had all the questionnaires tabulated as maintenance expenses, operating costs, development investments and costs of telecommunications.[6] The data were interesting but mostly useless. On the profit side, we had only the standard financial indicators, such as profits before and after taxes, *Return-on-Assets* and profits before allocations. These numbers fluctuated wildly, especially for international Divisions, because of currency, inflation and surprising differences in accounting practices. Information technology budgets and any conceivable measure of profitability showed no correlation!

We also obtained personnel counts by occupational classification, but they were of little help. The steady growth in the company's employment obscured whatever personnel reductions came through office automation. Our *Revenue-per-Employee* made little sense because inflation and currency changes made these ratios incomparable over time. We adjusted profits by cost indexes. This was not useful because many Divisions made major market or product investments and their profits were below normal.

To measure the physical output of our Divisions, we collected data about the number of copying machines installed and how many copies they were generating. We learned the number of service calls per week. We clocked telephone calls and counted invoices. Short of counting paper clips, we enumerated every conceivable measure of input and output.

Next, we examined several hundred ratios that were candidates for an indicator of effectiveness. Generating these indicators was easier than making any sense of them. A precursor of the electronic spread-sheet[7] helped us to calculate thousands of ratios. We labored with mountains of computer printouts but could not find anything that was related, even remotely, to Divisional profitability.

We found ourselves trapped when the Controller circulated to members of the Executive Committee a clipping from a Diebold Associates[8] survey reporting that manufacturing companies averaged a 2.1% *Information Systems-to-Revenue* ratio. Was the current level of Xerox information spending at 3.5% of revenue out of line with industry experience? What about the 4% projected spending levels for 1980? We had to find a way of responding to that challenge. No ratio would do us much good if the Executive Committee become convinced that our spending levels were higher than an industry benchmark.

COMPARING REVENUE-PER-EMPLOYEE

Inter-Divisional Comparisons

In our study we found that Divisions with above average *Information Technology-to-Revenue* ratios showed only average profits. That finding was inconclusive because it varied over a wide range. We needed another index that would give legitimacy to our growing expenses.

How about trying out correlations with a widely used indicator of productivity, such as *Revenue-per-Employee*? The respected annual financial performance tabulations by FORBES magazine listed 500 companies' *Revenue-per-Employee* figures as their measure of *productivity*.

If you assume that computers improve employee productivity and that higher productivity (as measured by *Revenue-per-Employee*) reflects computerization, then computer budgets and productivity should appear as an upward sloping line on a graph. We decided to explore this hypothesis.

Xerox, like many other global companies, has many Divisions that function as marketing organizations. Their *Revenue-per-Employee* figures are high, because they buy everything from manufacturing Divisions at cost and sell at list price. Most of the marketing Divisions' revenues pay for internal purchases. Another large portion of revenues pays for allocations from Group or Corporate staff services. Revenues from marketing Divisions are always large, as compared to their employment levels. Although they have high *Computer Expense-per-Employee* and high *Revenue-per-Employee*, their *Information*

Technology-per-Revenue ratio is small because the revenues dwarf payroll expenses.

Manufacturing Divisions need large amounts of computing power to support their complex materials-handling and production management activities. Their *Revenue-per-Employee* does not look good if inter-company pricing dictates the transfer of manufacturing output to marketing Divisions at cost. The wages of production labor are lower than the wages of marketing people, especially in Latin America. A large personnel count, even if employed at lower wages, will make the *Information Technology-per-Employee* ratio number look small, even if the *Information Technology-to-Revenue* spending ratio is high.

Huge amounts of computing take place in the research laboratories. The accounting rules define that each laboratory budget is equivalent to its revenue. Because the R&D Divisions have the largest concentration of high-priced talent, their *Revenue-per-Employee* suggests high levels of productivity.

The most anomalous cases were in our component Divisions. Some were merely assembly operations of motors and circuit-boards bought elsewhere. Others were vertically integrated, starting with raw materials and manufacturing most parts. Making a *Revenue-per-Employee* comparison was meaningless because the cost structure of each component group varied tremendously.

When all the productivity ratios were plotted against *Return-on-Assets* and *Profit-to-Revenue* ratios, the chart looked as though someone had fired a shotgun with a faulty barrel. The points were random, making the pattern unintelligible. These shotgun graphic displays were to plague us indefinitely. They appeared without regard to which profit indicator was compared with any measure of information technology.

Over-achievers and Under-achievers

To what extent were the Xerox internal comparisons unique? There must be a plausible explanation why so may researchers were using *Revenue-per-Employee* as a measure of productivity. Their rationale was that productivity of a firm derives from the revenue each employee generates.[9] If revenue is up without the firm hiring more people, then productivity should be increasing. If other influences are equal and if inflation in prices matches the inflation in costs, then the *Revenue-per-Employee* ratio could be a way of keeping track of a firm's gains.

To test the reliability of the *Revenue-per-Employee* productivity indicator I extracted the shareholder returns, for a ten year period, for the top-ranking ten firms in the service sector. Their average returns were a delightful 46.6% per year. For this group, the average *Revenue-per-Employee* in 1986 was $98,250.[10] The average returns for the ten bottom-ranking firms were an unsatisfactory -1.9%. Amazingly, the average *Revenue-per-Employee* in this group was higher, at $135,776.[11]

There was no relationship between *Revenue-per-Employee* and the financial performance of a firm in the service sector.[12] Price levels and the share of revenues allocated to payrolls change continually. You can not assume that you improve profits by increasing the *Revenue-per-Employee*. We concluded that the *Revenue-per-Employee* ratio was of no value in assessing the contributions of information technology.

COMPARING UNIT COSTS PER INVOICE

After failing with the *Revenue-per-Employee* ratios, we were ready to try anything. To our disappointment, every other measure of performance, such as *Computer Rentals-to-Revenue, MIPS-per-Employee,*[13] *Terminals-per-Employee, Lines of COBOL Code-to-Revenue* and *Computer Personnel-to-Total Employment* all produced shotgun displays.

We found that our organizations were just too different to be comparable using any of the measures that were reported in the Divisional questionnaires. This recognition came as a shock, since each of our operations were in the office equipment business, producing similar boxes, containing similar electromechanical equipment. Our divisions shared the same competitors, each in well-defined markets. If I could not compare ratios between Xerox Divisions, what chance would there be to come up with a valid relationship against companies such as IBM, AT&T, Pitney-Bowes, Olivetti, Fujitsu and Thompson?

A staff analyst suggested that we try proven industrial engineering methods to come up with measures of productivity. Why not analyze the effects of computers on costs of individual transactions? The industrial engineering tradition suggests that if you cannot understand something, you should chop it up into smaller elements until you come up with something that is unambiguous.[14]

Now, what was common to all operations? Clearly, it was the customer invoice. The invoicing process consumed a large share of computer expenses. We would search for a correlation between lower costs per invoice, clearly a measure of productivity, and higher computer costs. We would have a hard time proving the benefits of computerization in other functions if it would not show up in the writing of invoices.

We developed a corporate-wide reporting scheme for unit costs-per-invoice. Three months and another questionnaire later we were looking at another shotgun chart. There was no correlation between information technology expenses and efficiency in generating invoices!

Unfortunately, this inconsistency made sense after we gave more thought to it. Unit computer costs per invoice ranged widely. For instance, the Brazilians used their computer primarily as a fast typewriter. Because of currency restrictions, their costs of computerized printing were sky high.

The Western Region had extra computer capacity and allocated their sizable data center overhead by pages of printout. No wonder their cost of invoices were twice the other U.S. Regions, because invoicing generated more sheets of paper than any other application.

The Publishing Division's invoice cost was a fraction of everyone else's. They billed for low-priced subscriptions and not for complex equipment. Invoicing and the book-handling were inseparable and not comparable with any other Division's business.

Our Tokyo contingent reported the highest invoicing costs. They misunderstood our instructions and assigned a large chunk of customer administration costs to invoicing. They could not conceive of analyzing only direct computer expenses for generating invoices. The Fuji-Xerox organization included the costs for resolving billing discrepancies and adjustments in their figures, because their data processing personnel included all corrections in their jobs. In Europe and the U.S. these administrative functions were in the budgets of other Departments and not reported as a data processing expense.

We did not succeed in correlating invoice unit costs with a Division's administrative expenses, and surely not with Divisional profitability. That was disappointing. Although Xerox believed it was a homogeneous organization, the computer costs per invoice were not.

After this experience, we stopped trying to find the benefits of computers by microscopic examination of procedures. The more we examined the details, the greater the differences and the less significant were any comparisons. Increasingly refined analyses led nowhere.

COMPARING INFORMATION TECHNOLOGY-TO-REVENUE

We still had to deal with the controller's clipping showing that our *Information Technology-to-Revenue* ratio was much higher than suggested by the Diebold survey. The Diebold survey, like most surveys,[15] just reported average *Information Technology-to-Revenue* ratios. The names of the firms in the sample, and the ranges of these ratios were confidential. Yet, we had to compare precise Xerox numbers with an average of unknown origin.

It just happened that the chief information officer of IBM disclosed at a widely reported meeting that his company was spending 4.5% of revenue for information technology. We also found out that the IBM ratio was not in the Diebold survey. My boss did not think it was smart to parade the IBM's 4.5% benchmark because Xerox had just left the computer business. The Government classified Xerox in the *Scientific Instruments and Photography* industry. How about getting comparable ratios from Kodak, Perkin-Elmer and 3M? After four months of attending industry meetings and some consultant-mediated exchanges, we came back with another shotgun chart. Our industry peers were no different from us in that their internal *Information Technology-to-Revenue* ratios were as inconsistent as ours.

Despite the unresolved question of whether or not information technology spending was higher or lower than necessary, top management had lingering doubts. After 1975, executives came to believe that the information technology spending had expanded too fast. Budget planners latched onto the percentage of revenue indicator when comparing year-to-year cost increases. Our information technology managers responded by changing how they reported their costs.

CHAPTER SUMMARY

The quest for a simple comparative index for evaluating the spending levels for information technology is more than twenty years old. Top management would like to have the means for asserting budgetary controls over their fastest growing corporate cost. Computer researchers wish they could find one because that would make it easier to collect data supporting their theories. Computer sales representatives need one because they need to stimulate more orders. M.I.S. executives must have one to prove what a good job they are doing.

Unfortunately, simple comparative indexes of computer spending do not exist. If someone proposes one, it will be arbitrary, irreproducible and not amenable to after-fact verification.

If there is an urgent demand for something, there is enough ingenuity around to satisfy it.

Chapter 1 Comments

[1] You could ask why I received only half of what I asked for. Difficult disputes are often settled by splitting the differences. It has an aura of fairness. For the earliest precedent see also the Bible, I Kings 3:25.

[2] A good corporate staff can prove anything. Superior corporate staff can disprove everything. Good corporate management can disregard staff recommendations. Superior corporate management do not have staffs because they can find out what's lacking from customers who switched to the competitors' products.

[3] Nothing has changed since then. The inadequacies of academic research on measuring the effectiveness of information systems and on the contributions of information systems in the period from 1977 though 1986 are discussed by V. Grover and R. Sabherwal in An Analysis of Research in Information Systems from the IS Executive Perspective, *Information & Management*, 16 (1989). They note that while these managerial issues have been increasing in importance, the research on them has been slackening while research on technical issues, of lesser interest, has been increasing. They find that narrow technical issues are easier to research and more likely to be accepted for publication.

Gorla, Identifying M.I.S. Research Issues Using a Research Framework, *Information & Management Journal*, 1989 shows the percent distribution of 3,038 M.I.S. research papers, by method and topic:

	Behavioral Sciences	Computer Enginrg.	Operations Research	Functional Mgmnt.	Economics & Costs
Analysis	3.0	9.7	3.0	1.9	1.9
Design	3.8	20.2	3.9	2.9	2.0
Operations	2.1	6.2	2.2	1.8	1.0
Management	2.7	3.6	1.3	7.0	2.0
Applications	2.5	10.4	1.1	2.1	1.6
% of Papers	14.2	50.2	11.4	15.8	8.6

Only 1.6% of the total number of academic research papers dealt with the economics and costs of the applications of information technologies.

Is it reasonable to expect much from Business School research about computers? An article by J.L. Frand and J.A.Britt, Sixth Annual UCLA Survey of Business School Computer Usage, *Communications of the ACM*, May 1990 casts an interesting perspective on the amount of computing actually done by US business schools. The median computer operating expenditures, per MBA student, was only $78 per year. The median computer expenditures for business school research were only $36,000 per business school per year. One Wall Street financial analyst is likely to spend anywhere from $30,000-$40,000 of computer expenditures per year. The low levels of business school expenditures for computing may be one of many reasons why business school professors concentrate on topics which require relatively little actual business data, but yield a respectable volume of publishable articles.

[4] The corporate financial function lost direct control over the data processing activities a few years prior to these events.

5 Hospitals still do not try to prove this, a reviewer remarked. Why pick on proving something for computers that nobody does for advertising, market research or accounting?

6 The costs of copying were excluded because management did not wish to discourage it by highlighting its expenses. Internally installed copiers were handled by means of special accounting procedures which made it difficult to find out what they cost. As more firms manufacture information processing equipment, the policy of how you account for intensive internal use can make a major difference in what you report as "information technology" expenses. Only a few firms charge internal customers the equivalent market price for their own equipment or services. This is why cost ratio comparisons between information systems vendors are unreliable unless you know precisely what they exclude.

7 Our analysts were addicted to the APL matrix manipulation language.

8 The Diebold organization has reported on M.I.S./Telecommunications Budgets and Key Indicators for more than ten years. The indicators cover: M.I.S. budget as a percentage of revenues; M.I.S. staff as a percentage of total staff; and ratio of hardware to personnel costs. The latest Diebold Group measure of computing intensity (as percentage of sales) reported as follows: Banking=4.9%; Retailers=3.2%; Insurance=2.4%; Health Care=2.2%; Metal Products=1.9%; Consumer Products=1.9%; Electronics=1.6% (*Computerworld*, April 6, 1987, p.79).Before you apply any of these averages in your company, consider that others came up with different numbers. For instance, *Computerworld* in its special issue of 1989 PREMIER 100 Most Effective Users of Information Systems notes that the average ratio for Retailing is 1%, Metal Products is 0.89% and for Electronics is 2.14%.

Diebold is not alone in using the *Information Systems-to-Revenue* ratio as a norm for judging computer costs. Price Waterhouse (Price Waterhouse, Information Technology Review 1989/90, Price Waterhouse, London), A.T. Kearney and the Butler Cox Foundation use it as well. The IBM Corporation published reports that refer to *M.I.S.-to-% of Revenue* as an indicator for judging levels of effective spending. The BusinessWeek Newsletter for Information Executives features a *Spending Spreadsheet* for different industries. For instance, the February 16, 1990 issue shows *Information Systems Spending as Percent of Industry Revenue* for Amusement and Recreation, Hotels and Lodging sectors.

The persistence of gathering information about widely ranging revenue ratios is illustrated in a recent survey (E.K. Brumm, Chief Information Officers in Service and Industrial Organizations, *Information Management Review*, 1990, Number 3, Table 13) which shows the percentage of information technology expenses to gross revenues (or net interest income) as follows: for Service Corporations, mean value=5.1%, minimum=0.23%, maximum=15%; for Industrial Corporations, mean value=2.25%, minimum=0.10%, maximum=10%. I do not understand how such widely ranging information can be useful to anyone.

In a special report on economics of computers (R. Carlyle, Recovery! A 1990 IS Budget Survey, *Datamation*, April 1, 1990) notes that "...if you feel like your organization is spending less than its rivals, here is a way to make your point. By comparing your M.I.S. budgets against industry averages, you should be able to measure just how competitive you are." The article then proceeds to list *Average Annual Revenue-per Company* and *Average IS Budget* for 12 industry segments. For instance, the average percentage ratio of *IS-to-Revenue* for Banks and Savings & Loan Association is 0.22%. How you reconcile that number with Computerworld's September 1989 average ratio of 4.4% for banking is not clear. This difference shows that the percentage ratio of *IS-to-Revenue* for Banks depends on how you define revenue and IS expenses.

9 The idea that *Revenue-per-Employee* is a measure of the productivity of a corporation is perpetuated by annual tabulations, such as the Forbes 500 Annual Surveys. For instance, the April 28, 1986 issue of *Forbes* included 18 pages of tables about *Jobs* and Productivity.-*per-Employee* ratios and rankings of *Sales-per-Employee*, *Profits-per-Employee* and *Assets-per-Employee* are neatly arrayed. These listings

offer little help in understanding the significance of any of the measures. Revenue-, profit- or assets- rankings have no relation to market value, cash flows or any of the other profit measures. There is a bias to equate *Sales-per-Employee*-gains with productivity. In the *Forbes* 500 largest companies' review (April 29, 1985) the editors commented that the +5.5% gains in revenue as compared with –3.8% losses in employment during 1984 are "...good news for productivity." You cannot come up with that conclusion just from revenue and employment numbers.

10 The June 8, 1987 issue of *Fortune* magazine shows tabulations of financial data about service companies. The key indicator of profit performance is the *Total Return to Investors - 1976-86 Average:*

	Return	Revenues	Employees	Revenue/Employee
Subaru of America	54.6%	$1,939,286	980	$1,978,863
M.D.C. Holdings	54.4%	$674,564	1,217	$554,284
Charter Medical	51.0%	$666,186	13,400	$49,715
The Limited	48.7%	$3,142,696	34,900	$90,049
Wal-Mart Stores	48.4%	$11,909,076	141,000	$84,462
Comdisco	47.7%	$869,000	932	$932,403
Ames Stores	40.5%	$1,888,471	25,000	$75,539
Berkshire Hathaway	40.5%	$2,058,236	23,000	$89,489
Waste Management	40.0%	$2,017,775	18,135	$111,264
DCNY	39.8%	$273,365	354	$772,218
Top Ranking Totals	46.6%	$25,438,655	258,918	$98,250

11 The under-achievers' ratios are:

	Return	Revenues	Employees	Revenue/Employee
Pittston	-7.3%	$1,189,949	12,616	$94,321
National Intergroup	-6.5%	$4,166,294	6,965	$598,176
Tiger International	-1.7%	$1,110,948	6,200	$179,185
PanAm	-1.6%	$3,038,995	21,500	$141,349
Tesoro	-1.4%	$1,472,789	2,300	$640,343
Transcon	-1.1%	$343,393	4,120	$83,348
Emery Freight	-0.5%	$887,523	7,100	$125,003
Best Products	-0.2%	$2,200,517	20,500	$107,342
Frank B. Hall	0.4%	$438,392	7,000	$62,627
Haliburton	0.8%	$3,509,439	46,909	$74,814
Bottom Ranking Totals	-1.9%	$18,358,239	135,210	$135,776

12 This will be also proven for the manufacturing sector in Chapter 7.
13 Million Instructions per Second, a frequently used measure of computing capacity.
14 Similarly, if you do not understand how frogs jump, you cut them up and examine the pieces under a microscope.
15 The International Communications Association has made annual surveys of telecommunications budgets as a percentage of revenue for many years. The latest (1988) results, as reported in the July 17, 1989 issue of Computerworld, show that the percentage of revenue ranges from 1.8% (Office equipment firms) and 1.7% (Universities and non-profit organizations) to 0.8% (Manufacturing), 0.8% (Utilities), 0.7% (Government Agencies), 0.4% (Textiles), 0.3% (Steel) and 0.2% (Food Processing).

2

FLEXIBLE DEFINITIONS

Determined executives can produce whatever numbers they wish.

In an overwhelming number of companies, the computer departments are many organizational layers removed from revenues or profits. Unless computers generate revenues directly, such as in computer services firms, the measurement of their effectiveness comes only from some proxy indicator. The measurements you make will depend on what you are trying to evaluate. Whatever measures you come up with will be surely muddled by changing conditions because the applications of information technology are evolving rapidly. Few executives have accumulated enough experience to know what to ask for when approving information technology expenditures.

If you show interest in the performance of your computer department you will receive massive amounts of technical details. Systems managers have the capacity to generate enormous quantities of data about their own work. You will receive charts, grids and tabulations showing improvement relative to earlier results, but you will have no external yardstick to tell whether the gains are satisfactory.

In this book, I shall discuss many of the evaluation methods served up for executive consumption. In this chapter, I shall concentrate on the most frequently abused measure of performance: the ratio of *Information Technology Expense-to-Revenue*.

YOU CAN GET WHAT YOU ASKED FOR

Information technology costs are migrating to where they are not easily counted.

Every executive information system includes comparisons of current expense ratios against last year's ratios. M.I.S. managers can oblige with suitable numbers if top management feels more gratified with a declining ratio of *Information Technology-to-Revenue*. They will agree with "user" departments' purchases of mini- and micro-computers. Departmental personnel, not classified as M.I.S., will support this distribution of computing power. The result will be a reduction in the information systems budget.[1]

Recent trends in technology make the re-deployment of a computer budget not only feasible but also economically attractive. What used to be an identifiable central computer budget can go to diverse pockets where information technology costs cannot be easily ascertained.

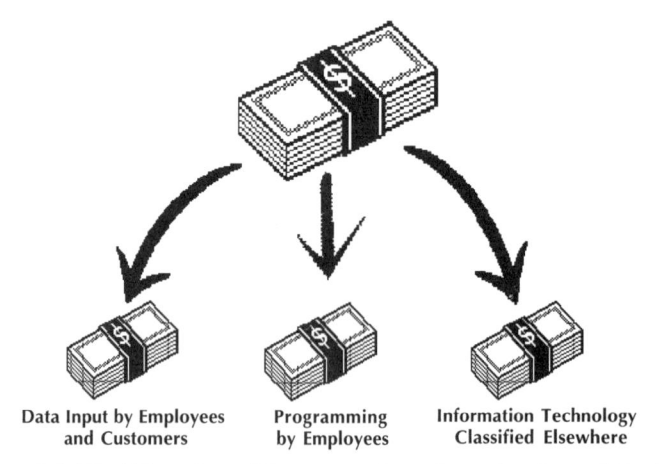

Figure 2.1: The Migration of Computer Costs from the Central Budget

The transfer of computing system responsibilities from the M.I.S. organization to customers is illustrated by studies that tracked the changing roles of systems staffs.[2] For instance, *Mainframe Computer*

Operations personnel declined from 28% of the total in 1978, to only 2% of the total in 1988. *Central Data Entry*, which absorbed 19% of the total personnel in 1978 had nobody in this category by 1988. Meanwhile, *Customer Computing*, which did not exist in 1978, employed 72% of information processing personnel. Though the compound growth rate of M.I.S. was 5.5% per year over a 20-year period, this average masks the transformation what these people actually do. The disappearance of a central data entry personnel category by merging it into "departmental computing" reflects changes in the characteristics of office work. What used to be done as a specialized, factory-like task becomes a by-product of administrative activities. The fraction of a clerk's activities now doing equivalent "information systems" work is hard to find. Only the group taking care of the central computer retains its original functions.[3]

These events do not tell the full story of what happens to the reported costs of corporate computing. There are other subtle ways to redirect the flow of expenses from the information systems budget into general operating expenses. To illustrate, Figure 2.2 show an allocation of the total cost of owning the hardware of a workstation bought for $9,700:[4]

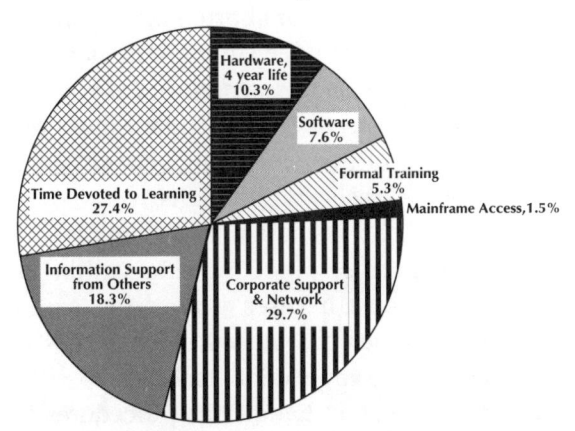

Figure 2.2: Elements of a $23,500/year Workstation

45% of the above costs (*Time Devoted to Learning* and *Information Support from Others*) will not count as information technology, because it is nearly impossible to track these efforts. Companies also will differ in accounting for *Corporate Support* as a computer expense. This leaves us with less than a quarter of the total included in every survey about a company's computer spending.

SHIFTING DATA INPUT TO OTHER EMPLOYEES

Give unto others what you do not want anyway.

Throughout the 1960's and persisting through the 1970's, a large chunk of a data processing budget covered data-preparation activities. These included key-punch operators and people who checked the data before the start of a processing cycle. Large data centers employed people with occupational titles such as data input auditor, data preparation specialist, tape librarian, customer liaison (to verify that missing inputs appeared), key-entry operators and input-verification specialists. Programmers spent their time writing and testing computer code. When finished with programming, they could spend an additional third of their efforts writing elaborate data preparation and data validation instructions. Unglamorous pre-production activities called for finishing meticulously checked procedural steps before processing any application.

As recently as ten years ago, even a sophisticated data center would have to commit 20–40% of its employees to activities that preceded computer processing. Errors in input data or input procedures would appear either as reruns or aborted processing. Every data center manager had to cope with sudden surges in demand when applications with tight deadlines *bombed, trashed, abended*[5] or "*unsuccessfully terminated for unknown reasons.*" If you knew where to look, you would find at least a quarter of the processing capacity on stand-by, just to take care of unexpected recovery situations.

A good applications systems manager made sure that programmers added to programs elaborate data-validation routines and consistency-checking logic. In cases where errors could be of interest to the President[6] the routines that precede such processing could contain 200% more code than the application itself.

How a computer center handles its procedures for accepting new programs, program changes and modification of master records reminds me of the elaborate rituals that exclusive sects institute to preserve their continuity. M.I.S. management responds by over-compensating on costly safeguards against the exposure to any failures because of risks from frequent software errors.

The harassed M.I.S. executive can easily reduce the *Information Technology-to-Revenue* ratio. He divests himself of the burdens of data preparation and data validation. A wide range of technology choices makes it now possible to transfer functions previously included in information technology budgets back to *users*,[7] where the functions become administrative overhead. For example, converting an application from *batch-processing* to *on-line processing* eliminates most of the central data preparation labor costs and moves all accountability to whoever is responsible for the remote data-entry terminal. *On-line* processing is also attractive for the advancement of the technologists' careers. It enhances their technological skills and status. It stimulates buying more advanced equipment. Reassigning lower-priced employees from the information systems department is ideal[8] when organizations rely on headcount control as a substitute for profit planning.[9] The M.I.S. department will comply with whatever employment targets are set by the financial planners.

Year-to-year comparisons of the *Information Technology-to-Revenue* ratios are misleading if a company is reassigning the responsibilities for data input and data control. It's a trend that computer departments follow for good technical and often for good economic reasons. If this is happening in your company, you should be cautious before you believe claims of productivity gains based on improved *Information Technology-to-Revenue* ratios.[10] You should ask probing questions whenever you hear claims that unit transaction costs declined.[11] Shifting costs may improve the ratios somebody is tracking, but it will not improve your firm's profits.

SHIFTING DATA INPUT TO CUSTOMERS

Enter information where it originates.

Passing on data entry responsibility to customers, suppliers or taxpayers is even more attractive than giving this task to your intracompany clients.

Take the example of banking ATM's (Automatic Teller Machines) or Banking-at-Home (from microcomputers). They offer to many customers added convenience and to the bank a reduction in data input costs. The bank realizes savings when a customer chooses from a bewildering array of transaction codes, enters his information and retains full responsibility for everything.

Passing your costs on to others is one of the justifications of Electronic Data Interchange (EDI). If you can take advantage of your customer's order in electronic form, you can save money, reduce errors and speed up order turnaround. By connecting your computers directly to those of your suppliers and customers, everyone stands to gain. However, linking your systems with others may not be an unqualified blessing.

I recently reviewed a small company's proposal to buy additional computer capacity and a software package because a primary customer insisted on EDI transmissions. The customer used to send, by facsimile, copies of his computer-generated purchase orders. The customer's systems people justified EDI by eliminating the job of feeding the facsimile machines. Nobody bothered to find out that the small company would incur a one-time cost of $45,000 to save less than $25 of monthly clerical expense.[12]

The tax collector is the greatest advocate of shifting work to the taxpayer. Regulations are now in place that call for the submission of payroll withholding and social security taxes in electronic form. This is an advantage for large firms, but there are millions of small businesses which cannot comply with government regulations without increasing their computer expenses.

Large companies and the government have the power to demand that suppliers and taxpayers assume their input-preparation costs. Before such programs claim any savings, you should consider who will receive the benefits.

SHIFTING PROGRAMMING COSTS TO OTHERS

Ultimately, everyone will be a programmer.

Programming backlogs are the source of a computer executive's greatest annoyance. Centralized monopoly over programming creates unmanageable client demands. Computer managers are besieged by requests, threats or begging for changes to existing reports[13] and the creation of new applications. In the first decade of computerization this annoyance was tolerable. It led to better control over programming, increasing budgets, elevated corporate status and new management positions.

When top management presses for cost reductions, getting rid of the most onerous program maintenance jobs is the preferred solution. If you are an M.I.S. executive, how will you accomplish that?

Information Centers

You offer to a particularly insistent customer a remote-access terminal. You also provide a report-generation software package.

Everybody will then show increased satisfaction with the computer service. The data center gets rid of the hated paper, and gains revenue that does not increase labor costs. Most of the requests for programming changes disappear. The customers get exactly the columns, subtotals or line items they need.

Very soon the customers find that their terminals understand only carefully coded instructions. *User programming* centers then come into existence, which includes additional support staffs. To legitimize their role, the people supporting the remote terminals take on suitable new designations, such as *information centers*[14] or *information services*. Administrative people learn how to do low-level programming, on a part-time basis.[15] Satisfaction increases because the most annoying customers now take care of their own requests.

The M.I.S. department gains as well. Demand for computer time increases because inefficient programs demand more processing power. The central information systems group can replace the most frustrated maintenance programmers with expensive systems programmers who can deal with more advanced applications.

A large share of program maintenance hours now will be in the general administrative payroll. The apparent gains in productivity can be very large. Consider, for instance, that in a manufacturing company with 10,000 employees you may have about 100 programmers. You will have as many as 40 to 80 separate organizational units, each with unique information requirements. If half of these units get an *information center* (with 1 to 3 employees each) you will increase your available programming staff by 50% without any apparent increase in programming expenses.

Departmental Computing

There are customers who need limited (less than a person-year) applications in a hurry. They cannot wait for the multiple approval signatures necessary for every project authorization from the central organization. They have no patience for ushering their proposals through the priority-setting systems review committees. They do not have the elaborate skills required for the preparation of feasibility studies. They see no benefit in completing phase reviews and securing the required audit approvals. They cannot afford the costly budget agreements that cover the costs of centrally-supplied terminals. They resent the cautious and time-consuming acceptance testing procedures whenever they wish to install even minor applications remotely from their terminals.[16]

Eventually, enough expertise accumulates in a few departments to start agitation against the central computer organization. Applications are function-specific and best understood by the customers themselves. Nobody has the time or motivation to explain to systems analysts how the business operates. The customers also do not like the monthly computer center charges for their terminals.

When a department buys its first microcomputer, it is usually from an under-spent budget category. Everyone in the department will work extremely long hours to make this first high-technology venture succeed. The new capacity is addictive, easily accessible and provides what appears to be low-cost computing. Very soon, every other department starts planning for even bigger savings.

Nobody mentions, when proposing the purchase of a departmental minicomputer or of a microcomputer local area network, that many employees may have to drop whatever they are doing to set up the installation and learn how to operate these devices. Additional employees may spend ten to twenty percent of their time adapting software packages to suit departmental needs.

In a manufacturing corporation with 10,000 employees, there may be as many as 4,000 information processing workers. As the number of microcomputers approaches the number of information workers, you will double and maybe even quadruple the programming hours consumed by your company. You will never uncover the total costs spent on these efforts. The programming and learning tasks become an inseparable element of each person's job.

Interactive Terminals

A way to harness latent programming talent is to offer programming capabilities to everyone who is willing to learn a specialized computer language. Interactive terminals with rapid response time and access to "third-generation" software will serve this purpose.

As noted above, in a manufacturing corporation with 10,000 employees you may have only about 100 full-time programmers. In the same company you would have at least 500 analysts, researchers, designers, controllers, auditors, coordinators and expediters. These staff employees have an insatiable hunger for data. Most are individual contributors, with unique analytic needs to extract data from large databases. Their needs are not satisfied by microcomputers. If you supply this group with powerful interactive terminals, you could easily double the programming hours in your company. You will not show any increases in information systems personnel. The demand for computational cycles will explode, but you can buy those at prices that decline more than 30% per year without much effort on your part. Over two-thirds of your total application development hours now will submerge into the general and administrative overhead and become an untraceable programming expense.

The effect of the widespread use of professional workstations is a proliferation of applications without a remarkable increase in costs. The most visible systems expenses, incurred in purchasing workstation hardware, are dropping precipitously. A low inflation rate of 5% to 8% will increase your revenues at a sufficiently fast rate to mask the 100%+ per annum absolute growth in computing power. Everybody now is using computers, but your *Information Systems Expense-to-Revenue* ratio shows a decline.[17]

How do you maintain a growth in technology without adding to your expenses at a rate that exceeds revenue gains? One way is to seek new customers who are not happy with what they are getting. You find new applications where spending habits are not subject to tight budget constraints. The most promising opportunities are *Executive Information Systems*.

Executive Information Systems

A typical financial, buying or market analyst will consume from $15,000 to $35,000 of computer center charges per year. For access to external data bases you may add another $5,000 to $8,000 per year. Professionals in these jobs need a wide array of information services because they are trying to satisfy non-routine, one-of-a-kind demands from senior executives who like instant answers.

The analyst requires an expanding collection of statistical programs, simulators, spread-sheet tabulations, text retrieval software, on-line data searching routines and graphic slide generators to be available instantly with little effort. Professional programmers, with little business knowledge, cannot support such variety and cannot support executive needs to deliver anything of value.

The business analyst, usually an M.B.A. who does not view systems as a career, cannot specify exactly what he wants until he sees what he gets. Even then, what he gets may not be what the executive can use. Executives cannot tell what is useful until they see a range of possible answers. Which answers are feasible depends on interaction with other executives who will have different data or divergent interpretations of the same data.

Executive Information Systems were conceived to keep up with the intensity of these rapid interactions.[18] They use easy-to-learn and highly stylized computer languages for answering an enormous array of standard questions, for the answers are largely pre-defined. *Executive Information Systems* depart from the traditional handling of inquiries by substituting customized computer languages instead of using general-purpose programming methods. They extract information from a dedicated "executive" database. They do not rely on the analysts' knowledge of generalized database management commands to do that job. Their essential feature is their easy-to-use output format.[19] You will recognize an *Executive Information System* if the top dozen officers of a corporation use it routinely, without intermediaries.

When evaluating information technology costs, *Executive Information Systems* represent the most refined form of overcoming the conventional limits of computing. They eliminate the financial analyst, who substituted for the information center specialist, who replaced the systems analyst, who automated a programmer. Despite this transfer and simplification of tasks, everybody is busier than ever before. The full costs of these efforts do not appear because they are indistinguishable from whatever else employees are doing. In such a setting the traditional definition of "information systems" is meaningless. Its ratio of *Costs-to-Revenue* is without significance in making historical comparisons with past trends.

When the president and every vice-president, division manager or department head "program"[20] complex searches, you will surely not charge their efforts as systems costs. Everyone is now a part-time programmer. Systems work is everyone's part-time occupation.

CLASSIFICATION OF INFORMATION TECHNOLOGY

Information technology will be everywhere and in everything.

Business and Personal Equipment

There is a copying machine[21] that incorporates a self-diagnostic computer, a paper-path control computer, software programs with over a quarter of a million lines of computer code, a cathode-ray display for instructing the operator and an expert system that prompts

CHAPTER 2—FLEXIBLE DEFINITIONS   25

the customer what to do. Inside the equipment, a high capacity communications network distributes commands to and from individual components such as collators, page feeders and book-binding equipment. This copier has also a direct digital connection to a diagnostic center. A remote diagnostic computer communicates with the copier for detection of incipient maintenance problems. Despite its impressive computing powers, this copier does not show up in reports as information technology.

My copier at home contains more computing power than my first personal computer ten years ago. The Oldsmobile in the garage has over twenty microprocessors and an elaborate digital display.[22] The microwave has three controller chips. The dishwasher has five. The washer-dryer combination has over 10. Telephones, burglar alarms, the oil furnace, the programmable thermostats, the dehumidifier, the air filter, the water softener, the refrigerator, the automatic driveway spotlights and whatever else there is around all have silicon chips with pre-programmed or programmable instructions. My household now has the equivalent computing power of a large 1960 data center. None of these count as computers.

Between electronic mail, writing letters, paying bills electronically and an occasional shopping trip, my daily consumption of computation cycles, as a consumer and not as a computer professional, was well over 1 billion when I stopped counting.

Production Equipment

To manufacture and service the pervasive computing presence in business and consumer goods, factories throughout the world started investing in information technology after 1969. By 1985, more than 35% of the total U.S. investments in producers durable[23] were for buying information technology. How much of this equipment is counted when companies report their *information technology* costs?

At Xerox, the manufacturing computers[24] were not included in the information technology totals for corporate reviews and consultants' surveys. Manufacturing computers were justified and bought as production equipment. Their amortization passed into direct production costs. Although they were computers, they were not *information technology* expenses, because they were production and process control tools.

To program and test the equipment used in the production processes and incorporated into products, engineering departments throughout the world started to fill with information technology devices after 1965. By 1988, an engineer without a workstation[25] was an exception. How many of these devices are reported as *information technology* expenses? The equipment used in product research, development and engineering are product expenses which flow into product costs. The accounting rules favor exclusion of direct product costs from *information technology* expenses. How typical is the Xerox experience in the treatment of computers that are in direct product costs?

I have checked enough information technology budgets to learn that every company has its own definition of what is included in their information technology spending numbers. When you probe for an explanation of the exclusions, the answers refer to precedent, expediency and control. I shall illustrate that with a few examples.

The automatic teller machine in the neighborhood bank, which dispenses cash before I go shopping, has 780,000 lines of code.[26] The ATM is included in the bank's information technology expense. Next to the bank is a supermarket equipped with a check-out scanner. It produces the bill for goods bought with the cash I got from the automatic teller machine and spent in the supermarket. The check-out machine has 90,000 lines of code that required 58 person-years of programming.[27] Supermarket chains often do not include check-out counters as information technology because they are a direct replacement of equipment that previously was a store fixture. Only the network that connects the local cluster-controllers and the central computers is in M.I.S..

A large manufacturing company contracted with a consultant to perform its systems work. The CEO decided that his company did not have the expertise to manage its information technologies and should concentrate on manufacturing automation. The company transferred all personnel with occupational titles even remotely resembling data processing to the contractor. They did not transfer any manufacturing engineering people who were programming computers that controlled factory robots. They did not transfer any of the publishing and documentation personnel, though they operate a fully computerized publishing plant. When the manufacturing company now reports its information technology costs, it recognizes only the external costs. Everyone avoids calling anything else information technology, fearing that they would move to the contractor's payroll.

A direct competitor of the above manufacturing company has a different information-management tradition. Its corporate systems staff controls everything related to computers, regardless of location or organization. The approval of computer purchases is under tight central supervision. When this firm reports how much they spend on information technology, there are no exclusions because the people who do the reporting also control everything. Comparing the *Information Technology-to-Revenue* ratios of these two manufacturers is misleading.

Recently, I examined the computer budget of a financial services firm. Their budget was on the extreme low side for comparable institutions. To verify the cost data, I asked for a list of their major computer applications. A few key applications were missing. Oh, said the vice-president of finance, we get this work done in exchange for other services. After some head-scratching, the vice-president came up with an additional cost that was equal to 55% of the reported numbers. The computer budget did not reflect the full extent of computing used in this business.

The military knows how to exclude from reports items that are open to exceptionally frustrating reviews.[28] For instance, modern weapon systems contain awesome computing power. The government insists on procurement regulations that single out administrative computer systems for a torturous approval and review process. This makes it attractive to classify all sorts of computing capabilities as "embedded systems."[29]

Managers of process control factories use similar tactics. In a paper manufacturing plant, I found process control computers with peripheral equipment and elaborate programs to handle employee timecards, production records and quality control readings. This business information passed to the accounting department to produce summaries. The process control computers were classified as paper-mill equipment. The low information processing costs of this firm did not reflect the full information processing costs.

In service industries such as in airlines, banking, stock-brokerage and merchandise distribution, you will find that the customer's terminals generate revenues. Terminals placed internally detract from revenues. How airlines account for the cost of delivering computing power to travel agents changes what they report as information technology expenses. You cannot compare the *Information Technology-to-Revenue* ratios of American Airlines with those of U.S. Air, because American Airlines is also a major computer services company.

Chapter Summary

The *Information Technology Expense-to-Revenue* ratio is still the most frequently used comparative index for assessing computer spending.[30] It is only as good as your definition of your company's information technology costs.

Budget pressures, performance problems and new technology solutions influence the definition of what is the expense for information technology. Previously well-defined central budgets are now redistributed, reallocated or redefined. In the new form they are not "information technology."[31]

Before you make valid inter-company comparisons of spending ratios you must have a standard method for accumulating data about information technology. This method must stay measurable and consistent over an extended period of time.

If nobody paid attention to the *Information Technology-to-Expense* ratio, this subject would not be worthy of discussion. The next chapter will show how organizations apply this index as a yardstick for evaluating computers.

Chapter 2 Comments

[1] According to a survey by the Diebold Group (reported in the *Office Magazine*, November 1989, p.19) user spending on information systems outside IS budgets was equivalent to another 64% of the IS departments' spending in manufacturing and 27% in service firms.

[2] P. Cinelli, Data Centers: Dropping Walls and Building New Identities, *Computerworld*, January 23, 1989, p.66. The case describes the transition in the deployment of M.I.S. personnel in an insurance company.

Another study tracked computer functions that have been turned over to departments (E.R. Greenberg, Close Calls: Lines of Authority Shift as Department Computing Grows, *Chief Information Officer Journal*, Summer 1988):

BUSINESS FUNCTION	% BY M.I.S.	% BY USER
Budgeting & financial management	23.6	43.3
Report generation	23.6	39.5
Systems project management	17.5	45.6
Text processing	9.9	57.9
Presentation graphics	9.5	44.9
Computer-aided design and production control	13.4	38.8

Functions not under control of either M.I.S. or users were classified either as under shared control, or "no responsibility clearly assigned."

[3] Central data processing personnel reduced from 115 in 1978 to the projected 44 in 1988.

[4] Based on data from Nolan, Norton & Co, as quoted in the January 12, 1989 issue of *Computerworld*, p.43. I estimated the costs of the professional's time devoted to learning about new features and about new applications.

[5] ABorted ENDing. An example of computer euphemisms for the initiated technical

CHAPTER 2—FLEXIBLE DEFINITIONS   29

priesthood. A message in IBM-talk to avoid terms like "disaster" or worse.

6 Such as under-payment of a salesperson's commissions, missing factory materials tickets and a delay in the monthly accounting close.

7 A term applied by information technologists to everyone who receives their output. One of the definitions (*The Oxford English Dictionary*, Volume XI) identifies a *user* as someone who consumes tobacco and drugs. It also calls an animal useful, such as "...a cow is said to be a good *user* when she yields abundance of milk." I prefer being a customer, a client or just an employee.

8 Public sector organizations have perfected this maneuver. The reductions in staff employed in most M.I.S. departments should not be taken as a reliable proof of increased productivity. Contracting out for labor-intensive information handling offers another means for headcount control.

9 Getting data preparation and administrative personnel out of the data center also reduces supervisory difficulties in dealing with technically untrained personnel. When you get a proposal to convert to on-line processing, check if it includes a thorough evaluation of all training, startup, error-correction, data entry and maintenance efforts. You should also guard against the technologist's built-in bias to favor all *real-time* processing.

10 One of our managers relied on short-term executive memory to claim (at budget time) that his ratio was *lower* than another Division's. Therefore, he deserved a hefty budget increase to upgrade his technologies. Six months later, during his performance appraisal, he claimed that because his ratio was *lower* he deserved a hefty salary increase because he was more efficient. This proves the versatility of all ratio-based comparisons unless they relate to cash flow.

11 This practice is most prevalent in insurance and banking. Before you can accept a decline in unit costs as productivity gains, make sure that the labor content and functions within the transaction are comparable.

12 Later, I saw the Chairman of the customer's company claiming that a *paperless relationship with suppliers* was one of his strategies for reducing his suppliers' costs of doing business.

13 According to a Gartner Group survey 75% of all software resources are consumed in maintaining existing applications (*Datamation*, February 15, 1990, p.66)

14 *Information centers* are a legitimized form for by-passing costly and inconvenient means to distribute information. They offer an acceptable avoidance of corporate standards such as elaborate database, data control, documentation, audit and applications cost-justification procedures usually specified for larger projects. *Information centers* that fit into an overall corporate systems architecture remind me of the discount, tax-free mail-order houses. Where such integration does not happen, *information centers* are more like the black market in some countries, where you can find goodies otherwise unobtainable from government-run stores.

15 It is an excellent way for clerical personnel to enhance their careers, on company time. Though this is an expensive way of programming, it is effective because the people who need information can now get it directly, without delays.

16 The typical approval lead-time in a large corporation is a year before any actual work begins. The project approval cycle, for small projects, in the U.S. Federal Government is ten times longer than it takes to do the work. Much of the customers' ingenuity goes into finding ways to bypass formal approvals. I think that this is the dominating reason why everyone wishes to own his computer and control his own programming. In the Soviet Union, this striving for independence extends to hardware technology. You must own your own maintenance engineers and somehow seize possession of a supply of components. I asked a Russian computer manager how he does that. "Simply," he said. "I have three computers and use two of them for spare parts."

17 Some of the earliest reporting about the migration of information technology away from the centrally managed information systems resources is in Minicomputers-An Industry Perspective (Gartner Group, June 1985). It shows that only 22% of the information technology assets were in the corporate mainframe, with 19% in Departmental or Divisional minicomputers, 25% in work-group minicomputers and 34% in personal workstations.

The shares of total information systems spending outside the Information

Systems function (*Computerworld*, April 6, 1987, p.83) average 57% for all firms and as much as 118% for retail firms.

18 When the time comes to make rapid computer-supported decisions, there is a chance that the business equivalent of an atomic chain-reaction may occur. As you know, atomic chain-reactions are controllable only within well understood limits. Too much information, acted on too quickly, can create excessive conflict. Runaway computer-generated escalation of data can produce the equivalent of a reactor melt-down. The growing instability of financial markets from computer-programmed trading is an example of this potential danger. As yet, there are no recorded cases of such a thing happening in government or corporations.

19 One of the early developers of EIS tested the ease of the commands by bringing in 6th grade students. If it required greater skills, it would not fit the low levels of executive patience.

20 "Programming" begins when you have to create instructions instead of just picking from a menu of ready-made choices.

21 The Xerox 5090.

22 The 1989 Lincoln Continental has 83,517 lines of code that required 35 person-years of programming at a development cost of $1.8 million according to *Fortune*, September 25, 1989, p. 102.

23 Equipment used to produce other equipment.

24 Circuit-board testers, assembly robots, numerical control machines, automatic inventory storage devices, assembly line monitors, process controllers.

25 Is the workstation the only computer device for actual work? Is a "personal computer" really personal if it does not even recognize my name? I am still searching for better ways of categorizing information technology devices. The spread of electronic work in the U.S. shows up in the following table:

	1979	1989
Number of Terminals	12M	32M
Personal Computers	0.3M	52.4M
Information Workers	54M	67.6M
Electronic Access	34%	125%

26 That required 150 person-years of programming at a development cost of $13.2 million.

27 B.R. Schlender, How to Break the Software Logjam, *Fortune*, September 25, 1989

28 The operating statement of a food company used to highlight the costs of scrapped packaging materials. Materials management made sure that scrap did not show up by filling the boxes with food and then writing off the surplus as "expired inventory."

29 The Warner Amendment to the onerous Brooks bill makes special allowances for the procurement of "mission critical" automatic data processing equipment. For instance, test equipment that generates parts orders would be "embedded." Similarly, banking terminals and super-market check-out counters would be "mission critical." An insurance salesperson's laptop computer could be an office expense and not data processing. The economics and administrative procedures are all driving information technology towards "embedding." Information technology, as an isolated functional specialty, will ultimately vanish because it will be inseparable from the conduct of the business.

30 E.M. Kass, HP Denies Outsourcing, *InformationWeek*, January 29, 1990 quotes the Chief Computer Executive for Hewlett-Packard "...IS staff succeeded in paring internal IS costs from 3.9% to 2.9% of the company's sales."

31 In January 1990, a survey of information systems executives revealed that only 20% of them kept a count of IS expenditures outside their own organization. (*InformationWeek*, February 19, 1990, p.37.) The survey showed that between 20% and 40% of total corporate spending is outside the IS department and that this number will increase significantly.

3

MAKING COMPARISONS

In the beginning Computers created control.

The compulsion to measure, evaluate and report resides deeply in our industrial society. The higher the concentration of decisions, the greater the emphasis on numbers that would give the executives a way of maintaining control. If your model of guiding a firm is that of an all-knowing clock-maker who designs how the mechanism works, your information systems will reflect this bias. You will rely on controls over key transactions to manage the business. You will keep discretionary decisions in the hands of a small management group. Employees will reach maximum efficiency by following well-defined procedures. Nowadays, you cannot run such an organization, in a free society, without computers. Information technology has the potential of delivering more complete control, at a lower cost and with fewer risks, than any other managerial method.[1]

The early alliance between computer technologists and financial controllers explains the first twenty years of business computing better than any study of electronics or computer science. The designations have changed from machine accounting to data processing and then to management information systems. Nevertheless, using computers for asserting control over increased business complexity continues to be the underlying rationale behind all hard-to-justify systems proposals.[2]

In later Chapters I will show that information systems are used primarily to address a company's internal management and coordination needs. Delivering customer value-added is not where most of the money is spent, especially in manufacturing industries. If that is so, how do you measure and then justify your controller's need for more computing? How much is an Executive Information System worth? How do you explain the costs of a research data-base? What indicators will guide your acquisitions of computing resources, without which your enterprise could degrade into chaos?

The most controversial aspect of budgeting computers concerns internal communications that are of no concern to paying customers. Therefore, most of this book will deal with the question of how to evaluate what you spend on electronic means to satisfy your control and planning aims.

CONTROLLING THE TECHNICAL MEANS

Since 1954, when I started on my first computer job, I estimate that over three trillion dollars were spent in getting and installing management information systems in OECD (Organization for Economic Co-operation and Development) countries. I have started, reviewed and approved hundreds of requests for more computer spending. Regardless of the phrasing of the various automation proposals, their financial justification was primarily cost-reduction or increased control. I got many proposals that promised revenue gains, competitive advantage, improved customer service and quality gains, but those savings always had the label "intangibles."

I find that not much has changed over the last two decades in how proposals are approved. The need for improved controls, especially after a bad audit report, will always get you the money. Direct labor displacement proposals will also get the funds. Opportunities for eliminating clerical labor have diminished. The hard-to-quantify benefits make up now the greatest share of new computer spending. That is the reason why there is suddenly so much interest in cost justification.

Initially, increased information technology spending was subject only to perfunctory examination to explain rapidly rising budgets. When computer managers worked directly for the financial controllers there was not much to discuss because new computer applications could deliver remarkable gains in central financial controls.[3] The 20 to 50% annual growth rates in information technology budgets were safe within the financial departments until everybody else also realized that computers could support their needs as well.[4]

The question of how to control information technology spending was born on the day when the M.I.S. organization acquired its own identity. It became a new corporate function, apart from finance, when it became expensive and when its services to manufacturing, marketing and personnel took up a larger share of its costs. Finance could not compromise its position as an independent guardian of expenses if it was also in the business of satisfying customers.[5]

To assert controls over rising information technology budgets, finance resorted to the same simple revenue-ratio methods it applied to budgeting and controlling manufacturing, sales and service. This did not work then and still does not work today because information technology, similar to finance or personnel, is not a discrete, isolated function. It is a phenomenon that penetrates everything, everywhere and in many guises.

Though the applications of conventional financial and budgeting measures are a resounding failure (see Chapter 10), M.I.S. departments continue to be subjected to the same analytic treatment for budgeting and equipment acquisition purposes as manufacturing. The rest of this Chapter will show how industrial-age control ratios persist as a way of thinking about information technology costs.[6]

THE FOOD INDUSTRY EVALUATION

If your thermometer keeps jumping from fifty to one hundred degrees during a hot summer day, you get another thermometer.

My investigation into the adequacy of revenue ratios began when the 1977 Diebold Group's *M.I.S. Budgets and Key Indicators* did not help to answer questions about expected spending levels for information technology. Xerox's wide range of definitions of what was counted as information technology, the company's rapid growth rate and inability to compare division revenues yielded too little consistent data to produce useful results.

From my previous nine years of directing systems work in the food industry I knew that their centralized information systems budgets were kept under tight control. Computer applications within the food industry were similar. If accurate revenue-related comparisons of spending levels were possible, the stable food industry would be a good testing ground.[7]

34 THE BUSINESS VALUE OF COMPUTERS

The assumption of comparability and homogeneity within the food industry did not hold up after examination. The range in the distribution of the *Revenue-per-Employee* was even greater than that discovered within Xerox:

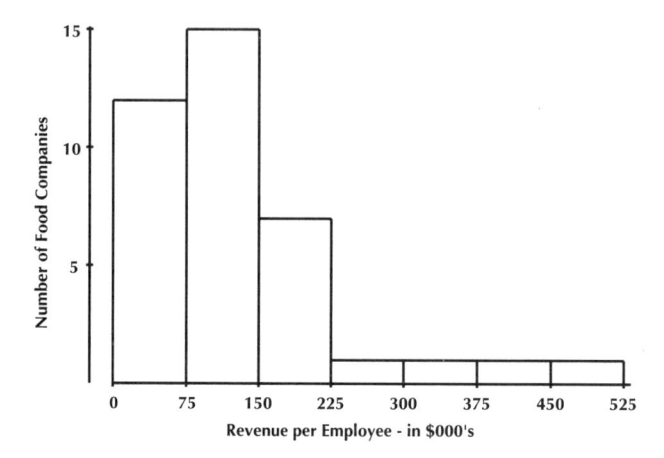

Figure 3.1: Revenue-per-Employee in the Food Industry

Companies with capital-intensive processing, such as edible oils, margarine, cornflakes and instant coffee had fewer employees than labor-intensive firms, such as frozen or canned food packers.

The share of revenues applied to wages in the food industry were also more diverse than anything we encountered in Xerox:

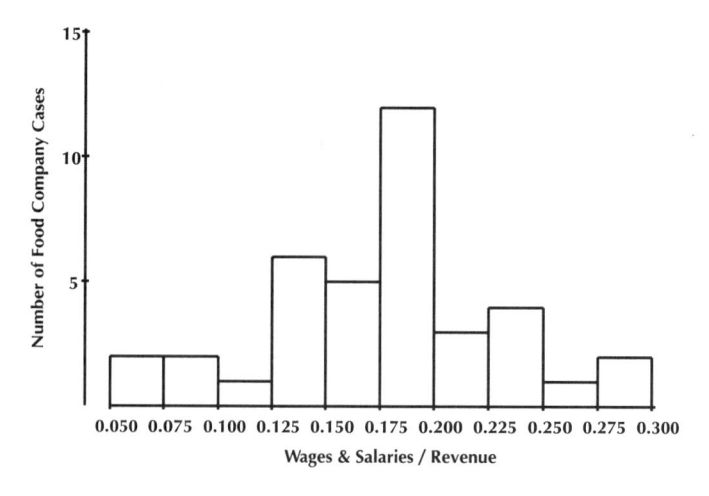

Figure 3.2: Wages & Salaries as % of Revenue in the Food Industry

Highly unionized meat-packers received wages that were many multiples of wages for seasonal labor picking fruits and vegetables.

To apply the Diebold survey results to the food industry, I computed the spending levels for each company, as suggested by the survey averages. Based on such theoretical budgets, I found that the A.C. Staley Company (highly capitalized and low-labor content) could afford spending ten times more on *Information Technology-per-Person* than the Gerber Company (low-asset, low average-pay but highly labor-intensive). I made similar computations of suggested spending levels for eight more food firms, and then compared their calculated information technology budgets with their actual 1977 spending.[8] The two sets of numbers were distinctly unrelated.

I concluded that an average revenue-based ratio for food companies is not a satisfactory predictor of how much information technology is necessary to operate a particular food company.

BANKING INDUSTRY EVALUATIONS

I made a presentation ten years later to banking executives on the evaluation of information technology budgets. I used my food industry statistics to illustrate the difficulty of using revenue-based ratios. The banking executives did not think that my conclusions were applicable in their case. My technique showed no regard for profitability. They felt that if I applied information technology costs as a ratio of some operationally important measure, a satisfactory correlation with financial profits would appear.

That sounded like a good suggestion, so I decided to check it out. Banking profitability and information technology spending as a ratio of money-on-deposit were unrelated.

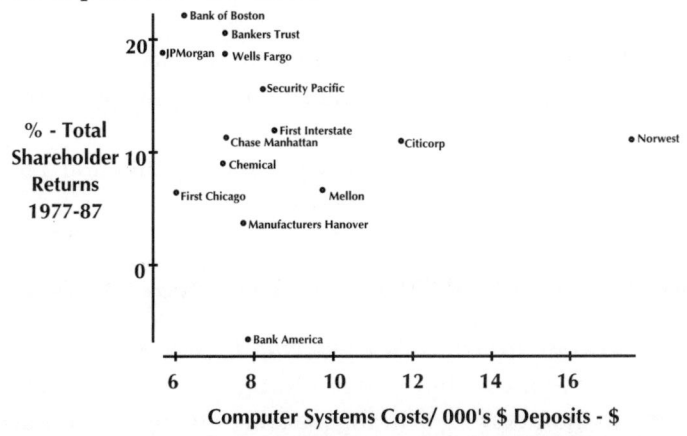

Figure 3.3: I.T. Deposit Ratios and Banking Profitability

Over-achievers (companies with better than 15% total shareholder returns, over a ten-year period) did not spend more on information technology than under-achievers (companies with shareholder returns below long-term bond interest rates):

All other operating ratios, such as those based on assets and loans, gave inconclusive results.

Next, I tested the hypothesis that information technology expenses relate to employment. A higher ratio of *Information Technology-per-Employee* would suggest intensive laborsaving automation.[9] Does automation-intensity produce greater profits? It seems that ten-year shareholder return is unaffected by how much money a bank spent on *Information Technology-per-Employee:*

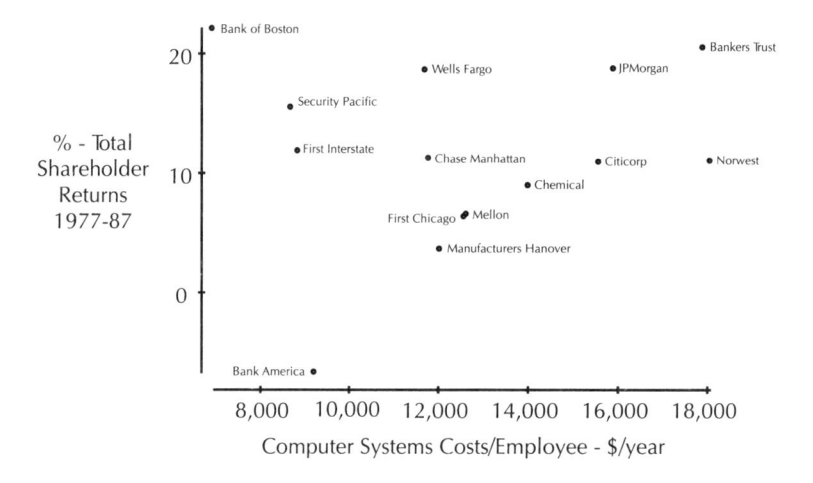

Figure 3.4: I.T. Employee Ratio and Profitability

I tried other ratios, but none of them produced the sought-after proof that banking had greater applicability for applying industry averages than anyone else.

What are some of the reasons why nobody could find a few ratios that would measure and monitor increasing costs?

REVENUE-BASED RATIOS AND BUSINESS STRUCTURE

The ratio of *Information Systems Expense-to-Revenue* may change because a company may change its financial structure. Consider a manufacturing firm that shows a steady revenue growth of

8% per year. The firm finds domestic labor expensive. It begins buying lower-cost parts from Singapore. This allows it to reduce direct labor costs by 5% per year.

It then happens that the savings from lower priced materials and from lower direct labor costs are offset by a 15% annual growth in overhead. New government regulations, international coordination and a more complex procurement process require a growth in staff. A new computer system will keep track of the longer chain of supply.

Suppose that before restructuring the company spends 10% of its overhead costs on information systems. After four years, information technologies are still 10% of overhead costs, because the factory-control investments are in Singapore to manage local labor costs. Singapore adds to factory capacity, reduces its costs and expands its volume, while New York adds staff and computers.[10]

The following shows what happens to the various percentages of revenue ratios, after four years:

	Year 1	Year 2	Year 3	Year 4
Materials	50.0%	52.3%	54.7%	56.7%
Direct Labor	30.0%	26.4%	23.2%	20.4%
Overhead	20.0%	21.3%	22.1%	22.9%
Information Systems/Revenue	2.00%	2.13%	2.21%	2.29%

Table 3.1: Demonstration of Changed Ratios over Time

At the beginning of the four-year scenario, the *Information Systems-to-Revenue* ratio is 2%, slightly above average for an electronics assembly industry. Four years later it is 2.3%, among the top three firms in the industry. The firm's M.I.S. Director can now claim that his company has advanced to a higher stage of development because he now is supporting more complex managerial needs instead of concentrating on the factory. In effect, he is supporting a larger overhead payroll. In four years, the overhead and information systems budgets increased 44.5%, while the revenues grew only 26%. There are more jobs and more promotional opportunities for managers and professionals. Meanwhile, the company became more vulnerable to competition.

A better indicator would be to compare information systems expense to the cost of people it supports. In the first year that was 4%.[11]

In the fourth year the ratio was 5.3%.[12] Information systems costs increase 44.5% while the costs that call for support grow only 9.1%.[13]

This example shows that changes in the financial structure of a firm also change the significance of its revenue ratios. You should not trust simple ratios for measuring changes without first knowing if the internal composition of costs remains comparable.

WHEN IBM SPEAKS YOU LISTEN

"...an IBM team of experts will work closely with your management to plan the information systems that will be most profitable to you."[14]

IBM's understanding and support of their customers' need for control is the most plausible explanation for their dominance in the computer industry. However, by 1984 the world-wide demand for computer shipments started turning downward, closer to the customers' revenue growth. The 20 to 30% yearly increases in computer industry revenues in the early 1970's have vanished.[15] Surveys by consultants, industry associations and researchers showed rising resistance to buying more computing power without corresponding gains in profitability.

The IBM marketing organization always paid attention to the attitude of their customers. With the rise in computer department budgets, customer executives demanded better assurances that they were making safe investments. IBM always had published instruction manuals on how to plan for investments in information technology.[16] However, the cost-justification issue did not rise in prominence until industry sales dropped once to zero growth.

The *Information Systems Investment Strategies* (*ISIS*) program[17] was launched by IBM early in 1988, during a slump in computer shipments. I had little doubt that what I would see would have been thoroughly tested tools for evaluating expense levels. Considering the prowess of IBM financial analysis staffs, you would have to be attentive to what IBM consultants say regarding the economics of computers.

ISIS has chosen the ambiguous *Technology-to-Revenue* index as one of the ways to assess the adequacy of the customer's spending levels. The *ISIS* texts contain a graph that compares a company's spending on information technology with an *industry ratio*.[18] After you get this graph for your firm, you should ask about the comparability of these ratios. IBM refers to surveys by the International Data Corporation, the Diebold Group and to their own research as the source for plotting your benchmark. Before you accept this, you should find out how the picked ratio applies specifically to your company.

I doubt if such comparability is possible. The definition of information technology is becoming more vague, as pointed out in the previous Chapter.

THE MOST EFFECTIVE USERS OF INFORMATION SYSTEMS

Computerworld 1988 Ratings

You can't use a rubber band for a yardstick.

IBM's reliance on information spending data from the International Data Corporation confirms IDC's eminent standing as the largest data-collection enterprise concerned exclusively with information technology. The IDC conducts surveys about the uses of computers, and has the largest research staff on computer installations in the U.S.A. It also has access to the world's largest group of reporters who concentrate on the computer industry.

It was a monumental achievement when the flagship IDC publication, *Computerworld*, published in September 1988 an 80-page supplement showing the ranking of the *Most Effective Users of Information Systems in the U.S.A.* Although similar tabulations were tried before, these were always based on opinion polls. None of the prior rankings showed the rationale for the results. The *Computerworld Premier 100* disclosed all the facts for deriving a *Computerworld Premier Effectiveness Score*. The *Score* is a proprietary formula for deriving a rank of relative excellence. Computerworld also included the procedure for computing your own *Effectiveness Score*.

The disclosure of the *Computerworld* ranking method reflected high professional standards. The data sources were credible. The effort exceeded anything tried by any consultant or academician. The extensive publicity heaped on the top-scoring firms suggested that considerable know-how was backing an innovative concept for evaluating the effectiveness of information technologies. Was it possible that an acceptable yardstick for determining the business value of computers had arrived?

The *Premier 100* companies included 38 service sector businesses and 62 manufacturing companies. My earlier research showed that the revenues of food, electronics, paper and oil companies bore little relation to their employment or capital. Therefore, I decided to see how well the *Effectiveness Score* related to service company profits and their information technology spending. My tests used the premise that a company that IDC finds excellent in using information technologies would also have superior long-term financial results. An examination of service companies, as a separate group, would allow the *Effectiveness Score* to appear in the most favorable light because these firms are more labor- and information-intensive than manufacturing companies.[19]

THE INFORMATION EFFECTIVENESS SCORE

To come up with their evaluations, the *Computerworld* researchers collected the following information:
- Estimated information systems budget.
- Information systems budget as a percentage of revenue.
- Estimated value of the installed equipment.
- Value of the installed equipment as percentage of revenue.
- Percentage of the information systems budget applied to staff.
- Percentage of the information systems budget applied to training.
- Total number of personal computers and terminals.
- Percentage of *Personal Computers and Terminals-per-Employee.*

The staff of *Computerworld* decided to use a combination of the above data for judging effectiveness. They said, "...these criteria were developed after consultation with leading industry experts, to take into account current methods of determining systems effectiveness." They defined the *Information Effectiveness Score* as follows:

Weight	Criteria
30%	Information Systems Budget as % of Revenue
15%	Current Market Value of Installed Equipment
15%	Profitability During the Past Five Years
10%	Below Average Level of Spending on Staff
15%	% of Total Budget Spent on Training
15%	% of Employees with Terminals, Personal Computers

Table 3.2: Information Effectiveness Scoring Components

The choice of the rating criteria looked plausible. The *Computerworld Effectiveness Score* is a mixture of some related and some unrelated criteria, although it is not obvious why the *Percentage of Revenue ratio* is twice as important as *Profitability*. However, the examination of the *Computerworld* multi-criteria's scores offered an opportunity to test a technique widely used in information systems research studies.[20]

You cannot validate multi-factor ratings that use opinion-based weights unless you also match them against an independent, objective measure, such as long-term profitability.

The values of the *Information Effectiveness Score* for service companies ranged from 6,000 to 16,000. When plotted against *Shareholder Returns*,[21] you get another shotgun diagram:

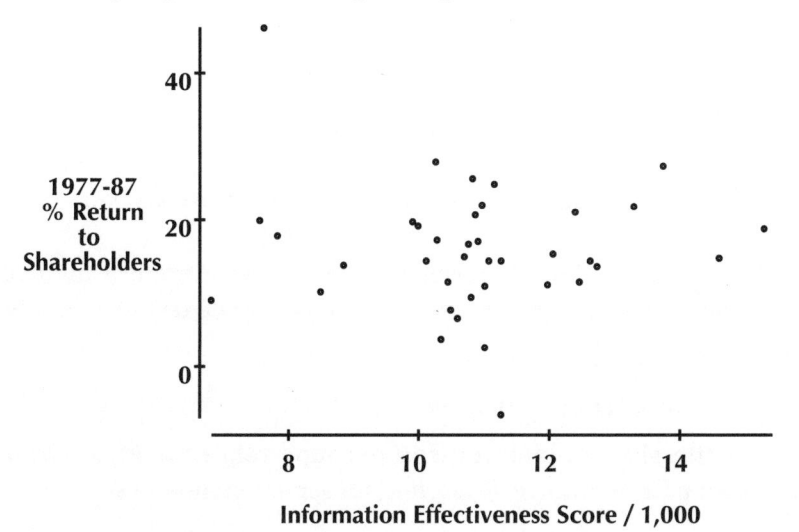

Figure 3.5: Service Company Profits vs. Effectiveness Scores

This comparison shows there is little correlation between the *Information Effectiveness Score* and ten-year *Shareholder Returns*. The correlation coefficient is mildly negative, which means that a lower *Information Effectiveness Score* tends to have higher *Shareholder Return*. This anomaly occurred because the best company (Wal-Mart) earned the third lowest *Effectiveness Score* rating.[22] Despite the experts' views of how to measure effectiveness in the service sector, the 1988 *Computerworld Effectiveness Score* could not identify effectiveness when compared with profitability. Therefore, it measures something other than effectiveness.[23]

Next, I tested whether the *Effectiveness Scores* among manufacturing companies were more conclusive. The correlation results were disappointing. They displayed the same random pattern as found for service industries:

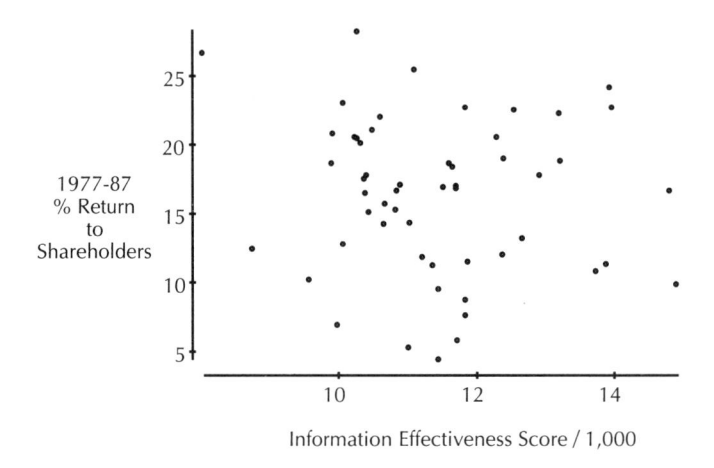

Figure 3.6: Manufacturing Company Profits vs. Effectiveness Scores

If the Information Effectiveness Score does not reflect financial performance, maybe the *Computerworld* data can be restated, in other terms, to give us better results.

THE % OF REVENUE INDICATOR

Do the shareholder returns perhaps relate to *Information Technology as a Percentage of Revenue*, for service companies?

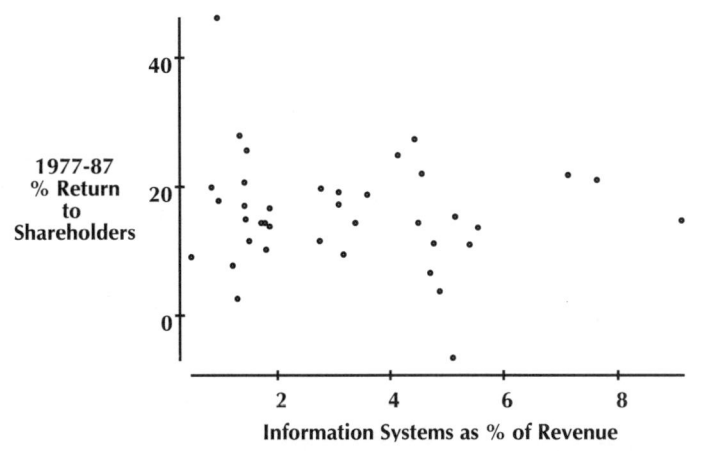

Figure 3.7: Service Company Profits vs. I.T. % of Revenue

The relationship of information systems spending (as a percentage of revenue) and profitability is random. There is no correlation between these two measures. The persistent use by consultants, vendors and M.I.S. executives of the revenue ratio as a comparative indicator thus loses credibility.[24] Why is that so?

The statistical technique[25] of correlation tests whether two or more variables are related. It helps to search for possible causes of observed consequences, although it cannot prove causation. I analyzed the *Computerworld* data from the services sector to seek hidden patterns.[26] There was only one set that corresponded to the *Effectiveness Score*. It was the information systems budget as a percentage of revenue, which we already had found to be of no value:[27]

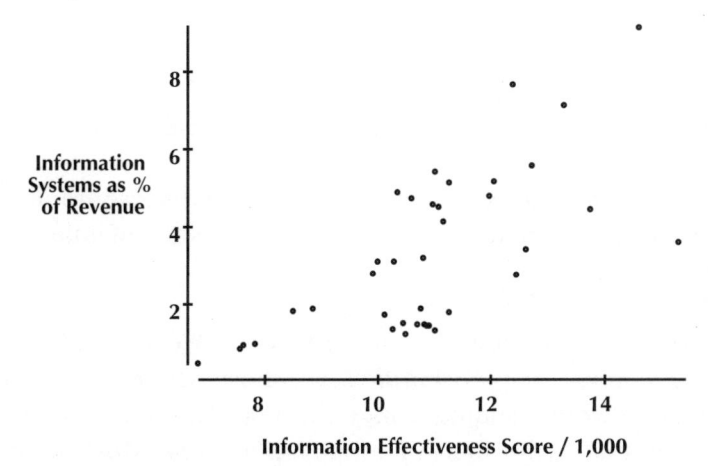

Figure 3.8: Information Effectiveness and I.T. as % of Revenue

44   THE BUSINESS VALUE OF COMPUTERS

The impressive sounding *Information Effectiveness Score* therefore delivers the revenue-based ratio in new clothing. The addition of the *Current Market Value of Installed Equipment* to the *Information Systems as Percentage of Revenue* ratio explains 78% of the reasons why a company comes up with its *Effectiveness* ranking. The other criteria in the *Score* contribute only random noise. The *Score* ranks spending, not effectiveness.

EXPENSE-PER-EMPLOYEE

The *Computerworld* tabulations are valuable because they provide data for testing other measures of information effectiveness. The leading candidate for a comparative indicator is the ratio of *Information Systems Budget-per-Employee.* We add another randomly scattered graph, signifying nothing, to our collection:

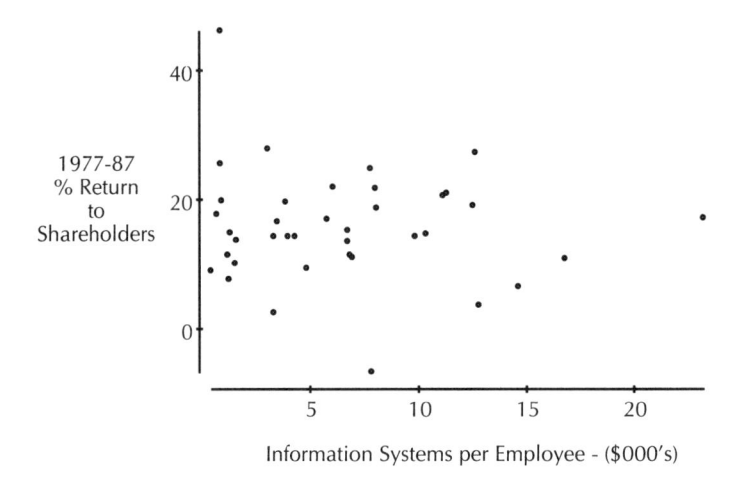

Figure 3.9: Information Systems Expense-per-Employee and Profits

Average *Information Technology Expense-per-Employee* are only randomly related to shareholder returns and therefore is also of little use.

EMPLOYEES-PER-WORKSTATION

One of the factors used in the *Effectiveness Score* computation is the count of *Employees-per-Workstation.* For those who believe that every information worker should work electronically, it must be disappointing to see that having more or fewer *Employees-per-Workstation* does not deliver superior financial results:[28]

CHAPTER 3—MAKING COMPARISONS   45

[Scatter plot: y-axis labeled "1977-87 % Return to Shareholders" ranging from 0 to 20; x-axis labeled "Employees per Installed Personal Computers, Terminals" ranging from 1 to 5.]

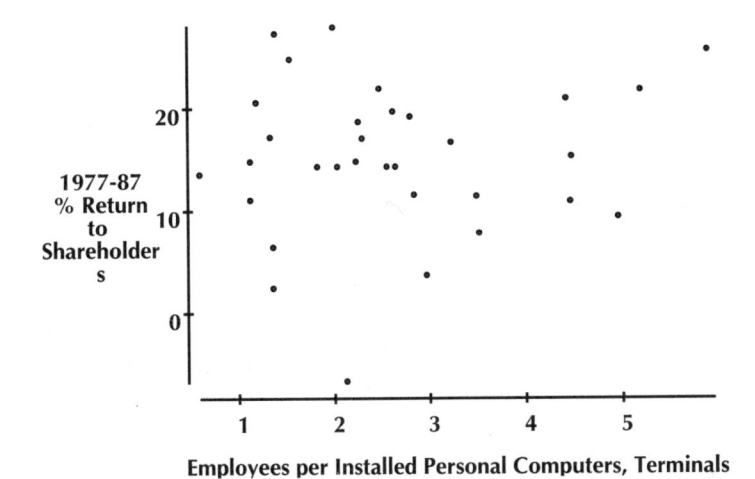

Figure 3.10: The Penetration of Personal Computers vs. Profits

EXPLANATIONS

The 1988 *Computerworld Effectiveness Score* rankings finish as a celebration of companies that allocate more cash to computers than companies that do not.[29] The *Effectiveness Score* does not uphold the view that obtaining superior profits, while spending less than anyone, is the correct meaning of the word "effectiveness." It has little to do with the business value of information technology or with profitable uses of computers. It assumes big spenders must be excellent because they would not be spending more money than others without getting better results. The *Score* rating scheme makes sense only if companies' revenues and information technology expenses directly reflect a company's profitability. We have shown that this is not the case.

The premise that the computer budget indicates *information effectiveness* is deceptive. The most profitable company in the services sample, Wal-Mart, received its bottom ranking. The *Computerworld* formula does not recognize that successful merchandisers incur only a small amount of value-added for each dollar of revenue.

The top *Computerworld Effectiveness Scores* went to utilities whose revenue comes primarily from their capital investments. The utilities' information activities are large relative to their total employment because their administrative and billing departments are more labor-intensive than their plant operations.

The *Computerworld* effectiveness formula also suffers because it assumes that it is possible to make valid comparisons of information technology spending across different industry sectors. As I found at Xerox, that assumption does not apply even within the same organization. The occupational profile of each company's workforce, the assets required for the production of revenue and the proportion of internal costs bought from outside suppliers differs greatly from firm to firm. You cannot assume similar needs for information technology among those firms that have comparable variables as were used in the formulation of the *Scores* ranking.

I plotted ratios for all service sector companies in the *Computerworld* listing to show that information systems ratios were as divergent as I found in other companies.

The wide range of these numbers, from less than 1% to just under 10%, suggests that computer spending follows something other than differences in individual effectiveness. If that were so, then it would be inconceivable that you could survive in the banking business by spending only one tenth of the ratio as compared with your competitors:

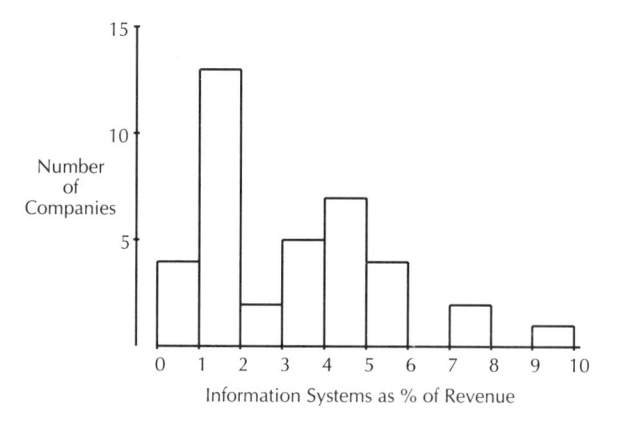

Figure 3.11: Information Systems Spending in the Services Sector

Before you can compare the information effectiveness of firms in different industries, you need to know much about their financial structure.

Other Measures of Effectiveness

Long-term financial results are the most reliable measure of company performance. One way of detecting the potential influence of information technology is to find whether firms with higher computer budgets show greater profitability than those who spend less. If profit *under-achievers* differ in their information technology spending habits from profit *over-achievers,* you may get a clue as to what could be a better measure of effectiveness.[30] To define the classes of *under-achievers* and *over-achievers* distinctly from *average* companies, I took the cumulative distribution of shareholder returns among service companies and identified the top and bottom 20%:

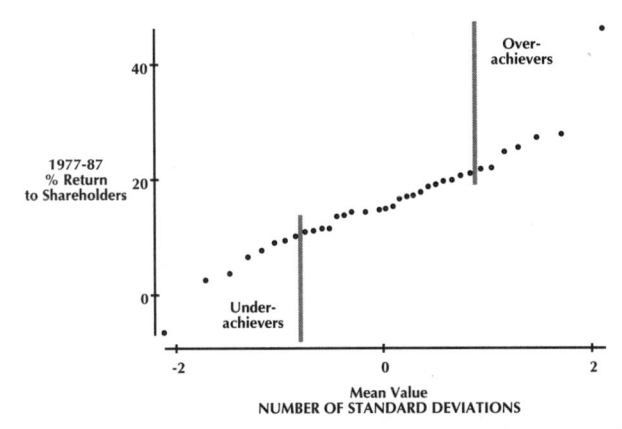

Figure 3.12: Classification of Service Firms According to Profitability

The above figure shows the distribution of investment returns[31] for service firms in the *Computerworld* sample. The mean values of factors contributing to the scoring method are as follows:

	Under-achievers	Average	Over-achievers
% Returns to Shareholders	5.2%	15.5%	27.0%
Systems budget, $ millions	$271	$261	$111
System Cost per employee	$5,801	$6,775	$6,300

Table 3.3: Information Technology and Mean Measures of Performance

Ironically, the above table shows that *over-achievers* have smaller budgets than anyone else.[32] Their *Systems Costs per-Employee* are below average. The *Systems Costs per-Employee,* for *over-achievers,* are 7% below those for *average* firms and only 9% higher than the expenses by *under-achievers*. These differences do not explain why the *over-achievers'* average shareholder returns are 300% greater than the *under-achievers'* and 175% greater than those of *average* firms.

Large computer expenses therefore are not an indication of favorable financial results.

48   THE BUSINESS VALUE OF COMPUTERS

Re-packaging Revenue-based Ratios

If the facts do not fit, change the calculations.[33]

In September 1989, *Computerworld* published an updated ranking of *The Premier 100 Most Effective Users of Information Systems*.[34] The publicity given to the top-ranked companies overshadowed the prior year's hoopla.[35]

The new *Information Effectiveness* scores ranged from 23,000 to 30,000. The rankings used a new scale that differed from the one used in the prior year. The rank order of the top-rated 25 firms in 1989 did not resemble the 1988 top 25. This does not suggest that a firm's *Information Effectiveness* could change dramatically within twelve months. The re-positioning of the firms' ranking resulted from calculating the 1989 ranking differently from the year before.

It appears that the *Computerworld* editors worried about the diversity of ratios. They decided to adjust the offending revenue ratios.[36] The ratios of companies in sectors consuming a greater share of revenue for computers, such as the 4% in banking, were adjusted by a fixed amount. Every industrial sector changed by a different amount to make their ratio resemble companies that expend less money, such as the 0.89% in metal products.[37]

Although this truncation made the revenue ratios look more alike, the scoring had to contend with different financial structures in each industry segment. *Computerworld* analysts added another refinement common to many subjective ranking schemes. The already truncated numbers were further adjusted to fit into another measuring scale.[38]

Except for the inconsistencies within the prior years' ratings, the 1989 nominations of the *Premier 100 Most Effective Users of Information Systems* reflect the same point of view as before: more is better. The *Computerworld* editors believe that if your information systems *Budget-to-Revenue* ratio is materially higher than everybody else's in your industry, you merit a higher *Effectiveness Score*. Higher levels of budget spending, higher ratios of your commitments to computer staffs, higher expenditures on training and education, higher market values of installed equipment, and a larger percentage of employees with terminals and personal computers will improve your ranking.

Statistically, the new version is an improvement. In 1988, it would have been impossible for a retailer, with typically lower spending ratios, to receive a top effectiveness score. The new truncation and rank-slotting scheme makes it possible for overspenders, regardless of industry, to claim a higher *Effectiveness Score*. If you torture any data enough you will get the exactly the results you want.

If the 1989 *Computerworld* ranking evens the chances of less computer-intensive industries to compete for the top effectiveness positions, are the new *Effectiveness Scores* any better than before? Here is the comparison with the latest ten-year average shareholder returns:[39]

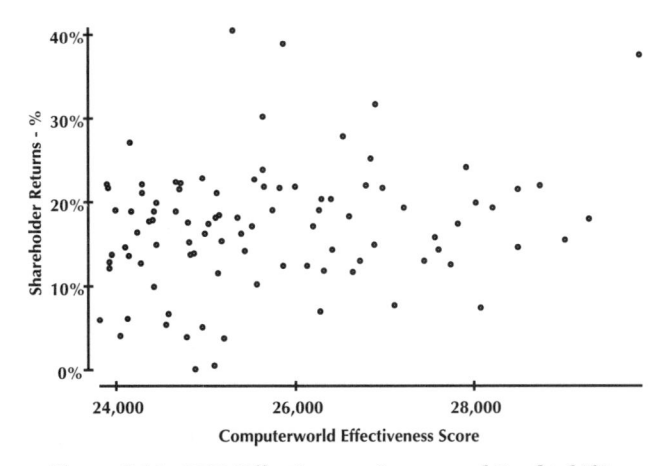

Figure 3.13: 1989 Effectiveness Scores and Profitability

We get another shotgun diagram which indicates there is no correlation of the revised *Effectiveness Scores* with *Shareholder Returns*, or with any other measure of profitability.[40]

THE BANKING CASES

Have the elaborate efforts to adjust data to fit industry averages improved the correlation between the *Effectiveness Score* and profitability?

Not surprisingly, the banking industry is over-represented among the top 100 *Computerworld* companies. In this sector, computers are the principal means of production.[41] Any cost census will report full costs of banking computers because of their high centralization. Banking automation is also the key to keeping operating costs competitive. Because of regulatory limits placed on banks, performance is more valid than in any other industry sector. It would be interesting to see if the *Effectiveness Score* rankings track the profitability of its top-rated banking firms:

50   THE BUSINESS VALUE OF COMPUTERS

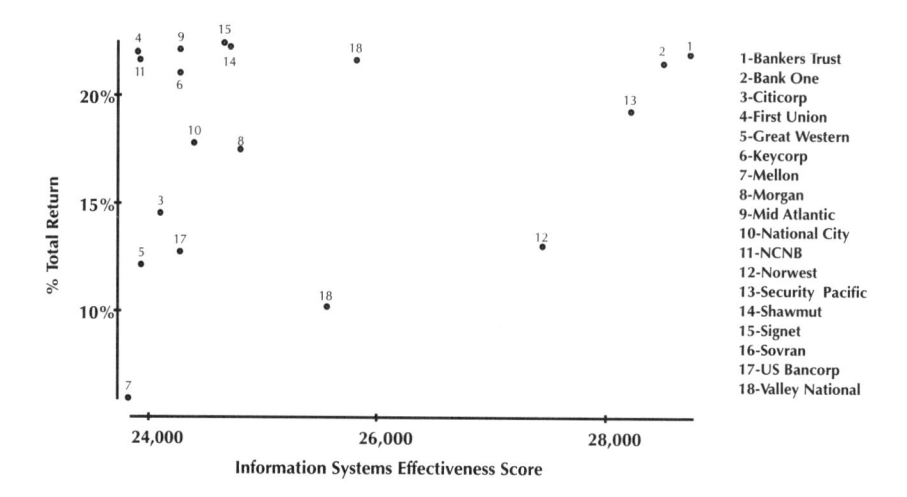

Figure 3.14: Profitability and Information Effectiveness in Banking

The above diagram is again a disappointment. The bank with the #1 ranked *Effectiveness Score* (Bankers Trust) does not show noticeably higher shareholder returns than banks ranked #11, #14 and #15 out of a total of 18 banks.

There is only one strong statistical relationship. If you assign points based on the extent to which a firm exceeds the industry average, you get a good statistical fit. I can now predict (with reasonable accuracy) the *Computerworld Effectiveness Score* for a major bank based simply on its revenue ratio, its employment and its number of personal computers.[42] Almost all of your *Score* comes from spending more money on computers per dollar of revenue, than your industry peers and whether you install more personal computers.[43]

RANKING EXCELLENCE

If you can rate others people will assume that you are an expert.

Since 1985, *InformationWeek* magazine has featured special annual issues devoted to the 100 largest users of information technology. In 1989, the magazine editors decided to tackle a more ambitious task. They would list the 100 *best* users of information technology in the U.S. *InformationWeek* had the difficult job of how to identify the

"...elusive but all-important quantitative approach to determining the measure of information technology effectiveness."[44]

I found the *InformationWeek* attempts an advancement over any prior rating efforts. The 1989 special issue is a source of new data about corporate spending on information technology.[45] It places into a proper focus the debate about the value of information technology because it concentrates on financial results. It introduces the *Profit-per-Information Technology Expense* as the indicator for judging the importance of computers.

The tabulation of the ratio of *Profit-per-Information Technology Expense* shows that the costs of computer systems are comparable[46] to profits for half of the top-rated companies:

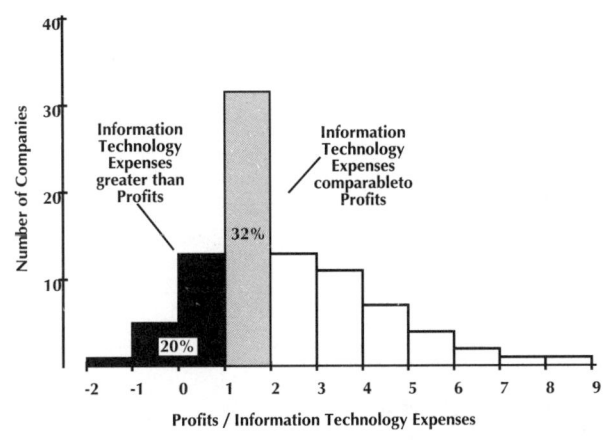

Figure 3.15: Distribution of Companies by Profit/I.T. Expense Ratio

The editors of *InformationWeek* and their principal researcher[47] came up with a simple number that reflects how well a corporation uses information technology. Their method for ranking the "best" was supported by valid arguments of how to define excellence in the use of information technology:[48]

- "... Ranking that is based on *Profit-per-Employee* places all companies on an equal footing for comparison."
- A ranking ratio based on profits "...underscores the intended purpose of the technology, which is to build a more effective corporation."
- Ranking ratios based on employees "...serves as an aid to identify corporate resources, people first and foremost."

- The management of information technology resources "...is inextricably intertwined with overall performance."

These principles define a refreshingly innovative agenda for judging the value of information technologies. When M.I.S. chiefs were asked what they thought about the *Profit-per-Employee* measure, the magazine editors heard much agreement with the idea that information technology should be judged by how it helps a company to do better, as defined by profits.

How well do these ideas hold up?

In the *InformationWeek* approach, *Profit-per-Employee* is the measure of the *Output* of information technology. It follows that *Information Technology Expense-per-Employee* is the measure of *Input*. There is a simple test to find whether *Output* and *Input* are related. If that relationship holds, we have proved that information technology generates productivity, because the ratio of *Output/Input* is a restatement of the meaning of "productivity."

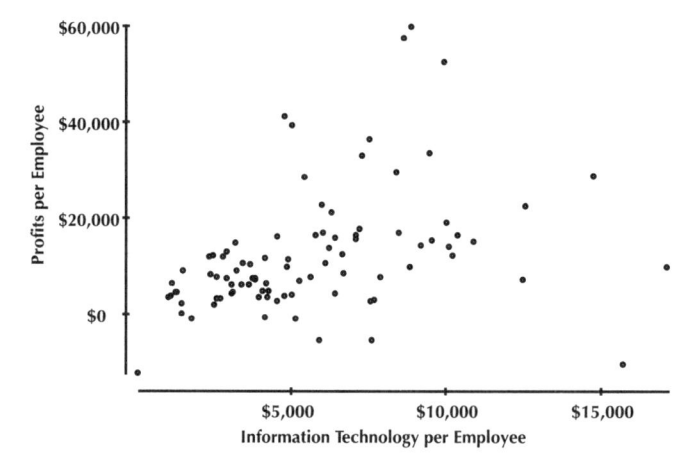

Figure 3.16: Excellence Rating and I.T. Spending

When plotting *Profit-per-Employee* vs. *Information Technology Expense-per-Employee*, the pattern you get is not completely random. The graph shows a small positive trend for companies with *Information Technology Expense-per-Employee* below $7,000 per year. For *Information Technology Expense-per-Employee* over $7,000, the *Profits-per-Employee* are either random or negative. Notice there are a few heavy spenders on computers who are losing money. The total picture is one of inadequate correlation between information technology spending and *Profit-per-Employee*.

Although the *Profit-per-Employee* is not an adequate predictor of the influence of information technology, it is superior to other measurement attempts. Its shortcomings come from the following:

- Employment headcount is a poor predictor of the profitability of a firm. For example, oil companies incorporate huge amounts of purchased raw materials into their output. Their employment will be always lower than employment in manufacturing establishments with similar profits. This is why the *InformationWeek* ranking favored petroleum companies over manufacturing and certainly service companies.
- Reported profits are the result of not only the effort of labor but also from the contributions of capital assets. Depending upon the industry, companies use widely ranging amounts of capital to gain similar revenues. The role of capital must be recognized before you attribute all the profits to employees, which is what *InformationWeek* used as their measure. This is why the top *InformationWeek* ratings went to a few communications companies. These firms have relatively low levels of employment and very high capital needs.

CHAPTER SUMMARY

Despite the occasional bias, stretched logic and omission by the researchers behind *ISIS, Computerworld* and *InformationWeek*[49] their evaluations stimulate a better understanding of the economics of computers. The readers of published rankings get conflicting and inconclusive valuation schemes. Such rankings raise more questions than they answer, which is the essential beginning to all learning.

The efforts discussed in this chapter are positive contributions to a better understanding of information technologies. They provide full disclosure of what they are trying to accomplish. They disclose previously private data. Study of the *ISIS, Computerworld* and *InformationWeek* methods is useful because it tells us how little we know about measuring the value of information technologies, regardless of any measure of excellence. They confirm that existing measures for evaluating the effectiveness of information technology are inadequate. The question is not if the best available measures today are any good, but whether we can do even better.

Computerworld and *InformationWeek* confirm the observation first published in 1985 that there's no simple correlation between the money spent on computers and a company's financial results.[50] Correlations do not show up because information technology is not an independent variable. It is an arbitrary percentage of a company's revenues used to purchase what's affordable. Computers are not a direct cause of profitability, but a contributor. They may be an essential but surely not a sufficient ingredient of success.

What then differentiates between superior and inferior results in the use of information technology? Factors such as overhead, market share, pricing, taxation, capital intensity and overhead costs are far more decisive. The influences of computers on organizational behavior and financial performance involve more aspects of a firm's well-being than any other technology, but that effect is indirect and subtle.

Opinions or simple profit ratios comprised of only a few variables do not yield useful insights into how to manage information technology resources for greater profitability. Financial analysts' attempts to evaluate and control computer expenditures by means of a few simple ratios can not succeed.

CHAPTER 3 COMMENTS

[1] Computers can be manipulated to give the appearance of control while the business is in total disarray.

[2] This idea found its flowering in the writings of cyberneticians working for centrally planned economies. As the economic performance stagnated, these theoreticians proposed computer networks as the solution for salvaging an unworkable economic system. Real-time computer terminals, credit cards and the elimination of all cash transactions would allow perfect control of prices, supply and demand at the retail level. Although the cyberneticians of the 1960's and 1970's failed, their ideas stay dormant and ready to germinate whenever political conditions would favor a planned economy again.

[3] During my 30 years in corporate America, I have never seen or heard a justification of the size of the financial staff. The full costs of financial controls are unknown and never compared. As much as half of all overhead staff hours are for taking care of control-originated demands, which include budgeting, financial planning and responses to financial reports.

[4] In 1969 finance and accounting personnel, accounting for perhaps 5% of total employment, owned 80% of the computer budget in Xerox. The service department, with close to 40% of employees, received only 3% of the computer budget.

[5] 40.7% of chief information executives in industrial corporations still report to the Finance function and another 15.2% report to the Administration function (see E.K. Brumm, Chief Information Officers in Service and Industrial Organizations,

CHAPTER 3—MAKING COMPARISONS   55

Information Management Review, 1990, Number 3, Table 3). Out of a sample of 111 firms, which includes service companies, only 50% of information systems functions were an "independent function."

6 How you measure and evaluate a subject is the clearest way of expressing what you think about it. If the M.I.S. function is evaluated as a factory (and some M.I.S. groups aspire to nothing more than that) M.I.S. will assume the identity and the ambitions of high-technology factory management. On the other hand, if you assume the title of CIO (Chief Information Officer, which is eponymous with the more exalted titles of Chief Financial Officer, Chief Operating Officer and Chief Executive Officer) you are really saying that you are trying to be evaluated like those who occupy the executive suite. That means escape from cost justification because you are now "strategic." Though an exceptional individual, supported by a small staff, can aspire to the coveted Chief Officer status, that is not a defensible position into which to place the entire M.I.S. function. If M.I.S. costs account for 5–30% of the total labor value-added, they are an important, sophisticated and expensive factory, but not much more. The CIO who tries to model the economics and the privileges of his function to imitate the CFO's operations cannot succeed. Finance is and will remain in the circle of top management. There are only a few M.I.S. functions, such as policy, planning and architecture, that can be construed as an extension of top executive powers.

7 Financial data about 38 food companies obtained from C.N. Athanasopoulos, Corporate Productivity Atlas, *Delphi Research Center,* Lincoln, Mass.

8 From associates in the food industry.

9 D. Vincent explains the lagging profits of BankAmerica by pointing out that its IT *Expense-per-Employee* trailed Wells Fargo and Citibank by 40%. (D.Vincent, The Information Based Corporation, *Dow Jones-Irwin,* 1990). Figure 3.4 shows that such a selective comparison is not conclusive.

10 The following table illustrates how a changing mix of principal cost elements will influence the ratio of information systems as a percentage of revenues:

	Year 1	Year 2	Year 3	Year 4
Revenue	100.0%	108.0%	116.6%	126.0%
Materials	50.0%	56.5%	63.8%	71.4%
Direct Labor	30.0%	28.5%	27.1%	25.7%
Overhead	20.0%	23.0%	25.8%	28.8%
Information Systems	2.00%	2.32%	2.58%	2.89%

When industry opinion leaders report that "breakaway companies spend more on information technology as a percentage of their sales" (R. Nolan, Breakaway Strategies for Investing in Information Technology, Nolan Norton and Company Symposium, Innisbrook, January 1987) they may be tracking the ratios of companies breaking up their production capacity.

An interesting insight into the tendencies of increasing overhead costs and reducing direct payroll comes from the 1986 Profit Sharing Survey by Hewitt Associates. Contributions to employee profit-sharing funds are based on a specific percentage of total profits. Since foreign workers do not share in profits, the remaining employees receive a larger share of profits when a company reduces manufacturing employment.

11 ($2 for information systems)/($20 + $30 for overhead and direct labor).
12 ($2.89 for information systems)/($28.85+$25.72 for overhead and direct labor).
13 ($28.85 for overhead+ $25.72 for direct labor in year 4) minus ($20 for overhead+ $30 for direct labor in year 1) divided by ($20 for overhead+ $30 for direct labor in year 1).
14 From a two-page advertisement in *The Wall Street Journal* of January 29, 1988. Similar advertisements appeared elsewhere. This campaign announced the launching of the ISIS Program (Information Systems Investment Strategies). By the end of 1989, more than 8,000 IBM marketing people knew how to use this technique. Thousands of IBM customers have been coached in how to apply ISIS. ISIS had been over five years in development and employs a large full time staff supported by an impressive array of outside consulting help.

[15] From 1974 to 1984 the outlays for information technology grew at an annual rate of 15%. Since 1984, the current dollar spending has risen only 6% per annum (Has High-Tech America Passed its High-Water Mark? *Business Week*, February 5, 1990, p. 18). As late as 1987 (D. Ludlum, The Information Budget, *Computerworld*, January 5, 1987) the firm of Nolan, Norton and Company predicted the average growth rate for information technology expenses to be at least 20% until year 2000. It is unlikely there will be average growth rates greater than 10% per annum except for cyclical perturbations balanced by periods of lower growth.

[16] Such as the consultant-imitated BSP (Business Systems Planning) and EPDP (Executive Planning of Data Processing) methodologies.

[17] To be discussed in greater detail in Chapter 15.

[18] IBM Advanced Business Institute, I/S Investment Strategies: Making a Difference on the Bottom Line, IBM Corporation, 1988, Publication G520-6497.

[19] The service sector organizations include:

Utilities: GTE Corporation, Northeast Utilities, Texas Utilities, Middle South, Pacific Gas, Southern Company, MCI, Duke Power, Contel.

Insurance and Financial Services: Travelers Corporation, American Express, Primerica, Salomon, American International.

Other Services: McGraw Hill, CBS, Time, American Airlines, Dun & Bradstreet, Capital Cities.

Banking: Banc One Corporation, Norwest Banking, BankAmerica, Corestates Financial, Citicorp, First Union, First Chicago, Manufacturers Hanover, First Wachovia.

Retailers: J.C. Penney, Sears Roebuck, Carter Hawley, Dayton Hudson, Federated Stores, May Department, Wal-mart, Kroger, K-mart.

[20] For example, the subjective project priority and investment payoff rating, with arbitrary weights, is the core of ISIS. It originates from Marilyn M. Parker and Robert J. Benson, Information Economics—Linking Business Performance to Information Technology, *Prentice Hall*, 1988.

[21] There are many indicators of company profitability. I prefer using the *Fortune* magazine annual compilation of industry results which includes figures for the ten-year average percentage return to shareholders. The long-term average offers the most realistic view of the systemic effect computers may have on company profitability. The long development lead-times for strategic applications dictate taking a long-term view of profitability to detect their effects. Shareholder returns, rather than accounting profits, also reflect the reliability of earnings and the consistency of revenue growth as indicators of a firm's strategic advantage.

[22] The Wal-Mart merchandising organization has the reputation of being effective users of information technology (see E. Booker, IS Trailblazing Puts Retailer on Top, *Computerworld*, February 12, 1990, p. 69). The effectiveness formula commits Wal-Mart to their bottom ranking because Wal-Mart does not spend much money on computers as compared with its revenues.

[23] Additional correlation studies to find whether there is a statistically valid application of the *Effectiveness Score* in a more restricted segment, such as in banking. Nothing was found.

[24] The 62 manufacturing firms in the sample also exhibited the same lack of correlation.

[25] Regression and correlation analysis.

[26] Odesta Corporation's *DataDesk* software. It is analytic software, with extensive graphic output, for finding if masses of apparently unrelated data hide any discernible patterns.

[27] Not surprisingly there is some correlation ($R^2=0.43$), especially for the lower values, because of the heavy weighting of the percentage of revenue factor in the effectiveness-scoring formula. That does not work for the top "winners," where the relationship is again random and inconclusive.

[28] To avoid cluttered graphs, we are displaying only the 38 service companies from the 1988 ratings. The 62 manufacturing companies and all the 1989 indicators are equally inconclusive.

CHAPTER 3—MAKING COMPARISONS 57

29 This critique was published in P.A. Strassmann, Financial Earnings Don't Measure Up to I/S Payoff in Services Sector, *Chief Information Officer Journal*, Vol. 1, No. 3, 1989.
30 This approach is the standard technique for testing the effectiveness of pharmaceuticals. Drugs are administered to subjects in varying doses. Finding out which subjects thrive and which do not allow pharmaceutical companies to make valid claims about the value of a particular drug.
31 As reported in the Directory of the Largest U.S. Non-Industrial Corporations, *Fortune*, June 6, 1988. The total return to the investors includes both price appreciation and dividend yield in the company's stock. The ten-year figures are compound annual averages.
32 Over-achievers are smaller companies with smaller budgets. The presumed economics of large computer installations do not seem to make any difference.
33 That's the art of "...patching up a program..." It is deeply ingrained in the computer software community as the preferred way of fixing faults without addressing a possibly faulty design. The art of patching is held in high esteem among computer professionals in trouble while they are trying to meet a deadline and salvage the software already in place.
34 The editorial for this special issue notes that "...we rank the most effective I.S. users not by how much they spend but by how they rate according to six carefully picked and researched criteria."
35 Including a celebrity-attending prize-winning dinner.
36 "Find your company's industry below and subtract the industry average percentage of estimated M.I.S. budget as a percentage of corporate revenues. Subtractions: For Aerospace, 1.38%; for Automotive, 2.28%; for Banking 4.4%; for Building materials, 1.2%; for Chemical 1.46%; for Consumer products, 1.15%; for Diversified financial services, 3.42%; for Diversified services, 2.24%; for Electronics, 2.14%; for Food and beverages, 0.97%; for Forest products, 1.2%; for Industrial & Farm Equipment, 2.24%; for Life insurance, 2.52%; for Metal products, 0.89%; for Petroleum and Mining, 0.68%; for Pharmaceuticals 1.2%; for Publishing & Printing, 2.14%; for Retailing, 1%; for Rubber Products, 1.2%; for Scientific and photographic equipment, 1.96%; for Textiles and Apparel, 1.2%; for Tobacco 0.97%; for Transportation 4% and for Utilities 1.3%."
37 This technique has an early precedent in the ancient Greek story about the inn-keeper, Procrustes, who shortened his guests' legs with a hatchet if their limbs were too long for his average beds.
38 If you subtract the industry average from your actual *M.I.S. Budget-to-Revenue* ratio, you add the following points to your *Effectiveness Score*: For -3.0 you get 110 points; for -3.0 to -2.0 you get 120 points; for -2.0 to -1.0 you get 130 points; for -1.0 to -0.84 you get 165 points, for -0.84 to -0.64 you get 175 points. At the other extreme, if your actual *M.I.S. Budget-to-Revenue* ratio exceeds your industry's average by more than 6%—an incredible yet possible number—you will get 320 points added to your effectiveness score. Why a 1.5% favorable variance, as compared with your industry's average, rates only 130 points and an unfavorable variance gives you 320 points is unclear.
39 Using the 1989 edition of *Fortune* magazine 500 Service and 500 Industrial companies. Our database includes, besides the ten-year average shareholder returns, information about revenues, assets and employees for each of the *Computerworld* top 100.
40 I tested for correlation with *Return-on-Assets, Return-on-Shareholder Equity, Earnings-per-Share* and *Earnings-per-Share Growth*.
41 The Midland Bank in London has a $650 million M.I.S. budget representing 16% of the bank's total operating budget for 1990.(R.Carlyle, Getting a Grip on Costs, *Datamation*, July 15, 1990).
42 Effectiveness Score = 19,663+ 1,076*(I.T./Revenue) + 10*[(# of PC's) /Employee]. Similar equations apply to other industries, with only minor changes in the coefficients.
43 This point of view is consistent for a computer vendor or a recipient of large advertising revenues from computer vendors.

44 Editors, *InformationWeek*, September 18, 1989. Special issue, 136 pages.
45 Such as information technology spending, *Profit-per*-dollar spent on information technology, *Information Technology-per-Employee* and the count of information technology-personnel.
46 This comparison suggests one possible way of getting more attention from top executives on matters related to systems management.
47 Professor E. A. McLean of the Georgia State University.
48 The editors of *InformationWeek* rejected what they called "...strange arithmetic formulae that examine a string of unrelated elements, from a corporation's total number of PC's to the percentage of revenue it spends on information technology."
49 Consulting reports that try similar evaluations are too numerous to mention. It is noteworthy that a newsletter dedicated to information technology financial and budgeting matters (the *DP Budget* Monthly) consistently uses the percentage of Corporate Revenues as a budget indicator. Its 1989 year-end issue projects average information systems and telecommunications spending for U.S. companies to rise from 4.3% of revenues in 1989 to 8.68% of revenues by 1995. 4.3% of revenue for a manufacturing assembly company would bankrupt it, whereas 8.68% would not support essential transaction-processing in a retail bank.

The rise of information systems spending from 4.3% to 8.68% of revenue implies 18–22% per year budget increases for US companies. Without high inflation, such a forecast would make sense only if you foresee a sharp reversal in the average 11% expense growth since 1980, a scenario unsupported by any current industry forecasts. Budget projections based on average percentage extrapolations are more understandable if also examined in dollar terms.
50 In my book Information Payoff, *Free Press,* New York, 1985. Similar conclusions seem to apply to other favored endeavors. Of 65 studies about instructional costs per student and scholastic achievement, 75% found no effect and 5% found a negative relationship (J. Hood, Education: Money Isn't Everything, *Wall Street Journal*, February 9, 1990, p. A10).

4

TOWARDS EXPERIMENTATION

You see only what your brain recognizes. Data make sense only if you have a good theory.

There are good reasons why there is a random relationship between information technology and various financial measures. The researchers could extract only limited amounts of information because their analytic tools did not encompass the complex nature of the relationship involved in the application of information technology.

I considered two possibilities after reviewing publications concerning this subject:

- The lack of correlation between information technology expenses and profitability could originate from the choice of unrelated measures. Pre-Newtonian experiments could not predict the motion of a pendulum because nobody thought about the concepts of mass and acceleration.
- The effect of information technology on profitability could be too subtle for detection by simple means. Medieval medicine

could not explain the causes of the Black Death plague because they did not have the means to detect bacteria.

I had to devise new ways of measuring the effects of information technology. I needed to find, through experimentation, where and how computers coexist with improved productivity.

ABANDONING REVENUE RATIOS

It's harder to hit a moving target from a moving position.

Accounting practices that calculate the *Value-added* of a company offer a more stable platform for analyzing the benefits of computers than revenue-based ratios.[1] A company uses management systems to take care of its employees' information needs. When that company purchases materials, parts and energy from suppliers, the purchase price already includes payment for the supplier's own information systems. There is no reason to add the supplier's output into the evaluation of the company's own information technologies. Therefore, revenue is not a relevant measure of the extent of a firm's economic activity. In the remainder of this book all my evaluations are based on ratios of *Value-added*, defined as:

Value-added = **Revenue − Purchases**

The above simple equation means that the proper measure of the scope of an organization is only what's left after the suppliers are paid. For example, *Value-added* would include the cost a firm's purchasing department or the costs of the advertising department that makes media purchases. Well managed purchasing or advertising departments will operate on a relatively low budget, will be able to purchase outside products and services at an advantageous price and will make decisions that will improve the capacity of a firm to earn additional *Revenue*. Most importantly, effective purchasing will lower the cost of doing business without an unfavorable effect on *Revenue*. Since purchases of goods and services are the single largest expense, our measures of productivity will have to capture this important influence. Counting only *Revenue* will give the mistaken appearance of greater importance than conditions warrant. To justify larger budgets managers always prefer to inflate the importance of their activities. *Value-added* measures will always deflate these claims.

In the early 1980's it was difficult to test the utility of *Value-added* ratios as compared with *Revenue* ratios. I only had information about U.S. information technology spending and no data about purchases. The published accounting reports of U.S. companies do not show purchases as a separate item. The available reports incorporate bought items in the *Cost-of-goods sold,* without separating them from other costs. Component purchases disappear into standard manufacturing unit costs, and then pass from one cost center to another as *direct cost.* Professional services, advertising expenses and contract programming costs can end in accounts that classify the costs, but not their sources. Divisional and departmental operating statements do not identify what is subcontracted out.

At this time, another researcher[2] had just published a large collection of financial data about U.S. corporations. This information included data about payrolls, taxes, depreciation and profits.[3] From this data it was possible to estimate business *Value-added* for 143 major corporations.[4] The data supplied a clear insight into how the cost structures of companies, in diverse industrial sectors,[5] changed from 1972 through 1975, and from 1980 through 1982. To illustrate these findings, I shall use only the latest data for major food companies.[6]

Purchases are the Largest Cost Item

The distribution of average costs helps to understand why *Value-added* instead of *Revenue* reveals the true scope of a company's activities:

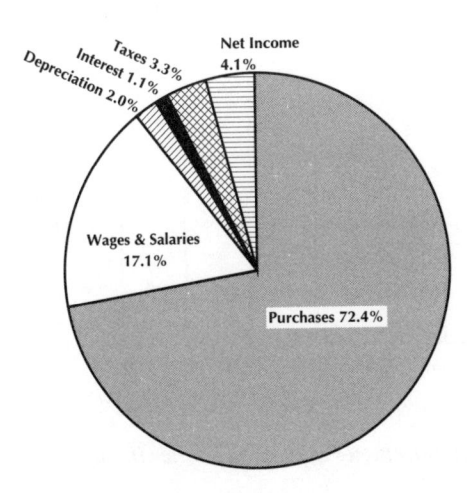

Figure 4.1: The Composition of Food Companies' Revenues

External purchases of raw materials and advertising services dominate the disposition of reported *Revenue*.[7] The information processing costs for accounting, billing, scheduling, dispatching and controlling the supplier's own deliveries is already in the purchase price. Therefore, a realistic understanding of a firm's information-handling expenses would concentrate on those functions that support the 27.6% portion of the *Revenue*, the *Business Value-added*, that remains after purchases.[8]

Similarly, when judging the size of a firm's information technology staff, you must exclude the costs of external purchases of information technology. For example, if the company is outsourcing most of its data processing, software maintenance and telecommunications services, then the budget for managing the remaining MIS personnel should be measured against its *Value-added* and not against the total size of a firm's information technology expense.

Purchases Vary Depending on Vertical Integration

Each food company's buying patterns is different. Firms that produce highly processed, packaged food will employ more labor and make smaller purchases than firms that sell basic commodities, such as flour or salt. The ratio of purchases to *Revenue* range widely around the industry average:

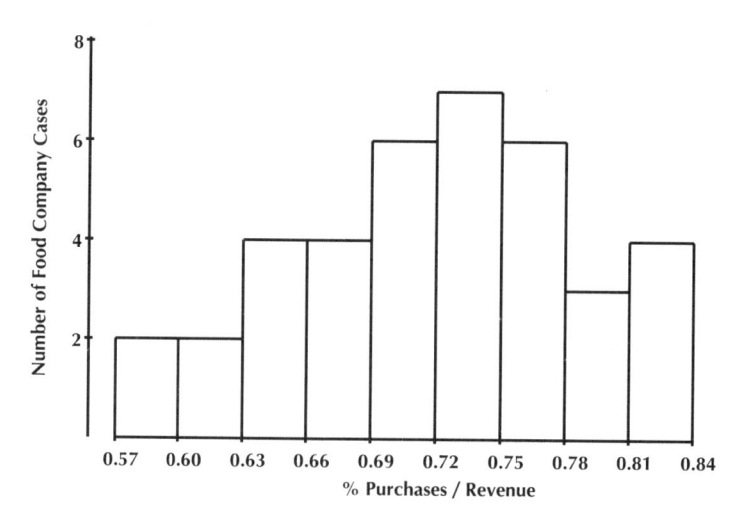

Figure 4.2: Purchases as % of Revenues in Food Companies

A company's needed amount of computing power will differ depending on a firm's *Business Value-added*.[9] If the management information systems need to cover only 16% of *Revenue*, for the same type of business, you probably will need to spend less on computers than if you manage 43% of *Revenue*.

I constructed similar bar charts for other industrial sectors. In each case the purchases of the companies in the sample, as a percentage of *Revenue*, varied widely from the average of their respective sectors. An industry's average purchase-to-revenue ratio lacked meaning. Each firm seemed to follow a different approach as to how much vertical integration it could afford in order to produce its unique product mix.

Tradeoff Between Labor and Capital Spending

Most of the justification of management information systems comes from substituting capital for labor. If labor costs are high, the purchase of more computers becomes attractive. In the food industry, the average wages and salaries per employee vary from $9,000 per year for seasonal agricultural labor, to $39,000 per year for skilled labor with large fringe benefits.[10] Non-unionized companies that ship agricultural products pay lower wages than highly unionized meatpackers.

The rationale for information technology spending would differ for companies at either end of the pay range. If a firm has automated processing plants, the compensation levels may not be as critical a consideration as the total number of employees. For example, your high-wage and fully automated plant will use very few workers if you produce cooking oil. The labor costs will be comparable to those of a petroleum refinery.

High labor intensity will always demand more information technology. Therefore, it will make a difference if you are making margarine or preparing individually packaged beef stew dinners.

Production and Distribution Determine Assets

Owning more assets always calls for more information. Inventories must be managed. Machines must be maintained. The acquisition of property and of equipment requires engineers, accountants and lawyers. It matters whether you need 90¢ of assets to produce a dollar of *Revenue* or if you can manage to do that for only 22¢:

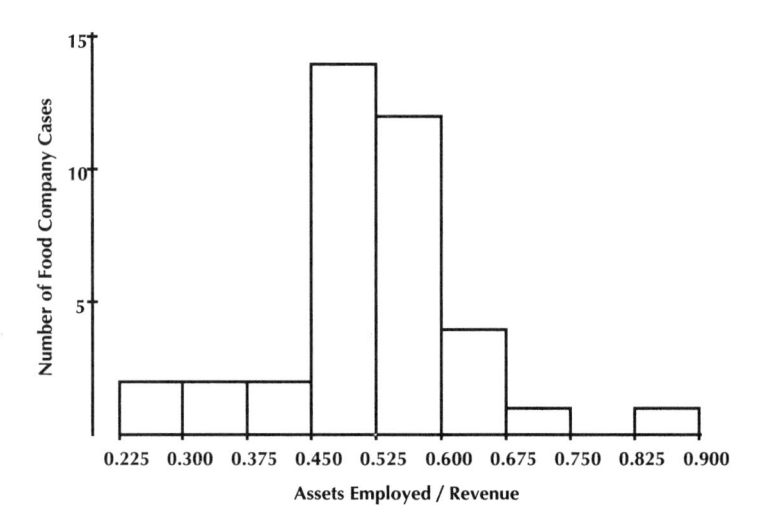

Figure 4.3: Distribution of Food Companies by Assets

If you are capital-intensive, you will need to manage more information and therefore, you can justify buying more computers. For this reason the concept of *Value-added* must include not only elements that show up on the profit & loss statement, but must also provide an allowance for what is found on the balance sheet.

The Dominance of Overhead Costs

A survey of 350 U.S. manufacturing companies gives us a good insight into manufacturing overhead costs.[11] The survey collected product costs broken down into materials, direct labor and overhead categories. Materials are external purchases. Therefore, the ratio of overhead to direct labor expenses indicates the relative importance of internal managerial costs. This ratio could provide an insight into how much computing is necessary.

The average distribution of costs found for manufacturing companies was 53% for materials purchases, 15% for direct labor and 32% for management overhead. This gives a management/operations ratio of 213%, consistent with what I have found in later research.[12]

When searching to improve efficiency, large overhead deserves more attention than direct costs. You cannot expect to realize productivity improvements by squeezing only direct costs. Overhead represents the largest share of a company's discretionary expenses. You can always manage to ship goods and deliver services for several days without the President, the accountants, the personnel staff, market researchers, planners, supervisors and coordinators. Overhead reduction offers superior opportunities for productivity gains. Overhead people handle information, not physical goods. Computers are the choice tool for aiding each information worker to do a better job.

Overhead people dictate the buying of the right materials. Overhead staff plan, engineer, schedule, dispatch, invoice, collect, account and control. They hire, train, encourage, coordinate and guide. Overhead provides the funds for the most important source of productivity: competent management. In examining the need for computers, we therefore must isolate overhead costs from other financial aspects.

TESTING RETURN-ON-EQUITY

Profitability has many definitions.
To measure it you must pick one.

Before proceeding further with my explorations I had to adopt a measure of profitability. The most frequently used indicator is *Return-on-Assets (ROA)*. This is a troublesome measure because company debt, depreciation policies and tax accounting can make this ratio vary depending on the accountants' choice of valuation methods. I also rejected *Return-on-Investment (ROI)* because high inflation rates make this number look too favorable if the investment is on the balance sheet at acquisition cost. I disregarded the possibility of using *Return-on-Sales (ROS)* because it uses the misleading *Revenue* number instead of the more applicable *Value-added*.

This left *Return-on-Equity (ROE)*. I find that ROE is more reliably consistent than any other published measure of profit. It also relates to shareholders' interests. Even though *ROE* is the best among the indicators common to corporate financial reports, it suffers from several defects.[13] As a result, I had to extract from the ROE a better measure of profitability. Any new measure would have to:

- Relate directly to the shareholder's *Return-on-Equity*;
- Remove the effect of external purchases on measuring the productivity of a firm;

- Recognize that shareholders need compensation for equity financing. Subtracting only the cost of debt from the financial statement does not give a complete picture of the performance of a firm;[14]
- Adjust for differences in currency, inflation, capital structure and labor uses.

RESTATING ACCOUNTING INFORMATION

In a rapid river you must swim upstream to get across.

In previous chapters, we found that graphs of individual revenue ratios show shot-gun patterns when plotted against profitability. We have seen also that the scatter of points stems from the inherent diversity of the data.

If ratios using two variables are deceptive, could a combination of several ratios using many variables be less misleading? Is it possible that the effects of an unusually high ratio would offset the influence of a low ratio?

I decided to test the idea that profits, and ultimately the effects of information technology on profitability, arise from multiple compensating factors. I applied multivariate analysis to the *Value-added* and its associated financial measures. The results were gratifying. Three variables[15] were sufficient to explain 72.5% of the actual values of *Return-on-Equity*, despite the great diversity in the food industry:

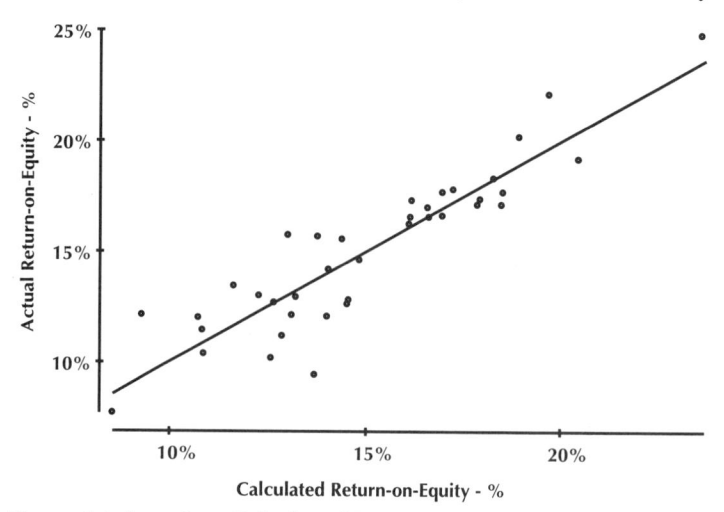

Figure 4.4: Actual vs. Calculated Return-on-Equity in Food Industry

Next, I incorporated data about food industry computer budgets. Multiple regression illuminated why some budgets were larger than others. High levels of vertical integration, high capital intensity and high labor content correlated favorably with information technology budgets. The answer for which I was searching, the correlation of computer budgets with profits, did not show up.[16]

As a result of this exploration, I decided to study the relationship between *information technology spending* and *profitability* through multi-factor techniques and not by means of any single ratio. The effects of information technology had to compete with too many other financial influences.

My research would be anchored in published financial data. A Chief Executive would find it unconvincing if I showed a favorable effect and could not relate it to published accounting reports. Unfortunately, conventional financial reports do not show *Business Value-added*. Standard accounting data would, therefore, require adjustment to come up with such information.

The equations that fit the *Return-on-Equity* also contain another term, *Equity Costs*. This does not appear on financial statements and it would be necessary to calculate it. In conventional financial reporting the costs of depreciation and interest payments are subtracted from *Revenue*. If a firm had little debt, its reported *profit-after-taxes* would not reflect the large equity costs that are backing its productive capacities. Standard accounting data therefore would have to include the costs of the capital supplied by shareholders. A new way of looking at a financial statement would be to sort out the critical components of profitability, as follows:

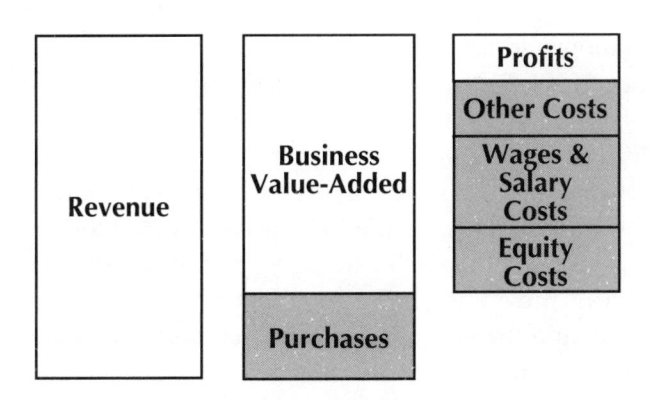

Figure 4.5: Restating Accounting Information

Conventional financial statements made it difficult to research the effects of computers. Therefore, it was necessary to obtain accounting information for analyzing financial data in ways not possible before.

The PIMS Method

*If every person is unique, how do you find
what people have in common?*

We had found close correspondence between *Return-on-Equity* and a composite of three ratios:
- *Purchase/Revenue*;
- *Equity/Revenue* (Capital *Value-added*);
- *Wages & Salary/Revenue* (Labor *Value-added*).

It was now necessary to construct industry-specific equations to show the relationships between *Value-added, Capital Value-added, Labor Value-added* and the *Return-on-Equity*. A closer examination of several industrial sectors[17] showed there were similarities between the ratios for the food, textile, paper, petroleum and pharmaceutical industries. There were food companies that had *Asset–to–Revenue* ratios that looked like those for oil companies. There were chemical companies that had wage structures similar to leading pharmaceutical firms. Although every firm could be categorized by its SIC[18] code, the financial ratios did not fall into such neat groups. The *Purchase/Revenue*, the *Equity/Revenue* and the *Wages & Salary/Revenue* ratios did not fit into any standard pattern. They were unique to each firm the way fingerprints are unique to each person.

The next step in the investigation called for deriving a multi-factor equation that would combine financial data for firms across all industrial sectors. This larger sample (116 cases) explained 82.5% of the relationship between *Value-added, Capital Value-added, Labor Value-added* and the *Return-on-Equity*.[19]

The high levels of correlation between a few *Value-added* measures and the *Return-on-Equity,* despite industrial classification, were similar to the cross-sectional research conducted by the PIMS[20] program since 1963. The PIMS program[21] showed that marketing and financial characteristics explain a firm's profit performance more accurately than its industry, demographics and size or any simple financial ratio.

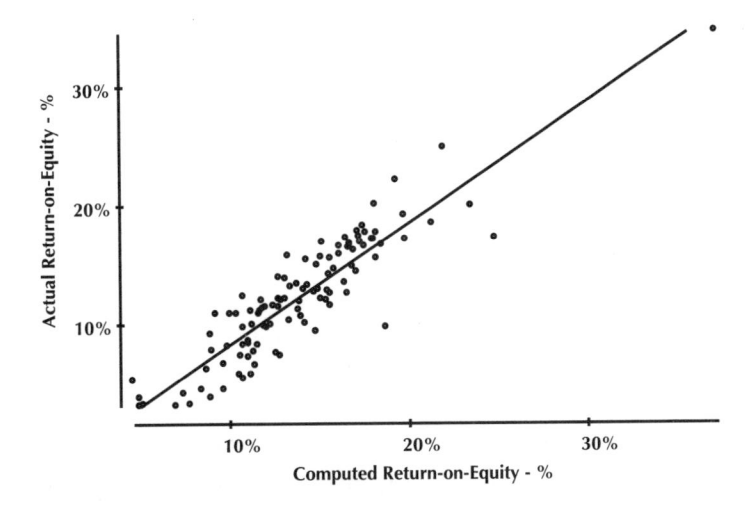

Figure 4.6: Predicting ROE Across Industrial Sectors

The PIMS researchers obtained insights and statistical techniques from methods used in health services. When it comes to judging a person's cardiac fitness, what matters is not his or her name, religion, wealth or artistic talent. What matters is a combination of their smoking habits, blood pressure, weight, age, cholesterol level and physical fitness. I needed to explore the accumulated PIMS knowledge and find if its extensive research findings would be applicable to evaluating computer investments. I had to stop thinking about computers as calculating machines. Instead, I had to start examining them as a remedy applied by companies with the hope of improving their financial well-being.

Early in 1978, I started talking about the business value of computers in terms used by epidemiologists.[22] I proposed a hypothesis that computers are analogous to prescription drugs. Their application, dose and therapeutic powers can be clinically substantiated before use. Adopting this point of view proved to be the conceptual turning point in my search.

CHAPTER SUMMARY

Complexity blocks the understanding of how the use of computers relates to profits. You first have to filter out those influences which are unique to each firm.

Using *Value-added* instead of *Revenue* helps to make companies more comparable despite how much they buy from others or how many resources they generate internally. You also must consider that differences in how they use capital, how much they pay in taxes and how much they rely on labor-intensive production can mask the business value of computers.

To find out how organizations, with or without computers, improve their profits I applied multi-factor analysis. This technique provides the statistical tools for finding out how computer expenses and a company's profitability are related. The principal disadvantage of this approach is in obtaining the large quantities of verifiable data needed to feed the enormous appetite of the statistical methods before you can get reliable results. The difficulties involved in acquiring adequate data are the reason for the rare use of this method to evaluate computer effectiveness.

The decision to follow well-established PIMS methodologies for data collection and data analysis turned our search from improvised exploration to experimentation.

CHAPTER 4 COMMENTS

[1] D.R.Vincent, The Information Based Corporation, *Dow Jones-Irwin*, 1990 arrives at the identical conclusion. In his Chapter 2, he shows how Value-added calculation is more reliable in evaluating the results of banking companies.

[2] Dr. C.N. Athanasopoulos. The latest and second version of his work is the Corporate Productivity Atlas—Gross Corporate Product Measures 1978–1982, *Delphi Research Center*, Lincoln, Mass. 01773. Professor Athanasopoulos made worthy contributions as a member of the Committee on White Collar Productivity, of which I was chairman for the White House Conference on Productivity in 1982. In one of our findings we recommended the adoption of *Value-added* accounting for dealing with the intractable problem of how to measure the lagging "white-collar productivity" in America. The recommendations appear in the President's Report on Productivity in America, *Government Printing Office*, 1983 and summarized in P.A. Strassmann, Improving Information Worker Productivity - The White House Conference on Productivity, *Information Management Review*, 1986, 1 (4).

[3] Such as number of employees, wages, salaries, and benefits. The database also includes: total net revenues, total assets, total equity, net income, book value per share, dividends per share, *Fortune* magazine rank, income taxes, interest expense, dividends, depreciation and retained earnings.

[4] Thirty eight companies in food and related products, 20 in paper and wood products, 18 in chemicals, 26 in petroleum refining, 14 in metal manufacturing, 14 in electronics and appliances, 10 in aerospace, 10 in pharmaceuticals, 21 in industrial and farm equipment and 90 companies in miscellaneous sectors.

[5] Textiles, paper products, chemicals, oil refining, metal manufacturing, electronics, pharmaceuticals, and industrial equipment.

[6] Dart & Kraft, General Mills, General Foods, Nabisco Brands, H.J.Heinz, Campbell Soup, CPC International, Borden, Quaker Oats, Carnation, Kellogg, Hershey Foods, Gerber Products, Amstar, A.E.Staley and Stokely-Van Camp.

7 The effect of purchases on the cost structure is amplified when an industry experiences a dramatic cost decline, such as the 46% reduction in product costs in the electronics industry from 1982 to 1988. As product cost decreased, due to advances in semi-conductors, low-technology components increased in importance. By 1988, material costs of the electronics industry were 80% of the total product cost, labor cost only 2% and overhead cost 18% (*Electronic Business*, June 26, 1989, p. 127). When the costs of materials are set by global competition the best opportunity for profit improvement is in overhead reduction or premium pricing, not in reducing direct labor.

8 EDI (Electronic Data Interchange) does not change that view. When I connect my computers directly into my supplier's materials management system, I lower my transaction costs. The supplier's savings should produce lower purchase prices.

9 The ratio of business *Value-added* to total *Revenue* is the *Vertical Integration* ratio.

10 For details see Figure 3.2 which shows the distribution of wages and salaries as a ratio of company *Revenue*.

11 R.A. Howell, J.D. Brown, S.R. Soucy, A.H. Seed, Management Accounting in the New Manufacturing Environment, *National Association of Accountants and Computer Aided Manufacturing-International*, Montvale, N.J., 1987. The overhead ratios come from Figure 7 in "Management Accounting in the New Manufacturing Environment." The "Ratio" of overhead to direct labor differs by industry segment:

Industry	Direct Labor	Overhead	Overhead Ratio
Consumer	14%	25%	178%
General Industrial	13%	37%	284%
High technology	16%	40%	250%
Electronics	15%	38%	253%
Aerospace	20%	36%	180%
Automobiles	14%	34%	242%
Machinery	15%	35%	233%
Metals	18%	22%	122%

These percentages come from a breakdown of manufacturing costs. Marketing and general administrative expenses come on top of that. The numbers are industry-wide averages. The overhead-to-direct labor ratios at the firm level can vary enormously. For instance, IBM's Proprinter plant produces more than $250 million sales with fewer than 200 plant employees. An Allen-Bradley plant produces $50 million of goods with only five operators.

T. Pryor of the Computer-Aided Manufacturing research and consulting consortium reports that overhead costs for U.S. consumer goods manufacturing companies increased from 22% of revenue in 1960 to 32% of revenue in 1986, while direct labor costs declined from 22% to 15%.

When the overhead burden in operations is 900% of direct labor cost, conventional cost accounting figures are misleading when estimating the benefits of further automating factory workers. R.H. Hayes and R. Jaikumar in Manufacturing Crisis, *Harvard Business Review*, September 1988, tell about managers who were eager to buy parts from suppliers. As justification, they include allocated overhead costs for each direct labor hour saved. Increasing purchases called for added overhead costs. As direct labor costs fell, they drove the overhead rate on the remaining products even higher. This forced the company into a deepening spiral to divest all manufacturing operations.

12 Rising overhead does not occur only in business. For instance, in the case of public elementary and secondary schools teacher's salaries (as a percentage of operating budget) have declined from 56% in 1960 to 40% in 1989, a 29% reduction (P. Brimelow, American Perestroika, *Forbes*, May 14, 1990, p.86).

13 The accounting (book) number for *Equity* is the cumulative consequence of entries under historical conditions of changing depreciation policies, differing inflation and fluctuating currency rates. The accounting valuation of *Equity* rarely

72   THE BUSINESS VALUE OF COMPUTERS

approximates the shareholders' valuation as expressed by the market price. It is difficult to attribute *ROE* to individual investments.

For a more comprehensive critique, see also Chapter 2 in A. Rappaport, Creating Shareholder Value, *Free Press*, 1986.

14 A company with a fine reputation for financial management, Coca-Cola, subtracts from after-tax operating profits the cost of capital employed to produce the earnings as a way of "...ensuring that operating people think like top management." (*Fortune*, January 29, 1990, p. 50).

15 Return-on-Equity = Constant + 1.55*(Purchases/Revenue) + 0.48*(Equity/Revenue) + 1.74*(Wages & Salaries/Revenue). Each of the terms in this linear equation adjusts (normalizes) the ROE for variations in the financial structure of the food companies.

16 If you want to check whether your company's information systems budget is comparable with your competitors', you should try multi-factor analysis. You had better be sure that your data definitions are consistent and that your data sources are reliable before you make any conclusions. For instance, it is easy to come up with the equation for a 1988 U.S. bank's expected information systems budget (in millions $) as equal to –6.58 + 0.6377*Assets + 0.0418*Revenue. This equation explains 93.1% of the budgets for 17 banks listed in the Computerworld 1989 tabulation (with Citicorp excluded because of its extreme size). However, if you include the percentage of PC's per employee in the banking equation, the budgets will decrease by –0.097*(PC/Employee), which suggests that costs may shift elsewhere.

Correlation studies introduce interesting questions for consideration by top banking management at budget time. For instance, the relationship between all computer budget ratios and the shareholder returns is negative. This could be a warning that even if your bank's computer budget is in line with your competitors', it may not do much for your profits.

17 Initially, 29 Textile and 44 Paper cases along with the 38 Food cases. Ultimately, the experiment was run for all companies in the database.

18 Standard Industrial Classification code. This is a classification used by the U.S. Federal Government in reporting economic statistics.

19 Return-on-Equity = Constant + 1.23*(Purchases/Revenue) + 0.26*(Equity/Revenue) + 1.03*(Wages & Salaries/Revenue).

20 Profit Impact of Market Strategies, a research program originated by Dr. Sidney Schoeffler in 1963, first at the General Electric Corporation and then continued at the Strategic Planning Institute of Cambridge, Mass. Dr. Schoeffler currently is continuing his work as the managing director of MANTIS (Management Tools and Information Services, Inc.) a research consortium in Boston, Mass. which offers business strategy diagnostics and consulting services.

21 For a comprehensive overview, see R.D. Buzzell and B.T. Gale, The PIMS Principles, *The Free Press*, New York, 1987.

22 The science which investigates the causes and control of epidemic diseases. The rapid spread of computers into business had assumed epidemic proportions by 1978. I am indebted for lessons in this specialized discipline to Vera Strassmann Dolan, who has worked on a wide range of epidemiological studies for life insurance companies.

5

RETURN-ON-MANAGEMENT

About Measurement

The essence of a corporate culture is the firm's measurement system. It is the lens through which reality is perceived and then acted on.

There is an entire branch of philosophy[1] that is concerned with the reliability of knowledge about proposed actions. People act to reach goals because they believe that they will get expected results. You may then criticize their actions on either of two grounds: the goals may be ill-chosen, or the supposed connection between the action and the consequences may be ill-founded.

You cannot begin a discussion of the value of information technology without clarifying the question of how much do we know when we insert computers into the workplace.

Goal-Setting and Measurement

Misapplications of technology occur when goals and actions are confused. All-embracing appraisals such as "reasonable," "right," and "necessary" are used in advocating a preferred solution. We find that organizations launch projects for "giving personal computers to all salespersons," "automating clerical labor," "converting from batch-processing to on-line systems," "introducing artificial intelligence into decision support applications" or engaging in the building of an "executive information system." By not separating the validity of goals from the implementation, the conflicts between ends and means will confuse even the best-intended schemes.

The problem is that complete goal-validation, such as a detailed commitment to getting specific benefits, is a painful process. It brings to the surface all the underlying problems likely to arise with the proposed venture. The appraisal of a particular goal is possible only if the goal is clear, measurable and supported by verifiable cases. Most importantly, verifiable goals specify how we will measure the result of our efforts after we complete the intended project.

Coming up with proof that the desired goals were reached is a tough assignment. That is hard to do, especially if the proposed technology project needs support from constituencies who have conflicting needs, opposing interests and diverse qualifications in considering the merits of the proposal. In the public sector, such projects are carried by contention between competing Agencies. In the business world, they are opportunistic compromises arising from the annual budget process which favors the dressing up of goals into acceptable projects.

Because of the difficulties in goal-setting and measurement, I have concluded that unless an information technology has measurable financial outcomes, the clarity of its goals is questionable.

Single vs. Multiple Goals for Information Technology

The effects of computers are systemic.

When introducing information technologies, you must be fastidious in articulating the principles used in goal-setting. All systems investments are inherently risky. Therefore, a good investment proposal also builds in a feedback mechanism which allows revising the project efforts when unforeseen conditions arise. Those with a background in servo-mechanism design know that mid-course corrections are impossible if the measurement standards do not exist, or if they change based on the latest exigencies. Playing around wildly with thermostat settings when your furnace has an ignition problem can blow it up. If your initial aim is to increase market share, and midway through the project you decide to maximize clerical savings, you will do neither.

In reality, goal-setting in the organization is more complex than suggested by the furnace analogy. Organizations, like the living body, do better when they try to deal with multiple variables at a time. Major corrections involving a single business function, such as transaction cost-reduction or elimination of processing delays, make sense only in situations when the defect has reached intolerable levels. In times of war, disaster and other hazardous conditions, basic goal-setting is necessary. However, since the environment I am discussing usually involves normal business conditions, the effects of information technology are more subtle than can be defined by any one tangible result.

When you introduce computers into an organization, their effects are systemic, affecting the working of the whole company. The consequences will modify the way the firm operates. Because of this, your measurements must encompass the aftereffects of many changes, instead of just one isolated improvement. It is relatively easy to achieve simple goals by sacrificing others.

As an example, the effect of increasing market share will ripple through every Department. Your production, personnel, manufacturing and distribution functions never will be the same. This raises the issue of goal-setting for information technology investments: what principles help us examine a proposal for changing systems that manage an organization?

My standard answer is that you should measure the *productivity* of organizations before and after automation. Gains in organizational productivity would tell us if the new system improved overall performance, perhaps because the overall advantages outweigh the overall disadvantages. What then is the meaning of organizational *productivity* in an information-based company?

The Productivity of Information Systems

The term *productivity* is about two hundred years old. At the start of the industrial revolution, factory owners needed a quick way to assess operating results without having to wait for financial reports. Productivity was output divided by input. For example, if a blast furnace produced 10 tons of steel per worker, and next year the same furnace produced 11 tons of steel per worker, labor productivity increased by 10%.

Physical Measures of Productivity

Under the influence of Frederick Taylor the measurement of efficiency and productivity came to the factory floor. Productivity was re-defined as the physical *output* produced with a given number of physical *inputs*. For example, the number of shafts, bearings or carburetors produced per work-hour or man-week would be a measure of direct labor productivity. The whole idea of physical productivity also applied to national economic measurements. Today, U.S. productivity is a weighted mix of physical outputs (tons of steel or paper, kilowatts of electricity, etc.) divided by a weighted mix of labor inputs, such as hours worked. In addition, national productivity includes an allowance for capital inputs, such as the reported financial value of physical assets.

This measurement of productivity was satisfactory when the country's main economic activities were agriculture or manufacturing and when physical outputs were comparable to similar physical inputs at an earlier time. A bushel of wheat or a ton of pig iron did not change much over the period when comparing productivity results.

During the 1930's quality began to displace quantity as a critical factor in advanced industrial economies. As a result, imperfections in the measurement of productivity started creeping in. Automobiles and convenience foods sold in 1960 or 1970 were not equivalent to those produced in the 1930's or 1940's. The labor-intensive assembly lines of the pre-World War II factories were not comparable to the highly engineered production processes thirty years later. Accurately measuring gains for the number of automobiles or tons of freeze-dried vegetables could not be done, because dissimilar outputs were produced with different inputs. Similarly, a computer in 1989 is not comparable with a computer in 1979 or 1969, regardless of how we try to define their equivalence in millions of instructions per second per dollar.

Lost Reliability in the Reporting of Physical Productivity

After 1970, serious difficulties in interpreting productivity numbers began to surface. In advanced industrial societies, the manufacturing sector had declined in importance to represent less than a third of the total economic product. Information-based trade, financial and business services were taking over. Economic structures were changing as the origin of *Value-added* shifted from production (reported in the manufacturing sector) to distribution (reported in the service sector). When a steel company shifts its warehousing to a distributor, this appears as a loss to the production sector and a gain in the services sector.

The automation of a factory reduced the direct labor force, and therefore presumed to improve productivity. But, for every factory worker displaced, there were now two other people employed in the company's offices. These changes appeared in corporate productivity calculations as gains in manufacturing productivity. The offsetting productivity declines from office work did not get reported, because no means were available for measuring the outputs of the rising office population. You had inputs (office costs) but no easily identifiable outputs. Without output estimates you cannot come up with useful measures of productivity.

Some banks and insurance companies have re-organized themselves on the model of paper-work factories. They began measuring the productivity of clerical personnel using the principles of industrial management. Detroit time-and-motion study engineers found employment in New York offices when computers were introduced on a massive scale. The industrial engineers succeded only in streamlining clerical labor. They failed in dealing with the rising costs of professional staffs which were excluded from productivity calculations because their output was intangible.

The 1982 White House Conference on Productivity in America concluded that the declining productivity[2] of "white collar" labor was becoming a large, but unquantifiable, economic liability for the economy. The traditional formula for determining "productivity" as a critical business indicator was at a dead end. Nobody knew how to calculate the gains, if there were any, caused by the growing costs of information work. Without a generally accepted correct measure of productivity, you could not support massive investments in computers. The stage was set for the approaching decline in the seemingly unlimited appetite for more information technology.

Omission of Management from Productivity Measurement

The fastest rising and the most expensive labor costs—executives, managers, administrators, professionals and officials—whom I designate as *Management*, were omitted from all productivity calculations.[3] *Management* was overhead, with "intangible" and "immeasurable" physical results, and therefore had been exempt from the measurement of their *outputs*. "White collar" productivity studies concerned only the work products of clerical and secretarial personnel. It was acceptable to claim savings from reducing fully burdened[4] clerical and secretarial labor hours, even if this added to the size of managerial and professional staffs.

The widespread adoption of computers made the misjudgments of productivity only worse. Computers generated outputs for which internal customers often did not pay. Computers also supported people delivering intangible advice to *Management,* whose output also was intangible. This meant that the economy began absorbing large quantities of information-processing capital unrelated to the generation of profits. Legions of specialists attending to the needs of overhead personnel joined the payroll. Productivity was no longer the traditional concept of a ratio of physical *outputs* to *inputs. Output* was indeterminate and *input* was an untraceable overhead expense.

The first twenty years of euphoric acceptance of computers ended when overhead costs (including supporting capital) surpassed direct labor costs (including their supporting capital) in the service sector. Since the immeasurable became the largest *input,* physical productivity ratios ceased to have any meaning.

Financial Measures from the Industrial Era

Capital is the essential input to productivity.

Because there were no valid measures of productivity, investments in computers were justified only in strictly financial terms. Corporate procedure already was familiar with filling out similar forms for the approval of fork-lift trucks, the building of warehouses and the buying of a new milling machine. Forms for acquiring information systems also took on the same appearance. These forms are much alike, regardless of the industry or the country. They differ only in detail as to calculating[5] and documenting *ROA* (return on assets) or *ROI* (return on investment).

Every method for computing *ROA* or *ROI* goes back to the eighteenth century, when capital was the most important element in organizing the industrial means for production. According to this view, all profits created by a company are possible because of capital. Labor was a commodity, according to the value theories of both the political left[6] and the conservative right. *Management* was overhead to the costs of labor. Therefore, *ROA* and *ROI*[7] are the essence of free-market, as well as Marxist economies, for they calculate the efficiency with which you use capital.[8] Following this outlook, the financial analysts, the stock market and your shareholders will judge you primarily by your capital efficiency and not by the efficiency of how you utilize your human resources.[9]

To come up with the financial measure of productivity is simple: you divide profit (the final *output* of any enterprise) by capital (the decisive *input* to any enterprise). Labor, management, land and material *inputs* are bought at commodity prices. What counts then, is capital. If capital is well invested, you get productivity.

This explains why management theorists until now have been primarily concerned with the efficiency of using capital.[10] I agree that before the introduction of large administrative staffs, management's concentration on capital budgeting was essential. The capacity to manage capital resources meant having access to more capital for large plants to produce steel, refine oil, generate electricity and make appliances. An adequate supply of inexpensive capital was a prerequisite for gaining market share through production and distribution efficiencies. The fascination with capital obscured the understanding that the annual costs of corporate bureaucracies were becoming more expensive than the annual carrying charges for capital assets.

A special case of a propensity for excessive capital spending comes from government-regulated businesses such as utilities, post offices, telephone companies, railroads, insurance firms, airlines and the defense industry. Regulated companies cannot make more than a "fair" return on capital. A regulated enterprise will not make efficient use of capital because that will reduce revenues and support a smaller management group. As a result, managers will have a bias to spend capital whenever that is possible.

THE PROJECT AUTHORIZATION BIAS

The concentration on capital investment changed the ways of managing innovation. Management focused on capital budgeting as the place where they could exercise maximum influence over the future directions of a business. Once a capital investment was approved, the operating expense would then follow from the initial investment decision. Therefore, the annual costs would not be amenable to major changes. As a consequence of such thinking, all innovation required estimation of expected benefits and costs with confidence.

When such investment-oriented logic was applied to computer projects, it resulted in elaborate, lengthy and tortuous approval procedures.[11] In the absence of reliable productivity measures, industrial-age executives became convinced that the preferred way to control computers was through project authorization procedures which reduced the risks of computerization to a minimum. This resulted in favoring projects that automated existing business procedures instead of changing them to take advantage of the new information-handling methods. Investment-oriented executives failed to recognize that computerization is an incremental, continuous and evolutionary organizational learning process that requires better controls over operating results for the entire business. Cumbersome project review procedures produced elongated development schedules, and created a tendency to combine long overdue incremental improvements into a single costly project. Emphasis on controlling new investments led to the establishment of the information system as a discrete and separate function, instead of integrating it into every manager's job.

Executives who rely primarily on project authorizations to control computer spending are focusing on a diminishing fraction of total costs. As soon as the annual growth rate in information technology spending slows down below 10%, I estimate that less than 20% of the total budget would be available for new development. The rest of the budget goes for ongoing maintenance and inflationary salary increases. The share of capital expenses for any new information technology development is also very small, because most of the cost of installing new applications is in systems analysis, coordination and training. Relying on project authorizations of information technology investments as the principal method to guide the application of computers becomes irrelevant.

The still prevailing emphasis on hardware and software procurement as the principal control check-point in many firms, and especially in the public sector, is an example of counterproductive practices. Do not manage information systems through a series of disconnected projects, but as an inseparable continuum of managing an ongoing business operation. Otherwise you end up with obsolete technologies, incompatible systems and inflated project budgets which include what should otherwise be a short-term operating expense.

Post-Industrial Development

Management is the essential input to productivity.

By 1980, global competition created excess production capacity for nearly every product or service. Rapidly accumulating profits were seeking out opportunities for re-investment. The globalization of financial markets created conditions where capital became a readily traded commodity, not a scarce resource. Hundreds of billions of dollars moved electronically, on a moment's notice, from country to country whenever there was a small change in the price of capital. When international financial transactions exceeded international trade by a multiple of 20 or more, finance capital ceased to be the prime explanation for value creation. Capital was now a commodity, like everything else.

The scarce resources today are people who can organize and motivate the productive capacities of their employees, and who know how to maximize the use of capital.[12] The scarce resource of the post-industrial world is *Management*. If a company is profitable, this is because of *Management*, and not because of capital. You determine *Management* costs by first identifying all *Operations* costs, which are all resources that are essential for serving today's customers. Everything not in *Operations* is, by definition, *Management*:

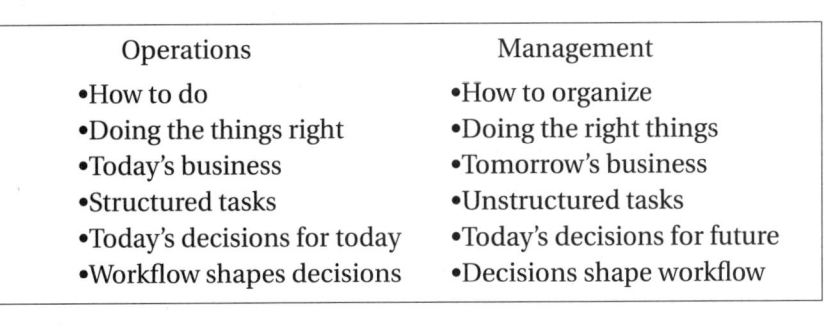

Operations	Management
•How to do	•How to organize
•Doing the things right	•Doing the right things
•Today's business	•Tomorrow's business
•Structured tasks	•Unstructured tasks
•Today's decisions for today	•Today's decisions for future
•Workflow shapes decisions	•Decisions shape workflow

Table 5.1: The Characteristics of Operations and Management

Companies in the same industry, with the same technology and same capital structure, can have widely differing profits. *PIMS* research found that high capital intensity is always harmful to profitability, unless this liability is overcome by superior labor productivity or a capacity to general additional *Value-added*. Therefore, measuring business productivity only by means of capital productivity ratios will not reflect the variety of influences that generate profits.

The modern enterprise employs large numbers of computer-supported managers. Measuring its capital productivity will not tell us much about this critical resource. Measuring the productivity of its direct labor is also insufficient. Reporting automobiles produced per worker per year does not tell us much about what cars are being produced with robots. Boasting about gains in clerical productivity will be equally misleading.[13]

If management is the scarce resource, and if management is the key to the productivity of organizations, why not measure "management productivity" instead of "capital" or "labor" productivity? This approach would be different from the way today's economists or accountants think about evaluating business results.

Most importantly, measuring *Management productivity* would open the way to exploring the benefits of computers used by their principal customers, the managers of information.

Individual, Business and National Productivity

Management productivity can be evaluated only in terms affecting the business itself. This implies that you should judge a manager's effectiveness only by the results of the people he manages. Personal efficiency, hard work or brilliance means little if the manager leads an organization to deliver below average financial results.

THE PERSONAL POINT OF VIEW

Personal productivity, such as physical output per capita, is a valid approach if we wish to find out about individual efficiency. There are many computer applications where personal productivity, measured by industrial engineering methods, is as applicable to the evaluation of gains as it was a hundred years ago. It is not the purpose here to comment on this well-documented topic.

What's missing is an understanding of organizations where the efficiency of individuals does not guarantee high levels of productivity. It is not possible to sum up individual or group efficiencies and prove that the entire organization also is productive. It is necessary, but positively not enough, for productive organizations to have hard-working and efficient individuals. Unfortunately, there are many capable, decisive and intelligent people buried within organizations that deliver dismal financial results. There are also companies using inauspicious people, with unimpressive credentials, who produce spectacular gains year after year. There are productive companies that meet local standards of excellence, but fall victim to international competition, to government regulation or to accidental financial misfortune.

CHAPTER 5—RETURN-ON-MANAGEMENT

THE SHAREHOLDER'S POINT OF VIEW

The measurement of organizational productivity is only possible if we consider how well a firm's leadership guides the business so that the employees' contributions remain constructive. How well management manages, over an extended period of time, is the aim of measuring *Management productivity*.

From a shareholder's standpoint, management—not capital—should be the most important investment that needs watching. From the shareholder's standpoint, the only evaluations that make sense concern the effectiveness of management. *Management productivity* answers the following question: for every dollar spent on management, how many dollars of net gain accrue to the shareholders? Boards of Directors could accomplish more by spending their time evaluating top management instead of discussing capital budgets.

People like to measure everyone except themselves. You cannot expect that *Management productivity* will become an acceptable yardstick unless somebody other than the affected *Management* asks for it.

SOCIETY'S POINT OF VIEW

A nation's productivity is not the sum of the productivity of individual firms. Productive businesses are a necessary but not a sufficient condition for increasing national prosperity. Government interference, legislative manipulation, military commitments, deterioration of health, poor education, a crumbling transportation infrastructure, environmental pollution and inflationary fiscal policies will detract from the gains made by businesses. Small changes in taxes, which now take 30% to 65% of the national income of OECD (Organization for Economic Co-operation and Development) countries, can easily nullify productivity gains, which usually are in the 1 to 4% range.

Today's macro-economic productivity statistics continue to view the world as though it were an industrial society. Scores of government commissions are searching for solutions to arrest their country's deteriorating "competitiveness" in the global market place. Lagging national productivity is always mentioned as one of the reasons for falling behind others. The inadequacy of current national productivity statistics becomes apparent when the published numbers are of little value for prescribing remedial action in the service sector of the economy.

The measurement of national productivity should not be confined to calculating the ratios of physical outputs to inputs. It also should address the achievements of the national leadership in freeing individuals and businesses to make their maximum contributions to increasing economic *Value-added*. That translates into measuring the lasting contributions of our political leaders. It would help if we start viewing our wealth-creation political processes as a value-producing managerial activity.

Before we can proceed with a national agenda we first must establish how to assess *Management productivity* for individual businesses because it is there where all *Value-added* originates.

MEASURING MANAGEMENT PRODUCTIVITY

In the next Chapter, I will show that computers primarily serve management and not operating personnel. Because the use of information technology is not evenly distributed among workers, we can get a better understanding of its effectiveness by separating its managerial uses from other applications.

I measure the value of computers by an index that relates directly to *Management productivity*. I can then evaluate the effectiveness of *Management* with or without computers. I shall isolate cases showing superior managerial productivity, and then examine their characteristics of computer use that differ from cases that show inferior managerial productivity.

My research led me to articulate the concept of *Return-on-Management*™. This ratio does a good job not only in evaluating information technology, but also in identifying excessive overhead costs. This ratio is calculated by first isolating the *Management Value-added* of a company, and then dividing it by the company's total *Management Costs*:

$$\text{Return-on-Management}^{\text{TM}} = \frac{\text{Management } \textit{Value-added}}{\text{Management Costs}}$$

Management Value-added is that which remains after every contributor to a firm's inputs gets paid. If *Management Value-added* is greater than *Management Costs*, you can say that managerial efforts are productive because the managerial *outputs* exceed managerial *inputs*.

Another way of looking at the *Return-on-Management* ratio (*R-O-M*™ *Productivity Index*) is to view it as a measure of productivity.

It answers the question of how many surplus dollars you get for every dollar paid for *Management*.

$$R\text{-}O\text{-}M^{TM} \text{ Index} = \frac{\text{Management Output}}{\text{Management Input}} = \text{Management Productivity}$$

To attribute all surplus value to *Management* instead of capital or labor, is a departure from classic economics. It is *Management* that makes the investment and pricing decisions. It is *Management* that motivates the employees. It is *Management* that chooses products and markets. It is *Management* that organizes the suppliers and the production and delivery of goods to customers. Good *Management* can get more of the capital it needs, at a lower interest, than poor *Management*.

The scarce resource of contemporary society is not capital or technology, but *Management*. The time now has come to begin measuring it explicitly. *Management productivity* is not apparent from capital-based financial ratios that only tell us something about *Management* by proxy.

The theory behind this concept comes from the idea that information (e.g., *Management*) is a disorder-defying phenomenon which assures survival of a firm in a competitive environment. Without continuous intervention by *Management* every enterprise must perish from chaotic conditions which arise when external information (about customers and competitors) and internal information fails to guide people in what to do. When that happens people can not cooperate in bringing in new revenues.

According to laws of thermodynamics, machines always produce less energy than they consume. *Management* has the capacity to construct a device—an organization—that extracts from a hostile environment *Net Value-added* (*Outputs*) in excess of total costs (*Inputs*). A well-managed organization is superior to any engine ever invented. A profitable corporation generates a net surplus of wealth. For effective organizations, *Output* always exceeds *Input,* which defies the law of physics that states that this is impossible and disorder must ultimately prevail. Our civilization has created an enormous accumulation of wealth, because *Management* has learned how to increase cooperation through organization of its productive resources.[14]

How to measure a phenomenon that must generate a positive *Net Value-added* to survive is central to the issue of what *Management* is all about. For the last two hundred years, management was evaluated by its capacity to extract new surplus (profits) out of past accumulations of profits (invested capital). Since smart management can get all the capital it can use, the old formulation can be now replaced by directly measuring the productivity of *Management* as an information-processing function. In my approach, I measure the *Output/Input* ratio by finding what's left after *Management* pays everyone, and dividing that by the costs of managing the *Net Value-added* creation process. This is why it is critical to find how much information (*Management*) is necessary to run an enterprise.

If you follow this approach, you will find that companies that can extract more *Net Value-added* from the marketplace, while consuming less information to accomplish this feat, will be the winners. The question of what is information effectiveness resolves into finding how much *Net Value-added* can be created with the smallest combination of managers and computers.

Measuring *Management Value-added* is then the key to evaluating organizational performance and to measuring the effects of computers on management information systems.

Finding Management Value-Added

Finding the *Management Value-added* is similar to extracting gold from rocks or from river sand. First, you sift out large pieces of matter that clearly do not belong. After that, you do not assume that whatever is left is gold because there is still too much extraneous matter. You concentrate on removing foreign material, making sure that in the process you do not accidentally discard anything that is valuable.

Management Value-added is the purified residue of a winnowing process. You obtain it if you have exercised good care in removing all variables that do not belong.

ADJUSTING FOR PURCHASES

As the first step in the cost-separation process, I remove from *Revenues* the costs of *Purchased Raw and Finished Materials, Parts, Energy and Services*. These essential inputs are managed by somebody other than a firm's management. Their prices already reflect the suppliers' management costs.[15]

Next, I subtract the cost of *Interest*.[16] I view interest payments just like payment for any other service. In this case, the supplier is usually a bank. Effective management will pay less for loans than an unreliable one. What matters is the incremental *Value-added* that management creates with loans. In this respect, the money that management obtains is not different than any other rental contract for equipment or services.

Next, I subtract all *Taxes*. Profit after taxes is the indicator that matters to the shareholder. I subtract[17] taxes directly from revenues—before, not after other expenditures—because government makes sure it gets paid before anybody else. In this way taxes become payments to the most insistent supplier. I consider that all taxes are an *involuntary purchase*.[18] Allocation from headquarters is also a form of imposed taxation and must be subtracted from *Revenue*.[19] What remains is the *Business Value-added*.

It is revealing to examine the enormous range in *Business Value-added* as a percentage of *Revenue* for manufacturing firms:[20]

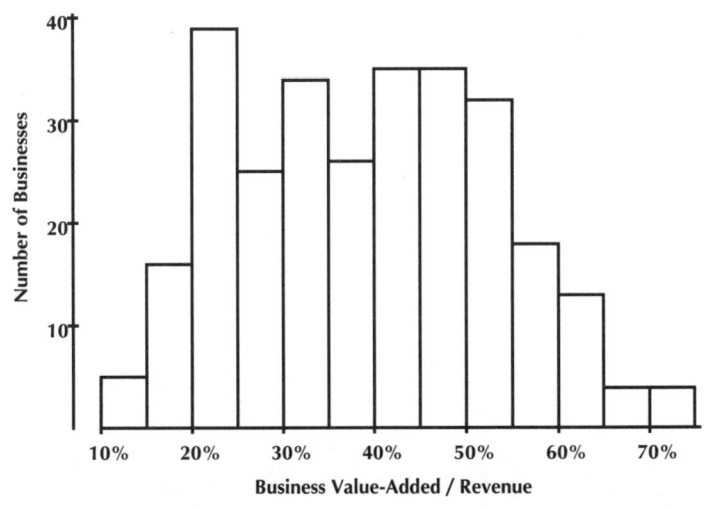

Figure 5.1: Vertical Integration Ratios for Manufacturing Companies

I base all productivity evaluations on *Business Value-added* instead of on *Revenue,* because companies with a high degree of vertical integration (a high *Business Value-added/Revenue* ratio) can justify more *Management* than those with a lower level of integration. Productive executives are likelier to make better choices on the mix of what to buy and what to make. They can then support the additional costs of coordination and integration, provided that the incremental *Value-added* is greater its incremental costs.

Superior management also can get better prices for their purchases. This translates into improved *Business Value-added*. Choosing efficient suppliers, especially in manufacturing, offers the greatest possible opportunities for profit improvement because purchases will be the largest cost element. *Value-added* analysis becomes the key to judging the worth of computer investments that support buying activities.

Focusing on *Business Value-added* gives an unobstructed view of the scope of a firm's managerial activities. It is unfortunate that accounting practices fold into the cost-of-goods an indistinguishable mixture of direct labor, overhead and purchases so that nobody can tell whether the company is increasing or decreasing *Value-added*. Whenever my clients begin a *Value-added* analysis, they must first extricate from their ledgers external purchases. Clients used to *Value-added* concepts do not have these difficulties, because taxation rules dictate *Value-added* financial reporting as a matter of routine.

ADJUSTING FOR SHAREHOLDER VALUE-ADDED

After paying suppliers for their share of inputs, *Management* has to account for the shareholders' *Value-added*. The major distortion in the *Return-on-Asset* calculations is that ROA for low-debt businesses will be higher when compared with high-debt businesses. Calculating the *R-O-M*™ Index adjusts such comparisons by subtracting from the *Business Value-added* the going rate of the costs of shareholder capital, multiplied by the market[22] (or book) value of shareholder equity.

Subtracting the going rate of shareholder capital costs from profits is another way of computing the economic "rent" for capital. This is not a new idea. It is also known as the "economic profit" of a firm, which is different from the usually quoted number known as "operating profit." According to this view,[21] shareholders' economic profit, or economic rent, is equal to operating profits minus interest costs, minus the investment revenues a company's assets could earn if employed elsewhere. Such rent can be also calculated by estimating the breakup value of a firm, and multiplying that with an interest rate that can be earned in a comparable investment.

Regardless of the technique used for computing the shareholder

Value-added, it is essential that it reduces reported accounting profits. Otherwise, the financial reports overstate the contributions by *Management* and could end up paying bonuses on *Value-added* which rightfully belongs to shareholders.

ADJUSTING FOR BUSINESS COSTS

Day-to-day *Operations* are paid for next. These include the fully burdened costs of employee payrolls, asset depreciation and interest.[23] *Operations* include everything that is essential for getting today's goods and services produced and delivered to today's customers.

Management Costs are calculated by considering that everything that's not in *Operations* automatically is placed in this category. The *Management Value-added* is *Revenue* minus *Purchases* minus *Shareholder Value-added* minus the *Costs of Operations* minus the *Costs of Management*.

The following diagram should help in understanding cost elements for deriving the *Management Value-added*:

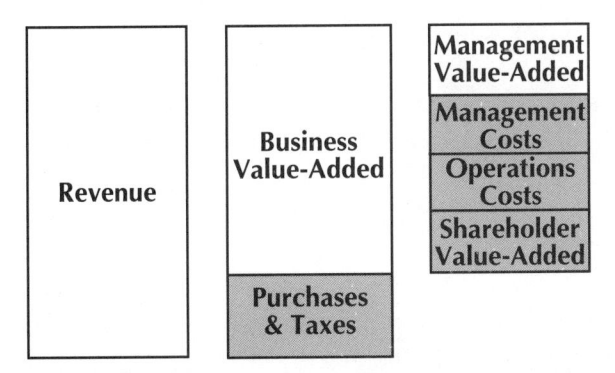

Figure 5.2: The Definition of Management Value-added

The good news is that the *Management Value-added* can be a large multiple of *Management Costs*. I have found firms where for every dollar paid to *Management*, they create two or more dollars of surplus *Management Value-added*. The unhappy aspect of *Management Value-added* is that it can be less than zero. Over 20% of firms I have examined show a negative *Management Value-added*, although more than 50% of those still report profits and a positive R-O-A, using generally accepted accounting principles.[24]

MANAGEMENT PRODUCTIVITY IN THE PUBLIC SECTOR

Services in the public sector do not charge prices based on quantity, do not offer options as to quality, do not account for invested capital, pay no taxes and do not compensate "shareholders." Consequently, the *Value-added* of a public sector agency is measurable only in terms of its cost ratios.[25]

Many public sector agencies act as distribution channels for public funds, such as social payments, money transfers to and from tax funds, and payments to contractors for public projects. Such purchases and transfers should be subtracted from the total agency budget to produce an estimate of the agency's *Value-added*. For instance, the total budget of the Social Security Administration is not an appropriate measure of its internal efficiency, since its payments to its clients are set by law. That agency's *Value-added* is the sum total of all costs that remain after the beneficiaries receive their payments.

The management productivity of the public sector is:

$$\text{Public Sector Management Productivity} = \frac{\text{Operations Costs}}{\text{Management Costs}}$$

because it evaluates how much *Management* is necessary to deliver to public sector beneficiaries *Value-added* services by personnel involved in *Operations*.

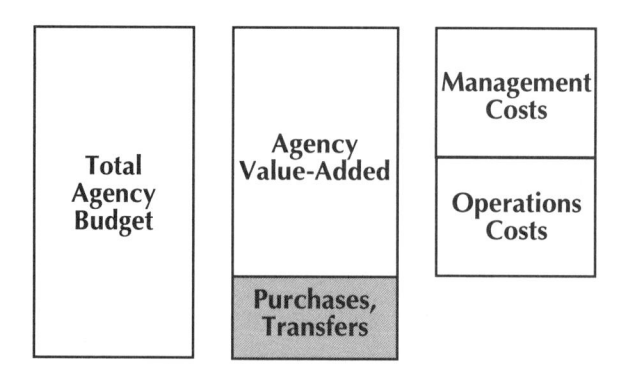

Figure 5.3: Classification of Public Sector Costs

An example will help to explain the *Value-added* approach to public sector productivity. One of the rare instances of public sector analysis comes from a doctoral dissertation accounting for every dollar of the

$1.4 billion spent on New York City high schools in 1988–89.[26] This involved reviewing the time sheets of 16,000 Board of Education employees to see which employees actually were teaching. I accept actual teaching time as a reasonable definition of *Operations* for a public school organization. Costs of the employees' salaries, hour by hour, were allocated either to overhead or classroom activities.

The study found that New York City spent $6,107 per high school student, per year. Only $1,972 per student was attributable to classroom activities.[27] This then yields the following estimate of *Management Productivity*:

$$\text{New York Board of Education Management Productivity} = \frac{\$1972}{\$4135} = 0.48$$

Operations Costs in this case are only 48% of *Management Costs*. When you see such a low ratio, consider that market-oriented firms in the services sector require at least 150% *Operations/Management* cost ratio to remain competitive.

USING THE *R-O-M* INDEX TO EVALUATE INFORMATION TECHNOLOGY

Before the Federal government approves a new pharmaceutical for medical use, exhaustive testing is necessary. Most often, two groups of eligible subjects randomly will receive what looks like the test drug. Only half of the drugs contain the new pharmaceutical. The other half has something that looks very much like it but is ineffective (a placebo). The experimenters do not find the result until the trial is complete.[28]

If the subjects who received the new pharmaceutical show remarkable improvement and those with the placebo do not, you have good proof of a benefit. You must also pass another test proving that the new pharmaceutical is not harmful for every other conceivable condition.

Can computer investments be subject to such stringent testing? In most cases, that is practically not possible.

PILOT TESTING OF COMPUTER SYSTEMS

Whether or not computers are beneficial to the health of firms could be settled if it were possible to apply clinical methods to their evaluation.

92   THE BUSINESS VALUE OF COMPUTERS

There are instances where you can approach such conditions, but they are imperfect and on a restricted scale. Instead of full scale implementation, computers sometimes serve only a limited group, while others would keep working as before. That is a "pilot systems installation."

Pilot tests cannot meet the rigor of "double blind" testing, for a bias toward the results is created when everyone finds out about the test. People involved in the pilot always receive extra management attention which creates an incentive for succeeding independent of the merits of the computer application. All the pilot studies I have seen were suspect of suffering from the "Hawthorne Effect"[29] in their reported productivity gains.

When it comes to testing large-scale system investments, clinical trial methods are impractical. The experimental testing of new work methods while retaining and comparing without bias the old ones is undesirable because of the large financial commitments necessary prior to starting any trials.[30]

Tracking comparable computer investments within the same corporation is very hard to do. There are only a few recorded cases where this was done successfully. Although such an approach may answer questions about specific applications, they still do not address the executives' interest in finding the right level of total spending.

CROSS-SECTIONAL ANALYSIS

Spending on computers from a large group of comparable companies can be collected and classified. Such data can be studied to find what usage patterns can be associated with superior financial results. We can approximate methods used in medical studies by taking a sample of companies and observing how the healthy ones differ from those which are not so healthy.[31]

The problem with cross-sectional analysis is that you have only the information you decided to observe at the time of data collection, unless you update the database. You also have to settle on one measure against which to correlate the information that you will collect. In *PIMS*, the definition of well-being is relative to the company's *Return-on-Investment*, although in special cases other measures are used as well. In the case of cardiac studies, often the single measure of well-being is an estimate of life expectancy. As I was setting out to hunt for a correlation between profitability and computers, I settled on *Return-on-Management* as the criterion to determine corporate health. To identify the productivity of computers, we will start with the productivity of *Management* who are the principal generators, distributors and users of computer-based information systems.

I chose *Return-on-Management* because it has the following merits:[32]

- It combines the effects of both Financial Statement and Balance Sheet entries.
- It is self indexing. The numerator and the denominator are in terms of current costs which means that the ratio is indifferent to currency or inflation.
- It isolates the productivity of the critical business resource, which is managerial.[33]
- It is particularly suitable for measuring service-based businesses, which use less capital to create revenue than manufacturing or utilities.
- It tracks performance during corporate restructuring when capital-intensive firms become increasingly dependent on purchased components and leased assets.
- It makes possible diagnostic evaluations, including cross-industry and international comparisons where there are major differences in vertical integration, *Debt-to-Equity* ratios and taxation.

Chapter Summary

The concept of *Management productivity* points the way to learning more about the effects of information technology. The *R-O-M* Productivity Index is not a substitute for capital-based or production-based indicators. It augments our understanding of how the productivity of enterprises changes when information management becomes the most important resource.

The formulation of the concepts of *Management productivity* was complete in 1979. Like all theories, the idea had no credibility without first being subjected to a reasonable test. That would be difficult, for data were not available in the required format. A cross-sectional analysis requires a sufficiently large sample collected under controlled conditions. Managers were uninterested in evaluating their productivity, afraid of what they might find. They were reluctant to disclose confidential financial data to Xerox.

94   THE BUSINESS VALUE OF COMPUTERS

Computer people worried that the lack of correlation between information technology expenses and their firm's profitability might spoil their next year's budget requests. Computer managers were also uncomfortable in dealing with financial data.

Researchers were pursuing topics that would lend themselves to articles that do not require many years of fact-finding. There were no research grants available for engaging in multi-year comparative studies of the economic benefits of information technology investments.[34]

The absence of any competition indicated that this was a good time to begin a long-term investigation into the business value of computers.

Chapter 5 Comments

[1] Epistemology.

[2] The frequently quoted assertion that "white collar labor" shows declining productivity comes from calculations where the physical outputs are attributed to "blue collar" labor. With automation and increased external purchases, it follows that "blue collar" labor will always show productivity gains because the numbers of "blue collar" workers are steadily declining. In the case of "white collar" labor it is very difficult to prove productivity gains, unless measured in factory-like terms such as numbers of checks or phone calls. In the absence of measurable outputs—which is most frequently the case—output is equal to inputs. For instance, the value of the output of a legal staff is equal to its costs. By this reasoning, most white collar labor will never show any productivity gains. If you allocate productivity gains between "blue collar" and "white collar" labor, your calculations will end up showing that "white collar" labor productivity is declining.

[3] I have searched for a better label to identify personnel that have the prerogatives of governing, guiding, counseling, coordinating, informing and deciding how a company operates. Governors, directors, bureaucrats, supervisors, guardians, superintendents, staff, overhead, controllers, the authorities, overseers, custodians, advisers, checkers, commanders and "establishment" were just a few of the candidates for the new label. None of the designations seemed appropriate because each word had a meaning rooted in earlier experiences of how to organize an enterprise. "Overhead" expresses best what I mean, but reflects the accounting practice of including all plant indirect costs as standard costs, whereas my interest is in information-handling. "Management" is what's reported on my data-gathering forms for computing "management productivity."

[4] Direct labor plus allocated costs.

[5] Some of the most popular methods include IRR (internal rate of return) and DCF (discounted cash flow). The IRR technique is not useful for information technology projects with a long life. For further discussion, see Chapter 10.

[6] It is ironic that the over-emphasis on capital, as the primary source of productivity, is the greatest in centrally planned economies which claim their legitimacy from Labor. Relative to their costs of labor, the Soviets have invested more in capital to support a unit of production output than any free market economy.

[7] Asset-based measures of performance are biased because book values of *Investment, Assets and Equity* reflect the consequences of past tax treatment. They are a composite moving average of a series of past accounting entries. What you get is a reflection of one-time depreciation policies mixed up with fluctuating inflation and currency rates. If you then divide your current profits by your asset valuations to judge management performance, you are using a number whose comparability with other firms is coincidental.

8 The *Economist* (July 28, 1990, p.55) put it well when they said: "The belief that profit depends on capital employed runs deep in businessmen's and economists' minds. It was the abiding theme of Karl Marx's *Das Kapital*. But, there is no more reason that profit should be expressed relative to capital, than relative to any other input."

9 CEO's often write in their Annual Reports that employees are our most important asset. I find that a paradox. None of the reports ever show "employees" as an asset. Only buildings and machines show up as asset entries. The financial statistics only disclose the firm's capital productivity numbers.

10 A noteworthy exception is E.G. Flamholtz, Human Resource Accounting, *Jossey-Bass*, San Francisco, 1985.

11 Current government practices illustrate industrial age thinking. Government control over its computer activities is primarily project oriented. The legislative and administrative emphasis on project management instead of long-term Agency or Department operating efficiency is the principal reason for huge budget overruns. That thinking also explains the lengthy delays in the installation of desirable operating improvements. The government's over-emphasis on controlling hardware and software procurement as the principal checkpoint in project control further detracts from its capacity to apply computers to improving its operating productivity.

12 You do not even have to own much capital for success. You can lease or rent it. You can pay for it in the transfer price from another Division. You can buy it from your supplier in the price you pay for a purchased item. One of the firms in my sample has negative working capital: they receive payment well in advance of deliveries.

13 For many years, AT&T disclosed in their annual reports the number of long distance calls per year handled by its telephone operators. The staggering labor productivity gains did not reflect the costs of the more than $50 billion of call-handling automation.

14 Management's principal tool in securing cooperation is through effective communication. The primary role of information technology is not computing but communicating. It is unfortunate that the word "computer" embodies the industrial age view of what information technology is all about. This industrial-age label suggests a superior capacity to perform calculations more efficiently. The preoccupation with calculations and computing goes back to seventeenth and eighteenth century philosophy which saw the universe as a giant clock that could be understood by calculating all variables.

The purpose of organizations is not primarily to calculate better, but to share information more effectively. It is ironic that the word "communicate" comes from the Latin "communis," or sharing, which is associated with the communist ideology. The failure of Marxism was pre-ordained when this ideology denied the role of *Management* as the organizing principle for all productivity. Karl Marx was just repeating what he heard about the role of capital as the decisive means for all production. The communist ideology never managed to shake its mistaken view that *Management* was synonymous with the ownership of capital. If you accept *R-O-M* as a measure of organizational performance instead of ROI, you also accept the idea that capital is a commodity. In that case the issue of the ownership of production is secondary to the question of whether such means are productive or not.

15 If prices are set by policy or monopoly, such as in inter-Divisional transactions, the purchased quantities must be valued at competitive prices.

16 I have a case where a firm accumulated large amounts of cash, instead of distributing it to shareholders or buying back stock. The firm proceeded to lend the accumulation of cash at interest rates which were lower than the costs of shareholder equity. In effect, this manufacturing company entered the banking business. I included their interest income as "other revenue." The resulting *R-O-M* was lower compared to paying out the accumulated funds as dividends, stock buy-backs or for another more profitable investment.

17 Tax credits, rebates and subsidies are added. There are some large corporations, companies such as IBM, Zenith and Xerox who not only did not pay any Federal tax,

but received tax credits. In 1987, IBM received $113 million tax credits, Zenith $11 million and Xerox $6 million (Electronic Business, October 1, 1988, p.62).

18 In some parts of the world this is "protection services," which is the basis of all taxation any way you look at it.

19 A client reported the distribution from corporate research as a deduction from its profits. It was equal to its profits. The Division maintained its own research staff and viewed corporate research as irrelevant. Corporate management justified keeping the operating Division largely because of its positive contribution to corporate overhead. Since the Division could operate without corporate research, the allocation was excluded from "purchases" for the *R-O-M* Productivity Index computation.

20 This data comes from the *MPIT* (Management Productivity and Information Technology) research, to be discussed in Chapters 6 and 7.

21 That's an easy calculation. Take a three to six months' average of your share prices and multiply by the number of shares.

22 E. Davis and J. Kay, Assessing Corporate Performance, *Business Strategy Review*, Summer 1990. I have some difficulties with Davis' and Kay's pricing of capital and the subtracting of "economic rent" from operating income.

First, I do not believe that the average long-term government-bond yield is a comparable alternative investment. The shareholders' price for keeping money in a company is the government long-term bond yield (a risk-free yield), plus a risk premium for keeping an investment in a risky stock (computed by adding the cost of investing in the stock-market) plus the cost of the risk premium that reflects the past volatility of a particular class of stock (also known as the Beta coefficient).

Second, operating profit after interest applies in all computations. Interest payments are for current debt that would have to be re-paid in case the firm breaks up. Debt is excluded in the valuation of the shareholders' equity.

23 Unless there are exceptional circumstances, the cost of borrowing is the cost of financing the working capital.

24 You may wonder how that is possible. If a company's return on invested capital is below the shareholders' cost of capital, *Management Value-added* will be negative. The subtraction for the *Shareholder Value-added* will exceed the reported after-tax profits. If the shares of a company trade below its book value, chances are that *Management Value-added* will be negative.

25 This approach may also apply to professional associations, trade unions and non-profit organizations performing some sort of public service. In the case of mutual insurance companies and quasi-government enterprises I can apply *R-O-M* methods using, as a simplifying assumption, *Management Value-added* equal to zero.

26 D. Wechsler, Parkinson's Law 101, *Forbes*, June 25, 1990, p.52

27 The central non-teaching staff of the New York City Board of Education absorbed $2,969 per student. Two more administrative layers (Division and School) absorbed the rest of the overhead.

28 This procedure is called the "double blind" testing method.

29 From a study where the personal attention devoted to the workers became more important than changes in the physical environment.

30 I reviewed the test results from a few branches that were the first ones to receive on-line terminals. Some branches reached the planned goals, others were doing worse than before. To meet business commitments, systems management added personnel, changed supervision in the lagging branches, put into effect revised clerical output targets and deferred implementation of some features. I would not call this a "double blind" pilot experiment, but the controlled execution of a plan. What management calls a pilot test is usually a carefully sequenced installation. For a true pilot test, you must be ready to discard your entire investment and restart the project in case you fail.

31 The most favored design in epidemiological studies report observations of the same population over an extended time period. The best known example of such a study is the Framingham Experiment, which showed how cardiovascular health relates to blood pressure, cholesterol, weight, age and smoking history. (Excellent health

for systolic blood pressure between 90 and 120, poor health with systolic blood pressure over 140. Excellent health for cholesterol under 144, poor health with cholesterol over 350, etc.)

32 Because *Return-on-Management* has many useful characteristics it can become an addition—not a replacement—to the existing indicators for judging business results.

33 Incidentally, this makes it a superior measurement method for incentive pay purposes.

34 During that period I served on the Advisory Committee on Information Systems Research, for the National Science Foundation, and obtained a good overview of what types of research in information systems received study grants.

6

GETTING THE FACTS

If all guesses fail, consider facts as an alternative.

A large accumulation of facts does not guarantee that they will be useful. More data does not necessarily lead to better understanding. Precisely the opposite may happen if an organization suffers from an excess of publications, declarations, notices, disclosures, conferences, accounts, forms, copies, reports, certifications, messages, statements, proclamations, notes, gossip, advice, memoranda, communications, letters, dispatches, news, stories, rumors, and announcements.

For instance, there are accounting rules that define sales reports. They are useful for accountants but of questionable value to sales people. I often have seen sales staff wading through piles of fan-fold printouts. They spent much time figuring out how to reconcile accounting revenues with marketing booking so that they could question the calculation of commissions. As another example, budget variance reports to Department Heads record what the accountants posted in the general ledger. Since they usually show no clues for understanding the differences between actual and planned amounts, such reports are ineffectual.

The design of systems must begin with the needs of the decision-makers. The decision-maker who determines the business value of computers is the executive who is accountable for profits. He or she has the final authority for signing off[1] on investment proposals. Executive decisions during project selection shape the expectations from computer investments. A measure of the business value of computers must give useful answers when top managers must cut next year's expenses. If company-wide spending must come down by 10%, how much will you trim information technology or customer service, marketing or product development? Do you curtail the systems budget by eliminating new projects or by postponing the finishing of existing work? Do you shrink operations or development? What information will you need to answer these questions?

Searching for Sources of Data

To collect facts about computers in business, I could tap into commercial data bases such as those provided by the International Data Corporation or the Gartner Group. This would provide the number and the models of installed computers. I could mail questionnaires to every M.I.S. executive and ask how many employees are information systems professionals. From published financial data bases such as Standard & Poor's, Dow Jones and FORTUNE magazine I could extract financial indicators useful to Wall Street analysts. From all these pieces, I could create a diversified data base about information technology spending and company results. Unfortunately, none of these sources report about the *Value-added* of a firm. In rare instances, when I was able to get good information about a firm's materials purchases, I could only estimate the costs of purchased services.[2]

While at Xerox, I accumulated this information for internal Divisions and for a few chosen competitors. The data were insufficient and inconsistent for figuring out what is a comparable level of information systems spending. I could never be sure that the scope of the information received from one source corresponded to another. This data collection was inadequate for estimating the tradeoffs among operating, development and non-computer budgets. Other researchers have tried all-inclusive surveys, but without tight controls over data definitions, and their inability to find out the dependability of their sources, they ended up with unreliable information.[3]

Information from government sources was not helpful. A periodic census[4] of government computer and telecommunications spending reveals little. It concentrates on capital investment, purchases and technology expenses as a percentage of total spending. No useful conclusions about desirable spending levels can come from this limited data because government agency spending includes large amounts of spending for capital.

There are also market research organizations with enormous data bases. They sell this information to computer manufacturers whose interest is in selling equipment. This data is usually an extrapolation of the latest trends in shipments. None of it reflects the customers' total operating expenses for information technologies. I have also seen a few consultants' proprietary data bases but found them either incomplete or excessively detailed. None of the data related to profits.[5]

This left me the laborious alternative of obtaining my data through tightly controlled data-gathering, directly from each business. I used data-gathering techniques applied by the *PIMS* (Profit Impact of Marketing Strategies) organization.[6]

THE *PIMS* APPROACH

You cannot measure what cannot be defined.

A firm's superior profitability is the consequence of favorable influences prevailing over unfavorable circumstances. *PIMS* researchers focused on determining the effects of marketing and financial relationships on profits. One interesting finding has been that market share and product quality can overcome the financial disadvantages of high wage rates.

My purpose was to find if increased spending on computers overcame cost disadvantages. I would search for characteristics found in firms with a high *Return-on-Management* using techniques developed by *PIMS*. The design of the data-gathering forms had to gain information suitable for conducting tests that would answer the following questions:

- When you compare high spenders on information technology with low spenders, can you isolate differences in profitability?

- What financial or operating characteristics explain how productive companies deploy their computer resources?
- Is there anything special about information technology that makes known measures of profitability unsuitable?
- Is it possible to accurately define what comprises *information technology* spending, and how it differs from *information resources* or from *information systems* costs?[7]

Since 1972, *PIMS* investigated similar issues. In their pursuit they accumulated an extraordinary data base of more than 3,000 businesses.[8] This data came from client firms that filled out elaborate forms which specified how to make each entry. This collection includes information about market conditions, competitive position, financial results and operating performance. Computer programs check each entry for consistency.[9] No analysis takes place without prior validation of all inputs.

I favor the *PIMS* approach to securing reliable research information. Clients pay *PIMS* a fee for a diagnostic report that gives feedback as to how they compare with their peers. It frequently happens that a client sees unexpected findings. *PIMS* staff check for possible misunderstandings whenever they enter the source data. This procedure ensures that only reliable data enter research findings. The gathering of data in medical research passes through the same validation process. The patient or the physician should not have a motive to give incorrect information.[10] As a safeguard, a firm's financial information is cross-checked against publicly available references, and compared with key ratios for equivalent businesses. Extreme ratio values suggest where the *PIMS* staff should make further inquiries.

Dozens of doctoral dissertations and hundreds of articles have their origins in the *PIMS* data base. For instance, the *PIMS* findings about the relationships between business strategy (such as capital intensity, pricing, market share, buying patterns, labor productivity) and financial performance are now guiding principles for many successful ventures.[11]

The *PIMS* approach defines strategic business units (SBU's) as organizations that operate in a *defined served market* and compete against a *defined set of competitors*:

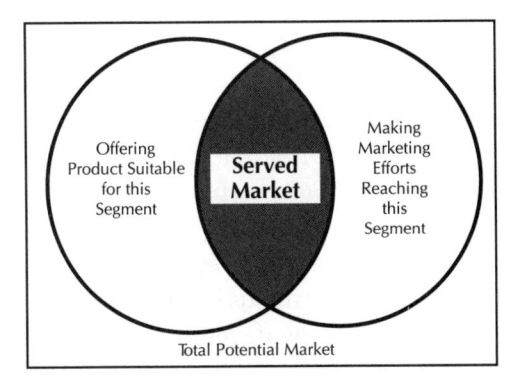

Figure 6.1: The Definition of the "Served Market"

The scope of analysis is not the entire corporation. Usually it includes several SBU's. The overall profit of any large corporation is the sum of profits from above-average and below-average business units. Averaging profits, assets or information technology expenses across several businesses would mask the effect I was looking for.

Difficulty in detecting the effects of information technology on profitability requires analyzing data at the lowest organizational level. This dictates that corporate data centers and company-wide telecommunications networks charge all expenses to SBU's. Corporate costs are distributed to the SBU's because you cannot measure the *R-O-M* of corporate staffs if they do not serve revenue-producing customers.

The *PIMS* principles—guideline ratios developed from experimental data—can tell why some firms are more likely to succeed than others. Was it possible to adapt what *PIMS* has learned about patterns of business success and failure to the analysis of the profit contributions of computers?

THE GAPS IN *PIMS*

The *PIMS* method originated in 1963, when Dr. Sidney Schoeffler developed the PROM (Profit-Optimizing) model for the General Electric Corporation. The model helped to evaluate Departmental[12] investment plans. Since then, Dr. Schoeffler and his colleagues have made many improvements in the collection and analysis of business results. Their findings have formulated principles about the effect of strategic decisions on profits.

The *PIMS* method reflects its GE origins, for it focuses on marketing and capital investment decisions. It measures the performance of an SBU most frequently in terms of its capital efficiency[13] as measured by changes in the *Return-on-Investment (ROI)*. Simple tabulations[14] display the effects of any two strategic variables on *ROI*, such as capacity utilization and labor productivity.

While the *PIMS* method helped to elucidate strategic issues during the 1960's and 1970's, several new trends have influenced the applicability of the *PIMS* approach. These new developments would challenge the applicability of *ROI*-based measures:

- The service sector of the economy became the dominant consumer of information technologies.[15]
- The most rapidly growing sectors of the economy, such as business services, were not capital-intensive.[16] Their *ROI's* could fluctuate widely as a result of the slightest change in earnings. *PIMS's* reliance on *ROI* is not adequate to evaluate such firms.
- Except where information technology applies directly to production[17]—an area where top management was comfortable with evaluating computer payoffs—information technology is primarily an overhead expense. *PIMS* forms did not collect enough data about overhead expenses, so it was not possible to analyze how information technology, applied as overhead, contributed to profits.[18] Financial analysis methods considered only cost cutting as the way to improve overhead productivity. However, imaginative and innovative investments in quality, product innovation and marketing intelligence—all in overhead—were increasingly the keys to a firm's success.
- Steadily rising overhead costs, not direct labor costs, not purchases, not assets, are the most prevalent cause of falling profits. There was no proof that computers, heralded for twenty years as the engines for improving productivity, reduced overhead costs. Proofs to the contrary were accumulating that indicated precisely the opposite.

To apply the *PIMS* principles to computers I would have to modify the *PIMS* method. The leadership of *PIMS* wished to sponsor innovative solutions if that led to a better understanding of computer investments which, until then, had resisted analysis. The *Management Productivity and Information Technology (MPIT)* project would now become a research activity funded and managed by the Strategic Planning Institute.

Defining Information Technology

The scope and applicability of information technology expenditures are changing rapidly, as pointed out in Chapter 2. To identify the effect of information technology and profits, the *MPIT* efforts would have to keep the definitions of information technology unambiguous and consistent. To fit the *PIMS* data-collection method, the *MPIT* approach would have to place a boundary on the scope of data gathering. There would also be limits on how much information could be collected. *PIMS* clients would not participate in a research study if that required more than 4–6 hours of data-gathering. The *MPIT* research applied the following rules:

- Exclude *embedded* computers from the definition of information technology and from the scope of the research. Examples of such devices are: production robots, numerical control machines, materials handling equipment, diagnostic devices, quality monitoring and testing meters, engineering workstations integrated with manufacturing processes and production control computers.[19] As this equipment is already in the costs of goods sold, established financial control techniques were adequate to monitor and to evaluate them.[20]
- Define all information technology—hardware, software, programming and telecommunications—applied to delivering revenue-producing information services as *embedded* costs. This dispenses with concerns about profit-making airline subsidiaries,[21] electronic publishing ventures or electronic data-base vendors where computers provide customers with direct access to information. Established financial control techniques are adequate to monitor and to evaluate these computer investments. The costs of *embedded* computers would not be separated from other production expenses because of lack in comparability among different firms for such uses.
- Define all information technology that is immediately essential for the production of customer revenues as *mission critical*.[22] These would include ATM's (Automatic Teller Machines), airline check-in devices that dispense boarding passes, supermarket point-of-sale scanners and cash registers which include credit validation, billing and inventory management functions. Since there is enough knowledge as to how to make

sound investment choices in these applications, established financial control techniques are adequate to monitor and evaluate such investments.

• Whatever information technology is not *embedded* or not *mission critical*, is a *management information system*, or *M.I.S.*

On the *MPIT* project only *mission-critical* and *M.I.S.* technology costs—plus software and telecommunications needed to run the systems—will be counted as "information technology":[23]

Systems Type	How System Identified	Examples of Systems
Embedded Computers	Not Identified Separately. Included in Cost of Goods or Services	Production robots; Equipment delivering commercial computer services; Process control equipment; Computerized products; Computer-aided diagnostics.
Mission-critical Computers	Included as Operations Information Technology Expense	Point-of-sales devices; Airline reservation systems; Banking terminals; Order entry devices; Warehouse automation; Decision-support in Operations.
Management Information Systems	Included as Management Information Technology Expense	Payroll; Invoicing; Sales reports; Accounting applications; Executive information systems; Electronic mail.

Table 6.1: Types of Information Technology Expenses

Mission-critical systems are essential for conducting business whereas *embedded* systems are the product or the service itself.[24] *MPIT* would concentrate on the relationship between *mission critical* and *M.I.S.* spending. The research efforts would find out if the money spent on *management information systems* delivers gains in *Management Productivity.*

To collect comparable information about information technology expenses we made sure to include only well-defined personnel costs. All expenses directly associated with using computers are in operating costs and not in information technology costs. For example, all personnel operating *embedded* systems would be an operating cost.

Personnel supporting *embedded* and *mission-critical* computers are not included in the *MPIT* definition of information technology costs. Their contributions can be understood only as a business case, not as an isolated information technology. Their costs are in the direct cost of goods and services.

People Managing	How Wages & Salaries Charged	Examples
Embedded Computers	Included in Direct Cost of Goods or Services	Operating personnel in computer services; Process control and robotics equipment operators; Users of computer-aided diagnostics; On-line data-entry.
Mission-critical Computers	Included as Indirect Cost for Business Function	Entering retrieval requests; Using computer applications such as word processing and spread-sheets; Training and installation costs; Customer support activities; Program maintenance expenses.
Management Information Systems	Included in Overhead, General & Administrative Expenses	

Table 6.2: Types of Wage & Salary Costs Associated with Information Technology

Personnel that guide, operate and support *M.I.S.* applications are excluded from the *MPIT* definition of information technology costs because their functions are now so widely distributed to everyone in the organization as to be untraceable. Their economic value comes from improving management productivity. Their contributions can be analyzed only as improving the value of *R-O-M*. Their costs are in overhead expenses.

DATA COLLECTION

Research is new understanding extracted from facts.

Where to Collect the Data?

The distribution of information technology spending in 1980 indicated where there are good sources of consistent and comparable data.[25]

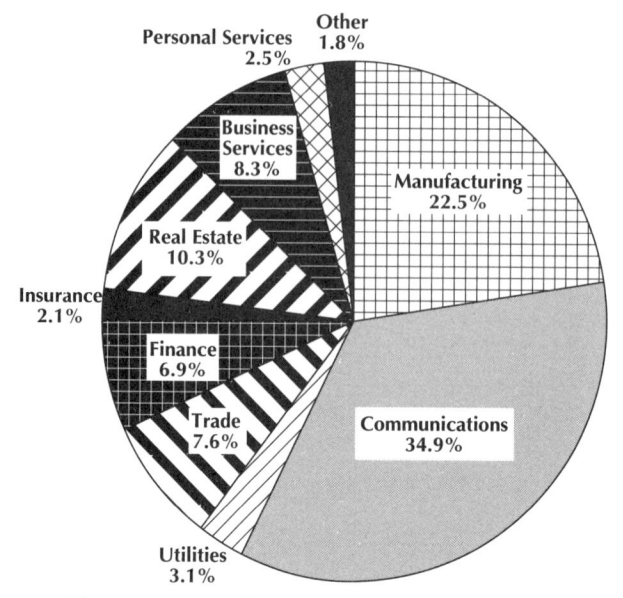

Figure 6.2: Distribution of 1980 U.S. Spending on I.T.

I eliminated communications companies from the study, even though they displayed the largest concentration of computer spending. *Embedded* and *mission critical* applications dominate this concentrated business. One company, AT&T, accounted for more than 85% of the total information technology spending in this sector. The telecommunications industry, as a regulated monopoly, was a poor candidate for measuring the effectiveness of management systems. *Value-added* computations would reflect more the decisions of Regulatory Commissions than of actual business productivity.

Banks and insurance companies were exuberantly expanding their computer installations in the early 1980's.[26] They would be poor subjects for studying the effectiveness of computers since they pursued a faster growth in information technology spending than for any other activity.[27] I also excluded real estate, finance and business services because their accelerated rate of spending would distort the influence on profits. When expenses for information technology rise at compound annual rates of 20–30%, it is possible to argue that current poor productivity may be ultimately offset by future gains.[28]

The manufacturing sector offered the best opportunity to collect data. Its rate of spending for information technology was steady during the study period.[29] Because of severe competitive pressures, manufacturing companies, who were already *PIMS* members, were eager to learn about strategic uses of information technology.

The Manufacturing Data Sample

The *MPIT* project succeeded in collecting reliable data for 292 cases.[30] Component manufacturing, consumer non-durables, and raw materials firms dominate the sample:

- Supplies Manufacturing 4.6%
- Consumer Durables 3.8%
- Components Manufacturing 39.4%
- Consumer Non-Durables 28.8%
- Raw Materials 21.9%
- Capital Goods Manufacturing 1.7%

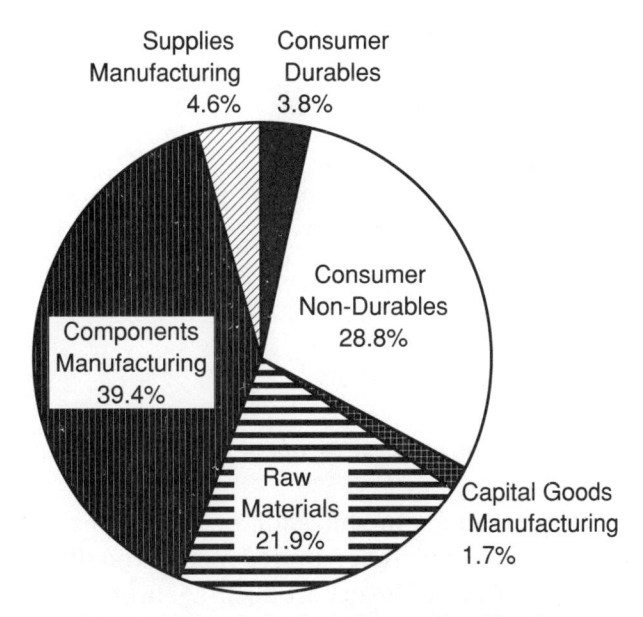

Figure 6.3: The R-O-M Database, by Industry Classification

It was not necessary to break up the entire sample into groups by industrial classification. After making adjustments for differences in capital assets and for differences in vertical integration, the *Business Value-added* ratios were comparable. High *R-O-M* firms processing raw materials were more like high *R-O-M* firms making components than low *R-O-M* raw materials firms. It is a testimonial to the power of the *Value-added* methods that they make firms comparable despite differences in their financial and marketing characteristics.

Geographical Origins

The global marketplace for manufactured products made it desirable to include European organizations.[32] There are international differences in currency, labor costs, labor practices and taxation that needed checking to test the suitability of the *R-O-M* method. There was also a belief that European businesses were slower in accepting information technology than comparable U.S. businesses. Including European firms in the data-base enriched the quality of the research and broadened the range of data for study.

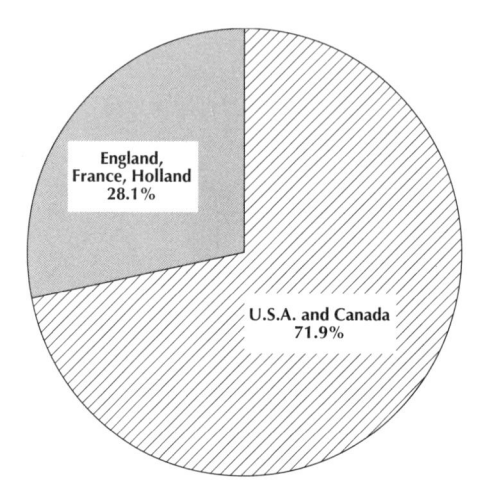

Figure 6.4: The R-O-M Database, by Geography

The European companies did not show enough atypical *Value-added* ratios to require different treatment. Even through they showed, on average, higher overhead cost than U.S. firms, these differences fit a continuum. European manufacturing companies are not a distinctive species warranting different treatment than anyone else.[31]

Since the completion of the *MPIT* project in 1984, two new data collection efforts are proceeding as by-products of consulting practices.[33] The sample size has grown appreciably, particularly in Europe. Although the latest findings have improved the reliability of the conclusions, they have not changed the fundamental ideas that have come from the *MPIT* research prior to 1984. Should new insights arise from the enlarged database, the results will appear in revised editions of this book.

Size of Organizations

When the *MPIT* project began, I worried about the bias contributed by companies with employment of over 10,000 and hundred-million dollar information technology budgets. Giant companies may indulge in excessive spending on computers because they can afford bigger bureaucracies.

The *MPIT* researchers obtained a nicely diversified sample:

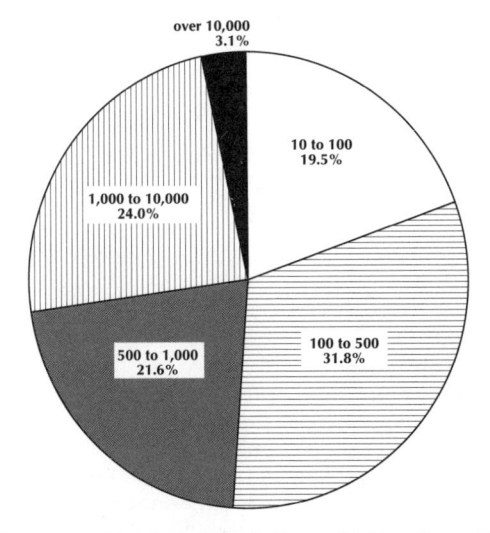

Figure 6.5: The R-O-M Database, by Employee Size

Small to medium size businesses (less than 500 employees) comprised approximately half the sample. Very large businesses (over 10,000 employees) were only 3.1% of the sample. The size of the company did not have a decisive effect on *R-O-M*, and therefore there was no need to treat big companies differently from small companies.[34]

THE DATA FORM

The original *MPIT* data-gathering form was 30 pages long. Included were 18 pages of instructions to explain how to fill out the desired information.[35] The broad scope of the *MPIT* data collection effort shows why other researchers always chose simple revenue- or asset-based ratios to study the effects of information technologies on profits. This was the first time that this type of comprehensive data was collected. The prior assumption was always that computer spending has a strong and direct influence on profits. Therefore, its effects would be readily discernible from studying only a minimum of data.

My research convinced me that computer spending had a weak and indirect relationship to profits. To detect these faint effects, I had to

112   THE BUSINESS VALUE OF COMPUTERS

collect the right kind of data, for a sufficiently large number of cases, to make the assumed "weak computer effect" show up.[36]

There was no way to foresee what effects would actually appear and which variables would correlate with information technology spending. The *PIMS* staff knew we had to collect data that was proven to have strategic significance. We also had to add data that did not exist currently in the *PIMS* database. To guide our search, we had the hypothesis that *Management* costs needed to be separated from other costs.[37]

Gathering Competitive Information

To begin, we picked a subset of variables already gathered by *PIMS* for conducting strategic analyses:

Market Share, This Business
Market Share of Largest Competitor
Market Share of Second Largest Competitor
Market Share of Third Largest Competitor
Industry Concentration (Share of Largest Four Producers)
% Ranking This Business as Having Superior Quality
% Ranking This Business as Having Equivalent Quality
% Ranking This Business as Having Inferior Quality
Price Index as Compared with Average of Three Largest Competitors
Forecast Growth in Selling Price, Next Five Years
New Products as % of Revenues, This Year, This Business
New Products as % of Revenues, Three Largest Competitors
Real Past Market Growth, Served Market, This Business
Forecast Real Market Growth, Served Market, This Business
Number of Immediate Customers Accounting for 50% of Revenue
% of Immediate Customers Accounting for 50% of Revenue
% of Customers Accounting for 50% of Revenue for Competition
Typical Purchase Amount by End User
Typical Purchase Amount by Immediate Customer, This Business

Table 6.3: Strategic Variables used in MPIT

The first four variables in the table above capture what we must know about a company's competitive position. Many advocates of increased information systems spending argue that competitive or strategic advantages are the primary justification for computers. It was essential therefore that these attributes be captured for further evaluation. In *MPIT*, we adopted the same approach as in *PIMS* of using *relative market share*[38] as an indicator of competitive and strategic strength.

Improving customer service and products are the most difficult variables to quantify when proposing quality-enhancing computer projects. Unless you can assign some worth to quality, omitting it means that it has no value. We used established *PIMS* procedures to make quality explicit. A ranking scheme compares the quality of a business against its competitors' quality.[39]

Organizational Information

I assumed that occupational and organizational characteristics of each firm's workforce would shape computer spending.[40] The *MPIT* forms would capture not only payroll data, but also details of where the personnel worked, by business function:

Executive, Administrative and Management
Professional Specialty
Technical Specialty and Related Support
Sales Workers
Administrative Support, including Clerical Workers
Service Occupations
Precision Production Occupations
Operators, Fabrication and Laborers
% of Employees in Unions
Organization Levels Between Chief Business Executive (CBE) and the CEO
Organization Levels Between (CBE) and First Level of Supervision
Organization Levels Between (CBE) and Immediate Customers

Table 6.4: Organizational Information Used in MPIT

There are many articles and books about the potential of information technology to simplify organizational structure. To check these theories our data-gathering forms requested a description of each company's organization structure. Four measures of *Organizational Distance* were collected by counting organization layers[41]:

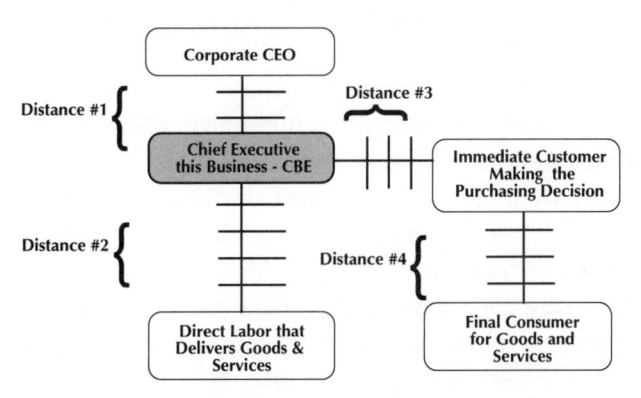

Figure 6.6: Measuring Organizational Complexity

- Distance #1: The number of reporting levels between the *Chief Executive Officer* of the corporation (for multi-divisional cases) and the *Chief Business Executive* (*CBE*) of the Strategic Business Unit;
- Distance #2: The number of reporting levels between the *CBE* and the direct labor that delivers the goods and services;
- Distance #3: The number of reporting levels between the *CBE* and the customer's buyer;
- Distance #4: The number of intervening levels between the immediate customer and the final consumer of goods and services.[42]

How to Differentiate Management from Operations

Information effectiveness is getting maximum results with the least information.

To distinguish between resources needed for running a company today and tomorrow is not a new idea. The concepts of *zero-base budgeting* and *overhead-value* analysis isolate the essential from the optional workforce. It calls for the discovery of the least amount of resources needed to deliver goods and services to today's customers. It assumes employees have the minimal skills and resources to cope with suppliers and customers on a daily basis without the Chairman, President, secretaries, supervisors, market research, product development, planners and coordinators.

To identify the essential *Operations* resources does not deny the critical role of everybody else. Everyone not essential for sustaining current *Operations* is *Management*. This covers planning, motivating, controlling, rewarding, researching, investing, hiring and marketing. If you can separate out who and what generates the immediate revenues, the remainder can be considered as the safeguarding of the future. The costs of providing for the future continuation of a business are mostly information-handling costs. This involves meetings, budgeting, hiring, promotional activities, research, legal actions, accounting, financing and other such activities that engage information workers.

In analyzing corporate costs, I make the distinction between the flow of goods or services, and the flow of information. Each of these has separate *Management* and *Operations* characteristics:

Figure 6.7: Defining Operations and Management Information

OPERATIONS FLOWS

Raw materials, semi-finished goods, parts, energy and services go into *Operations* to create *Business Value-added.* After a company adds its value, goods and services pass to customers. The key elements here are *Purchases* and *Sales.* In a market economy, they involve exchanges of money.

As previously discussed in this chapter, robots, on-line monitoring, process control computers, instruments and dials, and computerized product features will not be in "information costs," but in the costs of goods and services. An example of information technology inextricably *embedded* into the costs of *Operations* is the cost of programming and designing a microcomputer-driven automobile display. This cost would be in the price the customer is willing to pay for this feature.

There are information flows essential to the movement of goods and services in and out of *Operations:* purchasing places orders with suppliers; engineers pick vendors; production scheduling keeps track of incoming shipments; salespersons write orders; distribution schedules and keeps track of merchandise deliveries; service personnel answer the customer's questions.

Although such activities are *mission critical,* they are irrelevant to the customer unless they fail to meet the customer's needs. The customer does not care how much you spend on them, or whether you use computers or not. You know if an information system is *mission critical* when it malfunctions. When that happens, the delivery of products and services halts immediately and revenue declines.[43]

The business value of *embedded* systems can be judged only by the paying customers. They are a direct cost of sales. You can evaluate *embedded* systems in the same way as you do any other product offering or service innovation.[44]

The business values of *mission critical* systems should be judged by the line executives who are accountable for profits. The value of such systems involves making complex tradeoffs. Only the executive who balances employee skills, response time, product and service features, pricing and competitive strategies against computer applications can evaluate *mission critical* applications. The costs of such systems will appear as operating costs. Their effects are an integral part of the profit plan. The justification of a *mission-critical* investment is meaningless in isolation.

You may ask why I spend so much effort to distinguish between *embedded* and *mission critical* systems. I explained in Chapter 2 that the definition of information technology can change at will. You cannot gather useful data unless you verify that the information you get is consistent. Loosely interpreted definitions of what is in computer surveys are the reason why reported information-technology ratios are shaky.

MANAGEMENT FLOWS

Management flows include goods and services (chairs for the managers, consulting services for executives). Information flows consist of reports, meetings, sales summaries, budget statements and personnel records.

Of greatest interest are the costs of management information. This is where you find the most difficulty in identifying the value of computers. The customer does not care a whit whether or not you have any management information systems. The customer does not care if you use computers or a quill for your invoices, provided they are clear and convenient.[45] Only the Government seems to care if you use computers: it makes auditing by the tax authorities easier.

Information systems that are not *embedded* or *mission critical* are *management information systems* (M.I.S.). These includes sales reports, invoices, accounting records, inventory lists, production planning listings and personnel files. If a system does not cause an immediate stop in the delivery of goods and services to customers, it is a *management information system*.

The business value of *management information systems* can be judged only by managers who are directly accountable for their function's contributions to business profits. The value of management systems calls for the making of tradeoffs between employee skills, costs of communications, timeliness of responses, safety and security.

The costs of *management information systems* will always appear as overhead costs. As the initial step you should examine whether the systems make any contribution to operations. For example, your first reaction to a proposal to upgrade invoicing should be to check whether the improvement does anything for customers. Only after getting an answer you may consider whether the invoicing project will lower costs, improve reliability or speed up its timeliness at the lowest possible cost. You may not want to do something that does not create *Value-added.*

To study the contributions of management information systems (e.g., overhead) to *Operations* systems (e.g., direct costs, revenues and profits) you must evaluate *Operations,* not *Management* costs. Neglecting this important rule is the source of all problems in budgeting and controlling information technology expenses.[46]

DISTRIBUTION OF INFORMATION TECHNOLOGY AND LABOR COSTS

Those who put accounting data into a *management information system* rarely foresee its uses. Corporate charts of accounts usually reflect age-old management practices. It may take a long time before anyone will venture to change the recording of costs.

Spreadsheet programs make it easy to redistribute accounting data from established accounts into categories for making *R-O-M* computations. This allows keeping track of the allocations from existing accounting schedules, while maintaining the integrity of total costs at each step. The following diagram shows how to distribute information technology and labor costs:

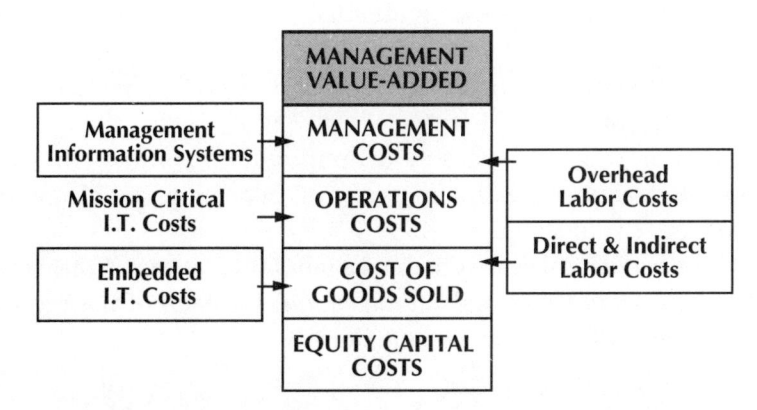

Figure 6.8: Allocation of Information Technology and Labor Costs

First, you remove all *embedded* costs from information technology expenses. Next, you identify all *mission critical* applications and assign them to Operations. Everything else is *management information.* A similar approach applies to materials and services:

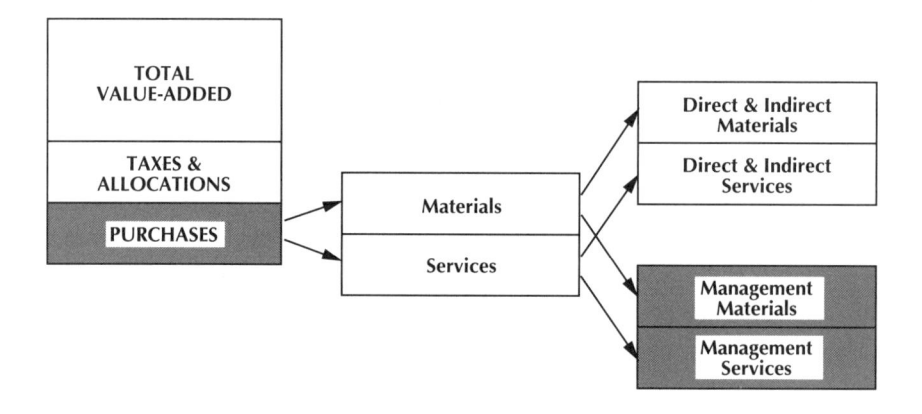

Figure 6.9: Allocation of Materials and Services Costs

The above figure illustrates the logic of distributing the cost of purchases, considered as either information or non-information purchases. For instance, computer maintenance, contract programming or bought software would be service purchases. Paper and supplies used in computer processing would be materials. All materials and services essential for the support of *mission critical* systems go to *Operations*. Everything else is in the costs of *Management.*

Accounting reports seldom identify how much money flows into purchases, as contrasted with internal costs. If you do not have good data for your company you can estimate your purchase contents from data available for your industry.[47]

Categorizing costs, assets or employment follows the same method illustrated above. If there is any misallocation, it is always possible to retrace your steps.

Using explicit rules, we obtained a tabulation of costs (further subdivided into *Operations* and *Management*) for each of the reported SBU's, by the following business functions:

Production—Total Employee Costs
Production—Non-information Purchases
Production—Information Purchases
Distribution—Total Employee Costs
Distribution—Non-information Purchases
Distribution—Information Purchases
Sales—Total Employee Costs
Sales—Non-information Purchases
Sales—Information Purchases
Marketing—Total Employee Costs
Marketing—Non-information Purchases
Marketing—Information Purchases
Research & Development—Total Employee Costs
Research & Development—Non-information Purchases
Research & Development—Information Purchases
Administration—Total Employee Costs
Administration—Non-information Purchases
Administration—Information Purchases

Table 6.5: Management and Operations Cost Categories

WHO USES INFORMATION TECHNOLOGY?

Data from 292 manufacturing company cases show that information technology expenses cover a wide range:

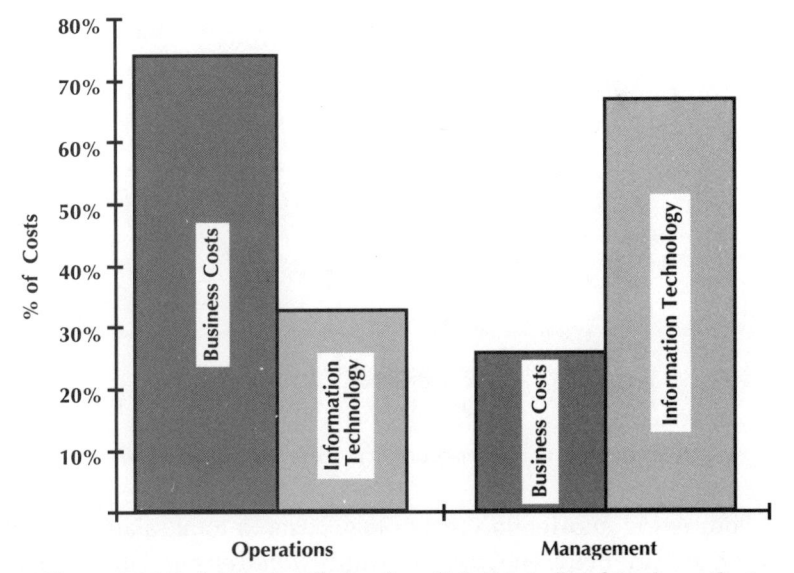

Figure 6.10: Information Technology Relative to Total Business Costs

120   THE BUSINESS VALUE OF COMPUTERS

Operations are all activities essential for delivering products and services to today's customers. They represent 69% of total costs but consume only 36% of the firms' information technology. *Management* is, by default, everything not in *Operations:*

**Operations = Costs of delivering goods and services to today's customers
Management = All costs not in Operations**

Management uses information technology more extensively. With only 31% of total costs, they absorb 64% of the firms' information technology budget.

I consider information systems as people-related activities. Process control computers and robots are in plant equipment. For the purposes of the *MPIT* study I excluded the costs of systems analysis, training, input creation and report-handling personnel from the definition of information technology costs. The widespread use of distributed computing and the diversity in organizational approaches for managing information technologies makes these costs indeterminable and incomparable.[48]

When I compare the per capita costs for information technology, the difference between *Operations* and *Management* is large:

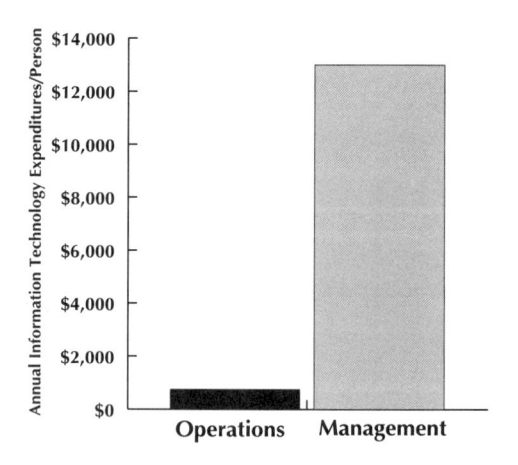

Figure 6.11: Comparison Between Per Capita I.T. Costs

Comparing information technology costs to total salary costs also show a disparity between *Operations* and *Management*. This is because a smaller number of *Management* people with higher average salaries use information technology:

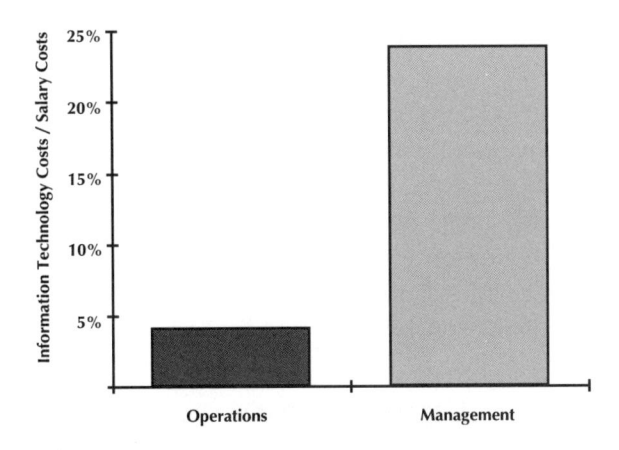

Figure 6.12: Comparison Between I.T./Salary Cost Ratios

Management people use 18 times more information technology dollars than *Operation*s. The *Information Technology-to-Employee Salary* ratio ranges from 4.1% for *Operations* to 23.9% for *Management*. This shows that information technology is primarily an intra-organizational activity.[49]

Who in *Managemen*t spends all the computer money?[50] *Administration* and *Sales & Marketing* show the highest concentrations:

Information Technology/Salaries	Operations	Management
Manufacturing & Distribution	8.8%	5.0%
Sales & Marketing	6.2%	26.9%
Administration	24.9%	32.7%
Research & Development	none	5.5%

Table 6.6: Importance of Information Technology Relative to Salaries

Manufacturing & Distribution and *Research & Development* activities showed no appreciable changes in their information technology spending for the five years of our data. The only heavily automated *Operations* function was administrative processing. The low penetration of information technology in *Manufacturing & Distribution,* field *Sales* and *Research & Development* suggests a potential for applying information technology where it creates customer *Value-added*. An examination of the balance sheet also shows that information technology assets work more for *Management* than for *Operations:*

	Operations	Management
I.T. Assets/Total Assets	3.0%	35.4%

Table 6.7: Importance of Information Technology Relative to Assets

The relatively large allocation of information technology to *Management* is the reason why measures based on revenues or assets give us puzzling results. Companies vary enormously in how much money they spend on *Management*.

CHAPTER SUMMARY

We gathered data from customers who had an interest in the accuracy of what they gave us because they would receive in return an evaluation of their own information technology spending. To make companies comparable, we collected information about competitive position, financial conditions, employment and how their costs apply to *Management*.

We also defined important distinctions between *Operations* and *Management* costs:

Operations	Essential for delivering products and services to today's customers.
Management	Everything not in Operations

Table 6.8: Definitions of Operations and Management Costs

Attributing activities either to *Operations* or *Management* was necessary to allow different approaches to justifying computer investments. *Operations* applications can be justified only as an integral part of a revenue-producing profit plan. *Management* applications can be justified only insofar as they improve *Management Productivity*.

Another important distinction is the classification of information technology costs according to their use. As the uses of information technologies evolve, an increasing share migrates into *mission critical* or *embedded* applications. Here they become indistinguishable from the processes of conducting the business. These distinctions are important. Expenditures which once were under the general heading of *Management Information Systems* migrate into *embedded* applications where they may cease showing up as "information technology."[51]

CHAPTER 6—GETTING THE FACTS   123

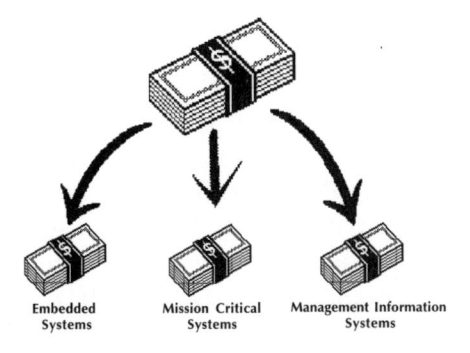

Figure 6.13: Migration of Computer Systems Missions

From an investment standpoint, computers are one of the direct costs of generating revenues. Their uses are not different from any other business resource. How to invest and manage them are integral to the ways you deal with any other investment decision. Information technology ceases to be a special case to which you can assign value in isolation from other costs of satisfying customer needs.

The careful definitions of data and the controlled collection of company information gave us a database that is, to my best knowledge, unmatched by any prior study of computer expenditures. This database supports two separate and distinct activities:

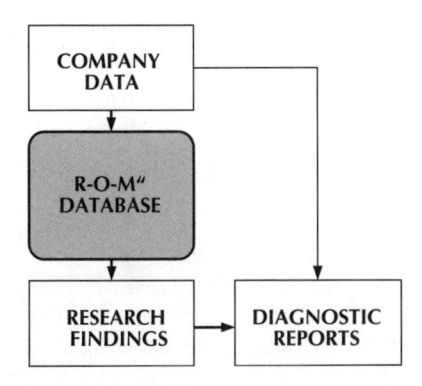

Figure 6.14: The Uses of the R-O-M Database

The research findings, which cover the findings extracted from *MPIT* data, will be discussed in Chapter 7. Meanwhile, I continue accumulating additional cases from my consulting practice. These are used to update the research database periodically.[52] My current efforts concentrate on improving the usefulness of diagnostic reports to Chief Executives, Chief Planners, Chief Financial Officers and Corporate Systems Review Boards. The better these reports serve client needs, the faster I can gain additional information to improve the scope of the research database.

The case studies based on my diagnostic findings are voluminous enough to warrant a separate book. Therefore, I shall illustrate only two of the 45 standard diagnostic displays in Chapter 8. These examples should explain how I apply the *R-O-M* database to the most critical aspect of any planning: the diagnosis of investment opportunities.

With a foundation of facts firmly in place, I could explore of the relationship between computers and productivity.

CHAPTER 6 COMMENTS

[1] A note for the public sector executive: although there is much fuss about the distinctions between for-profit and not-for-profit organizations, that is a score-keeping matter. One quarter of private businesses in the *R-O-M* database do not create positive management *Value-added*. In my approach to evaluating specific information technology investments I concentrate on expected differences in cash flows, with or without computers.

[2] From the *Electronic Business Magazine*, April 16, 1990 we have unusually detailed data about the internal cost structure of Japanese electronic companies:

Fiscal 1989 Results	Fujitsu	Hitachi	NEC	Sony	Toshiba
Manufacturing Materials	41.0%	42.1%	45.1%	77.2%	36.2%
Manufacturing Personnel	6.9%	13.2%	6.8%	6.4%	10.8%
Manufacturing Overhead	5.2%	20.1%	18.2%	5.9%	7.8%
Inventory and other adjustmnt.	-0.7%	-0.2%	-15.0%	-5.8%	-0.2%
Cost of Manufacturing	52.4%	75.2%	55.1%	83.7%	54.6%
Rents & leases	0.0%	0.3%	1.4%	0.0%	0.6%
License fees	0.0%	0.0%	0.0%	0.0%	0.6%
Taxes	0.8%	0.9%	0.7%	0.0%	0.0%
Depreciation	5.8%	3.9%	3.6%	3.2%	5.0%
Other Costs of Goods	2.4%	-4.6%	7.1%	-6.5%	12.0%
Costs of Goods Sold	61.4%	75.7%	67.9%	80.4%	72.8%
SG&A Personnel	3.5%	2.2%	2.9%	2.3%	3.5%
Advertising & Promotion	1.0%	1.0%	1.2%	1.5%	0.9%
SG&A Purchases (Calculated Estimate)	28.4%	15.9%	23.1%	11.9%	16.7%
SG&A Costs	32.9%	19.1%	27.2%	15.7%	21.1%
Operating Income	5.7%	5.2%	4.8%	3.9%	6.0%
Total	100.0%	100.0%	100.0%	100.0%	100.0%

Based on this data I could estimate the *Return-on-Management* for these firms. This estimate is an approximation only. To get a reliable and consistent value of *R-O-M* would require more detailed information:

Fiscal 1989 Results ($ billions)	Fujitsu	Hitachi	NEC	Sony	Toshiba
Revenues	$15.2	$24.5	$19.3	$9.5	$22.1
Purchases	$10.5	$14.2	$13.2	$8.5	$11.7
Taxes	$0.1	$0.2	$0.1	$0.0	$0.0
Total *Value-added*	$4.5	$10.1	$6.0	$1.0	$10.4
Capital *Value-added*	$0.7	$0.9	$0.8	$0.5	$0.7
Operations Costs	$3.0	$8.0	$4.3	$0.3	$8.1

Management Costs	$0.7	$0.8	$0.8	$0.4	$1.0
Management *Value-added*	$0.2	$0.4	$0.1	($0.16)	$0.6
Return-on-Management	25.8%	47.8%	13.9%	-44.1%	66.4%

The high-purchase, capital-intensive and low *Value-added* Sony shows a negative value of *R-O-M* which suggests that this firm has a productivity problem.

3 The *Computerworld* estimates of information systems expenditures are inconsistent because the scope and definitions are not uniform. For instance, some companies include in their reported systems spending their revenue-producing information services Divisions, such as in the case of Citicorp, whereas other banks' information systems expenditures support only their own internal needs.

4 By the Office of Management and Budget.

5 The information technology database of one of the largest consulting companies contains breakdowns of computer budgets by industry, departmental function, application, input source, output source, lines of code, machine run time, maintenance expense, data center utilization, etc. Clients can view this awesome collection as a four-dimensional diagram (a cube with its sides folded out). Each of the 50,000+ data classifications contains the average ratio for the data that intersects at that point. Artful graphic displays, in color, make this complexity more palatable. The information is so diverse, clients may use this information to support whatever argument they wish.

6 The *Management Productivity and Information Technology (MPIT)* project was funded by the Strategic Planning Institute and carried out under my direction. The original idea is in a letter of September 12, 1980 to Donald Heany, Principal of *PIMS*. Sidney Schoeffler, the *PIMS* Executive Director, deserves my profound gratitude for sponsoring the *MPIT* project and for allocating scarce research resources to large scale testing of the *R-O-M* concept. Dr. Schoeffler's support is admirable, because *MPIT* represents a departure from *PIMS*' ROI-based measurements. Without Sidney Schoeffler's faithful commitment and support, the *MPIT* project would not have been possible.

After the project started, the entire *PIMS* staff, and especially Bradley Gale and Donald Swire, made many suggestions about data definitions and data-gathering practices. Without their encouragement and support, the project would have stalled. The culmination of all this work was DataForm 8, *Special Research Project on Overhead Manpower Productivity and Information Technology*, released on April 19, 1982.

In mid-1983, M.C.A.(Gus) van Nievelt was appointed full-time project manager by *PIMS* to fulfill the research under my direction. Most of the actual data gathering and early data analysis were done by Gus in 1983 and 1984. He rightly deserves credit and thanks for his admirable persistence in eliciting finished data forms from *PIMS* clients, and for the early research findings. In 1984–85, two researchers from the MIT Sloan School (Dale Murphy and Charles Loveman) received access to summarized *MPIT* data. They published their findings as Master's and Doctoral theses at M.I.T.

The *MPIT* project was completed in 1985. *PIMS* released copies of the full *MPIT* data-base to myself and to Prof. Charles Kriebel of Carnegie-Mellon in the Summer of 1989. All the findings in this book come from a complete re-examination of the original data. Because management purchases are not in *Management Costs* for computing *R-O-M*, the numerical values shown in this book are not identical with those originally published by *PIMS* and later by van Nievelt.

7 There is a raging debate regarding the scope of "information technology management" and "information resources management." These are not idle disputes but organizational turf battles. In the Federal and State Governments, the concept of the IRM (Information Resources Management) is now a high-level civil service position. "Information technology management" has control over computer hardware, software, telecommunications devices, video, electronic mail, facsimile, and sometimes microfilm and copiers. "Information resource management" is more ambitious, because it also claims jurisdiction over the personnel and capital that concerns any information-handling activities. This includes librarians,

file-clerks, record-depositories, customer inquiry-handling, electronic publishing, mail-rooms, telephone operators, reservation clerks and whoever else attends to a computer terminal. Every executive, engineer, administrator and worker, including operators of robots, will ultimately end up working and communicating via computers. Therefore, there is much controversy as to how to confine the scope of an IRM executive. The IRM concept, if taken literally, is boundless, and therefore unfeasible as a functional approach. Ultimately, when everyone is an information worker, you can manage only through *Management*, not through a specialized function. The information resources management approach is a transient organizational solution for addressing the lagging productivity of information workers.

[8] A business unit (Strategic Business Unit, or SBU) is an organization with an identifiable set of competitors, selling in identifiable markets. It has a financial statement and a balance sheet. One corporation may have many SBU's.

[9] You cannot have escalating prices and a rising market share in a growing market while showing declining revenues.

[10] Research surveys are likely to be more reliable if participants have a verifiable interest in telling the truth. Most of the published reports from surveys are partial, non-random samples, unchecked for bias. Surveys not subjected to any testing for respondents' bias are the most frequent research method found in academic journals on information technology.

[11] For a list of doctoral dissertations, newsletters, textbook references see the bibliography in R.D. Buzzell and B.T. Gale, The *PIMS* Principles, *The Free Press*, 1987.

[12] The General Electric Corporation pioneered decentralized Strategic Business Units, then called Departments. It was the Departmental organization that generated the Strategic Business Units data that Schoeffler used in his studies. He helped to specify the measurements that would apply to market-oriented profit-center managers. The ideas developed by Schoeffler now permeate much contemporary management thinking about decentralization. The concept of mapping the strategic position of a firm in terms of two critical variables was reformulated and repackaged by extremely profitable consulting firms.

[13] Current accounting systems are subservient to the idea that executives, shareholders and the Stock Market are primarily interested in how efficiently a firm uses its capital. *Return-on-Assets* (e.g., Profits divided by Assets), *Return-on-Investment* (Profits divided by Balance Sheet Valuations) and *Return-on-Equity* (Profits divided by Book value of Shareholder Equity) always appear in annual reports. Consequently, executive bonuses and profit sharing are unrelated to the efficiency of people, but to the efficiency of capital. That is not the way financiers judge mergers and acquisitions, who now focus on the capacity of the new management team to generate improved cash flow.

Though *PIMS* analyses most frequently rely on the *Return-on-Investment* to measure the effects of strategic factors, it also employs measures such as *R-O-S* (*Return-on-Sales*) and *Shareholder Return*, as the situation warrants it.

[14] As 3x3 or 4x4 grids.

[15] In 1985, only 15.8% of the total information technology capital was in manufacturing, inclusive of computers used for business data processing. Although we do not have reliable statistics, production and process computers were less than a third of the manufacturing capital for information technology. The balance was in the services sector: 37.7% in telecommunications; 11.7% in business and health services; 10.8% in finance & insurance; 10.4% in real estate; 9.7% in wholesale and retail and the balance in others. For an excellent discussion see S.S. Roach, Technology and the Services Sector, *Technological Forecasting*, 34:4:1988

[16] I once computed the ROI's for Arthur Andersen & Co. and Peat, Marwick & Mitchell. The numbers were astronomical and could not be used for any practical comparisons.

[17] Defined as "embedded costs." The information technology-to-revenue ratio for an on-line computer services company in my post-*MPIT* database is 48%. A small

electronic company which engages in the business of testing weapons-control computers has 70% of its assets invested in information technology. To these firms computers are a manufacturing expense.

18 *PIMS* included most overhead costs as *General and Administrative Expense*. Such a large aggregation did not lend itself to isolating the effects of computers.

19 In Defense this would include weapon systems, such as target acquisition and missile guidance computers.

20 If the price of a product or service incorporates a customer-recognizable contribution of information technology, it is the direct result of *embedded* computers. *Embedded* technology is what the customer purchases.

21 For instance, I would exclude from the American Airlines' information technology those expenses for generating $455 million SABRE system revenues, because these include services to other airlines and travel agents. I would count as either *mission critical* or *M.I.S.* only those SABRE charges that support the American Airlines internal business needs.

22 If "mission critical" systems get funds with less resistance, project managers will find it attractive to give it that label. D. Vincent (The Information Based Corporation, *Dow Jones-Irwin*, 1990, p. 138) reports that the IBM Corporation has classified its general ledger application as "mission critical" because it "...standardizes the unique IBM culture at thousands of locations around the world." Unless the general ledger is directly essential for the production of revenues, I would classify it as a management system.

23 Voice telephone, facsimile and copying equipment are general overhead costs, like furniture and workplace conveniences, unless a firm has in place a costing method for distributing such expenses to revenue-producing tasks. For instance, in a consulting firm most of the billable telephone and reproduction costs would be *mission critical*. Whether a technology is directly attributable to a product or service determines how you will treat general infrastructure costs, such as data-bases and networks. Unless computer costs are variable, on a transaction basis, you should charge all fixed infrastructure to overhead as costs of *management*.

24 How to classify computing equipment in Xerox Computer Services (XCS) illustrates the distinction between systems types. XCS is a supplier of on-line applications to small firms. Its computers are *embedded*, because they deliver a revenue-producing service. The Xerox Supply Division is in the telephone-order supplies business. It purchases services from XCS. 80% of the applications support on-line order-entry, inventory control and delivery. These applications are *mission critical* because you cannot make delivery commitments to customers if the XCS system is down. 20% of the supply Division's applications from XCS are in accounting, sales reporting, productivity measurement and planning. These are *management information systems*.

The SABRE computers in the American Airlines seat-reservation business are *embedded* costs. When an American Airlines reservations agent uses SABRE services, the cost of that transaction is a *mission critical* expense.

A point-of-sale device is a convenience for the customer and a cost saver for the merchandiser, but is not a product itself. It is *mission critical*. The costs of information processing of data extracted from a point-of-sale device, for control, accounting and planning purposes, are *management information systems*.

In the Defense Department there are many arguments about whether or not to classify a computer application as *mission critical*, because nobody will admit that they are not essential. Only if it can directly assist soldiers in carrying out combat missions is a system *mission critical*.

25 As measured by the ratio of Information Technology Spending/Total Business Value.

26 Since 1980 the distribution of spending for information technology has changed because the manufacturing sector has grown at a much slower rate than the services sector (From Economic Perspectives, *Morgan Stanley Economic Research*, December 15, 1989):

128   THE BUSINESS VALUE OF COMPUTERS

	1980	1988
Manufacturing	22.5%	11.3%
Communications	34.9%	26.4%
Utilities	3.1%	4.3%
Trade	7.6%	11.5%
Finance	6.9%	14.8%
Insurance	2.1%	5.8%
Real Estate	10.3%	9.9%
Business Services	8.3%	12.1%
Personal Services	2.5%	2.8%
Other	1.8%	1.1%
Total	100.0%	100.0%
Total Spending ($ Billions)	$55.2	$114.1

	1980	1988	Growth/year
Manufacturing	$12.4	$12.9	0.5%
Communications	19.3	30.1	6.6%
Utilities	1.7	4.9	16.2%
Trade	4.2	13.1	17.7%
Finance	3.8	16.9	23.7%
Insurance	1.2	6.6	28.3%
Real Estate	5.7	11.3	10.3%
Business Services	4.6	13.8	17.1%
Personal Services	1.4	3.2	12.7%
Transportation & Other	1.0	1.3	3.4%
Total Spending ($ Billions)	$55.2	$114.1	10.9%

At the time of the *MPIT* research effort, it would not have been prudent to focus on banking and finance. When their extraordinary expansion stabilizes such a study will become more reliable because this sector will then represent the largest accumulation of information technology.

[27] People who have just bought a very expensive automobile are not unbiased sources of information about other vehicles. Never ask an employee who just got a personal computer after a long wait how he likes it.

[28] I tested whether a one, two or three year lag between expenses and several measures of profitability would improve results. No offset worked. In the manufacturing sector, nearly all information technology spending is committed to computing operating costs and software maintenance (estimated at 70%+ of all development resources). Year-to-year changes in budgets for new applications do not emerge from the statistical "noise" created by shifts in employment, purchases, assets and profits.

[29] *PIMS* membership is mainly in manufacturing, which would make it possible to compare any new data against the already accumulated findings. *PIMS* members also had much experience in dealing with the *PIMS* approach to highly structured questionnaires.

[30] The *MPIT* data came from 64 Strategic Business units reporting at least three years and a maximum of six years of data each. In Chapter 7 you will see that the financial and employment structure of this sample was inconsistent over the study period. During the study period, most of the firms showed employment shifts from factory operatives to professional and managerial labor. They showed a large increase in external purchases as total employment declined. Instead of averaging the histories of the 64 SBU's, each year's financial and employment profile had to stand on its own for coming up with a valid analysis of management productivity. The *MPIT* sample of 292 cases are statistically independent financial, marketing and employment SBU profiles.

[31] Negotiations have been proceeding for the past five years to include Japanese, Hong-Kong and Singapore companies in the database. An acceptable agreement does not exist because of the reluctance to share detailed financial information.

32 Before you come up with too many generalizations from the data shown in this book you must remember that the sample comes from *PIMS* members. Prior *PIMS* research has shown that companies in the *PIMS* sample deliver somewhat better results (as defined by ROI) than all firms. This makes sense because any management that will subject itself to an analytic diagnosis is probably better than those who do not.

When I do productivity analyses on a specific company in a particular industry sector and location, I use a small sample for peer-group comparison. Readers should resist the temptation to scale the charts. First, they represent averages and therefore could lead to erroneous conclusions when applied to a particular situation. Second, to protect the data, a few graphs show the general relationships but do not label the values of one of the scales.

33 By Strassmann, Inc. or by VN (VanNievelt) International, Montvale, N.J. Strassmann, Inc. also collects data through third party licensees. The 1988/89 questionnaires and analytic methods offer several improvements based on the experiences learned since the original data collection. The latest version of Strassmann, Inc. services also include strategic diagnostics supplied by the MANTIS (Management Tools and Information Services) organization, directed by Sidney Schoeffler and Joaquim Branco in Boston. This makes it possible to consider the profit effect of marketing and capital investment strategies (based on ROI) simultaneously with *R-O-M* findings.

34 A study of the relationship between company size and management productivity is currently under way. Our approach to all findings is that unless we get acceptable statistical proof, nothing gets published.

35 The latest version of the *R-O-M* data-gathering form is 28 pages long, including instructions.

36 This analogy comes from experimental physics. To give you some idea of the amount of the data, consider that the raw data input was 53,728 numbers. The *R-O-M* database may be the largest collection of information regarding computers. Four hundred five ratios (118,260 items) screened this mass of data using multivariate analysis. It is conceivable that a few new insights stay undetected which leaves room for further research.

37 The following balance sheet data came with each strategic business unit:

Cash
Net Receivables
Inventories
Gross Book Value of Plant & Equipment
Net Book Value of Land and Buildings
Depreciation Expense/Year of Land and Buildings
Net Book Value of Equipment, except Information Technology
Depreciation Expense/Year of Equipment, except Info. Technology
Net Book Value of Information Technology Related Equipment
Depreciation Expense/Year of Information Tech. Related Equipment
Other Assets
Short-term Borrowings
Other Liabilities
Cost of Capital

The following income statement data come with each strategic business unit:

Revenue
Purchased Materials
Revenue per Employee
Total Employee Costs
Non-information Purchased Services
Information Purchased Services
Taxes Applicable to this Business
Allocated (to Management) Net Book Value of Corporate Plant&Equipment
Allocation of Corporate Depreciation

% Allocation of Corporate Information Equipment
Allocation of Corporate Employee Costs
Allocation of Corporate Non-information Purchased Services
Allocation of Corporate Information Purchased Services
Net Income

38 Your company's served market share, as compared with your next three competitors' market share in your relative served market. The inability of company executives to articulate what is their served market is a frequent source of data-gathering error.

39 Quality is what customers vote on when they decide to buy your products or your competitors'. The market, and not a preferred-practices checklist, is the ultimate measure of quality. The most reliable source of information about quality is the customer who has switched to a competitor. Rapid gains in market share and evidence collected from customer surveys (by completely independent agents) can verify whether your concepts of quality relate to improved revenues and in better prices. Checklists filled by visiting experts, such as used in the fashionable Quality Awards, have a bias to infer quality (a result) from observations of company procedures (inputs). Formal ranking rules make it possible for a company to win a coveted Quality Award while losing market share, suffering a decline in profits and experiencing a dismal return to its shareholders. Though internal processes and procedures are important, I would assign to them lesser weight than votes from the marketplace.

40 Full-time equivalents of personnel in *Management* and *Operations*. This allows for part-time *Management* work by *Operations* people. For instance, Operators in training are a *Management* expense.

41 These counts were further adjusted to make the employment comparable. The adjustment assumes the "span of control" of every manager is 10.

42 We failed to get consistent data for this measure because the instructions defining this dimension were not clear enough.

43 Depending on business circumstances, I define "immediately" as one day to one week.

44 The ambitions of computer executives to extend their influence to revenue-producing strategic systems do not recognize the inextricable connection of such applications to "embedded systems." Including such systems within the functional scope of the Chief Information Officer or the Information Resources Manager shifts accountability for revenue-production from operating management to a specialized support function. That is ineffective and counter-productive; it cannot ultimately succeed.

45 Invoices using a fine calligraphy get more attention and get paid faster by a small company. There is no way to justify such methods for frequent transactions and dealing with large organizations.

46 How to resolve disputes as to whether a person is *Operations* or *Management* is easy. The King Solomon Rule from the Bible is a good precedent for settling this matter. If removal of an activity causes an immediate loss in revenues, you have cut *Operations*.

47 For example, for the food industry the ratio is Purchases/Revenue= 0.83+0.37*(Revenue/Employee)−0.43*(Equity/Revenue)−1.12*(Taxes/Revenue). The correlation between actual and predicted Purchases/Revenue is high, because the Revenue/Employee and Equity/Revenue ratios are reasonable ways to adjust gross revenues. Employee payrolls and shareholder equity in business are the principal elements of all *Value-added* calculations.

It is possible to estimate *Management Value-added* if you have a few clues about internal costs. During a conference with financial analysts, the Chairman of a large electronics firm disclosed the break-down of his company's manufacturing, service, sales and engineering employment. This data corroborated the company's reputation for excessive staffing. Using other published financial information it was possible to figure out that the firm's *R-O-M* was negative. Within 24 months, the price of its shares declined 60% from its peak and has not recovered over the past three years.

48 These costs do not disappear. They become non-computing *Management* or *Operations* costs. Some of my reviewers had difficulty with the exclusion of these costs because they felt that M.I.S. managers will find that unacceptable. During the *MPIT* study we tried to capture these costs, only to give up this effort when we found that firms differed in their approach to defining and measuring these expenses. In a 1988 revision of the data-gathering forms, I have finally dealt with this problem by classifying all "user/customer" related costs as a part of functional expenses. For the purposes of this study technology remains defined narrowly so that it can be measured with consistency.

49 If you follow business magazine articles and computer manufacturers' advertisements, you would come to precisely opposite conclusions. This shows that when it comes to computers, we are long on myths and short on facts. In manufacturing, I find that *mission critical* systems are few and inexpensive as compared with the costly *management information systems*.

50 We do not have the data to answer this question by occupation. What is the per capita consumption of information technologies for executives, managers, professionals, clerks, secretaries and engineers is an interesting research topic which deserves further study.

51 The evidence of migration of computer systems mission is only circumstantial. The reported annual increases in corporate information systems budgets (R. Carlyle, 1990 IS Budget Survey, *Datamation,* April 1, 1990) are substantially below the gains in computer industry shipments (Economic Perspectives, *Morgan Stanley,* December 15, 1989). If you consider that information technology makes up only about 40% of reported information systems budgets—the rest made up of inflation prone personnel and services expenses—the average corporate information technology budgets in the period from 1984–1989 grew only about 4–5%. The industry reported shipments have averaged 10% during the same period. Where is the unaccounted for equipment? It ends up where it is not "information systems" but as *mission-critical* or *embedded* applications.

52 I plan to release the results of my 1985–1992 data in about 1997. I do not think there will be many major surprises. New details will become statistically significant and will show up as new diagnostic ratios. The existing diagnostics will also have a lower margin of error.

7

RESEARCH FINDINGS

Information technologies now have penetrated all business activities. This makes a study of their economic effects very difficult, for it is hard to tell which effects came from computers, and which came from other causes.

Through the *MPIT* (Management Productivity and Information Technology) project, we successfully collected data from comparable businesses. In this Chapter, I will discuss differences in computer spending patterns after comparing high and low *Return-on-Management* cases.

IDENTIFYING OVER- AND UNDER-ACHIEVERS

What distinguishes the *Over-achievers* from the *Average* firms? Unusually high *R-O-M* companies—in the top twenty percentile of the sample—deliver exceptional results.[1] Therefore, they rightfully earn the designation of *Over-achievers*. Unusually low *R-O-M* companies—in the bottom twenty percentile of the sample—deliver dismal results. They deserve to be called *Under-achievers*.

I divided the 292 cases from the *MPIT* study into five groups of equal numbers according to their values of *R-O-M*:

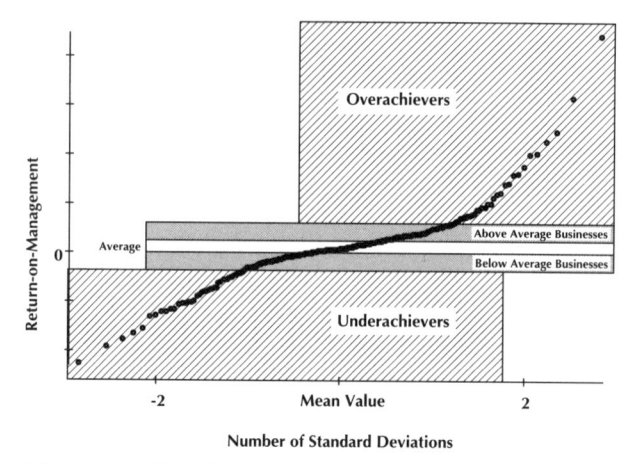

Figure 7.1: Classification of Company Groups by R-O-M

These five groups are:
- *Under-achievers* (with a *R-O-M* below –100%);
- *Below average* achievers;
- *Average* businesses (with a median *R-O-M* of 50%);
- *Above Average* achievers, and
- *Over-achievers* (with a *R-O-M* over 175%).

Companies which have *Management Value-added* that is greater than *Management Costs* will have a positive value of *R-O-M*. *Return-on-Management* is an absolute measure of performance, in contrast to *ROI* or *ROE*. If you see an *ROE* of 10%, you cannot be sure if that is good or bad. If you find an *R-O-M* of 100% you can be certain that the firm is above the average manufacturing firm on the basis of this study.

Companies also may have *Management Value-added* that is less than *Management Costs*. In such cases the *Management Value-added* is negative and *R-O-M* will be less than zero. Companies with a negative *R-O-M* are paying for their management out of their shareholder equity. If that continues, the company must get better management or eventually go bankrupt.

COMPARING *R-O-M* WITH OTHER MEASURES

Profits and Management Costs

Declining *Management Costs* are related to rising *Net Profits*. To make these variables comparable, these measures are shown as ratios of *Business Value-added:*

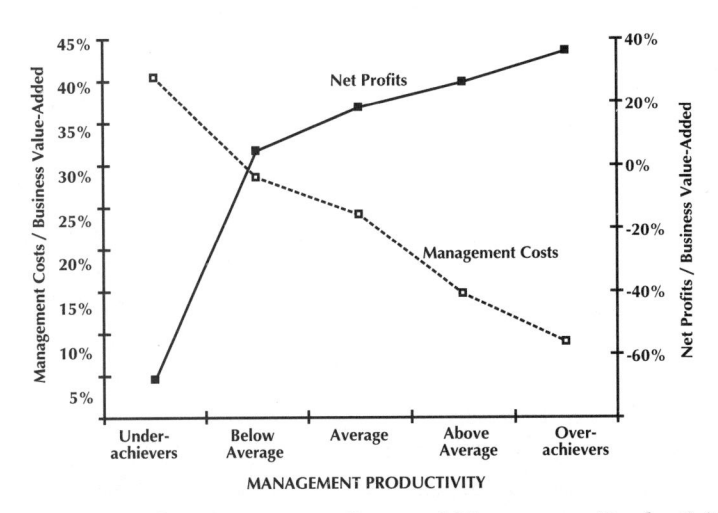

Figure 7.2: Profits, Management Costs and Management Productivity

The above figure displays the essential finding of *MPIT* research: *Over-achievers* spend less on *Management* relative to their *Business Value-added*. Improving *Management productivity* is not an empty phrase, but a matter of direct benefit to shareholders. Over-achievers have a high *Net Profit/Business Value-added* because their slimmer management knows how to extract more surplus out of their high *Value-added*.[2]

Management *Value-added* and Management Productivity

Return-on-Management shows that reductions in *Management Costs* can be translated into rapidly rising levels of *Management Value-added*:

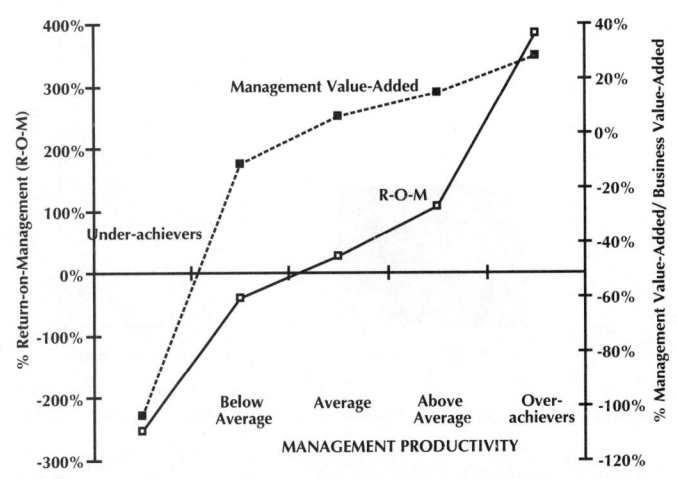

Figure 7.3: Management Value-added, R-O-M and Productivity

The values of *R-O-M* increase rapidly for *Over-achievers* and decline precipitously for *Under-achievers*. This makes the values of *R-O-M* a sensitive performance indicator.

Comparing *R-O-M* with ROA and ROE

For conventional measures such as *Return-on-Assets* or *Return-on-Equity*, the variability of results primarily is attributed to the numerator (e.g., *Profits*). The denominator (e.g., *Assets* or *Equity*) stays remarkably stable.[3] How reliable is the *Return-on-Management* measure as compared with conventional ratios such as *Return-on-Investment*, *Return-on-Assets* or *Return-on-Equity*?

Asset-based ratios reflect the 19th and first half of 20th century history of persistent capital scarcity.[4] Such financial indicators concentrate on the efficiency of capital investments. *Profit* (the output of an enterprise) is divided by *Capital* (the decisive measure of input). Conventional asset-based ratios reflect how well an organization uses its material *Assets,* instead of how effectively it uses its people.[5]

From the *MPIT* data, I found that average *Management Costs* were three times larger than the average *Shareholder Value-added*. Management costs therefore must be more critical as a resource. In a subsequent study of service businesses, which have relatively less capital to produce *Business Value-added*, I found that *Management Costs* were more than six times larger than *Shareholder Value-added*.

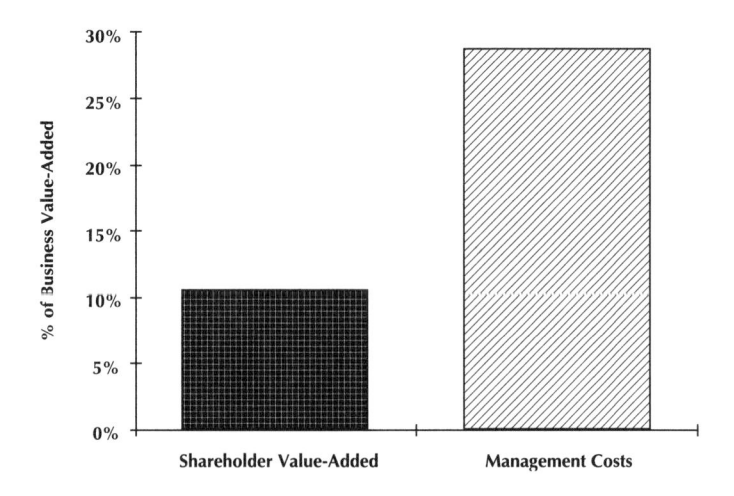

Figure 7.4: Shareholder Value-added and Management Costs

If your financial experts are concerned that the *R-O-M* measure conflicts with the customary financial ratios, the following compares *R-O-M* with the shapes of *ROA* and *ROE*:

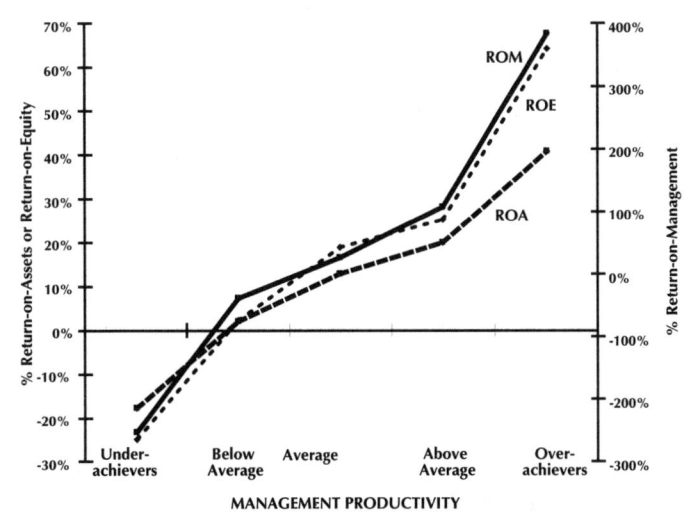

Figure 7.5: Comparing Values of R-O-M, ROE and ROA

The general trends for each indicator are similar. The valuations of these ratios have a wide ranging scatter because the ROE and ROA also mirror wide differences in accounting practices. This may be one of many reasons why prior studies have not produced useful correlations.

DO OVER-ACHIEVERS SPEND MORE ON COMPUTERS?

Less is more.

Overall Levels of Information Technology Spending

The most frequently used measure of the relative levels of information technology spending is the ratio of *Information Technology Expense/Revenue.* How does this indicator relate to management productivity?

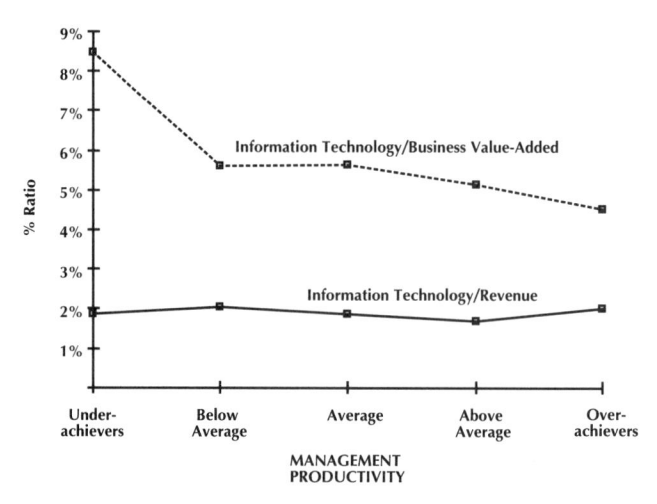

Figure 7.6: Information Technology Ratios and Productivity

The *Information Technology Expense/Revenue* ratio is remarkably constant over the entire range of *R-O-M* values. *Over-achievers* deliver their results with a level of spending equivalent to *Below-Average* performers. The *Information Technology Expense/Revenue* ratio is not a useful measure of computing intensity. The similar values for *Under-* and *Over-achievers* reflect averages of widely scattered values which make them useless for any comparisons.

You get more interesting results from the ratio of *Information Technology Expense/Business Value-added*. *Over-achievers* show the lowest levels of spending for information technology. I conclude that more technology does not necessarily deliver better results. I also infer from this relationship that moderately lower spending levels are related to higher productivity for the participants in the *MPIT* study.

Employee Spending on Information Technology

On a per person basis, *Management Information Technology* spending outweighs information technology spending in *Operations*. This is another major finding from our research. The people in administrative functions received higher levels of support from information technology than operating people who deliver products or services.[6] *Operations Information Technology* accounted for a smaller share of employee costs than *Management Information Technology*, as shown in Figure 7.7.

Over-achievers spent less money on *Management Information*

CHAPTER 7—RESEARCH FINDINGS   *139*

Technology than *Average* performers. *Over-achievers* also spent more money on *Operations Information Technology* than *Average* performers. When you add up all the information technology spending, the *Over-achievers'* total per person spending was less than that for the *Average* performers. *Over-achievers* delivered better *R-O-M* results, although they spent less per person on information technology.

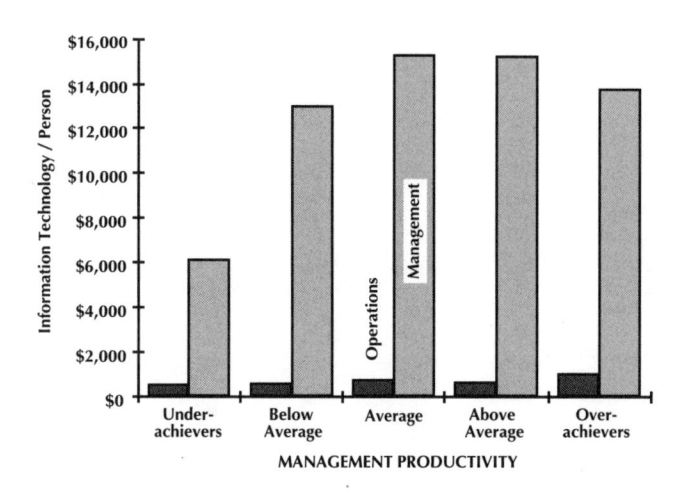

Figure 7.7: Information Technology Spending, per Person

I repeated the analysis shown in Figure 7.7 using the ratio of Information Technology Expense to *Wages and Salaries* because per person ratios could distort comparisons when pay levels differ among firms:

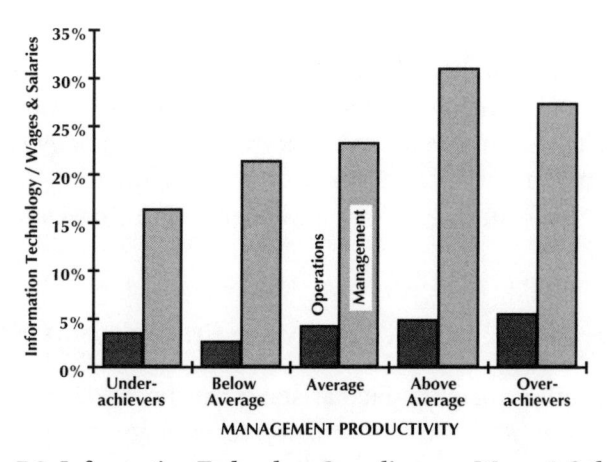

Figure 7.8: Information Technology Spending, per Wages & Salaries

The results are similar to those found for information technology spending per person. Although *Over-achievers* spent more than others on *Operations Information Technology*, their total spending does not grow beyond *Above Average* companies, because their *Management Information Technology* spending declined. I could not find that the *Over-achievers'* elevated status came from greater spending on computers.

I explored dozens of other relationships to find what made *Over-achievers'* uses of computers different from ratios found among *Average* performers. Only one distinction appeared and it describes how *Over-achievers* deployed their information technologies:

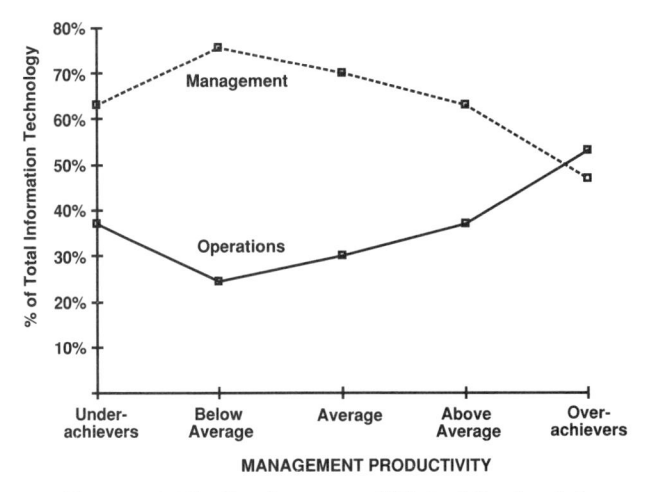

Figure 7.9: The Deployment of I.T. And Productivity

Only *Over-achievers* spent more of their total information technology on mission critical *Operations* systems than on *Management* information systems. This shows that information technology should apply where it has a direct and favorable effect on the generation of revenues.[7] Unfortunately, only a minority of our cases followed this principle.

INFORMATION TECHNOLOGY AND FUNCTIONAL SPENDING

What other insights have arisen from the *MPIT* research? *Over-achievers* spent heavily on information technology to support administrative staffs:

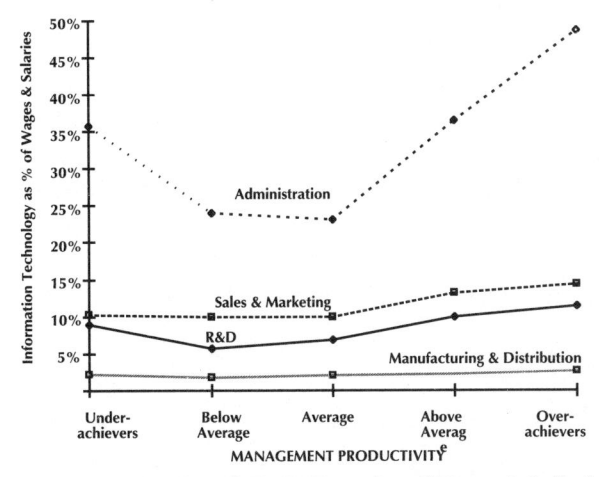

Figure 7.10: Ratios of I.T. To Functional Wages & Salaries

Non-administrative functions, such as *Sales & Marketing, Research & Development, Manufacturing & Distribution* did not show significantly increased computer spending as management productivity improved. When you invest in non-administrative applications, it seems that your success is not related to how much you spend on information technology.[8]

Before you hasten to give more information technology to *Administration,* you should examine why administrative applications are successful. I found that *Administration Information Technology Costs* rose with remarkable reductions in the administrative overhead ratio. The exceptions to this pattern were *Under-Achievers* and *Below-Average* firms who apparently spent increasing amounts of information technology on automating activities which did not add value:[9]

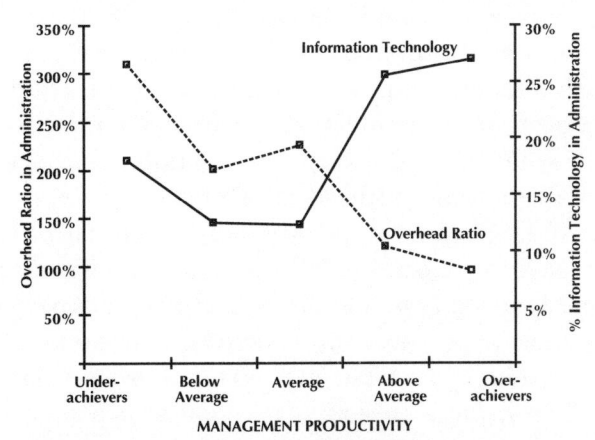

Figure 7.11: Overhead and I.T. Ratios in Administration

Administrative managers for *Average, Above Average* and *Over-achiever* companies have learned how to make better use of automation. They succeeded in reducing their overhead costs. *Over-achievers* spent relatively more money on administrative systems, because their lower overhead ratios made these systems affordable and profitable.

Sales & Marketing displayed a pattern similar to the *Administration* ratios. As the proportion spent on this function for information technology went up, the proportion spent on overhead decreased.[10]

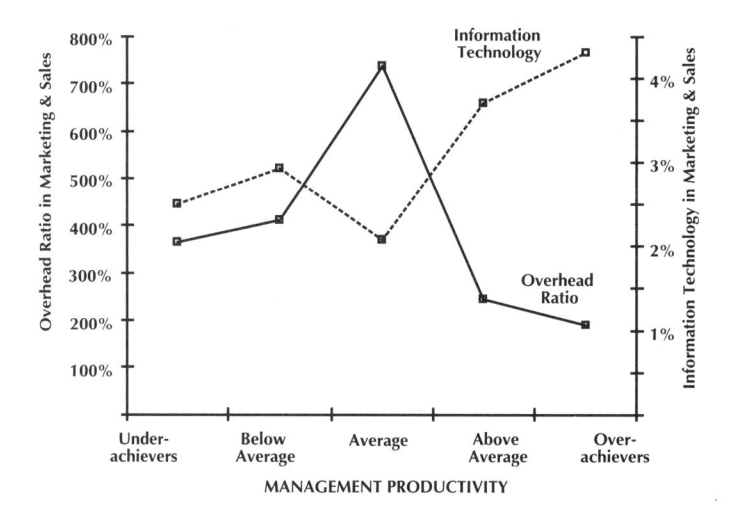

Figure 7.12: Overhead and I.T. Ratios in Marketing & Sales

We have observed how the *Over-achievers'* low overhead ratios in *Administration* and *Sales & Marketing* changed in connection with high computer spending on these functions. Do these favorable results also apply to *Production, Distribution and Research & Development?* I could not find such a relationship with the available data. These functions have been absorbing computers into *embedded* and *mission critical* applications where they show up as reductions in direct costs and therefore did not become overhead cost reductions.

Successful computer applications in *Administration, Sales & Marketing* seem to lead to a lower overhead ratio for the entire business. If corporate *Administration* staffs are small, you do not need more people in sales branches, plants and warehouses to respond to headquarters inquiries. Therefore, you do not need to add overhead staff to these functions.[11] *Over-achievers* need fewer *Management* people:

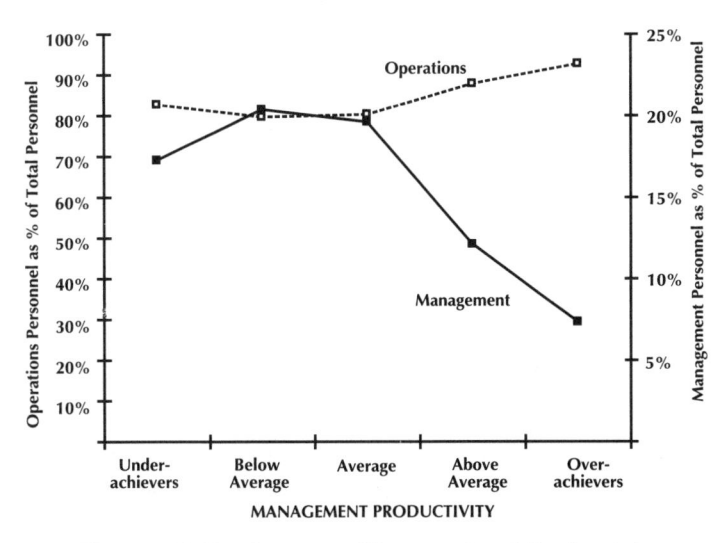

Figure 7.13: Deployment of Personnel and Productivity

One of the key findings from *MPIT* research was that the heavy concentration of information technology in *Administration* made it possible to operate *Over-achiever* businesses with less *Management*. I also found that the relatively high level of information technology spending by *Under-achievers* suggests that *Over-achievers* applied information technology to already reduced *Management* staffs. *Under-achievers* kept adding automation to inflated *Management* staff levels. This conclusion came from examining *MPIT* data for individual companies.

What comes first, low overhead or less communication? Statistical analysis does not tell you which are causes and what are effects. Therefore, I cannot give you a sure answer. However, I tested the hypothesis that low overhead is essential for over-achievement.

I examined every *Under-achiever* with above average administrative information technology spending. I also looked at every *Over-achiever* which had low administrative expenditures. There were no *Under-achievers* with low overhead but there were many *Under-achievers* with high information technology spending. Almost every *Over-achiever* had a low overhead ratio and a high level of information technology spending. There were no *Over-achievers* with high overhead costs.

After comparing these two groups on the basis of their *R-O-M*, I concluded that superior executives most likely reduced their *Management* costs before they made their information technology investments. This implies that if you need to increase business value, you should shift resources from *Management* to *Operations*. You automate the remaining procedures only afterwards.

The *Under-achievers'* high levels of information technology spending and high overhead suggests that they may be applying information technology to automating unnecessary work. Now you can understand why identical levels of information technology spending can produce opposite results. *Over-achievers* will improve and *Under-achievers* will get worse financial results.

These comparisons lead me to guess that overhead reduction is the primary cause of requiring less information. In other words: overhead people breed information irrespective of the work that needs doing. This only confirms what Professor Parkinson said 20 years ago.

To extract the benefit of information technologies, you must first simplify your conduct of business. Technical specialists are not very good at this mission. Simplification of a business requires close guidance from executives responsible for managing the business, not systems analysts. If your *R-O-M* indicates that you are an *Under-achiever* or a *Below-average* performer, you should deploy computers to minimize your *Management* costs. Only after you are successful in doing that, can you afford to make more venturesome applications.

INFORMATION TECHNOLOGY AND ASSETS

Consider the *Over-achievers'* lower ongoing spending levels for information technology with caution. Expense levels are never the full story. We also must check their uses of information technology assets:

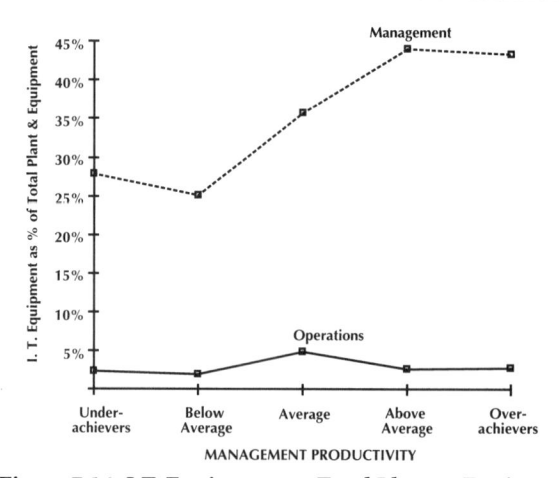

Figure 7.14: I.T. Equipment to Total Plant & Equipment

In the *MPIT* study all *Plant & Equipment* was allocated either to *Management* or to *Operations*. *Plant and Equipment* supporting the delivery of goods and services are *Operation*s assets. Computing equipment was only a small fraction of the total *Operations* assets.

Information technology assets for *Management* are different in that *Over-achievers* dedicated a large share of their total *Plant & Equipment* information technology assets to supporting *Management*. Other than computers, staffs need only an office, furniture and transportation equipment. If you can cut your overhead, the remaining staff can afford generous amounts of information technology.

The *Over-achiever's* high share of computing equipment for managers may tempt you to ask your Board of Directors for a bigger budget. Before you ask for more money, check whether you may already have already too much[12] investment in place to support your business. *Over-achievers* used less *Plant & Equipment* to deliver their *Business Value-added:*

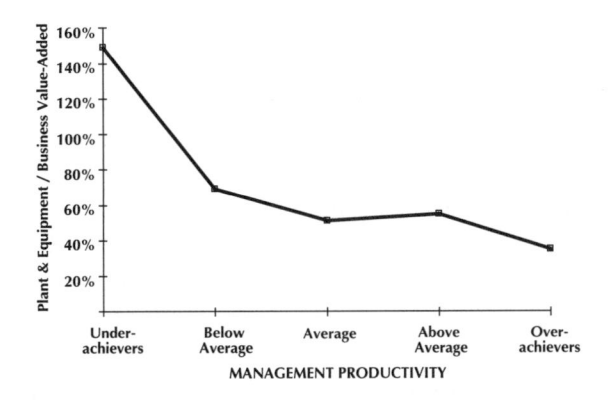

Figure 7.15: Capital Intensity and Productivity

INFORMATION TECHNOLOGY AND ORGANIZATION STRUCTURE

Are high performance organizations relatively less complex? Are *Over-achievers* with high levels of administrative automation any closer to their customers and workers?

The trends are modest but show that *Over-achievers* have somewhat shorter lines of communication. I did not find dramatic differences between *Average* and *Over-achiever* cases. I concluded that it does not matter how you draw your organization charts, but how many overhead people you put into them:

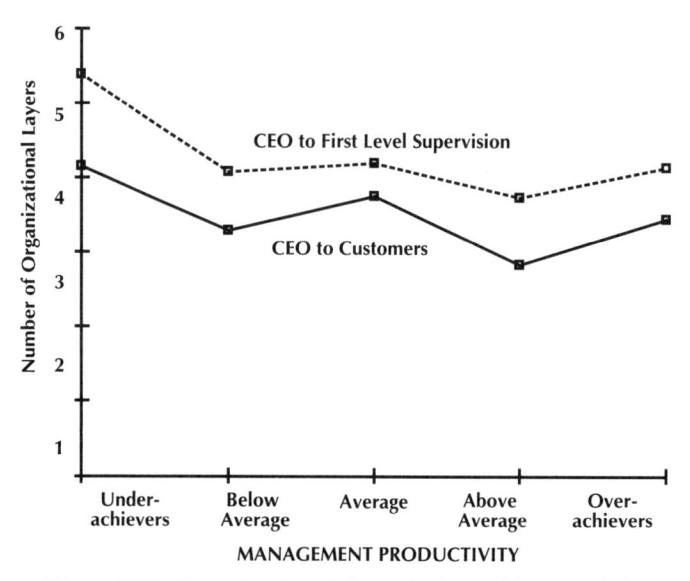

Figure 7.16: Organizational Complexity and Productivity

The effect of information technology on organizational structure is subtle. Information technology makes it possible to have less *Management*. It is hard to build up a large hierarchy if the potential administrators, controllers and checkers are taking care of customers. For improved performance, you should eliminate unnecessary managerial work before you simplify your organization structure. Information technology contributes to productivity after you streamline internal communications.

Rearranging organization charts to make them appear less hierarchical does not seem to make much of a difference. It is not how you organize your chain of command, but how much it costs, which distinguishes the superior organizations from the poor ones.[13]

I explored questions related to organizational structure, such as personnel ratios. Thirty years of working for large corporations have conditioned me to deal with the annual budgeting process in terms of "headcounts."[14] Budget examiners find it easier to control personnel than to evaluate costs. Department managers respond by removing low-cost clerical support people and replacing them with fewer higher-priced managerial, administrative and professional personnel. To what extent does the database reveal the presence of such practices?

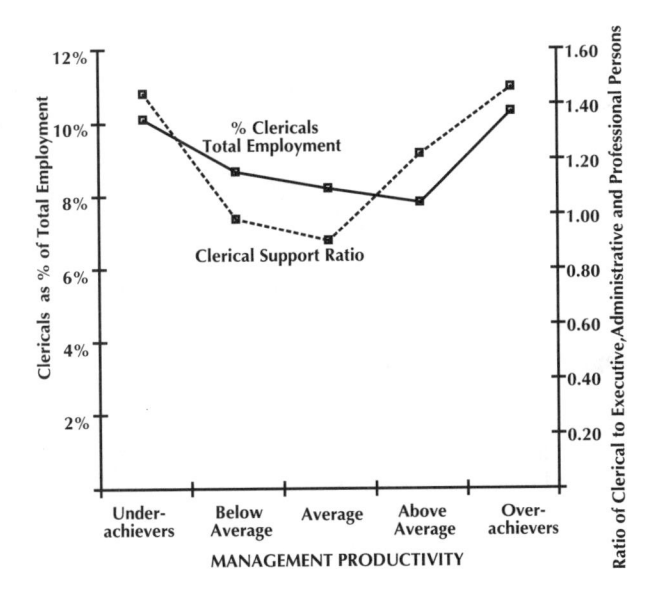

Figure 7.17: Support Ratios and Productivity

The above graph shows that *Over-achievers* have a higher clerical employment ratio and that their *Clerical Support Ratio*[15] is above that for *Average* firms. I conclude that *Over-achievers* tightly control their costs, and therefore distribute work to the least costly employees capable of doing the job. *Average* firms decrease clerical support and depress *Management Productivity*.[16]

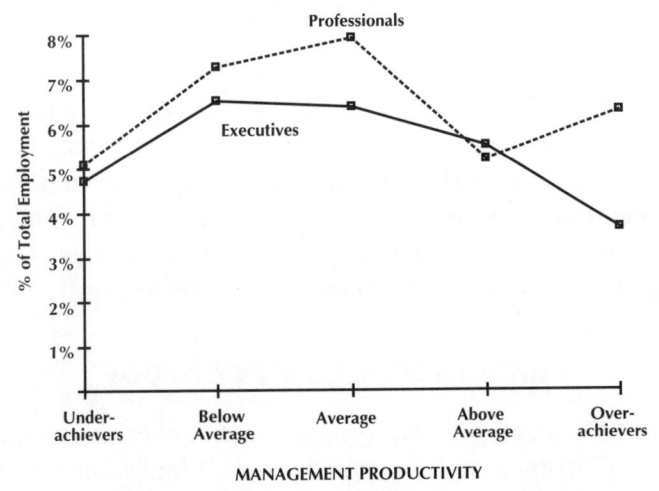

Figure 7.18: Knowledge Workers and Productivity

Over-achievers can manage with fewer executives and professionals. *Over-achievers* operate simply. They use information technology and clerical people more effectively. *Over-achievers* convert the increased productivity into *Management Value-added* gains. The *Over-achievers'* gain in professional personnel offsets the drop in executive employment. Every firm that uses high technology will call for increasing numbers of specialists.

Does the reduction in *Management* jobs offer a sure way to improve managerial productivity? You had better check before you end up paying higher salaries to those who stay:

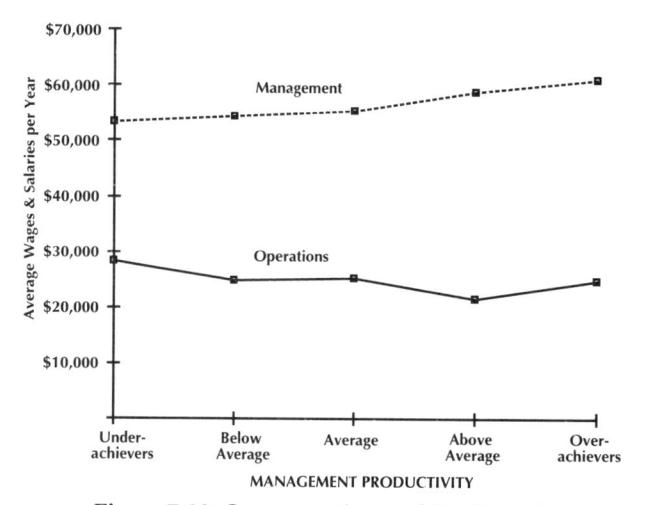

Figure 7.19: Compensation and Productivity

Over-achievers pay a slight premium for their average *Management* salaries as compared with *Under-achievers*. They also pay less for *Operations* wages. Salaries and wages for *Operations* personnel decreased while productivity gained. That is a good bargain because the ratio of *Operations* to *Management* personnel is about 8:1. *Management* surely earned their compensation premium because they delivered a 300% higher *Management Productivity* than *Average* firms.[17]

CHANGES DURING MPIT STUDY

The *MPIT* data span a six-year period. Some firms supplied only three years of history, others as much as six. I looked at statistics for firms with at least five years of history. Fifty-one companies satisfied this criterion. I wanted to know if the firms' critical financial ratios changed during the study period.

Whenever you compare ratios, you should examine your sources for evolutionary changes. Otherwise, averages for the same firm recorded over several years could be misleading. When I began my review, I did not expect to see any radical changes.[18]

Changes in the Financial Structure

The five-year histories showed some startling changes. Total personnel declined steadily. The rate of profit growth fluctuated wildly. The growth in revenues peaked in 1981 and then settled during the 1982 recession:

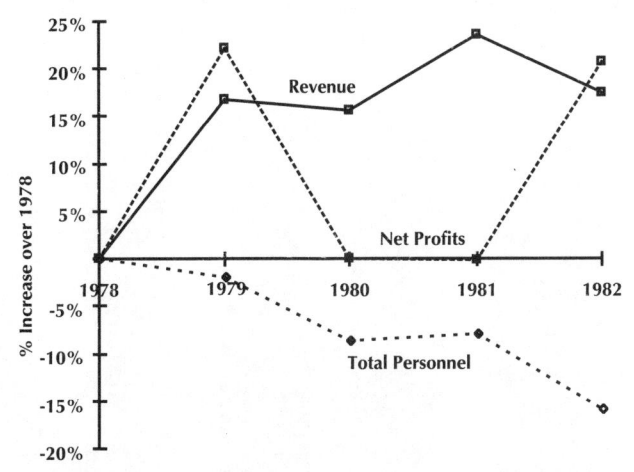

Figure 7.20: Changes in Financial Results and in Personnel

A decline in revenue growth associated with a temporary reduction in profits occurs during a recession. I could not reconcile the revenue increase with the reductions in employees. I looked at what happened:

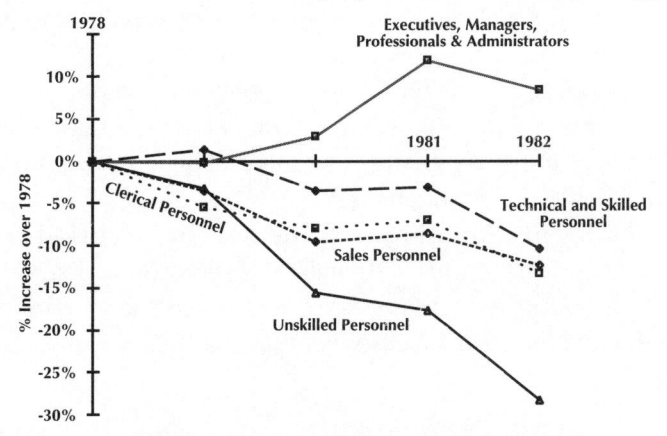

Figure 7.21: Changes in Employment

The 17% decline in total employment over the five-year period covered surprising changes in the composition of occupational groups. Executive, managerial, professional and administrative personnel increased by 8% while unskilled labor decreased 30% by 1982.

Why would fifty-one manufacturing firms try to increase overhead positions while direct labor was declining, profits were fluctuating, and revenues were steady? It appears that the businesses, which were mostly divisions of large corporations, were trying to manage their profits while improving their labor productivity. They succeeded in this goal:

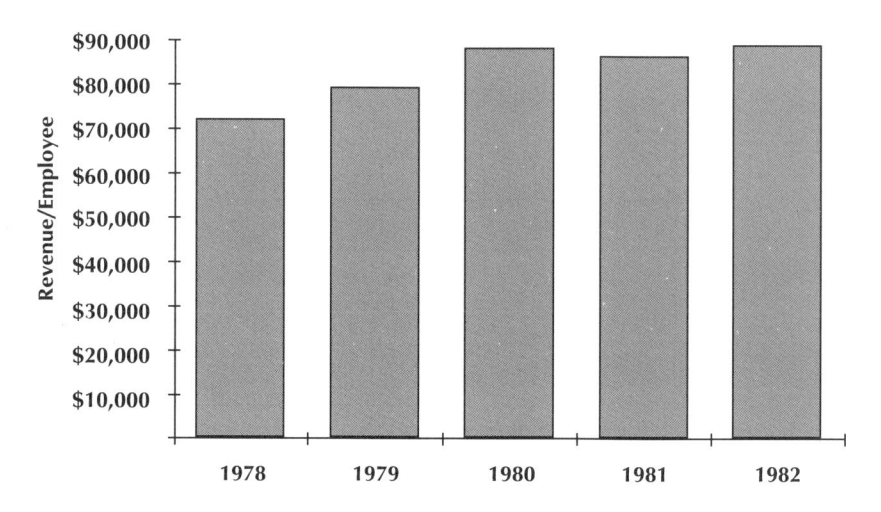

Figure 7.22: Growth in Revenue/Employee from Personnel Reductions

Despite the economic recession, "productivity" improved because the firms began replacing employees with services bought from others.[19] The substitution of purchases for internal business costs provided an instant recovery in "productivity."

The shifts to obtaining services outside occurred in both *Management* and *Operations*. Although revenues over the five year period grew 18%, *Management Purchased Service Costs* increased by 49%. *Operations Purchased Service Costs* increased by 58%:

CHAPTER 7—RESEARCH FINDINGS   151

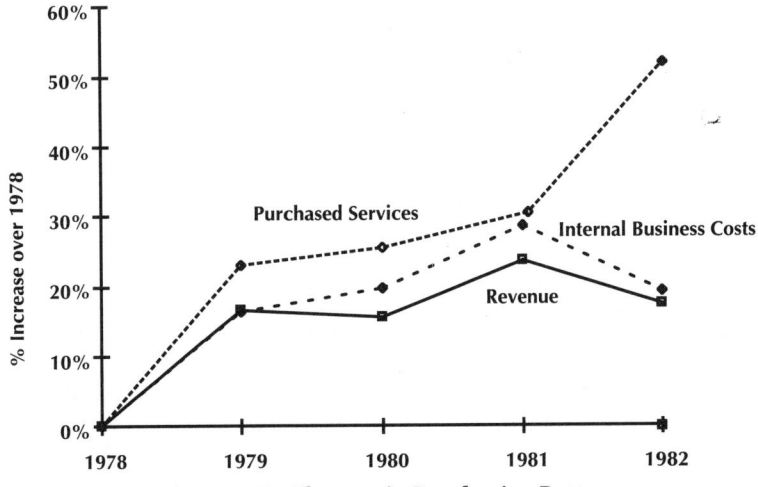

Figure 7.23: Changes in Purchasing Patterns

Another way of boosting productivity ratios[20] is to accelerate capital-intensive automation in the factory and in the office. Automation substitutes *Assets* and *Management* staffs for unskilled *Operations* people and clerical *Management* employees:

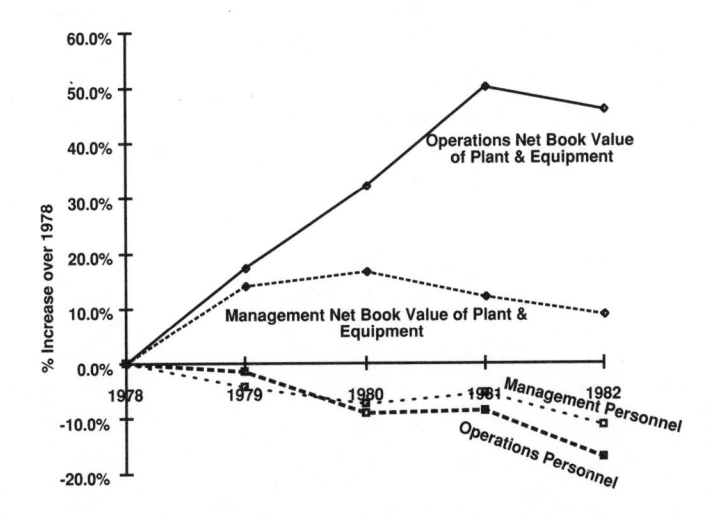

Figure 7.24: Changes in Employment and in Capital Structure

The five-year period shows a dramatic 50% increase in the net book value of plant and equipment dedicated to factory automation.

The capital assets supporting clerical automation grew by 15% in the first three years and then declined as the firms shifted to leasing computers.

These drastic effects on the financial structure of the businesses show how capital-based productivity ratios can lead to misunderstanding. The long-term viability of firms depends on the creation of *Value-added*, not revenue or tons. The previous figures show firms divesting their *Operations* capacity for creating *Value-added*. Despite increased capitalization, the fifty-one manufacturing firms studied reduced their vertical integration[21] and became more dependent on their suppliers.

The five-year analysis showed that as time passes businesses may not be comparable with themselves. Companies which show large year-to-year changes are really a separate case for each year under examination. Comparisons should be made among firms that have a similar financial structure, instead of against past records.[22]

Changes in Information Technology Spending

Changes in business structure will distort the validity of internal indicators that multi-divisional companies use to judge information technology expenses. You have seen how unskilled and clerical personnel left the payroll, and administrative or professional personnel took their place. The companies substituted users of computers of more than $15,000 per year for those who consumed less than $700 per year.

When computer-intensive staffs replace employees who do not use computers, a firm's computer budget will outpace revenue growth and increase faster than labor costs:

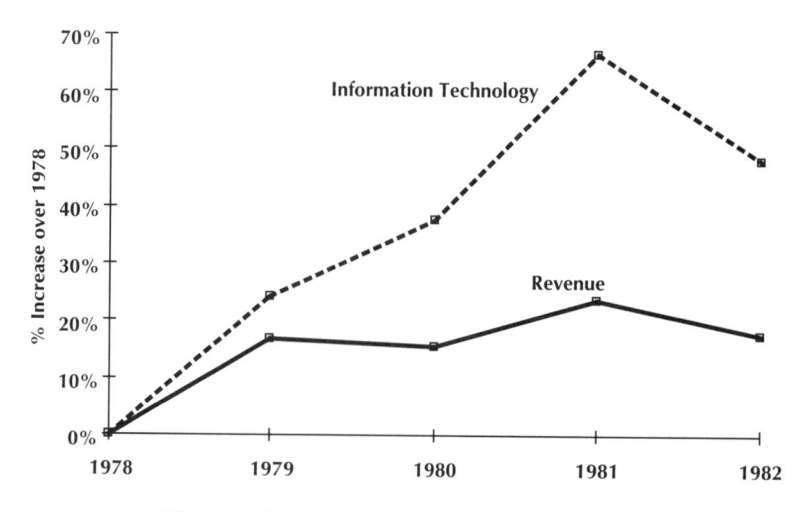

Figure 7.25: I.T. Expenses Grow Faster than Revenues

When businesses dismiss production workers, increase outside purchases and hire more staff, this increases the *Information Technology-per-Revenue* and the *Information Technology-per-Business Value-added* ratios.

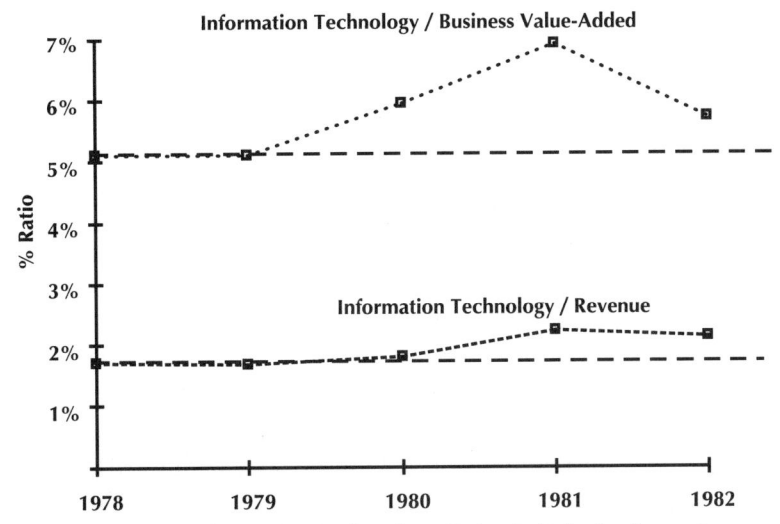

Figure 7.26: Information Technology Gains in Relative Importance

The above figure illustrates how the ratios of information technology costs can change because of changes in employment and *Value-added*.

External Influences and Management Productivity

So far, I have discussed only internal costs. There is always a possibility that external influences overwhelm what you do to improve internal affairs. To complete our picture, I shall discuss how some extrinsic variables affect *Management productivity*.

The Effects of Taxes

Taxes average nearly 50% of *Management Costs*. *Taxes* deserve attention because government policies will determine how much money will be available as *Business Value-added*.

The assumption is that the tax rate rises with profits. Do the *MPIT* results support this view?

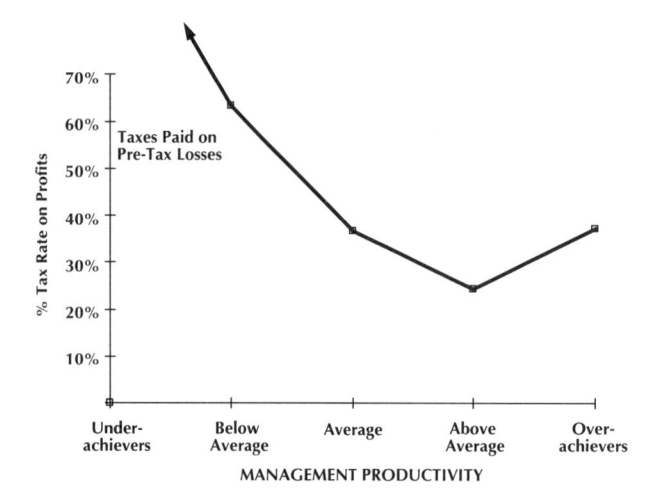

Figure 7.27: The Tax Rate and Productivity

Under-achievers who incur financial losses still pay taxes because they incur payroll, property, franchise, licensing and other levies. The tax rate then declines until it reverses for the *Over-achievers*. Figure 7.27 does not support the contention that above average companies incur higher tax rates than below average companies.

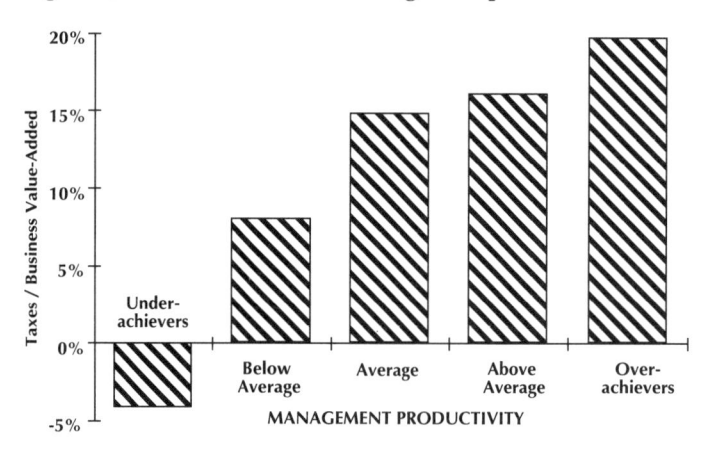

Figure 7.28: Taxes as % of Business Value-added

Over-achievers make impressive contributions to the public sector. For every dollar of *Business Value-added* they contribute increasing taxes.[23] The tax-paying capacity of superior performers is substantial. Taxation extracts a greater share from the *Business Value-added* than *Management* and collects more than the *Shareholders Value-added*. Despite this burden, *Over-achievers* deliver a large after-tax surplus. At the other extreme, *Under-achievers* receive tax subsidies. This does not make any difference in their *R-O-M* values, unless it also prolongs their survival.

Tax policy does not slow down *Over-achievers* and may not help *Under-achievers*. Productivity is the consequence of how well a firm manages its internal costs and how well it competes. Tax is a tribute that does not seem to change any of the business fundamentals.[24]

Checking the Strategic Position

Whenever a company scores poorly for some variables, you should not assume this means its doom. The financial health of a firm, like the health of a person, arises from a combination of favorable and adverse impacts. Some of these influences are internal and some are environmental. When *Management Productivity* is high, it comes from favorable influences outweighing the unfavorable ones. It is important that you consider all the effects before you can safely come up with a prescription of what to do.

A company's diagnostic examination must include good insights regarding competition. The *MPIT* database contains data about each firm's market share, its product quality, its new products and its customers' buying patterns. These variables are "strategic."

All strategic factors[25] are not equally important. Analysis of the *R-O-M* database confirmed prior *PIMS* program findings that the *Relative Market Share* and the *Relative Quality* have a dominant weight in predicting profitability. Whenever a firm has *Under-achiever* ratings for these two indexes, it takes unusual results for the other variables to show superior productivity results:

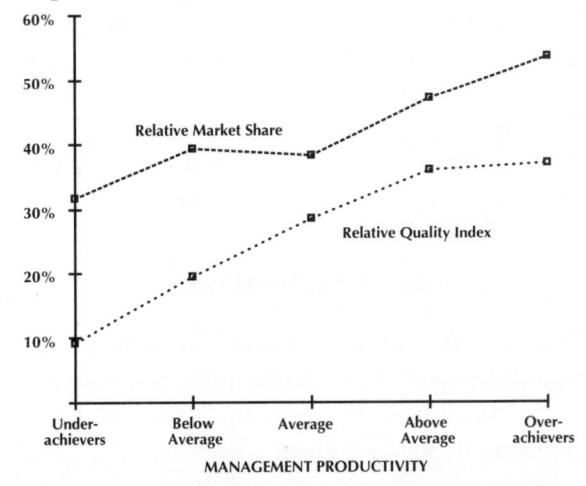

Figure 7.29: Market Share, Quality and Productivity

Over-achievers show consistently higher values for the *Relative Market Share*[26] and *Relative Quality Index*.[27] To understand a firm's *R-O-M* requires running checks on a list of up to forty-seven ratios to identify what may be causing substandard results. To illustrate what such checking involves the Figure 7.30 shows how *Over-achievers* and *Under-achievers* differ when you examine ratios such as *New Products percentage* and the rates of *Relative Market Growth*:

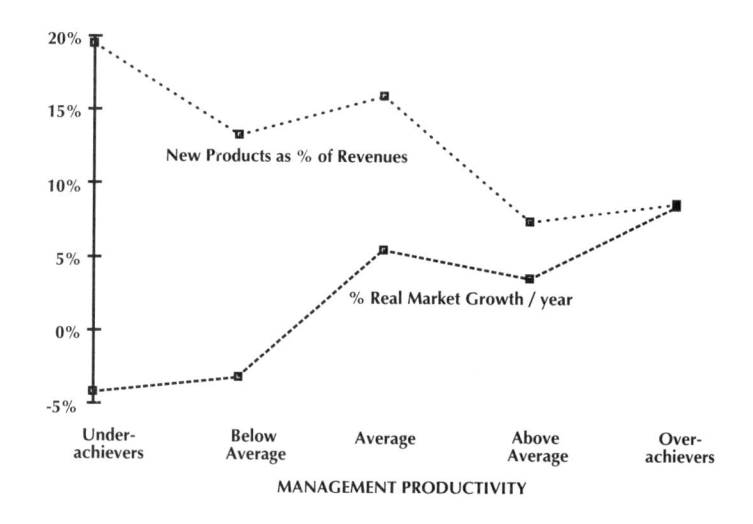

Figure 7.30: Market Growth Does not Need Too Many New Products

More than 10% of new products in a firm's portfolio do not seem to improve profits and productivity. New products call for concentrated management attention and incur expensive marketing efforts. If your firm tries to justify spending large sums on engineering work stations to increase the rate of new product introductions, you should first examine whether that makes strategic sense.[28] To come up with investment priorities for computer investments, you first must evaluate your firm's strategic needs.

CHAPTER SUMMARY

Management Value-added is a sensitive indicator of a company performance. *Management Value-added* reflects not only *Profits* shown on the Financial Statement but also the value of the *Shareholder's Equity* described on the Balance Sheet.

Return-on-Management is a more suitable measure than *ROI* or *ROA* when evaluating investments in management information systems because it focuses on the productivity of management, the principal user of computers.

The examination of the *MPIT* data base has been valuable. It confirmed that effective reduction of management costs is the key to increasing management productivity. It demonstrated that less management can mean more profits. It revealed that management costs exceed shareholder *Value-added,* and therefore are the resource that need close evaluation to judge results from investments. It confirmed that the information technology/revenue ratio is misleading. It described how the consumption of information technology varies by business function and operating mission. It showed how management costs drive the demand for management information systems. It suggested that shifting information technology from *Management* to *Operations* should be a top priority when choosing how to allocate information technology investments. It confirmed that superior administrative productivity is a prerequisite for a firm's financial success. It identified the importance of information assets in evaluating information technology spending. It checked the hypothesis that computers simplify the organizational structure of firms. It explored the effects of automation on support personnel. It provided insights into how managerial and operating personnel wages and salaries differ when a firm becomes more profitable. It examined the effects of taxation on corporate success. It verified selected *PIMS* findings regarding the influence of strategic factors. It came up with surprising findings about shifts in the deployment of resources. It highlighted the growing importance of purchases. It displayed the reduction in the vertical integration of manufacturing firms. It dramatized the rapid rate of substituting unskilled labor by assets. It confirmed Parkinson Law, that the number of managers increases regardless of the number of employees needing supervision. It substantiated the critique of existing information technology ratios.

The research findings in this Chapter suggest a few useful lessons:
- Do not compare your operating results with industry-wide averages. It makes a difference whether your firm is average or superior. When you compare your firm against firms in a radically different performance range your evaluations will be misleading. I dislike comparisons that suggest that you imitate American

Airlines, Citibank and American Hospital Supply in how they approach computers. Peer-group comparisons are more realistic. They will give you credible improvement targets.

- If your firm is under-achieving your approach to information technology investments should differ from firms where *R-O-M* exceeds 100%. *Under-achiever* information technology strategies are painful. You must self-finance overhead cost-reductions, innovate sparingly—with little investment—and deliver results in a hurry, without any margin for error.
- *Over-achiever* strategy options are challenging. *Over-achievers* rarely can sustain their elevated profitability positions. Invariably they gravitate toward the average. To sustain abnormally favorable results calls for a steady stream of innovations so that you hit a few that produce spectacular results. Extraordinary achievements are possible only by taking large but calculated risks. The *Over-achiever* winning strategy is to invest in adventurous applications while plowing back technology profits into a steady stream of rapid cost reductions. *Over-achievers* know how to cut losses ruthlessly and without delay.

Knowing where you are leads to improvement. An uncompromising diagnosis of your firm's management productivity—which requires a reliable diagnostic database—is the prerequisite to finding whether information technology can work for you.

The above results are not complete. As the database grows, I shall include new evaluations in revised editions of this book.

CHAPTER 7 COMMENTS

[1] I plotted *R-O-M* for each business on a scale that assumes that the values would fall on a "bell-shaped" frequency curve. If the distribution of the companies' *R-O-M* were "bell-shaped" it would appear as a straight line. What you see in Figure 7.1 is not a straight line. This leads to an interesting conclusion: the productivity of management does not follow a "normal" probability distribution.

Both *Over-* and *Under-achievers* are chosen by picking the points where the straight line bends. It just happens that this works out to be at the 20% point of *R-O-M* values.

Extreme *Under-achievers* perished or did not have the money to participate in *PIMS* studies. They are not in our data, although they exist. When you read business studies, you should remember that often the most instructional cases are missing. Business research favors success stories. As in military history it is the victors who produce most documentaries.

Are these characteristics unique only to the *R-O-M* measure? I plotted various profit ratios including long-term average shareholder returns. High performers always produce better results than expected and vice-versa. The reverse "S" shaped

curve in measures of profitability seems to confirm that success magnifies success and failure accelerates failure.
2 You could argue that *Under-achievers* have a high ratio of *Management Costs/Business Value-added* because they do not create enough *Value-added*. I will show later that this argument does not hold.
3 For established companies, the accumulated assets are much larger than any year's new investments in plant and equipment.
4 This observation applies only to OECD countries.
5 The Chairman of one of the largest U.S. corporations said in a recent Annual Report that improving *Return-on-Assets* was his #1 business aim. That was O.K., until he added a cliche pronouncement that "...our people are our most important asset." No major corporation has ever reported the financial worth of its people as an asset.
6 The ratio of *Operations* to *Management* personnel will most likely explain the wide range of per capita spending on information technology in the public sector. Personnel and computer budgets for 524 State Government agencies are in S.H. Caudle and D.A. Marchand, Managing Information Resources: New Directions in State Government, *Information Management Review*, 1990, 5(3):

State Government Function	Total Personnel	EDP Budget	Budget/Person
Commerce, regulation & development	624	$4,611,000	$7,389
Education	608	$1,714,000	$2,819
Employment & labor	824	$5,689,000	$6,904
Environment & natural resources	910	$2,626,000	$2,886
Health	3516	$4,088,000	$1,163
Human & social services	1887	$6,415,000	$3,400
Safety & criminal justice	1599	$1,905,000	$1,191
Transportation & utilities	2941	$14,462,000	$4,917
Average	1451	$4,850,000	$3,343

Regulatory agencies, such as Commerce, will have a higher ratio of management to operations personnel than Health.

Executives frequently ask about the application of *R-O-M* analytic methods to public sector or non-profit organizations. On the few occasions when I have done such analyses, I compared public sector companies to *Average* industrial companies with regard to their administrative cost ratios, the uses of information technology, etc. This approach makes public sector companies look better than the *R-O-M* theory warrants.

Public sector companies invariably have a 100% market share in their services segment, incur no balance sheet charges, have no marketing expenses, do not have compensate for shareholder equity, locate their assets on land usually acquired at no cost and pay no taxes. On the basis of these advantages they should compare with industrial *Over-achievers*. This view is not acceptable to public officials until some discover that they are administratively more efficient than the best industrial firms.

7 When critics examined Figure 7.10 they puzzled about the crossover between *Operations* and *Management* expenses for *Over-achievers*. Didn't *Operations* spend less on information technology than *Management*? The chart shows the distribution of the total computer budget. More people are in *Operations* than in *Management*, especially for *Over-achievers*. Increased costs for more people quickly add up.
8 Several reviewers have objected to this conclusion. They felt that the *MPIT* information was too old and did not reflect the large spurt in non-administrative spending after 1982. The most recent data has not shown that such a shift has happened. Recent large computer purchases in engineering and manufacturing primarily were for embedded systems which show up in the increase in capitalization and decrease in direct labor costs. If there was a shift to non-administrative systems, this first would occur among "leading-edge" *Over-achievers*. The 1982 numbers do not show this effect.

9 Defined as *Total Management Administration Costs per Total Operations Administration Costs*. The *percentage Information Technology in Administration* is the share of the total expenses for the administrative functions. I explain the "J" shaped graph in Figures 7.10 and 7.11 by noting that the overhead ratio for *Under-achievers* is exceptionally high, at 300%. Personnel classified as *Management Administration* consumes large amounts of information technology. They respond to failing profits by increasing the number of control reports and expediting applications.

10 There is a puzzling pattern in this figure which is open to several interpretations. It seems that *Average* firms do not pay much attention to information technology in marketing. They take care of their information needs by hiring more staff (e.g., end up with a higher overhead ratio). The *Better-than-average Performers* realize that excessive staffs are a burden and follow the success patterns set by *Administration*.

Can I prove the above conjecture about the causes for the up-and-down patterns? That is one of many subjects for more research. The firms contributing to my database will be answering other questions before I can produce proof of the effect of computerization on overhead ratios in marketing and in sales. Whenever a new anomaly appears I always need more data to understand it.

11 Having a small corporate staff now warrants mention when magazines write about successful companies. An indication of how small corporate staffs could become is in T. Moore, Goodbye, Corporate Staff, *Fortune*, December 21, 1987, p. 68:

Company	Sales ($ Billion)	Employees	HQ Staff	Staff/1000
Burlington	$6.9	43000	77	1.8
Transamerica	7.1	15200	100	6.6
CSX	6.3	52000	100	1.9
Heinz	4.4	45000	175	3.9
Hanson	3.8	33000	89	2.7
Dana	3.7	36000	72	2.0
Borg Warner	3.6	82000	175	2.1

Before you accept the headquarters ratio as signifying effectiveness, you should first check Divisional overhead. One of the above firms decided on the size of its corporate staff by the size of their new headquarters building. The rest of the huge staff relocated to the largest Division where they are counted as Divisional staff.

12 The answer to what is "too much" or "too little" can come by comparing your company's financial data against its peer group in the R-O-M™ data base.

13 There are Group Executives with a staff of three and Group Executives with a full complement of functional staff, including legal, finance, personnel, planning and research. Just from an examination of the organization chart, you cannot tell how many additional reviews and reports they impose on Divisional staffs that must respond to each request.

14 Budget exercises are rituals in which a manager tries to explain why he always needs more people. The financial analysts must counter the manager's requests, though they cannot match the manager's specific knowledge about the work the new people would do. In such an uneven contest, the budget analysts construct headcount ratios to prove that the requests deviate from irrelevant averages.

15 The number of clerical people for every executive, administrative and professional position.

16 Why do *Under-achievers* have a *Clerical Support Ratio* which is comparable to the *Over-achievers*'? *Under-achievers* are unprofitable and must squeeze every expense to survive. They cannot afford the luxury of employing executives and professionals, but still need to get their work done. The financial duress of the *Under-achievers* appears in other U-shaped curves not included here. I tell my especially talented students to seek their first job with small companies in trouble. In the first few years, they would get a better chance of getting diversified business experience than working for a tightly structured profit-maker.

17 This raises the question of how the 10% compensation premium should be distributed to the people in *Management*. Only a handful of people make investment and organizational structuring decisions. If those few shape a firm's management productivity, there is a good argument that the entire pay premium belongs to members of the Executive Committee. Paying a few million dollars to the CEO of an over-achieving billion dollar company then makes sense. Similarly, a CEO of a billion dollar company who causes huge losses in shareholder value would not be worth a clerk's wages.

18 I considered averaging two or three years of data to smooth out annual fluctuations in the figures. The *MPIT* findings originally released in 1985 were from multi-year averages. Averaging annual figures for each variable turned out to be a mistake. As shown in Figure 7.21 the companies changed during the time of the *MPIT* study.

19 A dramatic example of this trend is Firestone Tire & Rubber. They sold their radial tire factory to Bridgestone Corporation, their arch-rival, and then continued to buy tires made at the plant they previously owned, operated by their ex-employees (*Business Week*, March 3, 1986, p. 62).

20 Such as physical quantities produced per employee or per work-hour, the basis for most government productivity statistics,

21 The ratio of *Business Value-added* to *Revenues*.

22 This is called "competitive benchmarking." Without providing at least a few external competitive measures, all internally generated performance numbers are suspect.

23 As corporations reduce their *Business Value-added* through purchases, they diminish their tax-paying capacity. When the Treasury wonders why corporate taxes have fallen behind expectations (see D.E. Rosenbaum, Big Shortfall in Corporate Taxes Thwarts Key Goal of 1986 Law, *The New York Times*, March 6, 1990, p. 1) they should examine what structural changes in American business are doing to the assumptions built into their revenue-estimating models.

24 Taxes may, however, affect the costs of competing with someone who enjoys a more favorable tax structure.

25 See Table 6.3 for a complete listing.

26 The company's market share as compared with the most frequently encountered three competitors. To test a client's interpretation of his market share, I ask for an analysis of recent proposals and orders. You gain or lose market share when you win or lose against a competitor whom you should be able to identify.

27 The company's relative quality ranking as compared with the most frequently encountered competitors. To test the client's interpretation of how to calculate a quality index, I ask for an analysis of the reasons for lost orders. Was the cause price, product quality, service reliability or styling?

Why a firm may gain competitive dominance through market share and quality improvement tactics is well beyond the scope of the *MPIT* research. The reader interested in these topics should consult the *PIMS* bibliography summarized in R.D. Buzzell and B.T. Gale, The *PIMS* Principles, *Free Press*, 1987.

28 A client asked me to perform a post-installation review of gains realized from a massive investment in engineering workstations. In that business, a faster rate of product innovation was strategically undesirable. Engineers could now produce engineering changes and product enhancement at a rate that was ten times faster than the factory or marketing could handle. The escalating friction between engineering and manufacturing damaged the firm. Yet, engineering met all the goals first set in their investment proposal! This is a prime example that even in the rare instance of meeting all cost and productivity targets, a firm could end up being worse off.

8

STRATEGIC INVESTMENTS

An organization must gain strategic advantages over its competitors if it is to succeed. Strategic planning is the process for getting ready to compete.[1] It is a matter of style whether strategic planning occurs through informal understandings, improvisation or a formal procedure. However, strategic planning for information systems requires meticulous documentation. You cannot improvise commitments that establish long-lasting programming code, database layouts and telecommunications procedures.

Integrating management information systems into a business demands articulating systems strategies. Chief computer systems executives must promote and establish consistent technical and applications design rules, sometimes known as "computer systems architecture." This is important, since data-base commitments now have a life-cycle of over 10 years and communication network decisions often are binding for more than 15 years. You cannot afford to tamper with such designs frequently. The inter-dependencies among equipment, networks, data bases and applications make it necessary to specify a detailed technology strategy. The penalties for changing the basic design architecture for a major system after its recent installation could exceed its initial acquisition cost.

The technical systems strategy cannot be separated from business needs. Do you need to run each factory as a market-competitive profit center, or do you wish to operate them as cost centers that transfer the product to your marketing organization at cost? The management information systems that support these choices will be different. Does the CEO insist on retaining the option to change factory pricing methods on short notice? You can design infinite pricing flexibility into a system, but it will cost more than if pricing methods remained stable. Costs, implementation schedules and systems controls will be different depending on the organizational strategy that top management will dictate.[2]

Why does one firm gain strategic advantages while another wastes money using the identical software? The answer will not be apparent in their computer applications. Business executives asked about what they see as obstacles to using computers strategically give different answers from computer executives. Business executives see information systems as an interaction between competitive and organizational issues. The computer executives' horizon has a specialized focus and therefore they are likely to concentrate on technical questions. However, all agree that because it is difficult to assess tangible gains from "strategic" uses, using computers as a strategic weapon is much inhibited.[3]

Top computer executives are ambivalent about planning for the strategic uses of computers. They find that the customary two- to five-year business plans hinder them in developing the necessary long-range technology plan for data centers, software, databases and networks. The rise in organizational instability is one of many reasons that has made strategic planning for computers a frustrating exercise. Fortunately, well-planned technology strategies reduce costs. The ultimate outcome of systems projects forms at their inception, so good planning must occur.

PLANNING FOR STRATEGIC ADVANTAGE

Opinions

The consulting firm of Price Waterhouse periodically reports on planning practices for management information systems.[4] Only 40% of the survey respondents in the 1988 report said they have a system plan integrated with the corporate plan. For the banking and insurance respondents, where computer expenses are a major cost element, 55% have such plans. Among the retail and distribution respondents, only 33% have systems plans that reflect company aims.

It should not come as a surprise that companies without concrete plans tie up much time in meetings about priorities. If there are no such plans, anyone can disagree with anything. When Price Waterhouse asked if there was agreement among department heads on systems development priorities, only 49% of the executives replied affirmatively.

Justifying computer investments to gain a strategic advantage is the top-ranking topic of interest. Magazine articles and presentations frequently refer to cases where strategic advantage improved the business.[5] Companies presumed to be enjoying a "strategic advantage" shape current thinking of what information technology is all about.

Magazines and professional societies delight in citing which companies excel in the strategic use of information technologies. A recent list included: American Airlines, American Hospital Supply, BANC One, Citicorp, Dun and Bradstreet, Federal Express, McKesson, Merrill Lynch, United Airlines and the United Services Auto Club.[6] Articles and books about the strategic advantage of computers mention the same firms. There is a great demand from computer vendors and computer journals for inspirational examples substantiated by profit figures. Despite this attention, companies with successful strategic applications should think carefully about their publicity, for their competitive advantage can evaporate if an opponent imitates or improves such applications. Too much publicity lowers a competitor's risks in coming up with a better solution.[7]

Consensus Processes

Linking the information systems plan with a company's business strategy is an increasingly popular topic. It arises whenever increased spending stimulates declarations of "strategic" necessity to justify costs. Consultants and academics have generated volumes on how to establish a plausible linkage between expenses today and strategic gains tomorrow.

The critical success factor method is the most widely used approach to deal with this issue.[8] This method begins with a "strategic vision" that inspires the corporate business plan. The "vision" articulates a futuristic picture of the organization. Business strategy then becomes the means for achieving this dream. Strategic planning for computers begins when corporate goals define "...the context or frame

of reference for a subsequent and more specific means-end relationship." Critical Success Factors (CSF's) identify key business goals. The CSF's support the preparation of four strategic systems planning products:
- Critical Decision Sets;
- Value-Based Processes;
- Critical Assumption Set;
- Strategic Data Mode.

If you follow the contents and the logic of the entire procedure, you would find that nobody mentions the topic of profits. The CSF method is exploratory and conceptual. It stresses creativity and concurrence among the peer group. It emphasizes sociable interactions and the ability to get key people to think of new ways to use computers. The centerpiece of the planning process is the CSF's that are "...interviews from as broad a range of strategy stakeholders, as a means to establish critical factors. Focus groups or other mechanisms are used to validate and gain consistency and commitment among these stakeholders with respect to these CSF's."

Using these methods, facts are obtained by consent and not by analysis. For instance, one requirement of the strategic planning process is to test for "extrinsic validity." How do you get that? Commission market research? Ask customers? Verify nasty rumors about competitors? Nothing that complicated is necessary. An externally valid plan is "...one that does not suffer significantly from the collective bias of those involved in the process."[9]

The CSF orientation gives primacy to negotiated consent and stakeholder compromise.[10] The emphasis is on consistency and consensus. In an environment rife with dissent about long-term business goals, this approach is the least objectionable way to decide what to do next.

I call this method of planning "consensual." Its objective is to reach an agreement for changing budget priorities. How do you use this method to find what to do next? That is done by probing, questioning, confronting, comparing and searching for logical consistency. For such an exploration to work, you need a discovery process for airing stakeholder opinions.

The consensual form of planning is attractive to everyone with limited expertise. Corporate staff, auditors and financial analysts prefer it because no first-hand knowledge of business realities is needed.

Consensual planning works well for executives in multi-layered organizations. When you are remote from customers and competitors, you must rely on arguments among subordinates to crystallize an opinion. This probing and confrontational approach reflects our legalistic traditions of governance.

Consensual planning is an ideal consulting methodology. Since all opinions originate from stakeholders, it follows that a legally minded CEO will find it attractive to hire a similarly inclined consultant. You cannot use a person vested in the organization for steering debates and confrontations. Committee chairpersons would damage their rapport with their peers if they disagree. The CEO can manage confrontations whenever necessary. Strategic planning for information systems does not usually call for the CEO's involvement except for final appeals. As it stands now, information technology is not sufficiently critical to get much time from the Executive Committee or the Board of Directors. No executive aspiring to a position in the executive suite can risk a searching involvement to steer computer strategies. They could easily get bushwhacked on technical issues.

To elicit from a disarray of opinions harmonized planning priorities is an ideal assignment for computer consultants or government advisory committees. Getting an organization to agree to a "strategic plan" is worth whatever fees they charge. The consensual method does a good job under such conditions. The outsiders rarely get enough facts to recommend anything that is not already on the strongest insider's agenda.[11]

EXAMPLES OF STRATEGIC ADVANTAGE

Mission first, computers afterward.

Well-managed businesses can gain a strategic advantage from computers. Strategic applications of information technologies have in common high-level decision-makers who wish to improve how their companies compete. These people do not get up in the morning and resolve to put computers to strategic use. For an application to become a strategic advantage, technology follows mission. Form follows function, similar to good architecture.

The following cases illustrate how several firms have managed to leverage computer technology to gain a competitive advantage. In each case, the strategic advantage could have arisen without computers, because the significant gains came from different ways of doing business and better ways of using employee talents. Information technologies made the new competitive options less expensive and faster, however. Only a small fraction of the financial benefits came directly from computers. The gain attributable to computers was the difference between the actual costs and the next least expensive means performed without the added investment.

Engineering and production-innovation strategy: Atlas Door

This 10-year old company has grown three times faster than the industry average, is debt-free and its earnings are five times the industry average. How did it achieve so much against fierce competition?

Atlas's strategic advantage is quick and reliable delivery of its products. Competitors quote four months' lead-time when an industrial door is out of stock or if it must be custom-finished. The competitors have huge inventories and are out-of-stock often because architects demand great variety in sizes and shapes. Atlas has organized its order-entry, engineering, manufacturing scheduling and shipping systems for fast-response custom production, and for 100% reliable delivery. Because of its setup, Atlas has spare production capacity, giving it a remarkable 2.5 week manufacturing cycle.

Traditionally, customers had to wait for more than one week just to get a quotation. For special orders, the quotation lead-time could be much longer. Atlas first simplified and then completely automated its entire order-entry process. Order-entry ties in directly to engineering, pricing and manufacturing scheduling. This enabled Atlas to quote prices and confirm delivery schedules for 95% of its orders while a customer is still on the phone. The engineering of special orders has a very fast turn-around for design and production data regarding previous orders are in the database. In this way, re-engineering and re-estimating consists of modifications of prior models.

To save customers' time and effort, Atlas developed a method so that orders consisting of multiple parts leave the plant only after the correct parts are together in the delivery truck. Atlas can command a premium price because it creates extra *Value-added* from the customer's point of view. The additional costs to Atlas for an integrated information system are a fraction of the customers' savings when installation can proceed without expensive delays.

The role of computers in Atlas is critical because they record everything from the inquiry to final delivery. The Atlas sales representatives can quote specifications, prices and delivery dates using workstations that integrate engineering, production scheduling and transportation databases. Low cost computers are omnipresent, but the Atlas system could not boast of technical sophistication, because it meets only simple, essential needs. Competitors can buy those identical computers, and could imitate everything that Atlas is doing. Yet, the competitors keep losing market share.

The secret of the Atlas strategy is the skillful integration of business functions into a well-balanced approach to do things differently from the competitors. I talked with the Atlas CEO and asked who was the chief system architect and designer for his company. He answered that he had personally designed and supervised the installation of "the system." When he talked about "systems," he did not refer to computers but how his company delivers superior products and services to customers.

To the Atlas CEO, his unique approach to carving out a large market share is the strategic system, not the computers.

Organizational innovation strategy: Toyota

About ten years ago Toyota's manufacturing capability in Japan enabled the manufacturing of a car in 2 days. It took 15 to 26 days to get the order to the factory, get the car made, and deliver the car to the customer in Japan. The cost associated with selling and distribution was higher than the variable costs of making the car.

Emphasis then changed from cost-cutting in the factory to streamlining logistics. Toyota changed its internal communications system. It would not support passing orders from dealers to the sales offices, from the sales offices to the sales regions, from the sales regions to the plant, before proceeding with production. To shorten the time-consuming order entry procedures, a new computer system allowed sales people to communicate directly with factory schedulers. The expectation was that the new approach would cut the sales-distribution cycle in half. By 1987, Toyota reduced turnaround to eight days, including the time for making the car. The effectiveness of these new systems helps Toyota to retain its growing market share.[12]

To what extent are computers essential for improving Toyota's strategic advantage? What Toyota is doing now with personal computers in sales offices was possible with Teletype fifty years ago. Toyota's real innovation is organizational, not technological; however computers have surely lowered the costs of their order processing network.

To Toyota, the several related organizational innovations are the strategic system, not the computers.

Work integration strategy: Technical Publications

A Technical Publications department with a staff of 40 publishes 4,000 pages per year. The introduction of desktop publishing speeded up the production cycle from 12–16 weeks to 3–4 weeks. This shorter cycle facilitates earlier product launches, and has been identified by management and a consultant as a source of competitive advantage.[13]

To Technical Publications, the ability to manage its work is the strategic opportunity, not the computers.

Design for survival strategy: McKesson Corporation

In 1976, McKesson, a wholesale distributor of drug-store merchandise to independent pharmacies, realized that its customers could go out of business because of fierce competition from large drugstore chains. McKesson's customers—the independents—would disappear unless they could get similar advantages available to the large pharmacy chains. McKesson conceived a strategy of combining small-company focus with large company efficiencies, and helped its customers to compete.

Previously, the nation's 30,000 independent pharmacies and 7,000 hospitals spent excessive hours manually listing the products they needed to buy. They would mail or phone an order to a distributor, who maintained thousands of items in alphabetically arranged warehousing. Order pickers took the randomly arranged orders and searched through the warehouse to find the necessary items.

McKesson evolved a superior computer system which included portable data-collection devices which make it possible to check inventory, automatically process merchandise orders and schedule shipments. Ninety-nine percent of McKesson's customer orders come in an electronic format, allowing the central computer to specify the order picking sequence that matches the distributor's warehouse layout. The computer also directs the packing of the merchandise in the sequence for unloading at the store.

McKesson now has enough data about each store's demand patterns so that it can assist in pricing, store layout, shelving arrangements, employment scheduling and profit analysis. It offers to its customers a service, *Economost*, that gives each subscriber detailed reports showing how well the customer is doing with each product line.

McKesson has diversified into providing accounting services for its customers, tracking prescription histories of individuals, alerting the druggist about a patient's drug allergies, tracking payments by insured medical plans, products mix management, promotional planning and advertising strategies. The customers are independent private companies but receive the benefits of centrally accumulated management know-how.

McKesson has benefited from the strength of its customers. It receives fees for information processing services so that its merchandise does not carry excessive overhead costs. Its sales have increased from $900 million in 1976 to $5 billion in 1987. Profits have increased 17% per year.

Automation permitted the company to reduce warehouse personnel from 130 to 54, eliminate 500 clerical jobs and reduce merchandise buyers from 140 to 12. The average order size increased from $4,000 per month to $12,000 per month while inventory costs decreased. Ninety-two distribution centers were consolidated into 52 centers. The operating cost reductions from these systems also lowered wholesale prices to the independent stores, enabling them to survive.

McKesson's strategic advantage can be proven only indirectly. Most of its major competitors developed similar systems with similar capabilities at the same time. In the decade following the system's introduction, McKesson's market share stood unchanged, partly because of Government restraints on acquisitions. During the same period, smaller competitors, unable to develop competing systems, left the distribution business.

The number of drug distributors declined 50% from 1975 to 1985. The wholesalers gained market share from factory-owned distribution because of their superior capacity to serve the needs of local markets. In 1985, wholesalers distributed 65% of all pharmaceuticals as compared with only 45% in 1970. The McKesson system became a strategic necessity and its contribution can be evaluated only against the financial performance of the surviving drug distributors. The operating savings or benefits from sales volume increases do not count because they passed to the customers.

The McKesson case is necessary study for anyone who wishes to learn about the strategic benefits of computer systems. Here is an instance where employment, market position, competitive position and profit margins changed dramatically in less than 10 years. McKesson nearly sold off its business in the early 1970's because the prospects were so bad. Instead, it invested a cumulative $125 million in information technology with extraordinary returns.[14]

To McKesson, design for survival is the strategic system, not the computers.

Overhead cost reduction strategy: Kao Corporation

Kao is Japan's leading soap and detergent maker. In 1986 it embarked on a major cost-reduction effort to compete with imports that took advantage of the strong yen. Kao's campaign to adjust appeared under the banner of "Total Creative Revolution," similar to other Japanese firms, to inspire the employees' total participation.

The first aim of Kao's improvement program was to disband and replace the functions of central production control. A computer-based system now allows each salesperson to send orders directly to the plants from a hand-held terminal.

The second aim was to link Kao plants directly to raw material suppliers and thus shorten the delays in production coordination. Work-in-process inventories are dramatically lower than before. As a result, materials losses decreased by 50%.[15]

To Kao, overhead cost reduction is the strategic system, not the computers.

Strengthening bonds with customers strategy: IBM's LINK

Information technology can provide affordable around-the-clock local support services without on-site personnel.

The IBM Corporation has recently offered to 5,000 major accounts direct "on-line" access to its central database. The database contains a catalogue of the most often asked technical questions, technical specifications and special articles of interest. IBM's intent is to forge a responsive link with the customers' experts who support personal computer networks. One way to add value to a relationship with a customer is to make the customers' administrators look smart. The customer's "technical coordinators" now can take care of frequent questions that arise as computers get into the hands of novices.

Such communication between a customer and supplier initiates dialogue and feedback. It changes the traditional relationship in which the value of a product is greater than its purchase cost. The complexity of new equipment and services makes it necessary to provide a continual flow of education, training, supplies, improvements and guidance. A sale of a product is thus the beginning, not an end to a commercial transaction. This will maintain IBM's strategic advantage.[16]

To IBM, the strengthening of links with customers is the strategic system, not the computers.

Lowering customer support costs strategy: Microsoft's Online Network

Microsoft is the world's largest software supplier for microcomputers. It offers two "on-line" technical support services to improve its responsiveness to widely dispersed customers.

The first system, "Microsoft Online" supports software developers who use Microsoft products as an integral part of their applications. This system makes it possible for customers to get answers from central support staffs and search a diagnostic database for technical answers. The system handles the transmission of software libraries and sending messages to other subscribers of the service. Microsoft has recognized the desire of computer programmers to keep in touch with their peers and made the network open to all software developers. The customer pays a modest subscription fee for membership in Microsoft Online.

The second support service is for retail purchasers of Microsoft software. The G.E. Network for Information Exchange (Genie) provides this as a *Value-added* service. It offers to all comers an "electronic roundtable" for information exchange plus access to Microsoft's problem-resolution database.[17]

To Microsoft, the lowering of customer support costs is the strategic system, not the computers.

Capturing customer orders strategy: Akzo Coatings

Akzo Coatings is the paint division of a large Dutch chemical company. They addressed unreliable cost estimates for automobile bodyshop customers in Europe.

They developed a computer system that gives repair shops access to spare part listings, repair procedures and labor hour guidelines for 2,000 car models. Each repair shop has a personal computer and modem. Estimators specify the description of the car, its damage and the repair work it needs. A local printer then types out itemized parts, labor cost calculations and an order list for parts and materials. The listing gives detailed instructions on how to make the repairs. It gives particular attention to the application of Akzo paint and materials to save the customer's labor costs.

Generally, customers with damaged automobiles do not have much confidence in body shop estimates because they think that they get arbitrarily excessive charges. Shop owners worry about cost overruns resulting from inadvertent omission of repair items. Akzo's on-line system has improved relationships between consumers and shop owners. It also has improved Akzo's competitive position.

To Akzo, the capturing of customer orders is the strategic system, not the computers.

Distribution of expert knowledge strategy: Du Pont

The "Packaging Adviser" helps Du Pont customers to design food packages, such as plastic soft drink bottles or microwave food containers. It conveys to customers advanced knowledge of how to use Du Pont products with superior packaging properties at the least cost. Packaging design is technically complex, including considerations such as government standards, protection against humidity, oxygen barriers for longer shelf life, and packaging rigidity. Some packages need five different laminations to meet all requirements.

Previously, only a few technical experts were available to teach packaging design know-how to customers. This program makes it possible to offer more effective sales coverage to customers.

To Du Pont, the distribution of expert knowledge is the strategic system, not the computers.

Retention of irreplaceable know-how strategy: Campbell Soup

The most complex and critical piece of equipment at the Campbell Soup food company is the "Cooker." It is a 70–100 foot tall sterilization machine through which soup and soup cans must pass to kill bacteria. Down-time is very costly. Even an isolated sterilization malfunction can lead to enormous damages if customers refuse to purchase products bearing the Campbell Soup label.

Four maintenance and repair experts on the "Cooker" with an accumulated experience of 165 man-years were nearing retirement. Campbell contracted with an "expert" systems company to capture the maintenance experts' know-how specifically to solve complex maintenance problems with the equipment. The resulting microcomputer application has captured about 95% of the known maintenance and repair conditions as well as their solutions. The Campbell Soup company believes they made an excellent investment.

To Campbell Soup, the retention of irreplaceable know-how is the strategic system, not the computers.

Upgrading salesforce skills strategy: Rhone-Poulenc

The marketing of a plastic additive involves assurance that it will not change the physical characteristics of materials with which it combines. A problem occurs when a change in an additive's composition has a chain effect on other properties. Originally, questions about possible effects came from clients to experts in the central research laboratory. Sometimes this required that specialists travel to check local conditions.

A new expert system reflecting the laboratory's knowledge regarding additives is directly accessible to world-wide sales personnel. The sales people can give customers the ideal formula within 24 to 48 hours instead of several weeks. The expert system can deal with hundreds of chemicals and give the right answer in 80% of the cases based on a knowledge base of approximately 500 questions. A system consultation usually takes 15 minutes and finds the solution in fewer than 20 questions. Tests have proved that the expert system can answer correctly all routine questions leaving the human experts with more time to deal with new and difficult situations.

To Rhone-Poulenc, the upgrading of salesforce skills is the strategic system, not the computers.

Speeding up the sales cycle strategy: Fidelity Union Life Insurance

This Dallas life insurance company is encouraging its independent sales agents to use laptop computers as a sales tool. Previously, it took several visits from an agent before a potential client could receive an insurance proposal. During the first visit, the agent usually gathered financial facts for analysis back at the office. On the second call, the client would see the analysis offering potential solutions. At that time, the agent and client would engage in a conversation about different policy options. Very often, new facts surfaced that needed re-examination of the first analysis. It could take four and sometimes even more calls to sell a policy.[18] With a laptop computer and printer, it is possible to generate several proposals during the initial visit and change the assumptions as the conversation develops. This makes it possible to close sales more effectively.

To Fidelity Union Life Insurance, speeding up the sales cycle is the strategic system, not the computers.

Speeding up information strategy: Industrial Chemicals Company

The small field sales force of a successful industrial chemical company[19] struggled to deliver to customers information about its products. The firm had 200,000 customers and 2,000 products. In addition, 500 bulletins per year informed the 50 salespersons about new products or new uses of old products. The sales representatives suffered an information overload. There were too many bulletins, catalogues and fact sheets. Customers bought only a few products because they could not cope with the proliferation of products and uses.

The chemical company initially tackled the information overload by revising its organization. The sales force was organized around market segments. The head office issued costly and elaborate product catalogues without any detailed information on how to use the chemicals. Although there was a corporate product database, it was accessible only through specially trained secretaries. The sales representatives did try to request information directly from the central files but the entire process was just too cumbersome and slow.

Sales representatives then received personal computers. The central data base became electronically available. The database also includes customer sales histories, all technical materials about products, generic proposal templates and an electronic bulletin board with news about promotion-worthy ideas, success stories and competitive situations. It has now become easy for each representative to generate customized sales materials for each customer call, such as proposals and technical bulletins. Individual sales people can start customer-specific mailing campaigns based on local market conditions. The salespersons have traded a 20 pound computer for over 70 pounds of technical manuals.

The entire program met its objectives. For instance, management reported that six large dormant accounts started ordering products again. New business volume also increased, with sales volume increasing above expectations.

To Industrial Chemicals Company, speeding up information is the strategic system, not the computers.

Adding value to the sales call strategy: Genentech and Parke-Davis

An endocrinologist (hormone specialist) gains access to cases with characteristics similar to his patients when Genentech salespersons visit. This represents an extended set of services offered along with the standard line of hormone products.[20]

A similar application is available through the lap-top computers of the 800-member prescription drug sales force of Parke-Davis. Each personal computer stores comprehensive information about Parke-Davis drugs. It also has information about the physicians who prescribe the drugs, their educational background, prescription habits and when a salesperson can best call on them.[21]

To Genentech and Parke-Davis, adding value to the sales call is the strategic system, not the computers.

Increasing customer satisfaction strategy: General Electric

The General Electric central customer inquiry and complaint center in Louisville handles three million phone calls a year, for about $8 million. The operators can provide intelligent answers because they can refer to a giant database that stores 750,000 answers about 8,500 models and 120 product lines of G.E. equipment. Every representative thus appears to a customer as an "expert." G.E. reports that its people can solve 90% of complaints or inquiries on the first call. This produces a large saving in warranty costs, because most problems claimed as equipment defects are misunderstandings on to operate an appliance.

The personnel in the center also act as marketing representatives. About 700,000 callers get advice on how to contact the nearest G.E. dealer. Such prompting generates more sales.

To General Electric, increasing customer satisfaction is the strategic system, not the computers.

Maintaining central control strategy: Mrs. Field's Cookies

This 650+ store cookie chain has become a much studied legend of how to organize an enterprise with a simple product using sophisticated information management methods. A personal computer in each store supports the following applications[22]:
- Labor Scheduling: The computer optimizes each store's employee schedule, recognizing fluctuating labor requirements and changing costs for different employee categories.
- Production Planning: Hourly scheduling of product mixes for baking ovens.
- Employee Time Collection: Each employee enters time worked

directly into the computer. It takes only five employees to administer a 7,000 employee weekly payroll.
- Employee Screening: An expert system for validating applicants' qualifications, and identifying questions to be asked by an interviewer.
- Skills Testing: Administration of aptitude tests.
- Inventory Control: Data for central inventory management and supplies reordering.
- Intra-company Communications: Electronic mail for local problem resolution from a highly centralized management.

To Mrs. Field's Cookies, maintaining central control is the strategic system, not the computers.

Global production management strategy: Mattel

Customer preferences are notoriously unpredictable in the toy industry. Mattel, Inc. compensates for erratic demand by speeding up its information flow with a worldwide communications network that connects all sales offices, plants and suppliers.[23] This shortens its reaction time for critical business decisions[24]:

	Before	After
Inventory Update	30 days	1 day
International Demand Forecast	3-4 days	Interactive
Financial Consolidation	7-10 days	1 day
Production Schedules	10-14 days	1 day
Engineering Changes	7-14 days	1 day

Table 8-1: Speeding Responses to Customers

To Mattel, global production management is the strategic system, not the computers.

Decentralized gathering of intelligence strategy: Frito-Lay

This snack-food manufacturer, which relies on direct delivery of its products to retail stores, has equipped its sales force with 10,000 handheld computers. The sales people carry the equipment into stores, enter inventory information, key in orders and print out invoices. The sales people connect to the central computer and transmit sales information after finishing their rounds. Simultaneously, the handheld computers receive the latest information about new products or changed prices. The company estimates that it has realized large cost savings, smoothed the delivery process, reduced inventories and simplified customer billing.[25]

Frito-Lay used the introduction of the portable computers to make other changes, such as changing the structure of the routes, re-arranging pay procedures and enhancing the salesperson's role in dealing with customers. The result was a marked reduction in non-productive time.

To Frito-Lay, decentralized gathering of intelligence is the strategic system, not the computers.

Shop-floor autonomy strategy: Lockheed Corporation

Long production lines and lengthy procedures consume more labor, take longer, make more errors, make it easier to lose an item and call for elaborate tracking of what is happening. The longer the process, both in time and distance, the greater the number of managers and expediters needed to maintain order. When something goes wrong, it is hard to find the reason.

Lockheed Aircraft installed a "Computer-Aided Layout and Fabrication" system for aircraft engine parts. It reduced the average distance a part had to travel from 2,500 feet to 150 feet. Work takes place in a series of "manufacturing cells," where worker groups are fully responsible for completing an entire part. These cells are autonomous and flexible so the operators themselves can make changes either in the process or tooling. This autonomy would not be possible without access to schedule, materials availability and cost information.[26]

To Lockheed, autonomous production groups are the strategic system, not the computers.

TOO MUCH OF A STRATEGIC ADVANTAGE?

American Airlines' SABRE reservation system is the most frequently cited example of a "strategic information system." In 1986, it had over 45% market share of computer reservation terminals in the U.S.[27] How is it that SABRE offers an advantage if reservation systems of competing airlines perform identical functions? Reservation agents can connect to other reservation systems. For instance, a United Airlines agent using their *Apollo* computer system can confirm flights on TWA's *Pars* system and vice versa. Similar inter-connections exist between SABRE and *SystemOne* (Texas Air).[28]

Airline reservation systems favor bookings on their own flights, similar to attracting customers to stay in the same store once you get them there. When an agent tries to make a flight reservation on *SystemOne*, Texas Air flights appear first. Any attempt to search for a United flight is likely to meet switching delays as *SystemOne* connects to *Covia*. Whether or not reservation systems deliberately give unfair preference to their own airlines is hard to prove. Differences in systems design and technical problems with data transmission can explain differences in performance when processing inter-airline transactions.

Supplying computer reservations is good business for not every airline can afford its own system. Other revenue also comes from independent travel agents.[28] Transaction volume drives profitability in this business. Market share generates volume that increases the utilization of capacity which is largely a fixed cost.[29]

To profit from SABRE, American Airlines adopted a strategy of offering a technically superior universal service, including support to competing airlines. Here is a case where a vendor gets a strategic advantage from offering the same service to competitors instead of keeping any technology advances to itself. The customer—such as an independent travel agent or a re-seller of information services—will prefer SABRE because he will get a reliable, predictable and standardized product.

With a 46% market share, American Airlines has the motivation to keep its services equally available due to the threat of legal suits.[30] Since 1984, there has been a $300 million antitrust suit pending against American Airlines, alleging monopoly. In 1988, Texas Air filed complaints against American Airlines and United Airlines, arguing that software in both airlines' reservation systems deprives competitors of bookings. Too much of a competitive advantage may not be wise as the best strategy.

For American Airlines, the following dynamic seems to be working:[31]
- Early innovation occurs through product differentiation and superior implementation.
- The innovator gets a dominant market share.
- Competitors try to catch up through innovation which does not necessarily offer more value to customers.
- Customers get trained on the computer that has the dominant market share. This creates a reluctance to switch to other competitors.

- As the industry standard, the dominant service provider gains market share and becomes more profitable. Now the standard-setter cannot be dislodged except through incompetence or a radical innovation by a competitor or newcomer in the business.
- If the dominant provider takes advantage of his position through discriminatory practices or monopolistic pricing his position will become vulnerable to price competition and governmental intervention. The leader has to surrender some competitive advantages to prevent such action.[32]

Too much of a strategic advantage may be short-lived.[33] When you plan strategic information systems, you should establish that they serve your company's information needs even after the assumption of an overwhelming competitive advantage runs into regulatory restrictions.

COMPUTERS AND SMALL COMPANY OPPORTUNITIES

The traditional view of efficiency calls for economies of size, the advantages of vertical integration and the unification of planning under central management. Most business school courses teach that view of industrial organization. You do not get to hear much about the liability of excessive overhead, or about the inflexibility of the corporate hierarchy to react to customer preferences. Small business has supplied all the employment growth since 1970, yet computer magazines mostly quote what big company CIOs are saying. How should a small-company CEO view planning for computer systems?

Good communication with suppliers and customers characterizes all successful strategic systems. When confronted with excessive diversity, a large functional organization cannot cope. Large corporations fight their size disadvantage through standardization. This is why large companies are the proponents of:

- Data Standards. They lower transaction costs. Bar codes make it possible to reduce the error rates in electronic messages. Low-cost reliability makes coordination faster and economically more attractive, even across cultural and language barriers. For examples see the McKesson Corporation and Akzo cases.
- Information Networks. They can substitute for an elaborate organization. Networks make it possible to offer specialized advice and support. For examples see IBM's LINK Network, Microsoft's Online Network and General Electric cases.

- Computer-Aided Knowledge Transmission. Large companies benefit from having specialized staffs who inform customers about products and markets. Programs such as computer-aided design, computer-aided manufacturing, financial simulations, and expert systems can distribute staff know-how. For examples, see Du Pont, Rhone-Poulenc, Fidelity Union Life Insurance, Genentech and Parke-Davis cases.

Data standards, information networks and computer-aided knowledge allow large corporations to reap the benefit of global economies, while acting as local small-scale enterprises. How can a small company survive?

If a small company wishes to compete with large organizations, it must offer something that the big corporation cannot or will not do. Otherwise, customers will find it more attractive to deal directly with the large corporation.

The expansions of information networks that support dealerships, distributors and franchises show that economic realities favor hybrid organizations that are neither monolithic mega-corporations nor small-scale owner-operated businesses. These hybrids can offer world-class quality, at global competitive prices, using small company methods.[34] Through electronic communication, the small company can get the same materials and parts as the big company. Through information networks, the small company can benefit from the same services as large corporations at a marginal cost.[35] Through computer-aided knowledge, the small organizations can buy central expertise whenever it is necessary. For the negligible cost of a few microcomputers a small company can lower its break-even business volume to a point no large firm can afford.

The small company does not have the advantages of size or specialized resources of the big corporation. Information technology makes it possible to overcome most of these disadvantages. Information technology allows small-scale enterprises to get most of the benefits of large-scale operations at competitive prices. More gains come from its superior capacity to respond to customers who need specialized services.[36] Employee-owned businesses can take advantage of the skills and the motivation of people in flexible ways that big company standard policies do not allow.

If the alliance with a large supplier does not work, how does the small organization survive? A business that relies on standard electronic communications for managing its transactions has great flexibility in changing its relationships with suppliers and distributors. A new product or a new market can be added by changing the company's database or adding to its software library. Maintaining a specialized competence while serving the widest possible market is the key to strategic success for any small company.

The computer-supported small business fits markets where each customer is unique and where products have an unlimited variety.[37] Serving diversity while preserving the economics of mass production is possible by imaginative uses of computers. The Atlas Door Company case is an example of such an approach but there are thousands of others. The CEO of every small business must therefore become the chief information systems strategist.

For competitive advantage, the small company should use the same *mission critical* applications as the big corporation. It can save money by spending relatively little on *management information systems* since management knows what's happening anyway. The principal information advantage of the small company is its capacity to conceive and carry out a harmonious computer strategy that blends with the firm's business.[38]

COMPUTERS AND OPPORTUNITIES IN ADULT EDUCATION

Public education for adults is the prime candidate for value-enhancement through information technology. It is an employment-protected, capital-rich and tax-exempt industry. Its operating costs are a fraction of its full costs because of tax subsidies, endowment and free land.

Product quality is unknown except when management rates itself. Its labor force is not evaluated for the quality of services delivered to clients. Its capacity utilization is less than 30%. The average teaching hours are less than 10% of the total paid hours, because of a large non-teaching staff, holidays and long vacations. Its employees have the highest rate of paid absenteeism of any industry, while scheduled working hours are the lowest. The damage this business can inflict on its clients, by leaving them uneducated, may be permanent. This business enjoys a preferred licensing status, including immunity from all liability and negligence suits. Output quality, production capacity and price are unrelated. Its products are not readily transportable because they are custom-produced and instantly perishable.

The next decade will see major reforms occurring in this business. A larger share of revenues will come directly from its paying clients. This will shift the focus to free market competition. Customers will insist on choosing from a diversity of competing suppliers. To deliver a high quality product, the producers will need the means for distributing their services in national and even global markets. This will force much of the educational product to take advantage of network-based systems. Network-based education has the benefits of mass production and mass distribution. It can also work in a tutorial mode so that it can deliver specific answers to a student's questions. It combines the best of post-industrial production methods[39] with the capacity to deliver education in the best Socratic tradition.

An expansion in adult education for profit is already on its way. Competition will drive this sector to cost reduction and further value-enhancement. Just consider how much it costs a middle manager or professional specialist to attend a two day off-site skill-upgrading course in a central city. It costs about $200 per classroom hour.[40] This educational service costs less than $10 per student-hour by electronic means.

The next generation of personal computers will offer multi-media capacity including animation, full motion video and context-organized instructional databases. When high-bandwidth networks become easily accessible, adult education has a prospect of becoming the growth industry of the 21st century.

Managing Strategic Opportunities

Superior strategies may fail from poor execution, but superior execution cannot overcome poor strategies.

How do you recognize strategic opportunities and priorities before you leap into computer projects? How can you tell whether an application will help reach strategic goals?

Correct strategic diagnosis is an absolute prerequisite for successful use of computers. A misdirection in goals can doom a project before it begins. A diagnosis that pinpoints what needs fixing can tolerate unimpressive technical solutions. Picking the wrong priorities will nullify whatever sophisticated technologies and excellent people could produce.

Never compromise on the quality of the diagnosis! The scrutiny, examination, dissection, quizzing and testing of whether or not a computer project attacks the right problems needs the personal attention of top executives. Checking the diagnosis offers the best opportunity to influence the direction of computer investments.

For many years, I participated in systems review committees, project authorization boards and computer advisory task forces. The usual format of these sessions is listening to advocates of increased spending as they present their cases. The presenters have good motivation to show their projects in the best possible light. Cases without merit rarely get on the agenda.

Chief executives often find these sessions frustrating. Requests for money always exceed what is available. How can you judge the relative priority for a new marketing database, when manufacturing urgently needs a new application for scheduling engineering changes? Chief executives are even more concerned about the alignment of various projects with rapidly changing business directions. The launching into new strategic directions, such as those illustrated for Atlas, Toyota, McKesson, Akzo and Mrs. Field's Cookies, required inter-departmental applications and adoption of new technical solutions. No individual department could have proposed a new computer strategy.

How can you independently verify that you are pursuing the right mission? This is where *PIMS*-like diagnostics can help. The profiles of success or failure can suggest which strategic gaps need filling. Superior profits do not arise from only one exceptional achievement.

Over-achievers do not show any one spectacular ratio. They simply avoid below-average ratings for all ratios that matter. Business excellence comes from balancing the essential favorable indicators.

The *Under-achievers'* diagnostics are spotty. You will always find a few ratios where they are similar to *Over-achievers*. They lose, however, because a few strong negative influences overwhelm whatever is good about the firm.

My usual recommendation to *Below-average* clients is to first work on eliminating poor influences that weigh heavily on depressing the value of *R-O-M*. Overcoming a few disadvantages gives faster results at a lower cost, than working on improvements that aspire for *Over-achiever* ratings.

If you find a ratio in this book that suggests that you should take corrective actions,[41] do so only after checking to see if other indicators also support the same conclusion. When physicians examine a patient, they look at several aspects before deciding on a remedy. In a business organization, information technology is just one of many important signs and rarely the single major cause of poor performance. Its effects on profits are subtle and almost always indirect. It cannot apply as an exclusive solution to a business problem. As in the strategic cases above, information technology offers one of many means for strategic gains. Computers deliver excellent results if their contributions are verifiable. Clearly defined strategic opportunities rest on fact-tested reality. You cannot expect to get a workable strategy if it comes only from wishful conjectures.

Identifying Strategic Opportunities

The development of useful diagnostic aids was the primary purpose for research described in Chapter 7. The diagnostic reports that a client of R-O-M™ database services receives show his company's position (marked as ✚ for case #752 in Figure 8.1) as compared with its peer group:[4]

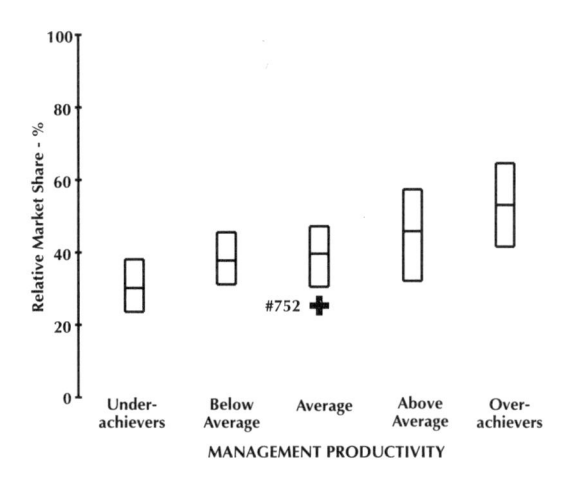

Figure 8.1: Diagnosis of Relative Market Share Position

The R-O-M calculation for this firm has categorized it as an *Average* firm. In its served market, it has a relative market share of 24.5%. The box plot in Figure 8.1 shows that more than 75% of *Average* firms[43] enjoyed a better relative market share. Though this diagnostic is not conclusive, the great weight of relative market share in explaining R-O-M value suggests that we pay attention to it. We will concentrate on marketing-

CHAPTER 8—STRATEGIC INVESTMENTS   *187*

related activities. Two considerations lead to that conclusion.

First, high values of *R-O-M* and high relative market share are closely related. A substandard relative market share in this industry sector is always dangerous. In this case the relative market share of client #752 is comparable to the relative market share at the bottom of the scale for *Under-achievers*. We shall therefore, look for every clue why relative market-share is so low. Is it price, an obsolete plant, inadequate distribution or poor service quality? The candidate for the largest improvement will appear on one of the *R-O-M* diagnostic charts as having the greatest substandard value. Different candidates for improvement will need different information technology solutions assuming the deficiency is amenable to a cure via computers. In the case of client #752, customers had switched to the competition because of poor product quality linked to inadequate plant information systems.[44] Plant management exercised excessive cost control and could not afford information systems.

Why did a company with an atypically low relative market share enjoy an *Average R-O-M* nevertheless? Did the company have materials supply, manufacturing cost, tax or overhead cost advantages?

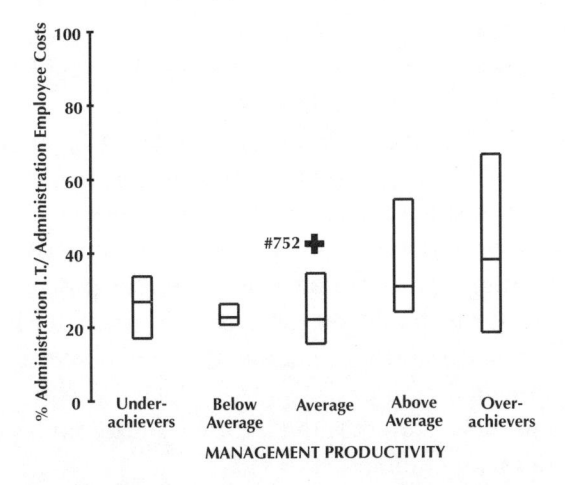

Figure 8.2: Diagnosis of Administrative I.T. Intensity

This firm earned its reputation for competent administrative uses of computers. That was the reason the client asked for *R-O-M* diagnosis. *Administration* kept producing impressive investment proposals that called for more investments in administrative automation. Top management wished to know if administrators' superb skills in preparing good proposals unfairly biased business priorities in favor of administrative applications.

I found that #752 was spending 42 cents of information technology for every dollar of administrative-employee costs. This high rate of automation placed it above the *Over-achievers'* average. Spending more money in administration could lower overhead costs, but has no effect on the company's market share.

I recommended that the most imaginative systems talent transfer from *Administration* to *Production*. I also recommended that the costs of strategic systems planning for new manufacturing systems be paid directly by the CEO. This would overcome the reluctance of Production Management to invest in an overhaul of its systems.

Avoiding Strategic Failure

The demise of the PeopleExpress offers the clearest case of strategic failure because of neglect of information technology. Donald C. Burr, the airline ex-CEO said that the competitors' skillful uses of reservation systems, while his airline had none, inflicted on his operations irreparable damage, ultimately leading to bankruptcy.[45] Burr explained his neglect of information technologies by claiming that it was not clear to the airline industry that computerized systems would become the primary distribution channel for airline seats.

Burr was asked what should be the role of a CEO in seeing to it that the strategic role of information technology remains important. He said that the CEO must have a personal and close understanding about the direction of information technology. This need not involve technical knowledge but a thorough comprehension about its potential competitive impacts. The CEO should set the broad priorities for information technology investments and then get the finest talent in the industry to execute the strategic directions. After that, the CEO needs to allocate sufficient time to make sure that the information resources do not fail for lack of attention and money.

I found Burr's sobering remarks sound advice on avoiding strategic failures.

Organizing for Strategic Opportunities

Whoever pays for strategic systems planning should also have the authority to decide on implementation. There is no point in devoting staff time to strategic systems planning if nobody will act on their recommendations. Only executives who have the direct accountability for long-term shareholder returns can articulate information systems missions. Planning for the technology architecture such as hardware and software standards may follow afterwards with greater assurance. Computer planning by experts from the M.I.S. function cannot hope to come up with actionable strategic programs to improve business profits.

Chapter Summary

What distinguishes strategic users of information technology from other companies? If everyone has computers, enjoys access to telecommunication networks and has a similar portfolio of computer applications, what makes the difference? Successful users are not technology innovators. They do not spend significantly more money on office automation than their competitors. Productivity and strategic advantages stem from other sources than information technology.

Strategic users cannot separately identify the contributions of computers from their innovative marketing methods, the way they improve production management and how they take better care of customers. To get superior productivity and strategic advantage, computers must support the capacity to compete. Spending more money and taking the most sophisticated technology does not increase revenues or market share without changing how the firm runs its business.

Using computers for productivity improvement and strategic advantage is like using pharmaceuticals to restore physical well-being. Improving health is the result of many correct choices. First, it calls for a good diagnosis of what needs fixing. Second, it calls for a thorough knowledge of the effects of the drug. Last, you must know when to begin and when to stop.

Computers are unlike any other machine. Since the strategic uses of computers are so new, many executives misunderstand how to blend them into their organizations. The prevailing executive view is that computers should be in the custody of technical experts who will somehow figure out what to do with them. This view will guarantee that computers will have a negligible strategic value.

If used in the wrong way on the wrong problems, computers can injure the health of your company. When directed by the top executives to line up with sound and clear strategic goals, you can expect remarkable gains.

Chapter 8 Comments

[1] The word strategy comes from the Greek word for the military rank of a general.
[2] Every company has a strategy. It need not be a formal plan. A strategy is what an organization does, not what it writes about.
[3] W.R. King, V. Grover, E.H. Hufnagel, Understanding the Strategic Uses of Information Resources, *University of Pittsburgh*, June 1987, describe their survey of 83 members of the Society for Information Management with the following top ranking scores on a scale of 1 to 5 ("greatly facilitating"=1 or "greatly inhibiting"=5) in applying information technology strategically:

Top Ranking Facilitators	
Strong Technical Expertise	3.4
Information Technology Leadership	3.2
Pressure from Competition	3.1

Top Ranking Inhibitors	
Business has Other Priorities	3.6
Difficulty in Assessing Tangible Gains	3.4
Lack of Appropriate Planning	3.3

[4] N. Statland, Big MIPS, Little Plans, *Datamation*, August 15, 1988, p. 74. Information collected from a panel of M.I.S. executives.
[5] The opening speaker at a recent executive conference about information systems promised, in his opening remarks, that nobody could mention American Airlines or the American Hospital Supply Corporation. The audience applauded.
[6] The Top Strategic Information Systems in Services, *InformationWeek*, December, 1986. Their profit performance is not impressive. None of the firms are in the top 10-percentile of companies as rated by FORTUNE, and one of the them is a below average performer.
[7] An interesting commentary about the origins of the American Airlines' system comes from Max Hopper, one of the architects of SABRE. He said that American Airlines started designing its own system only after United Airlines announced their plans. In those days, travel agents made about half of all airline bookings. As a reaction to the initiative by United, American started designing something that would be superior. United planned to give travel agents a system that would cover only the routes flown by United. American decided to counter with an offering that would serve a travel agent's complete needs. By fostering dependence on SABRE, American instantly gained market share and maintained its dominance since then, although when they got started that was not necessarily in their strategic plan. Donald C. Burr, the ex-CEO of PeopleExpress Airline mentions that as late as in 1979 American Airlines tried to sell a half interest in SABRE to Pan American for only $10 million (Interview with D.C.Burr, *Information Management Review*, 1990, 5, p.68).
[8] J.C. Henderson and J.G. Sifonis, The *Value-added* of Strategic IS Planning: Understanding Consistency, Validity, and IS Markets, *Center for Information Systems Research, M.I.T. Working Paper 145*, November 1986.
[9] The October 10, 1988 issue of *Insight* (p. 43) has a telling commentary about increasingly fact-phobic attitudes: "It used to be true that you could sell a product based on real and distinct differences. Now you can no longer sell products based on facts. There are so many facts out there competing for attention that people aren't willing to sort through them. It is more important to consider how people feel. The solution: offer an image that by-passes the consumer's analytic processes."

CHAPTER 8—STRATEGIC INVESTMENTS   *191*

10 A euphemism for company politics.
11 You can cut through the pre-arranged consulting agenda through direct experiences. A consultant who did a study of the New Jersey Turnpike toll-collection system showed up at Interchange #16. He worked, on a Friday night before Easter, as a toll collector. He got more useful insights in six hours than in four weeks of interviews and briefings.
12 G. Stalk, Time, The Next Source of Competitive Advantage, *Harvard Business Review*, July-August 1988, p. 41. It acknowledges Jay W. Forrester's work in "industrial dynamics" which explains how the slashing of delays can have a favorable effect on the performance of organizations. A further clue that Toyota may be pursuing the goal of close linking between the customer and manufacturing operations comes from the December 1988 issue of Computerworld. Toyota has begun installing very small-aperture terminal (VSAT) satellite dishes at each dealership in the USA. The new network will include all information about a customer's car, including complete maintenance history, and will be on-line and accessible centrally. A national, and ultimately a global, database about its customers will give Toyota a competitive advantage in its capacity to diagnose equipment reliability and performance for each car owner. This will allow Toyota to redefine its mission from car manufacturing to a more lucrative automobile transportation servicing business.
13 The Technical Publications/Desktop Publishing case is in Peat, Marwick, Main & Co., Macintosh Benefits Study (Privately distributed by Apple Computer, Inc., Marketing Department, May 29,1987) as a "strategic application." I am quoting this case to illustrate how far it is possible to extend the "strategic" designation.
  The Macintosh allowed reducing the staff from 40 to 35. However, most of the savings came from avoiding a corporate overhead allocation of $310,000 for typesetting. The Technical Publications department can do the job for only $25,000, using two Macintosh computers and a laser printer. Before you claim your savings always verify that reducing corporate overhead allocations are a real cash saving to the company.
  If you credit a "strategic" advantage entirely to your computer, you should check whether or not the entire improvement derives from the computer. It is difficult to understand how an $800 million sales company tolerates 9–12 weeks added to a product launch date because the Technical Publications Department follows a complicated publication procedure. It is always possible to cut the publication cycle without a Macintosh, though desktop publishing offers a particularly low cost way to create acceptable typeset pages. If you finally fix an unresponsive service, that does not give you the license to label such action as "strategic."
14 The McKesson case is in a report by R. Johnston and P. R. Lawrence, Beyond Vertical Integration—the Rise of the Value-Adding Partnership, *Harvard Business Review*, July-August 1988. The information about the 99% electronic order rate and the concept of strategic necessity originates from E. K. Clemons, Strategic Necessities, *Computerworld*, February 22, 1988, p. 79.
15 Tomohiro Akamatsu, *Tokyo Business Today*, April 1988, p. 18.
16 The IBM LINK case is a good counter-example of what a large organization can do to deliver customized answers that serve local needs. A well-designed and competently administered LINK application may help IBM retain the benefits of its large scale. It will give its customers easy access to centralized knowledge which otherwise would require supporting an unaffordable field organization. For more details, see A. LaPlante, IBM Enhances Support for Corporate PC Managers, *InfoWorld*, August 29, 1988.
17 The Microsoft Online service could be a prototype for similar offerings. It operates on a third party (G.E.) network. Microsoft's startup and operating expenses are minimal. The users do not take up excessive time since they have to pay for network time. Microsoft Online costs $495 per year plus usage time. End-user support charges range from $35 per hour (during prime time) to $5 per hour during off-peak hours. Access to the diagnostic data base costs from $10 to $35 per inquiry. Even a small to medium-size company now can afford supplying on-line support.

18 J. Webber, Laptops Save Salesmen Time, Spruce Up Sales Presentations, *InfoWorld*, August 22, 1988, p. 21.
19 Company name withheld.
20 R. McKenna, Marketing in the Age of Diversity, *Harvard Business Review*, September-October 1988, p. 92.
21 J. Ferreira and M.E. Treacy, It's More Than Just Laptops, *Datamation*, November 1, 1988, p. 127.
22 M.I.S. Holds Together A Crumbling Cookie, *InformationWeek*, March 13, 1989, p. 46.
23 *Fortune* magazine of February 13, 1989 covered the trend to computer-supported acceleration of business functions:

Company	Product	Old Cycle	New Cycle
PRODUCT INNOVATION			
Honda	Cars	5 years	3 years
AT&T	Phones	2 years	1 year
Navistar	Trucks	5 years	2.5 years
Hewlett-Packard	Computer printers	4.5 years	22 months
PRODUCT PRODUCTION			
General Electric	Circuit breakers	3 weeks	3 days
Motorola	Pagers	3 weeks	2 hours
Hewlett-Packard	Electronic testers	4 weeks	5 days
Brunswick	Fishing reels	3 weeks	1 week

24 E. Horwitt, Mattel Net Chases Xmas Blues, *Computerworld*, December 19, 1988.
25 J. Connolly, Handheld PC's Food for Thought, *Computerworld*, November 21, 1988.
26 G. Melloan, Making Gizmos, *Wall Street Journal*, August 23, 1988, p. 27.
27 When measured in terms of revenues, this was only a 35% market share in 1988 (Wanted: Co-Pilots for Reservation Systems, *Business Week*, April 9, 1990, p.78). American Airlines' SABRE 1988 revenues were $455 million as compared with United's Apollo of $299 million, Texas Air's System One of $234 million, TWA's PARS of $195 million and Delta's Datas of $117 million.
28 An operator of a reservation system usually collects about $2 per airline ticket from a travel agent. The cost per ticket for the leading operators is much less. Thus the net operating income of the two leading reservation systems—United Airlines' Apollo and American Airlines' SABRE—is $182 million on revenues of $600 million. The estimated ROI for these systems is 83%. The fully allocated cost per ticket for reservation systems with low market share (Delta Airlines' Datas and TWA's PARS) is over $2 and therefore these systems are not profitable (Global Distribution Systems, SRI International, 1989, Figure 4).
29 For further discussion of the economies of scale see Figure 11.3.
30 C. Phillips and P. Thomas, Texas Air Asks Transportation Agency to Examine Rivals' Reservation Systems, *Wall Street Journal*, August 19, 1988, p. 13.
31 Whether or not a company should offer an on-line service as a general utility always comes up when the initial proposal goes to management. I think there is a lesson in the origins of SABRE. First, you cannot assume that by giving your customers a company-preferred solution they will use it. Customers do not like being locked into a business relationship, regardless of how advantageous it may seem. Second, when you announce a new and advanced system, you may force your competitor to start with a superior design. Just like in the military, there is such a phenomenon as the systems escalation race. Equipment vendors thrive whenever that occurs.
32 The dynamic of American Airlines shows up also for U.K. tour operators. Thomson Travel successfully innovated in serving travel agents through an on-line service. Thomson did not have to tackle the difficult task of building a network. They cleverly added value to an already existing network service in making it user-friendly. Thomson's TOP system quickly secured a dominant market position. TOP is now the standard computer system for most tour agents.

David Feeny made an excellent study of what happened from a competitive

CHAPTER 8—STRATEGIC INVESTMENTS

standpoint. Feeny's report (Creating and Sustaining Competitive Advantage from Information Technology, *Oxford Institute of Information Management*, RDP 87/2, 1987) is unique because he has examined the competitive advantage through study of the entire industry, not just the leader.

33 As showed by the Cadillac automobile, Xerox copiers, the IBM Personal computer and Texas Instruments semiconductors.

34 Good examples (The Economist, March 10, 1990, p.30) of such hybrids are 3,900 Seven-Eleven convenience stores in Japan (no relation to the U.S. Seven Eleven Company). Less than 5% of these stores is company owned. Each store has a point-of-sale computer. The machine records the brand-name, the price, the sex and age of the buyer. The computer displays, on demand, sales of products by the hour or day. The clever store computer weeds out only the most profitable items from an offering of 8,000 products. Shopkeepers use computer-aided routines to send orders from their computers directly to the supplier. Replenishment orders arrive at the store within eight hours.

The parent Seven-Eleven Company controls the technical standards of software, hardware and telecommunications. The network, technical support and consulting to the store owners are their *Value-added*. The Seven-Eleven Company is in the information services business. Incidentally, it also sells summary statistics to manufacturers for market research.

35 Business services, such as supplied by Federal Express, DLH, Avis, Hertz, American Express, VISA, Master-Card, mail-order and distribution service warehouses, offer the variable cost economics of mature firms to startup firms.

36 A good analogy, suggested by J. F. Rada (in Information Technology and Services, *International Management Institute*, Geneva, Working Paper, January 1986) is the decrease in transportation and refrigeration costs in the last century. Before low-cost, rapid transportation and refrigeration there were natural barriers to trade in high-value agricultural products such as fruits and vegetables. They could produce only for local markets. The new technologies made it possible to market perishable products on an international basis. It allows local advantages to compete on a global scale.

Because of the difficulties in communicating and coordinating with other organizations, especially on a geographically dispersed basis, small businesses often serve only local markets. The limits on their serving capacity now have their origin in communications barriers instead of natural obstacles. As telecommunications costs decrease and knowledge is "preserved" through standard software embedded within a message, even small organizations will be able to deal with global markets.

I find the refrigeration analogy intriguing. If you think about it, you will understand that the problem in supplying any knowledge-based service is the perishability of existing business communications. Face-to-face contact, local culture, language, customs and informal understanding make it difficult for a remote expert to supply new knowledge that could be of value. Network-based software may be a form of "refrigeration" of ideas for global distribution. Using "Electronic Channels of Distribution" is an idea whose time came. In 1988, the Digital Equipment Corporation surveyed 75 largest U.S. corporations. One third planned to install computer systems for supporting their customers in the 1990's.

37 That describes the service-based markets of the future.

38 My favorite example is a local company that engages in the repair of wooden sail boats. The owner-manager of this tiny firm could not collect on his invoices because of endless disputes with clients. When you repair wooden boats you do not know what's rotten. You have to open the hull, which means that repair estimates are often way off. The manner in which you account for extras becomes important both financially and how you retain customers. The owner wished to know whether to buy an Apple or an IBM computer to do his billing.

I examined the operations and found that the problem was in his inventories and how he documented materials used in the repairs. The repair craftsmen—a persnickety bunch—had no interest in keeping detailed time cards. The owner's problem was not in the billing, but in data collection. I recommended that the owner reorganize the shop by treating each boat as a profit center. The craftsmen would participate in the profits from each purchase. Materials arrive, as needed, from a supplier who provides detailed accounting for each purchase. A computer keeps track of the profit margins and repair authorizations. The result was an enormous increase in profitability. The strategic advantage was work reorganization, not computerization.

39 For instance, a supplier of network-based tutorial services can use expert systems to track a student's capacity to cope with a specific educational experience. Computer-aided teaching is not only for students, but also a way of helping the tutor to interact with a student as needed.

40 $1,000 for tuition and supplies, $250 for transportation, $250 for meals, hotel expenses and incidentals, $800 for pay and benefits while away from work. The student will effectively receive less than 12 hours of instruction time.

41 Proceed with caution. What you see are broad averages, across industry and geographic region. A specific result may not apply in your situation.

42 The illustrations are for a European raw materials supplier.

43 The interpretation of the box plot is that the low end of the box shows the 25th percentile of the distribution, the line in the middle is the 50th percentile and the line at the top is the 75th percentile of all firms in each category.

44 The remedial actions using information technology and other measures are a case study in Chapter 10.

45 D.A. Marchand, Interview with Donald C. Burr, *Information Management Review*, 1990, 5.

9

RISK ANALYSIS

The more you are aware of a risk, the more you can do about it.

Risk rather than the difficulty of accounting for "intangible" benefit is the primary reason for the reluctance of top management to approve many investment proposals to launch innovative computer projects. To deal with such reluctance it is not sufficient to describe how the risk of a project will be contained. Instead, top management welcome the articulation of risk in financial terms so that the potential advantages of information technology investments can be balanced against the chances that predicted outcomes may not materialize.

The prevailing practice by M.I.S. project managers is to cut the *expected* net gains by 20-50%, and then claim that the prospective payoffs are safe. This discounting of the hazards of systems projects is unreliable. All systems projects have some element of risk because many things can go wrong. Reducing benefits or adding a contingency reserve to costs may be excessive or insufficient.[1]

Technical risks are manageable unless you buy the wrong hardware or your staff quits. Costs are also containable. You just stop spending, reassign the staff and sell the equipment. Although such extreme conditions rarely occur, management can reduce a budget instantly and redirect money from a project that has fallen into disfavor.

You will find your greatest risk exposures on the expected benefit side of the payoff computations. Examples include:
- A prolonged implementation schedule or employee dissatisfaction reduces your savings.
- A competitor comes up with a lower cost solution, forcing you to surrender expected savings by cutting prices.
- Your business changes, making your system obsolete.
- Your sales volume does not increase as expected, and you have excess fixed costs.
- Your implementation team concentrates on the technical aspects of a project and completely disregards the human element, sometimes described as "company politics."[2]

Experienced managers can foresee such events. To sell a project the simplest solution is to propose enough big up-side gains so that they will cover most contingencies.[3] Your insurance is the margin between expected benefit and what will prevent project cancellation. If you avoid risk analysis, the pessimists will reject your good projects because they will find out that you overstated gains. The compulsion to promise large potential gains as a way to compensate for risks can backfire. Optimists will drag you into ventures you ultimately will have to abandon when the unrealistic expectations become apparent during system installation.

How to perform valid risk analysis within the contention for limited resources is addressed in this Chapter. Business information managers need to understand technological risks. This becomes important as funding decisions migrate away from M.I.S. managers. Operating executives who are becoming dependent on information systems are intolerant of the tendency of their M.I.S. counterparts to over-simplify systems implementation issues by filtering out all uncertainty from estimated budgets and schedules.[4] The decision-makers, the individuals with accountability for profits, will not accept ignorance of the risks they are buying.[5]

Instead of inevitable risks, which may or may not be unforeseen, you are always in a better position when you can plan for risk containment. Formal risk analysis completed prior to finalizing a project proposal is the recommended way to prepare for contingencies. Performing risk analysis of computer opportunities is the most urgent challenge[6] facing executives who must make informed investment decisions.

CURRENT APPROACHES

Risk Classification

A horoscope is the most ancient form of risk classification. It may give satisfaction, but no realism.

Some consultants admonish their clients to identify risks by classifying projects according to levels of certainty. By locating your proposition on a grid with four squares, you may determine how to deal with the unknown. Cost/Risk matrixes[7] are one way of dealing with this complex topic, which categorizes projects using the following classes:[8]

- *Comfort* (Low Cost and Low Risk): Includes telephones and personal computers. Do not justify individually, but in aggregate.
- *Confidence* (High Cost and Low Risk): Traditional *Return-on-Investment* applies to laborsaving projects.
- *Caution* (Low Cost and High Risk): For these systems it is wisest to do experimentation, prototypes[9] and pilot installations before making investments.
- *Confusion* (High Cost and High Risk): There is no way of calculating value and therefore decisions rely on "gut" feel and intuition just as you make for new products or advertising.

This simple approach is appealing to someone with little experience in dealing with information systems investments, for you end up with few insights as to what to do in specific cases. Because these classes of risk include judgment calls, one person's "low" risk may be another person's "high" risk. Avoiding losses by being excessively cautious can mean foregoing all large gains.

The category *caution* is of little value. You should always proceed with caution whenever you invest in information technologies. You can get into some frightful trouble if your business depends on telephone orders, and you have a system that has no backup. In the above scheme, telephones are seen as low cost and low risk, which is not always the case.

Most exceptionally profitable computer projects fall into the "confusion" category. They incur high costs and high risks, so that relying entirely on intuition is the worst counsel you could give for managing a difficult venture.

Categorical Ranking of Risk

Because you can identify it does not mean you understand it.

Categorical rankings are presently the preferred method for analyzing risky situations. The scale of risks is defined by adjectives (such as high, medium, low; or disaster, dangerous, average, reasonable, excellent) which are subject to widely ranging interpretation. Risk types convert into numerical scales by assigning points or percentage weights to each category. In some situations, a formula adds or multiplies the risk scale to come up with a composite risk index.

One consulting firm suggested using a *Probability of Success Ratio* (PSR)[10] to pick projects whose lower-ranking payoffs balance their lower risks. The technique works best when management uses the opportunity of ranking risks to ask about the causes of the risks. Through increased awareness, a systems hazard can become a manageable event.[11] The problem with this method is its qualitative approach. A medium risk rating for a critical item could be less tolerable than a low risk rating for an optional feature. Words can describe risky situations but they are poor indicators of the potential damage to which you expose your company. Qualitative ratings are not comparable because one person's well-founded anxiety is not necessarily equal to another person's expression of ignorance. If you use categorical rankings there is no way to set up a research or audit program for after-the-fact verification. Categorical rankings are unmeasurable estimates, on an indefinable scale.

A more elaborate approach to risk assessment uses multiple risk indicators[12] such as:
- Project or organizational risk;
- Definitional uncertainty;
- Technical uncertainty;
- Information systems infrastructure risks.

Each of these risk categories is assigned a score ranging from zero (no risk) to five (high risk).[13] You derive these numbers from instructions given on a standard worksheet.[14] There is little you can do with these scores once you obtain them. For example, how can you compare the perils emanating from "five" (high) *definitional uncertainty*[15] against the offsetting confidence that you have "zero" (low) *information systems infrastructure risks*? Does it mean that a reliable communications network can compensate for my ignorance about business aims?

Despite the complexity of these scales, they are still categorical rankings, and cannot be compared. The scale for measuring *Competitive Advantage* can translate into marketing terms, such as year-to-year change in *Relative Market Share*. The scales for measuring *Skills Required* show up as *Years of Experience* of the programming staffs. However, neither measure is additive because their scales are different. This leaves us with the problem that we cannot tell what is the tradeoff between *Relative Market Share* and *Years of Experience*. The two ratings are interesting and descriptive, but are unrelated. If you add these numbers, the composite index explains nothing about the worth of a proposed computer project. To overcome this inconsistency, the rating scales are multiplied by arbitrary *weights*. You would get a new index that forms a third layer of untraceable abstractions.[16]

Risk indicators based on the ranking of risk categories are useful in general discussions about information technology. They highlight the extent to which a financial payoff is unreliable. However, they convey only a qualitative indication of the precariousness of your financial results. They are unreliable in choosing projects. They do not tell you how much a unit of *definitional uncertainty, information systems infrastructure risk* or *competitive advantage* is worth. They cannot help you make financial tradeoffs between the potential dollar damages of one risky project when compared to another.

The following case introduces financial simulation as a more useful way to understand investment uncertainty. My purpose is to show how the same facts can lead to different conclusions, depending on how you describe the sources of risk. The case study begins with a conventional Benefit/Cost ratio analysis. It then progresses to a statistical simulation that shows the probability of potential losses in dollar terms. The simulation approach can evaluate financial risks directly without resorting to proxy measures.

PAYOFF COMPUTATION BASED ON VENDOR'S TRAINING MATERIALS

There are many ways to make a promise, but only a few ways to deliver results.

IBM's *Information Systems Investment Strategies* (*ISIS*) program is the largest program ever launched to aid management in evaluating the payoff from computers. The case which follows a pattern from calculations[17] found in an *ISIS* tutorial. The *ISIS* approach starts a project evaluation by projecting benefits and costs:

In $000's	1986	1987	1988	1989	1990	1991
Cumulative Benefits	$0.0	$0.0	$83.4	$155.7	$237.9	$329.3
Cumulative Costs	$63.3	$94.8	$109.3	$124.3	$139.3	$156.5

Table 9.1: Financial Summary of a Computer Proposal

To compute the payoff for this project, the tutorial takes the cumulative benefits and divides them by the cumulative costs. This gives us a simple and easily calculated measure:

Cumulative Benefit/Cost Ratio = $329.3/$156.5 = 210%

Table 9.2: The Benefit/Cost Ratio of a Computer Proposal

The Benefit/Cost Ratio of 210% gives the impression of unusually favorable benefits. Conventional measures of payoff (such as *Return-on-Investment* or *Payback Period*) divide *net* benefits (e.g., benefits minus costs) by total costs or by time:

Cumulative Benefit/Cost Ratio = $172.8/$156.5 = 110%

Table 9.3: A Conventional Benefit/Cost Ratio of a Computer Proposal

The Benefit/Cost ratio properly should be 110% to be in line with generally accepted practices. How good is this second number? The purpose of financial risk analysis is to find out.

PAYOFF COMPUTATION BASED ON THE TIME VALUE OF MONEY

A dollar today is better than a dollar tomorrow.

Dividing cumulative benefits by cumulative costs, a frequent practice in the public sector, is misleading. Costs occur early in the life of a project when risks are more manageable. Benefits only arise after the technology is in place, usually when our ability to forecast is more difficult. The table below shows the projected cash flow for our example. It is negative for 3.5 years:

In $000's	1986	1987	1988	1989	1990	1991
Cumulative Cash	($63.30)	($94.80)	($25.90)	$31.4	$98.6	$172.8
Annual Benefits	$0.0	$0.0	$83.4	$72.3	$82.2	$91.4
Annual Costs	$63.3	$31.5	$14.5	$15.0	$15.0	$17.2

Table 9.4: Cash Flow Analysis for a Computer Proposal

The annual cash flow has a 25% discount, which is a number I find most often applied to U.S. computer projects. Financial controllers expect new risky investments to deliver higher returns than the average returns on shareholder capital, which average 15-18%.

The cumulative benefits are worth only $123 thousand after discounting by 25% per year, otherwise known as *Net Present Value*. The cumulative costs have a discounted *Net Present Value* of only $94 thousand. This gives us a Benefit/Cost ratio of only 31%, which is not as impressive as the 110% computed in Table 9.3 without the effects of timing of the cash flows. Yet, a 31% Benefit/Cost ratio is a very attractive investment. If I could borrow money for 12%, I would surely go ahead with this project.

Net Present Value of Cash Benefits @ 25%	$123
Net Present Value of Cash Costs @ 25%	$94
Net Present Cash Benefit/Cost Ratio = ($123-$94)/$94 =	31%

Table 9.5: The Effect of Discounting on the Benefit/Cost Ratio ($000's)

PAYOFF COMPUTATION WITH TIME VALUE PLUS RESIDUAL VALUE

The future does not end after the planning period.

The ratio of the cumulative benefits to the cumulative costs does not tell us enough. It implies that nothing after the end of the planning period could be of consequence because all benefits and costs suddenly stop. Analysts justify this approach by using a large discount percentage, such as 25%, because a high discount is supposed to make long-range benefit or cost projections irrelevant anyway. This view of the future is harmful to making good investment decisions.[18] Even if the future were predictable the use of high discounts serves no purpose except to avoid the question of what is the expected life of an investment. Most computer projects worth doing have a greater life expectancy than any six-year plan. Discounts of 25% or more do not substitute for long-term thinking.

Short-term planning, such as projections that cover only one-year payback should not be tolerated by business executives. This is contrary to practices in the 1960-1970 period when most applications had a woefully brief life of less than seven years and quick payback was desirable. The short life-expectancy of the early systems originated in the vendors' changes in operating systems and in conversion to on-line processing. The current state-of-the-art of software engineering allows for a much longer life of software. Program code does not wear out. With proper maintenance and evolutionary upgrading, it can be reused for decades.

Data definition standards, portable languages and "open" computing environments allow us to view new applications investments as an evolutionary sequence where the benefits are cumulative and not momentary. When you put a new application in place today you should expect its benefits to last during the time that function operates in your business. The function may change and evolve, but you will not have to relearn and re-systematize your business every time you upgrade your computer hardware, operating systems or communications.

Yes, applications can live longer than the 2 to 3 year payback time usually expected for risky investments. Most of the code that I supervised 10-15 years ago for major applications is still churning away because of sustained maintenance. You should be launching projects that will support your firm's basic business processes 15 to 20 years from now[19] although maintenance costs may rise after a while. Do not believe everything you hear about the advent of revolutionary changes in technology that will somehow fundamentally alter the ways in which you conduct your business. Though your organization and relationships with customers will certainly change, the underlying logic of most of the basic business processes will remain remarkably the same. From now on, you must insist on vendor-independent integration standards for operating systems and communications protocols. These should guide your technology strategies to extend the life of your systems investments well into the 21st century.

This brings us to the *residual value* of information technology investments. The *residual value* of a computer application is the discounted cash flow expected after the end of the planning period. To estimate this number you need more information about:

- The expected trends in benefits and costs.[20] In Table 9-4, you can see that benefits are escalating rapidly, whereas costs stay level.
- The foreseen life of the project beyond the current planning horizon. The positive cash flow in Table 9-4 is increasing rapidly. This makes it unlikely that someone would wish to shut off the benefits after 1991.

There are several techniques for computing the residual value.[21] Unless you have reliable information about long-term trends, you should use the simplest calculating method available. Take the cash benefits and the cash costs for the last year of the plan (1991), and compute the present value of this cash stream for 12 more years.[22] This implies that both benefits and costs will level off after the end of the planning period. That is the most unbiased statement you can make without specific knowledge about future business conditions.[23]

In $000's	1986	1987	1988	1989	1990	1991	Residual Value
Benefits	$0.0	$0.0	$83.4	$72.3	$82.2	$91.4	$340.5
Costs	$63.3	$31.5	$14.5	$15.0	$15.0	$17.2	$64.1

Table 9.6: Cash Flow Analysis, with Residual Value

The effect of the residual value, even after discount[24], is remarkable. Fifty-nine percent of the value of the benefits accrues from a cash flow beyond the planning period! Top management should demand large *residual values* from well conceived information technology investments.[25]

The inclusion of the *residual value* makes a big difference. It boosts the payoff ratio from 31% to 81%:

Net Present Value of Cash Benefits @ 25%, with Residual	$195
Net Present Value of Cash Costs @ 25%, with Residual	$107
Net Present Cash+Residual Benefit/Cost Ratio = ($195-$107)/$107 = 81%	

Table 9.7: Improving the Benefit/Cost Ratio with Residual Value ($000's)

Preservation of the *residual value* of your company's information technology investments should be your aim when specifying the operating systems, programming languages, database and telecommunications environments. The term *systems architecture* is a good label for such planning. Vendors currently are spending a great deal of money to promote the superiority of their own *systems architecture* solutions. Do not accept claims about "...easily upgraded and fully compatible software and hardware" until the vendor can prove residual values superior to the competitors'.

PAYOFF COMPUTATION WITH EXPLICIT RISK ESTIMATES

Payoffs Based on Risk-Free Interest Rates

One measure will not fit all risks.

So far, all payoff computations used the 25% interest rate to discount future cash flows as a way to compensate for future risks. Why use 25% and not some other number? For instance, the prime interest rate[26] is much less than the discount rate. Corporate debt costs more than the prime interest rate by about 4%[27], which is about half the rate applied to all risky corporate investments.

Your controller will readily admit that the high interest rate for screening out technology investments reflects his assessment of their inherent unpredictability. He will charge you 12% for the cost of money and another 13% as a *risk premium* that pays for an implied insurance policy against your project's failure. Such a rationale answers some questions but also leads to others. Should all projects have the same discount rate, suggesting the same probability of failure?[28] Should different rates apply, depending on a project's chances of success?

The annual budget planning process does not allow much time to discuss what discount rate is proper for which venture. Experienced managers find out what the rules are and then do their best to guide their projects over the hurdles. Because conventional financial forms define how to calculate *expected* returns but not *expected* risks, valuable projects may be rejected and marginal investments will be accepted.

The fault with currently practices for justification of investments in computers is the unfortunate combination of project returns and risks into a single *discount* rate. You will always find projects with higher average calculated rates of return that carry unreasonable risks for which the discount rate does not compensate. You also get projects which fail financial criteria but must be completed anyway because of legal requirements, or because an influential executive insists on an application regardless of costs.

To deal with this problem, I shall consider the *financial risks* separately from the *operating risks*. The *financial risk* of a project is the financial cost of future cash flows. It is the cost of risk-free capital, as seen from the corporate standpoint. Imagine that you take out a commercial loan at the most favorable rates available to your firm. You will repay the bank after the cash flow turns positive. In our case example, the costs of such a loan would be 12% (not 25%). The purely *financial* Benefit/Cost ratio, including residual value, would be 139%, and not 81%.

Financial NPV, Cash+Residual Benefits @ 12%	$352
Financial NPV, Cash+Residual Costs @ 12%	$148
Fin. NPV Cash+Resid Benefit/Cost Ratio = ($352-$148)/$148 =	139%

Table 9.8: Risk-free Benefit/Cost Ratio, with Residual Value ($000's)

With a lower cost of money, the residual value now displays superior financial returns. It increases benefits from $195 to $352 thousand (by 181%), which suggests that if I could manage the risks of cost overruns and unrealized benefits, my profits would increase. I therefore define the price of all risks other than the cost of capital as *operating risks*. What share of the future benefits do I have to surrender to pay for the ever-present *operating risk* interest premium?

The Classification of Risk

Risk will differ depending on what you do and how you do it.

Life insurance companies can quote reliable rates because they have good statistical information on how quickly individuals on the average would collect on their policies. Automobile insurance companies know what cash reserves to keep to insure motorists because they have accumulated massive data on the expected frequency of collisions and probable repair costs.

Computer people professionally engage in activities often as risky as climbing on a slippery roof or driving 30 miles an hour above the speed limit through a busy intersection. There is no systematic accumulation of corporate data about the success or failure of systems projects. Financial controllers have anecdotes from their audit reports. Congressional Committees and the General Accounting Office have a collection of reports about computer-related malfeasance. None of this information represents a concerted effort to evaluate the inherent risk of computer efforts. Without the equivalent of actuaries[29] who are experts in the morbidity of computer projects, management often relieves anxiety by subjecting computer project requests to more scrutiny than any other investment. Personnel or accounting departments do not need special review boards to examine their policies, procedures and expense levels. However, every major corporation has a Corporate Systems Review Board.

The best solution to handling risk is to acknowledge and manage it. To do this, you must insert risk analysis into every major computer plan. The time at which your capacity to contain risk is best before starting a project. After agreeing on the budget, schedule, scope and preferred technology solution, most of your options vanish. The best you can do after execution begins is to prevent the unforeseen from developing into a disaster.

To manage risk you must first identify it, then measure it and lastly express it in financial terms.[30] A fixed price contract with performance guarantees and an enforceable penalty clause is as close as you will ever get to a risk-free estimate. At the other extreme, imposing an "artificial intelligence solution" on a hostile and untrained labor force is an unbounded risk. Somewhere between are various grades of risk. Cost risks (e.g., supplier costs, internal technology costs, internal organization costs) differ from benefit risks (such as internal cost savings or productivity gains). External risks (such as market share gains, competitive response, service quality and opportunity for premium pricing) can be recognized only by an examination of a corporation's planning model.[31]

Here is an illustrative list of *classes* of standard risk exposures that I use in identifying the risks of information technology projects. This classification scheme is arbitrary. You may develop your own table to reflect how your firm carries out systems projects:

SUPPLIERS' COSTS	CLASS
Fixed Price Contract, Specified Performance Guaranteed	A
Fixed Price Contract for Specified Scope, Extra Options	B
Fixed Price Schedule, Quantities Known ≤10%	C
Fixed Price Schedule, Quantities Known ≤ 25%	D
Cost-plus Contract, Fixed Fee	E
Cost-plus Contract, Specifications Incomplete	F
Cost-plus Contract, Specifications to be Developed	G
INTERNAL TECHNOLOGY COSTS	
Known Technology, Demonstrated Cost Control ≤10%	H
Known Technology, Demonstrated Cost Control ≤25%	J
Known Technology, Difficult Cost Control ≤50%	K
Untried Technology, Demonstrated Know-how	L
Untried Technology, Know-how to be Acquired	M
INTERNAL ORGANIZATIONAL COSTS	
Known Organization Costs, Demonstrated Control ≤10%	N
Known Organization Costs, Demonstrated Control ≤25%	O
Known Organization Costs, Difficult Control ≤50%	P
New Organizational Methods, Demonstrated Know-how	R
New Organizational Methods, Know-how to be Acquired	S
INTERNAL ORGANIZATIONAL BENEFITS	
Known Organization Change, Demonstrated Control ±10%	T
Known Organization Change, Demonstrated Control ±25%	U
Known Organization Change, Difficult Control ±50%	V
Untried Organizational Change, Demonstrated Know-how	X
Untried Organizational Change, Know-how to be Acquired	Y

Table 9.9: Classification of Project Risks

The aim of this classification scheme is to attach a *risk profile* to each class of costs or benefits. Such a *profile* would show, based on experience, to what extent actual costs or actual benefits will vary from their mean *expected*[32] values.

How to Explain Risks

> *The future becomes more manageable if you can measure the consequence of present decisions.*

Actual costs[33] or benefits will never come out exactly as expected. If you plot on a graph the probability distribution of the percentage difference between actual and budget project costs, you will not get a *normally distributed* variable—a bell-shaped curve. Budget overruns will be more frequent than budget under-runs. Budget overruns will have a long upside "tail", because overruns can sometimes run into multiples of the initial estimates, whereas budget under-runs are usually only a small fraction of the budget. Budget variances will reflect how you manage information technology projects against established budgets.[34]

For example, a supplier's fixed price contract guarantees that actual costs will not fall below quoted costs. Depending on the contract terms, suppliers can expect that add-on work and extra features will increase their revenues. Therefore, their actual revenues would show a *truncated lognormal distribution*[35] if you plot their quoted prices against actual revenues. The customer's bills will cluster around the quoted estimate. The costs will truncate at that estimate because that's how one manages fixed price contracts. The costs above the fixed price may escalate to some upper limit after which you either cancel or re-plan the project.

In Table 9.9, you will find 17 cost classifications (A through S) characterized by different *truncated lognormal distributions*.[36] Consider what you can expect if your programming staff quotes a cost estimate that falls into the risk class J *(known technology, demonstrated cost control within a 25% standard deviation from first estimates)*. I would characterize risk class J as the typical case for major new applications. The *truncated lognormal distribution* for this example would show a cutoff at 90% of the cost estimate. You cannot expect more than a 10% under-run because all windfall savings will be reinvested to correct for the tarnished reputation of some other project.[37] The chance of an actual overrun decreases rapidly until it reaches 150% to 200% of the original estimate.[38] Any further escalation in costs will call for re-budgeting the entire project.[39]

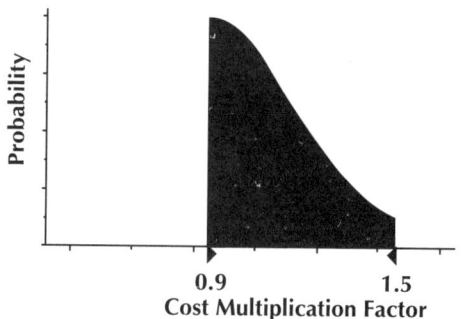

Figure 9.1: Distribution of Project Costs for Class J Risks

Describing the risk distribution of benefits is simple. Gains are never predictable and will fall only within a specified range. The benefit you get from a computer project is the result of many interactions among worker motivation, training, attitudes, workflow design, ergonomics, leadership, user participation in design, response time, data accuracy and other influences, given no predictable bias towards which would enhance or depress the benefit. If a large number of unpredictable interactions influence an outcome, this is a pattern described by *uniform distributions.*

Consider what you can expect if your operating management gives you a benefit estimate that falls into the risk class V (*known organization change, difficult to control the effects on future benefits within 50% of benefit estimates*). This is typical for a major new application that does not tamper with the established organizational structure and in which the employee roles stay unchanged. In Figure 9.2, the *uniform distribution* shows a cutoff at 50% of the benefit estimate, because I know that operating management has already committed the expected savings in their operating budgets. Therefore, benefits shall not fall much below the committed budgets for the next few years. The chances of realizing unforeseen gain beyond the budgeted expectation drops after 150% of the original estimate because management most likely stretched their benefit estimates to get the project through the financial hurdles.

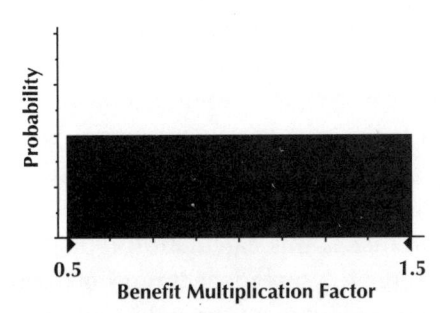

Figure 9.2: The Distribution of Project Benefits for Class V Risks

PAYOFF FROM VENDOR'S CASE—WITH RISK ANALYSIS

Every computer project has a chance of failing.

We have now seen in Tables 9.2, 9.3, 9.5 and 9.7 for the same project average Benefit/Cost ratios ranging from 210% to 31% depending on the computational method used. In Table 9.7 we finally settled on a Benefit/Cost ratio of 81% as the most realistic assessment. An 81% Benefit/Cost ratio sounds like a very attractive proposition. Would this finally satisfy management so that they can approve the proposed project with full confidence?

Top management ought to have an interest in average expectations and also in the risk of failure. For our purposes, failure means a negative Benefit/Cost ratio. It is conceivable that you will run into an unlucky combination of maximum cost overruns simultaneously with the smallest benefits possible. When you run into the worst possible outcome, what are the chances that cash costs will exceed cash benefits?

It is entirely possible that every computer project may meet circumstances, regardless of how remote, where discounted cash benefits will be less than discounted cash costs. If that defines failure, then *every* computer project carries a definite probability of failure. To get management approval, you somehow must show that the probability of failure for a computer project is tolerable. If every computer project is a gamble then management must be willing to take a gambler's view of all computer investments. You must find out how big are the potential gains that make it affordable to lose a bet. A high payoff for a huge single project may not give adequate safeguards against an improbable project crash. Compare this with many small projects that have a low average payoff, but a remote chance of failing. When an investment committee reviews a portfolio of potential computer investments, they need more information than simply average expected gains for individual projects.[40]

My preferred technique to examine and present information about the chances of project failure is by *financial simulation*. Instead of coming up with just one calculation of the Benefit/Cost ratio, a *financial simulation* makes this calculation repeatedly. In the illustrative case in this Chapter, the spreadsheet ran 1,000 times using different combinations of benefits and costs for each solution.[41]

Financial Simulation

An alleged low-risk proposition may hide severe perils.

To obtain the full range of payoffs for Table 9.8, each cash flow was assigned one of the *risk profiles* from Table 9.9. The risk profiles reflect

what we know about each item that makes up the Benefit/Cost ratio:
- It is always safer to introduce technology on a fixed price basis. We shall follow this policy. Based on this assumption, I classified the cash costs for the 1986-87 period as risk Class A expenses (*Fixed Price Contract, Specified Performance Guaranteed*).
- After installation operations, program maintenance and customer support will rely on internal systems staffs. I classify the expected costs after 1987 as risk Class J (*Known Technology, Demonstrated Cost Control $\leq 25\%$*) because the in-house staff has credible experiences in maintaining similar programs before.
- The new application does not call for changing the organization structure, business procedures or the roles of the staff. However, the installation will be difficult to manage toward predictable results. The operating staff may not have a sufficient background and experience with quick-response on line-systems. I classify the expected benefits as risk Class V (*Known Organization Change, Difficult Control $\pm 50\%$*).

The simulation produces the following distribution of benefits:

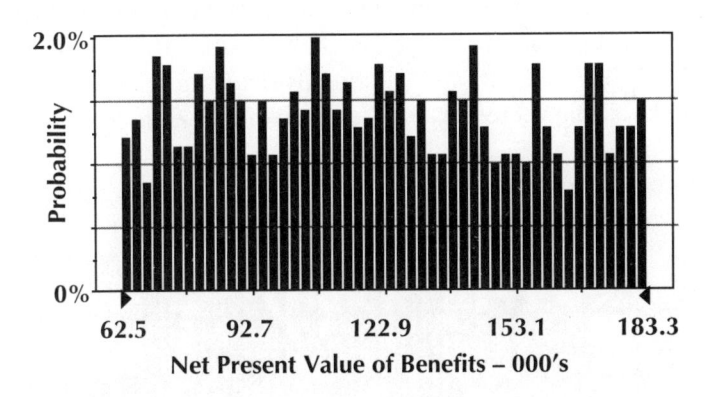

Figure 9.3: The Distribution of the Expected Benefits

The upper range of the expected benefits is three times greater than its lowest value. Next, we simulate project costs:

212   THE BUSINESS VALUE OF COMPUTERS

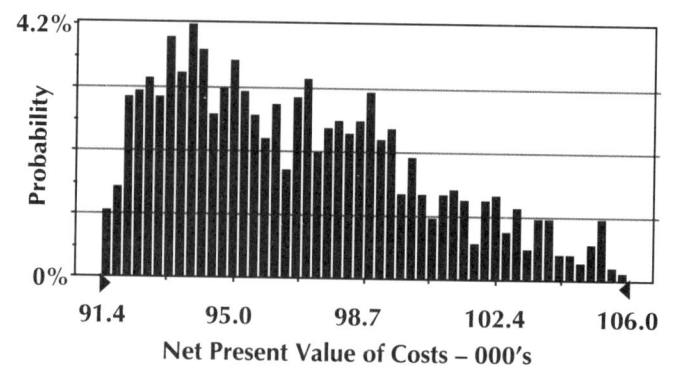

Figure 9.4: The Distribution of Expected Costs

The uncertainty about the long term operating and maintenance expenses shows a maximum cost exposure of $106 thousand. That is 16% above the least cost estimate of $91.4 thousand[42] and not upsetting as computer projects go, because long term computer projects usually require at least a 25% contingency fund. Unfortunately, the costs as shown in Figure 9.3 sometimes exceed the benefits shown in Figure 9.4. As a further complication, the costs tend to favor lower estimates. This makes it difficult to guess the chances of a negative Benefit/Cost ratio.

To find the probability of a loss, the financial simulator runs the combined effects of the uniformly distributed benefits with the left-skewed project costs. The result is a 70.9% chance that the Net Present Value of the Benefit/Cost ratio will be positive. The financial simulation also calculates that there is a 29.1% chance of project failure![43]

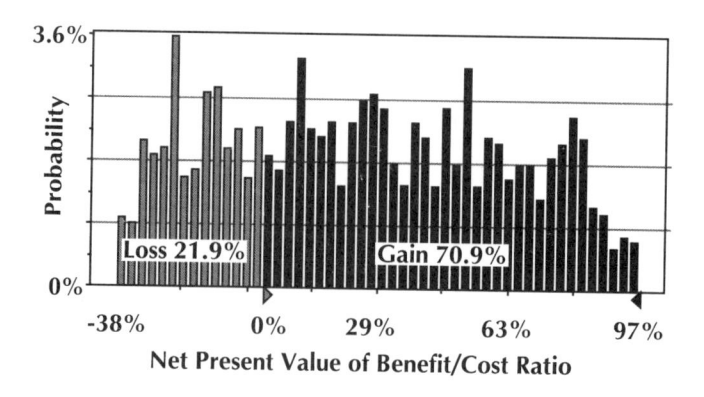

Figure 9.5: Probabilities of Gain and Loss for Low Risk Alternative

Given this information, management must decide if a 29.1% probability of coming up with negative results is acceptable for a "low risk" project. The original spread sheet analysis (see Table 9-4) shows a discounted expected ratio of 31%. Such a return is usually acceptable to capital appropriation committees. After the news gets out that the project harbors a 29.1% risk of failure, I doubt whether anyone will buy this deal.

You may wonder about the differences between the results obtained by *risk analysis*, in Figure 9.5 and *spreadsheet analysis,* in Table 9.4.

Risk Analysis vs. Spreadsheet Analysis

Spreadsheets overstate the payoff from computers.

Computer projects rarely cost less than their budget. Computer projects usually overrun their budget, sometimes by a large amount. This is why the actual costs show a skewed distribution, with large costs on the high end.

When you do payoff analysis using a spreadsheet program (see Table 9.4), you will enter your best estimates of average costs and average benefits. The result (in Table 9.5) will be the multiplication and summation of your average estimates. The expected costs produced by a spreadsheet do not consider the high costs included in the simulation. Therefore, the Benefit/Cost ratio in the spreadsheet will be always more optimistic than the situation warrants.

Despite the immense popularity of spreadsheet techniques to sell project proposals, you should be careful about their misuse.[44] If you do not attach a measure of risk to the spreadsheet numbers, you may be adding some very reliable small numbers to some very unreliable large numbers. The result you get could be an accurate number of dubious value. You deserve disappointment if you believe the impressive presentation graphics that convey the impression of thoughtful analysis. Spreadsheet computations should not be trusted without risk analysis that displays the entire range of possible payoffs.

Including Residual Value

High discount rates will deter high-payoff projects.

If we include the residual value in our computations,[45] the risks will decrease. As noted before, the steep rise in benefits—even after a

25% discount—will outstrip the gradual growth in operating and maintenance expenses. A new simulation will give us a different view of the expected returns[46]:

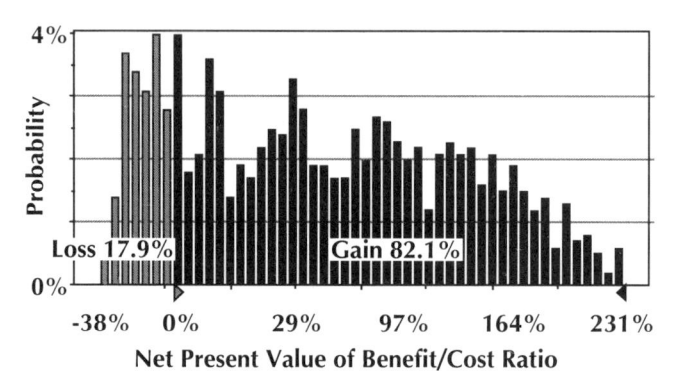

Figure 9.6: Probabilities of Gain and Loss for Low Risk Alternative

These results are more satisfactory. The mean expected Benefit/Cost ratio, after a 25% discount, is 75%. This is an attractive return by any standard. Like all high gains, it does not come without some peril. We should expect about an 18% chance of negative results.

Would you fund the project because of this analysis? Let me point out that the case still carries the 25% discount rate, which is higher than the 12% cost of capital. When the simulation shows a 17.9% probability of failure, this estimate already carries the additional 13% "risk penalty" that the controller built into the obligatory cost of interest.

With risk simulations, it is possible to identify the *operating risks* directly. It is possible to separate the *financial risks* (inherent in the cost of capital) from the *operating risks* (inherent in how we manage the project).

Analysis of the "Low Operating Risk" Alternative

Only operating risks are controllable.
It pays to know what they are.

To find out the actual *operating risks*, we shall make computations that pay only 12% for risk-free capital. The *net present value* of the rapidly rising future benefits now becomes more important. The following profile will tell us what to expect:[47]

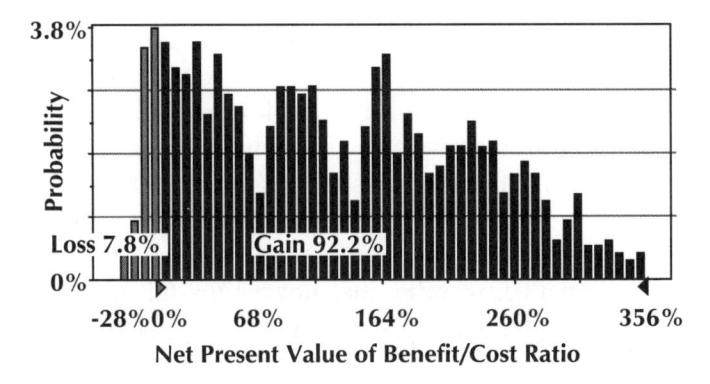

Figure 9.7: Operating Risk, Low Risk Alternative

The results are excellent. The mean payoff value as measured by the *net present value* Benefit/Cost ratio is an extraordinary 128%.[48] The probability of failure is about 8%. This means that only one out of thirteen similar high-payoff projects could end up as a failure. That is about what top management can expect from any well-managed information systems organization. If the stated corporate strategy is to pick investments from a portfolio of high-potential ventures, a summary profile will tell you how many projects can fail and still deliver superior overall results. For instance, if your projects average 100%+ *net present value* Benefit/Cost ratios, you can afford fumbling 20% of your projects without damaging long-term profits.

If losses occur, such experiences can become a cost of organizational learning. Failure need not be a penalty. You should never bury and forget the lessons learned from failed projects.[49] In a risk-prone environment losses always will occur. If you can salvage such knowledge and apply it to the next venture you will be able to reduce the risks of the next investment. In this way, technological losses can be converted into technological assets.

The High Risk Case

One person's high risk is another person's opportunity.

Our project, originally outlined in Table 9.1 and then defined further in the risk profiles in Figure 9.3 and 9.4 assumed the awarding of a turnkey project to a software vendor. If we proceed we will get an application that has more features than we need. A less costly custom-made application, involving greater risks, is another option: instead of subcontracting, we would prefer using our existing staff.

The planned expenses with the vendor are $63,300 in 1986 and $31,500 in 1987. A company-specific solution will cost only $38,000 in 1986 and $25,200 in 1987. The total savings are $31,600. Because costs would be lower in the first two years, the *expected* Benefit/Cost ratio increases from 139% to 193%.

The new Benefit/Cost ratio does not tell the full story. Top management must consider intangibles before it can agree with the lower-cost choice:

- The Cost risks would increase. If we proceed with internal development the lower internal costs would have to bear the higher risks (*Known Technology, Difficult Cost Control ≤ 50%; Class K Risk*).
- The Benefit risks would also increase because we end up with a customized solution that has only a limited scope. In-house development could be inadequate for dealing with unexpected market developments. I reclassify all benefits to *Untried Organizational Change, Demonstrated Know-how; Class X Risk*.
- Offsetting the above increased risks is the desire to retain the advantages from the new application. Internal development will enhance company know-how, and will not give the vendor product enhancements that could become available to competitors.

How should management weigh the increased risks against the gains in the Benefit/Cost ratio? Re-running the simulation model generates a new distribution Net Present Value of the Benefit/Cost ratio[50]:

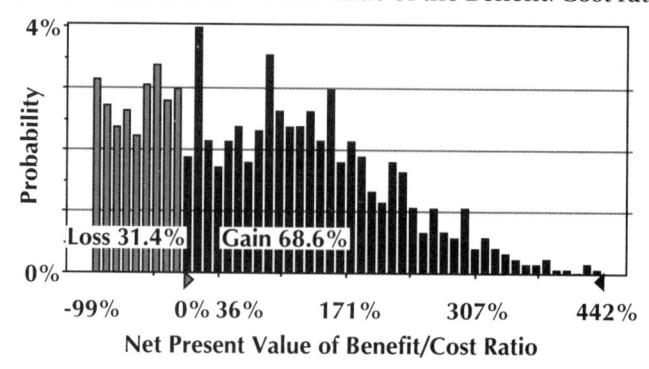

Figure 9.8: Benefit/Cost Ratio, Internal Development Alternative

The mean payoff value declines from 128% to 78%. The high range of the distribution climbs from 356% to 442%, whereas the lowest values descend from –28% to –99%. The probability of incurring a loss increases from about 8% to about 31%. Clearly, the low-risk alternative of using a turn-key software contractor is financially superior to the low-cost but higher risk internal development.

The Evaluation of Risks

To understand your risks, you need to know how much money you could lose.

What if management does not go along with the low-risk choice because they prefer to keep the company's know-how proprietary and its internal staff technologically advanced? What is the penalty (in cash terms) when the greater risk applies to a reduced payoff?

We must rerun the financial model to get this answer. The computer model has the capacity to evaluate interactions between costs, benefits, risks, the expected project life and other factors that influence the proposed investment.[52]

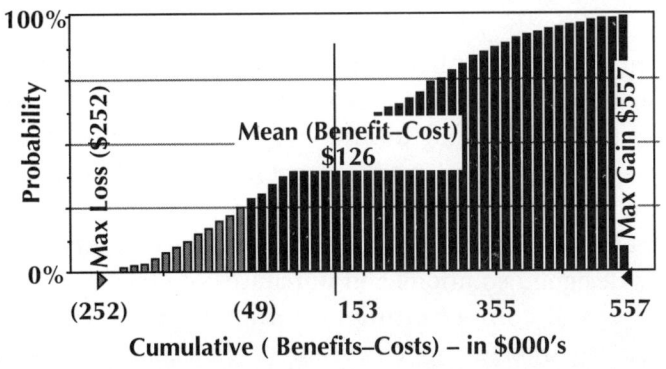

Figure 9.9: Finding the Maximum Loss or Gain, Internal Development

The maximum cash loss from pursuing the high-risk internal development alternative is $252,000. The potential for maximum cash gain is $557,000. Management now has the facts to judge the costs of the implied "tuition" bill for advancing internal staff know-how.

Your maximum loss exposure should be among the facts your management must know before making any information technology investments. An *under-achieving* firm, with few cash reserves, can risk very little. It must plan for lower average gains for every project, to assure that a disaster does not inflict an unrecoverable loss.

Over-achievers should play the investment game differently. You can remain an *over-achiever* only if you continue reaping spectacular results. Exceptional gains come with chances of big losses. *Over-achievers* can afford project failures, since their average gains balance the losses in the long run. *Over-achievers* must continue launching several high-risk, high-gain projects so that superior results will overwhelm an occasional streak of repeated losses. They must learn to tolerate losses so that they can manage their technical staff with patience.

Technical Staffs and Risk Management

Over-achievers who prematurely penalize risk-takers on their staff will lose their most venturesome talent to more entrepreneurial firms. *Under-achievers* who tolerate risk-takers may lose expensive talent only after discovering the damage. Companies between these two extremes have to manage information technology investments as a balanced financial portfolio. They must make their technical staffs sensitive to clearly stated expectations. Without explicit risk analysis you will not be able to communicate your expectations unambiguously to your technology managers.

Corporate and public sector bureaucracies penalize technical staffs who are risk-takers. They force their computer people to cultivate survival habits that include bizarre and ultimately self-defeating risk-avoidance schemes. They instill a propensity for risk-denial that persists even when an early warning could avert a disaster. Budget padding, cost reclassification, specification dilution, service degradation, over-designed solutions and purchases of obsolete technologies become ways of compensating for unmentionable risks. Control-minded management do not create anxiety-free conditions favorable to candid discussions about omnipresent risks, and therefore will always end up wasting their most valuable human resources.

Chapter Summary

Computer people, like everyone else, magnify small risks and ignore the big ones.

Managing risks is a prerequisite to increasing the business value of computers. If you know exactly what it is, what it will cost and when it will be finished, you can't be working on something very profitable. Risk analysis helps in making better investment decisions. By making the risks of technology more explicit, you create a framework for diagnosing, understanding and containing the inherent difficulties associated with technological and organizational innovation.

The introduction of computers is rarely risk-free. The best way to avoid failure is to anticipate it. Risk must be visible to everyone so that it can be eliminated, one exposure at a time. Do not obscure risk in averages, mean expected outcomes, implied assumptions and untested commitments, because it will not be manageable.

Computer people have a tendency to over-estimate short run gains and under-estimate long-run advantages. That is "macromyopia." Risk analysis is the correct analytic technique with which one can examine the uncertainty of information technology investments prior to implementation.

A few words of caution apply against potential over-use of computerized risk-models in striving for zero-risk investments. "We are not far from a situation where somebody develops a model ... and assembles a risk estimate without ever showing any cause and effect evidence. These computer models of risk have taken on a life of their own that has little relationship to reality."[51]

Computerized fiction is not a good substitute for the prevailing tendency of systems managers to avoid risk analysis of information technology investments.

CHAPTER 9 COMMENTS

[1] Airplanes may crash-land even at 10,000 ft. It all depends on the terrain over which you fly.

[2] A.D. Crescenzi, The Dark Side of Strategic IS Implementation, *Information Strategy Journal*, Fall 1988. Crescenzi's study of 30 strategic systems shows that only five achieved their objectives. Every failed system originated in organizational and not technical errors.

[3] "Typical accounting methods impose such high hurdle rates on systems...that instead of good analysis, exaggerated benefits are often the way to funding. A high level project champion might adjust the financial assumptions to ensure greater than expected gains and lesser expected costs." (G. Harrar, To Justify or Not to Justify, *Enterprise Magazine*, Digital Equipment Corporation, Winter 1990.

[4] I do not mean to pick on M.I.S. experts for their tendency to keep their customers dependent and ignorant. Auto mechanics, estate lawyers and physicians, just to mention a few other occupations, are also resented for the same reasons.

[5] "Fiascoes occur when senior management sees projects as low risk, but the M.I.S. director knows it is high but is afraid to say it." F.W. McFarlan quoted in *Computerworld*, April 19,1982

[6] Survival instincts should also help. According to a survey of 568 M.I.S. executives by Touche Ross & Co. (as reported in the November 20, 1989 *InformationWeek*,

220   THE BUSINESS VALUE OF COMPUTERS

p. 15), only one out of eight computer executives ever stands a chance of being promoted. Blown schedules and overrun project budgets chasing unrealized benefit commitments are the most common reasons for an MIS manager's dismissal or demotion.

7 A reincarnation of the ancient horoscope.

8 T. Davenport, Inter-corporate Measurement Program, *The Index Group* as quoted in W.M. Carlson and B.C. McNurlin, Measuring the Value of Information Systems, *United Communications Group*, 1989.

9 Prototypes are programs that can simulate the functions of a proposed application. Prototypes need to show only the most important business functions and do not have to run efficiently. There are software programs that generate display screens without any application behind them. Prototypes are useful in dealing with the greatest risk in any information systems design: the inability to predict whether the user will find the proposed information display of value.

10 PSR, the Probability of Success Ratio profile, is a proprietary technique described in V.M. Janualitis, Gaining Competitive Advantage, *Infosystems*, October 1984, p. 56. The five steps in PSR are: 1. Assess the competitive potential of technology in the industry; 2. Measure the risk relationships; 3. Develop the PSR profile; 4. Measure the risk ratio for M.I.S.; 5. Develop risk-management action steps. The steps use a simple risk-rating scale of "low", "medium" and "high" and a scoring technique in which "high risk" is -1, "acceptable risk" is zero and "low risk" is $+1$.

11 For instance, the success of a new application could depend on the ability of sales branches to enter customer orders correctly. Formerly, central administrative office performed this task. Risk analysis suggests that the expected savings may not materialize if the branches cannot train their people to deal with the established procedures. There are choices as to how to handle such situations. For instance, management can simplify the rules so the cost and complexity of training do not matter.

12 Parker, Benson & Trainor, Information Economics, *Prentice Hall*, 1988, especially chapters 13 and 14. This risk-analysis method applies to IBM's ISIS method and therefore deserves special attention.

13 For instance, the score for Technical Uncertainty consists of four scores (equally weighted) defined as: 1. Skills required; 2. Hardware Dependencies; 3. Software Dependencies; 4. Applications Software. Each of these four in turn has a scoring scale of five categories, from zero to five. To come up with a score for Technical Uncertainty, you pick average scores from a table of 20 risk categories. Project or Organizational Risk has five risk categories.

Besides risk factors this schema also includes: 1. Strategic Match; 2. Competitive Advantage 3. Management Information; 4. Competitive Response 5. Strategic Information Systems Architecture. Each of these has five rating categories to be chosen from a total of twenty-five.

14 For instance, the worksheet on *Project or Organizational Risk* give a risk score of five if one of the following conditions applies: 1. The business organization has no plan for implementing the proposed system. 2. Management is uncertain about responsibility. 3. Processes and procedures are undocumented. 4. No contingency plan is in place. 5. There is no defined champion for the initiative. 6. The product or competitive *Value-added* is not well-defined. 7. There is no well-understood market.

15 Described as "...Requirements unknown. Specifications unknown..." If somebody tries to sell me a project with unknown requirements and unstated specifications I expect an unmitigated disaster. In this rating scheme, the maximum penalty for such a situation is only a demerit of 10 points out of 100.

16 For instance, the maximum score for your *R-O-I* computation is +50, based on the evaluations range of 0 to 5 and the weight of 10. The maximum score of the organization risk is -5, based on the evaluation range of 0 to 5 and the weight of -1. The scores for ranking projects come from subtracting negative scores (with a maximum score of 35) from positive contributions (with a maximum score of 100).

17 The numbers are different, but the general approach is the same.
18 People readily accept a residual value when they buy shares or when they invest in rental properties. For instance, the price they pay for a share of a company does not come from discounted present value of planned dividends. A financial table from the ALCAR firm (for G. Hector, Yes, You Can Manage Long Term, *Fortune*, November 21, 1988, p. 65) illustrates this point. It shows that much of the stock price (in November 1988) came from the discounted value of dividends beyond five years:

Company	Stock Price	Present Value of Next 5 yrs dividends	% of Stock Price Due to Prospects beyond 5 yrs.
General Motors	$77	$19	75%
Exxon	$46	$9	80%
Ford Motor	$53	$16	71%
IBM	$124	$21	83%
General Electric	$45	$7	85%
AT&T	$27	$5	82%
Du Pont	$85	$16	81%
Boeing	$67	$7	89%

19 Technical implementation can take advantage of Computer-Aided Systems Engineering (CASE) techniques for specifying new systems. You should write functional specifications instead of technology-specific requests for proposals. By stipulating proprietary independence as a design goal, you will be able to make better choices from among the competing technologies. This will make it easier to extend the life of your systems. You should also specify systems that can integrate with many suppliers' offerings of hardware and software. You should not stay vulnerable to one vendor's technical decisions, as was true at the beginning of the computer era.
20 I omit calculations of how to treat inflation and currency for purposes of investment analysis. Investment decisions are *present* decisions. You should make the best use of intelligence about future trends. I use at least a 10 to 15% annual decrease in the per-unit cost of computing. I estimate inflation using the current price of long-term government bonds because historically the long term real cost of debt is slightly below 3% per annum. If your 30-year Treasury bonds are at 9%, then your expected inflationary cost increases in labor costs and labor-intensive operating expenses are at least at 6%.
21 The best discussion is in A. Rappaport, Creating Shareholder Value, *Free Press*, 1986, pp. 59-64. Also, the *Alcar Value Planner* (The Alcar Group, Skokie, IL.) is an elaborate software package which incorporates Professor Rappaport's ideas. It illustrates several methods for making residual value computations for shareholder valuation purposes.
22 This forecast comes from an assessment of the expected maintainable database technology and on the future upgrading of the operating system.
23 You can always change this assumption in case you expect a change in trends. It just happens that I have examined a rare case – a data center consolidation for a government agency—where an investment was justified on the basis of an 18-year forecast:

	1990	1991	1992	1993	1994	1995	1996	1997	1998
Costs	612	619	838	775	681	700	640	569	516
Savings	0	-7	-219	63	94	-19	60	71	53
Savings %	0%	-1%	-26%	8%	14%	-3%	9%	12%	10%
Savings+Replace	0	-7	-219	63	94	-19	60	71	53
Replace Savings %	0%	-1%	-26%	8%	14%	-3%	9%	12%	10%
Savings+Residual	0	-7	-219	63	94	-19	60	71	53
Cum.Savings	0	-7	-226	-163	-69	-88	-28	43	96

222   THE BUSINESS VALUE OF COMPUTERS

	1999	2000	2001	2002	2003	2004	2005	2006	2007
Costs	422	351	330	297	273	249	238	245	279
Savings	94	71	21	33	24	24	11	-7	-34
Savings %	22%	20%	6%	11%	9%	10%	5%	-3%	-12%
Savings+Replace	94	71	-86	24.1	37.7	-6.8	22.3	30.6	28.7
Replace Savings %	22%	20%	-26%	8%	14%	-3%	9%	12%	10%
Savings+Residual	94	71	135						
Cum.Savings	190	261	282	315	339	363	374	367	333
Average Savings/Yr.				3%					
NPV - Savings - $000				105					
NPV-Savings+Replacement- $000				85					
NPV-Savings+Residual- $000				127					

The projected cost reductions (benefits) were computed by starting with the "base case" cash expenditures of $612 millions in 1990, showing increased expenditures for making the consolidation of $7 millions plus $219 millions in 1991–1992, and projecting cumulative savings of $333 millions by year 2007. How good is this case and how accurately could we estimate the Net Present Value based on assumptions about residual value?

The proposal fails to meet a number of criteria. First, the average saving per year is only 3%. As will be discussed in Chapter 11, computer operations should deliver cost-reductions of at least 15% per year.

The future savings discounted to net present worth give us only a $105 million gain. This is less than the front-end investment although the government enjoys an unusually low cost of capital, 9% for long-term bonds. The negative cash flow lasts for 8 years which is just too risky for the governmental technology and management environment which revises its policies on a much shorter cycle.

The proposal also shows a drop-off in savings after 2001, which suggests diminishing returns from the consolidation. Current technology forecasts, especially with regard to telecommunications costs, suggest that data-center consolidations planned in 1990 will most likely not remain viable after year 2000. If we consider the possibility of having to replace the consolidated centers at that time, the Net Present Value savings shrink to $85 millions.

Projecting the residual value based on a level saving of $21 million/per year after year 2000 yields a Net Present Value of $127 million. This amount is an optimistic, but nevertheless an inadequate payoff.

The above case demonstrates that all proposals based on undiscounted cumulative cash savings are suspect, especially if they primarily rely on technology savings. Avoid investment proposals where the technology life-cycle is shorter than the reorganization cycle.

[24] A smallest *Return-on-Investment* percentage before approving any investment. Such a computation may include another discount factor for future cash.

[25] A few words about the prevailing practice of using the *payback period* as a substitute for discounted cash analysis are in order. Regretfully, there are still financial controllers who issue simplistic rules, such as "...I need less than one year's paybacks for projects..." Although such a short-term recovery of an investment may suggest there is a huge residual value lurking after the next year, this is not necessarily so. The short payback period reminds me of the story of three little pigs. The one with the straw house did not have enough time to build something that could cope with a permanent and deadly threat. Management in the systems business is always in a hurry to get things done barely adequately, but always finds the money to then re-do the poorly done job many times over.

Decisions based on time-to-break-even are short-sighted because they disregard prospects of any future beyond a few months. The allocation of investment money based on such a measure will damage shareholder interests unless you are trying to avoid imminent bankruptcy.

[26] The interest charged for short-term loans to established businesses.
[27] Early in 1990, for prime credit risks.
[28] "A single hurdle rate makes for bad investment decisions, overstating the risk of low-risk units and understating that of high-risk units" was noted by A. Rappaport,

The Staying Power of the Public Corporation, *Harvard Business Review,* January 1990, p.102.

29 Actuaries are well-paid specialists who collect, evaluate and set insurance rates. There is little likelihood that the computing profession will ever voluntarily consent to collect, evaluate and publish data about the mortality rates of computer projects. The closest we have ever come to such an institution is the promising *Software Engineering Institute* created by the Department of Defense at the Carnegie-Mellon University in Pittsburgh, Pa. Its methods to determine if an organization can expect to deliver a software project on budget and on time are an excellent foundation for the development of improved techniques. The *Software Engineering Institute* has found that overruns grow not from incompetent uses of technology but from faulty management processes. For instance, they found (as reported in the June 1989, *Electronics*, p. 74) that 72% of the Defense Department's software contractors have "chaotic management processes" for software development.

30 "...There are mosquito bites and there are snake bites. Good managers can tell the difference..." is one of the memorable sayings of my ex-boss, John Titsworth, Executive VP of Xerox.

31 External risks are unique to each company and therefore are not included here.

32 When computer people talk about expected costs or expected benefits, the definition of what they mean is fuzzy. You cannot tell, with any confidence, if they refer to an arithmetic mean, a geometric mean, the median, or the mode. These terms have precise meaning and different values.

Project proposals have a tendency to over-state expected implementation cost estimates by adding a hefty contingency factor although I can recall only a handful of projects that ever came in under budget. Benefits are over-estimated since companies rarely set up a method for checking what they are after project completion.

Management must know what is meant by what is said. Therefore, I use the term *expected value* as a statistician would define it: the arithmetic mean of the distribution of actual or hypothesized outcomes. Eventually, somebody will start collecting rigorous statistics about actual computer costs and benefits as compared with first expectations. Understanding the deviations from expectations is essential before you can start on systematic quality improvements.

33 According to a survey (D. Phan, D. Vogel, J. Nunamaker, The Search for Perfect Project Management, *Computerworld*, September 26,1988, pp. 95-100) 41% of respondents reported they always experience cost overruns, averaging 33% of budget costs. The survey polled software professionals, not financial controllers, and therefore may show a more charitable view of what happens.

When projects are overrunning, 46% of the survey respondents said that they postpone the delivery of planned features. Changing the scope of a project is a convenient way of reporting on-budget performance.

34 An extreme example of shifting budgets comes from the General Accounting Office, Audit of Internal Revenue Service Project, May 1988 (in $ billions):

Date of Estimate	Estimated Costs	Estimated Benefits	Target Completion
May, 1985	$1.0	$16.2	1989
January, 1987	$1.2	$42.7	1991
March, 1988	$1.8	$16.2	1995

35 The lognormal statistical distribution applies in situations where most of the values occur near the smallest value. This usually happens in financial transactions, such as in security valuations or in real estate valuation. For instance, stock returns exhibit this trend because the stock price cannot fall below zero but may increase to any price without limit. The long tail on the high end of all information project costs comes from faults (bugs) overlooked while rushing the software into operations to meet schedule and budget targets. The full costs for fixing a bug on a fully operational application can be 20 to 2,000 times greater than the costs of preventing it from happening altogether. Some bugs persist and cannot be fixed except by stopping the project for redesign. The usual solution is to proceed with a fault and then fix it as "ongoing maintenance." To improve the reliability of cost estimates calls for meticulous separation of quality

36 improvement (e.g., bug elimination) from feature enhancement (e.g., functional modifications to meet changing conditions). Programming organizations that use "maintenance" as a cover-up for low-quality software will never learn how to manage projects for the delivery of low-cost and reliable applications.

36 The distributions differ according to their *skewness* and the *lower or upper range* (which determine the expected truncation of the tails of the lognormal curve).

37 They will use any surplus to increase user satisfaction through better documentation, or by including extra features at no cost. Well-managed programming groups prefer to deliver their projects a few percentages under budget and then cover any overruns from supplemental contracts.

38 This rule applies only to tightly managed private corporations. 200% to 500% overruns in the public sector occur because Federal and State agencies cannot easily restart the same project under another designation.

39 These risk distributions exist in two computer programs which modify conventional spreadsheet analyses (LOTUS 1-2-3 for DOS cases and EXCEL for Macintosh cases) of project benefits and costs. What in these programs is "probability" is actually a "probability-density function."

These risk class distributions come from my own years of experience in managing application development and from reviews of projects that missed their financial goals. They are not statistically defensible empiric data. If my clients feel that their cost-control profiles are different, they can easily change the risk profile tables or introduce new risk classes.

40 Several prominent computer consultants have recently argued that management should not accept 20-50% payoff opportunities from computer investments. Instead, they should direct their attention to "blockbuster" projects that carry the potential of investment returns of 1,000% or better. In our economy, where shareholder returns averaging 20-25% are superior corporate performance, all extraordinary claims about potential profits are extremely risky propositions. Thousand percent profits are associated more often with illegal deals or gambling than with normal business.

41 For further details see the excellent tutorials included with risk analysis software, such as Risk Analysis and Simulation, *Palisade Corporation*, Newfield, N.Y. (for DOS) and Crystal Ball-Forecasting and Risk Management, *Market Engineering Corporation*, Denver, Colorado (for Macintosh). The calculations and illustrations for this chapter use the software from the Market Engineering Corporation. The computer simulates the probabilities of occurrence of costs and benefits by spinning an imaginary roulette wheel (that's why it is the Monte Carlo method). These computations randomly generate numbers that will look like the probability distributions shown in Figure 9.1 and Figure 9.2.

Risk analysis is also possible by calculating the joint probability distributions mathematically. Unless you are dealing with very simple projects, these analytic forms are computationally difficult. You also need advanced knowledge of statistical methods to get it done. This method does not work because your management will not understand the mathematical notation of how you came up with your results. However, I have displayed statistical simulations, in real time, in a conference setting. The audience could intuitively grasp the meaning of risk when they saw on a large screen each new payoff computation added to prior results.

42 Executives are not comfortable when project managers ask for a budget "somewhere between $91,400 and $106,000." I would request $99,000, with a $7,000 contingency to be spent only after giving an explanation. That's how you gain the reputation for trustworthiness.

43 The statistics describing the results of this simulation:

STATISTICAL INDICATOR	RESULTS
Trials	1000
Mean	26%
Median	25%
Standard Deviation	±36%
Range Minimum	−38%
Range Maximum	97%

44 The most prevalent form of spread sheet abuse is "back-to-front analysis" (a term suggested in D. Adams, Dirk Gently's Holistic Detective Agency, *Simon and Schuster*, 1987). In a conventional spread sheet you order and analyze the relevant facts to come up with the result. In a back-to-front spreadsheet you find out the numbers that will get the project past the financial reviews and then generate the facts accordingly.

Back-to-front features exist in a number of business modeling applications. For instance, MindSight Business Planning & Analysis (*Execucom Systems Corporation, Austin, Texas*) offers a "goal seeking feature" for its financial software. Its manual (p.4-10) includes, as an illustrative example "...you might want profit to reach $5,000, and you want to know the value for the number of units sold which makes that possible. Goal-seeking makes it easy to determine the necessary units sold."

45 Accomplished by simulating the possible outcome of cash flows in Table 9.6.

46 The statistics describing the results of this simulation:

STATISTICAL INDICATOR	RESULTS
Trials	1000
Mean, NPV Benefit/Cost Ratio	75%
Median, NPV Benefit/Cost Ratio	68%
Standard Deviation, NPV Benefit/Cost Ratio	±70%
Range Minimum, NPV Benefit/Cost Ratio	−38%
Range Maximum, NPV Benefit/Cost Ratio	231%

47 The statistics describing the results of this simulation:

STATISTICAL INDICATOR	RESULTS
Trials	1000
Mean, NPV Benefit/Cost Ratio	128%
Median, NPV Benefit/Cost Ratio	118%
Standard Deviation, NPV Benefit/Cost Ratio	±96%
Range Minimum, NPV Benefit/Cost Ratio	−28%
Range Maximum, NPV Benefit/Cost Ratio	356%

48 Coming up with enough projects with an NPV Benefit/Cost ratio over 100% is not easy. Chances are that any proposed list of projects will include labor-cost displacement and practical improvement projects that will yield only 10 to 15% over the shareholder's cost of money. If the risk for such investments balances against potential gains, there is no reason to hold back money from anything that delivers returns greater than the shareholder's average return on equity. As a rule, such low payoff projects can tolerate only extremely low risks of failure.

49 Projects that fail while they stay within the design limits are an educational investment. Any organization that wishes to increase its quality must engage in a thorough and uncompromising process of studying its failures clinically.

50 The statistics describing the results of this simulation:

STATISTICAL INDICATOR	RESULTS
Trials	1000
Mean	78%
Median	73%
Standard Deviation	±115%
Range Minimum	−99%
Range Maximum	442%

51 The scope of the model applies beyond random variables. It also handles discrete events such as estimated changes in tax law, adoption of standards, or entry of a new competitor.

52 W.T. Brookes, The Wasteful Pursuit of Zero Risk, *Forbes*, April 30, 1990. This article deals with environmental issues and emotional uses of misleading statistics.

10

PROJECT JUSTIFICATION

An Investment Case Study

Installing a new computer system is like performing surgery.

Cost elements of a project are easy to identify, although what is a "cost" is often debatable. Do you include training costs, work disruption and the costs of worker turnover? What about the costs of inefficiency and lost revenues while people learn the new methods? Is it possible to enumerate most of the cost categories that a prudent manager would consider in assembling a proposal? These would include hardware and software costs, supplies, site preparation and testing.

I have seen few proposals that omit anything of technical importance. You can be sure that Pareto's 80/20 rule will apply. This rule suggests that 80% of the pages in the proposal will accurately define less than 20% of the project that matters. It is therefore likely that the proposal will describe the easily identifiable costs of computer technology in great detail and gloss over the benefits.

The real problems lie in the 20% of the proposal's pages that try to describe the uncertain 80% of non-technology costs and unquantifiable benefits. The discussion of training and conversion expenses usually are perfunctory. The analysis of "intangible" benefit often is brief and not related to profits.

The toughest problems in preparing proposals concern credible and verifiable benefits. Through negotiation among all concerned parties, you must settle matters such as:

- Who will deliver the promised results? Will it be a "line" manager with profit responsibilities?
- How much time will pass before positive results must appear?
- How much of a negative cash flow will management tolerate?
- How many mistakes and of what kind will be allowed before management cancels the project?
- What parts of the benefits come from direct cost-reductions and what comes from "intangible effects," such as revenue and pricing gains?

I do not know how to come up with a general check list of benefits, for each investment proposal is unique. A case study is the best way to learn how to prepare justification proposals that align[1] information technologies with business goals. The term "alignment" means ordering, organizing, arranging and marshaling. It conveys the need to fit a new computer application into an organization and not treat it as an isolated event. Adding information technology is like performing surgery on a patient who continues to work at the same time. While you perform such surgery you had better be attentive to the patient's vital signs, not just to the operation itself.

If you are making investments that change the way a firm operates you need a comprehensive view of what's happening. You certainly need to manage how well the technology applies and how well it does the job. More important, you must monitor the environment in which the firm operates. You must check whether the firm is better off with or without your information technology investments.[2]

I shall demonstrate what I believe to be an appropriate sequence and method for evaluating computer projects in the following example. The recommended sequence is as follows:

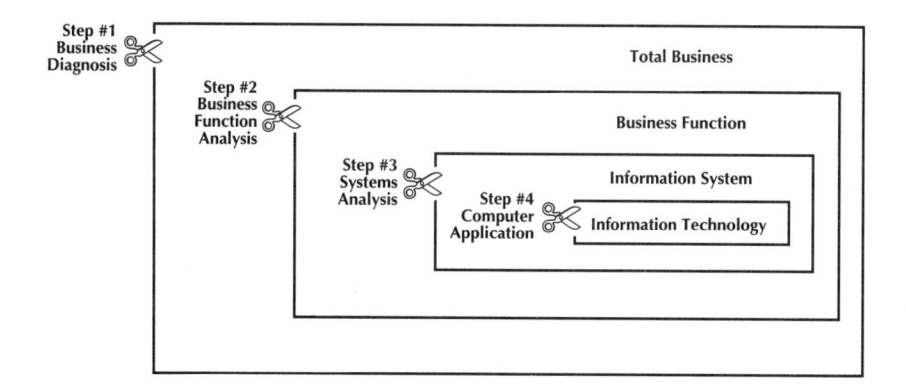

Figure 10.1: Sequence for Analyzing Information Technology Investments

The method of analysis begins with a discussion of the firm's competitive and financial conditions.

Conditions for Launching the Project

Early in the summer of 1987, I received an anguished call from the M.I.S. director of a mid-size corporation. He was told to freeze his spending at last year's levels for at least another two years. His company's latest five-year plan called for increasing the company's marketing expenses. The company plan proposed to handle a rapid erosion in market share by cutting everyone's budget requests, except for sales and advertising. The M.I.S. director would have to defer, for an indefinite period, the planned migration of existing applications to a common manufacturing, engineering and purchasing database. He would have to tolerate further proliferation of uncoordinated departmental computing, and a rapidly expanding patchwork of personal computers. Without any plan of how to integrate them into the existing network, each salesperson would get a laptop computer. These were promised as a morale booster because the competitor's salesforce made good uses of personal computers for rapid order entry.

UNSATISFACTORY BUSINESS PLAN

While I examined the best way to cut back the M.I.S. development plan, the CEO was reviewing the company's five-year financial plan for 1988–1992. The earnings over the next two years were projected to deteriorate but recover after 1990.[3] The earnings for 1988–1989 were not supposed to decrease at the same rate suggested by the previous two years. The profit would be lifted up by deferring of much needed improvements. Also, savings would be obtained from closing down one of three plants which would cut excess capacity to reflect the declining market share. However, the CEO concluded there were few reasons to believe that these short-term measures would produce the projected turn-around in profits after 1990.

The *Return-on-Management* diagnostics[4] were discouraging. Substituting overseas part purchases for internal production made the situation worse. The productivity of the firm would not improve since the *Value-added* of the firm was shrinking. The budget reductions did not make much of a dent in the large overhead staffs.

The main competitor could deliver products in less time by air-shipment than it took the firm to schedule customer orders. On top of that was the firm's lengthy production cycle for the delivery of what the customer wanted.

The competitor's products were neither better nor cheaper,[5] yet the competitor was gaining market share that would finance new products for introduction sometime after 1990. If the company could not compete now, soon it would have to fight for survival when the competitor's new products entered into the market.

The firm was not losing market share because of equipment quality or price. The company's products were selling at a discount and with promotional allowances to entice repeat orders from buyers dissatisfied with delivery schedules. The customers' shift to favor just-in-time method of production was the reason for their preference of the competitor's rapid deliveries. Timely responsiveness and rapid delivery were now the principal reason for choosing suppliers. The basis of competition had changed in favor of vendors who could react faster.[6]

The *R-O-M Productivity Index* diagnostics also suggested that the company's proposed five-year financial plan was probably too optimistic. The expected earnings would not materialize if poor delivery performance continued much longer. The relative market share was marginal and declining. Work-in-process inventories were too high. Overhead costs and marketing expenses were already excessive.

Meanwhile, most of the sales force spent their time expediting late deliveries and placating customers instead of bidding against competitive offerings. The new portable computers, which were cost-justified by the Marketing Department as saving the salespersons' unproductive time, speeded up expediting phone calls. Nobody gave much thought to the adverse effects of faster expediting. It magnified the disarray in the factories' production systems.

STRATEGIC DIRECTION

Before surgery eliminate the cause of the disease.

The CEO rejected the proposed corporate five-year plan and directed the Manufacturing Vice President to remedy customer dissatisfaction, reduce overhead and cut inventories, even if that called for more short-term expenses. The CEO decided to re-direct the company to fight for competitive survival instead of continuing business-as-usual with only improved marketing. He resolved to protect the value of the shareholders' investments from further deterioration.

The shareholder value of this company was considerable. At year-end 1987 this firm was worth $915 million.[7] The proposed five year plan (1988–1992) would add a further $356 million to shareholder value. Unfortunately, risk analysis showed that if market share dropped precipitously, the firm could lose most of its shareholder value within five years.

Confronted with the prospect of a potential $400–$600 million declines in shareholder value, the CEO decided to change the corporate plan. *R-O-M* diagnosis suggested what would be the long term gain in profits if market share recovered. The CEO could afford taking another $50–$80 million out of short-term profits to remedy the current decline rooted in unresponsive production management practices. The CEO would finance an additional 50% of the needed recovery expenses from overhead cost reductions. The CEO's goal was to reverse the losses in market share by regaining the leadership in rapid delivery of products to customers. He would redirect marketing people from administration to competition.

THE IMPORTANCE OF DIRECTION-SETTING

The chances of success for strategic information technology ventures are largely pre-ordained at project inception.[8] Faulty diagnosis makes for faulty prescriptions. If you are starting systems projects, make sure:
- The goals are simple and the aims are in sharp focus.
- Realistic financial analysis supports the objectives.
- The desired improvements are measurable.
- There is enough cash to afford to fix what needs fixing.

The analytic understanding of the competitive realities, the clarity of financial analysis and the articulation of operating priorities calls for greater skills than anything else that follows. Therefore, systems experts, vendors and consultants cannot possibly have a full understanding of what to do. They can only offer advice on how to install information technologies after the directions are clear.

The circumstances for launching a successful system project are never the same. There are no standard solutions, no dogmas. The same technology applied in the same industry can yield diametrically opposite consequences. Therefore, you can learn only from specific experiences, with occasional help from a few tools. Successful solutions are home-grown. They depend on the quality of the people who install and then operate what computer technology makes possible.

Major technical mistakes in project implementation do not occur often. There are too many safeguards available to protect against that. You also can fail if you choose incompetent managers. You can remedy that by rapid replacement. With well-defined and realistic goals the chances of project failure are rare.

Launching the Project

In our case, the unambiguous directions from the CEO had a forcefully motivating effect on the entire management team. The directions were clear, the limits on resources defined and a sense of urgency established. In a matter of days the M.I.S. Director teamed up with the Plant Manager to bring before the Manufacturing Vice President the following proposition:

- The order-to-factory-shipment cycle could come down from 14–35 days to 3–5 days by streamlining the clerical and administrative coordination among sales, materials buying, engineering and production scheduling. This would require a common database for goods-handling functions. A central, on-line computer would process all transactions. There would be no further batch processing for materials orders.[9]
- Major overhead cost reductions were possible by eliminating redundant clerical and accounting jobs. This would call for the consolidation of all data about materials and finished goods. In this way it would become readily accessible to everyone in the factory, in the warehouse and to key suppliers.

This aggressive proposal called for:
- A hastened conversion from batch processing to on-line transaction-handling;
- Reorganizing information flows from distributed processing to complete centralization in a fully integrated database;
- Moving most of the information-handling tasks from clerks and expediters to shop-floor supervisors and warehousing personnel.

The proposed technology strategy called for three radical and simultaneous transformations in business methods. How much would it cost, how long would it take and how risky would it be?[10]

THE COST ESTIMATE

It just happened that for three years the M.I.S. staff had been exploring the feasibility of on-line processing from a consolidated database. Visits were made to plants with a reputation for superior operations and similar business conditions. Two software vendors had made presentations how they solved similar problems in other companies. One vendor offered to receive payment that was contingent on satisfactory project completion. Except for the new company-wide data network, all cost estimates were reliable. Departmental batch equipment would be sold. Net operating personnel savings would be realized after 1990 by running unattended[11] dual-backup minicomputers:

$ Millions	1988	1989	1990	1991	1992
Operations & Development	−4.1	−4.5	−1.0	+1.4	+2.9
Network & Database	−0.3	−2.1	−0.3	−0.3	−0.3
Total New Systems	−4.4	−6.6	−1.3	+1.1	+2.6

Table 10.1: Proposed Increases in Information Technology Spending

THE BENEFIT ESTIMATE

The Plant Manager knew what to do. Overhead personnel reductions could be made soon after the first computer applications permitted much simplified production scheduling.[12] Half of the surplus personnel could transfer into sales after some training. Reassigning personnel would preserve jobs for long-term employees, diminish anxiety during the transition and reduce resistance to the proposed organizational changes. The biggest threat to installation of the integrated system would come from the inability of administrative supervisors to adjust to new relationships. The Plant Manager's entire staff would remain for the duration of the project to act as trouble-shooters. An *Administrative Allowance* would cover reorganization expenses, training, consultants and severance pay:

$ Millions	1988	1989	1990	1991	1992
Plant Overhead	0	+10	+22	+23	+26
Selling Support	–3	–8	–9	–10	–10
Administrative Allowance	–5	–20	–12	–2	–1
Total Business Impact	–8	–18	+1	+11	+15

Table 10.2: Business Effects of Plant Reorganization

Many benefits could arise without spending more for information technology. The challenge was how to find the least costly way of getting the maximum gains. From the plant manager's standpoint the proposed project was not a computer project. It was a long overdue overhaul of the plant's obsolete procedures.

The Plant Manager's aim was not to propose a computerization program but to come up with an affordable and low-risk financial justification. The M.I.S. Director wisely stayed in the background. He worked closely with the Plant Manager in getting whatever data were needed for a credible presentation to the Manufacturing Vice President.

THE CASH ESTIMATE

The Manufacturing Vice President prepared cash-flow projections for approval by corporate finance. This included the expected reductions in business assets and the projected cash-flow forecast:

$ Millions	1988	1989	1990	1991	1992
Information Technology	–4.4	–6.6	–1.3	+1.1	+2.6
Business Impacts	–8.0	–18.0	+1.0	+11.0	+15.0
Business Assets	–18.0	+5.0	+10.0	+15.0	+17.0
Total Project Impact	–30.4	–19.6	+9.7	+27.1	+34.6
Cumulative Cash Flow	–30.4	–50.0	–40.3	–13.2	+21.4

Table 10.3: Cash Flow of Plant Reorganization Proposal

The Controller was apprehensive about the 4.4 year break-even period. It was customary to get money back in less than two years. He

CHAPTER 10—PROJECT JUSTIFICATION   235

asked if reducing information technology expenses, by deferring the conversion to on-line systems could improve the payback period.

CHECKING THE INFORMATION TECHNOLOGY PROPOSAL

Before we examine the tradeoffs between various implementation schedules it is always useful to analyze computer spending in isolation. In our case such an analysis was worthwhile. The conversion to on-line processing created savings that would reduce the M.I.S. budget $2.6 million by 1992.

Would there be any residual value from the large conversion costs incurred during 1988 and 1989? In the collective judgment of the plant, finance and M.I.S. people, the benefits would continue for at least 10 to 12 years. The company-wide local area network would also have lasting benefits. Later upgrades could be justified as a much lower incremental expense. Therefore, the new computing and networking architecture could have a life of as much as 15–20 years.

The net present worth of the proposed information technology budget, at the current cost of capital of 12% would be:

$ Millions	1988	1989	1990	1991	1992	Residual
Total New Systems	−4.4	−6.6	−1.3	+1.1	+2.6	+16.1
Net Present Worth	+0.2					

Table 10.4: The Value of the Information Technology Investment

With information technology near break-even, would it make sense to prune some of these expenses further to shorten the payback time? A sample of the $22 million of clerical and administrative work, that would disappear by 1990, showed that 60–80% of the displaced work-hours would have to remain without an on-line database. Finance could not find anything else that offered a good rationale for deferring costs beyond 1992. The M.I.S. budget was trimmed to bare essentials. It had an allowance for contingency, but finance could not remove that as a savings before the project began.[13]

THE RISK PROFILE OF THE I.T. INVESTMENT

The next hurdle involved risks. What about potential budget overruns? The existing staff had little experience with on-line processing and no networking know-how.

Displaying the *risk profile* is the most effective way to explain the hazards of multi-year efforts. Risks are not always the same. Sometimes they occur during installation and sometimes they appear only after implementation. In Chapter 9 I described how you can simulate financial vulnerability at a point of time. The *risk profile* covering the life of a project reflects the distribution of risk at each year-end. In our case this appears as the band that covers ±95 percent of our confidence about the probable outcome:[14]

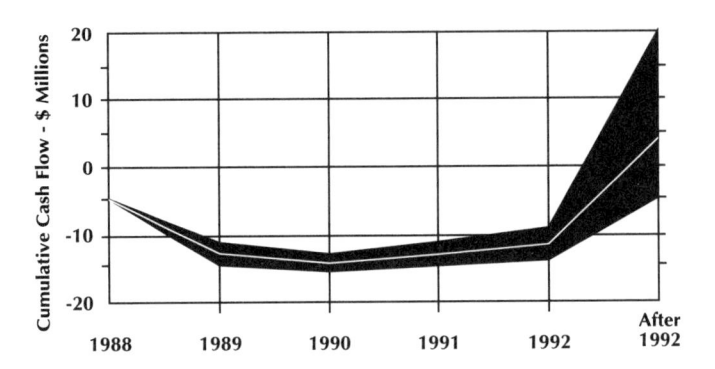

Figure 10.2: The Risk Profile of Cumulative Cash for I.T.

From 1988 through 1992 the risk profile would be within tolerable limits for the CEO. The M.I.S. Director helped to limit the risk exposures by writing fixed price contracts. A firm that had proven its capability got the contract to install the network. The new network would be similar to installations in comparable plants. The worst-case scenario (defined as 95% unlikely) showed a cumulative loss of $5 million after 1992.

As proposed, the project also had the advantage of short-term operating savings. These would start as early as 1989, producing $10 million in personnel cost reductions and $5 million in inventory savings. The M.I.S. Director and the Plant Manager did their homework and put together an excellent package that balanced risky long-term gains with more certain immediate cash savings.

Reducing the M.I.S. budget did not offer any advantages. The risks were under control. Was there anything else that could be done to improve time to the break-even?

Managing the Benefits

Without responsibility there is no accountability.

The benefits of the proposed project depended on the worth of residual values. The firm would realize savings only if it survived as a profitable concern. The plant would experience two years of wrenching changes. It would take two more years to recover the costs of fixing the past neglect. The results of the bold restructuring would appear only in the fifth year of the five-year plan. The value of the proposed project would be then an attractive $109.6 million:[15]

$ Millions Residual	1988	1989	1990	1991	1992	
Total Project Impact	−30.4	−19.6	+9.7	+27.1	+34.6	+214.3
Net Present Worth	+109.6					

Table 10.5: The Value of Restructuring the Factory

The CEO worried about the risk in his recovery plan. It would take a long time before the benefits of his investments appeared as a favorable 1992 financial statement. The Controller identified[16] three major project risks: higher re-training expenses, larger than expected severance payments and delays in building a warehouse for improved materials handling. The CEO decided to put in place special management reviews to establish that all critical events received his immediate attention. Constructing the risk profile for the entire project offered the means for monitoring progress:

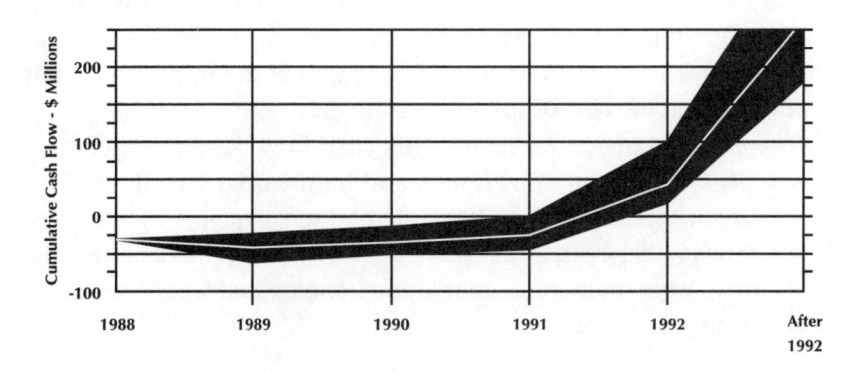

Figure 10.3: The Risk Profile of Cumulative Cash for Factory Project.

238   THE BUSINESS VALUE OF COMPUTERS

The risk profile shows that the expected payoff calculations were conservative. The chances of large cost overruns were not as great as the possibility that the benefits would be much better. As result, the CEO approved the project proposal late in Fall 1987. He informed everyone about the boundaries within which to keep all costs. He would not tolerate any schedule delays, even at the price of budget overruns, if the total cash flow remained within limits in Figure 10.2.

The CEO knew that the firm would get greater benefits from the plant reorganization than shown in the new plan. The recovery of the lost market share, the advantages of restoring pricing parity with competitors and the capacity to add new products would exceed the savings in payroll and in inventory. However, these benefits were not something the M.I.S. Director, the Plant Manager or the Manufacturing Vice President could influence directly. The manufacturing management team committed themselves to ambitious targets. They would deliver the results as promised. The CEO did not wish to divert their attention to matters they could not measure or evaluate. Therefore, he made clear that schedule took precedence over budgets.

The CEO would not allow Manufacturing to claim any of the benefits that would accrue to corporate Marketing. Similarly, M.I.S. could not make claims on savings from reduced plant inventories though computer systems made this possible. The CEO was an experienced operating executive. To get results he followed the rule that all accountability for commitments must follow the direct responsibility for results.

M.I.S. had to accept that the information technology project, taking only M.I.S. into consideration, would barely break even. M.I.S. would be accountable for meeting performance goals within budget limits for the project. M.I.S. was now on the critical path for reorganizing the business, and therefore could not fumble the implementation schedule, even at the cost of spending more money.

The Plant Manager knew that his cash flow would be negative until late in 1991, although with luck and hard work he could recover his investment as early as mid-1990. He had to manage a tight implementation schedule, even at the price of not meeting financial targets, because there were many more marketing benefits that were external to manufacturing operations.

How does the restructuring look from the CEO's point of view, which I equate to the shareholder's view?

The Shareholder Point of View

To keep his job the CEO must view the situation from the shareholder's standpoint as reflected in the price of shares. Besides the current profitability,[17] the stock market considers the stability of earnings, the long-term prospects of profit growth, the firm's competitive position and the general reputation of its leadership. The price of a share ultimately is the only method of valuation that generates continuous feedback about the value of a firm. It reflects the consensus of what sellers and buyers think about the company. Thousands of purchases and sales of the shares vote as to whether a profit-improvement program is realistic, even if it signals lower short-term earnings. The trend in the price of shares will show whether the loss in competitive position places future earnings in jeopardy.

How would the proposed plant reorganization appear from the shareholders' perspective? Earlier I noted that the unsatisfactory five-year plan triggered the proposal to overhaul Manufacturing. You will recall that the shareholder value was $915 million and the proposed five year plan to increase shareholder value by $356 million was too risky.

After the approval of the changes in manufacturing organization the company prepared a revised five-year plan. The revisions called for greater short-term borrowing and lower profits until 1991. Marketing would redirect its efforts to the retention of existing customers while preparing to regain market share. Improving the quality of customer service would have a positive effect on every business function.

By the end of 1987 all Departments finished a revised five-year plan. The estimated improvement[18] in the shareholder value would be (in $ millions):

Revised Present Value of Future Cash Flows	$1,797
Shareholder Value at Year-end 1987	$915
Value of Revised Long-Range Plan, 1988–1992	$882
Value of Original Long-Range Plan, 1988–1992	$356
Value of Improvement through Restructuring	$526

Table 10.6: Improving Shareholder Value through Better Systems

The Business Value of Computers

The business value of computers is the unlocking of Management Value-added.

Based on Table 10.6, what is the business value of computers in our case? Depending on which numbers you examine you will get different answers. Let us examine different interpretations (in $ Millions):

Total Systems Investment (1988–1990)	$12.3
Total Marketing Investment (1988–1992)	$40.0
Total Administrative Expense (1988–1992)	$40.0
Total Capital Investment, 1988	$18.0
Net Present Worth of Direct Savings	$109.6
Increased Shareholder Value	$526.0

Table 10.7: Costs and Benefits for Plant Restructuring Case

The advantage of spending $12.3 million on added computer systems is indisputable. Does that mean that the *Return-on-Investment* of our computer systems investment is $526/$12.3 or 4,276%? There are consultants who would have you believe that this is the right calculation method.[19] If you accept such logic, you would deny the efforts by plant management, purchasing and marketing. You also would nullify the role of the $18 million capital in the new warehouse. You would stay silent about everyone's efforts in the plant and in the warehouse. The commitment of the employees is essential for the new computer system to become a new way of doing business.

THE SYSTEM ORGANIZATION'S CONTRIBUTION

The CEO and the Manufacturing Vice President should thank the M.I.S. organization for coming up quickly with imaginative and affordable technical solutions. The M.I.S. Director should view the delivery of an integrated database and installation of an on-line network as a praiseworthy achievement. Doing all that at near breakeven is an exceptional feat.

After installation, the new systems become *mission critical*. They are inseparable from the costs of plant operations. If you buy a refrigerator, the value of electricity stops having any meaning except for its costs. Though a refrigerator cannot run without electricity, you can evaluate only the value of refrigeration, not the value of any part.

All that M.I.S. can do now is deliver the new *mission critical* system at the lowest cost and with high reliability. The *Value-added* of M.I.S. is the difference between its costs and the next alternative solution. That positive difference should be as large as possible.

THE MANUFACTURING OPERATIONS' CONTRIBUTION

The value of a *mission critical* system is in the increased *Operations Value-added*. In our case, that is ultimately $109.6 million. That is the Plant Manager's measure of achievement for the restructuring project. Only the Plant Manager can tell for sure if the M.I.S. contribution is worth the $12.3 million of net systems expense. He has two ways to test that proposition:
- He can try to cut the M.I.S. budget on an application-by-application basis and see if performance would suffer. That technique was used by Finance during the project approval process. M.I.S. substantiated that the proposed spending was essential. M.I.S. passed the credibility tests.
- He can benchmark the M.I.S. spending against comparable firms. If his M.I.S. budget were ultimately lower than the budget of his superior competitors then his computerization efforts could be judged as effective.

To the Plant Manager the new *mission critical* system is a cost of doing business similar to purchasing services, engineering, parts and materials. The computer support from M.I.S. has no value, taken in isolation, except for its costs. Though he cannot run the plant without the new systems, he can only evaluate it from gains in the *Operations Value-added* of the entire plant. The Plant Manager must treat information technology just as any other resource that would be judged by its competitive price. Without a competitive price, the contributions of the new *mission critical* systems would be attractive, but never known with any accuracy.

What about the $526 millions gain in shareholder value? Who can claim that as a benefit?

THE MANAGEMENT'S CONTRIBUTION

The creation of more shareholder value does not emanate solely from the presence of technology, redesign of the work in the plant or redirection of marketing efforts. Creating increased shareholder value is an act of superior skill in combining limited resources. It was the CEO who concluded that the company could not maintain profits by cost cutting and increased promotional efforts. It was the CEO and his immediate team who sorted out what needed fixing. It was *Management* that set the priorities for how and in what sequence to change the business. Therefore, the difference between the projected direct savings and the projected gains in the shareholder value ($526–$109.6 millions) is the measure of the newly created *Management Value-added*.

In our case the business value of computers, taken in isolation, was +$0.2 million which is the discounted net cash flow for which M.I.S. could be held accountable. Its decisive contribution in unlocking $109.6 million of *Operations Value-added* and another $416 million of potential gains in *Management Value-added* was acknowledged.

EMPLOYEE MORALE: THE ULTIMATE INTANGIBLE

An immeasurable part of excessive absenteeism, high employee turnover and increased sick leave is sometimes attributable to visual display terminals (VDT's). If office space and furniture do not fit, computer terminals may cause some visual and musculoskeletal discomfort. Improving offices to suit VDT's is expensive, especially if you have to upgrade unsuitable office furniture, lighting fixtures, power cabling, noise suppression and air-conditioning to overcome employee complaints.

There are only few documented stories of how to justify spending for ergonomics. I found a case study about ergonomic improvements in a telephone company.[20] It illustrates some of questions you may ask when you propose computers to improve employee morale.

The Case of the STK Company

A small telephone plant of the Norwegian firm STK is near Oslo. As is common in Scandinavian countries, worker health and good working conditions receive much attention. Workers did not seem to like working for STK. The annual employee turnover of 30.1% was unusual by Norwegian standards.

The workers' unfavorable attitude is apparent from absenteeism records. Long-term sick leave was 13.4% of work time in 1973 and 16.9% in 1974. Sick leave for "musculoskeletal" discomfort and injury were 5.3% of production time. Obviously, the workers were uncomfortable. The assembly stations had a fixed height, and illumination that could not be adjusted to individual needs. The workers had to assume awkward postures to get their work finished.

How would you justify spending the money for improved ergonomics?[21] This is one situation where computing the potential benefits was easy. All you do is add up recruitment costs/employee which include new employee training[22] costs and the direct costs of sick payments. You come up with an enormous sum of money. Next, you get the costs of the ergonomic improvement program. In STK these were the costs of improved ventilation, lighting and changing the height of the assembly tables. STK engineers figured that this would be only NKr 338,992.

What percentage of the enormously large benefit estimate should you use in computing the benefit/cost ratio? If you are the plant manager, you do not need extensive financial analysis to tell you to improve working conditions. However, procedures call for filling out the necessary capital requests before you can install adjustable tables and adjustable lights. The investment approval forms are for corporate financial purposes. Inserting the full calculated "potential benefits" into the specified line item would lead to a *Return-on-Investment* of well over 1,000%. You feel uneasy in submitting such a large number. You only need something better than 30% returns to get your money. With what number do you multiply 1000% so that you get something above 31%? Arithmetic will tell that you need to claim only 3.1% of your maximum savings.

We do not know how STK economically justified the ergonomic improvements. It seems that the situation was already intolerable when management requested the money to give each operator greater flexibility to vary working conditions. The results were immediate and gratifying. The tangible reductions in recruitment costs, training and sick payment expenses added up to net savings of NKr 3,226,194. This yields an excellent benefit/cost ratio of 9.5.

Alternative Approaches

All ergonomic projects do not have the same sense of urgency as in the case of STK. Coming up with credible benefits is always necessary for cost justification. There are alternative approaches you could consider.

COMPARISONS WITH OTHERS

You should compare ergonomic conditions in similar organizations.

The work-flow in the assembly of telephone equipment is similar, regardless of where it is in the world. What vary are local conditions that workers will tolerate. You could arrange to get employee turnover and absenteeism records for Swedish, Dutch and German telephone and electronics assembly companies. You could then ask about the ergonomic conditions in each company. Even competitors share such data freely.

Employee turnover and absenteeism rates in Swedish, Dutch and German companies can not be explained by ergonomics alone. If your ergonomic conditions, absenteeism and employee turnover rates are consistently worse, you should try to find an industry-wide correlation among these factors. It is a complicated solution but it is satisfying how well you can improve your proposal if you have comparable data from competitors or similar firms. Justifying investments entirely on internal costs is inadequate. You may be missing opportunities for greater gains.

SEPARATION INTERVIEWS

If you are in a hurry to get numbers for cost justification, you can always study why employees leave you. I believe that unbiased and properly safeguarded employee exit interviews are essential. Such interviews may be the most valuable source of insight about personnel management practices. It is ironic that when luring employees most companies spend hours interviewing an applicant. Can you imagine how much you could learn if someone spends as little as 20 minutes talking with a person who is leaving?

In the case of STK, it is interesting to note that the high turnover rate and absenteeism had persisted since 1967. The ergonomic redesign finally happened in 1975. You may wonder if anyone was listening to what the employees were saying. A small random telephone sample conducted by an independent pollster would quickly tell whether poor ergonomics was an adverse influence.

STUDYING DIFFERENCES

If you do not want to go to the trouble of getting the opinions of employees who have left the company you can try a simple experiment. From existing records get a distribution of sick leave hours by employee. A company-wide average of any employee indicator is the result of low and high performers. Which group has high absenteeism? Which group has an unusually good attendance record? Are there any dissimilarities in their ergonomic conditions? If you can identify how the ergonomic attributes differ, you can then explain how your proposal can deliver improved results.

EXPERIMENTATION

If none of the above fact-gathering works for you, try the direct approach. Use discretionary money, which every experienced manager knows how to lay aside, try a few ergonomic changes and see what results you get. Often, the solution to a very complicated problem comes from just trying out a new way. It could be the fastest and least expensive way to learn what will work. If a medication cannot do any harm, try it out!

CASHLESS PRODUCTIVITY GAINS

I have seen many computer justifications that claim "cash" savings for personnel replaced in the calculations, but not in reality. I have called these analytic gyrations the "farmer's horses" justification technique. If a justification calculation bothers your common sense, try applying the "farmer's horses" test. Just ask "How much cash will appear in my bank account?"

The "Farmer's Horses" Method

Here is the "farmer's horses" method: A salesperson tells a farmer that buying a new tractor will increase his efficiency and profitability. For only $50,000 he can buy a 450HP (horsepower) tractor that has a life of 10,000 hours. Running the tractor costs $20/hour. You can buy a horse for $2,000. Maintaining a horse costs $1/hour. Therefore, the salesperson claims, the tractor has a 450:1 cost advantage over horses. The tractor is then worth $898,000 (449 horses x $2,000). The operating cost advantage of a tractor over horses [(450 horses x 10,000 hours x $1/hour)–(10,000 hours x $20/hour)] is $4,300,000.

When the farmer hears the salesman's presentation, he is overjoyed. Before he signs the purchase contract, he pauses. "When can I deposit the $5,198,000 in my bank to pay off the loan for the tractor?" Unfortunately, we do not know exactly what happens after that.

The lesson in this story is that the farmer may need the tractor and has the money to afford it. The new tractor may be essential for the farmer to get his plowing done on time. The farmer should not base his expectations on fictional horses and cash that never comes.

The Time Savings Method

The most frequently applied variant of the farmer's method involves computations where time savings are equated to benefits. Suppose that you can shift 10% of professionals' work to clerical personnel by means of an electronic network. Suppose you can prove that for every hour of professional effort, you can get the same work done by a clerk. Will your savings always be equal to the differences in wage rates, minus computer costs? That depends on answers to questions rarely, if ever, asked.

Could you end 10% of the professionals' work completely through work redesign or simplification? If the work shifts to clerical personnel, will the professionals use the 10% more time available to increase the company's earnings?[23] If you have to hire more clerical personnel, what will be their full cost, including training and administration? Are the computer costs in your calculations incremental, average or full life-cycle costs?

The time-saving method is often used to justify laborsaving investments. Unless you can show how this produces more cash, you will only end up with promises.

You Find Out What You Have Only After You Buy It

The value of computers is what you are willing to pay for results.

Customers lament that they do not know how much they gain from computers. The solution to this problem is easy. Pay for information technology only after you have realized your savings.

This direct approach is not utopian. The Baltimore, Maryland public schools signed a contract with IBM to pay for its microcomputers only after there is an increase in the children's reading test scores.[24] Under a two year contract, IBM will receive $2.9 million if first graders' reading test scores meet expected standards. Otherwise, IBM gets its equipment back and receives only a small fee.

This is an elegant way of avoiding the justification conundrum. This will work if the reading tests are valid and the improvements stay permanent.[25]

A CAD/CAM Case

Direct labor cost-displacement is the preferred way to justify information technology. An illustration of payback computations for a

Computer-Aided Design (CAD) and Computer-Aided Manufacturing (CAM) system shows the following logic:[26]

- The life of the CAD/CAM system is 10,000 hours, which is equivalent to 5 years of single shift operations.
- 20% of the time the equipment will be used for product design to produce drawings.
- CAD/CAM has a 4:1 productivity ratio for design personnel. This translates into an assumption that 20% of the time a designer spends on the system (e.g., 2,000 hours) will be equivalent to his "finding" another 6,000 hours (10,000 hours x 20% x 3) of output during a five-year period.
- A designer/draftsman normally works 2,000 hours per year, of which 60% is productive time. The additional 6,000 hours are equivalent to five extra design personnel [6,000 hours/(60% x 2,000 hours)].
- If designers get $25 per hour, then the earnings of each of the "equivalent" five draftsmen would be $52,000 (52 weeks x 40 hours x $25).
- The five "equivalent" draftsmen (e.g., the draftsmen I do not have) are made possible by the CAD/CAM system. This represents a gross saving of $260,000 per year.
- The annual out-of-pocket costs for maintaining the CAD/CAM system is $185,000. The investment for the CAD/CAM system is $300,000.
- The net annual "cash" flow for the system is $75,000 ($260,000 – $185,000).
- The payback is then 4 years ($300,000/$75,000). With an expected system life of eight years, the internal rate of return is close to 20%.

Would you approve this carefully reasoned proposal? It looks perfectly logical, and therefore should be acceptable. You can simply ask if the entire proposition makes sense from what you know about the work of a designer/draftsman. Can you get 2,000 hours/year from a designer/draftsman? How much of this work is amenable to CAD/CAM treatment?

The core of the justification is in the assumption that you will get a four-fold productivity multiplier. Before you agree with this number, you should find out if it came from an independent source such as another engineering organization operating under comparable conditions. You also may ask about the learning costs before you get a 400% productivity improvement. It takes hundreds of hours before you can expect an engineer, without prior CAD experience, to make full use of it.

If you do not know much about potential productivity gains, you can ask how much cash you can expect to appear in your bank account after your purchase.

According to the proposal, a designer/draftsman working on the CAD/CAM equipment would produce in 368 hours an additional output of 1104 hours (368 x 3) valued at $27,600 per designer. How often can you multiply the $27,600 gain/designer? That depends on the work that needs doing, the capacity of the CAD/CAM equipment, how many individuals require training to operate the new system and how many people will not have to come to work. The proposal is silent on these matters. The $300,000 purchase price and the annual support costs show that you are buying five workstations. The best potential savings are only five times $27,600, or $138,000. That will not cover your annual out-of-pocket costs for the system.

This does not mean you should not buy CAD/CAM workstations. You may desperately need such a system to shorten your product cycle to match your speedier competitors. Do not buy workstations because a proposal claims to expect potential payroll savings of $260,000 per year ($52,000 x 5) when your real cash gains, at best, can be only half of that.

Who Justifies Computers?

Customers, not technologists, get the benefits from computers.

What systems are needed and what is affordable are not necessarily what is technologically possible. Benefits, not costs, are from now on the key to all computer investment decisions.

It is impossible for M.I.S. executives to be accountable for the cost justification of computer investments.[27] The benefits from information technology are realized by the customers, not the information systems function. If the customers own and operate their own computers, they are in a better position to explain why they traded increased computer expenses for other benefits or costs.

New computer applications frequently are intended to eliminate operating problems, correct errors and waste, limit losses or put in proper controls. This calls for someone to get up in front of top management and ask for money that will rectify an undesirable situation. For proper cost justification, somebody must estimate the costs of the losses. How would you like the company's computer executive to make a presentation describing how much money is lost by your department because of faulty management practices?[28] No other subject can create as much misunderstanding as who will propose budget increases for computers.[29] Information executives frequently assume that they should be advocates for innovative computer applications. It is unfortunate that "innovative" usually means greater spending. Why take such a perilous and indefensible position?

Computer executives have a tendency to believe that they have better qualifications to judge potential computer benefits than executives without technological knowledge. A 1988 survey from the Index Group[30] reports that functional managers, not computer executives, are increasingly making decisions about information technology. Yet only 38% of the computer executives believe that the non-M.I.S. managers understand the potential value of information technology in their business. M.I.S. executives also placed cost cutting within M.I.S. on low priority (#14 out of 20). Only 8% of the M.I.S. executives felt that their own budgets were too high.[31]

How Much to Spend on Project Justification

Clients often ask me how much time should be spent on project planning, including financial analysis, before proceeding with the implementation of a new computer system. I subscribe to the doctrine that you aim before you shoot. If you hunt for deer that can disappear in 5–10 seconds, you cannot afford more than one second for aiming. If you are planning a new *mission critical* system that will remain in place for a decade or more, you should not hurry with securing top management approval.

You should spend at least 5% of total life-cycle development plus maintenance costs (discounted) and more than 5% of total elapsed implementation time in the planning and justification phase. A two-year, $1 million project should have allocated to it at least $50,000 and five weeks to project planning prior to being submitted for approval.

Project planning must include the costs and the time for pilot or prototype testing. Prototype verification should be a major early milestone prior to securing approvals to proceed with full implementation. All that top management can reasonably expect from the project planning phase is to obtain the range within which project management will keep the financial projections to retain the go-ahead approval.

Money to fund project proposals should not require formal justification, only a general outline of intent and scope. Every systems organization should have at least 5% of its total development resources available for exploratory purposes of which at least half will not get approved (for *Average* organizations and more than that for *Overachievers*). Systems organizations incur cost overruns because they seek top management authorization prematurely. To justify spending on the planning phase the proponents find it necessary to guess at the costs and benefits on the basis of only scanty evidence.[32]

Management should consider requests for project funding only after the proponents can commit to keeping a project within the limits of a thoroughly explored risk profile.

CHAPTER SUMMARY

The business value of information technology is the present worth of gains reflected in your business plans when you add information technology. It is equal to the present cash value of the difference between:

Business Plan With Changes to *Information Technology* Costs
and
Business Plan Without Changes to *Information Technology* Costs

Each firm always will have many requests for added information technology spending. The benefits of improved management processes ultimately may appear as gains in market share, better prices, reduced inventories or highly motivated employees. Top management has the job of judging the merits of information technology proposals. Only top management can evaluate how information technology investments compare with other uses of money. The discipline of risk-adjusted discounted cash flow makes such comparisons possible.

Chapter 10 Comments

[1] The term "finding the alignment of IS with business goals" is acknowledged by information systems executives as their principal weakness. Since 1983 it has ranked consistently as the #1 information management issue, by a wide margin, as reported by D.L. Amoroso, R. Thompson, P.H. Cheney, Examining the Duality Role of I.S. Executives, *Information & Management*, 17, 1989.

[2] Bear in mind that according to the 1989 *Computerworld* CEO survey, 64% of CEOs in large companies did not think their firms were getting their money's worth from computers. A follow-up survey of managers in midsize companies has found that nearly half are unhappy with their information systems investments because information systems managers can't align information systems with business goals (*Computerworld*, June 11, 1990, p.2).

[3] This is the "hockey stick" plan because of the shape of the projected earnings. Hockey stick plans always promise great gains, but only in the more distant future.

[4] Completed early in 1987.

[5] This competitor was a one time-licensee who originally received the firm's technology to serve another market.

[6] The principal competitor's production methods were already well-tuned to supplying customers who carried no parts or semi-finished product inventories.

[7] The shareholder value is the price of a share multiplied by the number of shares.

[8] Poorly defined objectives or ambiguous goals have the most destructive effect on the capacity of project managers to deliver results. For a study of 100 projects see H.J. Thamhain and D.L. Wilemon, Diagnosing Conflict Determinants in Project Management, *IEEE Transactions on Engineering Management*, Vol. EM-22, February 1975

[9] How could the M.I.S. Director be so sure that the speed-up was possible? A year earlier a bootlegged Operations Research study proved that the Division suffered from archaic administrative practices and adherence to parochial departmental procedures, especially in Materials Purchasing. Large clerical staffs were kept busy expediting and coordinating delayed or mis-routed shipments. A model of the plant's information flow was constructed using the STELLA SIMULATION software from the *High Performance Systems Corporation*. The simulation showed that speeding up information and a few changes in materials buying policies would not only improve the logistics, but also reduce work-in-process and finished goods inventories.

[10] All cost and benefit estimates that follow are in summary form to show only *incremental* changes from *base cost* projections. To establish the integrity and credibility of all investment proposals it is essential that every projection begin with the current business plan, without the proposed investment.

[11] When the M.I.S. Director gives a tour of his data center, he takes pride in shutting off all lights when he leaves the room.

[12] He would impose on his own suppliers the just-in-time discipline.

[13] Telling your management how much contingency money you need is always a good policy. It improves your credibility. It ends the need to hide the risks of your venture. It is always better to deliver superior results for less money than to request budget supplements because you did not originally have the courage to tell what could possibly go wrong.

[14] The expected mean value of the cumulative net cash flows since the inception of the project. The 95% band around the mean expected value comes from assumptions about costs, benefits and risks.

[15] Discounted present worth at 12% cost of borrowed capital.

[16] Through financial simulation. Sensitivity analysis made it possible to rank the largest negative effects on cash flow.

[17] Measured in free cash flow instead of reported accounting profits.

[18] Completed in a few hours by re-running the ALCAR Group's VALUE PLANNER software. This is the most sophisticated and maybe most widely used package for analyzing the financial health of companies.

[19] N.D. Meyer and M.E. Boone, The Information Edge, *McGraw-Hill Book Company*, New York, 1987.

[20] The STK case is based on information from Schatz, *Datamation*, August 15, 1988

[21] The proposed ergonomic investments by STK will not reduce employee turnover and absenteeism to 0%. To come up with a formal justification, the STK manager would have to multiply the maximum benefits by a percentage of "achievable benefits" that is better than 30.1%.

[22] Half of the available time of new employees can go into training during the first three months on the job (E. Graham, High-Tech Training, *Wall Street Journal*, February 9, 1990, p.R.16). Only 5% of that would be in formal training. Graham finds that additional training comes from: 50 hours watching others, 80 hours informal training by managers, 50 hours informal training by other workers. High employee turnover rates either from new hires or from job re-assignments have a disruptive effect on productivity. This effect is rarely included in computer justification proposals.

[23] A mathematically elegant method for evaluating the best mix of work in a department comes from P.G. Sassone, A Survey of Cost-benefit Methodologies for Information Systems, *Project Appraisal*, June 1988. His "hedonic" wage model requires that the marginal values and the revenue contributions of a man-year of managerial, professional and clerical work be known. The work profiles (percentage of time each occupation expends on different types of work) are also a needed input. Case studies are necessary to show that the hedonic wage model applies to business applications.

[24] Wall Street Journal, November 15, 1989, p. B1. One third of first-graders will receive the computers.

[25] This contract needs imitation if the pre- and post-testing guards against the *Hawthorne Effect*. This effect has its origins in an experiment at Western Electric's Hawthorne plant, where productivity improved because the workers received special attention, not because physical conditions changed. I have little doubt that the *Hawthorne Effect* will be alive and present in Baltimore when the time comes in 1991 to pay up. Unless the Baltimore Board of Education sets up this contract as a controlled experiment, we shall wonder how much the reading scores would improve without computers. The experiment will be valid if the additional teacher training, the attention from IBM support people, the money and the parent's involvement equally apply to a comparable group of children who do not get personal computers.

[26] The CAD/CAM case is in Exhibit 1 of Cost Accounting for Factory Automation. R.E. Bennett, J.A. Hendricks, D.E. Keys, E.J. Rudnicki, Cost Accounting for Factory Automation, *National Association of Accountants*, Montvale, N.J., 1987.

In the same publication (p. 27) we find an interesting comment about the problems with traditional capital budgeting approaches: "...the study group readily admitted that their attempts to justify acquisition of a CAD/CAM system using traditional capital budgeting approaches fell short of the rate of return normally required to get approval. However, in most of the companies, top management was convinced that the qualitative benefits were so attractive that they approved acquisition despite the unsatisfactory performance shown by the capital budgeting models." Supplementary measurement tools are necessary to deal with the situation. For instance, "...the benefit of the CAD/CAM system is a reduction in the length of the product cycle. A shortening of this cycle must bring net cost savings and/or other competitive advantages." Applying the farmer's common sense approach, you would then justify CAD/CAM based on your ability to get business which otherwise would go to faster competitors. Computing the worth of losing market share is a complex calculation. If defending your market share is the reason you need CAD/CAM, then you do not need fictional gains in designers you will never have.

[27] Except for cost reductions within M.I.S.

28 D. Mattson, How to Educate Senior Executives, *InformationWeek*, February 13, 1989, p. 56 recommends that is what chief information executives should do. To sell projects Mattson recommends that the M.I.S. executive describe hidden problems and costs of past mistakes in other departments to "...get upper management's attention and approval for a systems project."

29 A survey of 100 M.I.S. executives and their counterpart General Managers found major disagreements about who should do cost justification (Ravinder Nath, Aligning M.I.S. With the Business Goals, *Information & Management Journal*, 16 (1989), p. 71). General Managers attached very low importance to cost justification by M.I.S. executives, whereas M.I.S. ranked it as their fourth among the essential tasks. The General Managers reflected a realistic view of what can be credibly done.

Two more recent surveys (1989 and 1990) of 243 M.I.S. Executives by the Index Group showed that "cutting IS costs" ranked #10 and #14 on their priority list—at the bottom (C.Wilder, Re-Engineering is IS Priority, *Computerworld*, February 5, 1990).

30 Critical Issues of Information Systems Management for 1989, *Index Group*, Cambridge, Mass. December 1988. Out of 3,500 questionnaires there were only 324 responses. I always wonder what is the bias of those who respond to questionnaires about their careers. I suspect that optimists who are not very busy are likelier to reply to a survey than harried realists.

31 The same M.I.S. executives admitted that 32% of their senior managers in the USA (39% in Europe) felt that too much money was spent on computers.

32 This practice is prevalent in the public sector and vendor-inspired ventures. Legislative Committees, auditors and some executives who never liked a project will always quote the early estimates as the benchmark against which they compare actual costs.

11

COST MANAGEMENT

Nothing in history is comparable to the dramatic and steady cost reductions available from information technology products and services. Since the advent of the industrial revolution, we have seen enormous gains in the efficiency of agricultural production, transportation equipment and machine tools. However, even the largest recorded gains in physical output per year are less than one tenth of the improvement we have witnessed in information processing over the last thirty years. Therefore, attention to cost management is necessary to secure for your company those gains that information technology suppliers have made available and will continue to provide in the foreseeable future.

INSTALLATION COSTS

When new models of computers appear, the prices of the equipment receive most of the attention. From the customer's standpoint, a decision to buy based only on equipment costs will always be incorrect, because the total costs of computing are much larger than the costs of computers:[1]

256   THE BUSINESS VALUE OF COMPUTERS

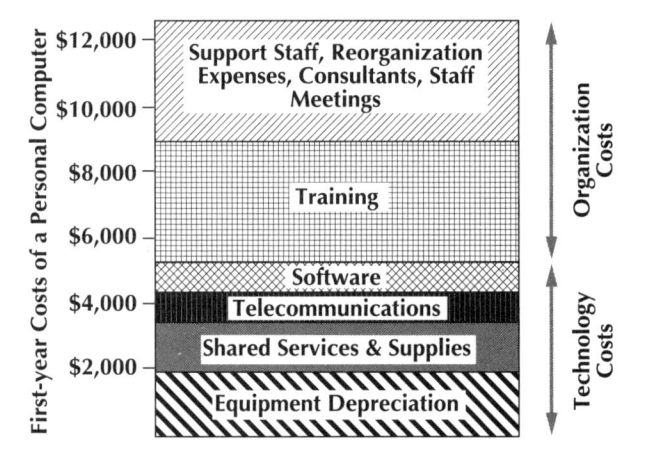

Figure 11.1: Organization Costs are Larger than Technology Costs

How you manage information technology has a greater influence on ownership costs than the price of computers. "Organization costs" will always exceed the depreciation expense for equipment. The "organization costs" vary depending on the quality of support for making the transition from manual to automated processing.

COSTS OF RESOURCE SHARING

The technology costs of ownership of clustered personal computers will change depending on resource sharing. Non-CPU expenses will dominate, as illustrated in the following comparison:[2]

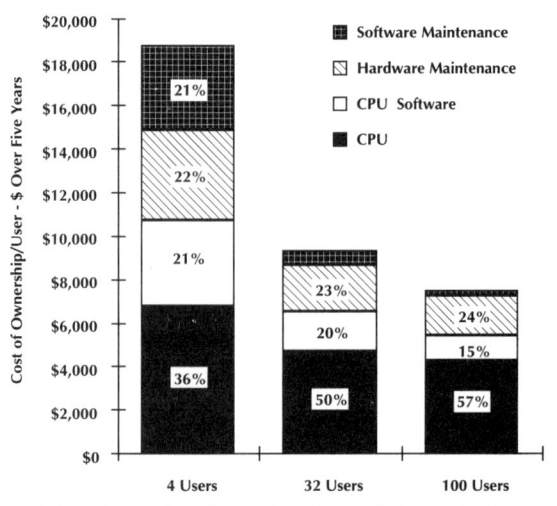

Figure 11.2: Example of Per User Cost of Network Ownership

There are cost advantages to sharing the ownership of information technologies, especially in lower software support and software costs. The technology costs of centrally managed computing[3] resources are potentially much lower than those for distributed computing.

For example, consider the costs of an IBM 4381-24 MVS-XA processor purchased from a third party for $950,000. The five-year cost of software[4] will run about $2.2 million. To that you have to add costs for operators, data control costs, telecommunications support, systems engineering expenses, hardware maintenance, electrical expense, air-conditioning, security and back-up expenses of at least $2 million for five years. It will pay to consider consolidating small data centers into super-centers.[5]

Airline reservation systems provide us with a case study of the economics of network computing. The scope and function of this application are comparable for each system. There is intense competition among airlines in offering their services to travel agents. Therefore, reservation systems managers are under formidable pressure to minimize their expenses.

Airlines differ, however, in their market share as defined by the percentage of penetration of U.S. travel agencies. I found that the average fully allocated unit cost, per passenger reservation, relates directly to the market share enjoyed by each competing system:[6]

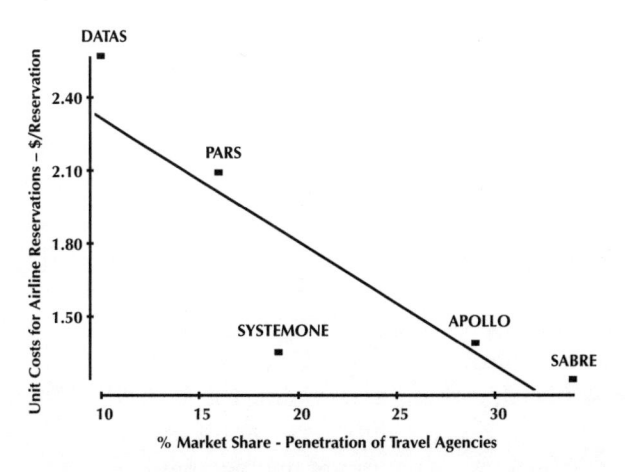

Figure 11.3: Economies in Airline Reservation Networks

You may then wonder why there are so many micro- and mini-computers that do not share software, filing, printing, support, security and telecommunication gateway resources. The following list offers a few explanations for the opposition to central computing:

- Central computing services carry a burden of overhead costs which does not occur with distributed processing. This makes central computing appear to be more expensive.
- Central computing services must distribute their overhead costs equally. Customers receive a share of overhead regardless of whether they benefit from it. This leads to the customers' resentment of arbitrary allocations.
- Central computing tends to subsidize applications and technology development, which some customers will find to be irrelevant.
- When top management constrains central computing budgets, the customers' own priorities may suffer.
- A steadily growing overhead in central computing[7] and its vulnerability to arbitrary budget limitations eliminates many of the intrinsic advantages of sharing resources.
- The advantages of direct customer control over decisions where, when and how to implement computer applications can far outweigh the benefit of lower technology costs for central computing. The cost difference between individual and shared resources of approximately $2,000–$3,000 per workstation per year can disappear in negotiations[8] with M.I.S. managers about schedules and priorities.

To maximize the business value of computers, the decision of centralization versus decentralization of computing resources should consider the full costs of each alternative. I find that individual customers and small functional groups justify the ownership of their own computers for reasons that have little to do with the economics of information technology. Their justification depends on their problems of coping with a bureaucratic institution. While "central computing" remains synonymous with "inflexible monopoly," customers will seek relief through alternatives that offer them greater control. Individual managers will seek to acquire their own computers even if this requires them to get into the costly business of computer management.

When top management confronts yet another emphatic request for a new stand-alone computer, they should insist on a full disclosure of all expenses. Such a review should be thorough, because I have yet to find a proposal for a new computer operation that reflects its full costs.

Cost Reduction

A penny saved is a penny earned.

A steady reduction in the unit costs of computerized transactions should be the key indicator that the information technologists are doing a good job. Whenever you receive promises about benefits from computers, lock the anticipated gains into lower unit cost targets. The achievement of promised cost reductions should show up when next year's unit costs compare favorably against a revised cost target.

Equipment vendors offer rapidly decreasing costs in electronics and telecommunications. Software companies are offering a steady stream of innovations that speed up processing and reduce maintenance costs. Consultants offer application redesign services to relieve the burden of costly and error-prone software maintenance.[9] Voice-input and optical scanning devices offer the potential of labor-savings in input.

Executives should demand that all investment proposals include, by major information processing activity, expected cost-reduction goals. Activity planning of productivity gains is necessary because conventional accounting does not break out expenses into categories amenable to setting cost-improvement targets:

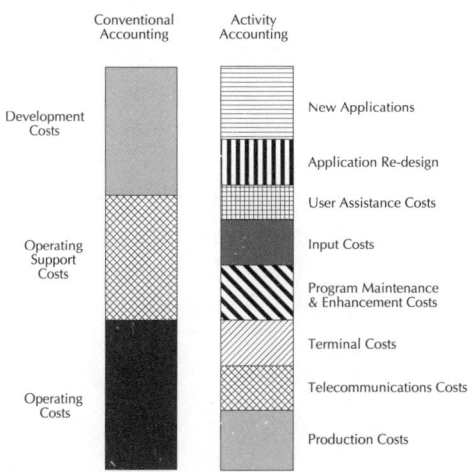

Figure 11.4: Example of Activities for Setting Cost Reduction Targets

M.I.S. staffs can apply proven methods for reducing expenses in ways that until recently were technically not possible. These include:
- Computer room and network automation.[10]
- Discount packages for voice and data networks offered by

telephone carriers locked into intense competition to win large accounts.
- "Tariff hunting" consultants offer their services to identify cost-reduction opportunities.[11]
- Improved reliability and maintenance of programs by using Computer-Aided Systems Engineering (CASE) methods.
- Buying software from a rapidly growing number of proven suppliers.[12]
- Instituting price-oriented buying policies by buying computing management services from facility management companies,[13] purchasing used equipment and contracting for turn-key applications.
- Moving specialized applications from mainframe computers to microcomputers. On interactive applications with small databases, large cost reductions are available by making such shifts in processing.

Despite the opportunities to reap the benefits of lower technology costs most information systems executives do not believe that it is possible to reduce spending.[14] Corporate management has not yet placed computer operating cost reductions high on the M.I.S. agenda, because development projects always seems to be of greater interest. Yet, operations and operations support costs always will dominate the budget. Consider the breakdown of the $1.6 billion annual budget for information technology of Merrill Lynch & Co. Only 2.5% of that budget is for new applications and 7.5% for program maintenance.[15]

The cost-reduction potential warrants management's concerted attention to this opportunity. To determine how large this is I can give you a suggestion of what the numbers may look like. For instance, the following lists the annual decline in the market price of used IBM computers over the last four years:[16]

Computer	1986	1987	1988	1989	4-yr Average
3090	-10%	-23%	-29%	-17%	-20%
308X	-52%	-32%	-57%	-53%	-42%
4381	-31%	-38%	-52%	-48%	-38%
Disk drives, misc.	-15%	-23%	-35%	-33%	-22%
Tapes, misc.	-15%	-23%	-31%	-34%	-16%
Printers, misc.	-13%	-22%	-42%	-15%	-27%

Table 11.1: Decline in the Market Price of IBM Computers

There are conditions when equipment depreciates faster than the industry average, such as when a product family comes to the end of its technological life. The projection of such reductions should be in all proposals and should influence the choice of technologies. The latest technology announcement may not offer the best value.

Take, for instance, the rapid advances in disk drives that have steadily driven prices down 30 to 50% per year. Buying equipment at full list price may be too costly as compared with waiting for a lower price. Well-maintained disk drives do not physically wear out as compared with other production equipment.[17] The current forecasts foresee the residual values, which equal market prices, to decline 40–45% per year. Disks are electromechanical devices that realize smaller cost reductions than computers made up mostly of semi-conductors. Medium-sized computer installations would have 10 to 20 disk drives. Taking advantage of the industry's cost declines has the potential of generating $200,000 to $400,000 savings in the first few years. This should show up as large annual price cuts to customers.[18] I do not think your management can find comparable unit cost-reductions without degrading quality anywhere else in your company.

Even bigger savings are available for mainframes and communications equipment.[19] Dramatic market price reductions are now taking place in mid-size computers which are being rapidly displaced by high-performance workstations. Large annual reductions in the market price of equipment are not unusual, as illustrated by the estimated residual values of the DEC Microvax 3500 computer.[20]

Competent M.I.S. executives, before making any other claims about their contributions to their firms, must show that they are tracking the declining cost/performance trends offered by computer manufacturers.

Very few M.I.S. executives have concentrated on cost reduction as a means for advancing their careers. Most of the time they can avoid accountability for increased costs by pointing to rising demand for computer services. They were safe in concentrating on more spectacular feats—such as promoting the competitive advantage and strategic opportunity of computers—because the overhead cost-accounting methods could not address the productivity of computing services.

Productivity Reporting for Computing Services

In a typical data center, the volume of work and costs will change rapidly. A monthly comparison of the charges for processing services will not reveal whether there were any productivity gains.[21] To show productivity improvements, the indexed method of analyzing data center charges should be valuable for executive reviews. Using inflation-adjusted prices for comparative purposes is an accepted accounting method for cost analysis in manufacturing. This approach is absolutely necessary for making sense of data services charges, which are a combination of mildly inflationary (for labor and supplies) and strongly deflationary (information technology) expenses.

The conventional method of cost analysis, noted in Table 11.2 as the *Current Price Method*, shows the cost of an invoice. A decline from 100¢ to 80¢ per invoice would suggest that data center productivity has risen 20%. Is that a realistic appraisal of actual productivity gains?

	1988	1989	Productivity
Number of Invoices	200,000	250,000	
Current Price Method			
Labor Cost	$50,000	$52,000	
Computer Processing Cost	$150,000	$148,000	
Unit Labor Cost	$0.250	$0.208	+16.80%
Unit Processing Cost	$0.750	$0.592	+21.07%
Total Unit Cost	$1.000	$0.800	+20.00%
Real Price Method (1989=100)			
Unit Labor Cost (Index=107.5)	$0.269	$0.208	+22.60%
Unit Processing Cost (Index=74)	$0.555	$0.592	−6.67%
Total Unit Cost	$0.824	$0.800	+2.88%

Table 11.2: Reporting Real Information Processing Productivity

Using the *Real Price Method*, which reflects changes in the cost structure, we obtain different results. With inflationary labor cost increases of 7.5%, the comparable labor cost of $0.250 in 1988 dollars is actually $0.269 in terms of 1989 prices. Therefore the real (inflation adjusted) productivity gain of labor is +22.60% instead of +16.8% computed by the *Current Price Method*.

The *Real Price Method* is unforgiving when it comes to reporting the productivity gains for computing. While the *Current Price Method* suggests that the data center has reduced unit costs by +21.07%, the real productivity change is a loss of −6.67%. $0.750 worth of computing in 1988 should have cost $0.555, in 1989 terms. The reason for this difference is the *Computer Cost Index* which I have set at 74 based on earlier technology improvement proposals.

A steady and consistent demonstration of real productivity gains in information services must be one of the key indicators that information technology resources are efficient.

Managing the Costs of Computing Services

Cost reductions do not occur easily if fixed-cost allocations, such as corporate overhead, support of planning staffs and expenditures for the technology "infrastructure," overwhelm your controllable expenses. What do you charge your customers for their share of a corporate database? How do you distribute the overhead expense for managing a data network? To whom do you pass the expenses for maintaining security, auditing, systems architecture development, standards and capacity planning? If you must convert to a new operating system to take advantage of new technologies, who will bear today's expenses to realize benefits that may come only in the future? Customers will view cost-reduction as a hopeless task if their costs go up anyway because they are allocated over a smaller base of direct expenses.

The economics of new systems will differ depending on the accounting methods used for allocating the costs of the computing infrastructure.[22] If a communications network is already in place, a new application would incur only a small incremental cost. This will reflect marginal costs but will not generate enough money for innovation when the time comes to replace or upgrade the network. Similarly, in the case of an installed database, the cost of making an additional inquiry is only a small fraction of the fully allocated average cost.

Pricing computer services at an incremental cost for new applications, a frequent practice to entice new customers, makes it difficult to use data center charges to make decisions concerning when to adopt new technologies. You will end up with dissatisfied customers, because older applications will now carry a disproportionate share of overhead costs. Customers will not trust their expense forecasts unless the prices for computing services are simple and consistently declining over many years. Their proposals to apply computers to improving productivity will be unnecessarily risky, and therefore they will tend to invest less.[23]

One of the most counterproductive pricing policies involves the monthly distributions of expenses to customers. Costs for the same work will fluctuate, sometimes wildly.[24] The customers will gain no experience in cost management. Their invoices will reflect not only changes in their own demand, but also the demand from others and how central overhead is allocated. The customers of computer services will not have much of an incentive to press for immediate cost reductions. Their invoices will not tell them if their efforts produced any results.

Competitive Pricing of Computer Services

Meeting the budget target is OK except when the budget 300% of what it ought to be.

"We want to compete globally, but before we can do that we have to become competitive internally..."[25] sums up the argument from Bell Atlantic that internal staffs should charge for inter-departmental services using competitive prices, not costs. This approach makes each business function a profit center. It calls for information systems, medical services, business research, training and development, and others to pay their expenses, including rent, office equipment, salaries and benefits with what they earn. They charge for their services at market competitive rates. Profits go back to the corporation. If a department does not break even, it could get a new manager, reduce its costs or be replaced by contract services. Bell Atlantic departments now haggle over prices and demand good service from internal suppliers. After seeing the price for a fancy computer program, one department manager decided she could make do with a simpler and cheaper one.

The Bell Atlantic experience is not entirely new. In 1971, I formed in Xerox the Information Services Division (I.S.D.), that provided internal services with prices set by competitive benchmarks. As a safeguard against monopoly control, customers were free to buy services from outside suppliers, as long as I.S.D. could return with a second bid. I encouraged excursions to outside suppliers because during periods of rapidly escalating demand we could not satisfy everyone's needs. In this process I learned that any internal monopoly that would have tried to provide 100% of the needed capacity would be exorbitantly expensive.

The cost of introducing new technology is always expensive. It absorbs large amounts of management attention, time of staff planners and training of personnel in new skills. All these are not chargeable overhead. The most effective way to introduce technology innovation is to find a supplier who has progressed far on his learning curve. This supplier will sell the new technology at an attractive price in the hope of building enough volume to reach his growth and profit goals. Such a vendor will accept mutually advantageous contracts in which cross-licensing and knowledge-transfer occurs between the vendor and customer if the volume reaches economically attractive levels for the customer. Such a deal made it possible for Xerox to introduce APL time-sharing for thousands of terminals, faster and cheaper than was done by any other major corporation.

After two years of healthy profits, we changed the pricing formula to *competitive benchmark price minus industry marketing expenses*. Taking marketing expenses out of the price made sense because I.S.D. enjoyed a preferred vendor status. We did not have the sizable marketing costs of computer services vendors who were competing for our business.[26]

We adopted pricing methods that imitated the cost accounting practices then in use by the most successful low-cost computer services firm we could find.[27] Investments in the computing and telecommunications infrastructure came from the Services Divisions' accounting profits. An internal Board helped to decide how year-end accounting profits would be reinvested into promising new ventures.

Pricing computer services at competitive rates makes it easier for customers to concentrate on the benefits of their proposals. They do not suffer from unnecessary anxiety that costs would escalate for reasons out of their control.

Activity Pricing for Computer Services

The Xerox Information Services Division charged a standard activity price for every product, such as screen transactions, reports, checks and invoices. The monthly invoice showed the quantities for each item, multiplied by the unit price. The price per item would not change for an entire year.[28] At budget time, these prices were expected to show year-to-year price reductions. Top management judged the productivity of the Division by its ability to take down unit prices at least 15% per year while showing a profit.

The activity price for each item was set at the start of each budget cycle. For each item there was a "bill of materials" sheet. This showed the breakdown of each "product" into its most elementary components, such as disk accesses, computer calculating cycles, lines of printing and even the cost of paper. The "service bill of materials" also would show the overhead burden, such as electricity and supervision, applied to each cost element. The customer could examine each item on the cost sheet. The customer receiving I.S.D. services could then decide on cost-reduction priorities. For instance, the customer could decide whether to spend money on maintenance or program redesign.

Internal customers had every incentive to invest in cost reductions. They could fund program re-engineering projects to cut run time or program maintenance costs. They could simplify on-line displays to stop superfluous disk accesses. They could switch from paper to microfilm to reduce the report-handling labor costs. The customers' unit prices would come down immediately after an improvement would go into effect. The customers saw the results of their cost-management efforts on the next monthly invoice.

The stable and predictable application of unit pricing policies made it possible for customers to submit their business proposals with confidence. They would be in control of their operating costs.

Facility Management

Exporting all difficulties to a "facility manager" is becoming an attractive solution for managing the costs of information technology. This involves a long-term contract, sometimes for 10 years. The terms of the contract provide for profit incentives for the contractor to keep his billings within prescribed budgetary limits. These arrangements always expect large cost reductions. In its simplest form, facility management calls for the contractor to take over the management of central data processing operations, administration of telecommunications networks and supply of systems engineering support to personnel who stay on the company's payroll. Sometimes the facility contractor also takes over the entire programming staff.

Until recently, facility management contracts were common mostly to government departments and health insurance firms. These are sectors that could tolerate contract awards based on a cost-plus fixed fee formula. Decreasing profits, especially among petroleum companies and savings banks, have made it attractive to hire facility management firms because these firms had built up excessive data processing capacity and expensive staffs. Their cost reductions were long overdue.

The reason for engaging a facility manager is not always cost-reduction. There are manufacturing firms that chose facility management after proving that they could cut costs without mercy. Executives chose to contract out for computer services because they were not comfortable with managing the downsizing of this large accumulation of fixed overhead. Operating computer services was not an essential managerial skill for meeting global competition. Top management could then concentrate on applying computers to improving decision-making and better support of customers. The facility managers offer not only cost reductions in running data center operations, but also the discipline of transaction-pricing and conversion of fixed costs to variable expenses.

Facility managers offer a more effective method for controlling the costs of information services. They give something that the company could have provided itself, if it wished to do so. Subcontracting (also called *outsourcing*) of information services is often a maneuver to shift control over information technologies from the M.I.S. function to the business functions such as purchasing, manufacturing and personnel. M.I.S. Departments that had the foresight to adopt competitive pricing for their services are in little jeopardy of being discarded.[29] Their companies would not be given the incentive to choose divestiture as a way of solving a festering financial and organizational problem.

The primary reason GM had for buying Electronic Data Systems (EDS) was the acquisition of expertise to manage GM's unwieldy multi-billion dollar per year internal computer establishment. The conflict between the EDS roles as a facility manager and its profit-making goals may frustrate GM from taking full advantage of the available technical know-how. Similar conflicts arose within every aerospace company when they spun off their internal computer operations as diversifications from their cyclical defense business. If a for-profit subsidiary does not get much business from external sources, it is difficult to allocate overhead fairly to internal customers. The inevitable pressures to push for higher profits from a computer service Division will make internal customers always unhappy about their bills.

An arm's-length commercial relationship between computer services and executives who wish to divest themselves of their computer operations seems to work.[30] Consider the $750 million ten-year contract from the Enron Corporation to EDS.[31] Enron's aims are clear. They expect to save $200 million over the life of the contract. Enron will get from EDS monthly invoices that show the prices and volume of computing services. Enron will not only get cost reductions, but also a clearer means to shift control over information technology to the ultimate customer who requests the computer services. Though buying computer services at a lower price was Enron's primary objective, they will end up with a different approach to managing information technology. They will shift control from the M.I.S. function to Enron line managers, who will have to learn to become smart buyers of information services.

Why Competitive Pricing Will Prevail

The financing of computer operations from central overhead or allocated "chargeouts" has evolved from practices that prevailed when computers first came into corporations. When central computers delivered pre-defined and pre-programmed output to users, all costs were made part of the fixed overhead. Central management and control offered the best solution.

New forms of computing are now emerging. Distributed systems having thousands of computing sites (including print, file, communications, gateway and database *servers*) and tens of thousands of workstations are spreading throughout the world. Any one workstation or node may communicate with many others, internally or externally from the organization.

Unlike stand-alone computers or company dedicated networks, future networks cannot be scheduled centrally. The allocation of computing resources will be unpredictable, because customers will have many choices of how to get a job completed. Computational tasks will seek out those computing nodes or databases that offer the greatest immediate advantage. All applications will reside within powerful personal workstations which will serve each customer by sending out intelligent computational "program agents" to obtain answers to a specific question. The innovative enabling technology for this approach to computing will be the availability of high bandwidth communication links that will be capable of transmitting information at presently available microcomputer data-channel speeds[32]:

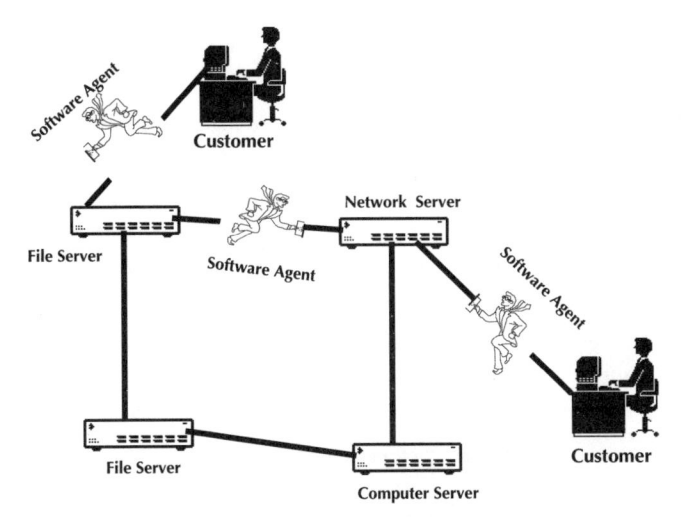

Figure 11.5: Control over Computer Costs is Discretionary and Instant

In addition to its technological feasibility, this approach to "asynchronous computation"[33] is possible only if there is a marketplace for computing resources in which real-time auctioning of computer services can occur. An idle processor at 4 AM in Singapore can offer a spot price for computing and message switching cheaper than someone operating in New York on a late Friday afternoon.[34]

In the existing closed corporate system the pricing for computer services is comparable to the ways medieval guilds, or East European command economies, regulated the supply of products and set prices. In each case, this required a central planner who had accurate knowledge (and control) of the supply and demand for goods. Such a system worked adequately only for economies that were slow to innovate. In tomorrow's global competitive environment, low-cost and rapid-response electronic communications will be a prerequisite for economic survival.

If you have an "open systems" architecture, and store your databases on widely distributed processors, the central setting of prices is not feasible. Complex networks depend on market-based pricing to remain economically viable. In our example, the "program agent" in the New York customer's computer will "contract" with the Singapore computing node following real-time "shopping" for the least cost and most reliable service.

Economic systems have evolved successfully despite imperfect knowledge of their markets. Economies that mandate central price and capacity setting stagnate after they try to advance beyond the most elementary levels of development.

A competitive pricing system must prevail if information services progress beyond their existing limits. Monopolistic pricing for computer services, whether you find it in intra-company situations or in legally protected cartels, will be uneconomic, costly and unresponsive to customer needs. Forward-looking executives should make sure that their companies begin the migration to market-based pricing of internal information services.[35] They may do so eventually, but in haste and without choice.

COMPETITIVE SIMULATION

Spreadsheets are the favorite planning tool to explore different scenarios for computer investments. You can use a spreadsheet to build elaborate models involving many variables. This works as long as the line items or columns of numbers do not interact as time passes. Spreadsheets cannot reflect "feedback" effects, when the result of a computation changes the rules for making the computation next time.

The dynamics of competition between high fixed costs and low marginal cost show up best in a simulation.[36] This technique recognizes that organizations react to changes in their environment, which is hard to do using spreadsheets.

Customers who are unhappy about the costs and delays of service from central computing operations acquire personal computers and local area networks. Transferring transactions from central computing to widely distributed microprocessors illustrates how to study what happens if customers have choices of where to process their computer applications.[37]

The diagram in Figure 11.6 is a simplified version of a cost-simulation model.[38] The block labelled *Total Customer Demand* generates a steady stream of transactions. The data center has a *Variable Cost* for processing each transaction. Each customer also gets a bill for *Variable Costs* plus a share of *Fixed Costs* which is proportional to the number of transactions.

One customer searches for cost reductions after reporting and budgeting delays (represented by the clock icon). He buys a few personal computers and removes from *Central Transactions* those demands that bear the highest share of overhead costs. After year #1 this customer finds that his unit costs for *Local Transactions* are less than the data center *Variable Costs*.

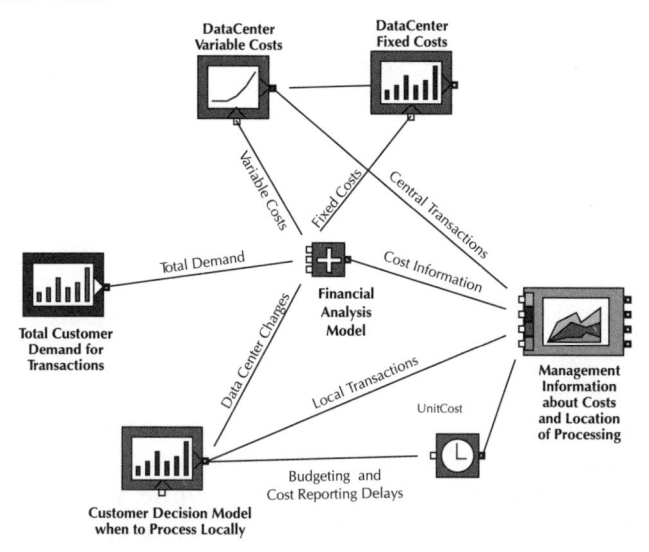

Figure 11.6: Logic of Data Center Cost Simulation

At the beginning of year #2, additional customers request immediate cost reductions from the data center. They plan to move their demand from *Central Transactions* to *Local Transactions,* based on the difference between the data center's charges and their own costs.[39]

To deal with the challenges from customers, data center management reduces overhead costs by 30%. This is the maximum they can do considering the limited time and large fixed costs.[40] The data center's projected unit costs for year #2 are now lower, but still do not meet the customer's expectations of unit costs realized by the first defecting customer in year #1.

Year #3 comes and the business does not generate the added volume of new transactions for the data center that would replace the lost business. Meanwhile, the transfer from *Central Transactions* to *Local Transactions* encourages the customers to simplify their *Local Transaction* workload. The effect on the data center is disastrous:

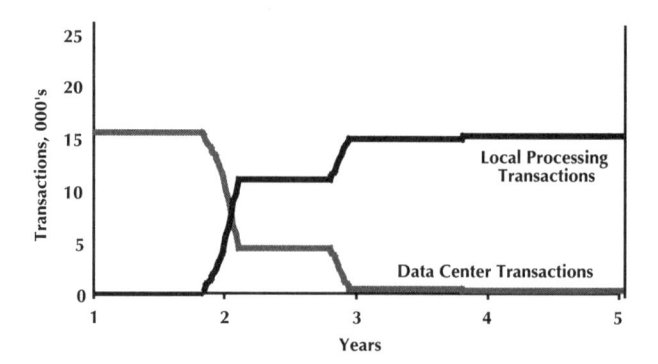

Figure 11.7: Results of Data Center Cost Simulation

Data center unit costs per transaction after year #2 are now much higher than before. More customers decide to transfer their workload to *Local Transactions*. Corporate staff now examines the prospect of a declining workload and high *Fixed Costs*. They recommend closing down the data center and "outsourcing" whatever workload remains.

It is a traumatic experience for everyone when customer-controlled computing on microcomputers competes against central processing managed by M.I.S:

- Data centers that fund exploratory projects, labor-intensive services, innovative technology and corporate projects become vulnerable to competition. Departmental or individual applications can always claim lower costs by charging their management and development costs to their general administrative accounts.
- Data centers that respond to customer requests for error correction, output delivery, acceptance testing, minor program changes and security services (such as back-up of files and recovery capacity) should bill for such work. This will alert the customer to the complexity of the services supplied by the central services.
- Marginal costs should not be the justification for decentralized investments. Any justifications of departmental computing should prove that overhead functions will not reappear under a different label. Almost every microcomputer proposal is faulty because of underestimation of security, file safeguarding, retraining, effort diversion, added managerial attention and technical support costs.

In other words, itemize and pay for every activity required to get the job done.

• High-overhead operations are vulnerable to catastrophic increases in unit costs if there is a sudden decline in the volume of business. There are situations where even dramatic cuts in overhead costs are insufficient to arrest such hemorrhage.[41]

CHAPTER SUMMARY

When you put together an investment proposal for new computer applications, your cost projections reflect how you expect to pay for them. Market-tested pricing of computer services is the key to forging the links between the customer and supplier. The business value of computers becomes visible not by financial analysis, but through interactions between value-creating customers and their technology suppliers. For a long time computers have served local technological monopolies. Without market competition and external cost comparisons, even the most impressive investment proposals may not be adequate to deliver what the business needs for success.

CHAPTER 11 COMMENTS

[1] For instance, H. Frost, Time for Change, *Computerworld Focus*, March 2, 1988 shows the following costs per MIP (million instructions per second) for different computers: Macintosh II=$2,000; Sun 3/2000=$4,000; HP 3000/930=$4,500; IBM 3090/120E=$7,500; IBM 3090/600E=$75,000. It does not follow that you should get rid of your IBM 3090's and put everything on Macintosh workstations. The total life-cycle cost of delivering computer services should be the proper criteria for your choice, not the calculating capacity of the hardware.

[2] Sierra Group, Cost of Ownership of DEC Computers, *Computerworld*, September 4, 1989, p. 110. Similar results, but in greater detail, were in a report about Data General computers in *Computerworld*, December 18, 1989, p. 90. The amortization of software purchases and the costs of software maintenance are 42% of total costs for a small clustered site and only 19% for a large clustered site. If you include the costs of back–up and security, the software support costs for a stand-alone personal computer will exceed hardware costs. Although vendors offer 25–40% discounts for multi-site software licenses, you will save the most if you have as few sites as possible.

[3] "Centralization" is a relative matter. Consolidating two large data centers can offer further economies. For instance, combining two data centers reduced systems, operations and programming support staffs by 55 people (J. Forsythe, The Efficient Frontier, *InformationWeek*, February 5, 1990, p. 48).

[4] MVS, JES, RMF, ISPF, COBOL, SMP, TSO, CICS, DB2 and VSAM plus miscellaneous software packages and software maintenance.

[5] The Midland Bank consolidated 30 data centers into three super-centers, instantly saving 22% of costs, 25% of the staff while at the time achieving a threefold

improvement in throughput (R. Carlyle, Getting a Grip on Costs, *Datamation*, July 15, 1990). You should know that without prior standardization in operating practices and technology, data center consolidation can be like walking barefoot through a swamp full of dangerous creatures.

[6] Global Distribution Systems: Emerging Trend and Strategic Issues, *SRI International*, August 1989. My correlation calculations use data tabulated in Figures 3 and 5.

[7] Fund research, standards and innovation as corporate ventures and not as data center overhead. This frequent practice acts as a surtax on existing applications. It drives customers to seek uneconomic solutions to evade excessive central charges.

[8] Customers find it particularly irritating if they have to pay central computing staff for the time technicians expend in understanding business needs.

[9] Guide International, Applications Re-engineering, MP-1411, Guide 72, offers seven case studies that illustrate how firms have successfully used re-engineering to get immediate cost reductions. A large installation with an average COBOL code age of more than four years should target 10% annual cost reductions in computer run-time plus program maintenance costs.

Designing new applications from modular and reusable computer code is the most rewarding application of re-engineered software. Software reuse involves transfer of subroutines from one application to another. For instance, in building a new application with 80,000 lines of code that tracks empty freight cars, only 5,000 of those lines were new (D. Todd, Code Recycling, *InformationWeek*, May 14, 1990, p.50).

[10] Except for two employees who stay to hang computer tapes, the Manufacturers Hanover Corporation has removed all other employees because it can now operate two data centers from one remote site. Automation is possible by passing supervisory messages to a central control board needing fewer operators, as reported in the November 20, 1989 *InformationWeek*, p. 14. Citicorp operates in a similar way, with lights out in one of its giant operator-less processing centers. Remote control consoles and robot cartridge loaders are making data center consolidation attractive again.

[11] Some of these consultants will work for a percentage of the money they claim as savings. For an excellent description of cost reduction practices, see Corporations Take the Offensive on Tariffs, *InformationWeek*, March 20, 1989. The ability to buy attractively priced corporate networks from service vendors offers opportunities to cut fixed costs and replace them with lower variable expenses.

[12] Providing complete software for hospital management is an example of the growing competition among software vendors specializing in a particular industry. The top five vendors of patient accounting and management software are: Shared Medical Systems (177 hospitals), Baxter/IBM (168), Amex/McDonnell Douglas (88), HBO & Co. (82) and Amex/SAI (69). The Information Services Division of the Hospital Corporation of America provides hardware and software services from a central computer installation in Nashville, Tenn. High speed data circuits lines connect to 1,400 NCR Tower distributed systems in more than 300 hospitals. The Nashville data center processes all base accounting functions for its clients. This includes billing, accounts receivable and individual patient information. The center also supports software for local processing of medical records, laboratory systems, operating room scheduling and nutrition applications.

Such competition offers management and technical know-how on an affordable basis. Similar trends are happening in software for municipal accounting, payroll services, savings and loan associations, credit unions, wholesalers and distributors.

[13] This is "outsourcing." It is a development that is rapidly gaining momentum. The estimated amount of these services is $25.6 billion worldwide in 1989, mostly in the U.S., which accounts for approximately 5% of total computer & business equipment revenues. This share will be increasing because computer equipment

CHAPTER 11—COST MANAGEMENT   275

revenues in the U.S. will increase at the rate of only 8.4%/year from 1989–2000, whereas computer services will grow by at least 20%/year during the same period.

More than one half of 1989 "outsourcing" revenues are provided by: Electronic Data Systems ($5.5 billion), IBM Corporation ($3.2 billion), Andersen Consulting ($1.5 billion), Computer Sciences ($1.4 billion), Digital Equipment Corporation ($1 billion), KMPG Peat Marwick ($0.6 billion) and AT&T ($0.5 billion), as reported by M. O'Leary, The Mainframe Does not Work Here Anymore, *CIO Journal*, June 1990, p. 34.

One example of the benefits of outsourcing is the American Ultramar Corporation, an oil refining and marketing organization. It has cut a $3 million per year processing cost budget by 50%. Other corporations have been able to claim instant 20–50% data processing cost reductions. (C. Wilder, Outsourcing: From Fad to Respectability, *Computerworld*, June 11, 1990)

[14] Critical Issues of Information Systems Management, *The Index Group*, December 1988, p. 16

[15] E.N. Kass, Merrill Looks to Outsource Overseas, *InformationWeek*, June 25, 1990. The article reports that Merrill is looking to outsource a part of their program maintenance to Singapore to achieve major cost reductions.

[16] Annex Research, CMS Bulletin, Volume VI, No. 89–69, December, 1989. The Annex Research corporation specializes in tracking declining costs of computer hardware.

[17] Computer Economics, Inc. Forecast of Residual Values of IBM Disk Drives, *Computerworld*, February 5, 1990, p. 146

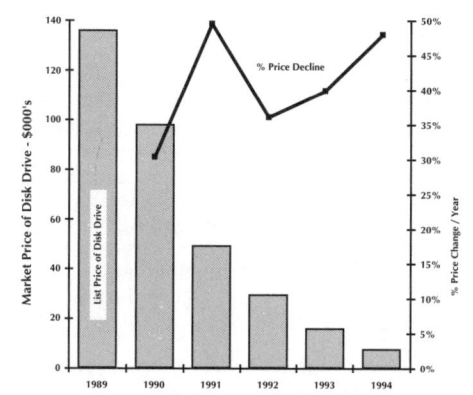

Medium-size computers appear to be depreciating at a faster rate than even peripherals. For instance, the popular IBM 4381–P91E with a list price of $512.5 thousand is projected to have a replacement value of only $6,200 by mid-1993. The widely used IBM 9377–90 with a list price of $239.4 thousand is expected to have a residual market value of only $3,800 by mid-1993. Replacement models for both classes of these machines are expected to appear in 1991. (Computer Economics quoted in *Computerworld*, June 4, 1990, p.126.)

In the case of UNIX workstations the projected cost reductions are even greater because of the keen competition in this market expected from a wide range of low-cost sources. A 1989 UNIX workstation with the power of 40 MIPS costs $175,000. The projected cost of a 1993 250 MIPS UNIX workstation is only $50,000! (M.R. Leibowitz, UNIX Workstations Arrive, *Datamation*, June 1, 1990, p.25.)

These unusually rapid declines in the commercial value of computer systems suggest that during the 1990's the technology of replacement systems will proceed at an accelerated pace. Unless the planning and procurement cycle are longer than one-quarter of the technology cycle, the purchaser will always end up buying more expensive technology than the market has to offer. An extreme case of always paying more for obsolete computers than anyone else is the Federal Government. The Defense Department is currently running at least a three- to seven-year cycle, if we count from systems studies until a system becomes operational. The approval and authorization process now consume about three years.

18 Management should set a minimum 15% to 20% cost-reduction target for highly automated computer services. The semiconductor industry delivers that potential to M.I.S. management through technological advances and from the consequences of cutthroat competition. Merit increases for superior cost-management should be earned only if computer services managers exceed what is already available without further effort. The Real Decisions Corporation which specializes in data center efficiency studies has been quoted (P. Krass, The Dollars and Sense of Outsourcing, *InformationWeek*, February 26, 1990, p. 26) that "...data centers that increase work volume, acquire more efficient hardware and work more efficiently can reduce their costs by 20% to 25% a year."

How to get such cost-reductions shows up in a large data center, such as in the FMC Corporation in Dallas. It has been reducing charges to customers by 15–20% per year and unit costs by 25% per year (M.L. Sullivan-Trainor, Positive Alternatives to Slash-and-Burn Cost-Cutting, *Computerworld*, February 26, 1990, p. 64).

When the Kodak Corporation announced that it would save 40% over the life of the long-term contract with IBM, that merely acknowledges the available cost reductions. In some cases the corporate flight to "outsourcing" is more a reflection on the company's M.I.S. management than proof of a vendor's technological superiority.

19 You cannot use annual projections of residual values to set the annual hardware budget for a small computer center. The decision to buy hardware from original manufacturers, buying secondhand hardware or the differences between short- versus long-term leases will lock in the technology costs for fixed periods. Ultimately the cost curve should track the industry falling prices. This is why small installations have greater exposure to error than firms with large pools of equipment. The current trend to third-party "outsourcing" of computer services rests largely on the ability of the information services firms to manage their equipment inventories. Corporations or government agencies are in no position to operate their equipment pools as if they were a leasing company. Large facility management firms can hedge their bets by trading their equipment in the global market for used computers. A large share of service company profits does not come from operations but from managing their equipment to follow the rapidly declining industry cost curves. Unless a corporation can negotiate a steeply declining rate for computer services, they will not get the full benefit from "outsourcing" services.

For a discussion of the advantages of centralized procurement see J.R. Taylor, C.C. Tucker, Reducing Data processing Costs Through Centralized Procurement, *MIS Quarterly*, December 1989. An estimated $12.4 million dollars were saved in 1987 on hardware and software procurements of $57 million (a 22% cost reduction) by the First Interstate Services Corporation, an information services subsidiary of the First Interstate Bancorp. It is interesting to note that the savings realized in software are substantially greater than those on hardware. A comparison of two years' results (in millions $) shows increased savings due most likely to increased experience in contract management and what I suspect to be a growing competitive environment, as the number of vendors increased from 7 in 1985 to 16 in 1987:

Year	Product	Purchases	Discounts	% Savings
1986	Hardware	$33.9	$3.7	11
	Software	$7.4	$2.5	34
1987	Hardware	$45.4	$8.4	17
	Software	$11.4	$4.0	35

Previously, each of the eight data centers bought hardware and software individually.

20 Computer Economics, Inc. Estimated Residual Values of DEC Processors, *Computerworld*, April 2, 1990, p. 122

21 Because of a fluctuation in the charges to a customer, regardless of the volume of work processed that month.

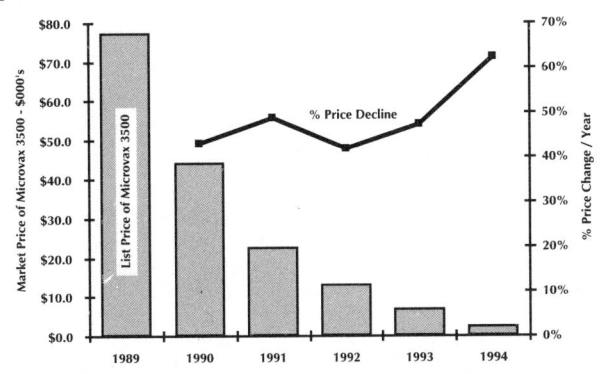

[Chart: Market Price of Microvax 3500 - $000's and List Price of Microvax 3500 (bars from $80.0 down to near $0 over 1989–1994); % Price Change/Year line labeled "% Price Decline" ranging roughly 40%–70%.]

22 R.A. Samuel and M.S. Scott-Morton in Information Technology and Major Organizational Change, *M.I.T. Management Review*, Spring, 1989 wondered about the possible causes of why information technology investments come out poorly. Much of it can be explained by the "...internal market failure by which managers are unable to value ... information technology." If you want to talk about an *internal market*, you must also address the question of proper internal pricing.

23 They can also opt for installing their own computing environment. This may introduce unnecessary elements of risk, which some Divisional executives prefer despite the disadvantage of higher costs. A financial company with one of the largest M.I.S. budgets in the U.S. had to scuttle its central computing services because customers were engaged in incessant warfare over budget allocations. The central service utility brought its demise upon itself by engaging in budget haggling. They never took the time to establish a sound pricing policy and then stick to it.

24 In any month there is always some unabsorbed overhead, a variation in the workload and a different mix of applications.

25 At Bell Atlantic, Competing is Learned from the Inside, *Wall Street Journal*, July 12, 1989, quoting R.W. Smith, Chairman and CEO of the Bell Atlantic Corporation.

26 Our pricing analyst learned from published ADAPSO (Association of Data Processing Services Organization) survey data that suppliers were spending up to 15% of revenue on selling and promotion. Buyers frequently fail to appreciate the great costs of preparing a complex proposal. I believe that time-consuming proposals should be paid for as *feasibility studies*. A superficial proposal will give you misleading intelligence about a technical solution. If you base your decisions on such data, your risk may be unmanageable.

27 The firm was Automatic Data Processing, now the ADP Corporation.

28 There was no need to offer quantity discounts because the bill of materials separated fixed and variable costs. There was a surcharge for fast response-time and peak-workload processing.

29 A good example is the Warner-Lambert Corporation. Its chief computer executive, Tom Hippe, says that his firm is making its I.S. staff more competitive by encouraging users to solicit project bids from both external and internal sources. (*Computerworld*, June 18, 1990, p.22)

30 An interesting commentary comes from P. Reynolds (*Datamation*, June 15, 1990, p.45): "When Shell's Belgium subsidiary decided to get rid of all its internal IT resources, its budget was growing at around 15% a year. Since farming everything out, IT-related expenditures have increased 75%." Reynolds attributes the growth to de-coupling of the IT expenditures from its overhead classification by making them a direct variable cost.

31 R. Layne and B. Caldwell, EDS Lands MIS Giant, *InformationWeek*, November 21, 1988.

32 The National Science Foundation will start installing a nationwide network linking super-

computers in 1990. The main communication links will operate at 45 megabits/second, which is equivalent to the internal channel speed of most small computers.

33 B.A. Huberman, The Ecology of Computation, *The Scientist,* May 16, 1988 and J.O. Kephart, T. Hogg and B.A. Huberman, Dynamics of Computational Ecosystems, *Distributed Artificial Intelligence,* Vol. 2, Morgan Kaufmann Publishers, 1989

34 Opportunities for new forms of collusive price-fixing will still exist. International airlines publish prices through a commonly owned computer network operated by the Airline Tariff Publishing Company. This network provides for instantaneous transmission of more than 100,000 daily fare changes. Many sources believe that this network provides a behind-the-scenes method for airlines to include codes that sometimes signal pricing intentions (A.Q. Normani, Airlines May Be Using A Price-Data Network To Lessen Competition, *Wall Street Journal,* June 28, 1990).

35 Tim Smith of Ralston Purina subscribes to this point of view. A one time executive vice president for manufacturing, he now runs all information systems (R. Carlyle, Getting a Grip on Costs, *Datamation,* July 15, 1990). Smith said he did not trust computer vendors and consultants to give him good answers about his competitive prices. "...You need this information if you want to run I.S. as a business. You have to be able to compare your I.S. utility to the competition, to others in your industry and even in other industries, if you want to really know what's going on."

It is noteworthy that Smith ended up making comparisons among his American, Swedish as well as U.K. data centers. After making the necessary improvements, the cost advantage of vendors such as McDonnell Douglas, Electronic Data Systems and Litton Computer Services disappeared.

36 The better the simulation, the greater the danger that the artificial will appear as the real thing. There are instances when simulations appear so real that decisions proceed without first checking the findings. Unless the results of such a mistake are quickly recognized, people will follow computer instructions that defy rationality.

During the 1960's the most widely discussed simulation model was the *Limits of Growth,* which predicted global starvation and exhaustion of natural resources starting in the 1990's. It was a very impressive model, except nobody ever bothered to run it backwards to see if it matched what had happened since 1900. Someone finally got the simulation program and tested it for fit with historical data. There was no fit. The simulation was an untested figment.

The most extreme case of taking a simulation for reality is the U.S. Navy Lieutenant T.W. Dorsey, who shot down an Air Force RF-4c reconnaissance airplane in 1987. Dorsey, an experienced pilot, was on a simulated exercise practicing attack maneuvers. He acknowledged verbally that he was in a practice run on a friendly plane, but guided by a computer display he instinctively fired live missiles.

37 Executives read that the average cost per million instructions per second on a mainframe is $200,000 while the same amount of computing is only $4,000 on a microcomputer (J.J. Donovan, Beyond Chief Information Officer to Network Manager, *Harvard Business Review,* September 1988). Million instructions per second is not a good comparative measure, but the dollar difference is big enough to give an incentive to take work away from the mainframe whenever possible.

38 The simulation uses standard "blocks" from the Extend simulator (*ImagineThat,* San Jose, CA). Many software packages are now available for building simulation models. As compared with the costly and difficult to use simulation languages, the new technology makes this technique available with remarkable ease. The diagram in Figure 11.12 uses a slightly simplified version of the actual Object Oriented Language to study the effects of competing prices on data center processing volume. The case used in this illustration represents an extreme and simplified condition.

39 For instance, 3000 transactions/day to be moved if next year's charges are $1 per transaction, and 10,500 transactions to be moved to local processing if the charges exceed $1.63.

40 A programmer once told his priest that he understood why Creation happened in only six days. There were no program changes and only one decision-maker!

41 A further 15% cut in overhead per year and the recognition that fully loaded costs of the microcomputers were larger than estimated would have preserved the central processing capacity at a reduced level. Scenario simulation can identify conditions where a small effort can divert a situation from potential disaster.

12

SUPPORTING ANALYSES

A good proposal makes its assumptions clear.

All business proposals get support from an array of fact-finding studies. The key to the credibility of any proposal to invest in computers is the quality and relevance of the evidence that substantiates the projected benefit or cost estimates.[1] Sometimes it takes months or years of data-gathering to accumulate such intelligence. Experienced executives rarely spend much time on the business proposal itself. Instead, they try to identify the pivotal two or three premises on which the solution rests.[2] They will check over a few familiar facts which support the principal assumptions. Afterwards, they may find it safe to proceed without examining every detail.

I would not presume to write a handbook that describes which analyses will substantiate the assumptions in any given systems plan. Each systems proposal is unique because it matches the specific business conditions that need improvement. Most proposal efforts will show that there is a gap between the proponents' beliefs and facts. The difference between what's stated and what can be verified can be enormous. This chapter will illustrate some methods for checking claims about expected benefits and costs.

Individual Productivity

Government Agency Case

Computerization will not improve productivity if most of a person's time has a fixed commitment to continue doing unproductive work.

The Chief of a Federal Agency was proud of his computer network. It connected all his Directors, Assistant Directors and their immediate support personnel. The Chief claimed that this network, connecting every employee, improved cooperative work. The network was to relieve the Directors of administrative minutiae and allow more attention to *mission-critical* activities. The employees' favorable reception to the proliferation of personal computers pleased the Chief. The Agency would proceed next with a costly expansion of the network to connect to Agency contractors. He requested that I make a brief assessment of the effectiveness of the existing computer network.

A Federal Agency accounts only for its expenses. You cannot compute its *Business Value-added* in the same terms as would apply to a competitive enterprise, because the Agency's customers have no choice of an alternative supplier. A good proxy measure is to find what the Agency employees do for the people they serve.[3] How do the Directors spend their time? What proportion of their time do they spend on their personal computer? What do they do when they use a computer? How do individuals differ in their computer-using habits?

Without a competitive market for the Agency's services, you cannot get conclusive answers about organizational effectiveness. You can, however, bring out facts that may not match the authorized pronouncements. I concentrated on checking the Chief's conviction that the computers allowed his key executives to devote more time to *mission-critical* activities that benefited the people served by the Agency. There was no difficulty in coming up with a definition of what was *mission-critical* work. In the case of this Agency it was the time the officials spent dealing with the public.[4]

If you wish to collect good information about anyone's work, you must assure them of complete anonymity. If you are dealing with executives, managers and professionals, the forms must be simple, understandable and take little time to complete.[5] The respondents must get rapid and personal feedback. The respondents must have an interest in the result of the study. The information must be subject to cross-checking by the respondents for consistency. I decided to sample the usage patterns of the 26 Agency Directors. They were accessible and their computer work habits were of greatest interest to the Chief. The total time from start to final briefing was 30 days.

The computers were in heavy use. The Directors averaged 25% of their total available hours working on their personal workstations:

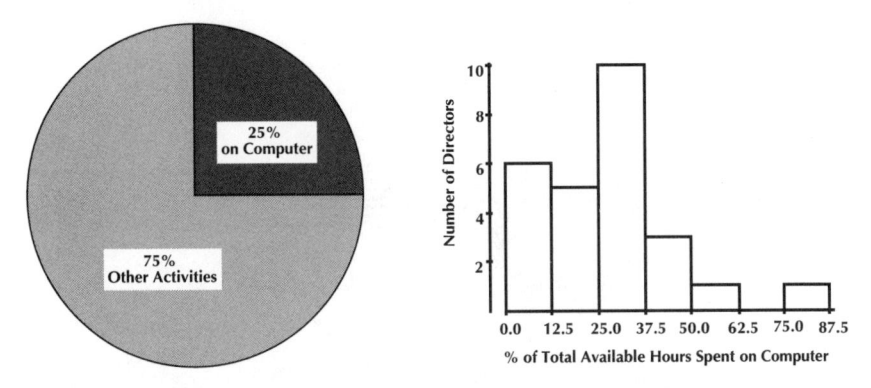

Figure 12.1: Percent of Directors' Time Using Computers

The average did not tell the entire story. A distribution of the percentage of time spent on the computer showed a diverse usage pattern.[6] You always need to have some diversity when making an evaluation of office work in order to compare different working habits.

Next, I decided to check out the Chief's assertion that the principal benefit of computers were better group collaboration. The Chief did not expect any measurable productivity gains from individuals.[7] An analysis of how the Directors were spending their time showed that the computers supported primarily the Directors' individual tasks. Inter-personal communication consumed less than one fifth of the available time:

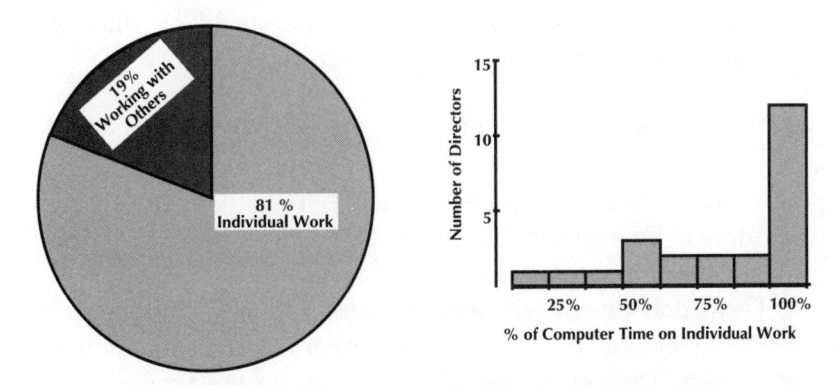

Figure 12.2: The Directors' Computer Activities: Communicating with Others

Half of the Directors did not use any of the cooperative features of networking. Their connection to the local area network was irrelevant to them.

Why did we get such a high concentration on individual work? A work profile, by business function, gave the answer:

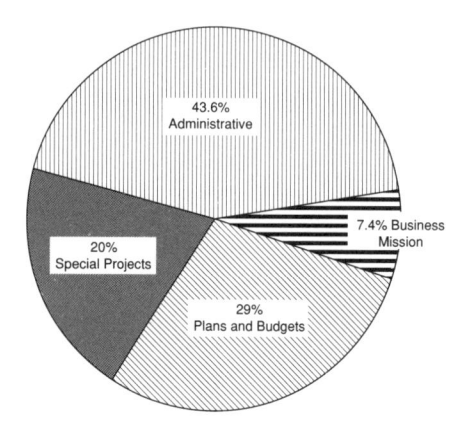

Figure 12.3: Computer Work Support - % of the Directors' Total Computer Time

Only 7.4% of the total computer time used by all Directors (on the average) applied to *mission critical* work for the Agency's constituents. The Directors used the computers primarily to cope with their increased administrative workload while their secretarial support was slowly disappearing. Cutbacks in the central financial support staffs further added to each Director's personal workload. The burden of continual re-budgeting shifted work from planning professionals to the Directors, whose training and knowledge were technical, not financial. The Chief's belief that computers made it possible for the Directors to devote a large share of their time to *mission critical* activities was questionable.

Twenty percent of the Directors' activities were for "special projects." I could not get a satisfactory answer as to what that meant. I inferred from the evidence that Directors continued their personal and professional career development while serving in their current posts. It was unclear how this activity related to the Chief's rationale for installing the computer network.

For widely diversified samples I always check whether there are identifiable relationships between computer use and some indicator of effectiveness. The percentage of hours spent on the Agency's business mission could provide some insights:

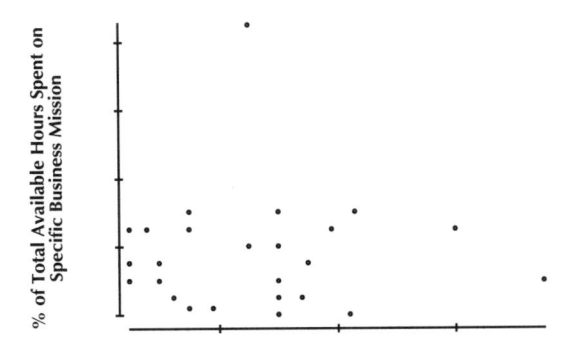

Figure 12.4: Time on Computer and Time for Business Mission

Individuals who used the computer more extensively did not find more time for carrying out *mission critical* work. Regardless of how much time a Director spent on the computer (with one exception), the percentage of time available for dealing with the public did not increase.

If computers did not help the Directors in getting to the Agency's essential business, perhaps the computers helped to reduce the Directors' administrative workload:

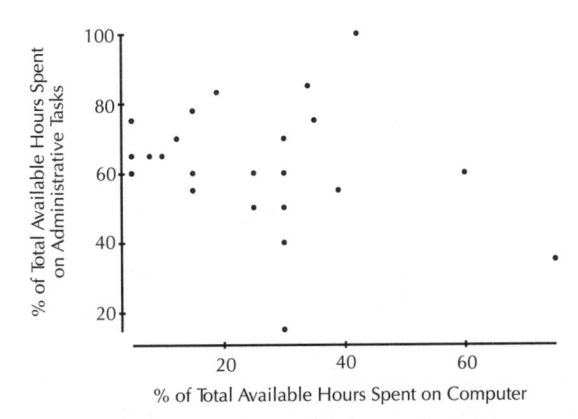

Figure 12.5: Time on Computer and Time for Administration

Regardless of the amount of time spent on a computer, the percentage of time required for completing the Directors' administrative tasks did not decrease.

From these patterns I did not find any consistent trends in usage that would suggest that time spent on the computer was beneficial. There were Directors spending little time on computers, with little time in administrative activities, and vice versa. Similarly, computers did not make more time available for dealing with the public.

Did the computer network support better communication within the Agency? Was more time available for cooperative work which was the Chief's original rationale for installing the network?

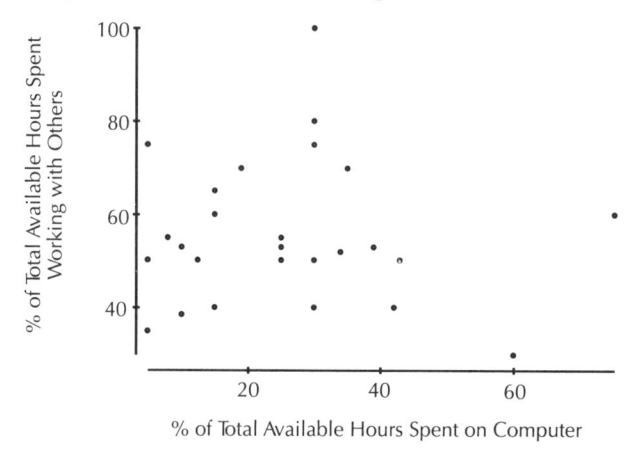

Figure 12.6: Time on Computer and Time Working with Others

Figure 12.6 is another inconclusive chart comparing time on the computer and time working with others. Just because a Director spends more time on a computer does not make a Director necessarily more likely to work with others.

I found these findings puzzling, as did the Agency's Chief. Somehow the personal computers and network were not delivering the expected work-patterns.[8] Was there a good explanation for our findings?

The issue was not what the Directors were doing while they were working on their computers 25% of their available hours. The explanation is in how the Directors spent 75% of their time when they were not on the computer. The pattern of computer usage reflected the general allocation of the Directors' time. They carried the burden of excessive administrative work, inadequate clerical and secretarial support, added burdens of financial analysis, incessant budget re-submissions and personnel matters. These diversions made *mission critical* work incidental to the Directors' activities, not their principal occupation.

To improve the Directors' effectiveness would take more than expanding the computer network.

Word Processing vs. Handwriting

Computer benefits do not arise when the methods of performing the work do not change. An example comes from a study where 41 clerical personnel received word processing equipment, and 38 continued to perform the identical work manually.[9] Although I do not doubt the benefits of word processing[10] for writing business letters or a book, here was a situation where the automated method was not superior:

	Handwritten	Word Processing
Minutes to compose	62	85
Words Written	561	632
Reading time, minutes	3.0	3.2
Redundancy count, words	38	42
Abstract verbiage, words	38	42
Longer paragraphs, lines	87	104

Table 12.1: Comparing Two Ways of Performing Identical Tasks

The hand-written text was more efficient. It took less time to compose. The hand-written letters had fewer words, took less time to read, the sentences had a lower redundancy, the ideas were less abstract and the paragraphs were shorter. The ease of text revision and copying gave the users of word processing equipment an incentive to write more elaborate messages. In this case, the application called for the preparation of brief notices.

A computer application is not necessarily the best for every situation. If word processing equipment makes legal secretaries more efficient, it does not follow that their gains apply also to others who have patterns of less intense use.[11] Making paired comparisons between users and non-users of a technology in the identical environment, under the same conditions, is the most trustworthy means for assuring that benefit estimates are realistic.

The Harris Corporation Case

The Harris Corporation widely distributed personal computers to its staff. When costs rose and somebody noticed that the machines were mostly idle, the CEO asked the top M.I.S. executive to find out if the computers were delivering any benefit.

The only reliable information about personal computers available was their physical inventory. Property records showed the location of every personal computer. The telephone directory indicated who occupied the desk where there was a personal computer.

This presented an opportunity to test the hypothesis of whether or not people with computers were more productive than those who continued to work without changing their work habits. The company's salary records offered the only way to measure such progress. Did personnel with personal computers show a faster rate of merit salary increases as compared with personnel who chose to work without personal computers? The findings were unexpected:[12]

- Salary raises of people without personal computers surpassed the salary raises of those who did.
- The more hours a person worked on the computer, the worse his salary growth, especially for managerial, administrative and professional personnel. The only gains from having computers were by people in clerical jobs.
- The more familiar a person was with advanced technical features of software, the worse his salary progression.

The approach used in the Harris study is unusual since it tried to infer productivity gains from records of salary advancement. There is a possible argument that performance appraisals are not a good measure of gains in employee effectiveness, except that top management found this approach perfectly acceptable.

I find the Harris findings intriguing. It raises doubt that the productivity of managers and professionals—at least in the early 1980's—could improve by giving them the capacity to make changes on spreadsheets, typing memoranda or making presentation slides.[13] If a manager's supervisory skills reflect his personal effectiveness, diverting him or her to perform clerical work with a keyboard will not earn him much advancement.

Measuring Quality

Customers can assess quality when they make their choices. Quality is tangible.

The director of a large metropolitan electric utility was proud of the 99.9% availability of his computer system that supported a system for responding to customer emergency calls. A tenth of a percent failure-rate sounds good until you consider that this gives you 8.8 hours of annual downtime. A system on which customers depend when trouble strikes cannot afford being out of commission 8.8 hours every year, especially if the incidence of failure occurs on only a handful of events.[14]

An indicator of system reliability has a different significance depending on whether you are tracking production errors, number of missed product release dates, police emergency calls, customer com-

CHAPTER 12—SUPPORTING ANALYSES   *287*

plaints or the monitoring of cardiac patients. Adhering to a meticulous procedure for reporting every system failure is essential for identifying what are the sources of systems malfunctions.

The critical question is how to set the standards which balance tolerable levels of system failure against incremental systems costs for preventing such events from occurring. If only 0.2% of the population suffers from a toothache at any time, it does not cease to be a pain. What is "acceptable" cannot be determined statistically.

I also do not always find that in the technical design of information systems "quality is free". This slogan that has been widely advertised by the leaders of the quality movement as the solution to the declining competitiveness of U.S. companies. Obtaining 99.99% network reliability is vastly more expensive than settling for 99%.

When problems arise, I like to take random samples of each incident type and classify each occurrence into a table with the following groupings:
- What is the cost consequence of each incident? Less than $1, $2 to $10, $11 to $100, $101 to $1,000, above $1,000?
- What is the cause of each incident? Are they coding defects, design errors, operator omissions, a break in power lines or a telephone failure?

Systems organization which strives to improve quality should first concentrate on incidents with the largest penalties. As the next step they should eliminate the most frequent causes for the costliest incidents. You improve quality by fixing one situation at a time.

If one delayed transaction causes the loss of a valuable customer, it does not necessarily follow that you should give all transactions a faster turn-around. You may be better off changing your service standards to deal separately with "sensitive" transactions. The evaluation of tradeoffs between quality and cost may lead you to influence your system design. You may decide to offer super-fast response time only for selected transactions.

When somebody shows you that his computers average one second response time and average 99.5% systems availability, do not conclude that this is necessarily a superior operation. You need to know more about the costs involved, and what happens in case of failure before you offer praise. Similarly, when you get a proposal that claims to improve the quality of customer services to 99.9%, as measured by some index, ask how much cash the firm will receive. The 99.9% target may be insufficient for some, and unaffordable for others.

The emphasis on reaching particular standards targets can lead to unwarranted complexity. It can add features which some customers may not be able to afford. The efforts to improve the quality of systems should lead to greater diversity, instead of narrowing the services available for everyone.[15] The pursuit of quality is a learning experience, and should not be merely a quest to improve some statistical indicators. The pursuit of quality is nothing more than a return to the fundamentals of how to run a business without waste and with satisfied customers. Unless a firm offers different prices for a variety of service levels, the quest for higher quality computer services can become an excuse for indiscriminate escalation costs.

COSTS OF CUSTOMER LOSSES

Giving the customer privileges to return defective products without penalty or a service cost is a powerful means by which to focus everyone's attention on quality. Return and service guarantees are very expensive unless you can be sure that few will use this privilege. Warranty claims also generate excellent customer feedback. Without a warranty, a dissatisfied customer will have little motivation to complain, unless the defect creates a financial liability. The customer will just switch to the competition. Losing such a customer will never appear in any sales statistics, though understanding why and where you lose a customer is the most informative source of competitive information.[16] A customer making a warranty claim cooperates in answering accurately all questions about the reasons for his displeasure.

The sources of warranty costs identify nearly everything about the quality of your goods and services. Computer-based systems that display the trends for warranty claims are essential to any "executive information system." Managers who do not review indicators of their customer's perceptions of quality, and pay attention to them, will eventually lose their business.

The Customer as a Franchise

Viewing a customer as a money-making franchise can be instrumental in coming up with the dollar value of improved customer care. The rate at which your firm is losing customers is a critical indicator of general performance. If your product is similar in features and price to your competitors', you can measure the effectiveness of your marketing efforts. You will be able to tell how quickly to write off the costs of today's marketing and sales expenses for adding each new customer. You also could compute the payoff from investing in improved customer services. Customer attrition affects your customer retention as follows:

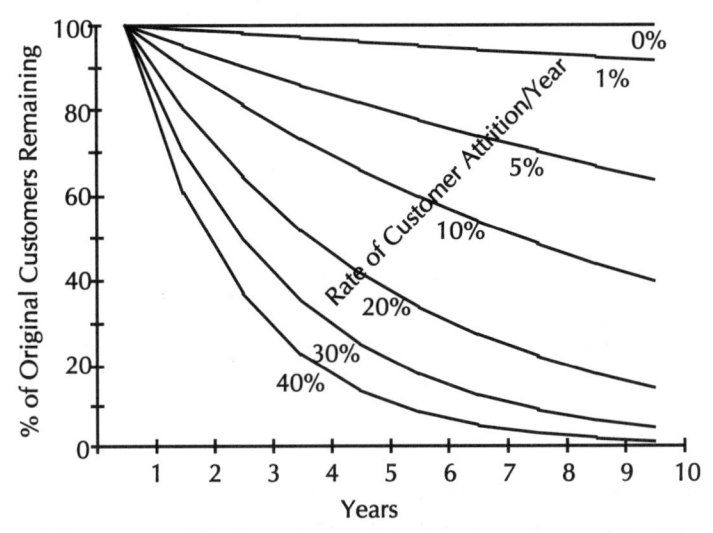

Figure 12.7: Different Rates of Customer Retention and Attrition

If the costs of adding new customers are high and operating business margins are large, you should compute your *Operating* and *Market Development Productivity* separately.[17] Otherwise, your managers may cut back on investments in market growth and skimp on customer support whenever they need to cover unexpected losses.

The effects of superior quality are quantifiable in financial terms. You can build financial tables that show the gains from different levels of improved services. If you consider your customer as a franchise, you can compute the money you would lose if customers switch to your competition. It also tells you how much money you may invest to overcome attrition from your existing customer base. You must verify why customers are leaving you, and effectively spend money trying to understand the customers you lose than the customers that you are courting. Statistical techniques are available to allow the calculation of the discounted present value of actions to retain customer loyalty.[18]

In Chapter 8, I discussed several cases where computers improved a firm's competitive position. In every instance, this involved a remarkable improvement in customer service. As computer applications shift from labor cost-displacement to "strategic" uses, you will need analytic tools for estimating the potential benefits of such applications.

Capitalizing Computer Investments

There are no past or future decisions. There are only present decisions, to be evaluated presently.

The idea that systems development costs are capital instead of current expense is a recurring theme at M.I.S. meetings. This topic comes up whenever conventional accounting methods, such as *Years-to-Breakeven*, do not get you the desired approval to proceed.[19] Depreciating a large sum of money over a five to ten-year span will always improve conventional payoff calculations for the *Time to Breakeven* will be shortened. *Return-on-Investment* will increase and today's budget pains will be passed on to your successor's operating statement. No wonder there are managers who find it more rewarding to advocate changing the accounting rules instead of improving the benefits shown in their proposals.

Whether you capitalize your computer investment or pay it out of current revenues[20] should have no effect on proceeding with a project provided that each alternative has a comparable cost of capital. Risk-adjusted discounted cash flow[21] is the only valid method for judging the profitability of an investment. If your net present worth of a proposed new application[22] is above zero, you have met the strictly financial criteria for spending your shareholders' money. A commitment to generate future net cash flows is the only reliable measure to guide long term investments in computer systems.

Spending time manipulating your calculations will only complicate your efforts to sell a computer venture that already has questionable benefits.

Software Valuation

You cannot revisit the past.

The sale price of a retail chain to an international conglomerate included software valued at $38 million. This valuation came from well-documented original acquisition costs. The $38 million reflected a large investment to develop a pioneering retail-management system. An early leader in point-of-sale automation, the company received criticism for over-spending on computer systems.

The acquiring company objected to the high valuation placed on the software. The conglomerate's M.I.S. staff estimated that their own point-of-sale system could be licensed for $2 million to the retail chain after the merger.

To come up with a correct valuation of the installed software was important. Whatever the value, it would reflect on the purchase price and tax treatment of shareholder capital gains. What was the proper valuation? Was it the software acquisition cost of $38 million or the software replacement cost of $2 million?

The lawyers for the conglomerate insisted on replacement valuation. They correctly concluded that the business value of any information technology is its replacement cost. Previously incurred costs, regardless of how large, are irrelevant. You can only consider today's replacement choices. The disputing parties asked for an expert opinion.[23]

The replacement cost was the correct way to value the installed software. If the new management chose to replace the existing software, they also would incur conversion costs plus large employee re-training expenses. This would cost about $18 to $26 million. Replacing the fully depreciated but specialized hardware in the retail chain would increase hardware expenses but also reduce maintenance expenses. The net present worth of these two cash items would be $25 million.

Replacing the current software would cost $2 million (for the software license) plus $18 to $26 million (for the conversion and training) plus $25 million (the net cost of changing the hardware environment). The least expensive alternative for getting rid of the installed software was $45 to $53 million. If the new management would decide to keep the installed system after the merger, they could avoid that expense.

The original valuation of $38 million of the retail chain software, based on acquisition costs, was irrelevant and too low. On a replacement-cost basis it was worth more. This example shows that every general principle is open to diverse interpretations. You do not find out the significance of these interpretations until you ask how much cash will end up in the bank.

Chapter Summary

Extracting the business value from information technology is not only a matter of what you do, but how you do it. Estimates of benefits depend on your approach to how you measure the quality that your customers experience. In many situations, you have to abandon focusing on the computer and examine how people go about conducting their business. Installing more computers may not be a sensible choice if the employees' efforts are wasteful.

What proponents of information technology believe and what the facts prove are not always in harmony. Exhaustive fact-finding that checks the key planning assumptions is a sign that a proposal is sound.

Chapter 12 Comments

[1] Extensive supporting data does not always relate to a proposal. Nowadays it is easy to include good-looking spreadsheets and tables with any plan. Casual reading of a laser printed, spiral bound report with appendixes, foldouts and listings can create the impression of exhaustive analysis even though the data supports unrelated premises. Several software packages are now available that automate the preparation of business proposals, including the generation of standard text.

[2] The distinguishing characteristic of all superior executives is their ability to focus on the few issues that matter. Experience positively contributes to that, but I think it is a cultivated talent.

[3] For further explanation see the section titled *Management Productivity in the Public Sector* in Chapter 5.

[4] It was not possible to gather data that distinguishes between useful and useless time in dealing with the public. Consequently, my findings present the Agency in the most favorable view.

[5] Using a matrix (Input/Output) format improves the quality of data collection on individual activities. It forces people to think not only of what they do, but also of how they apply it:

		INDIVIDUAL WORK Professional, Personal Tasks		INTERPERSONAL WORK Meetings, consultations, etc.		
OUTPUT \ INPUT		Under my Direct Supervision	Under Supervision of others, includes support services	Under my Direct Supervision	Under Supervision of others, includes support services	OUTPUT % Totals
AGENCY MISSION-RELATED WORK	Performance of activities that are directly relevant to delivering defined results	___%	___%	___%	___%	___%
	Performance of activities that are indirectly related but demonstrably essential for delivering defined results	___%	___%	___%	___%	___%
ADMINISTRATIVE TASKS RELATED TO AGENCY INFRASTRUCTURE	Activities that are essential for accomplishing defined results	___%	___%	___%	___%	___%
	Activities that are redundant, unnecessary, irrelevant and counter-productive for accomplishing defined results	___%	___%	___%	___%	___%
	Absenteeism, unproductive activities, time waiting for assignments, unused time for any reasons.	___%	___%	___%	___%	___%
	INPUT - % of Totals	___%	___%	___%	___%	100 %

A similar matrix allows gathering consistent information about the use of computers:

		INDIVIDUAL WORK Professional, Personal Tasks		INTERPERSONAL WORK Meetings, consultations, etc.		% of Total Hands-on time spent on computer work *
INPUT / OUTPUT		Under my Direct Supervision	Under Supervision of others, includes support services	Under my Direct Supervision	Under Supervision of others, includes support services	
AGENCY MISSION-RELATED WORK	Performance of activities that are directly relevant to delivering defined results					____%
	Performance of activities that are indirectly related but demonstrably essential for delivering defined results					____%
ADMINISTRATIVE TASKS RELATED TO AGENCY INFRASTRUCTURE	Activities that are essential for accomplishing defined results	Total number of paid hours/year totalling this table ____ hours		____% of Total hours for computer hours		____%
	Activities that are redundant, unnecessary, irrelevant and counter-productive for accomplishing defined results			Total number of Hands-on hours/year spent on computer work ____ hours		____%
	Absenteeism, unproductive activities, time waiting for assignments, unused time for any reasons.				Equals	____%
% of Total Hands-on time spent on computer work		____%	____%	____%	____%	100 %

6 When I first saw the distribution of these numbers I remarked about the one individual who claimed he was spending more than 75% of his total working hours behind a computer. Only a programmer could claim that. When I flashed this chart on the screen, the group broke into laughter. They turned to one of the Directors and acknowledged that he was unique.

7 The Chief was repeating a widely used and immensely popular explanation.

8 There is always the possibility that the desired work patterns applied to the Directors' subordinates.

9 Durand, Bennett, Betty, What Does Information Technology Do to Business Communication? *Information & Management*, Vol. 13, 1987

10 Word processing is the most frequently mentioned productivity-enhancing application on microcomputers according to Price Waterhouse, *Productivity Impact of the Automated Office*, 1984. Eighty-six percent of the respondents to the survey claimed substantial productivity gains from word processing.

11 Several vendors give you standard tables of percentage productivity gains from computer applications. For instance, a CAD/CAM vendor will tell you that you can expect a 40% labor saving gain in the drafting of structural drawings. Before you apply such a standard factor, you had better check its applicability. It may apply only to the detailing of steel shop drawings, not to the layout diagrams of concrete structures.

12 J.E. Gochenouer, An Empirical Study of the Impact of a Decision Support Language, Ph.D. Dissertation, University of Florida, 1985

13 The principal applications in this study.

14 365 days x 24 hours x 60 minutes x 0.001 = 525.6 minutes = 8.8 hours

294 THE BUSINESS VALUE OF COMPUTERS

[15] All public sector transactions, and especially those in defense, have a tendency to react to reported incidents by further tightening the quality standards for everything. That's why you end up with procurement regulations that apply equally to toilet seats, coffee pots and missiles. Systems become more complex, cumbersome, costly and therefore, more error prone.

I keep a folder with examples of excesses made by the inability of systems to deviate from standard procedures. A brokerage firm kept sending to me, by first-class mail, a monthly statement with a zero balance for 15 months although I wrote to them about the closed account. They explained to me that this was necessary "...to keep the file open for tax reasons."

[16] Just as in war, defectors and deserters have no incentive to report back to their units.

[17] These are adaptations of the *R-O-M* method of valuation as applied to a business function. *Operating Productivity* in marketing would be the gross margin contribution from current sales divided by the costs of supporting the current customer base. *Development Productivity* in marketing would be the discounted present cash value of the expected gross margin contribution from all new customers divided by the market development expenses.

One of the potential misuses of the *R-O-M* index—and as a matter of fact of any other productivity index—involves its use strictly as a short-term measure. Separating its short-term costs (e.g., cost of *Operations*) from long-term costs (e.g., cost of *Development*) offers a way by which to reconcile these conflicting elements. For a financial services company with unusually high costs of getting new clients but high follow-on gross margins, I recommended making such separate *R-O-M* computations.

[18] Such a table, per million dollars of new business, would look as follows:

Customer Attrition Rate/Year	Margins Realized from Customer
1%	$28,260
5%	$23,680
10%	$19,470
20%	$13,980
30%	$10,765

Alienating customers because of current neglect will depress future profits. If you expect to receive rapid promotions because you can show satisfactory short-term profits, you could double your accounting profits whenever you lose market share. Therefore, you should never trust accounting statements to reflect the health of a business. To evaluate business productivity you should penalize current profits for increased rates in customer losses. You should adjust profits if you are investing in reducing customer losses.

This approach suggests that price discounts should reflect not only new business but also the frequency of repeat business. In this way, repeat customers would receive lower prices every time they request more services.

[19] As reported by R. Moran, Treating IS As a Valued Asset, Not a Painful Expenditure, *Computerworld*, February 6, 1989, p. 94.

[20] An increasingly fashionable form of trading current expenses for future commitments.

[21] See Chapter 10 for elaboration.

[22] After considering the risk, the opportunity cost of capital and the expected life-cycle cash flows.

[23] The case is in its most simplified form.

13

PEOPLE AND SYSTEMS

All business systems successes and failures are the consequence of management actions. Every alleged computer failure, at our current level of technology development, is due to managerial errors. Only managers can make the right decisions about the choices of staff and technology.

FROM "SUPPLY" TO "DEMAND" ORIENTATION

Progress is making today's rarities tomorrow's essentials.

In the first twenty years of computerization, we spent much of our managerial energies trying to make the technology function as claimed by the suppliers. Our efforts concentrated on getting the computers to actually do work that vendors claimed to be feasible. All applications had to be uniquely hand-crafted by scarce computer specialists, on company payroll, to fit with each company's unique computer setup. The ability to buy complete computer solutions was not readily available ten to twenty years ago. The principal issue was how to control costs for delayed and malfunctioning applications. This was the reason why business executives delegated responsibility for managing information systems to technologists.

Nowadays, prudently chosen technology works as expected. The costs are predictable. If your company's technologists cannot deliver the applications they have promised, you can always find the needed expertise. You also have an active, competent and competitive marketplace to give your organization whatever information technology you need, when you need it, in whatever form you can use. There are a variety of computer services, facility management and turn-key systems solutions to satisfy your requirements. The risks are now in realizing the benefits. Securing the payoffs from investments in computers shifts the prime focus from technology to economic and organizational issues. That does not mean that computer technology is unimportant. Like gas, water supply, and electricity the computers are vitally important, but you pay attention to them only if they fail.

The management of computers now has less concern with unraveling of technological mysteries. It is rapidly becoming a matter of discovering benefits. Consequently, the responsibility for computers is now shifting from technologists to business executives.

Business executives have always asserted their influence by managing business practices. When the executives of the General Motors Corporation re-engineered their business methods in the 1920's, they did everything a systems designer does today. They had to design new accounting and reporting procedures. They changed transaction entry and reporting methods.

When the General Electric Corporation decentralized into profit centers in the 1950's, the actions were comparable to what happens today when a company does a major procedural overhaul.

The period from 1955 through 1975 was a time when executives temporarily released systems management to technologists because computerization promised to assure tighter compliance with established procedures. With a few notable exceptions where we found innovation in business practices, the technologists delivered exactly what they were asked to do. Analysts and programmers concentrated on teaching machines how to parrot the contents of elaborate procedure manuals that described complex business procedures. These manuals contained mostly unread pages, including the rules but excluding what people were really doing to get the job done. Executive management acquiesced to transferring controls to computers on the assumption that computer software finally could include what escaped the procedure manuals. Computerization also would replace the checkers who made sure that everyone was following the unread procedures.

It took twenty years for executives to figure out that it took a long time to encode business practices into computer programs. It also takes much effort to make any major changes once the procedures become software. In the 1970's, executives discovered that they owned costly systems which encapsulated obsolete business practices reflecting the best management know-how of the 1950's. Contrary to early assumptions, companies found computer systems increasing their administrative rigidity just when international competition called for accelerated adaptation to new business conditions. Customers became irritated when they received, as an increasingly common excuse, that the computer system did not allow for new or improved ways to transact business.

By 1985, it became apparent that systems design and systems management were inseparable from the essential managerial task of organizing people. Therefore, control over systems had to become part of every manager's job, and not be delegated to specialists.[1]

SYSTEMS MANAGEMENT IS EVERYONE'S JOB

A computer application is management by other means.

Managers are reasserting their role because the human element—the province of management—now dominates the costs of systems implementation and dictates the realization of any benefits. Information technology is still important, but will continue to receive less attention as the easy solution to solving the problems of a firm's declining productivity. We are rapidly approaching a stage of development where the acquisition and improvement of computer applications will blend into the routine tasks of organizations. Information will be readily available without fuss or unusual attention from top management.

The insertion of information technology into every managerial process and into most products and services is a magnificent achievement. Information technologists working in businesses have succeeded beyond their most optimistic forecasts. In 30 years they converted the business scene into one giant systems activity! No wonder the systems arena is now too big to remain solely in the custody of systems specialists.

Today, every child acquires the skills of the learned scribes who had served ancient kings as courtiers, which were positions of great prestige. With the widespread dissemination of literacy, every worker must know how to read, write and understand some mathematics. Literacy now is a pre-requisite in our society, not a condition warranting a position of privilege.

Similarly, every worker of the 21st century will need skills that used to belong exclusively to the small guild of computer professionals who introduced information technologies 60 to 100 years previously. Does that imply the demise of the computer technologists? Computer specialists always will be among us but may not be necessarily recognizable as they appear today. Ancient scribes, who could produce only a handful of documents, become in modern society authors, journalists, secretaries and lawyers who generate a profusion of written matter. The contemporary equivalents of the ancient scribes are a large and powerful group making notable contributions to our society and culture. They are a more productive and a influential group than their predecessors. Scribes could not stay an exclusive group forever, particularly when everybody acquired the skills and technology to do their work easier, better and faster.

Similarly, systems management cannot remain an exclusive occupation of a few highly trained analysts. When everyone's job depends on information systems, everyone becomes a consumer of information technology. Only paying customers are best equipped to decide what they need, when they need it and how much they will pay for it. In 1988, the total number of systems analysts in the U.S. was 479,000.[2] Contrast this with 68 million information workers[3] and an estimated 52 million computers.[4]

When everyone has a programmable workstation with the power of a large 1975 mainframe computer, the options are too numerous to filter choices through computer specialists. The most distinctive achievement of the nascent disciplines of "artificial intelligence" and expert systems will be the empowering of individuals to deal with networks and databases without the intervention of computer specialists. An intelligent "software agent" residing in each person's computer will be "taught" to complete needed tasks, on demand.[5]

The transformation of work into the electronically-based information age is well on its way. It will include everyone, because all work does include knowledge as a key ingredient. Wherever there is a need for knowledge you will find computers. They will become omnipresent, in the same way electricity is today in factories, offices and homes. In the age of electronically transmitted knowledge, the payoffs come from organizing people to extract that knowledge from computers and apply it to the creation of *Value-added*.

The business value of technology materializes only through people who are skillful enough to create wealth from a combination of computer-aided knowledge and all other resources. I view information technology only as means for disseminating information to people who know what to do with it. The future of information technology lies in its mastery by everyone.

THE CHIEF INFORMATION OFFICER

When there is no satisfactory management process for creating value-based computer applications, companies usually try to solve their problems by reorganizing the systems function. It is no surprise that executive discussions about the declining payoffs from computer investments invariably jump to the short-cut answer: if we only had the right person in charge of M.I.S., most of our problems would go away. This "Gordian knot"[6] approach is seen as the most practical way of cutting through conflicting interests.[7]

The new person in charge of computers inherits the task of clearing up whatever confusion may exist about the mission of information technology. Top management has great hopes. The charisma of the new information chief ought to catalyze workable solutions and unravel long standing conflicts about computer investment priorities. To signify the importance of such trust, the existing position is elevated, sometimes with the lofty title of Chief Information Officer (CIO) or Information Resources Manager (IRM). The announcements that usually accompany such appointments proclaim that the charter covers directing all information resources in the organization. In fact, the appointees have only limited powers over the management of information technologies.[8] The appointment of a CIO or IRM implies that an expert in managing computers can guide and control the evolution into the "age of information."

I have come neither to bury the CIO nor to praise him—but only to understand the philosophy he represented when this position emerged as a key information mangement solution in the early 1980's.

Reasons for Appointing a CIO

The rise of the CIO and IRM concept coincided with the need to get departmentally conceived computer applications to communicate with each other. Computer systems of the 1960's and early 1970's mirrored the existing organizational structure, and were unique to each business function. Marketing information systems supported the marketing department, but only rarely passed data to the computer applications in the sales department. Manufacturing systems usually required the manual entry of sales forecasts from sales department printouts. Distribution staff did not know what they would be shipping because the production planning schedule was not in a form compatible with the needs for truck dispatching. Purchasing systems passed only summary data to manufacturing so that finance could not analyze how buying decisions affected delivery costs.

Government systems functioned by application, such as vehicle registration, tax collection or individual welfare programs because legislative procedures dictated acquisition on a case-by-case basis. Industry applications could share data only within a business function (such as in marketing, finance or manufacturing). This assured that every major application operated in isolation, which ultimately resulted in an accumulation of technologically obsolete, disjointed and costly computer installations.

The CIO and IRM position gained legitimacy as the preferred solution for securing a smooth flow of inter-functional data. Appointing a CIO to apply a systems solution to what had always been an organizational problem seemed like a sensible way to restore a corporate-wide vision of cohesive teamwork.

The basis of a CIO's power was the establishment of cross-functional ("corporate" or "enterprise") information systems that transcended departmental boundaries. A company with delivery difficulties could not rely on improving the situation through departmental systems but needed to tie together marketing, sales, distribution, transportation and production data. The theory behind inter-functional systems was that the contending departmental fiefdoms would somehow learn to cooperate if they had access to the right information. Therefore, the appointment of a CIO usually coincided with highly publicized announcements launching long term "corporate information" or "enterprise information" projects.

CIO—Commanding Impossible Operations[9]

The job of a master designer for information flows in a corporation—who gets what information, when and how—places the CIO in an untenable position.[10] Irrespective of advisory and "steering" committees, only line management has the authority to decide the arrangement of information flow. To gain benefits from information technologies, organizations must restructure (sometimes radically) responsibility and accountability. Jurisdictional conflicts are the primary source of all inter-departmental disputes. The CIO can, at best, merely carry out top management's wishes how to run a company. Without a clearly defined organizational design which originates and is implemented through line management, the CIO who attempts to act as a master architect for streamlining information flows must fail.[11]

The CIO's position becomes more precarious due to built-in conflicts of interest if he also provides central computer services to the contending departments. Wasteful and costly skirmishes between the advocates of "centralization" and "decentralization" of the corporate computers will naturally occur as an assault to scuttle the CIO's position of influence.

When it becomes clear that the embattled CIO cannot produce the desired results, the CEO must decide how to get inter-functional systems into his company. This usually occurs when systems task forces keep meeting without a conclusive outcome, or when the costs of redundant and ineffective systems become intolerable. This typically coincides with a corporate-wide reorganization into individual businesses, or the creation of a newly defined business function.[12] The focus for specifying and managing systems now moves from the CIO to the operating management, who can now afford their own systems staff. Whether a company decentralizes into strategic business units, or centralizes into super-departments, such actions invariably dictate the redistribution of corporate overheads to the new organizations. The CIO's power base, nurtured largely by generous allowances from corporate overhead, then suffers a serious setback.

When systems management know-how and control over systems costs migrate away from the corporate organization headed by the CIO, the role of the central systems organization becomes more restricted. The CIO's traditional power base of managing one of the largest Departments in a corporation disappears.[13] What's left involves matters such as standard-setting for telecommunication networks, applications design and databases. The CIO's influence becomes confined to an area of technical specialization similar to any other central staff expertise. The prospect for such special-purpose corporate staff position as a power base for entry into a top executive position is remote.

Whenever executives with direct profit responsibility take over the job of linking information technologies and information resources to business strategies, the CIO's membership in top executive councils becomes superfluous.[14] A company that has successfully decentralized the management of information resources surely needs a senior computer executive to set policy and standards. However, a CIO in such a job cannot expect to be projected as a heroic role-model.[15] He or she cannot aspire to being a president-in-waiting. Most senior computer executives do not have the background to become one of the firm's top business strategists.[16] Nevertheless, they have a challenging job of assuring the lowest costs for information-handling technologies that meet the firm's competitive needs. Such a job is sufficiently difficult to merit one of the key corporate staff appointments such as the chief information technology officer or head of policy staff, to set information resources management policies.[17] Frequently, the jobs of chief information technologist and chief of information manager coincide. It's an important policy-setting job, but certainly not a direct stepping stone to a senior operating appointment.

The Progression from CIO to CEO

One articulate exposition of the heroic view as to how to manage computers is "...the chief M.I.S. executives must lead the reorganization of their companies, creating new corporate structures and innovative ways of doing business."[18] According to this view—echoed by heads of consulting firms specializing in information technology—it is important that the Information Systems function embraces its new role as a leading revolutionary change agent because "...too often companies have used information technology to achieve incremental changes—to automate what is rather than create what could be."[19]

I doubt that there are computer experts who can offer magical solutions to deeply rooted organizational problems using computer systems as a platform for organizational reform. All management systems—whether computerized or informal—are a reflection of accumulated managerial practices. It takes more than one executive, holding a specialized job, to change that. Newly appointed Chief Information Officers, especially if brought from another company or industry, hold a discouraging record of not being able to change deeply ingrained organizational habits.[20] How can you expect miracles from a transplanted CIO with a technology career, with no record of ever managing a profit-making business and no prior company-specific know-how?[21]

A systems-based turn-around may be more plausible as executives are rotated from or through administrative and M.I.S. positions as they progress into top management. A *Harvard Business Review* survey of executive mobility shows there are already a few Chief Operating Officers who reported progress into their present jobs via the administration/M.I.S. function. For instance, 9% of Chief Operating Officers stated that administration or M.I.S. was their background. But moving computer people into the top jobs will continue to be very difficult. Right now only 7.7% of all CIO's report to the CEO or to the president.[22]

Interpret with caution stories about the origins of company presidents. The CEO's of Citicorp (John Reed) and American Airlines (Robert Crandall) are rare examples often cited as the systems professionals' entry into top executive positions. Their direct involvement with system design early in their careers was transient. They quickly moved into "line" appointments with direct responsibility for revenue-producing profit centers. Another example of a CIO's progress, Robert Dryden, the ex-chief of Boeing Computer Services, earned his operating Division Presidency because for many years he was running a successful revenue-producing business. Chief Information Officers will not qualify for promotion into top executive positions unless they move out of servicing internal organizations into jobs where they deliver direct contributions to profits.

STAFFING THE INFORMATION SYSTEMS FUNCTION

Constricted jobs produce people with confined understanding.

Which people do you pick to manage and implement information systems? The answer to this question is becoming easier. Do not engage managers who have a record of developing original technologies which add to the company's overhead. Concentrate your investments in people who can deliver revenue-producing information technologies (e.g., *Operations*). Buy as many of your management information systems as possible competitively from proven off-the-shelf packages, contract services or turnkey projects. Establish your own technology subsidiary if your company is big or unique enough to need proprietary technology. You then can run and evaluate such a subsidiary as if it were a commercial business. Following these simple rules will make your hiring choices easier because you will not end up with highly specialized technologists—people unrelated to your main business—in vulnerable overhead jobs. Outstanding computer professionals will not seek such jobs anyway, without a path for technical career advancement. Your systems development staff should excel in systems integration skills which provide a capacity to link diverse and often unrelated technologies to satisfying specific business needs. These skills will make them prime candidates for promotion into business positions that involve innovation and new ventures.[23]

The same reasoning applies to data centers. A computer operation, especially if its budget is over $10 million per year, can become an uncontrollable sink for dollars. This happens when the employees conclude there is little opportunity for getting promoted because growing data center automation steadily reduces available opportunities. The feeling of being locked into data center operations also arises when employees believe that they cannot get promoted except by quitting and finding better pay from someone seeking more advanced skills.

Stagnant or declining employment conditions in large data centers dictate that improved job opportunities are available primarily by switching jobs. The problem is that employers with few job openings prefer to hire only technically advanced talent. Therefore, the potential job seekers will press for accelerated technical innovation. Ambitious data center personnel without internal career growth opportunities will recognize that bigger and more sophisticated equipment is beneficial to their career advancement. Guess what will happen under such conditions? You will get proposals for more expensive and more sophisticated equipment whenever possible. This condition explains why unceasing computer obsolescence is advantageous, both for the data center staffs and vendors, to an extent never encountered with any other technology. Data centers are always a source of institutionalized discontent with whatever equipment is available. You can verify this observation by making a trip to a for-profit computer services vendor. Such vendors make their living by selling computer time or computer application services. You will find out how effectively they use fully depreciated equipment that your own data center folks would consider ancient.

If you must hire highly technical computer talent or operate your own data center, confirm that the employees' careers may enter your revenue-generating business. There are individuals who truly wish to stay narrowly specialized and may not aspire to advancement, but this condition may not last forever. Unless you have a large operation, there are practical limits to how much growth you can provide for such specialists. You should be always in a position to offer opportunities for personal advancement because information technology demands that people should not stagnate. Continued personnel development, job rotation[24] and diversification in technical skills will keep your personnel innovative and productive.

Organize information systems jobs so that individuals have an opportunity to obtain business-related experiences. Everybody talks about job rotation for computer programmers or data center people. I have rarely seen it done because the salaries of computer people are much higher than those offered in non-computer positions for which they would qualify.

You can also achieve the goal of skill diversification by offering job enlargement for computer people which will prepare them for new opportunities. Disregard narrow job definitions by rotating data center personnel into customer support jobs. Sacrifice some efficiency by giving programmers an opportunity to do some systems analysis, end-user documentation and heavy doses of user personnel training. I have tracked the careers of some of my programmers as they advanced through transient training assignments into top production management jobs. They had access to the kinds of opportunities I described.

Do not accept the widely promoted theory that a data center should run as a factory with the sole purpose of generating calculations and database access. This may appear technologically efficient, but it will be destructive from the human resources perspective. A data center should be responsible not only for calculating and printing invoices, but also for their distribution, error handling and routine inquiries. In corporate jurisdictional conflicts, there are too many technically-minded computer executives who avoid any involvement with the imperfections of the non-computerized world. For instance, a computer technocrat will be glad if some marketing function takes over the handling of complaints about lost invoices, misprints, wrong mailing addresses and missing postage. By drawing a distinct line between computer operations and the revenue-producing business, he keeps his staff from understanding that there are customers outside the walls of the data center. Data center people who must deal with the ultimate customer, regardless fo how tenuously, receive experiences that may lead them into a variety of sales administration positions. For example, a trainee who started as a tape-station operator in a data center is now Senior Vice President of Administration for a large Texas bank. I have run an operation where the information function was not only responsible for calculating and printing payroll checks but also for managing all the entries, cash and reporting. Several of the people who were staffing this operation have now progressed into senior personnel administration positions.

THE MANAGER AND THE TECHNOLOGIST

The Manager and the Technologist are like different tribes, with different cultures.

Managers often say about computer specialists: "They only care about the computer, not the company. I am afraid of being so dependent on them. Can't talk with them. Their answers are in jargon I do not understand."

Information specialists' views about management are equally skeptical: "Their expertise is in manipulating people, not in substance. I cannot get their attention unless I mention dollars or company politics. Whenever I need a direct answer, I hear only generalities."

The above extreme views demonstrate the polarization of how people in different roles see each other.[25] Nevertheless, for each point of view there is justification. The causes are primarily economic and social.

Managers have a much broader perspective about the business than the computer specialists. Their education is primarily in finance, social science, liberal arts and law. Their skills are verbal and idea-manipulative. They know something about customers, competitors and the production processes because they have held multiple company assignments. A manager reads the Chairman's latest press release with care, looking for hints about the latest change in direction.

Conversely, the computer specialists rarely, if ever, know anything about the company's customers or, in the case of government, the agency's missions. Their skills are in numbers and logic. They enter into a specialty and rarely leave it. Reading the Chairman's latest press release or even the Annual Report conveys little information that would benefit their careers immediately.

Managers concentrate on results and their career advancement. They think: What will it do, how much will it cost and how will it promote me? When will it be ready and how much can I risk with it? The managers' promotions depend on successful avoidance of trouble and aversion to even a taint of failure.

The technologists concentrate on mastering technology. Their salaries depend on how much indispensable, technical know-how they can accumulate. Their egos get satisfaction from getting access to new (meaning risky) technology. They learn from what does not work.

It is easier for a computer expert to find a comparable job elsewhere than a manager. Managers and technologists usually envy each other's position.

Managers are probably older and more experienced in how things really work around the company. Technologists are probably younger and confident that they positively know how things should work.

No wonder a clash in attitudes is inevitable. A skillful executive will not precipitously force a technologist to act as a manager or vice versa. The technologist and the manager have to acknowledge their differences as a source of their respective strengths. The organization will gain if there are processes in place for channeling diversity into constructive cooperation. That means leaving to managers what managers can do best, and asking technologists to concentrate on their unique capabilities unless the technologists have begun a migration that will ultimately lead to a managerial career. Technology and management are indeed different cultures and you should not try to force them into molds they do not fit.

Adapting the Culture

Analysis is the disciplining of speculation with facts.

The image a company projects to the public and its employees reflects its culture—the values, standards and convictions which guide the ways in which it expects to work. Organizational culture should include an attitude towards information technology.

An organization may permeate its rhetoric with positive pronouncements about computers as a symbol of modernization. However, if organizations have a bias against access to information, such as in government bureaucracies, computer applications will concentrate on checking employees' actions for compliance with rules and regulations.

If organizations try to place responsibility where people do *Value-added* work, the way they design and operate computer programs will reflect their decentralized culture. If organizations try to concentrate all discretionary decisions in just a handful of people, such as in control-oriented bureaucracies, the computer applications will concentrate on checking employees' actions. The computer applications will then mirror the control culture.

You cannot effectively design and operate information systems unless the systems are in harmony with the management style of dealing with problems of responsibility and accountability. Systems designs can exhibit schizophrenia the way people do, if the systems designers follow unfocused generalities that emanate from executive speeches. Computer projects ultimately fail when managers apply them as a covert tool to force an organization into new ways of managing the business. Cultural change must precede, not follow, computerization.

Organizations cannot cope with broad generalizations in order to deal with their difficulties in extracting benefits from computer investments. They have specific maladies which call for proven cures. The changing of a "corporate culture," similar to the alteration of personality, comes only through steady achievement in every activity, not just in those affecting information technology.

Giving employees electronic access to information about product quality, costs or profits can have an enormously favorable effect on the ways in which people will relate to their jobs. However, providing data will be meaningless unless the employees will be able to do something with the newly acquired knowledge, such as making discretionary decisions. The important ingredient in such a cultural change is not the availability of data, but the change in the ways by which individuals learn about their relationships with others.

Reforming a corporate culture begins with the selection of a project that is enormously profitable. The job of the agents facilitating change is to find this application and get it installed. People can then learn from their accomplishments, instead of speculating about possibilities.

This pragmatic view is not always welcome because it deprives staff and consultants of opportunities to engage in feasibility studies, working parties, surveys, discussion groups, presentations, quality circles and priority reviews. There are many schools of thought which say that the effective use of computers is primarily a "cultural" matter. The head of one consulting firm criticized the emphasis on the creation of economic value. He felt it was too simplistic. "...I would only spend 20% of my time on economics. I would spend the other 80% creating the culture to make it happen."[26]

The frequently voiced admonition from speeches and magazine articles to "change the culture" as a prerequisite to effective computerization is sufficiently broad to cover a multitude of sins. It is a sweeping generalization which calls for a license to leave nothing untouched. When consultants, teachers and researchers stress the creation of the right environment to nurture information technology, this includes:[27]

- Linking information technology with overall business strategy.
- Visible and active support from senior managers.
- Changes in the culture and structure of organizations before introducing changes in technology.
- An investment in people and their development.
- Disciplined project management and accountability for the delivery of commitments.
- Multi-disciplinary design teams, with varying skills and backgrounds.
- Sound methods for monitoring and reviewing progress.
- Emphasis on spreading the benefits from one project to other parts of the organization.
- Recognition of the need to continue developing and innovating the business as circumstances change.
- Supplying clear policy guidance on accountability and responsibility of personnel.
- Participative, non-threatening management.
- Job security and advancement opportunities without discrimination.

You can continue indefinitely preparing lists of good management practices. However, these are not unique to the use of computers. Most of the items would apply equally well to research, engineering, manufacturing, personnel, marketing and good housekeeping. Studies about creating a favorable business culture are more suitable to an examination of general management practices than as a precondition for using computers. Supportive, humane and well integrated environments are a prerequisite for effective and profitable acceptance of any innovation, including computers. Unfortunately, experts take advantage of the organizational disturbances created by information technologies to elevate themselves to telling CEO's and Boards of Directors grand strategies of how a company should operate.

There is only one good reason to defend the listing of all conceivable influences as an acceptable technique for coping with information technology. Recent developments in "chaos" theories suggest that in highly complex systems there is always the possibility that very small changes will generate enormous consequences. A consultant may just happen to include in his list the one effect which will magically prevent disaster or miraculously deliver fantastic gains.

Unhappily, a technical expert who tries to solve major business difficulties by listing brilliant insights will soon find there are as many favorite prescriptions as there are lists of desirable "cultural" changes. Lists drawn up without supporting evidence are only speculations. Factual analysis, especially in financial terms, should precede all explorations of the intangible. In other words, financial analysis is the disciplining of speculation with facts. When conceptual frameworks and cash are in conflict, the theories must yield.

Behavioral and social effects are extremely important to the success of computer investments. However, until behavioral and social approaches have shown greater consistency, subject to reasonable verification, technical experts should apply them only after completing their analytic work.

Tampering with organizational culture is for the acknowledged leaders of a firm. Computerization and work automation, especially when they are controversial, are not a suitable platform for launching the crusade to reform "cultural" habits. To guide changes in admittedly bad organizational habits, the computer experts must first remodel themselves from technical experts into general managers. Unless they arrive—after metamorphosis—into the executive quarters, they had better tend to their demanding roles in making computers deliver the best results that the existing organization will allow.[28]

Computer Literacy

It is now a generally accepted proposition that employees should be "computer-literate" and management must learn how to apply information technology. It is hard to argue against the need for more education. You should never deny to anyone the opportunity to learn something new.

So far, nobody has produced a shred of proof that executive or employee proficiency in BASIC or MS/DOS relates to intensity, profitability or superiority in the uses of information technology.[29] Most of the successful applications of computer technology are in organizations where employees receive only a minimum of training in the technology they are using. Most of the 30 million electronic terminals in the U.S. call for only ordinary "literacy": how to read and count. The specific technology applied in a cash register or a reservation terminal is irrelevant.

When it comes to top management, too much technical knowledge about computer hardware and software may be dangerous. Of the top ten most messed up internal information systems I have seen, two belong to vendors of information systems equipment.[30] Technical knowledge about computers is not a substitute for knowing how to manage computers.

Transfiguration of Organizations

U.S. organizations are in an unprecedented turmoil. One in five workers leaves his or her job every year. One in ten leaves a job involuntarily. One in ten must make a career change each year.

This turmoil has many dimensions. Job creation opportunities vary depending on the size of the organization. Over the last 20 years, large organizations have lost jobs whereas small organizations created jobs. The number and growth of small organizations have not remained constant. For instance, to create 0.5 million new jobs in the 20–99 employee category 3.2 million jobs materialized from startup businesses. Over 2.8 million jobs disappeared due to business closing. Companies upgraded or downgraded, which resulted in more mobility.[31]

The job losses in large companies disguise further structural changes. "Big" companies are not monolithic giants any more. Large companies are now trying to act as small businesses through increased decentralization. From a systems standpoint, the concentration of new systems development is shifting from a few to many autonomous units.

The implications of these trends on information technology are far-reaching. New companies and rapid turnover in organizations demand systems easy to install and easier to replace. Employee turnover and migration in and out of enterprises require systems that will install without delays for use by a volatile workforce that has little time for acquiring on-the-job training.

This environment does not tolerate significant errors in systems choices. A defective inventory, cash management or ordering system can wipe out a small firm before management has a chance to replace the offending applications. This is particularly important for the smallest companies which have the potential of becoming very successful. Slow-growth companies comprise 85% of the economy but create only 16% of the jobs. The fast growers, who represent only 7% of all establishments, create 67% of the jobs. Most of the fast growth companies start very small. 61% of the fastest growers are companies with fewer than 20 employees. If they do not install the right computer system from their inception, they will cripple their takeoff.

This instability also opens opportunities. It allows a late comer to choose the best and latest technology to gain a competitive edge over everyone else. This is why the Atlas Door Company case in Chapter 8 is my favorite story of how a relative newcomer can gain instant advantage over long-established companies. The innovator can use computers aggressively if management makes information technology an active ingredient in the formula of how to seize a business opportunity. This is why the Chief Executive, especially of a rapid-growth services-based company, must become the chief information decision-maker.

Today, you cannot restructure an old business or enter into a new venture without involving systems in your action plan. When a small company doubles in size every year, the Chief Executive may have good reasons for why he or she is not paying attention to information systems needs. This neglect could cause irreversible damage.

COUNTER-PRODUCTIVE EFFECTS

Invasion of Personal Privacy

"Computers could turn out to be the ultimate weapon in solving the case of the $10 prescription that led to a $10,000 hospitalization bill."[32] Such news offers computerization as examples of productivity. Computer service companies have entered the business of accumulating individual patient histories from health claims data filed with insurance companies. The computer generates a patient profile whenever it finds a pre-established risk threshold. A warning letter then goes to the patient's doctor or pharmacist.

The advocates of civil liberties do not applaud such practices. They will disregard economic gains and raise the issue of privacy invasion. They consider passing personal records to a third party without consent a violation of individual rights. People may feel offended and even injured in situations where employers, government authorities and institutions could use information about them without an individual being made aware. Litigation on charges of privacy invasion can nullify whatever economic gains are available through computerization. Databases containing personal information must have safeguards against misinformation and must carefully protect access privileges.

Databases that contain private personal information will continue to expand. Such databases will be increasingly accessible from everywhere. Personal workstations can scan many databases to come up with recommendations of what to do about a personal transaction, such as deny credit, grant a mortgage or admit for medical treatment. I have constructed an economically and technologically plausible scenario in which there are no cash transactions. Only credit cards authorize payments. Business communications can take place only by means of electronic mail. All education is computer-mediated. Such an arrangement could allow a totalitarian state to exercise unlimited economic and thought-control power over what each person can do.[33]

How society will ultimately protect individual civil liberties against the intrusions of an all-powerful computerized State is one of the major risks of a computerized society.

Monitoring Clerical Work

The timing of every activity and recording of every keystroke by an operator is commonplace in the insurance, banking and airline industries. Most supermarket check-out systems track every action of the clerks.

Reactions to computer monitoring have been hostile from labor unions and mixed from workers. Opposition to on-line performance monitoring culminates in trade union actions where it serves as a focus for other accumulated grievances. Organized labor sees in computer monitoring a return to sweatshop conditions. Behavioral scientists say that task-monitoring by computers creates implicit anxiety and depersonalizes the workplace.

Supporters of monitoring argue that the tracking of output substitutes clear quantitative measures for subjective, unreliable and stressful performance evaluations. Computer monitoring enhances the ability of managers to motivate employees to greater productivity. Opponents are vocal in their hostility. They tell distressing anecdotes about employee demotivation. There is, however, no research-based evidence which shows if any of these views are valid.

Proponents and antagonists agree, however, that monitoring encourages employees to concentrate on whatever the system measures and reports. Since the systems usually measure only the quantity of output, employees will deliver exactly that. Hard-to-measure ancillary qualities, such as courtesies and problem-solving are often discouraged in such a set-up.

I could find only one study that gathered data about monitored and unmonitored employees in the same company. A university team examined a large Canadian insurance company.[34] They came up with unsurprising results. Eighty percent of the monitored workers said that the essential factor in their work was the quantity of output. Eighty-six percent of the unmonitored workers said that quality, service, accuracy and teamwork were more important than quantity.

The study also examined whether supervisors relied on computer-recorded indicators in their performance evaluations. The researchers found some, but not convincingly strong, correlations between what the supervisors said and what the records showed. There was also no indication of whether the monitored employees were more or less productive as compared with some internal or external measures of output. Most importantly, customers did not say whether they could tell the difference.

The debate between opponents and proponents of computerized monitoring always ends up in calls for government regulation because there are no facts to prove either point of view. Meanwhile, everyone appears to be quite comfortable with their current positions, because no facts substantiate whatever anyone alleges, which allows the arguments to continue indefinitely.

Spending on Ergonomics

Demoralization can be the largest automation expense.

The capital costs per person for good air-conditioning, a low noise level, new office furniture and improved lighting will exceed the costs of a personal computer. The temptation is to defer the essential improvements of the office environment because the investment proposals justify their gains from the application of technology, and not from people's attitudes.

This orientation found in most computer proposals implies that operating management should worry about sustaining morale if employees react adversely. The penalties for such protracted neglect can be considerable. Employee dissatisfaction stemming from poor ergonomics can demolish the economic benefits expected from an otherwise profitable new computer system.

If you are making financial payoff calculations to justify added expenses for ergonomic comfort, hazard elimination, employee health and safety you should always apply a negative discount rate.[35] The penalties for correcting a demoralizing condition escalate as time passes.

Bad ergonomics is bad business. A little care and small amounts of money will produce considerable improvement. Whenever the ergonomic conditions are good, their hidden benefits are not directly measurable. Their costs always appear as an added overhead expense, such as higher office rental or higher furniture depreciation. The liability of bad ergonomics can be proven only when the penalties are high, such as was shown in the STK case in Chapter 10. Do not wait for unfavorable incidents, such as litigation, to generate the rationale for fixing disastrous ergonomic conditions. The following may help:
- Make the justification of ergonomics of any information system an integral part of the entire proposal.
- Keep track of ergonomic disasters that have happened in similar conditions such as yours.
- Learn about causes of dissatisfaction during exit interviews.
- If employees complain about adverse ergonomic effects, try to find out if they have unique characteristics as a group.

- Install pilot versions of all new office environments, and ensure that you have a competent observer studying the employees' physical comforts.

SPENDING ON TRAINING AND GUIDANCE

The validity of paying attention to ergonomics applies even more forcefully to adequate training and skillful management. Personnel working with computers need a fairly wide amount of knowledge to cope with the variety and speed of a computerized business. Variety, speed and complexity are precisely those attributes that make computerized work more productive than manual work. You cannot calculate your benefits just by multiplying theoretical gains from the acceleration of computer-automated work. Before you get those, you have to invest in employee skill-development and managerial support. After your staff reaches the needed skill levels, you will continue incurring expenses for the retraining of new employees, and further upgrading the employees' skills whenever procedures change.

I once commissioned a study tracing all efforts to correct a faulty invoice sent to a customer. The cost of correcting a mailed invoice was twenty to thirty times the cost of an error-free invoice. We could not find any computer errors.[36] The machines added and multiplied correctly. The output printers printed exactly the amounts specified by the programs. All errors were human errors, which in each instance originated from inadequate training or poor management practices.

Do not wait for major foul-ups to occur in order to prove why you need more money and time for more training and better supervisory guidance. In case of cost overruns or schedule slips, everyone will find it more acceptable to blame technical mistakes such as faulty hardware, software errors or contractor delays. This will depersonalize the real causes of failure and prevent organizations from learning about the human aspects that lie behind every real or alleged "technical" failure. The following may help:
- Include training, guidance, consulting and management development costs as a direct cost of implementing a project. If I do not see training costs exceeding the costs of hardware, I always wonder if I am seeing a realistic proposal.

- Allow enough time and money so that people can adapt to the changes in the working environment if your project calls for displacement of employees or for work redesign.
- Require that the employees who will have to operate an automated system have a great deal of influence from inception until completion by keeping them informed about expected systems characteristics. Circulating to employees survey forms or conducting "focus group"[37] interviews during the feasibility phase of a project is insufficient. In case of an innovative system the employees may not have sufficient insights to understand what is possible.
- Set up a randomly picked group of employees to participate with the technical project team in pilot studies and especially when final system testing begins.
- Give employees participating in systems testing the veto power to stop further systems implementation if they find the early results unacceptable. It is vastly more expensive to make major revisions in a project after full scale implementation than during early testing.

Chapter Summary

The business value of computers comes from the people who manage and use them. This is the principal rationale for insisting that managing the benefits takes precedence over managing the costs of information technologies.

In case of cost overruns or schedule slips, everyone finds it more acceptable to blame technical mistakes. This depersonalizes the real causes of failure and devalues the importance of the human element for all systems successes. Emphasizing managerial responsibilities for information technologies makes it possible for organizations to learn from mistakes, which is the only way to master computers.

If you accept this view you will cease looking to any magic agent, such as a Chief Information Officer, for leadership in guiding how a company's management should use its information. Instead, you will make information systems management an inseparable element of every manager's daily work.

CHAPTER 13 COMMENTS

1 B. Caldwell, Is M.I.S Losing the Factory Floor? *InformationWeek*, July 17,1989. This article carries the provocative subtitle "In the unending wars between information chiefs and plant-floor managers, MIS may have irrevocably lost both ground and credibility." It quotes cases where the initiative for systems development shifted from the experts to line management.

2 The Information Technology Industry Data Book, Industry Marketing Statistics, *CBEMA*, Washington, D.C., 1990, Table 3–3.

3 There were 14.6 million executives, administrators and managers and 15.9 million professionals in the U.S. in December 1989. These people spend their time almost exclusively in dealing with information that cannot be pre-programmed. (Monthly Employment Report, *U.S. Department of Labor*, December 1989, Table A-11.)

4 *Forbes*, June 11, 1990, p. 20.

5 The best way of learning something is to teach it. The monopoly of systems analysts and programmers cannot continue forever. Computerization has contributed to the de-skilling of people who are the end-users of centrally designed systems that leave no options open for adaptation to local conditions. It deprived the operators of systems of important learning experiences. Instructing a machine in what to do is a way of bringing a sense of innovation into everyday affairs so that end-users can learn how to structure and program their individual computer environment.

6 In this legend, the knot tied by King Gordius could not be undone. A Delphi oracle (a precursor of management consultants and executive recruiters) predicted that the future Master of Asia would undo the knot. Alexander the Great cut it with his sword. An example of cutting through technical complexities, such as voluminous systems plans, comes from the new M.I.S. Chief of the Unum corporation. He junked all systems design documentation and replaced it with a three-page statement of "business theology" (July 10, 1989 issue of *InformationWeek*).

7 An example of this thinking is in the following quote: "...the real key to the turnaround that banks need to achieve lies in a re-definition of the role of information systems management. The critical link...is a person—the CIO—with a vision for technology, access to top management and the ability to explain how technology can be used to lower operating costs." (Bill Hewitt of the First Manhattan Consulting Group, in A. Alper, Banks Seek Higher Yield from Info Systems Investment, *Computerworld*, August 15, 1988, p. 65).

8 I have checked with a number of CIO's and IRM about what escaped their influence. The technology list covered: desk-top publishing, records management, corporate archives, engineering computing, factory automation, all computing for research and development, external services (especially in advertising), all legal files, "office automation" (a catch-all term that includes copiers, microfilms, facsimile), voice telephone, all printing services, office mail and courier services. CIO's and IRM's rarely, if ever, guide costly information-intensive activities such as meetings, company publications, advertising or training and education which accounts for more than half of all information costs. A CIO or IRM cannot claim having responsibilities for managing "information" if he or she has direct influence for less than one fifth of total information costs.

9 The IRM equivalent could be Impossible Relationships to Manage.

10 A realistic indication of the actual involvement of CIO's in influencing business strategy comes from G.L. Hershey and J.L. Eatman, Why IS Execs Feel Left Out of Big Decisions, *Datamation*, May 15, 1990. Only 12% of chief IS executives were "very involved" in corporate planning—the key to promoting strategic uses of information technologies. Fourteen percent of the I.S. executives acknowledged being "involved." The remainder were either "mostly uninvolved" or "somewhat involved."

11 This generalization also applies if a corporation relies on a vendor, consultant, or services contractor to design its internal relationships.

12 A. Pantages, The New Order at Johnson Wax, *Datamation*, March 15,1990 is a good example showing how a change in organizational structure makes it easier to design and implement cross-functional information systems.

[13] Such as in insurance, banking, airlines, utilities and other business services.

[14] This view coincides with the comments by M.D. Hopper in the *Harvard Business Review*, May-June, 1990. Max Hopper is senior vice president of information systems at American Airlines. Some people consider him the most successful CIO in America. In his closing remarks, titled "Who Needs the CIO?" Hopper says "...as technology reshapes the nature of work...technology itself will recede into the strategic background....In this world, a company trumpeting the appointment of a new chief information officer will seem as anachronistic as a company today naming a new vice president of water and gas." In the subsequent issue of the Harvard Business Review a chorus of disagreement showed up in Letters to the Editors. However, nobody presented any arguments why Hopper's view of the computer utility (like water or gas) was unrealistic.

Another version of the diminishing importance of a chief information executive shows up in the shuffle at Chrysler (Chrysler IS Stalls, *Informationweek*, June 25, 1990). "The old guard in the finance department have won the war. Two top IS managers, tired of the struggle, have left and a finance executive has taken control. It appears that IS had constant clashes with finance over the M.I.S. headcount. Finance would approve a business unit plan that depended on a major IS project and then deny MIS the resources it needed to carry out the project." This case describes a prescription for CIO failure. If MIS depends on funding from central overhead to fund its operations, it becomes an unreliable supplier. I am sure that Chrysler MIS would be less frustrated if its funding had come from the operating unit as an inter-divisional purchase.

[15] W. Synnott, credited with articulating the CIO concept, did not retain that title for long. Synnott's replacement as chief information executive was a banker.

[16] E.K. Brumm, Chief Information Officers in Service and Industrial Organizations, *Information Management Review*, 1990, Number 3, Table 14 shows that only 15% of chief information systems executives in service companies have a marketing background, and only 16.4% have this background in industrial companies. 78.7% of chief information systems executives in services and 58.2% in industrials have progressed only through the M.I.S. function.

[17] An articulate argument that the most senior computer executive of a firm should concentrate on questions of technology strategy is in K. Melymuka, Say It Ain't So, *CIO Magazine*, March 1990. It features an interview with Bruce Rogow of the Gartner Group.

A realistic view of the role of the chief information executive comes from John O. Watson of British Airways, one of the most influential executives holding this title: "...to be the business systems visionary, the infrastructure designer, the data manager, the systems integrator, and the mechanic who will tune the performance of the information systems organization." (In letters to the Editor of the *Harvard Business Review*, July 1990.)

An even more subdued role is suggested in C.H. Deutsch, Treasuring the Technology Guru, *The New York Times*, July 22, 1990, p.F23. The following is a listing of what chief information technology officers do: 1. Play liaison between scientists and top management, 2. Incorporate technology into strategic plans, 3. Transfer technologies among autonomous divisions, 4. Interact with universities, national laboratories and other scientific groups, 5. Hammer out technological joint ventures or strategic alliances with other companies, 6. Act as mentors to younger researchers and scientists.

[18] Michael Hammer (quoted in the July 3, 1989 *InformationWeek*, p.37) said that M.I.S. chiefs are uniquely qualified to lead the reformation of corporations because "...information systems people know intuitively how to structure and solve large, complex problems. MIS executives can realign a world-wide corporation because of their ability to think about systems. The information systems executives' mission is to transform and redeem stagnant businesses and in this way become agents of corporate innovation." This exuberant view is well received by computer executives seeking legitimacy for their aspirations.

[19] D. Stamps, For Good Measure, *InformationWeek*, April 16, 1990, p. 54.

[20] The public sector equivalent of the CIO is the information resources manager (IRM). This position has arisen as the result of recommendations from government commissions and consultants. It is a solution that deals with the disarray in computer management because of increased centralization. The limits on the contributions of the CIO do not equally apply to the IRM executive because government and university organizations are centralized, hierarchical and functionally specialized. Such executives are especially prevalent in the Department of Defense which makes complete decentralization inapplicable for any long-term planning. Wherever the public sector or universities become market-oriented, the viability of the IRM approach to information management must erode.

[21] B. Caldwell, M.I.S: Expense or Asset? *InformationWeek*, February 5, 1990, p. 28, reports about a survey by the prominent executive search firm of Heidrick and Struggles. Half of chief information systems executives either resigned or were dismissed.

J. Rothfeder and L. Driscoll, CIO is Starting to Stand for Career is Over, *Business Week*, February 26, 1990, p. 78, report that the CIO dismissal rate was 13% per year.

InformationWeek reports (April 16, 1990, p. 50) that the current exodus rate for CIOs is "...anywhere from 13% to 30% annually, depending on which survey one believes."

A July 1990 report by the J.J. Davis & Associates executive recruiting firm specializing in M.I.S. reports that the average tenure of a Vice President of M.I.S. or CIO is about two-and-a-half years, down from three years during the mid-1980's. A Digital Equipment Corporation publication quotes a survey by Touche Ross & Co. that 30 percent of 538 CIO respondents said their predecessors were dismissed or demoted, and that the average tenure of a CIO is about 3.5 years (CIO's in Sea of Change, *Enterprise Magazine*, Spring 1990, p. 4).

[22] A survey of CIO's by Heidrick & Struggles reported in *Business Week*, February 26, 1990, p. 79.

[23] You will need a handful of technology "architects" to evaluate the wide range of standards-setting options in the marketplace. The best place to find these rare skills is precisely where they originate, which is with vendors, consultants and universities. After serving for a few years in the rarefied atmosphere of evaluating and setting policy, their careers will lead wherever they choose.

[24] For reasons of security.

[25] "Cultural difference" shows up in how different people react when confronted with the identical situation. An allegorical tale illustrates that. Four computer experts were in a hurry to get to a meeting but could not get their car started. The salesman said "Let's buy a new car." The maintenance engineer said "Let's rotate the tires, then change the carburetor, and keep swapping parts until we find the fault." The software expert said "Let's turn the ignition key while pressing the windshield wiper." The manager said "Let's take a taxi."

[26] Quoted in *Business Week*, October 14, 1985, in an article on Information Power.

[27] This list comes from Christine Howarth of the Work Research Unit, London.

[28] N. Seligman of the influential *Research Board* said "...the Chief Information Officers are paid to be good at providing the company with the right technological opportunities...they are not paid to act as a business generalist or set an overall business strategy." Quoted by A.E. Alter, Intelligent Networking, *CIO Magazine*, February 1990, p. 58.

[29] P. Ein-Dor and E. Segev, Information Resources Management for End User Computing, *Information Resources Management Journal*, Fall 1988, p. 44. The authors concluded that "...A CEO's personal use of computers has no effect on funding levels of the Data Processing budget or on the relative number of employees engaged in Data Processing." *Computing, Information Resources Management Journal*, Fall 1988, p. 44.

[30] One of these firms, managed by exceptionally talented and successful technologists, explained their profit decline by the failure of their computer applications in accounting.

CHAPTER 13—PEOPLE AND SYSTEMS   *321*

31 D.L. Birch, The Rise and Fall of Everybody, *INC. Magazine*, Sept. 1987, p. 18. Birch illustrates the uneven distribution of new jobs, by company size:

Company Size	Net Jobs Created
0–19	+536,000
20–99	+518,000
100–499	+183,000
500–4,999	-146,000
5,000+	-342,000

The net job creation does not show how this affects individuals. To create a net of 518,000 new jobs in the 20–99 employee companies the following movements happened:

	Employees affected (000's)
Jobs gained from startup businesses	+3,206
Jobs downgraded from bigger businesses shrinking	+398
Jobs upgraded from smaller businesses growing	+2,150
Jobs lost from business closing	-2,867
Jobs upgraded from smaller businesses getting bigger	-968
Jobs downgraded from businesses getting smaller	-922
Net jobs gained for 20–99 employee companies	518

32 S. Kerr, Information Systems: the Best Medicine for Drug Monitoring, *Datamation*, August 1, 1988, p. 41. Health Information Designs Inc. of Arlington, VA. is operating a computerized DURbase (drug utilization review) tracking individual patients' drug uses. Major corporations, such as General Motors, are also subscribing to DURbase. The goal of this operation is to reduce the costs of drug-induced hospital stays. An estimated 7% of all hospital stays relate to the misuse of pharmaceutical drugs, estimated to cost $5 billion. Another company, Health Data Resources, has gained access to every hospital record in Rhode Island and to 90% of all retail drug prescriptions.

33 I still hold the view that George Orwell's nightmarish "1984" was technologically incompetent. Big Brother, as defined by Orwell, could implement full controls by year 2000 with help from competent systems designers.

34 R.A. Grant, C.A. Higgins, R.H. Irving, Computerized Performance Monitors: Are They Costing You Customers? *Sloan Management Review*, 1988, Vol. 29, No. 3, pp. 39–45. Seventy-nine clerical employees engaged in claims processing were interviewed. Fifty-five were subject to computer monitoring and received information about the daily number of settled claims after each month. A corporate unit consisted of personnel who were not monitored. It appears that the work of the monitored and unmonitored personnel was incomparable in scope and location, and therefore the findings are of questionable validity. Nevertheless, the researchers came up with interesting conclusions: 1. Performance monitoring promotes bureaucratic behavior. 2. Computer-generated counts are not a fair measure of results. One group of clerks explained how they could routinely by-pass standard procedures to produce null checks. Such activity was also counted as "output" by the diligent computers. "Faking the counts" is a widely prevailing practice to be found in organizations that over-concentrate on transaction counts as a performance measure. For instance, a flaw in the software of a check-out register made it possible for the clerks to show increased transaction counts by opening and re-opening the cash drawer.

35 A positive discount rate means that the present worth of a future dollar is less. A negative discount rate means that the present worth of a future dollar is more.

36 "It is a computer error" has become the culturally most acceptable excuse for mismanagement. It absolves everybody because a computer is inanimate and irresponsible, though a powerful symbol. The readiness with which clerks offer these explanations to the public is a sign that computers have now assumed an identity of their own. Computers become objects that are separate from the people who are responsible for them. Institutions that have no accountability for their actions must ultimately fail.

37 Convening a specially picked group of customers for a session where they receive encouragement to express uninhibited opinions about a company's products and services.

14

LEARNING FROM MISTAKES

You learn best from your own mistakes.

A book about the business value of computers would be incomplete without a discussion of *runaway* projects. *Runaways* are the black holes of computer budgets. Cash, long hours, personal careers and potential returns of business value disappear without hope of recovery. Here are a few glimpses of this frequent, but rarely reported phenomenon:[1]

- Allstate Insurance in 1982, with software from Electronic Data Systems, started building an $8 million computer system that would completely automate the company by 1987.[2] An assorted number of problems developed, delaying completion of a redesigned system until possibly in 1993. The new budget is $100 million and there is a new contractor.
- In 1984, the City of Richmond hired the consulting firm of Arthur Young to develop a $1.2 million billing and information system. After paying out close to $1 million, Richmond has cancelled the contract, alleging that it has not received a system.
- The State of Oklahoma hired in 1983 a major accounting firm

to design a system for $0.5 million. It cost nearly $4 million.
- Blue Cross and Blue Shield of Wisconsin hired in 1983 Electronic Data Systems to build a $200 million computer system. The project met schedules but the system did not work. For instance, in the first year, the system disbursed $60 million in overpayments or duplicate checks.
- The firm of Peat, Marwick Mitchell & Co. has successfully promoted runaways as a new consulting discipline. Their survey of 600 of their firm's largest clients found 35% currently have major runaways in process.

Runaways arise from a combination of mistakes. Even though each error may contribute only a small percentage to the incapacity, the cumulative and combinatorial effect can overwhelm even the best laid plans. In this chapter, I shall discuss ways of avoiding some common mistakes that decrease the chances of success of computer projects.[3]

ANTICIPATE THAT ALL COST ESTIMATES WILL BE UNCERTAIN

In systems development it's not what you do but who does it.

Development costs for projects are not identical, but depend on contract conditions, skills of the development team and the bidder's financial incentives. What you are likely to end up paying is uncertain. The actual costs will reflect more who performs the project than what you plan:

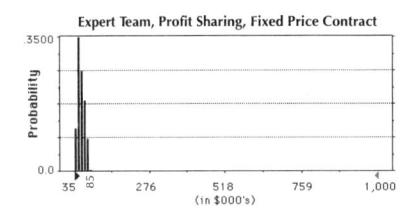

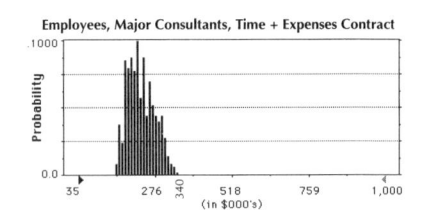

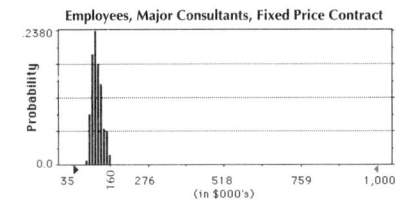

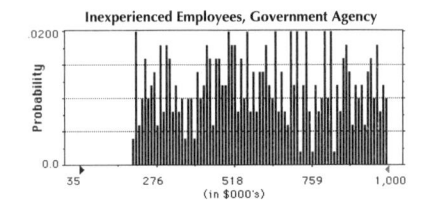

Figure 14.1: Development Costs for an Identical Application

In Chapter 9, I pointed out that estimating the expected project cost is difficult. Cost overruns are more likely to occur than cost underruns. Before you concentrate on cost controls, consider if you are approaching the implementation of the project in a prudent manner.

For example, you may have to live with a defective acquisition process that forces you to overpay whatever you buy. You may find yourself in a situation where you must purchase services from only one supplier.[4] You may also engage in a lengthy procurement procedure in which technology life is shorter than the time to install the system.[5] In such cases, you need not make extraordinary efforts to tighten project management or improve expense monitoring. Even if your project comes in under budget, you probably have wasted some of your money. Devote your energies to extricating yourself from having to pursue an undesirable solution. A few dollars spent on avoiding an ineffective approach could be worth millions in project expenses.

Evaluate a cost overrun not only against the project's budget but also against the least costly way that somebody else has delivered the same results.

NEVER INSTALL SOFTWARE WITHOUT ADEQUATE TESTING

Systems Conversion at Bank of America

Computer errors repeat themselves and accumulate penalties.

A part of many bankers' anxieties about computers comes from the recognition of how dependent banks are on computers to run their operations. Some insight into banking industry computer problems comes from a few cases which became public scandal. The near bankruptcy of Bank of America, once the largest and most powerful of U.S. banks, is an infamous case.[6] In 1983, their computer system for recording security sales failed. Billions of dollars of security transactions remained unaccounted for. How did that happen?

In 1983, the Bank of America installed a new computer system to handle the rapidly expanding volume of security trading. The application involved conversion from an existing system, but also required switching to a new accounting method. Such conversions are a frequent occurrence because the technical limitations of hardware and software generally do not allow for expanding operations without a complete overhaul.

Computer managers did not run the new system and the old system in parallel to correct faults. Then, the Bank of America executives switched to the new programs without any backup. The new system failed. The new system and the old one were sufficiently different so that mistakes remained uncorrected.

It turned out that on any day only a small percentage of the trades was improper, but nobody could tell for sure which transactions were good and which were bad. Meanwhile, trading continued at an accelerated pace, accumulating an enormous number of doubtful records worth billions.

Similar foul-ups occur often, but such events usually remain a company secret in order to maintain public confidence in a financial institution.

The Berserk Computer at United Education & Software

In case of systems failure stop and think. Do not run.

The computer system blunders at the United Education & Software Company may cost banks $650 million in unaccounted for loans.[7] United Education, originally a trade-school operator, began handling repayments for student loans in 1983. It grew rapidly, developing a portfolio of over $1 billion in loans. Its data processing service Division received management contracts from banks and the State of California to provide accounting and computer billing services. The computer problems apparently stemmed from switching to a new system in 1987. United Education's programmers introduced major software errors and failed to test the system before proceeding with conversion.

Instead of reverting to the old system, managers tried to fix programming mistakes while processing regular business transactions. As a result, delinquency notices went to students who did not owe anything. Many who lagged in their payments did not find out about their delinquencies. The computer system rejected payments from overdue borrowers. The system also logged fictional telephone calls and did not account for actual phone calls. Payments intended to repay loan principal showed up as interest.[8] The defective computer programs continued processing faulty accounts for at least eight months.

MAKE SURE THE COMPETITION DOES NOT WIPE OUT GAINS

Automatic Teller Machines

You may view the use of information technologies as weapons in a competitive race. You may not wish to invest in it, but competitors will force you to do so just to keep up. Ted Freiser, President of the Diebold Group, summarized this when he said: "If you wait until others make the technology work and only then do it, you are left without the benefits and with all the costs."[9] Is it true that you must rush with innovation in order to gain all of its benefits?

The experience with Automatic Teller Machines (ATMs) is a useful lesson about the economics of computer systems. Initially promoted as a major cost-reduction technology, the ATM is now a necessary cost of doing banking business. ATMs have added to the banks' costs of doing business, according to Elaine Bond, the chief computer executive of the Chase Manhattan Bank. Bond said "...ATMs are a convenience that someone has to pay for."[10]

When Citibank pioneered the installation of ATMs in New York, it was to gain a competitive advantage. This advantage disappeared when other banks offered the identical technology and equivalent services. Citibank's desire to lower its costs by means of ATMs also did not seem to work as expected. Citibank has recently begun to charge fees for ATM users who do not have sufficiently high balances. This suggests that the volume of ATM transactions is insufficient to recover their substantial costs. When everyone offers the identical technology, it ceases to have an advantage for everyone. It becomes difficult to price services to recover the increased costs.

Professor Michael Hammer noted that "Citibank so successfully terrorized its New York City competitors with its advanced ATMs, that, herding together for warmth, they formed the New York City Cash Exchange. This shared network involves the participation of virtually all major New York banks, except for Citibank. Such twists and turns make a mockery of attempts to build a competitive advantage from a proprietary technology."[11]

Professor David Teece of the University of California holds a similar view.[12] Teece said that ATMs have become a commodity, equally available to everyone. All competitors will end up with similar strategies and will develop similar systems. If the customers do not perceive greater value from such a service, it is difficult to recover the increased costs of the new technology through pricing.

Computerization of Clearing Banks

You are efficient if you produce more with less.
You are effective only if you can pocket the gains.

Eight clearing banks enjoyed substantial operating profits from their clearing business, which involves the settlement of inter-bank balances for checks written by their customers. In 1981, the profits from this business were $922 million. About that time, a few of the banks realized that major cost reductions were possible through the automation of manual paperwork. Heavy investments in computerization reduced massive amounts of low-priced clerical labor. As a result, a serious over-capacity developed by 1987. Pricing eroded and the same banks were losing $100 million per year.[13] The ensuing intense competition drove the banks to add costly enhancements which added new clerical work[14] that did not exist prior to automation.

There is a lesson here concerning cost-justification of investments in labor-reducing automation. Any one of the clearing banks examining their non-automated paperwork—in isolation—would have shown an excellent payoff from investing in computerized processing. Unfortunately, an expectation of large gains would be premature.

Every executive who conceives of a profitable investment in information technology must also consider that every other competitor will be examining exactly the same rationale, roughly at the same time.[15] Therefore:
- If a proposed investment will change the industry's cost structure, anticipate price erosion as imitators try to use reduced costs to increase market share.
- New features (such as improved reports) and new services (such as faster delivery time) will not deliver revenue gains if the innovation becomes accepted as a new way of doing business.
- Added convenience (such as additional support and maintenance services) will not bring premium prices if the customers will not pay for it.

Price erosion from excess capacity will be perhaps the greatest threat in the future planning of profitable computer investments, especially in financial services.[16] To understand the fundamentals of the economics of computers, you must realize that in the short run over 85% of operating expenses do not vary. This includes specialized buildings, utilities, hard-to-replace operating staff, programmers with accumulated know-how and a management team that understands the firm's business. The marginal costs of adding to computer processing capacity in this setup are very small. Perhaps as little as 2 to 4% of incremental cost that removes a bottleneck resource can add another 25% of processing capacity.

Every successful computer project will change the relationship between cost and volume. The high fixed cost combined with a low marginal cost will drive management to push for greater sales volume or to propose data center consolidation. Serving additional markets or providing incremental services initially will appear extremely profitable. That works well if the total markets are expanding faster than the industry's processing capacity. That's not the case in most businesses nowadays. With rapid access to computer technology and distance-independent telecommunications, everyone's investments into expanded computer capacity will run into difficulties, because surplus capacity will appear overnight. If your business lends itself to heavy computerization, this leads to drastic price competition for gaining market share, ultimately on a global scale.[17]

Service-based businesses should analyze investment payoffs from "strategic" computer investments by first studying and then modeling competitive retaliation scenarios, instead of contemplating only their own costs and benefits.

Similarities to an Arms Race

Comparing computer-based competition with an arms race concerned Michael E. Treacy, a professor at M.I.T.'s Sloan School.[18] He believes that everyone overstates the competitive advantages of information technology. He cited the effects of computerized reservation systems where a few companies gained an advantage, but in the process have decreased the profits throughout the entire industry.

It seems that regardless of how much you try to extract increased profitability from strategic deployment of information technology, the harder it becomes to achieve. It's just like striving for military security through modernization of weapons. Professor Michael Scott Morton from M.I.T. said that there is no correlation between the amount spent on information technology and payback.[19] He and other researchers at the M.I.T. Center for Information Systems Research have looked carefully at the evidence. No matter how hard they examined the data, they concluded that the intensely competitive marketplace is driving innovation and constantly is demanding new services because everyone is doing it.

The idea that the escalation in the use of computers is from a marketing-driven mania is interesting. To test this proposition, I asked the editors of INC. magazine to survey the 100 fastest-growing small public companies. The CEO of each of these companies responded to the following question: "In your opinion, has the use of computers played a significant role in explaining the success of your company since 1984?" From what I know about the make-up and the motivation of the INC. 100 companies' CEOs, you will accept their answers as motivated by growth and profit. These CEOs have little room for self-deception or imitation for the sake of imitation.

Out of 87 responses, 77% replied that computers indeed made a significant contribution to the growth of their businesses. Twenty three percent said that the help they were getting from computerization was immaterial to their success. The CEOs mentioned "overhead cost reduction" most frequently as their principal benefit. "Unique competitive advantage" or "offering innovative new services" were only a rare occurrence.

The INC. survey confirmed that information technology makes sense only when it solves a company's specific problems, such as overhead cost control, production management or support of customer services. Imitation, especially when adopting another firm's "strategic" uses, wastes money. Next time a business speaker begins with the alleged competitive advantages[20] of American Airlines or Citicorp, disregard most of what you hear. Your firm is not like American Airlines or Citicorp, or like your competitor. You must fit computers into your particular environment so that they will deliver profits in ways that reflect your own circumstances.

The deployment of computers in business is not like the deployment of weapons on the battlefield. Computers do not fire data at each other. They support competitive strategies which should differentiate competitors' tactics as much as possible. The arms race analogy sounds plausible but is misleading because it may lead you to blind imitation when you should be trying to do something that is unique.

Make Only One Major Change at a Time

Computer faults are not additive, but multiplicative.

The busiest time for using bank credit cards and automatic teller terminals occurs immediately after Thanksgiving when customers discover urgent needs for cash for holiday shopping. You can imagine the disappointment when 700 automatic teller terminals from Oregon to California malfunctioned on a Sunday after Thanksgiving due to changes in processing procedures. The failure arose just as the Bank of America mailed out notices regarding a new charge of 30 cents for "improved services" for every automatic teller withdrawal which until then was free.[21]

All changes are risky. Combining a change in marketing or organization with the introduction of a new computer system compounds the probability of failure. One of my traumatic checklists is a catalog of 25 potentially deadly sins in systems management.[22] They are traumatic because I have committed every one during my career. When I look at a business proposal, I count the incidence of deadly sins. If the number is greater than three, I consider that equivalent to a hurricane warning. You could benefit from using a similar approach because I am sure that you can supplement my list with a long catalogue of your own transgressions.

Anticipate Changes

Computer systems are infinitely adaptable.
It's computer management that is not.

Early in December 1989, the U.S. Social Security Administration announced that it would not be able to program its computers until "next Spring." As a result, 27 million pensioners would continue receiving higher medical coverage charges for an extended period. The total amount of excess charges was over $1 billion.[23]

As an explanation, the Social Security Administration offered that they ordinarily take nine months to make annual changes involving additions to their disbursement system. "We have never had to remove an adjustment."

This case reveals one institution's exceptional insensitivity to public needs. You can anticipate systems modifications if you follow the process for approving changes. In recent years, Congressional changes to the Social Security System came with increasing frequency which should have alerted the Social Security Administration to increase its responsiveness. The repealed catastrophic medical coverages in this case were subject to lengthy debates following an electoral campaign where this issue attracted much attention. The changes occurred only after extensive Committee hearings, which provided sufficient warnings that a change would be forthcoming. Therefore, the Social Security Administration had ample notice to get their act together.

Every company has at least one system, usually in marketing, which suffers from the vagaries of customers who keep changing their minds about what they want. A competent systems organization will respond by designing systems that can quickly change, even at the cost of increased operating expenses.

At General Foods, I first experienced what I call "procedural instability" when suddenly launched marketing promotions of products became an instant cure for budget shortfalls. Unfortunately, the normal inventory system could not keep up with the sudden spurts of product demand. We revised the computerized inventory system so that planners could manually override automatic warehouse replenishment rules with as little as a day's notice about a new marketing promotion.

At Xerox, the "procedural instability" manifested itself as frequent tampering with the sales staff's compensation formulae. As price competition became more intense, the sales commission application grew to a few hundred thousand lines of COBOL code. This system became one of the early examples of "structured programming." The systems organization adapted this innovative software technology to accommodate compensation schemes of labyrinthine complexity.

There is no reason to berate computer systems for poor adaptability unless you are looking for an excuse to make irresolute management appear blameless. Computer systems can change overnight if management wants it and is willing to pay for it.

Expect Operator Errors

A Big Error from Two Mistakes

Simple neglect is a better explanation than computer error.

The U.S. Federal Reserve Bank of San Francisco routinely transmits funds electronically to other banks. On January 21, 1986, the Fed operators erroneously transferred $2 billion to each of nineteen banks. Employees failed to erase a dummy test program with large numbers to test new software.[24]

The moral of this story is that major mishaps can precipitate from a combination of errors, none of which can cause much damage if they occur in isolation. Forgetting to erase a test program is not a calamity. However, when it was combined with an operator's mistake in running the wrong application, the result was a $38 billion error.

Can careful training, back-up computers and redundant commands prevent the occurrence of combined errors? The next case will cast doubts about our capacity to assure perfectly faultless results.

The Case of Compounding Errors

A computer on board Russian spacecrafts must calculate the position of the horizon to fire re-entry rockets. During day landings the cosmonauts just look out the window to check their settings. For a 1988 evening landing of a Russian manned craft, the crew had to rely on computer computations. When the commander of the capsule fired the re-entry rocket the computer halted the firing because its program rejected inconsistent readings from a dimly lit horizon. Seven minutes later, the computer accepted valid readings from the horizon sensors. Unfortunately, the astronauts forgot to clear the previous "fire" order and the computer fired the rockets improperly.

After two additional orbits, the landing sequence used a backup computer because the prime computer could not function after two aborts. The backup computer started executing a program which had remained from a spacecraft docking maneuver three months earlier. The engine burned for six seconds and then was shut down manually when the cosmonauts realized they were flying away from the Earth. The commander re-ignited the engine to reverse the thrust but the backup computer turned it off again because its program called for docking instead of landing. Finally, the re-entry began manually, under visual control. The cosmonauts landed with only a few minutes of oxygen to spare.[25]

I use this story to explain to executives that "computer errors" are not always the result of willful neglect. They can be a result of poor design so that even superbly trained operators do not understand what computer messages reveal.

You should never automate systems which have potentially catastrophic consequences without facilities to provide for easy personal detection and manual overriding of errors, so that common sense can prevail.

EXPECT UNCRITICAL ACCEPTANCE OF COMPUTER RESULTS

It's human to err, but it takes computers to produce awesome foul-ups.

Despite numerous horror stories about computer errors there still persists a tendency to accept computer printouts uncritically. Consistent large mistakes may go undetected for a long time because people are afraid of questioning of what they get from computers.

In a recent experiment 117 college graduates had the task of scheduling production for a fictitious company to meet sales forecasts while minimizing inventory costs.[26] One-third of the subjects got costs too high by a factor of 10, another third received costs too high by a factor of 100 and the remaining one-third received costs too high by a factor of 1,000. Only 11 out of the 117 detected the errors in the computer printouts and questioned the results. The group with the 1,000-times errors received special warnings about possible mistakes. Yet, only three individuals questioned the computer output.[27]

The above experiment proves only that educated and even properly warned people will disregard what they know when acting on computerized information. We do not have any research findings of what happens when personnel get misinformation under operating conditions. I think the results would be identical as to those experiment, unless the people receive proper training, understand the physical reality and have a direct personal interest in the correct answers.

Executives should not assume that operating people will catch major computer errors and act as a safeguard against disastrous misuses of information. Defensive shields must be present in all computer applications, including the signalling of every answer that falls out of an expected range.

Protect Against Computer-Controlled Damage

If a computer-controlled disaster is possible, it will happen.

A 63-year old patient undergoing radiation treatment at the Kennestone Oncology Center in Georgia mistakenly received two bursts of radiation that were 125 times greater than prescribed.

The 25,000 rads from each of those pulses burned a hole in the patient's chest, destroyed a nerve controlling the left hand and required a mastectomy. The error came from software in the hospital's radiation device, controlled by a PDP-11 computer.[28]

Full automation of risky decisions is always perilous. Controls must be subject to exhaustive safeguards that cover all damaging acts. There are legal precedents on the basis of which the managers of information systems are liable when a defect harms a person or property.

If your company produces a potentially dangerous computer program, hire outside experts to test the system in order to locate every hazardous risk. This precaution also must apply to all modifications of software or hardware, because that is where most errors slip through quality control.

In addition, you should devise a training program for your operators to sensitize them to the possibility of danger and the need for personal intervention when the system malfunctions. Disqualify operators who follow computer instructions mindlessly[29] in tests.

Do Not Count on Luck to Catch Your Mistakes

It takes an unconventional mind to locate systems faults. That's why systems designed by conventional employees will have faults.

A chance event prevented an attempted computer crime from becoming possibly Europe's largest recorded theft.[30]

A manager at the London branch of the Union Bank issued an instruction to transfer 82 million Swiss francs ($54 million) to a branch of

Credit Suisse. The payment instruction came over the Swift international network, which handles nearly a million payment messages per day.

A computer breakdown at the Swiss end forced the bank to make manual checks of payments which normally would pass automatically. Manual checks revealed a suspicious transaction which led the bankers to alert the Swiss police who were waiting for the man when he came to collect the cash. Everyone involved in perpetrating this elaborate fraud involving collusion at both ends of the transaction went to prison.

The system did not fail because its design could not deal with collusion. In this case the security was inadequate since it should not have been possible for only one person to enter fraudulent instructions.

MAKE SURE THAT TESTING CORRESPONDS TO THE Risks

A system test that tests itself is insufficient. It only proves consistency, which may be consistently wrong.

An error in a program cost American Airlines $50 million lost revenue in one quarter in 1989. The system involved American Airlines' SABRE reservation system, which may be the most sophisticated commercial application of computers.[31]

A software modification was to improve the automatic allocation of discount fares. The purpose of the allocation program was to juggle supply and demand on routes to produce a ticket mix that allowed the company to maximize revenues. An undetected flaw in the software enhancement caused errors in the discount fare tables. Travel agents querying the system ended up recommending that passengers seek discounted fares on other airlines.

American Airlines discovered this mistake only after reviewing operating statistics that showed below budget revenues. The incorrect fares remained in effect during peak travel times. The CEO of the American Airlines told stock analysts, "...we gave away $50 million of revenue. If we had done more thorough testing we would have discovered the problem before the new software was ever brought on-line."

American Airlines uncovered the loss because of a good financial audit. All systems changes should include an independent check for validating that software which passes a technical acceptance test also meets its performance goals.[32]

WATCH OUT FOR COST OVER-RUNS AND UNWORKABLE SYSTEMS

U.S. Patent Office Case – Part 1, Unrealistic Design

For many years, the advisory committee to the Assistant Secretary of Commerce advised that the U.S. Patent Office needed superior information technology. By 1983 the situation deteriorated to scandalous proportions, so the Patent Office finally secured Congressional approval for a major and costly overhaul of its business. The original goal was to install a completely new system using the most advanced technology available on an accelerated schedule. The new system would increase the efficiency of document handling that accompanies each patent inquiry or application. The Patent Office handles about 125,000 patent applications every year. For each application, a patent examiner must examine at least 1,500 pages of documentation.

The project plan originated in 1982 and called for creating a completely "paperless office." The initial contract for this effort was $289 million. By 1986, this cost escalated to $448 million. Whenever this system finally will operate, its cost may reach anywhere from $600 to $800 million.[33]

Nobody disputed that the Patent Office automation was necessary. The archaic manual system was incapable of dealing with the flood of new applications. Everyone agreed that the 1,500 patent examiners worked under strenuous conditions. However, investing about $500,000 in computer support per examiner and having to wait nine years until completion of the project does not appear to be the best solution. Furthermore, the estimated future increase in the operating costs from computer automation is $50 million per year. This is equivalent to increasing the number of patent examiners by 66%. Originally, the reason for automation was to reduce the number of Patent Office personnel and keep operating expenses low.

Most worrisome is the risk of the system not meeting the expected goals, even after delays and cost overruns. An outside team of experts commissioned by the Commerce Department reported that the patent examiners found the computer approach difficult to use and often slower than searching through paper files. As is frequently found with ambitious computer projects, the experts also noted that the Patent

Office staff's level of skill was inadequate for a project of this scale and complexity.

The Assistant Commissioner of the U.S. Patent Office for information systems is not very hopeful about productivity gains either. "...We really get no short-term increases in productivity. The real gains...are in improvement of the quality of the work."

Meanwhile, the quality of service has further deteriorated.

The moral of this story is that even the best reasoned intentions may lead to failure if not backed up with a practical approach to implementation. Accumulated neglect offers no excuse for making unrealistic leaps to achieve instant reforms.

New Jersey Motor Vehicle Department

A report by the New Jersey Commission of Investigation provides an example of how not to implement a computer application. It concerns the New Jersey Motor Vehicle Department's project to upgrade its computers.[34]

The history of this project follows a pattern similar to the Patent Office situation. A consulting firm received a $6.5 million contract to supply software, training and startup of a new computer system after completing a brief feasibility study. The Department of Motor Vehicles (DMV) adopted the following approach to managing the project:
- Awarded the contract on a sole source basis. There was no competitive bidding.
- Turned over complete technical project control to the consultant. Removed DMV personnel from supervision of the technical implementation.
- Appointed as the DMV Project Manager a lawyer with no prior computer experience. The DMV Project Manager in turn delegated his job to a person without any prior experience in data processing.
- Accepted billings from the consultant for expenses without checking work progress.
- Accepted unaudited time records from the consultant.
- Allowed the consultant to choose a new and insufficiently tested database software package for the key application.
- Accepted the consultant's staffing of inexperienced programmers with a very high turnover rate.

- Did not find out that in case of a database "crash," the entire computer complex, including 200 remote terminals, would become inactive and then require at least 60 hours for restarting.

Despite these disabilities, the computer system went "on-line" in June 1985 to support the registration of all motor vehicles in the state. The system immediately collapsed, because it could not process the necessary transactions.

The moral of this story is that removing all checks and controls on the implementing of an ambitious new system is likely to produce a technical solution which the customer will find unworkable.

Internal Revenue Service

The largest portable microcomputer contract ever awarded was the purchase of 18,000 computers by the Internal Revenue Service. Field tax auditors were to increase their productivity and find large additional sources of tax revenues with their enhanced analytic capabilities.

The IRS made just about every conceivable error in software development.[35] Inadequate hardware capacity and cumbersome software development by multiple contractors made it necessary for an agent to feed 18 different diskettes into the computer before completing an audit.[36] Software errors, inadequate training and incompatible versions of instructions increased the confusion so that 77% of the field agents did not like the new tool. Only one-third ended up using it at all. The financial consequences of these mistakes are in the following tabulation:[37]

Date of Estimate	Costs	Benefits	Completion Date
May 1985	$1.0 Billion	$16.2 Billion	Fiscal 1989
January 1987	$1.2 Billion	$42.7 Billion	Fiscal 1991
March 1988	$1.8 Billion	$16.2 Billion	Fiscal 1995

Table 14.1: Estimates for IRS Laptop Project

It does not improve the confidence of executive management when they hear about a computer project that increases costs by 80% and delays a four-year program for ten years. Even after making allowances for public sector circumstances, such a case does not boost confidence in the ability of some managements to manage information technology projects.

The moral of this story is that you never buy large quantities of hardware before you have tested your software.

Manage Your Risks

The costs of prevention should be commensurate with the costs of potential failure.

The Bank of America Case

Max Hopper, one of the architects of American Airlines' much acclaimed SABRE system, found a mess when he became the Chief Information Officer of the Bank of America. Systems were technically obsolete, poorly organized and incompatible. Auditors accumulated a long list of deficiencies, some of which threatened the integrity of the Bank of America business. To solve the problem in one giant sweep Hopper proposed to install the Transaction Processing Facility (TPF) as the master system for all Bank of America processing. TPF was an improved version of a system running the American Airlines' reservation system. The proposed budget of $4 billion, the largest non-military computer project ever reported for modernizing the bank's computers appeared in magazine articles as an imaginative move to restore the bank's "competitive edge."

TPF had the reputation for being an exceedingly fast and expensive system built to handle thousands of transactions per second. TPF also mandated centralizing computer resources on a scale that was unprecedented in the banking industry. Such a concentration did not fit well with the highly decentralized traditions of the Bank.

Hopper proceeded to install TPF, taking money from existing systems that already were performing poorly with the hope that the replacement systems would finally deliver much needed improvements. The problem was how to justify the massive expenditures for TPF. Bank of America's current transaction volumes did not need that sort of computing power. To gain the expected benefits, the bank would have to reach the ambitious marketing objectives established by business planners. If the projected volumes missed, TPF was the wrong solution. If TPF was not available, the new markets could not materialize using the existing systems.

Plans for a large number of new products, such as banking by phone, banking by computers and terminals in all client stores, never materialized. Hopper resigned and the CEO of the Bank retired. Afterwards, the systems investments were redirected to patching up existing malfunctions.[38] The risks of organizational, procedural and technical failure were too great to add to the already precarious financial position.

The Bank of America case offers an excellent study of information systems strategies that got ahead of the capacity of an organization to commit and execute a business plan.

The moral of this story is that information systems strategies cannot serve as the vanguard in attempts to reform an otherwise reluctant organization.

The AT&T Long Lines Case

The worlds largest and technically most expert computer network—AT&T's interstate and international network—could not fully function for nine hours on January 15, 1990. There was a faulty modification to a software program installed four weeks prior to the crash.[39] The rapidly cascading failure originated from a routine malfunction, on proven hardware, controlled by presumably well-tested software. Normally, such a common computer failure repairs itself instantly by re-routing messages.[40] The failure originated in self-inflicted interactions within the complex network and not because of anything wrong within anyone's computer.

A programming oversight triggered the crash. One of the network computers experienced a minor failure. It sent out the usual trouble messages to other computers across the country to divert calls. The faulty computer recovered quickly but without informing other computers that it was back in operation. It then sent out a burst of backlogged calls. That burst overwhelmed the next switching computer which shut down. The second computer again sent out trouble messages to others thus magnifying the number of trouble messages circulating in the network.[41] Soon, more than one hundred message-routing computers could not function. They kept interrupting each other with distress calls programmed to cope with local failures. Instantly, the network became filled with priority trouble signals. Only a limited capacity was available to handle customer calls. AT&T management finally cured the problem by sending out a program modification (a "patch") to all of the computers.

The error within the offending software modification eluded three stages of thorough testing. The chance of undetectable chain-reaction failures keeps growing as computer networks gear up to faster response times and interdependency. The possibility of a spontaneous collapse also grows with decentralized processing in which computers interact with each other in ways that are unpredictable and uncontrollable. As computer networks grow in complexity, organizations will have to incur the costs of dealing with interactions which no testing can anticipate.

Electronic interconnections make it possible to propagate a local failure into network-wide chaos before any human can intervene. The financial losses from such a failure can amount to billions of dollars. AT&T's systems-wide crash damages their claim to superior reliability which they believe to be their competitive advantage.

How do you manage these enormous risks which derive from highly improbable events? How can you deal with effects that are comparable only to biological mutations or a new virus strain for which a vaccine does not exist? Until recently, questions like these concerned only catastrophic situations involving missile attacks, nuclear power melt-downs or new epidemic diseases. There are useful lessons from electric utilities that live with the prospects of a nuclear melt-down:

- Do not try to increase your savings by cutting down on competent monitoring personnel. Operators at controls always should stand by to disable automatic control features and restore network stability, even at a degraded level of performance.
- Invest in instrumentation that detects and reports all unusual occurrences.
- Design your network for graceful degradation into a diminished capacity. It is always preferable to survive with only high priority messages or slower response times than to fail completely.
- All network stations should have another path for connecting to critical information, even if the alternative path operates under degraded conditions and at an excessive cost.
- Small episodes often precede catastrophic failures. Recovery from these small incidents can be a rehearsal for

the big ones. The record of every network malfunction should include a complete explanation for every failure. "Unknown" causes must get special attention from a staff that does not carry the burdens of day-to-day operations. The incidence of "unknown" failures deserves attention from top management.
- Practice for network failure. Testing component breakdowns is not enough. You may have to put in place costly exercises, usually at times when traffic is at its maximum, that should exert stress on the entire network with transactions far exceeding expected capacity.[42]

Millions of dollars can evaporate in a few moments of failure. To prevent the loss of the benefits your precautions should reflect to some degree the magnitude of your financial exposures.

The moral of this story is that all complex systems will fail regardless of what safeguards you use. Therefore, you ought to design all systems not only for when they work, but also for when they fail.

Contracting Out Isn't a Substitute for Management

It is now possible to contract for design and delivery of a complete system. This offers a "turnkey" solution and isolates the costs and results from other activities. Turnkey solutions are often the only way to install a major new system without a massive hiring of new personnel. This approach offers the advantages of separating objective-setting, performance-measurement and the delivery of a system. If managed well it forces the clarification of the scope of work. After all, you cannot make a binding contract for a system which does not have adequate specifications. If managed poorly it will create legal disputes that will force a postponement of systems implementation indefinitely. For a worthwhile system the damage from lost benefits is always more severe than that from cost overruns.

Failed turnkey contracts in the private sector remain hidden from public view, since everyone is interested in forgetting the fiasco as quickly as possible. A U.S. Government Agency cannot always hide its aborted systems contracts and therefore offers to us a rare view for understanding how to manage turnkey contracts. The Patent Office case, mentioned earlier in this chapter, is an instructive case which shows what can happen when trying to remedy accumulated neglect by means of a single contract based on compounding errors.

U.S. Patent Office Case – Part 2, Unrealistic Implementation

Because of the delays in the systems overhaul the Patent Office wanted to use a turnkey vendor who could deliver the system rapidly. The new system would place all of the Patent Office documents "on-line" for search and retrieval.

The Patent Office issued a 2,500 page request for a proposal outlining its wishes. Because of the urgency and uniqueness of the task, the Patent Office obtained a waiver so that it did not have to follow established Federal vendor selection, vendor evaluation and competitive bidding procedures.[43] The Patent Office proceeded to select one vendor who seemed to be the most responsive to their need for a rapid product delivery.

Shortly after the contract award the Patent Office decided to change the scope of the project because paperwork efficiency gains did not show up in the budget savings. The emphasis shifted from clerical efficiency to improving the quality of the patent search by the patent examiners. The contractor then spent 18 months negotiating changes in contract terms and systems specifications. Meanwhile, money continued to flow for software for which there was no agreement, and for which the hardware was not as yet available because of a lack of supplemental funding. Four years, a new project manager and $448 million later, it is still not clear what benefits the Patent Office will be getting from its new computer system.

This case offers useful lessons in managing computer projects. The biggest cause of systems failure is an inadequate definition of expected gains and a too hasty rush to buy technology for speedy start-up. Management disagreement about objectives or redirection in goals midway through the effort will destroy all of the benefits one can get from turnkey contracting. There must be a thorough, independently validated and unambiguous demonstration of the clarity of the desired end results prior to any contract award. Top management also must limit the unavoidable minor modifications in the original specifications from accumulating into a different design. When top management hands over systems execution to a project manager, they court disaster if everyone tries to accommodate changes without thinking about their cumulative consequences.[44]

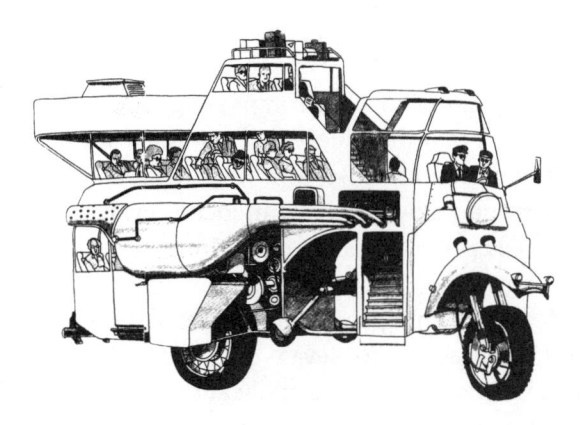

Figure 14.2: A Motorcycle Designed by a Committee to Satisfy All Requests

My biggest management failure occurred when I delegated too much freedom to a project manager. My instructions were to please the client since the client was paying the bills and knew the applications.

For a while, everyone was happy. My project manager pushed innovative technology to its limit because he wanted to demonstrate how sophisticated we could get. The customer generated glowing praise month after month about the exemplary flexibility in taking care of their rapidly escalating demands. These accommodations placated the customer's managers who did not have the budget to get their own systems projects completed. The President approved of what was going on, and focused on accelerating the completion schedules.

This collective joy lasted until a new President, with different priorities, looked at a prospective $12 million overrun in the project budget and shut down the entire effort. The tragedy of this experience was not only the loss of jobs and the large expense write-off. The abrupt termination of the project resulted in deferring for many years to come the much needed improvements that would reduce the cost of the Company's administrative system.

The moral of this case is that in a volatile organization you should deliver what you promised in your original commitments before adding new ones. Major changes in the scope of a project require justification and approvals as if they were new ventures.

Keep Away from Grand Designs

The idea of pursuing an all-encompassing "grand design" traces its origin to the concept that the Chief Executive is like a watchmaker. This 18th century view of the universe, as a well-ordered clockwork mechanism, offers an emotionally gratifying model to every computer executive. The watchmaker role offers the penultimate satisfaction of a single mind determining who gets what information, when and how. The idea of a centrally designed "integrated information system" is the Holy Grail of systems designers seeking to elevate their status. A centralized design of all databases and control over all applications would make it possible for a small group to impose controls on how an organization operates.[45] Centralization proposals always will claim avoidance of wasteful incompatibilities, elimination of overlapping efforts, efficient uses of scarce resources and the capacity to prevent technological obsolescence.

In the grand design scenario (also called the "Big Bang" solution), a company undertakes an all-encompassing project that combines all business requirements into a single multi-phase project. This includes data processing hardware and software, telecommunications, applications definitions, method improvement, job redesign and organizational changes. Such a unification of means and ends looks good in a presentation but fails dismally in execution.

The grander the scope the longer will be the effort to define the system. Even with the assistance of CASE (computer-aided systems engineering) tools, the bottlenecks will be organizational because current employees rightfully will feel threatened by any system that will rearrange relationships. It is not entirely a coincidence that "grand design" projects originate in organizations that are overripe for internal streamlining. Long postponed improvements and accumulated neglect are the most frequent reasons why top management buys radical modernization proposals. The proponents of the "grand design" approach to systems management may receive, at least temporarily, a sympathetic welcome in the Board Room.

You can easily recognize a "grand design" project by the hoopla that usually accompanies its launching. The Chairman or the Agency Head offers his version of the computerized cure for a chronic affliction.

Sprinkled into such announcements you will find references to the uses of state-of-the-art technologies[46] as an explanation for the hefty budget.

The initial goal of the "grand design," as with perestroika, receives applause from everyone. You do not argue with initiatives that come from the top. The "grand design" becomes unglued during the systems specification phase when existing obsolete practices enter as additional "user requirements." To maintain harmony, the systems requirement team accepts as legitimate needs whatever the users request. Sometimes it takes one to two years[47] before the specifications are complete. Such specifications are a melange of the desired ideal diluted by the perpetuation of the undesirable.

This eventually produces a computer system that is the equivalent of old vinegar mixed with good new wine in expensive new bottles that carry a designer label. As result, project costs escalate, schedules elongate and the expected benefits do not materialize until the "grand scheme" is finally reorganized into manageable projects or abandoned.

"Grand design" is not a bad idea if you use it for long term strategic guidance and if it reflects continually changing circumstances. It is not feasible as an all-embracing, unified technical design conceived and planned from its inception. No group of systems planners can anticipate how organizations will adapt when computer-managed processes arrive in the workplace. Evolutionary implementation that reflects organizational realities is much more pragmatic. This approach fits better within the usual capabilities of organizations to absorb the introduction of information technologies, given manageable limitations of how quickly organizations learn.

The Houdaille Industries Case

Conditions for extracting success from computers come from management, not from technology.

In 1977, Gerald Saltarelli, Chairman and CEO of the multi-billion dollar Houdaille Industries[48] conglomerate became taken with books describing a new concept of manufacturing management called-*Materials Requirements Planning* (MRP). Saltarelli was a believer in tight financial controls and a practitioner of the numbers-only approach to dealing with all problems. He believed that imposing the MRP discipline on his operations would become the unifying managerial scheme for the control of Houdaille. It would replace the incompatible systems installed prior to his acquisition of owner-managed enterprises. It would dictate order where informality and flexibility frequently got in the way of neatness or accounting discipline.[49]

The MRP would turn over the detailed control of plant schedules to a central computer. The computer would specify work assignments for each shift, for each machine based on a master schedule. Such discipline required that the computer's database contain comprehensive information about the amount of material and labor required to produce any of thousands of machine parts. The computer would also need perfect data about labor efficiency, labor skills, on-hand materials, the delivery schedules of purchased components, inventories and the status of all work-in-process. The database would include standard cost information and wage categories. It would then generate comparisons of actual against planned costs, by operator, by machine, by shift, by department, by product line and by contract. Saltarelli saw the installation of a MRP system as a crusade for restructuring the business so that he and his staff could understand it in financial terms.

After a rapid conversion to the MRP, the craftsmen who produced the machine tools developed a deep-seated antagonism to its disrupting effects. Everyone became flooded with paperwork to keep the MRP system informed of what was going on. Otherwise, the MRP would generate materials tickets and production orders that made no sense. If the system did not get data about what actually happened, it would print out reports showing meaningless deviations from planned performance. Every machine breakdown, each delay due to a scrapped part, a machinist's sickness, late material receipts and reworking of parts for salvage required entry using complex identification codes. Small human errors immediately became magnified as the all-encompassing MRP detected inconsistencies or gaps.

Theoretically, there was nothing wrong with the concept of an MRP except for its implementation. In a machine tool manufacturing plant, you produce only a few machines of great complexity. This requires parts produced to extremely tight tolerances. Engineering modifications are frequent. Productivity in such a plant is the result of the flexibility of the individual craftsmen, their sense of workmanship and their adherence to uncompromising quality. There are just too many variables, such as unpredictable lead-times, to presume that there will be any resemblance between the master and the actual schedules.

The implementation of the MRP also was hasty. Within three months there was no resemblance between what the MRP required and what was happening on the shop floor. Management insisted that the plant comply with the MRP in every detail which is an essential prerequisite for success according to the consultants. Consequently, the assembly department ended up with both excess and missing parts. To complete a machine tool, production people entered large numbers of expediting orders into the computer system to avoid showing idle time waiting for the corrected schedules. Production interruptions became more frequent and production runs became less economical. To satisfy the MRP, machine operators tore down machine tool setups for one-of-a-kind uneconomic machining.

Plant costs became "astronomical" after the installation of the MRP systems. Production output slowed down to a fraction of its previous capacity. Machine shop foremen "...literally begged management to release them from the MRP." Management never gave up pushing for compliance with the MRP. The product line was simplified to fit better into the MRP, just when foreign competition started encroaching on their customers with more complex and less expensive products. Management also initiated payroll cut-backs in manufacturing while increasing non-productive staffs to cope with the increased paperwork.

What were the results? The company closed down the machine tool Division after a few years of accelerating losses. A new owner ultimately sold off what remained of the parent conglomerate, Houdaille.

Did the MRP system cause the demise of a flourishing enterprise? Certainly not! Was MRP a misapplied technique that aggravated entrenched mismanagement? Surely that's the case.

The point of this story is that inexperienced and enthusiastic management, in search of easy solutions, will make conditions worse if they latch onto inappropriate computerization. Applications that deliver superior results, under favorable conditions, can destroy a company that suffers from chronic mismanagement.

Conditions for extracting success from computers originate from management, not from technology. The moral of this case is that a fundamentally sound MRP technique was hoped to substitute for experienced management, which is something you never should allow to happen. A fool with a fancy tool is still a fool.

More abuses of information technology has been generated by excessive zeal thany by deliberate misdeeds. Computers are economically neutral. What they deliver is more a reflection of management than of their information processing capacity.

INSTITUTIONALIZE LEARNING FROM OWN MISTAKES

The only problems worth talking about are the lessons for doing better next time.

Can you learn enough from others to avoid repeating their mistakes in your Company?

In this Chapter, I paraded before you a number of undesirable practices. I doubt ifr circulating a copy to your staff will create much change in how you manage your information systems. Lasting learning experiences come from dealing successfully with immediate occurrences in your own environment. Your own projects will have enough faults so that you need not depend on other companies' stories to discover what needs fixing. To do better, you need to create an environment that will direct everybody's attention to solving immediate, specific problems which reflect your organization's weaknesses, not somebody else's.

The most practical approach to institutionalizing an uncompromising search for improved systems quality is through ongoing and post-implementation assessments. Although Audit has a role in this process insofar as you may need the independent verification of facts, the purpose of assessments is organizational learning and not the conduct of audits. The best auditors can do is to transform hidden despair into public unhappiness. You should guard against witch-hunts. You will destroy the educational value of any assessment if you use it to find sacrificial victims. You do not get a post-implementation assessment when the project manager hands over test results to a customer and walks away with a memorandum certifying a completed technical job.[50] Post-implementation assessment takes place a few months, and sometimes years, after systems installation when the actual economic benefits finally show up.

Post-implementation assessments should be an integral part of a process where every participant should have a say in how the job should improve next time. People responsible for delivering the expected project benefits should have a particularly prominent role in speaking up during such discussions. However, there is no gain from spending too much time going over past events. A constructive post-implementation review will focus on immediate corrective actions and not dwell on past circumstances or future eventualities.

The product of a helpful post-implementation meeting should be a list of actionable improvements, including schedules, people and money. Here is a sample of resolutions that came from a practical review:

- What lack of skills that slowed down progress should now become available?
- How much additional training is necessary to overcome the gaps that persist in the project so far?
- Which technologies are necessary to reduce the cost overruns?
- When should customer management intervene to make sure that correct data is available for testing?

These points came from actual experiences but from different companies. They have meaning only in the context of a particular firm under specific circumstances. When it comes to learning from mistakes, you can do that most effectively if you act on the new knowledge without further delays. Presiding over post-implementation assessments and seeing that they deliver results is one of two[51] essential roles that top management may not delegate.

Chapter Summary

The capacity of individuals and organizations to learn is the key to successful use of information technologies. Executives must ensure that learning from mistakes, which is the best source of all educational experience, remains uninhibited. An organization that buries its mistakes does not learn anything.

You can alleviate the pain of learning by studying what others have done that you do not wish to repeat. Instead of attending vendors' and other conferences about the merits of computers, always reserve some time to study the rare instances when you find a report about somebody else's computerized misfortunes.

A busy executive can never learn enough to become a computer expert, but he or she can certainly acquire sufficient expertise to know what not to do.

CHAPTER 14 COMMENTS

1 J. Rothfeder, It's Late, Costly, Incompetent—But Try Firing a Computer System, *Business Week*, November 7, 1988, p.164
2 Obviously a *Grand Design*. To recognize the characteristics of such a hole into which you can pour money without anything coming out is discussed at the end of this chapter.
3 Each incident of malpractice in this chapter can contribute at least a 10% cost variance. From engineering analysis we know that systems unreliability is multiplicative, not additive. All you need for a cost runaway is to suffer from four or more incidents of mismanaging a project element. Your control will become 65% unpredictable. Every runaway I have seen had more than four foul-ups. It is amazing to see how long management tolerates faulty projects before such projects disintegrate from within instead of being terminated by direction.
4 A captive, in-house programming service.
5 For some government contract awards.
6 G. Hector, Breaking the Bank - The Decline of Bank America, *Little, Brown and Company*, 1988.

To know how much testing and what kind of testing are necessary before you can safely cut over to a new application requires seasoned judgment and a great deal of common sense. Experienced programmers certainly will exercise all new computer systems for logic and features in a synthetic and isolated test environment. Many of the problems that plague large systems originate not in logic, but in the interactions among programs, databases and telecommunications when an application operates with huge numbers of transactions. Replicating full operating conditions during a systems test can be difficult and expensive. Therefore, establishing the operational validity of any systems test requires much care.

To illustrate a laboratory experiment "proved" the cancer-inducing properties of a pesticide by feeding rodents all they could eat of food laced with the suspect chemical. The rats ended up dying from overeating, not from the exposure to the carcinogen. Programmers can claim that they have identified (and corrected) the cause of potential program faults. Frequently they discover that under full operating conditions the causes of errors are different than those rehearsed in the test environment.

7 United Education's Computer Blunders, *Wall Street Journal*, March 10, 1989, A6
8 Following a devastating audit, the president of United Education said "...software companies have problems all the time."
9 Quoted in *Business Week*, October 14, 1985.
10 The Executive Report on M.I.S. in Banking, *Computerworld*, August 15, 1988.
11 M. Hammer, Strategic Systems: Right From Wrong, *InformationWeek*, September 28, 1987.
12 E.K. Clemons, Strategic Necessities, Computerworld, February 22, 1988, p.79.
13 D. Teixeira, Productivity Efforts Must Focus on Boosting Systems Output, not Trimming Input, *Chief Information Officer Journal*, Winter 1989, p.8.
14 Requiring higher-priced personnel.
15 Computer salesmen thrive on "sharing information" about the latest industry developments. This reminds me of the exploits of Basil Zaharoff, who became one of the richest men in the world prior to World War I. Zaharoff was able to sell large quantities of new model machine guns immediately after he delivered samples of a few machine guns to a neighboring country.
16 Financial industries experienced the largest growth rates in computer investments between 1970 and 1985. They are more labor-intensive than any other sectors in the economy and have shown negative gains in labor productivity.
17 Electronic transaction service organizations with a global reach will have cost advantages in the delivery of improved banking, security and insurance products. Like the consolidations of many national automobile businesses into larger global enterprises that occurred in the 1970's, similar developments are likely to occur faster in the financial services businesses in the 1990's.

CHAPTER 14—LEARNING FROM MISTAKES 353

[18] Treacy, quoted by Business Week of October 1988.
[19] J. Kelleher, Companies Can't Live on Technology Alone, *Computerworld*, June 25, 1990.
[20] See Table 17.1 for a list of financial returns realized by companies nominated as superior strategic users of computers. Neither Citicorp nor American Airlines—the most frequently noted examples of strategic superiority—show noteworthy shareholder returns.
[21] C. Pelton, Bank of America ATM's Go Down, *Information Week*, December 5, 1988, p.20.
[22] Twenty-five potentially deadly sins in systems management:
 1. Never introduce a critical new application using totally new technology.
 2. Never install for immediate operational use early shipments of new hardware or software products.
 3. Never commit both to a budget and to a schedule for an application you have never delivered on budget or on schedule previously.
 4. Never estimate employee training costs without a pilot test.
 5. Never assume you have the capacity to restore an operation from back-up files without first trying it out during an unscheduled test.
 6. Never base your implementation schedules on vendors' promised delivery dates for software.
 7. Never assume that organizations with conflicting objectives will be able to agree on systems specifications, database definitions or standards.
 8. Never hire as a project manager for a critical project a person who lives in a trailer hitched to a pick-up truck. [I did, to my regret.]
 9. Never convert an old application to a new one without being able to retrace your steps in case of failure.
 10. Never use an operational database for testing program changes.
 11. Never give programmers direct access to the computer console that controls a large computer network when there is a program failure.
 12. Never program an application in a programming language known only to 1% of your staff.
 13. Never allow your staff to modify the vendor's operating system.
 14. Never allow the same crew to control a money disbursement application for more than one year.
 15. Never fully automate anything that does not have a manual override capability.
 16. Never design anything that cannot work under degraded conditions in an emergency.
 17. Never rely on 100% availability of a single communication link or a single database.
 18. Never operate a computer system or network that has not failed during an independent test.
 19. Never trust a customer's request for systems changes if somebody else will have to pay for it.
 20. Never commit to project schedules that take longer to implement than your customer's average time to reorganize.
 21. Never take over and consolidate data centers that operate with obsolete technology, dissatisfied customers and excessive manual intervention.
 22. Never assume responsibility for running an undocumented system.
 23. Never take over responsibility for running an application involving money unless previous management is audited by an independent party.
 24. Never hire consultants to deliver an application on a time-and-materials basis.
 25. Never start up a system without a prior acceptance test from the paying user.
[23] E. Booker, Social Security Systems Can't Handle Law Repeal, *Computerworld*, December 11, 1989, p.8.
[24] C. Hammer, Is Today's Office Receiving Full Value from its Computers?, *Information & Management*, (15), 1988, p.19.

25 A minute-by-minute rendition of the various misfires and computer malfunctions during the descent of the Russian spacecraft is in the *The New York Times*, Sunday, September 11, 1988, p.6E. This story is not about a business application. However, it dramatically illustrates circumstances when even exceptionally well trained operators are in peril when relying on pre-programmed routines.

26 J.A. Ricketts, Powers-of-Ten Information Biases, *MIS Quarterly*, March 1990. I found it of interest that the people who were "detectors" examined all data before using any of the information. Non-detectors checked information only during or after using it.

27 Intensive training will increase the chances of detecting large errors somewhat, but not sufficiently to assume that adequate training will catch over half of the errors.

There is another class of disasters where the computerized data is accurate, but the operator's bias causes a misreading. There is one well documented case of such an event. It involved shooting down a departing passenger airliner mistaken on a computer screen for an attacking bomber.

28 A. Kornel, When Computerized Disaster Strikes, *Computerworld*, June 4, 1990, p.90. There are numerous recorded cases where computer operators adamantly refuse to believe their own senses when they are in conflict with a computer read-out.

29 A training program can include a wide range of simulated disasters, some of which should evade detection by the computer program. My accelerated military training, at the age of 15, consisted of disabling a mine which was planted as a demolition charge. At the time, I did not know that it was set up as a dummy.

30 P. Hunter, System Crash Foils Swiss Bank Theft, *InformationWeek*, July 11, 1988, p.20

31 The $50 million "glitch" is in N. Andrews, Software Bug Costs Millions at Airline, *New York Times*, September 12, 1988.

32 In 1962 I designed and operated for the General Foods Corporation a comprehensive inventory management and plant scheduling system that ran on an IBM 7090 computer. This giant application finally worked as planned and I thought the job was complete. One day I noticed that a few warehouses consistently reported no out-of-stock conditions for any products. Our system aimed to deliver only a 98% product availability. On-site visits revealed that marketing personnel misinterpreted the computer reports and stopped offering to customers any products that were out-of-stock. They did not book any back-orders. The measures of performance looked better than expected because there were no measures in place to find out the customers' opinions.

33 E.L. Andrews, Patent Files versus Computer Age, *New York Times*, September 12, 1988, p.D1. The Patent Office automated project is an interesting case of trying to solve acknowledged problems by means of large-scale and enormously expensive multi-year contracts. This effort overlooked simplified, evolutionary steps and opted to leap into the ultimate "paperless office" in one giant step. I suspect that the origins for such behavior have roots in the appropriation process that favors big programs rather than incremental improvements or additional staff.

Andrews noted, when he interviewed an experienced patent lawyer "...what I would do is shut down the whole proposed system and buy desk-top computers with modems for each patent examiner." He would also hire a small army of additional clerical workers for the badly under-staffed Patent Office to cure the chaos in the existing paper files. We will never know whether or not this approach is right. Large organizations have a bias favoring centralized technology and will spend enormous sums on it while scrimping on funds necessary to make individuals more effective.

34 *Data Communications Journal*, November 1988, p. 153

35 General Accounting Office, Report on IRS Laptop Project, May 1988.

36 J. Angus, IRS Falls To Cost/Benefit Bunk, *Computerworld*, January 1990 gives an inside story of some of the mistakes. IRS bought the laptop hardware a full year before software design began. The contractor finished the software before IRS completed systems design and standardized data definitions. User requirements came from contractors without experience in dealing with the complexities of the IRS. The

system code is in Turbo Pascal language, but IRS had laid off programmers skilled in that language. The system was then converted into another language which is even more difficult than starting coding from the beginning.
[37] M. Betts, IRS Laptop Gains Not Realized, *Computerworld*, August 21, 1989, p.39
[38] G. Hector, Breaking the Bank - The Decline of Bank America, *Little, Brown and Company*, 1988
[39] Glitch Imperils AT&T Advantage in Long-Distance Marketing Wars, *Wall Street Journal*, January 17, 1990 and The Day that Every Phone Seemed off the Hook, *Business Week*, January 29, 1990. The purpose of the software modification was to speed up the transmission of signals between computers. Someone forgot to write a few lines of code (J.J. Keller, AT&T Tells What Caused January's Glitch, *Wall Street Journal*, February 14, 1990, B.4) which would notify the network whenever restoring an out-of-service condition. Pre-installation testing, under stressed conditions, should be able to catch such an unforgivable oversight.

Despite the public attention given to the network collapse in January, four weeks later a similar event occurred, though on a much smaller scale (*InformationWeek*, February 16, 1990, p.16). A service technician forgot to program routine changes into a network computer. Failures are inescapable. The only question is how quickly can you recover without causing excessive damage.
[40] There was no physical damage to the network.
[41] The technical term for a cascading failure, in which the back-up systems fail for the same reasons as the main system, is "*common mode failure.*" Mechanical systems rarely experience this form of collapse because their back-ups are not a duplicate of the original. Computer back-up systems which run identical software as the main computer are hazardous.

The back-up for this book is on a physically separate cartridge, using different copying software than offered by the text editor. Only after testing for a combination of power, disk and software failures would I be sure that this text would be safe.
[42] You cannot ever be sure if your data center has a back-up until you have paced everyone through several successful recoveries. You must induce failure and then demonstrate speedy restoration under a variety of conditions before you can go to sleep without that worry.
[43] U.S. Federal Government systems procurement follows explicit systems planning policies. The private sector could learn from the Office of Management and Budget (OMB). However, good policy does not guarantee good implementation. Neither does the application of excessive bureaucratic zeal that insists on compliance with every detail of regulations even if it makes a mockery of their original intent. In the case of the Patent Office Automation, the Commerce Department obtained a waiver from having to abide by OMB policy which requires users to adopt a phased systems acquisition strategy. This policy calls for explicit criteria for selecting a turnkey vendor such as the fit of the technical solution to the objectives, relevant experience in delivering comparable systems, track record in project management, ability to demonstrate a pilot-scale application and the total contract price. The OMB policy is useful in defining how the request for a proposal is a method for negotiating a tight agreement about the scope of the proposed project. The OMB policy insists on multiple proposals as a way to improve the quality of the bids and as a means to uncover possible misunderstandings about the scope of the job. How the discarding of the OMB policy led to the Patent Office situation is described by Keene, Jessel and Hagel, Solving the Systems Puzzle, *Datamation*, November 1, 1988, p.119.
[44] There are situations where there will be many changes in business strategy or a prospect of a technology breakthrough. For such conditions a turnkey approach (e.g., commitments to both budget and schedule) is unrealistic and only phased implementation with risk-containment checkpoints offers a prudent solution.
[45] Consultants offering multi-million dollar systems studies and vendors selling large central computers contributed to such views through publicity and executive education.
[46] Read this as risky technology which sometimes works, on a small scale, for companies that have lots of cash to spare.

47 Lee Mercer, Deputy Under-Secretary of the Department of Commerce, made a telling observation "...In the time it took to have a contractor deliver seven volumes telling us what kind of work we did here and how we might automate it, we automated it," quoted in the March 6, 1989 issue of *Computerworld*.

48 A manufacturer of high-precision tool-making equipment and simple metal stamping.

49 M. Holland, When the Machine Stopped, *Harvard Business School Press*, 1989. The contributory role of MRP to the demise of an entrepreneurial organization is on pp.145–148. The book is a clinical study that reveals how a business succumbed to Japanese competitors as a result of self-inflicted wounds. This story is essential reading for students of international competition.

50 K. Kumar, Post-implementation Evaluation of Computer-Based Information Systems: Current Practices, *Communications of the ACM*, Volume 33, 2. Kumar points out, with regret, that "...contrary to the widely-held view that post implementation evaluations are performed to assess and improve the information systems...this study suggests that...the primary reason for such activity seems to be technical project closure."

51 The other is approval of systems plans and budgets.

15

COMPUTER-BASED COMMUNICATION

The transition to an information technology-dominated age is already taking place. The direction where it will lead is a much debated puzzle. I shall examine one of the key productivity-enhancing tools of the new era: computer-based communication. What is it? How useful is it? Is it an evolutionary step or has it already evolved into its final form?

If you examine electronic mail (e-mail) that is used for sending messages from terminal to terminal, in actual form and content it is not much different from what goes by pigeon, lettermail, facsimile or telex. Most forms of e-mail show all sorts of arcane notes and protocols which make it less pleasing than an old-fashioned letter. The format of a typical e-mail message does not suggest that it originates from a machine that has intelligent powers. What you see is basically typing performed on a remote terminal, surrounded with all sorts of administrative notations necessary to safeguard the computer-to-computer connection.

If the e-mail message is only another means to convey coded characters, why pay attention to it? Can we improve business productivity by using e-mail more frequently?

What is E-mail?

In 1988, there were approximately seven million business e-mail subscribers. Seventy-five percent of these customers were connected through private networks.[1] In most cases, e-mail requires a modem at the users' personal computer and a switching system for network control. It is now easy for a corporation to set up its own e-mail network. The set up cost is low, though the transmission cost remains a relatively expensive $0.50 to $1 per page.[2]

There are about one thousand nationwide networks in the U.S. Bulletin boards, company-owned local area networks and government non-defense networks bring that number to well over 50,000. In addition, there exist a few hundred limited-feature versions of e-mail known as *videotext* aimed at consumer markets, but as yet have to be commercially a financial success. Overall, the 1988 volume of public net e-mail messages was about 4 billion, which is about 4% of the total volume of first class mail.

Belonging to a national or global network does not always open channels to a free flow of communication. More than half of all private users circulate messages only within their own organizations. Only a few networks are sufficiently compatible to take each other's transmissions without administrative intervention because each public network uses its own coding schemes. For instance, to reach me on any of my eight subscribed services you would have to use a unique address code to connect to each of my eight mail boxes. As an example, on one network P.A.Strassmann is StrassmannP:SINC@SDL, so that Paul Strassmann, Strassman and other variants are undeliverable.

E-mail studies show that the fastest growing e-mail load is not a substitute for free-form telephone, facsimile or memos. E-mail works predominantly in applications that use standard mailing lists, such as schedule or price change notices, shipping papers, sales reports, meeting announcements, and in shuttling documents back and forth between businesses. In this respect, today's e-mail service improves on other media because copies of messages can be delivered to multiple recipients rapidly and reliably.[3]

Current Status of the Technology

To use e-mail requires special software purchased separately, either as a microcomputer application or as an integral part of a comprehensive central processing system.[4] Integrated applications include text creation, text filing, proofreading, distribution lists, directories, calendars, appointment scheduling and access to stock market or news services. The ease with which messages are readily dispatched using mailing lists is a great source of irritation, because such practices fill up incoming message queues with more mail than anyone can handle. One of the problems for e-mail users, especially in large organizations, is how to stop the distribution of *junk* mail.

On the positive side, e-mail makes it easier to communicate independently of the social constraints of status, background or organization. It also has the positive effect of reducing the barriers to contacts across functional, cultural and geographic boundaries.

Over 50 companies have entered the business of providing e-mail services. They also offer applications such as weather forecasting, stock market reporting, bibliographic searches, employment opportunities, business news, marital advice, sports and home-based shopping. Banks are starting to offer e-mail as an add-on to banking-at-home services.

For each network, the subscriber must learn unique characteristics as well as the idiosyncrasies of each application. The lack of transferability of training is the severest inhibition to growth of this industry.

Recent innovations, such as higher resolution screens, color displays, faster modems and application integration, are the by-products of advances in personal computing. This does not solve the problem of how to transfer messages from one network to another. Little change has taken place in the handling of e-mail except for better access to individual networks and software for setting up e-mail on local area networks. I think that the cause for this relatively slow headway is the inability of existing e-mail services to satisfy a fuller range of information needs.

THE OPPORTUNITY WAITING FOR A SOLUTION

Analysis of office work shows that only a small share of business communications are handled by electronic means. Studies of office work consistently show that managers, professional specialists and administrators spend as much as 30 to 70% of their time in personal discussions and meetings in addition to making telephone calls.[5] Only a fraction of this involves contact with customers or suppliers.[6] Most of it concerns internal coordination. In dollar terms, spoken contacts are the costliest office activity. Professionals, managers and administrators prefer face-to-face oral conversation as the way to conduct business instead of written or computer-aided activities. Top executives often experience no more than 30 minutes a day without interruption for phone calls or meetings.

Document distribution, which is the primary role of electronic mail, occupies only a negligible amount of time for office employees. Calculation, where the overwhelming investment in office automation exists so far, is less than 5% of office hours. Document creation, the object of all word processing, takes less than 8% of office hours. I estimate that the time consumed in all office activities which are clearly eligible for economically justifiable automation is only about 15% of total hours. Coincidentally it just happens, the average cost of all office automation is about 15% of average payroll costs for office workers.[7] This leads to the startling conclusion that, on the average, the costs of automation are comparable to the current labor costs of getting computerized work accomplished.[8] This suggests to me that unless a company succeeds in altering the contents or quality of automated office work, new automation investments from now on will be at best a break-even proposition.

Compare the time spent on already automated office activities with the time in business meetings, which consume anywhere from 20 to 40% of total office costs. To that, add travel expenses and preparatory costs, such as phone calls or e-mail messages which are necessary to arrange a meeting.[9] I concluded that major new investments in information technology that will address the excessive costs of meetings will most probably come from exceptional gains in the form and contents how business meetings are conducted.

To date, the limited economic success of video-conferencing supports that view. Video conferences try to attack the rising costs of meetings. So far they have captured only a minuscule share of this activity. Having meeting participants stare at television cameras while they continue cultivating their ancient rhetorical and debating skills may save travel expenses but will not make a noticeable dent in the total time a company devotes to meetings. Without a change in habits that recognizes that the electronic medium makes it possible to conduct business differently, any cost savings from video-conferencing will be rapidly offset by the newly found convenience to schedule meetings with greater frequency, involving more people.

At present, computer technologies offer only a negligible contribution to increasing effectiveness or reducing the costs of meetings. Even the best computer-generated slides cannot solve the problem of how to share new ideas or solve problems. Visual aids are of little help in explaining how a meeting relates to preceding events, which arguments remain unresolved, or which statements are conjectures rather than facts.

Regardless of the proliferation of electronic means such as e-mail, on-line graphic presentations or video-conferencing, group cooperation arises from traditions not much removed from tribal habits. Instead of squatting around the campfire and looking for nonverbal clues from the Chief, the contemporary executives recline around the conference table searching for hints about everybody's motives. The airplane and the automobile will remain the primary transport means for securing group participation. To substitute for physical presence, the electronic means must also convey the context of a message which people get when they observe the interplay of ideas, hints, images and sound.

In the next twenty years the electronic message will overcome its current limitations in form and ease of use. When that occurs, we can expect that meeting activities will receive the next big wave of information technology investments. It is inconceivable that the computer industry would not exploit the single largest business information activity that is notorious for its inadequacies, once the communications and software industries realize that vast improvements in the methods how to secure group cooperation are feasible.

Electronic Conferences

Electronic conferences offered the earliest means to deal with inefficient meetings. Essentially, they are e-mail services repackaged for group use. A telephone line, a modem, a personal computer and telecommunications-handling software are all you need if you wish to explore these means. Comments, usually composed on separate word processing software, go into a central conference file arranged either by time of receipt or topic. Participants may connect to a conference whenever it is convenient, review the proceedings, respond to group or personal messages, ask questions and attach their own commentaries to any prior entry. Participants can also take advantage of a variety of features, such as searching for key words, reviewing who said what, referring to other conference text and rearranging the messages into a more logical order.

For instance, I have used an electronic conferencing facility provided by the New Jersey Institute of Technology (EIES) to bring forty-two experts together over a four-month period to prepare a report for the U.S.

government. The final report came out without delays, simply by editing the transcript of the participants' comments. The group met only once at the inception of effort.

An effective use of computer conferences is the construction of a single negotiating text. It is a process where all parties seeking an accord agree to maintain a mutually accessible file for all documents and commentaries while negotiations are under way. Several global corporations, such as Digital Equipment Corporation, Xerox and Texas Instruments, have managed for many years to run international taskforces and interdisciplinary design teams at distant locations to accelerate decision-making.

A special application of having an electronic conference involves the use of remote communications software. You can use such software to control other computers as if they were yours. For instance, you can call a customer who is having trouble understanding your financial proposal. While the customer is viewing his terminal, you may bring up identical message windows on both screens and take control of each application while talking with the customer on the phone.

Remote communications software also allows geographically remote groups to link their computers and use them as a chalkboard for sketching ideas and exchanging comments.

Electronic conferences embody attributes which are not achievable in conventional meetings. There is no time or geographic restriction on participation. All costs are direct (e.g., everyone is not idle while listening). The conference is self-documenting, because all messages can remain in each computer's memory. It allows adequate time for thought and responding to a query. It is self-paced. It maximizes information receiving speed (from the verbal maximum transfer rate of only 200 words per minute to the visual equivalent of 2,000 to 5,000 words per minute, depending on graphic capabilities).

An electronic conference is time-sharing (e.g., you may participate in several conferences simultaneously). Your own participation in an electronic conference is essential if you wish to understand how computer-based communication can evolve as a new communication medium.

Electronic Mail as a Shared File System

Relative to the growth of facsimile, e-mail has been a laggard. For casual uses it cannot compete on the basis of transaction cost or simplicity of use, because facsimile currently is superior for text and simple graphics. This situation has arisen because facsimile traffic is also benefiting from the universal acceptance of transmission standards, while e-mail vendors still are struggling to install 1984 standards[10]. In the absence of document interchange conventions, the transmitted text and graphic codes in e-mail are useless for most archival purposes. The primary advantage of facsimile is its simplicity. It requires at most five elementary procedures to set up an office for sending a page of text anywhere. To set-up a personal computer to send a page of text by e-mail could easily consumer fifty complex steps involving hardware, software and telecommunications. Yet, computerized transmission of text and data will ultimately prevail because facsimile has a fatal flaw: although its is almost always created digitally, it cannot be stored in a digital form and become a retrievable or manipulable as shared knowledge. The best you can ever do with incoming facsimile pages is to store them in bigger or better filing cabinets. Placing facsimile records on an optical disk does not alter the fact that this achieves nothing more than save the clerical costs of retrieval, while preserving information in a vastly impoverished format as compared with its digital original.

Facsimile will continue prevailing over e-mail as a business communications means as long as owners of personal computers print out their e-mail messages and conference proceedings on their printers, placing the printouts in file cabinets where their value instantly degrades. In this manner the expensive e-mail users regress to the level of inexpensive facsimile users, where e-mail cannot compete. Information workers and particularly knowledge workers can hardly ever find and then readily reuse any of the information they ever received.

I consider business files, in facsimile or printout form, the graveyard of organizational knowledge. Filing cabinets represent to me a mechanism for the destruction of reusable information assets. Perhaps as much as one half of the administrative costs of our private and public organizations are consumed in replicating, reentering, copying, retransmitting, rephrasing, restating, recoding and reinventing information that already resides in somebody's files unless it has already been discarded as garbage.

I have participated in dozens of conferences and acted as moderator in quite a few, but can rarely reuse any text because it is hard to isolate, locate and then relate the ideas in one message with arguments advanced in another. The proposition that electronic conference files and notes should be easily shared among diverse working groups is hopeless with the current electronic conferencing technology. The present electronic communications do not offer the capacity to group participants to browse through shared files with ease.

E-mail and electronic conferences have gained only limited acceptance because they concentrate on transmission, where they have only a limited advantage, rather than on reusable information storage, where they have an absolute superiority. Easy and rapid access to accumulated information is the key to making the electronic medium a viable substitute for meetings. When people assemble they carry just about all of their useful knowledge in their heads, so that they can apply what they know in rapid, interactive verbal sequences.

If you sit behind a keyboard you cannot keep up with events that take place when the drama of words, text, graphics and motion happens around a conference table.[11] Existing technologies are inadequate to bridge the chasm between the private knowledge of decision-makers, which resides in their individual heads, and organizational knowledge, which is distributed among specialists and their files. Reducing this costly gap offers an enormous potential for future gains in management productivity.

Central Shared Files

To ease the difficulties of limited real-time communication channels, e-mail vendors keep all message traffic on central files and will store it for as long as you wish. Electronic conferences do not take place in real-time (e.g., synchronously), but whenever a participant can conveniently send a message or inquiry to the central files (e.g., asynchronously). Vendors can also provide you with key-word search software for locating long forgotten text. Vendors favor the centralized model of filing, because they derive attractive profit margins from central storage charges.

Centralized filing systems are slow, expensive and incur message hauling costs between the customer and the central site whenever you make a search of prior messages. As long as most e-mail transmission speeds are in the 1,000 to 10,000 bits per second range, asynchronous file-sharing of central text files is the most economically attractive solution, especially if this involves frequent searches. Video, color, sound and interactive problem-solving are economically unfeasible thus far because they require large transmission capacity, and are therefore too expensive for most uses.

It requires skill and training to find your way through an electronic archive, even when your network uses graphic interfaces, such as shown below.[12]

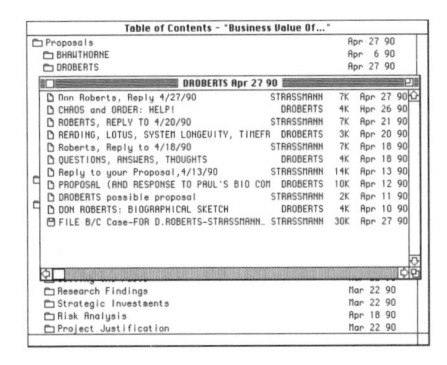

Figure 15.1: Display Showing File Structure of a Tutorial

Familiarity with the organization of the files and messages is essential before a participant can use this communications method in lieu of a meeting.

Distributed Shared Files

The desirable model for storing the exchanges that take place in a computer conference, as well as for all software known as *groupware*, is cooperative filing. Each personal computer or local file would have a copy of the portions of the shared database that is of interest. For instance, such group files would be set up to deal with a specific situation, such as a contract, project or a negotiation.

Cooperative filing requires that the network software automatically updates (synchronizes) all private files. This makes it possible to maintain the integrity of the distributed files without relying on a central control.[13] The future availability of high-capacity networks, low-cost gigabyte memories and document format standards will speed up the acceptance of cooperative filing. Meanwhile, new *groupware* applications offer immediate opportunities to improve the utility of e-mail. I encourage you to experiment with this new software, because it will help you learn about the next wave of profitable computer applications.

FROM INDIVIDUAL TO GROUP PRODUCTIVITY

It is possible to forecast probable new use of computers by studying what's wrong with what we have now. An understanding of those current inefficiencies which are amenable to improvement provides the best indication of where technology may move next. If something is potentially profitable, some innovator will surely figure out a workable solution.

By far, the most costly information-handling process is the business meeting. Presenters explain their ideas while everyone tries to interpret what they say. After much distillation, the final output is a written statement that may reflect most conclusions, but few of the arguments leading up to it. If this outcome arrives by e-mail, it may communicate what someone recorded, but includes none of the context or understanding leading to it. Most of the value of meetings is in what people remember. Unfortunately, the memories of business people are selective and brief, which usually means that additional meetings must convene to correct whatever misinterpretation arises.

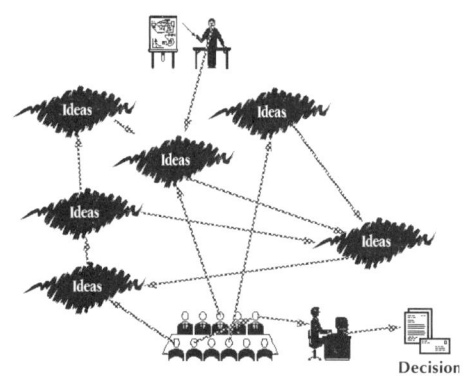

Figure 15.2 The Flow of Ideas in a Business Meeting

If the conclusions are simple, the decision-making clear, the participants follow accepted rules, and the execution of the decisions is competent, then the management-by-meeting will work.

If you have cultural and linguistic diversity, geographic dispersion, complex issues, a changing organizational structure and unclear guidelines for managing change, then every new decision will require re-interpretation to fit local circumstances. The decisions that come out of these meetings are vulnerable to error and misunderstanding. The meetings also consume large amounts of time and effort which in the end may be of little value.

Distributing meeting notes and presentation graphics used in such meetings by e-mail does not help much. The recipient understands only a part of what shows up in writing, which is only a fraction of what the presenters said, and even less than what the presenters wish to communicate. There are always ideas that are said, but never heard. There are also ideas which were not spoken, but are reported as heard:

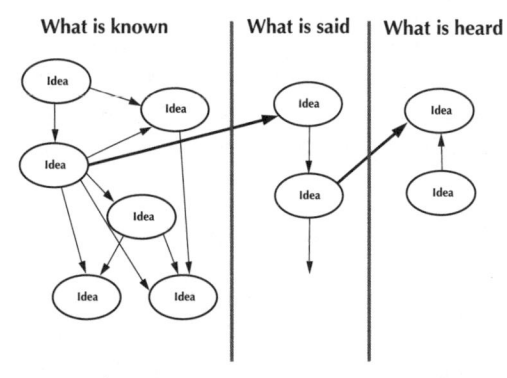

Figure 15.3 Filtering Ideas in a Business Meeting

You can get software to assist in explaining assumptions or revealing the consistency of logical statements.[14] Such software are "decision support" aids. Although the use of these techniques presently applies mostly to stand-alone applications, I expect that the logic of these routines will become attached, as readily accessible routines, to individual conclusions to improve the recipient's understanding. Embedded "decision support" programs will improve the understanding of an idea. For instance, instead of simply sending the image of a risk profile, such as illustrated in Chapter 9, for a software development project, it is better to include with it the underlying logic that generated the entire range of estimates. This makes it possible for anyone to run the program and to examine what are the sources of risk. In this way another manager can examine the assumptions which support a proposal and apply the originator's own expert reasoning to coming up with an alternative option.

Computer-aided Collaboration Meetings

There are experimental conference sites[15] where large screen video allows the participants to examine the logical rationale that supports what each participating individual is saying. The focus of such a meeting is to probe the assumptions that support each person's point of view. This allows exploring alternative views of the individual arguments. Organizational learning takes place when a group can discover new ways of rearranging and harmonizing the participants' assumptions, and subsequently articulate new conclusions.

Group participation becomes a discussion of multiple points of view. A tour through the presenter's mental model, which the displays represent visually, reveals not only what is in the proposal but also what options are open for further exploration. Once you get a chance to participate in such an experimental conference, it does not take much imagination to visualize non-sequential access from remote workstations.

REPRESENTATION OF KNOWLEDGE

Techniques that are used to effectively represent knowledge by means of electronic displays have emerged from several unrelated disciplines.[16] We are starting to see computer applications that not only distribute raw data, but also provide the context in which to understand it. Such applications have the attributes of "knowledge representation."

In 1990, already 35% of the U.S.A. information workers use communicating workstations, although most of them are only special-purpose terminals. They will have to begin using software that improves their ability to cope with related messages. The strongest incentive for using knowledge representation comes from multinational businesses. Cultural differences in word usage, even if translated, always keep senders guessing if recipients will understand what they see.

Professor Marvin Minsky from M.I.T. said "...the secret of what anything means to us depends on how well we have connected it to all the other things we know."[17] This formulation makes it possible to define knowledge in terms on which we can act:
  • Observe existing connections, and
  • Make new connections.

Computers have a superior capacity to act as logical devices instead of being used only as numerical calculators. Computers especially are suitable for recording and keeping track of related messages, dates, projects, personalities, locations and whatever make up your experiences.

As Minsky sees it, the goal of "artificial intelligence" is to mimic how the brain processes information to come up with understanding of what is happening. Your brain does not neatly file what you see alphabetically or by date. The mind is a large collection of mostly disjointed logic and bits of memory that learn, through adaptation, how to co-operate in the integration of individual elements into a coherent pattern. The human mind solves problems by successfully connecting everything that it perceives to that which it understands. Perception is then the act of making connections.

The essence of all intelligence is the capacity to construct *knowledge-gaining webs* that provide useful answers for coping with specific situations. The uniqueness of each person's electronic message reflects how its content relates to other ideas. According to this theory, displaying a person's *connections* that make up his or her *knowledge-gaining webs* would improve the capacity to communicate with others and be understood.

Reflecting this theory, a wide range of software packages is now available to display *connections*. They assist with the conversion of tangled information webs into improved understanding. Versions of such knowledge-representation software include outliners, thought-organizers, hypertext processors and reverse dictionaries. An example of a reverse dictionary illustrates how the logical context of a word can be displayed by graphical means:[18]

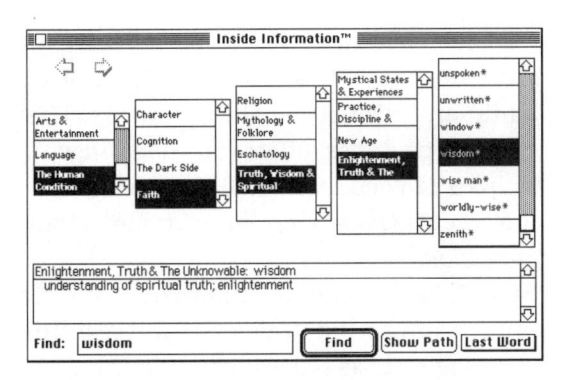

Figure 15.4: Graphic Display of Context

The application of such software to group collaboration assumes that:

- Participants connect electronically before, during and after a collaborative experience.
- Participants can view, through shared networks, each other's multi-media links (e.g., text, graphics, video, synthetic animation and sound) which represent each participant's knowledge that is relevant to the collaborative effort.
- Connections can be either real-time (synchronous) or off-line (asynchronous). They may be in a common language (e.g., business English) or interpreted to recognize the recipients' native language, level of education or cultural background.

The economic advantages from group collaboration, by electronic means, will not come easily. The mastery of interactive conferencing methods will require much training and learning new ways of presenting information. The biggest obstacles will be behavioral. In many meetings the presenters may not wish others to know the reasons for a proposition. Consultants and suppliers also may be reluctant to transplant know-how electronically, because this raises issues concerning copyright and proprietary rights. Many executives will object to the electronic communication of assumptions as interference with their need to hedge with opaque arguments against unpredictable outcomes.

Establishing trust and motivation to cooperate, not technology, will ultimately enable the reaping of benefits from computerized collaboration. Cultural conditions that favor undisguised sharing of information may become essential for the survival of every global enterprise.

Hypertext Software

Out of a large collection of available software, hypertext methods offer the most promising solutions to the display of logically linked text, graphics, audio and ultimately video sources. There are dozens of hypertext software packages, offering a wide range of capabilities. The guiding principle of hypertext is to allow the reader to copy the author's information elements (*nodes*) into his own files, along with the author-specified *connections*.

The reader then can edit the information and retain only relevant ideas for connection to the nodes already residing within his own *knowledge-gaining web*, as illustrated in Figure 15.5. The reader then may *browse*[19] in his own files, but would not connect again to the author's *knowledge-gaining web*. The reader cannot ask further questions concerning any *connections* that the author did not originally include in the hypertext:

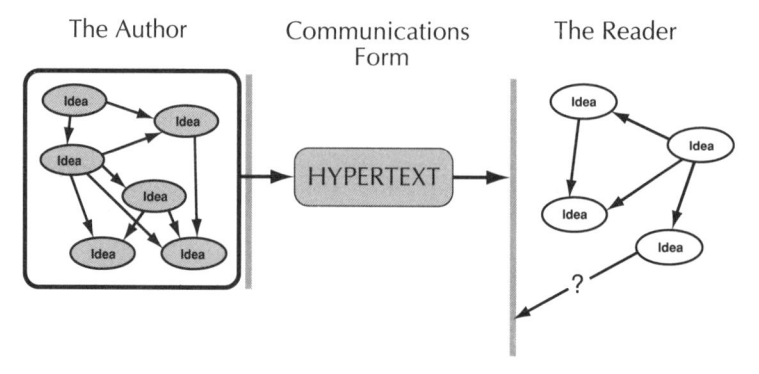

Figure 15.5: Hypertext: Reader Examines Nodes and Links

Although the idea of hypertext is at least 20 years old, it only recently has become popular.[20] The rapid acceptance of hypertext is evident from the size of the catalogues offering collections of *nodes* priced at $3–$8 per application.[21] A flood of hypertext software packages is now in the marketplace, offering a variety of techniques for displaying relationships among information nodes.

Advanced hypertext software[22] offers multiple *map views* of the information in a file or database. Each view offers a different logical path or sequence for information access. The development of hypertext methods is progressing rapidly and suffers only from the limited computing capacity of existing personal computers. To browse through text and graphics—in color and with sound—requires much computing power. For instance, the system with the longest history of graphic multi-node linking requires a fast workstation and tens of megabytes of memory before it can work.[23]

Hypertext Applications

To make a hypertext application useful in business, the software must solve the difficult problem of representing information in ways that diminish dependence on meetings. The major distinction among the various products concerns the strategy of describing the individual nodes. If the search semantics and display choices rely entirely on the users' visual discrimination, the screen has too much detail overwhelming the viewer. If the text is hierarchical and relatively simple in its structure (when organized into chapters, sections, paragraphs and subparagraphs), then hypertext is easy to follow. However, the simpler the organization, the less the advantage of using an electronic representation as compared with a well-indexed file drawer or an instruction manual that has a good table of contents.

The possibilities for applying the hypertext approach to business applications are without limits. In a corporation, there may be randomly arriving messages consisting of millions of documents, electronic messages, scanned images and voice recordings which must fit into the recipients' databases in an orderly way. A typical military intelligence or customer-support application in financial services has such characteristics, since it involves thousands of documents, ten-thousands of numerical expressions and hundreds of diagrams. Individuals will use the hypertext-embedded context within each message to integrate this flood of information into their own databases.

In situations such as business acquisitions, new product launching or preparing for a controversial shareholder meeting, the response to queries must be rapid and completely reliable. Legal cases and public hearings also may require an accumulation of background information in which purely hierarchical filing is impractical. Nobody can ever anticipate the form or progression of a query.

Knowledge-Sharing and Organizational Learning

The rate at which organizations learn how to learn provides their best competitive advantage.

The future of hypertext methods will be a compromise between the enormous power of this knowledge-representation technique and the capacity of collaborating teams to make use of it. When sociologists talk about group or company cultures, they are inferring the presence of conventions that simplify the sharing of ideas. The computer protocols adopted by companies to foster collaboration will become new sources of competitive advantage when electronic networks become the most frequently used channels for managing global businesses.

Organizations that will be able to share knowledge faster will be able to move innovative products and services into markets more rapidly. They will have shorter product development and manufacturing cycles, and will be able to respond to competitive actions with few delays. Ray Stata, the CEO of *Analog Devices* said it perhaps better than anyone else: "...the rate at which individuals and organizations learn may become the only sustainable competitive advantage..."[24]

All management processes in a competitive marketplace have a systems life expectancy. After the limits of the useful life are reached, the systems must be replaced before a competitor takes advantage of the system's weaknesses. The life-death cycle of organizational systems places an enormous strains on group learning. For instance, to cut manufacturing lead time from 15 weeks to 5 weeks, or to improve time-to-market from 36 months to 6 months, does not arise by making everybody work longer hours or faster. Changes in organizational behavior only occur by learning how to organize cooperation differently, which means sharing information with greater simplicity, without errors and without delays. Increasing the speed and volume of e-mail or facsimile will not overcome the limitations of the recipients' capacities to understand and then to react.

New forms of communication ultimately must make it possible to inter-connect each person's *knowledge-gaining webs,* as the need arises, to make error-free communication flow across organizational, cultural, geographic and conceptual boundaries. Knowledge-gaining networks will have to replace many of the current methods for making routine business decisions which limit the capacity of organizations to cope with rapidly shrinking systems life expectancies.

Future Prospects

Metatext

At present, most hypertext applications are analogous to electronically shuffled index cards. Speeding up the display and arrangements of the electronic equivalent of scraps does not always justify incurring the costs of recording and maintaining all business information inside a computer.

The real power of hypertext applications lie in their *browsers.* These can apply complex criteria toward the search for useful knowledge. For example, it is possible to apply an "expert program" to display the structure of assumptions that support an argument. This is important, because when people dissent, the causes of their differences are based not as much on contrary facts as on divergent assumptions. The display of each participant's logical argument structures will someday take place as a real-time display during a computer-mediated debate.[25]

Collaboration suggests the sharing of knowledge between authors and readers. Consider a meeting that takes advantage of knowledge-representation software. Participants face multiple display screens. They have the capacity for reviewing not only their own formal reasoning, but also everyone else's. The meeting may be synchronous, where the presenter talks while the participants listen. The meeting may be also asynchronous, where the participants read and participate in the exchanges whenever they are ready. Regardless of the timing, the participants will be consulting information available using remote files to compare how their own views match with the presenter's own *connections.* This arrangement describes a major use of *metatext:*

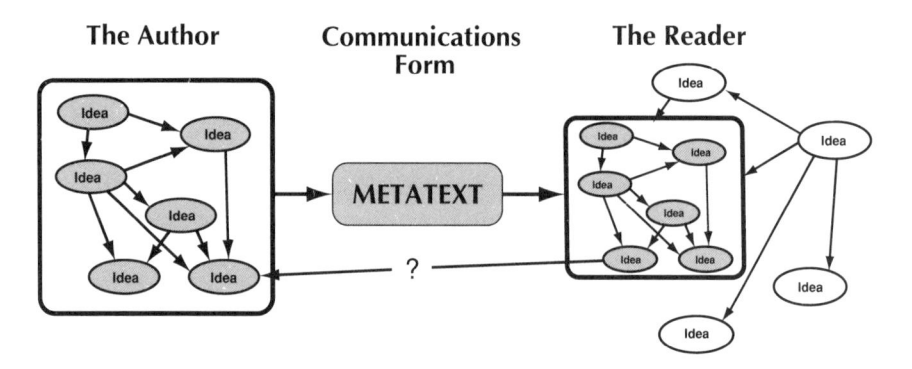

Figure 15.6: Metatext — Reader Interacts with Nodes and Links

The facility to browse through shared files and create links that extend beyond the reader's own files—illustrated in Figure 15.6 by the line that connects the "?" from the reader's *knowledge-gaining web* to the author's—differs from hypertext. It introduces a new dimension in the activity of knowledge-gaining. In *metatext,* what is the author's or what is the reader's is indistinguishable. The ideas exchanged by the author and the now active reader merge into a new integrated whole. The capacity to leap the boundaries that presently separate what is personal and what is the group's will change the concept of how groups work together.

What may be the economic and social consequence of such a working environment is only a guess. Certainly, it will change the legal doctrines of what is intellectual property, copyright and privacy.

Thought Control vs. Anarchy

One should not view the electronic message that reveals, in a prescribed way, assumptions, links and the structure of supporting nodes, as an unqualified benefit. I can conceive of conditions where modifications of information can take place on a scale that does not approach even the wildest Orwellian nightmare. Network access to individual personal files will make it possible to reprocess and reedit collective memories which will guarantee the removal of all nonconforming or undesirable facts. In its most objectionable form, *metatext* could reduce personal privacy through unwarranted intrusions into personal files. The antidote against such abuse is to design collaborative systems using only distributed filing of all personal information so that individual permission for access to data can allow or deny access.

Access privileges would require personal permission and possibly a one-time de-encryption key.[26] In this way distributed filing and privacy rights become synonymous. Some of the alleged conomic advantages of central filing may have to be sacrificed to protect constitutional rights of individuals.

Group cooperation can disintegrate if the overload of out-of-context messages, links and nodes makes the electronic traffic humanly intractable, despite the best efforts to reconcile logical inconsistencies. Well-meaning groups may engage prematurely in electronically supported cooperation if they first do not reconcile fundamentally opposing views of their goals. I have found two "excutive information systems" that were rushed into operation to foster improved group communications among a widely dispersed executive group. The long festering disagreements on key issues were magnified by the unforgiving format of electronic displays. The top management would have been better off spending its time and money addressing some the basic unresolved issues – or changing the roles of individuals – than proceeding with a showplace, but hollow, executive information network.

When attractive tools are available, especially in their computerized form, this tends to create an unthinking compulsion to use technology as a substitute for common sense. If a group has deeply conflicting views, it may be advisable to resort to emotionally healthier forms of communication. A good shared meal, before plunging into the details of programs, plans and projects, may be more productive than sending electronic messages. When a group loses sight of its objectives, amplifying the efforts by computerized means will accelerate its failure.[27]

New Forms for Knowledge-gaining

The designer of computer-driven visual models must provide the problem of what is intuitively the most lucid way to display conceptual complexity. Traditional computer applications, such as word-processing, spread sheets and hypertext, address this issue by constructing screen images which are analogues of paper forms. There are only a few disciplines, such as bibliography, mathematics, chemistry and astronomy, where there are established conventions for describing knowledge. Knowledge-representation structures that make group decision-making possible in business are still waiting for graphic innovations like those currently used in biochemistry, nuclear physics, structural engineering and meteorology. The complexity of business situations would call for color, sound and animation for visualizing concepts that lead to better insights.

One enabling technology for full-motion simulation of shared visual experiences is interactive digital video. It enables entirely new uses of computers. For instance, instructional sequences showing the image of a tutor can accompany a training program. The synthesized tutor—in fact an expert program—responds to the student's queries.

As another example, it would be possible to improve the understanding of the potential consequences of a production proposal by playing back a synthesized computer-generated video sequences of what one could expect to encounter when production schedules change for a new product.[28] Simultaneously, a project team could explore scenarios representing the competition's response to the new product and advise factory management for what contingencies to prepare.

A far more advanced technology is description-driven computer-generated graphic sequences which allow excursions through *simulated* plants, warehouses and retail stores, without ever leaving computer workstations.[29] There are no limits to the imagination when technologies will allow in exploring of alternative future scenarios. However, the danger arises when imagination becomes more attractive than facts. Plausible simulations have the tragic tendency of leading the mind to conclusions that deny reality.[30]

Interactive digital video technology will change how business people communicate electronically. Just think about the existing difficulties of imparting to a globally dispersed team the full implications of a new product. In the future, all participants will get access to programmable scenarios about the product launch. The connections between budgets, schedules and events show up on displays so that individuals or teams can explore how their roles are affected. Annotations of shared files and scenario improvements can become the means to secure commitment without requiring excessive time devoted to unproductive meetings.

CHAPTER 15 — COMPUTER-BASED COMMUNICATION

CHAPTER SUMMARY

To communicate means to share. To share means to understand.

The critical element in successful communications is the human being at either end. It requires a receiver who understands what the other is saying or writing. The efficiency of contemporary media to distribute messages has increasingly forced listeners into passive communication—you cannot talk back and explore what is seen or what is hear. Therefore the most common cause of breakdown in business communication is the denial of the recipient to participate.

Today's use of electronic mail originates in the traditions of hierarchically organized writing. Its structure, content and use differ little from an inscribed parchment, a typed letter or a telegram, except that it distributes information faster. Apart from the speed, convenience and sometimes cost, person-to-person computer communication does not take advantage of the logical powers of personal computers. Electronic mail and computer conferences transmit messages that use the efficiencies of the electronic communication channel but take no advantage of the potential capacity of computers to make a message more understandable.

Electronic mail has made only a small contribution to handling the increased load of business information. Person-to-person computer communications will become economically important when their emphasis shifts from the efficiency of message conveyance to and from individuals to the effectiveness of knowledge-sharing by groups.

Since Gutenberg, the emphasis in communication has been on reducing the unit cost of information dissemination. Electronic mail can distribute to designated mailboxes 1,000 copies of an announcement just by entering a code for each mailing list. These developments have created a surplus of information while magnifying the scarcity of understanding. We have arrived in an era when the amount of data is overwhelming while we lack the tools to use it. This is a dangerous development, because such an overload leads towards the rejection of understanding that based on evidence. It encourages relying on much simpler emotions in business affairs.[31] The increased complexity and quantity of data threaten the capacity of our executives to convert relevant information into careful reasoning.

The outlines of the solution to this conundrum seem to be emerging in the form of knowledge-gaining software that support the intelligence-aiding capacities of a personal workstation. This approach is diametrically opposite to the uses of electronic mail until now. In addition to emphasizing the dissemination of information from one to many, future initiatives must shift to the demand-side for acquiring useful knowledge, from many to one. This elevates the prominence of the recipient, as contrasted with the hierarchical view in which the sender dominates.[32]

Technological innovation will be needed to make the new relationships possible. We will require networks that have the capacity to carry the *connections* which encapsulate the context of all messages. Today's workstations, operating systems, applications software, display technologies and information-retrieval methods are grossly underpowered for this purpose. People speculate as to what to do with pocket supercomputers, terabyte memories the size of a sugar cube and gigabyte per second networks. I submit that even such awesome capabilities are barely adequate for the massive use of knowledge-gaining systems.

Despite these prerequisites for change, technological innovations will be necessary but will not be sufficient for success. The limits on whatever progress is likely will be organizational because the structure of a computer system reflects the structure of the organization that builds it. A fundamental change in the relationship between information suppliers and consumers will bring a transformation of how to create, own and control information. It will alter how corporations and government agencies organize. Freely accessible, assumption-revealing and knowledge-gaining computer communications in business will mark a new epoch of societal development. The most likely outcome will be that an expansion in global institutions will match the current growth in global trade.

Until then, the best you can do is to experiment and then learn from innovative forms of communicating by electronic means. Profit will come to those who will research better and learn faster. Delay is not advisable, because many new tools are ready to be explored right now.

CHAPTER 15 COMMENTS

[1] Private networks within individual companies serve only their own internal needs. For instance, at Xerox we set up in 1969 a Sigma computer to switch messages among all global locations and a few individual terminals. Those not connected

by private network had support from public network vendors, such as Western Union (EasyLink—175,000 mailboxes and 7.5 million messages per month), Telenet/U.S. Sprint (Telemail—165,000 mailboxes and 4.8 million messages per month), Dialcom (+Mail—140,000 active mailboxes and 3.8 million messages per month), CompuServe (InfoPlex), MCI (MCIMail) and 20 to 25 other resellers of services.

[2] To figure out e-mail costs per page you have to consider: connect time, monthly subscription fees for telephone lines, minimum usage charges, storage charges plus amortization of equipment and local area networks.

[3] For example, Boeing sends out 15,000 messages per day to suppliers. Continental Holdings, a food distributor, receives 4,000 e-mail orders from its customers every month.

[4] Such as IBM's (PROFS), Data General's (CEO), Wang's (Office) and DEC's (All-in-One).

[5] Travel time to and from meetings, often involving unpaid hours, and the personal time allocated to meetings is greater than is usually reported.

[6] For a more detailed discussion of office habits, see P.A.Strassmann, Information Payoff—The Transformation of Work in the Electronic Age, *The Free Press*, 1985.

[7] Based on *MPIT* project findings. For additional references about office time-studies see my earlier book, Information Payoff.

[8] Without computers, the hours consumed in document distribution, calculations and document creation would certainly add up to a much larger figure. The theoretical amount of labor needed to do office work by obsolete means is irrelevant and should not figure in computing productivity gains. You should not compare the cost of a cross-country airline ticket with the expense of taking the same trip in an ox-drawn wagon.

[9] For instance, a typical corporate staff 12 person meeting would cost about $13,000, or about $55 per minute (Presenter's preparation, $4,000; Organizing the meeting, $1,000; Participants' time, $7,000; Post-meeting follow-up, $1,000). It is noteworthy that a manufacturing firm would have to earn incremental revenues of at least $150,000 to generate sufficient gross margin to cover these costs.

My fascination with the costs of meetings goes back to 1974 when W.W. Simmons, former Director of Strategic Planning for the IBM Corporation, developed for me a customized version of his *Concensor*™ feedback device. The computer display recording the participants' reactions also showed a clock that tracked the dollar value of the participants' time. A low cost software version of the same idea is now available (from the Institute for Better Meetings, Palo Alto, CA). An eight-person committee would show the following accumulated costs when they adjourn after 39 minutes of deliberation:

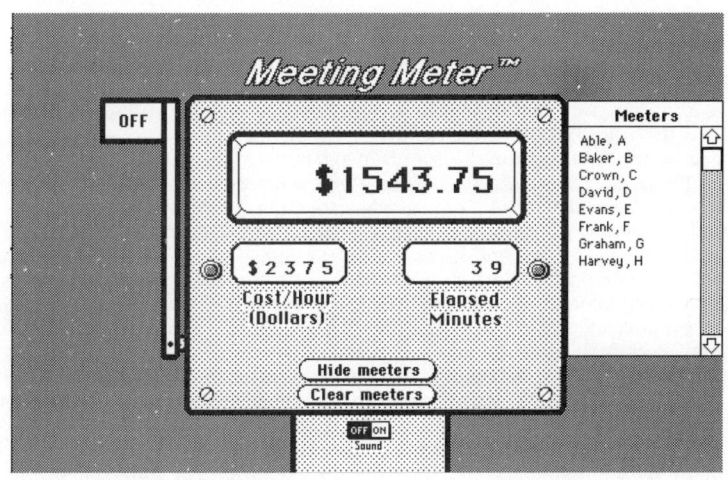

Sometimes I open my remarks to a large audience by figuring out the per minute cost of the occasion. My alltime record was the address to the global meeting of the world's largest auditing and consulting firm. There were 2,300 partners present. My words had to be worth at least $13,800 per minute (@ $300 per hour plus 20% for expenses), which I found difficult to do.

10 The CCITT (the *International Telegraph and Telephone Consultative Committee* in Geneva, Switzerland) X.400 standards for e-mail reveal the complexity of e-mail. The standard must provide for different grades and speeds of service, security levels, priorities, multi-destination delivery and message cross-referencing. Data encryption, message forwarding, access protocols to existing telex or teletext terminals, and address verifications are just a few of the features that need resolution before universal message interchanges become possible. The problem of achieving standardized e-mail is very difficult, because new features continually are being added by software and hardware vendors. Standard protocols can cope only with a limited number of variables to achieve satisfactory interconnections. For example, a new e-mail requirement calls for a standard method for converting from text to synthetic voice, where voice-annotation to text will be in use.

11 To provide an illustration about the amounts and portability of various information media, I have charted the following (based on *MacUser Magazine*, August 1990, p.239):

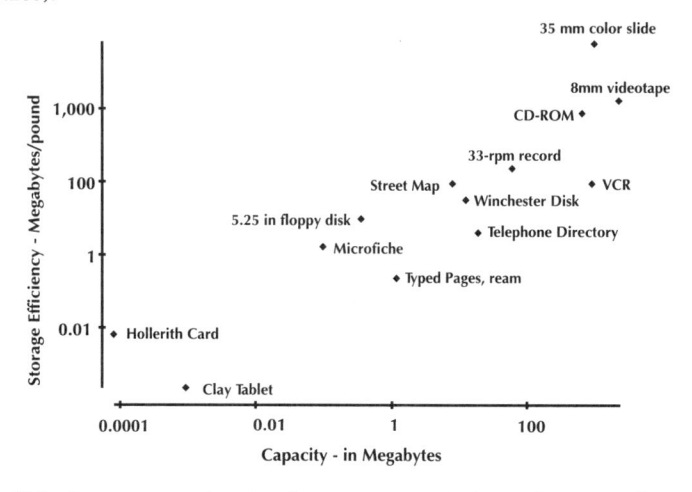

This chart suggests that simultaneous transmission and storage of sound, color and motion that convey the same content and form as face-to-face meetings will require electronic channels of far greater capacity than is currently available. The collective information content of even a small meeting involves exchanging messages that originate from thousands of gigabytes of the participants' knowledge. Any future electronic substitute for meetings will need awesome computing capacity to keep up with what's going on when members of a group engage in a debate.

12 Offered by *Connect, Inc.* of Cupertino, CA 95014. The example is from my tutorial on The Business Value of Computers, for the *International School of Information Management* in Santa Barbara, California. Each student prepares a business proposal for a major computer investment. This accredited course consists of coaching executives on how to come up with acceptable financial justification of computers. In the illustration, the folder of DROBERTS contains all of the messages and files exchanged between himself and the tutor (STRASSMANN).

13 The newly announced *Notes* product from the Lotus Development Corporation has these characteristics.

14 One of the most interesting tools for displaying qualitative preference-ranking of multi-factor judgments is the *Apian Software* Decision Pad software. Another one

is the Decision Analysis package by *Tree Age,* which is helpful in displaying the risks and probabilities of alternative propositions.

I have used *Decision Pad* to recommend to my clients which projects to include within a limited budget. Although project proposals usually include a payback figure, you will always get requests for money that have insufficient financial justification except that they claim intangible benefits such as "improves the company's image", "essential for future growth", "reduces risks", "responsive to potential competitive threat" and so forth. When 50 proposals worth $400,000 compete for $200,000 of available funds, I use *Decision Pad* to construct a table to derive customized criteria for rating each proposition. Tangible indicators such as payback period and expected project life are usually given about half of the rating points. However, risk factors such as an unpredictable competitive situation, can completely dominate simple Benefit-to-Cost calculations and strongly affect whatever you may do because of tangible savings. This software has helped to sort out clearly inferior projects. I can then concentrate on the 5–10 projects which require a careful assessment of payoffs against risks by applying financial criteria, such as the discounted present-worth risk-adjusted method.

Intuitive thinkers, which include just about all CEO's, find it difficult to weigh payback dollars against competitive risks. They readily accept, however, the idea that focusing their attention is the best way to make sure that momentary emotion does not sway their judgment. In practice I find the *Decision Pad* method preferable to engaging in debates. Experimental psychology has demonstrated that people have only a limited capacity for simultaneously evaluating as few as a dozen variables. Ultimately, intuitive insights about the value of a project will prevail over strictly financial methods. However, getting to the final decision by formal means puts into place a structure for making the choices reasonably comparable.

[15] The most thoroughly studied facility of this type is the Colab experimental meeting room to study support of real-time group problem-solving at the *Palo Alto Research Center* of the Xerox Corporation. For further details see Stefik, Foster, Bobrow, Kahn, Lanning and Suchman, Beyond the Chalkboard, *Communications of the ACM*, 30/1.

Other sites are the Collaborative Management Workshop at the University of Arizona in Tucson, The Capture Laboratory at the General Motors Center for Machine Intelligence in Ann Arbor, Michigan and the University of Michigan Collaboration Technology Center in Ann Arbor, Michigan.

In these installations, each participant sits at a conference table with a built-in personal workstation, usually in a near-horizontal position. The participants manage their own agenda and files which are available to everybody either individually or on a shared basis. The images from any of the workstations can be projected to screens for viewing by the group.

Unless you experience such a conference you would find it difficult to visualize how a collaborative group of individual workstations offers a completely different environment than a single overhead display.

[16] Such as applied linguistics, hypertext concepts, cognitive mapping, decision-tree analysis, structured design and object-oriented programming.

[17] M. Minsky, The Society of Mind, *Simon and Schuster*, 1985.

[18] For a literate person, a thesaurus in the identical language usually suffices. If someone does not have the necessary verbal skills, or comes from a different culture, a graphical display of a word's context will be better. The software package illustrated is *Inside Information* by Microlytics.

[19] "Browsing" is the capability of traversing links while examining the contents of nodes. It is also the ability to define logical templates for easing the burden of information searches. The availability of retrieval agents (e.g., software agents or software robots) ultimately will be essential to all large collaboration networks. They will possess the attributes of a librarian that has familiarity with the contents of all available databases.

[20] Through introduction of the Macintosh Hypercard system, offered without cost to all Macintosh customers. It may have well over one million users.

382   THE BUSINESS VALUE OF COMPUTERS

[21] The *Educorp Corporation* of Solana Beach, CA and *Heizer Software* of Pleasant Hill, CA offer hundreds of Hypercard applications.

[22] Such as ArchiText by *BrainPower, Inc.* of Calabasas, CA.

[23] NoteCards came from the *Xerox Palo Alto Research Laboratories* in 1980 and is now available from the *Envos Corporation*, a Xerox spin-off.

[24] From A. Schneiderman, Performance Measurement and Organizational Learning, An Analog Devices Private Report, July 1990.

[25] B. DeKoven, Connected Executives, *Institute for Better Meetings*, Palo Alto, CA. 1990 develops the concept of "technographic support" for meetings as a means to capture and edit group arguments into a consistent format. His book includes a collection of illustrative cases.

[26] I am impressed with the approach of the Lotus *Notes* "groupware" for allowing different levels of access to files: No access; Depositor access (can submit only documents); Reader access (can only read documents); Author access (can read all documents but only edit his or her documents); Editor access (can read and edit all documents); Designer access (can change database structure and edit all documents) and Manager access (can design the database and control the access list). Individuals may have Manager access privileges for their own files.

[27] One form of insanity is when a person keeps redoubling effort every time he does not know what he is doing.

[28] This technology delivers a realistic level for infantry combat, flight and navigational simulations. In its most advanced form tank battles involving thousands of vehicles take place through a totally distributed image-generation network in which every workstation can react instantaneously to actions taken by every participant.

[29] This idea comes from Steve Strassmann's Ph.D. dissertation in the M.I.T. Media Laboratory.

[30] The latest jargon for describing these methods is "artificial reality," "virtual reality" or "virtual worlds." If misused, they become habit-forming toys that distort the differences between fantasy, fiction and exploratory analysis.

[31] This thinking has been aptly summarized in an article about marketing in the 1990's, *Insight Magazine*, October 10, 1988, p.42: "Provide a product with a design image that avoids reliance on verbiage and by-passes the consumer's analytic processes. You can no longer sell products based on facts."

[32] Currently the sender pays the charges for electronic mail. This ignores the economics of information that the major cost is not in sending but in receiving and using. The price of a partner of a major consulting firm now runs about $5 per minute wheres e-mail networks cost only about 10¢ per minute. Company networks should add to the menu of e-mail commands an option "returned unread, to be paid by sender" as a way of providing feedback to originators of surplus messages.

16

OPINIONS AND RESEARCH

The Importance of Measurement

If you do not know where you are going, how can you tell if you arrived?

If you read what experts are saying about computer investments, you could become severely discouraged:

- "...the most commonly mentioned obstacles to successful use of automated office technologies were budget restrictions combined with the inability to measure effectiveness and to quantify benefits."[1]
- "...the main barriers to further uses of information technology are the lack of appropriate cost–benefit techniques."[2]
- "...while firms acknowledge the importance of I.T. to organizational performance, they do not have a satisfactory way of assessing that relationship."[3]
- "There is no well-defined method for cost/benefit analysis. Such strategic planning techniques as IBM's are expensive and time-consuming. It is very difficult to

associate information systems with a strategic role because these benefits might not be visible."[4]
- "The inability to measure productivity was the top-rated obstacle to implementing systems. Yet, only 34% of the companies plan to work on overcoming this obstacle. The survey showed that users are very much interested in measuring and increasing productivity. 78% see it as a major factor in their justification process."[5]
- 75% of surveyed top information systems executives in the U.S.A. and 78% in Europe agreed that they have yet to find a way to measure the value of information systems.[6]
- "...in the next five years banks will spend approximately one quarter trillion dollars on information systems. There is no cogent evidence of gains in profitability or productivity."[7]
- "...after 40 years of applying computers to business operations, there's no way to measure the business value of information technology."[8]
- "...there is urgent need for new cost/benefit formulas and measurements that go beyond the usual *Return-on-Investment* (ROI) evaluations to take into account the total impact of automation on the business."[9]
- "...the area of measurement is the single biggest failure of information systems while it is the single biggest issue before the Board of Directors. I am frustrated by our inability to measure costs and benefits."[10]
- "...$343 million hardware procurements are not justified. It is not clear what needs these procurements would address, what benefits would result or whether alternatives have been adequately analyzed..."[11]
- "...very few companies have gone through a process of planning and managing successful systems. In 80% of success stories the researchers concluded that existing information systems planning and project selection procedures were either purposely circumvented or simply ignored. Traditional cost-benefit driven planning was considered to be an obstacle to the timely implementation of strategic systems."[12]
- "There is simply no methodology that can be used to link computer technology to white collar productivity payoffs.

Many, if not most, successful computing projects actually raise direct costs and do not decrease the labor force at all."[13]

Figure 16.1: A Critical View of Computer Justification Methods

- "72% of the users were unhappy with the justification process or said it needed improvement. Only 47% of those filling out the forms felt that way. Similar levels of dissatisfaction persisted about performance measurement systems. 69% of the users and 57% of the preparers did not like what they were using."[14]
- A 1987 survey of 350 executives found that the absence of after-the-fact evaluations contributed to their unease about high technology. Only about one tenth of the respondents indicated that they evaluate all projects. Half of the survey participants said that they check up only on selected cases and one-fifth said they check on none.
- 77% of chief information executives and 70% of CEO's agreed that decisions regarding resource allocation for information systems are typically based on promises of benefits that are seldom achieved.[15]

Unless we change the way we judge automation's effectiveness, we might deny ourselves the biggest part of the payoff. The measurement system that will finally gain acceptance and support will relate the improvements from information technology to the performance and success of the enterprise.[16]

OPINIONS

A week does not pass without a consultant, publication or professor announcing survey findings about computers. Such opinions shape what people end up believing. They communicate what is the prevailing, and therefore popularly accepted, thinking. I believe that survey results influence the swings in purchasing habits, management practices, technological priorities and organizational ideas about computers. Therefore, paying attention to opinion surveys is essential if you are trying to follow what's going on.

Before you place too much reliance on surveys, you should realize that what appear as authoritative responses are actually reactions to questions asked of a carefully selected group. The method of asking also influences the results. You can get different answers depending on when you perform your survey. To illustrate, compare replies to two identical surveys taken in two successive years:[17]

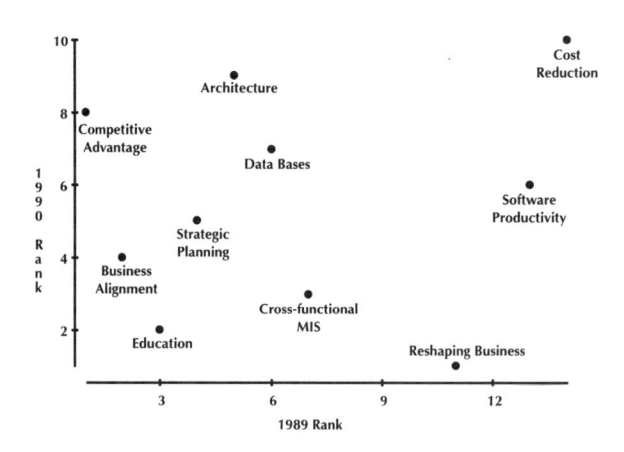

Figure 16.2: The Rapid Shifts in Top Systems Priorities

Figure 16.2 shows how the 1990 rankings of top systems priorities differ from 1989 rankings. For instance, *Competitive Advantage*, which ranked #1 in 1989 ranks only #8 in 1990. Since it takes many years of concentrated effort to create a noticeable effect on competitive advantage, it is curious that the relative importance of such a fundamental policy could change so rapidly.[18] There have been no economic or technological developments to explain why the previously fashionable *Competitive Advantage*, which concerns responding to external threats, passes into low priority. The newly fashionable phrase, *Reshaping the Business*, concerns internal efficiencies. You cannot flip top priorities from external to internal without disorienting people and wasting lots of money in a one year turnaround!

Another example of the influence of timing on survey results comes from a study by the consulting firm of Deloitte Touche. Early in 1990, they surveyed the opinions of 759 manufacturing executives. The consultants found that fewer than 30% of the executives believed that each of their companies was getting an adequate return on its information technology investments. A 1987 survey of a comparable sample showed that more than 60% of manufacturing executives took a positive view of their information technology expenditures.

If survey results are so changeable, why should you pay attention to them? First, you should keep up with what your peer group is thinking about so that you can be alert to the latest trends. Second, you ought to track opinions over an extended time so that you can pay attention to only those few insights that remain consistent. Unfortunately, I find that only computer equipment vendors have remained consistent in their views that computers will improve productivity regardless of where applied.

General Surveys

A study of seventy-one chief executives of large corporations expressed mostly optimistic views about the benefits of computers.[19] Twenty-two percent were extremely positive, seeing no barriers to implementing information technology. At the opposite end, two percent were skeptics who seriously doubted the benefits of computers. In-between was the majority (57%), who saw that there are benefits to using the information technologies, but realized that excessive costs and organizational resistance must temper expectations. Nineteen percent of the executives were ambivalent. They saw some advantages to computers but also were doubtful of their value.

I find that surveys, with negligible exceptions, do not demonstrate that they are querying a representative sample of subjects. Survey questionnaires always query accessible prospects. In this way it is easy to end up with similar but hard to interpret results.

For example, the Imperial College of London asked 50 managers in 34 companies the question, "How does the *Return-on-Capital* of your information technology (I.T.) investment compare to other investments?"

Sixty percent of the respondents said that their I.T. investments yielded average or above average returns. Only 12% stated that their IT investments delivered below average returns. Twenty-eight percent of the respondents did not know what returns they were actually getting. This research report[20] also quotes fourteen I.T. surveys that have shown that investments in I.T. often fail to deliver acceptable returns. Therefore, the Imperial College research could appear as an optimistic view of information technology investments. However, these conclusions obscured the fact that respondents in the same company did not always agree with each other. Furthermore, 28% of the managers acknowledged that they were not strictly calculating how the *Return-on-Capital* of their I.T. investments compared with their other investments. With such findings, you never can be sure what to conclude.

A survey of matched pairs of 92 Chief Executive Officers and 92 Chief Information Officers showed that 66% of the pairs agreed that "...the success of our company links to our ability to gain competitive advantage using information systems."[21] Whether or not they were actually realizing such an advantage did not show up in the replies.

Banking Executives

Knowing the costs but not the value leads to mismanagement.

A Touche Ross International poll of 50 banking Chief Executive Officers traced successful instances of computer use when linked with marketing strategies. All successful users also adopted comprehensive programs to achieve operating cost reductions.[22] Surprisingly, the executives generally believed that information technology has had little strategic impact in banking, despite massive investments by the industry. After all, technology enabled the banking firms to process an enormous volume of transactions at a lower unit cost and reduce the amounts of funds in "float". The executives expressed disappointment with the financial returns from their technology investments.[23] The technology did not give them a capacity to achieve a lasting competitive advantage because all competitors followed each other in using computers in the same way. Competition did not allow getting a price that would compensate for additional services.

The *Executive Report on M.I.S. in Banking*[24] starts with an eye-catching headline: "Banks seek higher yield from information systems investment." Why are the bankers looking for bigger profits? Simply because "...after spending tens of billions of dollars in the last decade on a potpourri of information technology, banks are facing a critical challenge: payback after years of negligible returns." The report then summarizes its findings by noting that although banks have spent an enormous amount of money, they are not sure they are getting their money's worth.

The survey concludes that not one of those interviewed said that results from information technology exceeded expectations. The survey's findings are a discouraging commentary about the bankers' capacity to analyze what they do with their computer investments. It appears that even the bastions of financial prudence are not certain whether they are gaining satisfactory returns from their largest non-financial asset.

If we assume that banking executives are conservative in their expectations, their replies imply that results were not good. Interviews by Klynveld Peat Marwick Goerdeler, the world's largest auditing firm, with 150 senior banking executives, echoed earlier findings: "...few of those interviewed could see any benefits from their huge spending on technology."[25]

Accountants

The National Association of Accountants, in a 1987 study of automation investments, reports that "...participating companies have difficulty evaluating the performance of their CAD/CAM (Computer-Aided-Design and Computer-Aided-Manufacturing) systems. While they are convinced that they could get greater benefits than expected, managers do not have the evidence to support that belief..."

Lack of demonstrable benefits is then a major problem in introducing automation into factories. Users overwhelmingly believe that the justification process needs improvement, while those who fill out the justification forms were indifferent.[26]

It is interesting that the accountants' survey notes "...the traditional accounting measures of performance, such as budgets and standard costs, were not in extensive use by systems management." This suggests that accounting data, which is the primary source of information for running a company, is considered to be mostly irrelevant in addressing automation investment decisions.

The dissatisfaction with current methods of explaining the

benefits of advanced technology originates in the conflict between qualitative and quantitative measurement criteria. The cost factors which are not decisive in CAD/CAM investments, such as lower direct labor costs and lower materials costs, are easy to explain in dollar terms. However, these are not the reason why engineering executives purchase CAD/CAM. The explanations include competitive advantage, consistency with business strategy and improved delivery and service. Yet, these qualitative "intangibles" rarely are translated into dollar terms.

Convincing Top Management

The way used to sell information systems projects to top management illuminates what computer executives think about their roles. Computer executives consider it a mistake to view the introduction of computers into business as amenable to financial analysis. This perception is important to understanding why the business value of computers is not simply a matter of finding improved analytic techniques.

Lederer and Mendelow[27] interviewed twenty top information systems executives to find out the source of their difficulties in persuading their bosses of the benefits of strategic information systems. They elicited the following three reasons why business executives are reluctant to commit money for such purposes:

- Top management lacks awareness about information technology. They are uncomfortable with the computing function.
- Top management sees strictly operational uses for computers and perceives information technology as an evil because of its exorbitant costs.
- Top management perceives a credibility gap because previous systems failed to live up to their expectations. Computer projects did not meet benefit, cost and schedule commitments.

The Lederer and Mendelow survey shows that the need for better financial justification is not a priority item. What did systems executives then do to improve their chances that top management will accept their proposals to spend money?

Overwhelmingly, they voted to solve their difficulties by concentrating on "educating top management." The computer executives preferred making regular presentations to top management and persuading them to attend seminars "...by such firms as IBM." The computer executives also wished to produce more "white papers" which describe the strategic impact of new information technologies.

The extent to which Lederer's and Mendelow's findings are representative of current thinking by top computer executives is debatable. However, I find that the "public relations" school of thought for counteracting the sinking credibility of computer departments has widespread acceptance from computer executives. Unfortunately, operating management finds this approach insufficient and unacceptable.

The transfer of control from experts to operating managers is taking place not because operating managers have suddenly become enamored with information technology. Line managers, with tough cost reduction targets, have concluded that computers are an equally essential resource for delivering expected operating results as any other resource which they can control. For tactical reasons, line management requires considerable flexibility in trading off resources as the need arises. Line executives cannot tolerate the special rules and procedures with which the computer departments have surrounded the information technology which remains in their custody.

Computer executives, who presume to become management educators and strategic thinkers, are pursuing a perilous strategy. Executive management does not gladly tolerate lectures from managers who have not made demonstrable contributions to company profits.

RESEARCH

M.I.T. Sloan School

The most devastating critique of information technology investments comes from Gary Loveman,[28] associated with the M.I.T Sloan School Research Program on Management in the 1990's. Among the results of this five-year multi-million dollar investigation, which concentrated on the effects of computers on organizations, Loveman found that "...expenditures on information technology capital were less effective in improving productivity than any other type of expenditure considered."[29]

The *MPIT* database, provided by the Strategic Planning Institute, is the source of Loveman's findings. He focused attention on the effectiveness of capital investments.[30] Loveman concluded that "...for profit-maximizing firms, the marginal dollar would have been best spent on non-information technology inputs into production."

Although this agrees with my own findings as applied to average and below average achievers, Loveman is too severe in his condemnation of all computer investments.[31] Using the identical data from the *MPIT* research database, I showed in Chapter 7 that Loveman's general rule does not apply in every case, especially for over-achievers.

New York University

Peter Weill's 1988 doctoral dissertation at New York University's School of Business[32] is an extraordinary contribution because it develops and tests a model for finding if information technology improves business performance.[33] Weill collected six years of a wide spectrum of data (1982–1987) from 33 valve manufacturing firms. Separate information came from the Chief Executive Officers, the controllers and the production managers.

The study divided information technology spending into three categories: *Strategic* (systems for gaining a competitive advantage), *Informational* (management information systems and reports) and *Transactional* (systems that reduce the administrative workload through mechanization).

To deal with the qualitative aspects of information technology, Weill proposed a new measure of effectiveness, a *Conversion Effectiveness*. This composite index results from combining the following survey results:
- The extent of top management's commitment to information technology.
- The firm's prior experience in managing information technology.
- The user's satisfaction with systems work in the firm.
- The turbulence of the political environment within the organization.

The following summarizes Weill's research findings:
- There is no correlation between *total* information technology spending and any other measure of performance. This is consistent with everything else you read in this book.
- There is a good correlation between the amount of spending on *transactional* systems, the *Return-on-Assets* and the productivity of non-production labor. Money spent on these systems had the specific objective of cutting operating costs. Again, this is consistent with my findings that spending money on laborsaving systems pays off.

- High levels of spending on *strategic* applications (averaging about 25% of total information technology expenditures) have a strong correlation with *low* organizational performance. Was this only a transient effect? Weill tested three- and six-year moving averages in search of more encouraging results. None showed up.
- Spending money on *information* systems (averaging about half of total information technology expenditures) makes no difference in any measure of organization performance.[34]
- Firms that already enjoyed superior labor efficiency in prior years continued to increase their expenditures on information technology. Firms with inferior efficiency show no relationship between past and present expense levels.
- *Conversion efficiency,* the scale Weill created to measure intangible managerial influences, is high in firms showing high productivity levels. Interestingly enough, firms with a high index of *conversion efficiency* were able to get some benefit out of *strategic* applications.

Weill's work is a noteworthy contribution to the small body of research based on the analysis of actual business results. Most of his findings go counter to the popular lore based on hope, adventure and salesmanship. Nevertheless, this academic work establishes a precedent for every researcher who wishes to study the elusive business value of computers.

Claremont Business School

Harris and Katz made a thorough examination of the relationship between information technology and other measures of organizational performance.[35]

Using 1984–1986 life insurance data, they showed that different measures of efficiency each suggested that there are significant economies of scale associated with the size of organizations.[36] The large firms also enjoyed relatively lower *Total Operating Expenses.*[37]

The implications of these conclusions could be far-reaching. Your primary objective then would be to consolidate operations, since gross averages suggest that you get substantial unit cost reductions as the size of your operations increases. Harris and Katz support this view when they say that, "...concentrating on attaining greater economies of scale may be more beneficial and less risky than attempting to implement major new product innovations."

Harris and Katz elaborate this point when they state that they view the *Operating Expense Efficiency* (e.g., the ratio of *Total Operating Expense* to *Premium Income*) as a proxy measure of profitability. The prescription is simple: to expand profits, increase the premiums processed through your information technology![38] This research continues beyond advocating larger business scale. Harris and Katz also grouped the life insurance companies by *Operating Expense Efficiency*. What do we get?

The 16 firms with the highest efficiency (e.g., the lowest average *Operating Expense Efficiency* ratio) also have the highest ratios of *Information Technology Expense* "efficiency" of 17%. Firms with lower *Operating Expense Efficiency*, averaging 14%, 20% and 28% spend less on information technology.[39]

The implication of these findings is noteworthy: here is the only known documented claim of a positive correlation between computer expense and profitability for firms in the same industry. Such proof has until now escaped all other researchers. Of course, this claim is credible only if one can show that *Operating Expense Efficiency* is a good proxy for profitability. If you manage information technology for a life insurance firm you could go before your management and claim that more money for computers is likely to improve profits.

Since everything rests on the question of what is a good indicator of profitability, we will examine this idea by referring to a source that tabulates actual life insurance financial results.[40] Unfortunately, running a correlation between *Net Gain from Operations* and *Premium and Annuity Income* does not produce a positive relationship, but a random one:

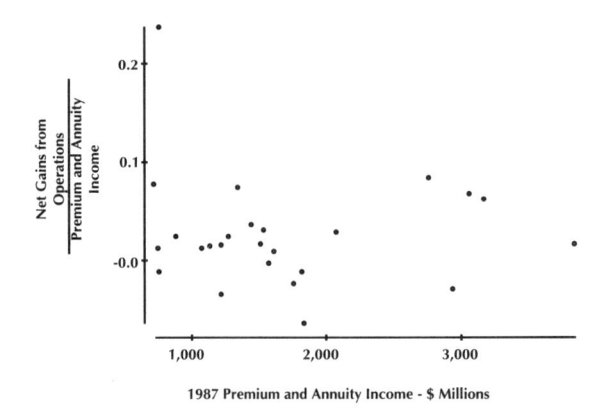

Figure 16.3: No Economies of Scale Among Insurance Companies

Therefore, *Operating Expense Efficiency* may not be a good proxy for profitability. The carefully constructed argument that there are economies of scale relating information technology to profitability must wait for further proof.

Cambridge University

Chef Sing Yap studied 638 U.K. service sector companies to find out what are each firm's characteristics in using computers.[41] This included users and non-users of computers. For each firm he collected data about revenues, average *Return-on-Capital*, growth of the business, classification of work complexity, percentage of information workers, formality of internal communications, degree of central decision making, a measure of competitiveness and a measure of customer predictability. With this data, he tested a number of hypotheses regarding whether or not organizations are more likely to use computers if they:

- Were bigger in size, as defined by revenue and employment;
- Were engaged in information-intensive activities;
- Enjoy higher profitability than average;
- Experienced higher growth rates;
- Had more routine work activities;
- Employed a higher percentage of information workers;
- Engaged in more formalized internal communications;
- Were more centralized in decision-making;
- Operated in a more competitive environment;
- Conducted business in an environment where customer requirements were more unpredictable.

The research explored the above hypotheses by correlating each characteristic with the use of computers.[42] The findings revealed the following:

- Computer users and computer non-users did not experience different levels of profitability, as measured by *Return-on-Capital*;
- More profitable organizations did not have a relatively large diversity of computers applications;
- Organizations with a high proportion of information workers relied on computers more often;
- More formalized organizations were more likely to use computers;

- More centralized organizations were not more likely to use computers.

Yap's work is useful, because it explores a range of variables to test commonly accepted hypotheses about the characteristics of computer users. It shows a rare combination of qualitative and financial data.

Research Surveys

What you believe influences what you see.

Surveys are currently the most favored research methodology in exploring the effects of information technologies. This is especially true in research oriented graduate schools of business, where they provide an affordable opportunity for students to complete their dissertations in a limited time. Surveys also generate papers which have acceptable levels of scholarship needed for publication in academic journals.

University of Pittsburgh

A survey performed at the University of Pittsburgh began with an expression of concern that gains from "strategic systems" applications are largely anecdotal and prescriptive, rather than diagnostic.[43] The researchers proceeded to interview 84 members of the Society for Information Management[44] whose job titles indicated that they held an executive position in managing the information systems function. The purpose of the survey was to determine the extent to which information technology applies in the pursuit of strategic objectives. 95% of those surveyed indicated that their firms were using information technology to achieve strategic benefits.

If you give questionnaires to chefs in highly advertised restaurants to find out if they offer a superior cuisine, they are likely to check off the box with "yes" in it. Such conclusions are not necessarily of value to someone looking for a good meal.

Index Group

The Index Group – a leading consulting firm that concentrates on information management issues – studied 30 strategic systems implementation efforts and found that only five (17%) achieved intended business objectives.[45] The five successful systems produced tangible, measurable business results.

For the other 25 companies, the promised results remained undelivered and the benefits stayed hidden. The reasons for failure were unique in each situation, such as the case of a system that passed all acceptance tests, but nobody wanted to use it. The Index researchers concluded that the reasons for failure were not in poor systems conception, but in poor implementation. In each case the causes were organizational, not technological.

The Index survey is useful, especially from an executive standpoint, because this organization has good high-level contacts for exploring facts that otherwise would remain hidden. The Index approach of examining specific projects rather than collecting opinions from a biased sample of respondents, is a noteworthy contribution to appropriate methods for finding out what is the reality of systems implementations.[46]

The "Hawthorne Effect" and Computers

A study of physicians using computers to improve their diagnosis of abdominal emergencies showed that physicians did increase their skills.[47] The proportion of perforated appendices fell from thirty-six to four percent during a test monitored with great care. However, after the completion of the study, the proportion of perforated appendices among patients rose to twenty percent. Telling the doctors that their skills were subject to research led to the observed improvements.

I suspect that many of the reported "productivity gains" from research studies may result from improved assistance to office workers or from changing office procedures based on the employees' suggestions.

When my staff interviewed clerks while preparing systems proposals, they often heard that "...this is the first time anybody has asked me how to improve my work." When productivity increases subsequent to installing a new computer application, you can never be sure whether the gain comes from the computer or from the change in work methods. When measuring the payoff from computer investments, you should take care to filter out the "Hawthorne Effect."[48] You may have to ask people to work in the new way, but without computers.

The study of the physicians with the abdominal diagnosis program is the only documented case I could find that is a statistically valid study of a computer application. The statistically more rigorous medical discipline knows what it takes to conduct an unbiased experiment by testing explicitly for bias.

CHAPTER SUMMARY

Advocates of computerization never discuss precautions to identify or prevent bias in studies of information technology. I suspect this is the reason for the generally low executive opinions about promised gains. The irony is that even when the promoters of computers deliver superior results, top executives remain skeptical. The students of computer effectiveness must improve the reliability of their research to include study designs commonly applied in medical studies.

Chapter 16 Comments

[1] Productivity Impact of Automated Office, *A Price Waterhouse Report*, 1984.
[2] A.T. Kearney, The Barriers and the Opportunities of Information Technology, *The Institute of Administrative Management*, London, 1984.
[3] P. Weill and M.H. Olson, Managing Investment in Information Technology, *MIS Quarterly*, March 1989, p. 16.
[4] A.L. Lederer and A.L. Mendelow, Convincing Top Management of the Strategic Potential of Information Systems, *MIS Quarterly*, December 1988, p. 530.
[5] A. Mayfield, Half-Truths and Statistics, *Datamation*, August 15, 1986, p. 86.
[6] Critical Issues of Information Systems Management for 1989, *Index Group*, December 1988, p. 27–28. Note that the same respondents also believed that the information systems organizations will play a significant role in reshaping operational and management processes through the use of information technology. They also believed in the integration of business and information systems planning.
[7] Steiner and Teixeira, Technology is More than Just a Strategy, *The McKinsey Quarterly*, Winter, 1988.
[8] B. Belitsos, Can We Measure What We Do? *Computer Decisions*, August 1988, p. 60
[9] F. T. Curtin, Factory 2000, *Iron Age*, June 4, 1984.
[10] William Garrett, information chief of AT&T, quoted in *InformationWeek*, September 19, 1988, p. 38. In 1988, Garrett had a staff of 13,000 and ran 120 IBM 3090-class mainframes supporting 120,000 terminals.
[11] United States General Accounting Office, Report to Chairman, Committee on Government Operations, *House of Representatives*, August 1986
[12] Oxford Institute of Information Management, quoted in *Business Computing & Communications*, March 1988, p. 22.
[13] A.P. Schwartz, When You are Asked to Cost-Justify Systems, *Computerworld*, August 3, 1987, p. 47.
[14] R.E. Bennett, J.A. Hendricks, D.E. Keys, E.J. Rudnicki, Cost Accounting for Factory Automation, *National Association of Accountants*, Montvale, N.J., 1987.
[15] United Research Corporation. Survey of 92 CIO's and their CEO's, as reported in August 22, 1988 issue of *Computerworld*.
[16] Quoted from J.J. Connell, *Return-on-Investment* in Information Technology, *Information Center*, October 1986.
[17] C. Wilder, Re-Engineering is IS Priority, *Computerworld*, February 5, 1990, p.6. The Index Group survey came from 243 U.S. and Canadian IS executives. The influential and widely respected large Index Group frequently publishes results of opinion surveys.
[18] In statistical terms, there is no correlation among the 1990 and 1989 rankings.
[19] D. De Long, Computers in the Corner Office, *The New York Times*, August 21, 1988, p. F4. The most interesting finding is that 34% of the executives made "some personal use" of computers.
[20] B. Hochstrasser and C. Griffiths, Regaining Control of IT Investments – A Handbook for Senior UK Management, Kobler Unit, Imperial College, London, 1990.

[21] D.A. Ludlum, What do Executives Really Want from MIS? *Computerworld*, August 22, 1988, p.59.
[22] Touche Ross International, The Impact of Technology on Banking, published by Touche Ross International, 1985.
[23] The negative opinions of top banking executives are not consistent with their spending habits. Finance and Insurance show a growth rate of spending for information technology 2–3 times greater than the average for other sectors of the economy (Economic Perspectives, *Morgan Stanley Economic Research*, December 15, 1989).

U.S. Sector	1980	1988	Growth/yr
Manufacturing	$12.4	$12.9	0.5%
Communications	$19.3	$30.1	6.6%
Utilities	$1.7	$4.9	16.2%
Trade	$4.2	$13.1	17.7%
Finance	$3.8	$16.9	23.7%
Insurance	$1.2	$6.6	28.3%
Real Estate	$5.7	$11.3	10.3%
Business Services	$4.6	$13.8	17.1%
Personal Services	$1.4	$3.2	12.7%
Other	$1.0	$1.3	3.4%
Total Spending ($ Billions)	$55.2	$114.1	10.9%

View the growth rates shown in the above table with caution, because they average high and low growth intervals. From 1974 to 1984, the outlays for information technology grew at an annual rate of 15%. Since 1984, the current dollar spending went up only 6% per annum (Has High-Tech America Passed its High-Water Mark? *Business Week*, February 5, 1990, p.18). In 1987, the firm of Nolan, Norton and Company predicted that the average growth rate for computers would be over 20% until the end of the century. (D. Ludlum, The Information Budget, *Computerworld*, January 5, 1987.) My opinion is that it is unlikely that the average growth rate will exceed 8–10% per annum.

[24] The Executive Report on MIS in Banking, *Computerworld*, August 15, 1988.
[25] The Economist, June 11, 1988, p.75.
[26] R.E. Bennett, J.A. Hendricks, D.E. Keys, E.J. Rudnicki, Cost Accounting for Factory Automation, *National Association of Accountants*, Montvale, N.J., 1987. The responses in the accountants' survey came from 260 "preparers" of justification proposals and 64 "users." The indifference of the "preparers" suggests that innovations will have to originate with the "users." This survey is commendable for concerns expressed about the information gathering procedures and the characteristics of the respondents.

The large accounting staffs—invariably exceeding systems staffs— should not be allowed to distance themselves from investment analysis.

[27] A.L. Lederer and A.L. Mendelow, Convincing Top Management of the Strategic Potential of Information Systems, *MIS Quarterly*, December 1988, p. 525.
[28] G.W. Loveman, An Assessment of the Productivity Impact of Information Technologies, *Sloan School of Management, Management in the 1990's Working Paper*, July 1988.
[29] R.A. Samuel and M.S. Scott-Morton, Information Technology and Major Organizational Change. Results from the Management in the 1990's Program, *M.I.T. Management*, Spring, 1989, p.3
[30] Making the *MPIT* (Management Productivity and Information Technology) database available to qualified researchers is in the charter of the Institute. Prof. Charles Kriebel and his associates from the Carnegie-Mellon Graduate School of Industrial Administration have also received copies of the database I am describing in this book. Because my *MPIT* findings may be controversial, I encourage other researchers to validate this data source.
[31] The observations that information technology investments, on the average, are not productive is not a helpful argument. I have shown in Chapter 7 that conclusions about the effectiveness of computers, when based on conventional average measures, have little value. The averages included a few awful losers and some outstanding winners. This just proves the yarn about the professor of economics

(or statistics) who was run over in a parking lot where the cars were mostly standing still.

32 P.D. Weill, The Relationship Between Investment in Information Technology and Firm Performance in the Manufacturing Sector, Doctoral Thesis, School of Business, *New York University*, 1988.

33 Weill used three different measures to evaluate business performance: Revenue growth, *Return-on-Assets* and Labor Efficiency (non-production workers required per million dollars of revenue). As noted earlier in this book, there are many defects in applying each of these measures. One can only assume that the 33 valve manufacturing firms were reasonably comparable. Unless you check that proposition, you can never be sure that you have good ratios for using Weill's approach.

34 This largest element in information technology spending is investment in the "infrastructure" of the firm, rather than increasing sales or cutting costs. Weill acknowledges that ROI or ROA is not appropriate for evaluating the contribution of these investments.

35 A partial version of the same research is in S.E. Harris, J.L. Katz, Differentiating Organizational Performance Using Information Technology Managerial Control Ratios in the Insurance Industry, *Office Technology and People*, Elsevier Publishers 5:4 (1989).

36 The 16 firms with average premium incomes of $7,800 million required only 13% of *Total Operating Expenses* devoted to information technology. Firms averaging $1,500 million, $542 million and $144 million premium incomes required respectively 17%, 15% and 18% for information technology.

37 For instance, the 16 firms required only 16% of Premium Income devoted to *Total Operating Expenses*. Firms averaging $1,500 million, $542 million and $144 million premium incomes required respectively 13%, 20% and 23% for *Total Operating Expenses*.

38 Not since the days of Grosch's Law (Herb Grosch from IBM stated that processing efficiency of computers grows as a square of the equipment costs) has anyone produced a study favoring large scale operations. Harris and Katz surpass Grosch who did not claim that there was a relation between the scale of information technology and business profitability.

39 Their respective *Information Technology Expense* efficiencies are 17%, 15% and 14%.

40 Every year Fortune magazine publishes The Fortune Service 500 rankings which defines *Net Gain from Operations* as the direct measure of profits.

41 C.S. Yap, Distinguishing Characteristics of Organizations Using Computers, *Information & Management*, 18, 1990.

42 A firm was either a computer user or not. This approach to measuring computer use is the major weakness of the Yap study. We cannot find out the relative importance of information technology as the intensity of use varies.

43 W.R. King, V. Grover and E.H. Hufnagel, Using Information and Information Technology for Sustainable Competitive Advantage, *Information & Management*, 17, 1989. The results confirm the deep-seated beliefs of the purveyors of information systems that their activities are "strategically" important. To test the validity of such a presumption conduct in-depth interviews with their respective Presidents and chief financial officers.

44 The leading U.S. organization for professional managers of information systems.

45 Index Group, Implementing Strategic Information Systems, *Indications*, August 1987.

46 Busy executives receive an endless series of questionnaires. These get passed to the lowest level in the organization that cannot find anyone else to do the job. The replies you see as "executive" opinions most likely are not. You should also wonder about the accuracy of the responses. The bias will be always to make the company look good. Whenever the researcher collects and validates data independently, you are likely to get more reliable answers.

47 F.T. DeDombal, D.J. Horrocks, et al., Human and Computer-Aided Diagnosis of Abdominal Pain, *British Medical Journal*, 1:376–80, 1984.

48 The "Hawthorne Effect" comes from research by W.J. Dickson and F.J. Roethlisberger, Management and the Workers, *Harvard University Press*, 1939. When researchers observed workers, productivity increased because someone was paying attention to the people, not because of changes in physical working conditions.

17

A GUIDE TO ADVICE

SYSTEMS ASSESSMENT INDICATORS

IBM spent about $3.6 billion in 1987 on internal information processing, which was 8% of its operating expenses. With such high levels of spending, IBM has worked since 1983 to come up with measures of effectiveness that would satisfy corporate management about the value of these expenditures. By 1988, managers at 90 processing sites were filling out a 24-page report to Corporate Information Systems to explain how well they were doing.[1]

Adopting IBM's appraisal method could offer a solution to your problems in communicating with top management. It is unlikely that you could readily duplicate the five years of staff effort that IBM devoted to a solution. Besides, IBM's guidelines are available, which makes this option attractive.

The IBM measurement framework consists of the following topics: contribution to the business, resources alignment and business alignment.

Contribution to the Business

Sound principles are essential for success, provided you also know how to put them into effect.

In the IBM protocol related to contribution to business, each operating unit reports on the value of its information technologies using only two numbers[2]:

- Controller-approved *Planned Gross Benefits from Business Cases.*
- Controller-approved *Information Processing Costs from Business Cases.*

This approach has several advantages. It asks an independent party who has responsibility for maintaining the financial integrity of plans and budgets—the controller—to attest both to savings and costs. Controller concurrence is essential to any evaluation scheme that links computer projects with business plans. This presumes that financial concurrence takes place only if the costs and benefits are already in a unit's profit plan.[3]

From an executive's standpoint, the proposed method is simple and understandable although it does not allow for costs or benefits beyond five years. This makes it possible for each business case to fit all information technology plans within the framework of a business planning cycle.

Unfortunately, the IBM guidelines are silent about the tough issue of how the controller keeps track of benefits for projects that are part of a plan that extends beyond a five year horizon. IBM revises profit plans frequently to reflect changing business conditions. The mechanics of how the controllers sort out information processing benefits and costs from the other cost streams are the key to evaluating the business value of computers. However, this problem is not unique to the evaluation of computers. If your firm's budgeting and planning system does not keep track of all changing commitments, you should not expect that it will be able to do that for information technology.

Resources

There is corn for eating and there is corn for sowing next year's crop. You had better treat them differently.

In the resources area of the evaluation protocol, IBM does not waste much effort on exhaustive cost breakdowns. They introduce a

useful perspective in viewing the information processing budget as made up of two kinds of expenditures:
- Those which introduce business changes, such as new functions, new capabilities, altered business processes and experimentation, and
- Those which provide ongoing support for existing business processes.

Executives should find much value in analyzing the information processing budget in these terms. In the case of ongoing support, the goal should be to extract productivity gains from today's operation, today. In the case of business changes, investments should generate a steady stream of innovation, which is critical to future productivity gains.

If ongoing support can demonstrate steadily declining unit costs, executives will have more confidence when investing in new applications that will pay off only in the future. The proportion of money allocated to present and future productivity missions is a pivotal matter. It is therefore essential that there is a consistent scorecard that keeps track of this distribution.

Business Alignment

No assessment of information technologies is complete without understanding how their applications link to a unit's business strategies. IBM requires its general managers to verify one of the following planning methods:
- Level 0: There is no formal information technology strategy.
- Level 1: There is a formal information technology strategy but it largely serves the internal needs of information processing operations. Business management, with profit responsibility for a unit's results, has not approved the strategy.
- Level 2: There is a formal information technology strategy and business management has approved it. However, the plan covers only internal information processing matters. There is no explicit linkage to the business except as added operating expenses.
- Level 3: There is a formal and approved information technology strategy which has explicit links to business needs. The stated strategies only react to stated business

needs and originate primarily from computer management. This separate plan covers only the information services function.
- Level 4: There is a formal and approved information technology strategy which came into being through joint participation of line and staff management. The information processing strategy is indistinguishable from other business strategies. Every document of integrated business programs ought to include information technology as one of the required resources. The contribution of information technology is explicit only insofar as it is a critical element in accomplishing specific and measurable business objectives. The review of information technology takes place at each management level where approval of business programs is necessary.

I applaud the approach where a general manager's rating of his information processing department reflects the above progression. It forces recognition of what will foster improved relations between business people and information technologists. It requires acknowledgment of undesirable budgeting practices. It raises questions about the adequacy of management skills to achieve Level 4 practices.

I do not know of a single organization, especially in the public sector, that would not gain immeasurably from such candid self-assessment.[4]

SAMPLING OF CUSTOMER OPINIONS

Good intentions do not necessarily make a good proof.

Probably the most widely advertised report ever published about the benefits of computers is the "Macintosh Benefits Study," produced by KPMG Peat Marwick in 1987.[5] Multicolor inserts in business magazines summarized the study and listed a free telephone number for ordering a copy. The executive summary said that Peat Marwick's "80-20 OA" measurement methodology was the basis for the report.

What is the "80-20" method? It is an application of Pareto's principle, which states that a disproportionately small number of events will usually have disproportionately large effects. To illustrate, Peat Marwick notes that 20% of customers generates 80% of revenues, 20% of products account for 80% of sales and 20% of daily work efforts provide 80%

of the value of a job. For the study of Macintosh computers, the "80-20" method applied selective sampling of selected opinions of a selected group, to find out how they thought the Macintosh improves their work.

How did this work in practice? The "80-20 OA" work-plan diagram outlined the procedure:
- The study began by identifying "Key Success Stories" and "Key People" for interviews. Clearly, this was not an unbiased sample. Its purpose was to limit the study only to cases where the Macintosh looked good.
- Interviews then took place with selected users. Work-flow diagrams show how work patterns have changed.
- Data gathering then began. Three to four workers, specially chosen, participated in structured interviews. The consultants selected employees identified as "best of their type." They quantified their views of Macintosh benefits. The estimates were a result of discussions with other best users. They filled out data-gathering forms that listed all critical items. The group then agreed and recorded their consensus estimates of Macintosh gains.[6]
- The data from the forms provided the basis for the expected performance improvements.

In the Benefits Study, there was only one detailed case study which illustrated the application of the "80-20" method. Forty-two Macintosh customers applied it to estimate average possible savings of 56 hours per person, per month. They said they would be able to deliver the identical work at the same quality level as before. The projections ranged from 28% possible savings for managers to 50% possible savings for professionals.

At this point, the Benefits Study introduced a table showing a comparison between "Possible" and "Actual" gains. The "Actual" numbers did not describe operating results validated by work measurement, job cost tickets or accounting records. The "Actual" gains were an estimate of "Preferred Actual Time, Same or Better Activities, Higher Quality."

The critical test of the applicability of the "80-20" method comes when you try to convert the estimated benefits of the Macintosh technology into cash. The Benefits Study did not tell whether an independent party verified the actual results, or if quality improved after removing the 56 hours per person. It also did not show if the existing staff absorbed the additional workload of 56 hours per person.

If you wish to prove the benefits of a computer investment, you should expect your methodology to provide:
- Verifiable actual costs prior to and after the change in work methods. Cost data prepared by auditors or an independent financial organization are always preferable. Never accept after-the-fact "estimated actuals" from the same people who have an interest in showing how well they are doing.
- Diligent precautions to obtain a random sample, especially if you are collecting data from only some of the companies or employees involved. You will discredit your conclusions by picking mostly enthusiasts to make your case, regardless of the merit of what you could show. If you have good proof anyway,[7] there is no need to spoil it with bias.

BENEFITS ESTIMATING SOFTWARE

Some vendors supplement their promotional materials with software that helps a prospective customer to justify a purchase. If used with caution, such software can be very helpful to the customer.

For example, *Action Technologies, Inc.*[8] offers a customized Lotus spreadsheet. You fill in tables with well-defined cost categories, such as training, coaching, current mailing costs and costs of meetings. The spreadsheet already contains most of the unit costs for installing and operating an *Action Technologies* network. With little effort a customer can get a quick indication of the benefits from an application that would otherwise seem to offer only "intangible" gains.

The *Action Technologies* benefit estimator software is useful as the basis for organizing network application proposals. It addresses only directly measurable and displaceable costs. It accurately reflects the fact that not all network users have the same habits or skill levels. It deals with questions that are missing from most proposals, such as training and startup expenses. It demonstrates how a vendor's considerable know-how and experience can help a prospective customer in ways that benefit everyone.

Overall, however, you should be cautious of benefit-estimating software used primarily for promotional purposes. An example is General Electric's Calma *Board Series Payback Analysis*.[9] The vendor provides "productivity factor" multipliers. The customer then inserts the number of workstations, the number of work shifts and percentage of the employees' time spent on activities such as schematic drawings, layout, bill of materials and assembly drawings. The "productivity factor" multipliers calculate an "equivalent annual labor cost."[10] The software's computed *Return-on-Investment* is the ratio of benefits (derived equivalent labor costs minus hypothetical labor costs) divided by the purchase price of the system (not including training, conversion and startup costs). You get an attractive number, but certainly not a valid estimate you can take to the bank.

"Blockbuster" Projects

Many consultants recognize that the traditional project-justification approach does not predict sufficient profitability. They find that project by project, machine by machine, "microscopic paralysis by analysis" usually limits investments to opportunities that barely exceed the cost of capital.

Justifying a single project is short-sighted because it ignores the business environment, according to this view. A too narrow focus would rule out "blockbuster" advances with a potential of 10 times the costs (e.g., 1,000% returns).[11] This reasoning usually leads to a recommendation to top executives to demand extraordinary investment returns from information technology.

How do you achieve such ambitious goals? This requires exploring new business opportunities, such as entry into new businesses. It also calls for servicing other businesses and customers, expanding the range of services to existing customers, and connecting customers or suppliers by communication networks to expand the global scope of the business. Most importantly, it makes it necessary to change the rules of competition.

The inspirational value of such pronouncements is attractive because everybody likes to hear an optimistic view of the future. When competitive pressures shrink prevailing profit margins to less than 20% (for good companies, with long-term earning records), potential 1,000% gains will get immediate attention.

There may indeed be opportunities for 1,000% gains. So far, nobody has produced hard evidence that anybody has actually pocketed 1,000% cash returns from computer investments. Such huge profits fall to individuals who buy and sell entire businesses, and who make their gambling decisions using non-computerized means.

Realistic targets for investment returns come from examining companies that are superior users[12] of "strategic information systems":

Company	Investment Returns	Percentile Rank
Dun & Bradstreet	25.6%	21%
Banc One Corporation	22.4%	28%
McKesson Corporation	22.3%	27%
American Airlines	15.6%	36%
Merrill Lynch & Co.	15.2%	60%
Citicorp	10.9%	79%
Federal Express	10.7%	46%
United Airlines	8.6%	54%

Table 17.1: Investment Returns for Superior Users of Computers

The above results for the most celebrated "leading-edge" companies are not impressive. Five out of eight organizations show ten-year investment returns that are below industry group medians. I would define this as "substandard performance," not as "leading edge." Only one company – Dun & Bradstreet – is in the top quartile rank of its group. No firm considered a "superior user" is in the top ten percent of its group. You may wonder what the leaders in the top 10% of financial performance use as information systems.

The magnitudes of the actual investment returns are noteworthy. The median total return to investors for all service industries, for the 1976–1986 period, was 18.6%. For all industrial companies, the median total return was 15.6%. With such averages, you cannot expect your top management to demand 1,000% profit returns as an objective. If you can demonstrate risk-adjusted investment returns over 35%, you will be welcome as a worthy contributor by most Boards of Directors.

FAITH AND VISIONS

Faith is what you substitute for evidence. Visions are a substitute for what you cannot see.

Belief, rather then evidence, is a very strong ingredient in making decisions about investing in computers. Theodore Freiser, president of John Diebold & Associates said once: "You have to be willing to make the investment without having a correspondingly measurable return. There is no measure we can construct that can isolate the contribution of information and not be also attributable to some other factors. It is subjective."[13]

This view is widespread.[14] An example is the pronouncement of a Chrysler executive: "Computers are absolutely not cost-justifiable. You are talking about an initial purchase of 600 to 700 machines and they are very expensive. Chrysler had a vision of the way we wanted to change the culture of our field force. We did it because we were trying to change the way we were doing business."[15]

Eric K. Clemons, Director of the Wharton School Project on Strategic Information Technology, is also distrustful of analysis. "The most interesting information systems projects suffer from the double whammy of uncertainty and intangibles, and if you insist on the numbers you end up with analysis paralysis." Clemons cites Bell Canada that spent "...tens of millions of dollars on increasing the flexibility of its systems, all without an explicit cost and benefit analysis."[16]

Cost justification is an obstacle to "visions." Thomas Pettibone, Senior V.P. of Information Systems for the New York Life Insurance Company said "...one can spend much time trying to figure out dollar-for-dollar values and ending up missing opportunities. Time I spend cost-justifying things is time I am not spending thinking up new ways to help the business."[17]

It is always hard to argue against faith and visions, because it is bad to favor disbelief and shortsightedness. Faith and vision are essential to investment decisions, because nobody can predict the future. Even the most sophisticated juggling of numbers can mislead. Therefore, analysis and credibility are not at opposite ends of imagination and inspiration, but complementary virtues. Extremes are perilous.

Advocates of faith and visions rarely offer any evidence, and hardly any accountability. I find such individuals suspect, especially when they counsel spending somebody else's money. You cannot buy computers with "vision". Only cash will do.

LOSS AVOIDANCE ANECDOTES

An anecdote is not a proof.

A Good Story Does Not Necessarily Equal Profits

A prominent consulting firm always cites the case of an Electric Utility to illustrate the linking of business strategy, performance and information technology.[18] The Electric Utility is a medium sized midwestern power utility with revenues of $200 million. Its rates come from the State Public Utility Commission. Because of political influence on utility rates, good customer relations are critical to profitability.

The power company decided to improve the speed of complaint-handling, telephone answering and tracking of customer service. It increased its information technology expenditures from $3,000 per year per employee in 1979 to $14,000 per year per employee[19] in 1984, for a total of $7.5 million per annum cost increases. That is a hefty gain of 36%, compounded per year.

At the end of this period, the power company received a $20 million rate increase. The chief executive attributed the revenue gains to computerized customer administration, because of improved customer care. The M.I.S. budget in the five-year period grew enormously. Is it then correct to conclude that there was a good payoff from the increased expenditures for information technology, based on the claim that computers made it possible to obtain a rate increase?

The consulting firm claimed that the increased expenditures were profitable, because information technology focused on the "key leverage points" of business strategy. The consulting firm also used this case to illustrate how the traditional project-by-project approach would never uncover such dramatic opportunities for revenue gains.

Although I favor improving the care of customers, I do not think that it follows that the money spent on computers was wholly responsible for the good returns. From a financial standpoint, the consulting firm must first show what portion of the $20 million rate increase was due to better service. Public Utility Commissions base their grants of rate increases primarily on the basis of increased fuel and labor costs. Only after allowing for added operating costs, including the $7.5 million per year incremental computer costs, can you count your net gains.

Magazine articles are full of good stories of computer applications that increase revenues. These articles are merely attractive advertisements for computer applications unless they are supported by credible benefits.

Phenomenal Valuations

The foremost proponents of phenomenal calculations are N. Dean Meyer and Mary E. Boone, who have compiled 54 cases that show *Return-on-Investment* results ranging from over 50% to over 100,000% per annum:[20]

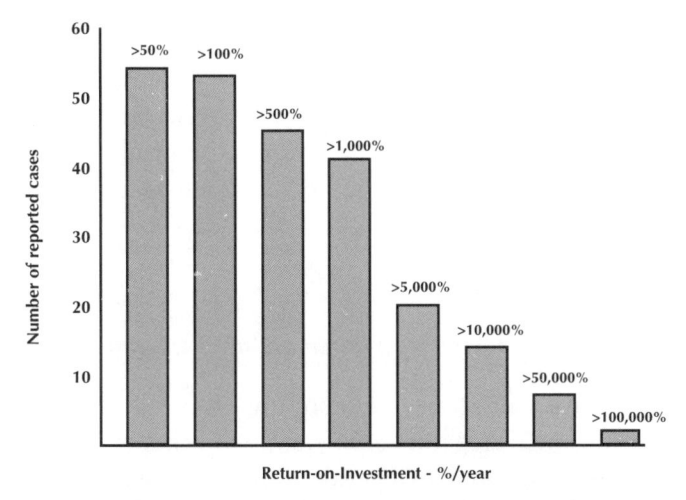

Figure 17.1: Profitability of After-the-fact Anecdotes

How does one get a *Return-on-Investment* of more than 100,000%, in a legitimate business? You use the techniques of over-attribution and retrospective valuation.

OVER-ATTRIBUTION

If you slice an apple into quarters, you still have only one apple.

Over-attribution is a method whereby the sum of all the claims for gaining benefits exceeds the total available benefit. Over-attribution could allow office automation to claim 80% of the profits because of imaginative market research. Shareholders could claim another 50% of profits for their capital investment. Top management would believe that they should get all the credit for leadership. Research & Development will claim at least 62.92% of all gains because of their innovations.

To understand over-attribution reasoning, consider the case of the startup venture in which the entrepreneurs originally spent $5,000 for an on-line search of potential market opportunities.[21] The venture proved to be successful with revenues projected in the $20 to $25 million dollar range eight years after startup. The gain in the value of the firm was $85 million, of which 80% Meyer and Boone attributed to spending $5,000 for on-line search prior to making a critical marketing decision. They came up with a staggering *Return-on-Investment* of 830,000% by dividing the huge gains by a trivial expense. The arithmetic is acceptable, except for assigning business gains to computers. This neglects the value of all the other efforts. The appropriate value of the $5,000 on-line search is not 80% of $85 million, but the least expensive amount needed to obtain the identical information without the benefit of an on-line computer search. The next best alternative would have been a consulting fee.

RETROSPECTIVE VALUATION

You cannot place a bet on a horserace after the race is over.

Retrospective valuation is a technique that looks backward to computer payoffs by disregarding the element of chance. Retrospective valuations have the advantage of perfect knowledge which comes out of perfect hindsight. They offer numerically overstated benefits. You can always hand-pick success stories or loss avoidance situations after they occur and disregard their original prospects of cost overruns and benefit under-achievement. Since the laws of probability no longer apply, you can always show how computers deliver superior profits. Retrospective valuation would allow an aircraft mechanic to value his services (or his screwdriver) as worth a billion dollars after an airplane crash. This could be a plausible retrospective claim if a loose pin caused one of the engines to fall off.[22]

To understand retrospective valuation, consider the case of a $10 million dollar item omitted from a budget proposal. A subsequent check of totals using a spreadsheet program found the error before it was too late. Meyer and Boone estimated that there was a 60% greater chance of catching the error by using a personal computer costing $10,000. By dividing the huge gains for catching the error by a small expense for a personal computer, Meyer and Boone came up with an amazing one-year *Return-on-Investment* of 59,900%.[23]

The arithmetic is faultless except for the implausible use of retrospective valuation which gave a microcomputer the credit for "saving" $6 million. The value of the microcomputer is not 60% of $10 million but the cost advantage over having another accountant check the budget proposal. It actually may be less costly to pay an accountant to go over the numbers than to spend $10,000 on a computer. Even better, employ someone who can assemble a budget proposal without making a $10 million dollar mistake.

The practice of over-attribution and retrospective valuation proliferates in computer vendors' brochures and magazines that get advertising revenues by describing the advantages of information technologies. For example, a widely quoted report[24] claimed that a computer system "...identified the strongest performing accounts and then reallocated a multi-million dollar budget accordingly." As a result, the computer system[25] allegedly increased profits by $2.4 million.

I think that it was not the computer system which increased profits, but the people using it who did. Could the marketing managers have identified the strongest performing accounts by some other means? The data about account performance was there all along but could not be retrieved easily. The advantage of the computer system truly was not $2.4 million, but the difference in cost over obtaining the identical result by other means, which would be a much smaller figure. You can always consider the cost of having junior analysts marking up with a red pencil all the good accounts.

In the fast-moving world of brand management, there are many justifiable opportunities for employing a wide range of computerized systems to assist in marketing decisions. Computers do not increase profits, only management decisions do. We should therefore evaluate the cost of improved *Management* as related to *Management Value-added*, not profit generation by a "data interpretation system."

THE ATTRACTIONS OF PHENOMENAL VALUATIONS

You will find over-attribution and retrospective calculations everywhere although sometimes it takes peeking behind the facade to discover what they really are. Because they are so popular, I should say something in their favor. Conclusions based on this technique are effortless to compose and pleasant to read. Imaginative people create them in cheerful and enthusiastic prose, in contrast with the uninspired analytic narrative of the fact-plodders.[26]

Although phenomenal calculations are logically and technically in error, they are much easier to make than preparing risk-adjusted financial alternatives. Financially astute executives often find that many promising computer investments are only artful science fiction that disguises unwarranted assumptions as prophetic facts.

The Group Estimating Method

You find the most useful information in the extreme values, not in the averages.

A few years ago I reviewed a Federal Government agency proposal for a $400 million computer systems acquisition. To comply with procurement regulations, the agency hired a prominent consulting firm to conduct a Delphi study of the potential savings. The consultants' report was 350 pages long and contained 210 triple fold-out spreadsheets. The agency submitted the report to satisfy Office of Management and Budget (OMB) procedures which require that formal financial analysis must support all benefit estimates.

Here is the consultants' methodology:

1. Divide the agency's work into nine functional categories. Within each functional category identify activities.
2. For each activity, identify factors that will explain the volume of work expected for the next ten years for the new system.
3. Take activity factors and multiply with each activity. This will yield the estimated "savings" for one activity.
4. Add up all of the savings and check if they exceed the estimated acquisition and operating costs of the new system.

The following illustrates how to do such analysis:

Activity Factor	Activity Factor	Basis of Factor
Average time allocated to activity	8%/Day	User Estimate
Estimated average savings per activity	13.8%	User Estimate
Learning/acceptance factor	73.2%	User Estimate
Number of Personnel affected	8070	Agency Plan
Growth in the Number of Personnel	–2%/year	Agency Plan
Average Salary, including Benefits	$62,600	Agency Plan
Salary Growth Multiplier	+6%/year	Agency Plan
Rate of Workload Increase	+15%/year	User Estimate
Function Availability on System	47 to 95%	Technical Estimate

Table 17.2: Method for Computing Activity Savings

The method looks logical but deserves further checking because the credibility of the savings estimate depends entirely on the credibility of the user estimates.

The consultant had seventy agency employees (less than 1% of the staff) come to Washington to participate in six estimating sessions.[27] This involved filling out forms for each activity within each functional category. Each person made 162 numerical estimates. The consultant then took this information and tabulated it in his report as "...empiric data..."[28] Next, the consultant calculated the average values for the 70 x 18 x 9 = 11,340 numbers and sorted them by activity. Taking the average values as multipliers, the consultant showed that the results added up to a seven-year break-even, which was a strong argument for approving a $400 million budget appropriation.[29] Additional arguments about safety, security and national interest assured the funding for this project.

I was suspicious of the procedure. There were no safeguards to protect the estimating process against bias. The employees selected for the benefit-estimating sessions had a commitment to obtain modernization funds for the agency. Nobody who made the estimates would ever be accountable for delivering any of the savings. Nobody could ever be accountable for the estimates, which were anonymous.

I examined the diversity of responses concerning an activity that would deliver the largest savings. Details from the employees' individual rating sheets revealed a disturbing lack of agreement:

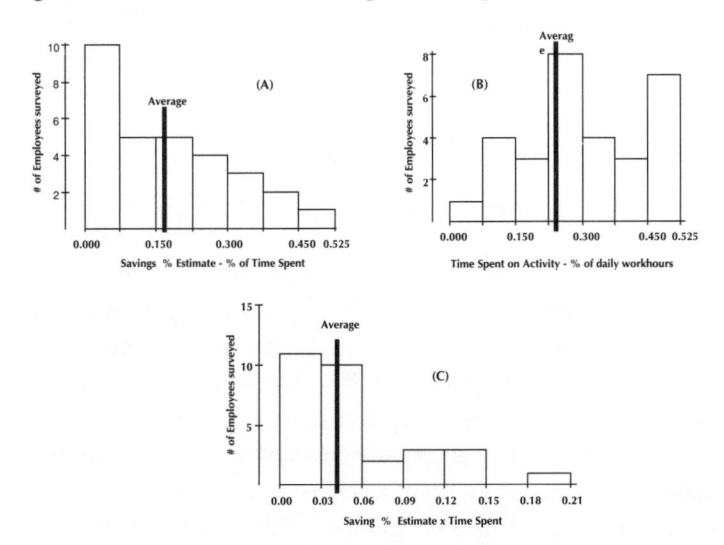

Figure 17.2: Savings Estimates for a Government Project Proposal

The estimates of savings ranged from zero to 52.5%, as shown in (A) in Figure 17.2. The consultant averaged it to 16.8%. Averaging such estimates of savings will likely hide informed opinions. The consultant did not reconcile the reasons for the participants' widely diverging expectations regarding the prospective gains. The consultant used averages in all calculations, which made the results from the spreadsheets appear to be accurate.

The second critical factor in estimating the proposed saving was the "time spent on this activity" factor. We see, in (B) above, estimates ranging from zero to 52.5%. This raises doubts of whether or not the seventy employees fairly represented the scope of the agency's activities. The consultant averaged out the estimates by recording them as 23.4%. Covering up diversity when estimating savings is dangerous, because you cannot tell if the proposed computer application will help people who devote much or little time to any specific activity.[30]

Cross-multiplying two widely-ranging numbers results in a greater range as shown in (C) above. By multiplying only the averages, the consultant's number was 3.93%. When the variability of numbers that make up what appears to be a very precise result covers a wide range, the result is always suspect. The consultant's benefit estimates could be off by $150 million either way, making a mockery of the elaborate financial analysis.

My interest concerned those individuals who spent 50% of their time working on an activity that could save 50% of their work, as compared with those who did not spend any time on it. The rationale for extreme work patterns provided a good insight into the economic potential of the proposed system. I concluded that the projected savings were higher than stated in the proposal.

CRITICAL SUCCESS FACTORS

The *Critical Success Factor* process is the most widely adopted method for deciding how and where to use information technologies. It requires holding extensive private interviews between consultants and business executives. Outspoken staff individuals representing forward looking ideas are always included in such interviews. The firm's acknowledged opinion-makers are always on the list. Each person's view about the company's business mission, objectives, critical management tasks and priorities is recorded and cross-tabulated.

The interview results first are shared with the CEO and then with the top executives to establish overall directions for holding group meetings where divergent opinions are open to debate. An alignment of views and a clearer set of priorities then emerges though group participation, with the consultant usually acting as the moderator and discussion facilitator.

The entire process usually concludes with individual managers publicly assuming responsibility for implementing agreed-upon tasks. This works well in situations where top executives do not wish to commit their own prestige in dealing with the organizational conflict that usually surrounds the information systems function. The external consultant serves as a surrogate executive in doing the painful fact-finding that top management prefers to avoid.

When consultants apply the *Critical Success Factor* method, they usually make a valuable contribution in changing a group's attitude about computers. Invariably, it results in a reorganization in which the present head of information systems gets a promotion or a demotion but is rarely left alone. It is a technique that has more in common with group psychotherapy than with any other discipline. The *Critical Success Factor* process is perhaps the most socially acceptable method that may produce remarkably favorable effects. This is particularly true in cases where the leadership of the computer function becomes unacceptable to the rest of the organization because of management's neglect, a frequent occurrence nowadays. Charismatic practitioners of this technique will deserve high consulting fees even in the absence of sufficient technical knowledge to understand the actual operating problems.

CLASSIFICATION FRAMEWORKS

An explanation is more useful than a description.

There are numerous classification schemes which can place their tersely phrased labels within rectangular 2 x 2, 3 x 3 or even 5 x 5 grids.[31] These matrix *frameworks* can be useful in describing how business circumstances and information technology relate. They are helpful as descriptions. Unfortunately, they end up as prescriptions, which detract from their value.

Descriptive Frameworks

Frameworks arise in lectures, tutorials and presentations as a way to explain complex ideas. As visual aids, they are effective in overcoming the limitations of hard-to-follow logic. They are particularly helpful in group discussions when people from different functions do not understand each other, particularly when a technically-oriented person speaks up. University professors and consultants with strong academic ties find much delight in inventing new word-classification schemata as new ways to look at an old problem. The philological opportunities are unlimited while the effort of drawing up a new schema is negligible, especially if you own good graphics software. They are inexpensive to construct and even easier to forget. An example of such a grid is one that tries to explain "key factors affecting executives' demand for improved information support."[32]

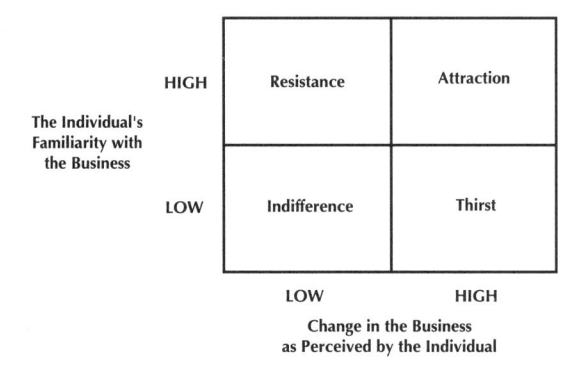

		Change in the Business as Perceived by the Individual	
		LOW	HIGH
The Individual's Familiarity with the Business	HIGH	Resistance	Attraction
	LOW	Indifference	Thirst

Figure 17.3: Example of a Descriptive Framework

How does one explain a new point of view? Just draw up a new grid. Audiences are always grateful for a new "framework." As compared with an uninterrupted stream of words, these simple graphics offer welcome visual relief during a presentation. Follow-up questions from the audience also become more focused.

Frameworks stimulate the imagination. Any group of reasonably bright systems people will rephrase the meaning of a diagram so that it will convey a different personal message. Several frameworks have achieved widespread popularity precisely because of their vagueness. Each interpreter's imagination is sufficiently unconstrained to give wide latitude to the interpretation of such grids. If used for tutorial purposes, the authors, usually academics, will fulfill their educational objective.

Prescriptive Frameworks

Taking an untested prescription may be dangerous to health.

An example of a prescriptive framework is the Index Group's much quoted Beneficiaries/Benefits framework. It displays how three different types of "benefits" (e.g., Efficiency, Effectiveness and Transformation) relate to three different types of "beneficiaries" (e.g., Individual user, Functional unit and Entire organization). This way of looking at systems opportunities makes it possible for the designers of the framework to associate new meanings with old words. For example, the word "transformation," a recent addition to systems jargon, labels the prescriptive recommendations of what you should do in case you have problems in managing computers. If you, as an individual user, are in a "transformational benefits" category, then you should pursue "role expansion." If you are in "transformation benefits" as a functional unit, then you should pursue "functional re-definition."

No research back up is necessary for the presentation of a new prescriptive framework. Frameworks also defy the test of any validation, since they are unscaled and unmeasurable. When does "efficiency" cease and become "effectiveness"? Nobody may know the answer to that, since the words themselves are imprecise. In the real world, both efficiency and effectiveness coexist and overlap over a broad range of experience.

The real hardship in understanding the limit of new classifications occurs when old words are recast into new forms, such as when "effectiveness" evolves to become "transformation." Trouble arises when the means for improving the comprehensibility of a presentation become a template for directing executives toward action. It's like astrology which initially attempted to describe the heavens. Astrology evolved into the horoscope business for giving specific advice when soothsayers got hold of it.

Classification frameworks, over the years, have suffered from an erosion of meaning and an escalation in complexity to compensate for their defects. A whole generation of managers learned the pristine simplicity of the Boston Consulting Group's framework for describing investment opportunities. The intuitive attraction of a 2 x 2 matrix that related competitive strength with market growth became a tool for identifying the financial condition of a firm. The Boston Consulting Group simply inserted easily remembered zoology into the 2 x 2 square and left it at that.

The universal popularity of this approach became apparent when within one generation of MBAs the terms "cash cows" and "dogs" became accepted as linguistic surrogates for more complex concepts.[33] In the same way, astrologers substituted "Pisces" and "Leo" for astronomical phenomena to deal with matters such as compatibility of partners engaged to be married. Unfortunately, competition in the consulting business could not leave it at that. Proprietary matrixes going up to 6 x 6 dimensions have appeared to match the complexity of business conversations, just like today's complex horoscopes which feature the latest jargon from astrophysics. You can always find people who suffer from a deep-seated belief that manipulating symbols can affect the realities that the symbols claim to represent.

An important study of the various conceptual frameworks concluded: "...most of the literature in the area [of strategic information systems] continues to be anecdotal...There is little evidence of an accepted or validated theoretical framework, although a myriad of conceptual and analytical frameworks have been suggested to be useful ...there is even less empirical evidence concerning the validity and utility of these notions."[34]

Frameworks attach labels to complex ideas. Labels may classify into neat categories what you already know. Clever descriptions may be helpful but are not necessarily good explanations of why something happens. None of the frameworks, which is the most frequently mentioned methodology, reveals why information technology has the perverse characteristic of having not correlating with profitability.

I find that the increasing size and proliferation of various "frameworks" stimulate thinking. It ultimately leads frustrated executives to the awareness that real systems problems do not have solutions in the form of simple tables containing terse phrases.

Grid Positioning and Ranking

Beware of guides who muddy shallow water so that it may appear to be deep.

Information executives often receive suggestions such as: "...each company should have a summary of the Information Systems plan of about three pages that vividly communicates to the Chief Executive Officer ... why Information Systems expenditures are allocated as they are, and what explicit type of competitive business benefits the company might expect."[35]

You may wonder how you can achieve such brevity while conveying insights regarding complex information systems activities. The suggested solution is to draw a *Resource Allocation Priority Matrix* for each business unit and then use the accompanying text to convey what the matrix means. A 3 x 5 matrix then defines both the priorities as well as the goals of information systems expenditures. For example, if you are a company "growing in a highly competitive industry," then rehabilitation and maintenance of your systems are your #1 priority. If you happen to be in a "static or declining industry," then the goal of achieving a *Return-on-Investment* should be only your #4 priority.

The "grid" method, like other classification schemes, may be a useful way to introduce a better understanding about systems priorities. It is also a superior teaching device to explain the realities of computers. However, to account for the behavior of businesses in terms of a few categories runs the risk of writing fiction.

Dollars never show up as a dimension when using this approach. Therefore, these methods are of little value to operating executives because they will not convey information about benefits or costs.

Decision Trees

You cannot fit more than two variables into two-dimensional grids. Some consultants have used perspective drawings of cubes to represent more variables. With color, you can represent four dimensions. Unless the illustration is very clever, the presence of too many or superfluous cells will distract the viewer. There are limits to what graphics can convey in explaining complex interactions.

Decisions concerning computers also can take advantage of a technique known as *decision trees*. Although they are in some ways superior to grids, they are less common because they must reveal what information is necessary before reaching conclusions.

An example of this method concerns what organizational strategy to use in implementing information systems.[36] It places variables into three dimensions:
- An assessment about the management of a company *(Adequate, Inadequate, Slow, Fast, Small and Large)*;
- An assessment of the situation in which implementation takes place *(Is the context and concept adequate? Is the pace of change slow or fast? Is the gap between current and required behavior small or large?)*;
- What strategy to pursue *(Traditional, Participative,*

Authoritative, Authoritative or Traditional, Participative or Traditional, Participative or Bail-out, Bail-out).

This graphic technique does not answer the more basic difficulties of how to make the distinctions among *Adequate, Slow* and a *Large Gap.* If the decision tree ends up prescribing the use of *Participative or Traditional* methods, I still cannot tell what to do next.

INFORMATION ECONOMICS

The inadequacies of common techniques for analyzing information systems activities, such as ratio methods (see Chapter 3), sampling of customer opinions, faith and vision, loss avoidance anecdotes, critical success factors and classification frameworks, have stimulated researchers to come up with more refined techniques.

The foremost example of a wide-ranging methodology is the work by Parker, Benson and Trainor, which they labeled "information economics,"[37] but which I will call the P.B.T. method. Their objective is to come up with practical recommendations regarding which projects to approve for implementation given a long list of plausible candidates. Their primary audience is information systems planners who are responsible for identifying the most valuable M.I.S. projects and then "...through methodology persuade management to provide the resources for these projects."[38]

The P.B.T. method has received extensive financial support from IBM's Joint Study in Enterprise-wide Information Management. IBM adopted it, with only minor modifications, to support marketing efforts[39] to teach customers how to make better investment decisions.

The P.B.T. method offers a positive and praiseworthy outlook: "...the value of M.I.S. to the business is based on improved performance at the line of business level of the enterprise. Decisions regarding information technology investments are linked to and driven by business planning."[40] This is the language of financial analysis that involves profits and cash flow. How well does the P.B.T. method achieve its objective?

Economic Impact Score Worksheet

The application of the P.B.T. method begins by calculating an *Economic Impact Score*, which is a "simple *Return-on-Investment.*" Fifty percent of the total *Score* points you may assign to any project derive from the ratings you get from the *Economic Impact Score.*

How do you come up with such a simple *Return-on-Investment?* The P.B.T. method divides the five-year average cash-flow by the required investment amount.[41] This technique does not recognize that the investment occurs at the start of the project, and that benefits occur only after implementation. In Chapter 9, I demonstrated that neglecting the cost of money will overstate all simple *Return-on-Investment* calculations. Not computing the net present value of money, and including only five years of cash flow, will lead to investments that do not maximize long-term profits.[42]

How about the *Economic Impact Score?* This is one of many implausible techniques found throughout the P.B.T. Method. The *score* comes from a scale that does not fit practices of financial analysis and planning. A score of zero indicates if the simple *Return-on-Investment* is zero or less. A score of 1 occur when the simple *Return-on-Investment* is between 1% and 299%. Every additional 200% gain in *ROI* adds 1 to the score.

In the discussion of "blockbuster" projects earlier in this chapter, I showed that even the most advanced users of strategic information systems yielded overall investment returns of only 8.6% to 25.6%. To assign to every project that has a *Return-on-Investment* between 1% and 299% the identical score of 1 presumes there are many projects with *Return-on-Investment* in excess of 299% that merit scores from 2 to 5. I do not believe that a project with a simple *Return-on-Investment* of 150% (a rare event) is the same as a project with a simple *Return-on-Investment* of 3%!

Benefits Estimates

No refinement in the method of computing the *Return-on-Investment* will matter if the technique for estimating benefit is doubtful. P.B.T. illustrates its approach to benefit estimation in the BEAM Parcels (a parcel delivery service) automation project.[43] Management expected additional revenues of $2,155,400 as a result of installing an information system for $111,000.

This yields a neat simple *Return-on-Investment* of 388%. That is not bad, until we remember the sins of benefit over-attribution. Is it legitimate to assign all incremental revenues to the installation of a new information system? I do not think so. Some of the new revenues must pay for gasoline, truck depreciation, management salaries, administrative overhead, taxes and so forth. The computation of the *Return-on-Investment* of $111,000 should consider as a benefit only the incremental net cash[44] rather than total revenues. My guess is that the proposed investment is still a good one for BEAM Parcels, but certainly is not responsible for a *Return-on-Investment* as high as 388%.

Risks and Intangibles

My greatest difficulty with the P.B.T. method concerns its treatment of risks and intangibles which fall into the following categories:

Business Domain Assessments:
- *Strategic Match,*
- *Competitive Advantage,*
- *Management Information,*
- *Competitive Response,*
- *Project or Organizational Risk.*

Technology Domain Assessments:
- *Strategic IS architecture,*
- *Definitional Uncertainty,*
- *Technical Uncertainty,*
- *Infrastructure Risk.*

For each of the above factors, there is an elaborate table which requires groups of evaluators[45] to fill out scoring forms according to established rules.

To illustrate the problems with the P.B.T. method, I will explain how you score for *Definitional Uncertainty.*[46]

Score = 0	Requirements are firm and approved. High probability of no changes.
Score = 1	Requirements moderately firm. No formal approvals. Low probability of changes.
Score = 2	Requirements moderately firm. Reasonable probability of nonroutine changes.
Score = 3	Requirements moderately firm. Changes are almost certain immediately.
Score = 4	Requirements not firm. Specifications not firm. Area is quite complex. Changes certain.
Score = 5	Requirements unknown. Specifications unknown. Area complex. Ongoing changes.

Table 17.3: Assigning Score Values of Definitional Uncertainty

What do you do with a project that gets a score of 5, which means that nobody knows what needs doing? The P.B.T. method applies a weighting scheme to translate subjective opinions into "corporate strategy." This technique is similar to the one I have already described in Chapter 3, where you multiply one arbitrary scale by a number from another arbitrary scale:

Individual Assessments	Relative Weight	Maximum Score
Economic Impact Score (ROI)	10	50
Strategic Match	2	10
Competitive Advantage	2	10
Management Information	2	10
Competitive Response	1	5
Project or Organizational Risk	-1	-5
Strategic IS architecture	-2	-10
Definitional Uncertainty	-2	-10
Technical Uncertainty	3	15
Infrastructure Risk	-2	-10

Table 17.4: Assessment Weights for P.B.T. Method Project Scores

The basic premise of the P.B.T. method is that the higher the Project Score, the better a project's contribution to corporate strategy. The maximum score a project can earn is 100, if there are no negative influences. The maximum negative contribution to the overall score is only 35 points, in which *Definitional Uncertainty* contributes a maximum of 10 negative points.

If you are completely unsure of what a project should accomplish you should not proceed. Investing without an objective is not prudent, regardless of 20 positive points for *Strategic Advantage*, 20 positive points for *Competitive Response* or 50 positive points for *Economic Impact*.

Furthermore, the P.B.T. method offers no reason why *Project or Organizational Risk*, possibly a deadly defect, receives at maximum only 5 negative points. It makes no sense why *Competitive Advantage*, possibly a prerequisite for survival, receives at maximum 10 positive points.

Equating 10 positive points for simple *Return-on-Investment* (up to 299%) with 10 negative points for the incompatibility with the approved *Strategic I.S. Architecture*[47] defies prudence. If I can really get a *Return-on-Investment* of 299% on a competitively urgent application,

I will concentrate on getting the benefits in a hurry before I consider following an approved *Strategic I.S. Architecture*.

The lofty goals of the P.B.T. method to link project selection with improved business performance erode as I examine the details. The P.B.T. scores that originate from arbitrary weights on a one-to-five scale are impossible to link with a profit plan. The P.B.T. method offers a technique that gives a logical, though questionable, consistency to project priority rankings. It leaves unanswered the question of how the profits and cash flows will improve, in a verifiable way, as a result of the proposed investments.

How Difficult is the P.B.T. Method to Perform?

Some of the assessments require further worksheets to show supporting details behind the summary scores. For instance, Technical Uncertainty calls for separate ratings of Skills Required, Hardware Dependencies, Software Dependencies and Application Software.

The P.B.T. method would require 15,000 data entries if a company has to come up with scores for 100 projects, and if the Systems Review Committee consists of 10 people.[48] Where opinions diverge, the ratings would require individual resolution because averages are misleading. What we have here is a highly formalized group estimating method which can experience as much bias as the case I mentioned earlier in this chapter.

COMPREHENSIVE SOLUTIONS

The first glimpse of *Information Strategies for Information Systems* (ISIS) came in November 1987, when the press reported that it was "...IBM's new marketing effort aimed at swaying the expenditures of its customers away from other capital expenditures and toward investments in information systems."[49] IBM salespersons went through training at IBM's Advanced Business Institute to offer ISIS services to selected customers.

The launching of ISIS coincided with a barrage of full-page advertisements in leading business newspapers and magazines stating: "...an IBM team of experts ... will work closely with your senior management to plan the information systems that will be most profitable. This doesn't mean selling you a piece of hardware here and a piece of software there. It means sitting down with you and understanding your goals, and demonstrating the financial return of our solutions."[50]

ISIS requires, on the average, two months of data collection and analysis by a joint IBM-customer team. There are no fees to the participants. It is the most comprehensive package of techniques for making computer investment decisions available thus far on the world market. It includes extensive training support, instruction manuals and comprehensive data-gathering forms.

The ISIS Methodology

The backbone of ISIS is the Parker, Benson and Trainor (P.B.T.) project rating method previously described in this chapter. However, ISIS also incorporates a variety of other approaches.

ISIS consultants collect information from outside sources such as Value-Line, Dun & Bradstreet and the International Data Corporation to come up with Information *Technology-to-Revenue* ratios using the same approach as used by the *Computerworld* studies discussed in Chapter 3.

ISIS calls for an inventory of all equipment, including computers manufactured by IBM's competition. The data forms catalogue the age of each application, identifying all applications older than five years as candidates for replacement.[51]

To get a better understanding of top executives' wishes, ISIS borrows heavily from Critical Success Factor practices.

ISIS makes much use of classification frameworks and grid positioning. It takes the P.B.T. scores and places them in 2 x 2 tables that have adopted imaginative new ways of describing projects. For example, the plot of *Project Benefits Rating* against *Project Doability Rating* has the following colorful categories:[52]

- *Dud* (Low Doability, Low Benefits);
- *Bread & Butter* (High Doability, Low Benefits);
- *High Wire Act* (Low Doability, High Benefits);
- *Blockbuster* (High Doability, High Benefits).

A *Strategic Opportunity Grid* has the following categories:
- *No Investment* (Low Importance Rating, Low Information Systems Rating);
- *No Emphasis* (Low Importance Rating, High Information Systems Rating);
- *Maintenance* (High Importance Rating, Low Information Systems Rating);
- *Key Investment* (High Importance Rating, High Information Systems Rating).

428   THE BUSINESS VALUE OF COMPUTERS

The classification frameworks and grid positioning exercises are useful for group discussions. An ISIS financial model then takes the conclusions derived from the qualitative ratings and converts the general logic into expected investment payoffs.

ISIS requires the construction of a financial model that uses a Lotus 1-2-3 spreadsheet template for receiving the results from a variety of ISIS analyses.[53] This model projects the company's financial performance for at least five years, using its current and proposed information systems plans. The model includes comparisons of internal financial data, such as revenue ratios, with companies in the same industry. Industry experts participate in discussions of how a particular customer applies computers as compared with the industry's practices. At the end, the customer receives three to five specific recommendations of what projects to fund to increase profits.

The ISIS approach is a skillful repackaging of a collection of consulting practices already mentioned in Chapter 3 and in this chapter. Each of these practices has some redeeming value as well as major pitfalls. The ISIS approach incorporates all the faults and fallacies associated with each method. The bias towards technology solutions of business problems shows up in its rating methods and classification frameworks. However, it is more complete in considering all of the computer investment issues than any other published approach for determining the business value of computers.

Many customers welcome IBM's free assistance in planning information technology investments because they do not get better answers from other sources. I do not know of any major consulting firm that offers standard financial analytic tools as an integrated element of their systems development methodology. Nobody can match IBM's educational support in promoting ISIS as the answer to questions about "bottom-line" results. IBM efforts are a significant contribution to the computer industry because they published their methodology and have trained customers to alter the model assumptions. By giving customers complete access to the financial models, they have neutralized potential allegations of prejudiced results.

Concerns about Bias

Perhaps the best way to understand the origin of ISIS is to realize that it was a major element in reorganizing the IBM sales force. ISIS is one of the tools for reorienting IBM from selling hardware-based products to offering complete solutions to customers' problems. ISIS thus became a way for retraining IBM's salespersons to pursue industry-based (e.g., vertical market) solutions.[54] IBM marketing management understood that offering free consulting assistance was the fastest means to teach its sales force to learn more about applications selling.

IBM's top marketing executive made the pivotal role of ISIS clear when he said that "...the new sales direction is the Information Systems Investment Strategy program, which will provide Information Systems consulting help and will enable IBM sales representatives to tie new applications specifically to the customer's bottom line."

Customers must now decide if they can accept equipment salespersons as unpaid consultants who are a reliable source of allegedly unbiased advice. If there is legitimate concern about an equipment vendor's consulting role it must address the issue of competitive uses of information technologies. I noted before that the introduction of information technologies within an industry is comparable to an arms race. The first competitor will innovate with an expectation of substantial gains and a rapid payoff. If this becomes the source of a strategic advantage, other competitors will have to adopt the innovative technology regardless of expense or payoffs. The imitators will then justify additional computer spending to protect their competitive position.

Regardless of technological innovation, every computer project will propose the installation of excess computer capacity during startup. Such a tendency is present in all established mainframe computer installations since the marginal cost for buying additional capacity is only a small fraction of the average current processing costs. Additional capacity is often necessary during the initial phases of any major new application because M.I.S. managers wish to be sure that their systems do not fail because of unpredicted excess demand.

A problem arises when everyone follows the leader with the identical technology and builds up excess information processing capacity. The predictable consequences of such development will be that everyone's profit margin will decrease and nobody's expected payoffs will materialize.

A vendor's marketing organization has motivation to whip up such capacity-building frenzy by accelerating the dissemination of competitive information. Competitive comparisons are one of the key investment-evaluation criteria for judging ISIS-justified projects. An organization with ideas of how to gain a competitive advantage from computers may not wish to disclose their plans if they suspect that their new application becomes an ISIS competitive benchmark.[55]

Chapter Summary

The huge expenditures for information technology are unmatched by corresponding efforts to make better investment decisions in computer applications. As long as the entire process remains technology-driven, there is little hope that we will see much improvement. Many methods for giving advice about computers have one thing in common. They serve as a vehicle to facilitate proposals for additional funding. They also reflect the centralized view that information technology needs to be rationed out of a pool of centrally managed overhead funds. The current techniques ultimately reflect their origins in a technology "push" from the experts, consultants and vendors, instead of a strategy "pull" from the profit center managers.

Many of the techniques for giving advice discussed in this chapter will lapse into oblivion when computer budgets become inseparable from every manager's plan to improve productivity. Operating managers with direct profit responsibility and accountability do not need to give special treatment to information technology apart from whatever other methods they use to justify any other resources. Loss avoidance exercises, group estimates, classification frameworks and economic impact grids will be unnecessary for deciding what to do next. The financial and control methods for decentralized management should apply equally to information technology, because it is a resource just like every other resource. Information technology does not require unusual analytic methods and does not deserve special treatment.

Chapter 17 Comments

[1] IBM Corporate Information Systems, 1988 Information Processing Indices, Internal IBM Document, November 30, 1988. Reproduced in W.M. Carlson and B.C.McNurlin, Measuring the Value of Information Systems, *United Communications Group*, Bethesda Md. 1989, pp. 69–92.

[2] The precise definitions are in the IBM guidelines.

[3] The guidelines recommend that the method to be used for defining benefits and costs should use the work of M. Parker and R.J. Benson, H.E. Trainor, Information Economics–Linking Business Performance to Information Technology, *Prentice-Hall*, 1988. The difficulties in implementing this method also are discussed in Chapters 3 and 10 of this book.

[4] In 1988, I evaluated seventy pounds of 33 Divisional systems planning and budgeting documents compiled by an organization with annual computer expenses of over

$1 billion. Applying the IBM assessment scale produced the following ratings: Level 0=22 Divisions; Level 1=5 Divisions; Level 2=3 Divisions; Level 3=2 Divisions; Level 4=1 Division. Only three Divisions included in their plan an explicit relation between information technology and proposed business plans.

In the public view, this firm has acquired the reputation as a leader in the application of computers. In reality, its M.I.S. departments accumulated a dismal record of aborted careers, failed projects and cost overruns. Although the company suffers from a long list of defects, I placed defective planning methods for information technology investments at the top of the list of what needed to be fixed.

[5] In response to advertisements, the Apple Computer Company distributed only a 24-page synopsis (Peat, Marwick, Main & Co., Synopsis of Macintosh Benefits Study. Distributed by *Apple Computer, Inc.*, July 9, 1987) of a much larger report (The Macintosh Benefits Study, May 29, 1987).

[6] The line items listed on the "Discussion Group Data Gathering Questionnaire" are as follows: 1. Description of Work Effort. The assumption here is that the group has agreed to discuss only 20% of their efforts isolated as "key efforts." 2. Hours that it took to do this work manually. 3. Hours that this work would take on an "other terminal," implying a competitor's computer. 4. Hours it takes to do this work on a Macintosh. 5. "Personal Effectiveness Rating," on a scale of zero to five. 6. "Group Effectiveness Rating" on a scale of zero to five. The entire effort of filling out these forms takes about two to four hours of group discussion.

The projected average possible savings of 56 hours per person per month were not based on taking a very bad situation and then demonstrating remarkable improvements by doing only slightly better. It did not employ a technique which I call "poverty benchmarking," in which you take the lowest possible output level you can find, such as demotivated clerical workers, and then show fantastic gains when new equipment and training are introduced for a different labor force. Even a small increase over prior poor output levels is a very large percentage improvement.

In the Macintosh case, a footnote states that "...the workers participating in this case averaged over 13 years in the industry and had competing technology available to them for over five years before the installation of Macintosh." This approach is correct in evaluating the benefits of an incremental investment. Within 10 years, all businesses will have to use the incremental benefit method to justify new computer purchases. The Peat, Marwick study is the only one that has applied this method properly.

[7] It just happens that I find my Macintosh more productive than my IBM/AT computer, by a wide margin. For example, I compared the time required to install the most recent update of two popular spreadsheet software packages. The one running on the IBM equipment required more than one hour to complete and was accompanied by an 80 page manual. The other, for the Macintosh, was installed in six minutes because the instructions were only two pages long.

[8] Action Technologies, 1145 Atlantic Avenue, Alameda, CA 94501. They market a complex group-cooperation software package, *The Coordinator*.

[9] I tested the version released on August 5, 1987.

[10] This is another application of the *The Farmer's Horses Method* discussed in Chapter 10.

[11] I do not wish to embarrass by naming the head of one of the largest information systems consulting firms who elaborated on his "blockbuster" theory in widely publicized talks.

[12] The June 8, 1987 issue of FORTUNE magazine has a detailed tabulation of the largest U.S. non-industrial corporations. The most useful indicators of relative profit performance are the last two columns: 1976–1986 Average Total Return to Investors, and the Rank of Average Total Return in the Investment Category. Since some of the categories list 50 companies and others 100, I adjusted each order ranking by listing it as a percentile of the total. For example, Merrill Lynch, ranked as #30 among the 50 companies listed in Diversified Financial Services, would be in the 60th percentile.

The "Total Return to Investors" includes both the price appreciation and the dividend yield to an investor in the company's stock. Of the many imperfect ways of measuring financial performance, this indicator gives the most meaningful

432   THE BUSINESS VALUE OF COMPUTERS

approximation of results. It is a ten-year average and thus eliminates objections that it may be too volatile to be of value.

The identification of the top ten "strategic information systems" comes from an annual poll of senior M.I.S. executives as reported in the December 15, 1986 issue of *InformationWeek*, page 45. This list has remained remarkably stable for a number of years. It is noteworthy that all top users of "strategic systems" were in the FORTUNE 500 service companies. None of the largest U.S. industrial corporations were chosen. To check on what an experienced researcher would consider a "leading industrial company", I looked up the FORTUNE rankings of Scott Paper and Pillsbury. Both companies were singled out in *InfoWorld* (August 1, 1988, p.34) by the director of the Center for Information Research as good examples of leaders in the strategic uses of computers that boost their ability to compete. Pillsbury came out in the 34th and Scott Paper in the 36th percentiles. Both were above average, but certainly not "leading" by financial standards.

A few technical notes are also in order. Two companies, The American Hospital Supply Company and The Federal Express Company were also among the top ten "strategic information systems." The American Hospital Supply Company merged with Baxter Travenol Laboratories in 1985, and its comparable financial data are not available. However, in 1984, its rank was in the 14th percentile, the highest of the 1986 group in our tabulation. The Federal Express Company had only a few years' results because of its youth.

[13] Freiser was quoted by *Business Week* of October 14, 1985.
[14] The consulting firm of Booz, Allen & Hamilton reported in the *Insights* #17 newsletter the results of their 1987 survey of how executives measure the *Return-on-Investment* for information technology projects:

Company Practices	by CEO	by CIO
Do not measure. Based on subjective view	52%	45%
Only measure costs, not benefits	31%	24%
Project by project justification	10%	29%
Evaluate against approved plan	7%	2%

The subjective "faith and visions" school has a clear majority over other methods. Relying on evaluations against approved plans, as advocated in this book, occurs only in a small minority of customers.

[15] M. Brody, Laptop Computers, *Fortune*, March 28, 1988, p. 112.
[16] D. Freedman, The ROI Polloi, *CIO Magazine*, April 1990, p. 30.
[17] D. Freedman, The ROI Polloi, *CIO Magazine*, April 1990, p. 35.
[18] A privately published case but widely used in the firm's executive seminars.
[19] According to the Bureau of Labor Statistics, the average wage for utilities was $27,500 in 1984. Computer expenditures of $14,000 per employee would be 51% of payroll. This is one of the highest reported technology over payroll ratios I have ever recorded other than in computer services.
[20] N.D. Meyer and M.E. Boone, The Information Edge, *McGraw-Hill*, 1987.
[21] For details, see the case summarized in Table 4.2 of N.D. Meyer and M.E. Boone's book.
[22] An aircraft crash caused by an improperly installed single pin in the engine mount actually occurred.
[23] For details, see the case summarized in Table 3.5 of N.D. Meyer and M.E. Boone's book.
[24] The Impact of Data Interpretation Systems On Business Performance, *Metaphor Computer Systems Corporation*, Mountain View, California, 1989
[25] In this case it was a "Data Interpretation System" which takes its data from existing databases and makes such data easily accessible and more understandable.
[26] Retrospective evaluations lend themselves to good story-telling. My favorite is the one that takes William Shakespeare's play Richard III (Act V,iv) literally. In this passage King Richard of England falls off his horse during the critical moment of the battle of Bosworth in 1485. Just before he is slain, Richard exclaims the memorable "A horse! A horse! My Kingdom for a horse!" If you give Richard's desperate offer to a financial analyst experienced in the arts of retrospective valuation, you could come up with the following *Return-on-Investment:*

1. The price of a good horse in 1485 was 5 shillings (20 shillings = 1£).

2. We also know what was the market price of the English Kingdom, since one of the two popes claiming title to all of Europe (Pope Clement VII in Avignon) offered to sell England to the Spanish King for £4 million.

The retrospective *Return-on-Investment* of saving Richard III with another horse would be 1,600,000%. This only shows that with a calculator you can prove just about anything you wish. This led George Herbert (in Jacula Prudentum, Antwerp, 1651) to compose what is now a model for all retrospective and over-attributed computer claims:

> For want of a nail, the shoe was lost;
> for want of a shoe, the horse was lost;
> for want of a horse, the rider was lost;
> for want of a rider, the battle was lost;
> for want of a battle, the kingdom was lost.

In this way you can equate the value of a nail to the value of a kingdom. The logic is the same as when you can equate the value of a critical computer search to most of the shareholder value ten years later.

27 The sessions advertised using "Delphi" methods, although the consultant did not use any of the usual precautions involved in a "Delphi" approach, such as reconciliation of divergent estimates.

28 Webster's Unabridged Dictionary defines empiric as "...relying or based solely on experiments or experience." Since the system was still in the proposal phase and had no pilot installations, it is hard to conceive how Simply Widely Assumed Guesses (SWAG in Washington parlance) is empiric.

29 As is usually the case with government proposals, the break-even period is on the basis of cumulative benefits minus cumulative costs. The cost of capital was zero. This gives risky projects with a large initial negative cash flow unusually favorable treatment.

30 The consultant should have first pre-tested his survey sample using a simpler questionnaire to find out what the people were doing. Then, he should have grouped employees by activity and sampled each group separately for potential savings.

31 The skillful use of a good thesaurus is the only limitation on the invention of new typologies. For instance, Mintzberg and Waters classify strategies as either Planned, Entrepreneurial, Ideological, Umbrella, Process, Unconnected, Consensus or Imposed. Galbraith and Schendel propose Low Commitment, Growth, Maintenance or Industrial Niche. Wisseman and Messer propose Explosion, Expansion, Continuous Growth, Slip, Consolidation or Contraction. The most prolific typology is the SUCCESS method proposed by Eli Segev and Paul Gray (*Information Resources Management Journal*, Winter 1989). Twenty-eight equally weighted types, such as "Environmental Complexity" and "Proactiveness of Decision Style" were rated on a scale of 0 to 100. The scores entered by each rater were added up and averaged. Next, these values were matched to pre-defined solutions. What fit best was the prescribed action. Unless there is good evidence showing that such recommendations can be associated with patterns of financial success, these techniques look very much like a sophisticated horoscope. Unfortunately, none of the reported typologies show the data on which they base their findings except in the case of Segev, who mentions using 25 graduating MBA's as judges to establish the standard against which firms are evaluated.

32 C.F. Gibson and B.B. Jackson, The Information Imperative, *Lexington Books*, 1987, Figure 5-1.

33 In the same way astrologers managed to substitute "Pisces" and "Leo" for ideas that came out of astronomy.

34 The critique of the myriad of frameworks comes from W.R. King, V. Grover and E.H. Hufnagel, Using Information and Information Technology for Sustainable Competitive Advantage, *Information & Management*, 17, 1989.

35 W.F. McFarlan, Information Technology Changes the Way You Compete, *Harvard Business Review*, May-June 1984. The grid has 15 cells. In each cell there is a number where #1 indicates highest priority.

36 C.F. Gibson and C.J. Singer, New Risks for M.I.S. Managers, *Computerworld*, April 19, 1982.

434   THE BUSINESS VALUE OF COMPUTERS

37 M.M. Parker, R.J. Benson with H.E. Trainor, Information Economics – Linking Business Performance to Information Technology, *Prentice Hall*, 1988 and M.M. Parker, H.E. Trainor and R.J. Benson, Information Strategy and Economics, *Prentice Hall*, 1989.
38 See Preface to Information Economics.
39 Information Systems Investment Strategies (ISIS), described in Chapter 3.
40 See Preface to Information Economics.
41 See section 8-4-2 of Information Economics, p.97.
42 In a later example, P.B.T. compares a simple *Return-on-Investment* calculation with a discounted computation based on discount rates ranging from 4.5% in year 1 to 7% in year 6. The authors conclude that discounting cash flow makes little difference in the example they studied. I agree that if you use sufficiently low discount rates, such as 4.5% to 7%, the differences in the two computations may not be decisive. However, the current cost of equity capital ranges anywhere from 12% to 22%, which makes discounting a much more powerful influence.
43 See Section 12-3, p.140-141 in Information Economics.
44 Variable contribution margin is Revenue minus Direct Expenses (wages, gasoline, maintenance cost per mile) plus any overhead costs which are activity related, such as the increased number of shipping papers required to bring in the added revenue.
45 Usually a corporate systems review committee.
46 Section 14-2, p.163 in Information Economics.
47 I am a strong proponent that each organization must adhere to well-defined standards for defining, engineering and implementing information systems. The judgement of whether or not to allow a project to proceed if it does not follow all of the standards is largely a matter of payoff and risk. I would be reluctant to apply to every project, regardless of whether it is a short-term pilot experiment or a major long term investment, the identical standards.
48 The BEAM Parcel Company, a relatively small enterprise, had over 100 projects to evaluate.
49 The earliest report about ISIS was by Michael Sullivan-Trainor, The New Team Approach with Users, *Computerworld*, November 18, 1987, p.17.
50 The newspaper quotation is from a double-page advertisement in the *Wall Street Journal*, January 29, 1988.
51 The hypothesis that maintenance costs for "old" programs are higher than those for newly developed programs cannot be supported, as noted by F. Lehner, Cost Comparison for the Development and Maintenance of Application Systems, *Information & Management*, 9, 1990.
52 IBM Advanced Business Institute, I/S Investment Strategies: Making a Difference on the Bottom Line, IBM Corporation, 1988, Publication G520–6497. A widely distributed internal promotional booklet by the IBM Advanced Business Institute, I/S Investment Strategies, A Powerful New Approach to Identify, Analyze and Validate Major I/S Investments, displays the strategic opportunity grid.
53 The proprietary ISIS model is a standard Lotus 1-2-3 spreadsheet with data layout templates and pre-defined computational routines.
54 The insight about the tie-in between ISIS and the reorganization of IBM's sales force comes from G. McWilliams, Selling IBM on Solutions Selling, *Datamation*, January 1, 1988, p.58. The use of ISIS for a massive retraining of the IBM sales force reveals a sophisticated understanding by IBM's top executives of how to reorient the "culture" of an organization. Giving salespersons tools for becoming "consultants" shows a recognition of the most effective teaching techniques. Children learn best if they have to teach some other child new skills. The teacher always learns more than the student about any subject.
55 G. McWilliams, Selling IBM on Solutions Selling, *Datamation*, January 1, 1988, p.58. This case history about the success of ISIS notes: " ...in a previous consulting arrangement IBM sales members conducted a study on the use of the Universal Product Code (UPC) for the Carter Hawley Hale department store chain....that study was later taken by IBM to Allied Stores to help Allied decide on its UPC strategy."

18

COMPUTERS AND NATIONAL PRODUCTIVITY

The measurement of performance shapes what people will do.

PRODUCTIVITY COMPUTATIONS

"Productivity" is a ratio of *Output* over *Input*. As long as the *Output* is simple, such as quart containers of milk, there is little difficulty in counting the containers to come up with the productivity of the milk-filling machine. It gets more complex if the same machine fills also half-gallons and pints with orange juice. When products, costs and units of output vary, companies usually construct a proxy measure of factory *Output*, such as equivalent quarts of milk.

If a company produces not only drinks but also detergents, salad oil and mayonnaise, the determination of "equivalent outputs" becomes intricate if you wish to know what is the company's overall productivity. You have to include in your calculations the costs of transportation, sales and administration in order to compare year-to-year productivity gains for the entire enterprise.[1]

Productivity Indicators

When confronted with the difficulty of measuring diverse physical *Outputs*, somebody will suggest abandoning quarts, gallons, jars and cans to express everything in terms of labor hours or dollars.[2] A new problem then arises whenever there is a change in prices of either *Input* or *Output* components. If the price of milk goes up while the volume produced remains constant, does that mean that the *Output*, now expressed in dollars, increases? Also, price-based measures do not reveal if an item's quality changed, such as by increasing the shelf-life of milk through irradiation. Aggregate dollar measures of output will not reflect comparable *Outputs* over time if product quality changes.

NATIONAL PRODUCTIVITY BASE PERIOD INDEXING

To cope with these inconsistencies, economists have devised "base period" indexes. Each index requires elaborate calculations to derive a multiplier which will adjust for current prices. Current prices would become comparable to prices in the "base period" ten or twenty years ago. You can then evaluate productivity changes during which the prices of raw milk, packaging materials, labor and transportation are as if they were constant. For example, indexing was used when statistical reports state that the numbers are "in 1969 dollars."

Problems with output measurement arise when a product radically changes its production process or its uses.[3] I do not think it is possible to restate the purchase price of 1990 computers in terms of 1960 computers. Similarly, there is no sensible way to evaluate the output of a 1990 software spreadsheet and figure out the equivalent number of 1960 accountants it would take to do the identical job.[4] Although these two examples are extreme cases of why the computation of "base period" indexes can be misleading, government economists rely on indexes for reporting on national and industry productivity.

COMPANY PRODUCTIVITY BASE PERIOD INDEXING

The practice of computing equivalent units of output, defined in terms such as "equivalent clerical positions," is prevalent when making productivity estimates for specific industries. For example, AT&T used to feature in their Annual Reports computations based on how many 1920 telephone operators it would take to handle telephone traffic fifty years later. The labor productivity gains were astronomical, until you realized that the productivity came from huge capital investments in switching technology, with a minor contribution from operator efficiency. Whenever someone quotes impressive labor productivity numbers, you should examine the "base period" mix of labor, capital and service quality before you accept any claims of productivity improvement.

"Base period" indexing is often used to justify computer expenditures and audit productivity gains. Watch out for comparisons involving work that does not remain the same. If a financial analyst can construct 140 spreadsheets per day in 1990 where he could make only one in 1960, this does not necessarily suggest a 140-fold gain. You cannot claim as a benefit of productivity gains the salaries of 139 additional analysts.

Productivity Calculations

Base-period productivity computations are attractive, especially if you have a computer to convert just a few numbers into impressive-looking and elaborate schedules. You can take unit costs for each of a thousand products or services and break them down into innumerable labor categories, material costs, overhead allocations and capital cost. You can then compute price, cost and volume variances, by quarter, in three or four different ways depending on the formula you used to calculate the base-period index.[5] This creates elaborate and impressive looking statistical tables that show productivity variances by product and cost element. However, such effort has little meaning if the products and services of interest keep changing rapidly.

Computing the ratios of physical *Output/Input* can be useful for businesses that deal with unchanging products or services over an extended period. Operations such as bakeries and iron nail manufacturers may be able to use the *Output/Input* method for keeping consistent productivity records. Difficulties arise when analysts apply this approach to an information-rich environment in which variety is enormous and procedures change all of the time. Nevertheless, banks, insurance companies and government agencies keep using simple *Output/Input* methods to report on productivity because they are always under pressure to show measurable gains. They may produce plausible numbers showing productivity improvements if they select the right "base period" index for making comparisons.[6]

Insisting on physical *Output/Input* productivity measurements of clerical and administration personnel gives an incentive to break work-flow into tightly defined and discrete tasks. Office procedures would become oriented towards task-specialization instead of work-enlargement. Zealous applications of physical *Output/Input* measurements will increase the reliability of *Output* measures, but will hinder efforts to improve the quality of services. Customers do not organize their problems in ways that conveniently appear as orderly and measurable elements. If the transaction counts penalize employees who perform knowledge-based work on computer terminals, the measurements may have a detrimental effect on work quality and on morale. To stimulate people who perform complex tasks to improve their productivity you must use complex indicators to describe what they do.

Applying Value-Added Productivity

> *How to measure productivity gains: Find everyone's Value-added.*

Useful computer work is knowledge-enhancing work. Organizations that wish to increase the business value of computers should not rely on factory-like measures to evaluate results from their investments in information technology. *Value-added* indicators are more trustworthy in showing if individuals or groups are improving their efficiency and effectiveness. In this view, people are not cogs in a production machine but actors who create wealth when their net *Value-added* exceeds their expenses. The methods for making such appraisals are similar to profit-center accounting.

The ultimate consequence of easily available computing power at each workstation will be the capacity of knowledge-workers to maintain their own profit and loss statements. The measurement of productivity and the realization of business results then will be linked directly. This will dispense with the artifice of physical counts which, in knowledge-enhancing work, do not measure results and do not resemble *Value-added* estimates.

NATIONAL PRODUCTIVITY INDICATORS

All commentators on the decline of U.S. productivity base their arguments on the same productivity estimates. Productivity indexes originate from the U.S. Department of Commerce or the U.S. Department of Labor. If these numbers are not reliable you may have to re-examine whatever you hear regarding "information worker" productivity.[7]

CHAPTER 18—COMPUTERS AND NATIONAL PRODUCTIVITY   439

How Reliable are the Productivity Indicators?

The current method for computing national productivity numbers requires tracking the volume and prices of all *Outputs* and *Inputs*. For instance, the estimated tonnage of paper comes from its sales divided by its price. The effects of the changing mix in paper products (the relative decline in low-priced newsprint as compared with the steady growth in high-cost coated papers) on year-to-year changes in calculated productivity require statistical adjustments. The *base period quantity* must compare with the *current period quantity*, and the *base period price* must be compared on the same basis with the *current period price*. Additional adjustments are necessary to account for differences between *base period* and *current period* quality.

The reason for going through such elaborate adjustments is the doctrine that changes in productivity must translate into physically measurable quantities. This industrial age view holds up reasonably well when output occurs in tons of paper, number of freight cars loaded, barrels of oil or work-hours. Such measures are numerically consistent. When making short-term comparisons, there are few dramatic shifts in the ways how the economy consumes these resources. The premise that productivity needs physical measures of output became invalid when economies shifted towards services which now account for 50 to 75% of the economy. Services are hard to define and even harder to measure consistently over a period of several decades.

Government statisticians have concentrated on evaluating the productivity of the industrial sector because it is easier to quantify *Output*. Industrial statistics also are more complete because a small number of companies account for a disproportionately large share of *Output*. Large industrial corporations have the staffs to fill out government questionnaires and therefore the information about industrial output is more reliable. The service sector contains many small enterprises that account for a large share of its activity.[8] The government surveys cannot cover them adequately.

When you examine the details of national productivity statistics, you find that *Value-added* estimates of the service sector are hard to define. A large part of the service sector depends on government or government subsidized operations such as health services, social services, safety, transportation and education. In the absence of reliable ways to estimate the value of these *Outputs*, government statisticians assume that *Output* is equal to *Input* costs. This simplification automatically depresses any estimates of productivity in the services sector whenever the public sector or public subsidies expand.

Productivity indicators for individual Standard Industrial Classification (SIC) categories are also misleading. *Output* is continually shifting from one SIC grouping to another. Products can substitute for services and vice versa.

For example, on-site maintenance for copiers was always a "service." With the introduction of replacement cartridges, a large share of service costs is now an expense classified as industrial "products."

In another example, consider a manufacturer of fabricated steel products who sells directly to retailers. The steel company's total revenues, including the costs of distribution, are part of the steel industry's contribution to the economy. When the steel manufacturer later decides to handle sales through distributors, a large share of the distribution costs would now show up in the "services" sector of the economy. Such events have occurred often in recent years, especially as distribution costs started exceeding direct manufacturing costs.

Government statistics cannot keep track of these rapid shifts in economic activities. The statistics will be much more reliable about the easier-to-track changes for physical products than for the less tangible services.

Difficulties in Productivity Measurement

To illustrate why current national productivity indicators are dubious, examine those which deal with computers. Productivity statistics now adjust for the number of *equivalent computers* you can get for the same price as five, ten and twenty years ago.[9] Government analysts have attributed enormous productivity gains to computers based on precipitously dropping costs per calculation. However, there is no evidence that customers have realized comparable productivity gains from using computers. As computing equipment becomes a larger component of total U.S. manufacturing capital, these adjustments tend to overstate manufacturing productivity. Manufacturing gains will depress the calculated contributions of the service sector because the sum of all gains and losses must equal the net improvement.

National productivity measures do not recognize shifts in industry categories due to technological changes. In 1954, a $4,000 teletype machine was part of the telephone and telegraph category. It is now a $1,500 communicating word processor, classified as the output of the computer industry.

The U.S. statistical system does a good job in measuring large manufacturing companies which are a declining part of the economy. Since 1970, most of the growth in the U.S. economy took place among small private companies, especially in the services sector. Only 5% of the small companies in the United States have public shareholders.[10] The reporting about small firms' contributions to economic growth therefore is less accurate.

"White-collar" Productivity

What you do to create Value-added matters more than your job title.

Some researchers[11] have used occupational data as a proxy for comparing the efficiency of the industrial and services sectors. Employment data provides the basis of computing the changes in the ratio of "blue collar (production)" to "white collar" workers, and the ratio of "knowledge workers" to "information support workers."[12]

This approach loses validity when engineers, technicians and clerical workers become direct contributors to the *Value-added* of services. A large number of "white collar" employees work for firms which sell personnel services to manufacturing companies where they become direct product costs.

It used to be true that "white collar" occupations were unproductive overhead added to the cost of goods produced by "labor." That distinction does not hold any more. Only some people in "white collar" occupations[13] are in overhead work, which may or may not be "productive" depending on the *Value-added* of the firm. A large number of "white collar" personnel are as much a direct cost of labor, such as in financial and personal services, as any factory worker in manufacturing. An increasing share of personnel classified as professional and administrative "white collar" workers work in a consulting capacity. They bill their time on a hourly basis just as if they were punching a time-clock in a factory.

Many studies have highlighted the increasing reliance of post-industrial society on information occupations. This increased the awareness of potential adverse effects of information-handling personnel on national productivity indicators because "information" is not considered a consumable good.[14] To determine the magnitude of changes in the information sector using personnel ratios, based on occupational categories, is unreliable and inconclusive. A society where robot factories and capital-intensive farming employ only 10–15% of the population as strictly "production" workers could be a more productive economy than we have today.

"White collar," "information worker" and "production worker" ratios tell nothing until we measure the *Value-added* of the businesses where they work. Executives should not accept productivity improvement proposals which exclusively rely on projected changes in occupational ratios.[15]

A Micro-economic Point of View

I find the work of economists ambiguous when they try to estimate the contribution of computers to national economic performance. They express concern about the apparently poor contribution of information processing capital. They attribute price indexes to computers that show gains for the producers of computers, but not for their customers. The published statistics reflect the economists' assumptions rather than what computers actually accomplish.

Official productivity statistics reflect a bias favoring the industrial point of view of measuring productivity by means of physical factors. They are also not helpful in evaluating the productivity of the entire country. Such methods cannot prove that lagging productivity comes from the misuses of computers in the service sector. Bureaucratization, increased taxes, excessive costs of capital and government regulation can nullify all gains from information technology.

Proxy physical measures such as airline reservations, checking account transactions or occupational ratios cannot capture the rapid shifts in the conduct of business. Without consistency and stability in the measurement methods, productivity comparisons in physical terms lose all meaning.

The definitions and measurement methods currently in use are also inadequate for tracking changes in the structure of the economy. Numbers representing the "services" component of GNP in 1967 are not comparable to those in 1990. Only *Value-added* measures of productivity based on accounting adjustments to the reported profits of firms can serve as the basis for making valid comparisons.

Proposed government measures, such as the frequently mentioned "industrial policy" initiatives, always refer to falling productivity, which comes from questionable productivity statistics. To come up with credible and constructive policy decisions we need to make improvements in how we measure and report business productivity. Legislators need to discriminate between productivity *over-achievers* and *under-achievers* when recommending tax or regulatory measures. National productivity solutions proposed on the basis of problematic averages are not only suspect, but also lead to simplistic policies that are likely to damage *over-achievers* without necessarily aiding the *under-achievers*.

Measurement Reforms

There are suggestions on how to reclassify output. One proposed reform is to establish an "information sector" that would cut across existing Standard Industrial Code categories and include all occupations engaged in the production, storage, retrieval and distribution of information. This sector would include "knowledge workers", such as teachers, engineers, lawyers, journalists and accountants.[16]

Such a move would further confuse our understanding of the value of information-handling activities in the economy. The product of "knowledge workers" has no intrinsic meaning isolated from the delivery of associated goods and services. Separating the costs of "information" from the rest of the economy as a mere accounting device would make GNP-based measures of productivity meaningless. The wages and capital base of "information workers'" must be combined with the costs of non-information workers before assessing any gains with *Value-added* measures.

The economist Juan Rada acknowledges the difficulty of classifying and measuring the "information economy," especially its services component.[17] He suggests a number of alternative approaches, including "...to use value-added, regardless of whether it is obtained by the production of goods, services or a combination of both." Rada, like too few other economists, suspects that measuring *Value-added* would provide the unifying basis for understanding changes in the structure of the economy.

Value-added must become the basis for reporting economic results. *Value-added* productivity will then measure how organizations create wealth for the society. The improved approach should reveal the diversity of the net *Value-added* created by individual firms.[18] In Chapter 7, I have shown how vastly different *over-achievers* are from *under-achievers*. If the measures of performance shape what people will do, then we need to understand how business-level practices deliver superior productivity.

Productivity Comparisons of U.S. vs. Japanese Firms

REVENUE-PER-EMPLOYEE COMPARISONS

Commentators credit the Japanese with a competitive advantage because their ratio of direct to indirect personnel is more favorable than the U.S. ratio. I always examine the ratio of *Operations* to *Management* costs before I analyze a company, although I believe there are problems with personnel ratios that are taken out of context. The definitions and accounting for direct and indirect labor are not comparable because the structure of Japanese companies is different from American companies as I will show below.[19]

The Japanese release little information about their internal costs. In the absence of reliable and comparable data, experts on Japanese productivity resort to quoting comparisons based on *Sales-per-Employee, Workers-per-Car* or similar physical ratios. Such ratios always show that Japanese steel, automobile and electronics industries are superior to those of the U.S. The advantage of such measures is that they are readily available. The disadvantage is that they always are misleading because the Japanese businesses tend to rely on subcontractor and supplier manpower to a much greater extent than U.S. firms. If most of your manpower remains on your supplier's payroll, your revenue per remaining employee always will be very high.

This point shows up in a recent comparison of 20 top U.S. based companies with collective sales of $123.9 billion, and 20 top Japanese electronic companies with collective sales of $118.3 billion.[20] The conclusion was that the Japanese, averaging $267,100 of *Sales-per-Employee*, are vastly more productive than the Americans, with sales averaging only $88,700 per employee. Is the presumed 201% Japanese advantage a meaningful comparison?

CONVENTIONAL AND VALUE-ADDED COMPARISONS

The *Electronic Business* magazine has analyzed the financial statements of the 20 top Japanese electronic firms reported by the Bank of Japan.[21] Based on manufacturing cost ratios, Japanese factories produced less than their U.S. counterparts. Materials and component purchases made up 62% of the cost of sales, whereas for the American firms outside purchases were only 23% of sales. The Japanese rely much more on their suppliers in producing their output. They manage the cooperation from suppliers so that their supply of materials, components and subassemblies is reliable.

Labor cost differentials are not significant. Both countries' labor expenses were similar, 7.2% of sales in the U.S. and 7.8% in Japan. This small difference is not sufficiently important to warrant an exhaustive study of comparative labor costs in the electronic industry, which is a favorite topic for every expert on Japanese productivity. Since the factory throughput for the American electronic firms (defined approximately as revenue minus purchases) is almost three times larger than the throughput for Japanese firms, I could argue that in this case the American industrial worker is vastly more productive than the Japanese worker! Unfortunately, that's not the case because you cannot use any one ratio to make valid conclusions about productivity.

Overhead costs deserve a closer examination. American factory overhead is nearly twice as large as that for the Japanese which suggests that the Japanese may classify as direct labor what the American electronic companies identify as management. American *Selling* and *General and Administrative* costs are three times bigger as compared with Japan's firms. Japanese companies sell much of their output through trading companies, whose costs do not affect the financial statements of the electronic firms.

U.S. taxes are 150% of Japanese taxes. Because U.S. electronic companies add more value in their operations, they end up with larger reported profits. Such superior financial results can occur only if U.S. companies realize better prices for their products. As a result, U.S. companies have a higher *Return-on-Shareholder Equity* (by 4.3%) and enjoy a better *Return-on-Investment* (by 4.2%). Using conventional financial measures, U.S. electronic companies are more productive. Is that correct?

Not exactly. To support operations that have a higher level of vertical integration (e.g., lower outside purchases), the 20 U.S. electronic companies require more capital than their Japanese competitors. U.S. electronic companies use more equity capital to finance their capital needs. I assessed both U.S. and Japanese firms for the cost of using shareholder capital using the procedure outlined in Chapter 5. This analysis shows the Japanese advantage to be decisive. The smaller amount of shareholder capital and their higher debt gave the Japanese a competitive edge, because their cost of capital is less than half of the American cost.[22]

Using the identical data as provided by the *Electronic Business* magazine I recalculated the comparison of the top U.S. and Japanese electronic companies, using *Return-on-Management* as a better measure of comparative productivity:

$ Millions	U.S. Companies	Japanese Companies
Sales	$123,895	$118,291
Purchases	$28,000	$72,867
Operating Costs	$16,974	$7,689
Management Costs	$63,682	$29,809
Taxes	$6,566	$3,785
Net Income	$8,673	$4,140
Capital Value-Added	$9,129	$2,300
Management Value-Added	($456)	$1,840
Return-on-Management	-0.72%	6.17%

Table 18.1: Comparing Productivity for Top Electronic Companies

The Japanese produce a greater amount of *Management Value-added* (after payment for capital) while spending less money on management overhead. Despite their apparent inferiority using conventional U.S. financial measures, the Japanese electronic companies are superior on the basis of *Return-on-Management*.

PRODUCTIVITY COMPARISON METHODS

The U.S. electronic companies' performance relative to the Japanese is unfavorable when using a revenue-based measure of productivity (e.g., *Revenue-per-Employee*). It becomes favorable using conventional methods of financial reporting and then again unfavorable using value-added metrics (e.g., *Return-on-Management*). This illustrates that performance measurements founded on different underlying assumptions do not necessarily yield the same conclusions. Which of these three measures is the most revealing?

During 1985, when the above comparisons apply, the Japanese electronics industry was gaining market share and improving its global position, as the U.S. electronics industry was relatively declining. There is something amiss if one set of measurements indicates superiority and results in large executive bonuses, while another approach signals negative results.

The need to measure macro- or micro-economic productivity is a pragmatic issue. What stimulates management to become more productive gives us more realistic criteria of what to measure than any other approach. It is interesting to note that Japanese companies see productivity reporting measurements more as the means for motivating management and operating personnel than a method for reporting results that are consistent with public accounting practices.

Indicators that guide how people receive their rewards shape how people behave. Simple physical productivity ratios always will be misleading and can lead individuals to counter-productive acts such as meeting unit cost targets while sacrificing product quality. Most current reporting systems compare actual with budgeted amounts that are on the average more than eight months old, which does not motivate quick corrective action. Conventional accounting reports to shareholders take many years to reflect how well an entire organization is competing which lulls management into complacency while they may be losing their competitive position.

To make valid international comparisons among firms that have radically different ways of organizing production and distribution, the only common denominator is management. Management productivity, e.g., management *Value-added*, should supersede conventional physical output ratios or financial accounting measures for tracking business productivity.

INFORMATION TECHNOLOGY AND U.S. PRODUCTIVITY

Steven Roach, a senior economist for the investment firm of Morgan Stanley, has written extensively about the lagging productivity of U.S. information workers and the ineffectiveness of information technology capital.[23] Roach's writings have shaped what is now the generally accepted view that information technology has not made a positive contribution to the U.S. economy, despite its growing importance:[24]

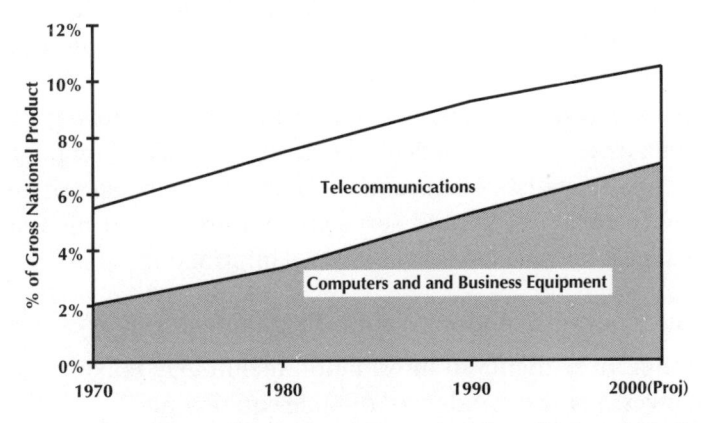

Figure 18.1: Information Technology as % of Gross National Product

448   THE BUSINESS VALUE OF COMPUTERS

Roach compared shifts in U.S. productivity (by major economic sector) with the "relative information technology ratio" (an indicator of the relative importance of information technology):[25]

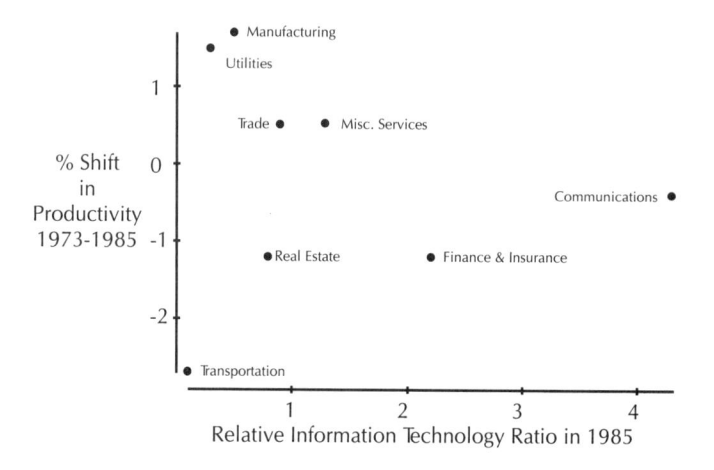

Figure 18.2: Information Technology and Productivity Gains

According to the above pattern there is no correlation. *Communications* and *Finance & Insurance* are profuse users of information technology but showed no improvement in productivity from 1973 through 1985. *Manufacturing* and *Transportation*, which had comparable spending, had widely diverging gains in productivity.

Roach's views about low productivity, particularly in the services sector, have also received much attention. Since 1982, Roach has noted consistently that many of the productivity problems relate to accounting measurements which do not show the full costs of the information technology and do not adequately measure productivity. "...Productivity is the ultimate benchmark by which we must gauge the success of a investment."[26] Roach's conclusions are based on published U.S. government statistics. His caution about the inadequacy of existing productivity measures should serve as a reminder that his findings could change if he had access to additional information.

The Effectiveness of Computer Capital in Manufacturing

Capital investments in information technology make up a large share of investments in producers' durable equipment:[27]

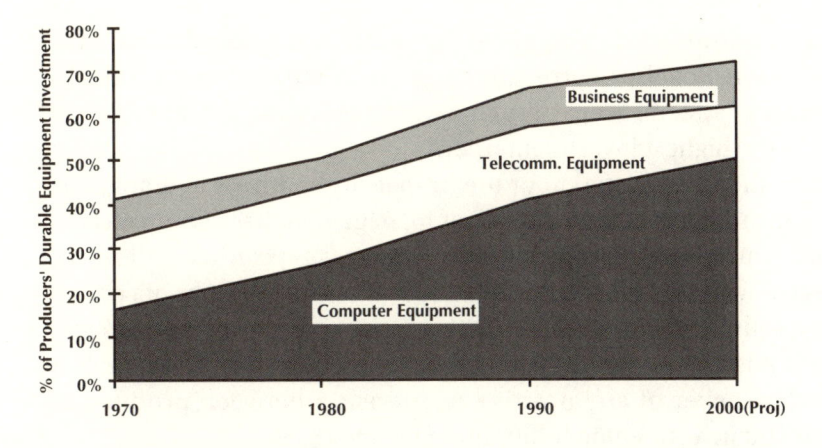

Figure 18.3: Importance of Information Technology Capital

In his comments about falling U.S. competitiveness and dropping market shares Roach is particularly critical of the changing composition of capital expenditures as the rate of growth in capital investment declined. He reports that "...fully 98% of the total rise in manufacturing capital comes from increased outlays on computers, telecommunications equipment and other information technology items."[28] Meanwhile "...the core components of factory capital have gone through an unprecedented period of virtual stagnation." For example, Roach says that early in 1988, information technology capital accounted for 42% of total equipment outlays in the U.S. It was the largest line item in the capital spending budget. About 60% of that amount was spent on computers and office automation.

Roach noted that since 1980, although business fixed investment has risen as a percentage of GNP, the share of the investment committed to the manufacturing sector has actually declined.[29] Roach found that the funds in the manufacturing sector were applied predominantly to replacing of increasingly antiquated equipment rather than for capacity expansion. Whatever overall growth in capital investment has occurred mostly has been due to accelerated spending for computers in the service sector rather than from increased capability to produce manufactured goods.[30] Roach concluded that U.S. firms must improve their capacity to manufacture competitive products.

Roach's critique of the manufacturing sector's spending on computers suggests that management finds it apparently more profitable to invest in administrative applications than in improved production processes. If Roach is correct, it suggests to me that manufacturing information systems were in such a deplorable state that they needed fixing as the highest investment priority.

Another interpretation of the propensity to invest in administrative applications of computers is that management has accepted claims that computers are superior means for increasing control. Just in case you agree with this theory, Roach adds that "...the evidence of computers as a source of improved productivity is not particularly promising. A recent statistical analysis of 60 manufacturing business units reveals no sign whatsoever of any positive relationship between productivity growth and investment in information technologies..."

The Effectiveness of Computer Capital in Services

In the July 1988 Morgan Stanley Economic Letter, Roach pointed out that 80% of total capital investments in the U.S. ($120 billions in 1988, defined in 1982 dollars) were spent in the service sector where computers accounted for 15.5% of total capital:

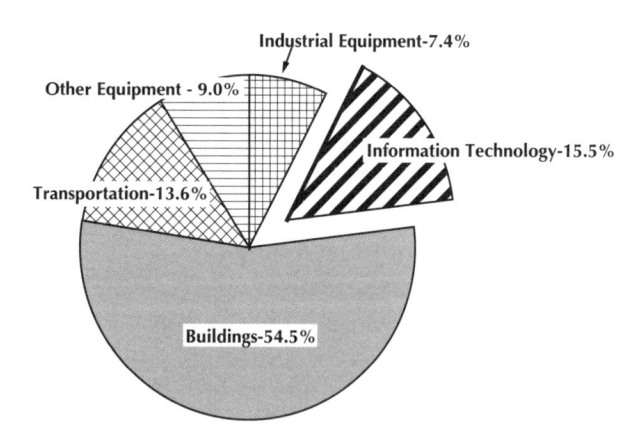

Figure 18.4: Distribution of Capital in the Services Sector

However, the productivity of the service sector as defined by Roach, where information technology purchases dominate, has grown only 0.5%. There is no evidence that information technology improves productivity in the services sector. Roach said "...I dispute the idea that we need ever-increasing computational power to get work done by white-collar workers in the service sector. American business managers are hooked on technology." The lack of productivity gains is particularly noticeable in the finance and insurance sectors which in 1986 spent about 43% of their total new capital spending for computers and office machinery, or $46 billion. Finance and insurance showed a negative productivity growth from 1979 through 1986. The next largest spender on computers – 12% of total spending – has been in the business and personal services which include hotels, health care and recreation. Likewise, this sector also had a poor productivity growth from 1979 through 1986.

Views About Productivity and Computers

Researchers at the Brookings Institute offer a plausible hypothesis of why productivity has not improved, despite the fact that computer equipment has made up 21% of purchases for non-residential durable equipment in 1973 and 44% by 1983. "...It looks as if the administrative bureaucracies have swallowed a large share of total investment without making corresponding improvements."[31]

You will find this point of view in what is perhaps the most influential article that attracted the attention of executives to the lagging contribution of information technology: "...U.S. business has spent hundreds of billions of dollars on computers, but white-collar productivity is no higher than it was in the late 1960's. Getting results usually entails changing the way work is done, and that takes time."[32]

To explore this hypothesis, let us examine the single largest source of information work, the Federal government.

Administrative Effects of Government

When the Government mandates what to do, economic justification becomes meaningless.

THE INTERNAL REVENUE SERVICE

One of the most labor-intensive activities performed in the U.S. involves taxes. To pay taxes you must first learn how to conform to the law, keep records, fill out the forms and mail the statements.[33]

Legislation has mandated that all Federal agencies must show the estimated time it takes someone to fill out their forms. The IRS reported that it would take an average person 9 hours and 5 minutes to fill out the basic income tax form (Form 1040). For supplemental schedules, such as those concerned with capital gains or the sale of property, the time spent on each schedule could range anywhere from 77 minutes to 17 hours and 40 minutes.[34] These time estimates originate from a three-year study conducted by the consulting firm Arthur D. Little for the IRS. The study found that Americans, including individuals and businesses, spend a total of 1.5 billion hours on Federal tax filing. Two-thirds of this burden falls on business.

How much additional time is necessary for State and local tax filing is unknown but it may be a substantial proportion of the time spent on the Federal total. If you make an allowance for other business tax reports that consume an additional 25% of the income tax hours, the total business cost for preparing all tax returns may be about $25–30 billion. That amount is about half of the net income for U.S. industrial corporations. It is also equivalent to 880,000 people doing nothing else for a year except filling out tax returns!

According to a report in the New York Times, businesses spend 3.7 billion hours every year on preparing income taxes.[35] That is equal to 1.5 million employees. On the basis of this estimate I calculated that business compliance with government-mandated tax reporting consumes perhaps as much as 3% of business wage and salary costs. This estimate excludes the wages and perquisites of tax experts and does not include direct expenses, such as computer costs.

It is hard to estimate the overall economic effects of escalating government demand on the costs of information processing. We have only isolated evidence about the costly demands imposed on employers by the regulators. For instance, the Tax Reform Act of 1986 contains a rule requiring corporations to show that health benefits are equitable.[36] Employers must prove that they pass "non-discrimination" tests. This requires complex analysis of personnel and benefits data which is practical only with computers. Large employers may offer more than 100 different benefit plans. For instance, the City of New York examined 7,000 different benefit plans for an additional data processing cost of $400,000.[37]

THE SOCIAL SECURITY ADMINISTRATION

The Social Security Administration requires all employers with more than 250 employees to report wage data electronically. This amounts to approximately 100 million statements per year. The Social Security Administration has benefited by eliminating paper-handling clerical labor. The electronic wage data report (Form W-2) produces estimated savings to the Social Security Administration of about 2 million hours per year, which is equivalent to 1,250 clerical employees or 35 million dollars.[38] The employers' incremental computer costs certainly match or exceed the savings realized by the Social Security Administration.[39]

When a government agency imposes added reporting requirements on business, it rarely finds out what are the employers' full costs of compliance. To illustrate this point I have included a few examples below. When the employer's computer manager needs additional computing equipment, or must allocate programmer's time to meet a new government regulation, economic "justification" is never an issue.

FOOD AND DRUG ADMINISTRATION

Computer executives in pharmaceutical companies have few difficulties in justifying expenditures for computers that support new drug applications (NDA's) to the Food and Drug Administration (FDA). A pharmaceutical company may spend up to 10 years and over $100 million in research on a new drug. A drug can have a revenue potential of billions of dollars. The drug cannot go to market until approved by the FDA, which may take a few years.

The documentation requirements for an NDA are exacting. A recent drug filing consisted of 600 volumes, each 350 pages thick.[40] The company shipped the application by trailer truck. It is no wonder that the pharmaceutical industry has a program to reach agreement with the FDA as to how to handle the massive amounts of data by direct computer transmission. Some companies, such as Syntex, have not waited for a government sanctioned program and have begun keeping their own NDA information on large and costly computer databases.

PENSION ADMINISTRATION

The Employee Retirement Income Security Act (ERISA) sets elaborate rules for managing private pension funds. To comply with ERISA guidelines, "...companies are forking over some $30 billion each year in fees to a growing gaggle of experts, pension fund consultants, brokers, money managers, lawyers and actuaries..."[41] Each of the 870,000 pension funds must keep elaborate records before it can operate legally. Even the smallest corporate pension fund is sufficiently complex to require elaborate computer programs. The total administrative costs of

ERISA, including the employer's costs, are unknown. The current approach to government regulation does not require a "bureaucratic impact statement" before imposing an added information workload on business.[42]

MEDICAL CARE

The entry of government into financing health care has expanded the amount of medical paperwork performed in the U.S. From 1970 to 1986 the number of professional health administrators in the U.S. increased by 400%, not including clerical and secretarial personnel. During the same period, the number of doctors increased by only 50%.[43] The health administrators are essential to managing the personnel and computers that are processing government-mandated documentation of insurance claims.[44]

Legislative Cost-Generation

The real cost of bureaucracy is the damage it does.

New legislation increases the costs of operating businesses if it adds complexity. Alas, legislation that simplifies or eliminates complexity is rare. The amount of legislation seems to be independent of political pronouncements, occurring only at election time, that the new Administration will reduce its regulatory burdens.[45]

When legislation adds to the administrative costs of the government, the additional agency budgets come from taxation. Taxes are involuntary management fees that have precedence over claims from creditors, employees or shareholders.[46] To a factory manager, the overhead cost allocation from corporate headquarters differs little from the tax bill. For both cases, the charges increase the overhead burden. The company recovers increased costs by increasing prices or taking any productivity gains and spending them on administrative costs instead of plant modernization.

The costs of new legislation pass through to the taxpayer, preferably through wealth-producing organizations such as partnerships and corporations. The costs are either in the form of direct taxation or shifting the government's administrative expenses from the government's payroll to an organization's payroll. The latter technique is by far the legislator's and the public's preferred option, because the full costs of government regulations then remain obscure.

CHAPTER 18—COMPUTERS AND NATIONAL PRODUCTIVITY 455

The most extreme example of legislatively-imposed costs is the Federal procurement system.[47] Federal agencies are the nation's largest buyer. They buy $200 billion of equipment and services per year. At current rates, this would be about one fifth of all U.S. purchases for goods and services.

Federal purchasing rules amount to over 45,000 pages and are subject to over 4,000 different laws. Every year, Congress passes additional laws that result in increasing contractors' costs for dealing with the largest customer in the country.

The Defense Department is an extreme case of a procurement process burdened with controls. More than 134,000 of its employees out of a total civilian employment of 1,150,000[48] work on procurement. 26,000 people watch them, which includes 29 Congressional committees, 55 subcommittees and multiple audit staffs to make sure that everyone complies with every procedure. In a typical year, the Defense Department responds to 720,000 inquiries related to procurement matters from Congress.[49] These inquiries must properly fall within the limits set by law and regulations issued by 79 different offices.[50]

Recent Congressional hearings made much fuss about the discovery that a hammer in a maintenance kit was $400. A coffee pot cost $600 and a toilet seat, $800. These numbers may appear to be ridiculous until one considers the vast amounts of bidding, administrative and legal costs involved in getting these items proposed, approved, delivered, explained, audited and paid for.[51] All of these transactions involve substantial amounts of data processing.

Each piece of legislation begets regulations which beget administrative staffs, which beget forms, which beget procedures for supplying information, which beget information systems, which beget computers and copiers, which beget additional legislation to correct the omissions begotten by the original legislation. It also begets legislative and administrative staffs with jobs interest in safeguarding the source of their livelihood.

The Effects of Litigation

The chairman of a large chemical firm told the Conference Board[52] that the company's legal department is the "fastest growing group within the firm." Concerns about product liability complaints have a major impact on a company, regardless of whether or not it loses legal suits. More than 20% of firms polled by the Conference Board believe that they lost market share to foreign competition because of added costs to protect against litigation.[53] Companies are potentially hostages of the courts due to a change in the legal code (e.g., the tort system) in 1965. The legal adversary system, which consumes extraordinarily high costs for lawyers, has now become the ultimate arbiter of whether or not products are fit for public use.

Prior to the 1965 change, an offending company was guilty if someone could demonstrate negligence or lax methods. The complaining party had to prove that the manufacturer was at fault. Under the present system, judges and juries hold the power to decide if a company is liable for any cause of injury. If a product is unsafe for any reason or uses, its maker is at fault. A product is never free of liability, even if it wins case after case. The manufacturer can be sued over and over again. All it takes is to find a single jury that believes that the technical design of a product is unsound. The legal profession has a strong motivation to initiate liability suits because lawyers take 42% of all damage awards.[54]

As a consequence, all businesses now maintain elaborate records of test results to anticipate all conceivable legal challenges. To keep track of such information, companies install database applications which index huge masses of documents, transactions and events. Companies also have invested in elaborate litigation support systems to cope with legal suits. Since jury awards can amount to billions of dollars, even multi-million dollar computer investments get authorized without much hesitation, thus adding to information technology expenses that increase overhead expenses.

The Costs of Variety

Another way of looking at a company's cost structure is to separate costs into two categories: those that respond to volume and those caused by variety.[55]

Operations costs respond to volume and the "learning curve" effects of volume. As the volume of production expands, experience has shown that unit costs decrease by 15% to 25% every time output doubles. This would apply not only to the production of gaskets or electrical motors, but also to office transactions such as invoices and bills of lading. Industrial engineers, financial analysts and accountants expend much effort to make sure that these unit cost reductions materialize.

Conventional accounting systems, especially those that deal with standard unit costs, track costs that respond to volume. Capital investments support these measurable objectives. Textbooks about cost control tend to deal exclusively with linear models of unit costs whose objective is to reduce direct labor costs.

Management costs reflect the cost of business variety, which is synonymous with complexity. Such costs in manufacturing would include manufacturing set-up costs, inventory costs, quality control and expediting costs because management has ordained that the plant will operate with a greater variety of products. In the financial services business the increased costs of variety would include the choices of where to keep your savings. Years ago my bank used to offer only two types of savings accounts. I now can consider at least 25 options before I decide exactly what accounts will serve my needs best.

Management costs also include supervision, engineering, safety, personnel, finance and all sorts of staff experts who justify their presence due to changing work practices. The variety of business activities requires watching, coordination, measurement and correction. As variety increases, so does management complexity. Complexity requires complex systems according to *Ashby's Law*.[56]

While volume-related costs always are watched, the costs of variety get little attention. Overhead costs can increase at a rate of 15% to 25% per unit each time variety doubles. For instance, doubling the number of SKU's (stock-keeping units) will increase administrative and computer costs per SKU because of increasing difficulties in keeping track of choices, avoiding errors and training personnel. Doubling the number of sales territories increases management costs per territory because of increased costs of coordination. Doubling the number of suppliers increases procurement costs per supplier. Doubling employee turnover (e.g., doubling employee variety) will increase employee costs per unit of output.

The growth of variety received attention only recently because conventional accounting systems hid the costs of creeping complexity. Accountants allocate the costs of variety uniformly, based on easily measured volume-related variables, such as direct labor costs. Management, especially staff personnel, favor variety because it makes their coordination roles more important. Complexity calls for more managerial positions which improves the prospects for advancement. Complexity calls for more computer applications, which managers often justify for that reason.[57]

Unless a continuous effort is made to simplify business processes, business productivity will tend to decline. The cost of coordination will exceed whatever additional revenues come from variety. I suspect that the decline of U.S. industry during the 1970's coincides with the proliferation in unmanageable variety. I also suspect that companies have not realized the attainable cost reductions in information technologies because they increased software, database, applications and systems options whenever new choices became available.[58]

The computerization of complexity may be helpful in temporarily restraining the escalation in business costs while keeping existing managerial practices in place. To gain lasting competitive advantages computerization projects should set as an objective the simplification of decision-making. Steady simplification of the decision processes is essential because customers will continue escalating their demands for more sophisticated products and services.

Complexity arises from creeping additions to the variety of products and services. Productivity gains arise from new ideas of how to add to variety while decreasing costs.

COMPUTERS AND THE BUSINESS CYCLE

Computerized inventory management has received much credit for lessening the impact of economic recessions which in the past had an origin in the manufacturing-inventory-sales cycle. Lower inventory levels and the capacity to respond to shifting demand reduced production-based economic oscillations. Can we say that computers have improved the economic stability of post-industrial nations?

Since the 1890's, most of the economic recessions in the U.S. were precipitated from inventory over-accumulations. An "inventory recession" is one of the causes of fluctuating manufacturing output levels. Computer simulations can demonstrate how a recession can arise by perturbing the inventory-manufacturing cycle with only negligible changes in final consumer demand.[59]

I suspect that the diminishing effect of inventories on economic fluctuations would have taken place without computers and other logistic innovations. The cost of carrying manufacturing inventories is now only a small component of the Gross National Product. The "flywheel" effects of inventories are less significant as the manufacturing sector, which carries inventory, has given way to the services sector (now about 78% of GNP), which does not carry inventory. Since we are no longer a predominantly goods-oriented economy, we should not be satisfied that we overcame one of its debilitating diseases.

What is the potential contribution of computers to stabilizing a service-based economy? The bad news is that we now have shifted to something called "debt" as a dominant form of storing up the capacity for consumption. You can stimulate consumer demand through debt because everybody can then afford increasing demand for goods and services. You can shrink the economy when debt accumulation gets out of hand. This occurs when debt repayment exceeds earning capacity, or when interest rates increase to retain foreign loans. Excessive generation of debt beyond the productive capacity to support it creates conditions for squandering resources, as occurred in Latin American economies. This further deteriorates the credit-worthiness of the debtors.

When there is a huge amount of debt, and especially if a large portion of the debt is foreign, computer networks contribute to making this situation inherently unstable. In an industrial economy it took a small inventory adjustment (maybe as little as 2 to 3% of GNP) to cascade an accumulation of unsold goods into plant layoffs, unemployment, deficits and stagnation in consumer demand. Because inventories are physical, it takes a while for the falling demand to ripple through the economy. Therefore, inventory recessions were fairly flat and had a long period of oscillation, something like 2–4 years (from peak to trough and back again).

Today's computer networks have the awesome capacity to move funds and collapse paper valuations of assets with a speed that may approach 10 to 25% of a country's GNP in a few days. What happened in October 1987 could be a preview of what can happen if there is a flight from financial assets in a panic. This can arise if the global financial equilibrium suffers a catastrophic jolt during a period of temporary instability. Examples of such a shock are a major cutoff in supplies of oil or an accident of cataclysmic proportions.

On a computer network, the difference between a million and a billion is just a few electrical changes in voltage. There are already hundreds of autonomous currency and bond traders who can punch these zeros in a matter of seconds. These people have their hands on the economic triggers, the transaction terminals, which are everywhere and are uncontrollable by any government, perhaps not even by their nominal organizations.

Recent economic policies pursued by governments, corporations and individuals over the past twenty years have resulted in an enormous accumulation of debt. This makes our economies more vulnerable to financial instability. It is not possible to predict at what point our global financial dealings could evolve from self-adapting institutions into a condition where a major perturbation precipitates an uncontrollable liquidation of debt.

Rapid feedback by means of computer networks is economically necessary in a society which operates with self-adapting stability. Rapid feedback can also create self-generating and destructive excesses if a society enters the domain where its debt-balancing systems can overreact and panic. Instant-reponse global computer networks can be the source of enormous productivity gains when balancing the supply and demand of goods and services. They can also bring us closer to uncontrollable economic instability because their rapid responses will magnify fluctuations that previously were inherently self-healing.

Computers have helped to solve many of the problems of the industrial economy, such as dampening inventory recessions in the last few decades. We cannot base our expectation of future benefits on solving only old problems. Advanced industrial countries have now entered into a phase of development where global currency trades of $200 billion per day are common. What will happen when our global computer networks become loaded with persistent trillion dollar per day currency transfers is anybody's guess. At that point we would enter the twilight zone where the behavior of financial and government institutions is without precedent. Computers have diminished the reasons for worrying about inventory recessions. The same malady may appear reincarnated in a new and more virulent form as uncontrollable currency transactions over computer networks.

When corporations begin thinking about the long term implications of global computer networks, it may be useful to pause and think about the unforeseen and the uncontrollable. Those will be the challenges for information systems planners who will have to search beyond the boundaries of their firms to anticipate what is presently unthinkable.

CHAPTER SUMMARY

Computers have become a major national asset, and have attracted a disproportionate share of new investments in tools and equipment. I have shown that at the national level the correlation between information technology and productivity, as measured conventionally, is as yet unseen. There are studies that suggest that computers may depress productivity, especially in the service sector. However, these findings may not be sufficiently conclusive because government reporting of national productivity indexes in the services sector may not be trustworthy.

Whether or not computers improve societal productivity relates to the growth of bureaucratic workloads that increasingly depend on computers. Automating bureaucratic activities may be an efficient application of information technologies, but unless deployed wisely may not contribute to delivering *Value added*. Performing unnecessary work faster does not increase the living standards of a country.

When evaluating the contribution of computers to business you must consider the potential effects of international economic relationships. Global financial networks will change the handling of matters that nowadays are only on the agenda of sovereign nations. It would not be the first time in history that inventions originally conceived as solutions to local problems become the means for altering the economic order.

CHAPTER 18 COMMENTS

1 The president of one of the largest packaged foods companies once complained that his sales force manipulated the productivity statistics to their advantage. The company had established equivalent units of sales for its entire product line of over 2000 items and used this composite index for setting sales quotas and awarding bonuses. The "unit of sale" was a half-gallon can of an item on which the firm's Founder built this business over 80 years ago. Neither profit margins nor customer demand patterns related to the standard unit. For instance, the shift to smaller households favored small-size packages, whereas the equivalent units for fractional-weight products did not reflect their greater perceived value. To make the unit sales quota, the sales force frequently compromised profitability and customer satisfaction by pushing "units" instead of profits. This example illustrates how improper measures of productivity can cause people to engage in counter-productive acts because people respond to rewards.

   An extreme example of counterproductive behavior comes from the Russian steel industry, where plant managers get rewards for the thousands of tons of steel pouring out of their furnaces. Sometimes they take a share of their output and just re-melt it to make the quota.

2 Revenue per labor hour or revenue per total cost of inputs is a proxy measure of productivity.

3 Consider the difficulty of evaluating the productivity of a potato grower who is diversifying, as suggested in the *Wall Street Journal* of July 25, 1985:

Bag of potatoes	$0.40/lb
Frozen cottage fries	$0.85/lb
Potatoes au gratin, packaged	$1.93/lb
Giant stuffed potatoes, frozen	$2.13/lb
Au gratin potatoes with herbs, in pouch	$2.88/lb
Gourmet cottage fries, delivered to restaurants	$4.35/lb

4 The American Productivity Center in Houston has promoted several enhancements in the uses of physical Output/Input measures. A "Profitability" index is constructed by multiplying the physical Output/Input ratio by a Unit Price/Unit Cost ratio defined as "price recovery." The Profitability Index is then a composite of four indexes: Quantity Output/Quantity Input multiplied by Unit Price for Output/Unit Price for Input. A base period is defined for each of these factors, and the percentage gains in the cross-multiplied ratios are compared. An excellent case study illustrating this technique as applied to banking is by J.B. Strom, Bank Profitability: A Function of Productivity and Price Recovery, *American Banker*, February 29,

1980. This method will work if the patterns of banking services during the comparison periods remain reasonably comparable. Otherwise, all of the ratios will reflect the bias of the definition for the base period.

5 For one of the most elaborate schemes, see R.D. Banker, S.M. Datar and R.S. Kaplan, Productivity Measurement and Management Accounting, *Journal of Accounting, Auditing and Finance*, 1989, pp. 528–553.

6 The staff in my invoicing operations at Xerox showed large gains in productivity until auditors discovered that they were separating invoices that previously were in the same envelope to save on postage. The measure of output was the envelope count.

7 An excellent summary of the questionable reliability of government-generated national productivity numbers is by L. Mischel, Of Manufacturing Mismeasurement, *The New York Times*, November 27, 1988.

8 That's like equipping airplanes with reliable ways of measuring the distance flown because the altitude is harder to determine.

9 R.J. Gordon, The Postwar Evolution of Computer Prices, *National Bureau of Economic Research*, Working Paper 2227, Table 21. The base reference is the computing power that could be purchased in 1982 for $100. Using technological measures such as MIPS/dollar and memory cost, the identical computing power has the value of $1,264 in 1970, $11,739 in 1960 and $93,046 in 1950. Such adjustments are irrelevant for national productivity purposes. I would not survive a budget review claiming efficiency gain if in 1990 I were able to spend only $100 million for what used to cost a billion dollars ten years before.

10 D. Birch, The Rise and Fall of Everybody, *INC. Magazine*, September 1987, p.18

11 M. Porat, The Information Economy, Ph.D. Dissertation, *Stanford University*, 1976 and S.S. Roach, White-Collar Productivity: A Glimmer of Hope? *Morgan Stanley Special Economic Study*, September 16,1988.

12 Knowledge workers are executives and professionals. Information support workers are technicians, salespersons and administrative personnel, including secretaries.

13 Socialist theoreticians especially are ambivalent about this matter. There are also economic fundamentalists who maintain that unless labor is physically discernible, it is not productive work.

14 Direct purchases of services from the information sector for books, newspapers and entertainment represent only 8% of the consumer budget, according to Charles Jonscher, Models of Economic Organizations, Ph.D. Dissertation, *Harvard University*, Cambridge, Mass., 1980.

15 The earliest reference to a white collar ratio is in Chronicles 2, Chapter 2:2 "...Solomon resolved to build a house...he engaged 70,000 hauliers and 80,000 quarrymen and 3,600 men to superintend them." It would be risky to reconstruct the Temple in contemporary Jerusalem with only a 2.4% overhead allowance.

A contemporary version of the white collar ratios for the U.S. economy comes from *The Bureau of Labor Statistics Publication*, USDL News, January 1990. The following are extracts from the Occupations Status of the Employed Tables (in millions):

Employment Classifications	Jan. 1982	Jan. 1990	Growth
Executives, Managers, Administrators	10,427	14,972	44%
Professional Specialists	12,567	15,852	26%
Technicians and Support Personnel	3,059	3,665	20%
Sales Occupations	10,843	14,293	32%
Administrative Support, Clerical	16,465	18,554	13%
Service Occupations	13,154	15,313	16%
Precision Production, Craft, Repair	11,543	13,462	17%
Operators, Fabricators, Laborers	16,689	17,123	3%
Farming, Forestry, Fishing	3,060	2,803	-8%
Total Employment	97,807	116,037	19%

It shows that Executives, Managers and Administrators grew faster than any other occupational category. This produces the following Supervisor-to-Worker Ratios:

CHAPTER 18 — COMPUTERS AND NATIONAL PRODUCTIVITY

	Jan. 1982	Jan. 1990
Supervisor/Worker Ratio	12%	15%

[16] The idea originates in Marc Porat's monumental doctoral dissertation on The Information Economy, *Stanford University*, 1976 (available from University Microfilms, Ann Arbor, Michigan). Since then a number of researchers have pursued the same thought.

[17] J. Rada, Information Technology and Services, *International Management Institute*, Geneva, Working Paper, January 1986.

[18] Using calculations as outlined in Chapter 5.

[19] T. Miromoto, Another Hidden Edge – Japanese Management Accounting, *Harvard Business Review*, July-August 1988, p.22.

[20] P. Doe, U.S. Versus Japan in The Year of the High Yen, *Electronic Business*, April 1, 1987, p.72. The comparative 1985 *Sales-per-Employee* were:

In $000's	Top U.S. Companies	Top Japanese Co's	Difference
Sales	$124	$118	-5%
Employees	1,397	443	-68%
Sales-per-Employee	$89	$267	201%

Cost analyses show that the large Japanese electronic companies in the sample operate differently from their principal U.S. competitors. Japanese purchases are +173% of U.S. purchases, cost of goods +60%, while overhead is –46%, selling, general and administrative is –65%, taxes –40% and *Return-on-Investment* –40%:

All Costs in % of Sales	Top U.S. Co's	Top Japanese Co's	% Difference
Sales	100.0	100.0	
Purchases	22.6	61.6	+173%
Labor cost	7.2	7.8	+8%
Overhead	18.4	9.9	–46%
Adjustments	0.0	–2.4	
Cost of Goods	48.2	76.9	+60%
Gross Margin	51.8	23.1	–55%
Selling, G&A	25.8	9.0	–65%
Other charges	7.2	8.7	+21%
Overhead Costs	33.0	17.7	–46%
Operating Income	18.8	5.4	–71%
Non-operating costs	6.5	–1.3	–120%
Pre-tax income	12.3	6.7	–46%
Taxes	5.3	3.2	–40%
Net Income	7.0	3.5	–50%
Dividends paid	3.0	0.9	–60%
Return-on-Equity	13.3%	9.0%	–32%
Return-on-Investment	10.6%	6.4%	–40%

[21] P. Doe, U.S. Versus Japan in The Year of the High Yen, *Electronic Business*, April 1, 1987, p.72.

[22] G.N. Hatsopoulos, The High Cost of Capital, *American Business Conference*, 1983

[23] Similar views are in New Technologies in the 1990's – A Socioeconomic Strategy, OECD, Paris, 1989. "...Information Technology has so far failed to provide that major spur to economic growth normally associated with sweeping technological changes."

[24] The Information Technology Industry Data Book, *Computer and Business Equipment Manufacturers Association*, 1990, Table 2-2.

[25] S.S. Roach, Technology and the Services Sector, *Technological Forecasting*, 34:4, 1988

[26] Morgan Stanley Economic Letter, July 1988.

[27] The Information Technology Industry Data Book, *Computer and Business Equipment Manufacturers Association*, 1990, Table 2-4. Producer durables are investments in tools and production equipment. They are perhaps the best indicator of what is important when it comes to equipping the economy.

464   THE BUSINESS VALUE OF COMPUTERS

[28] The following data are from the July 14, 1988 Economic Perspectives published by Morgan Stanley: The business fixed investment, as a share of GNP, has averaged close to 12% since 1980 as compared with 10.8% for the period from 1950 to 1987. The manufacturing share has declined from the average of 45% (for 1950 to 1969) of the total Plant and Equipment Spending, to about 38% (for the period from 1970 through 1987). However, capacity expansion since 1983 has averaged only 5% of the total of manufacturing investment as compared with an average of close to 20% for the period from 1950 through 1980.

[29] The following data are from the July 14, 1988 Economic Perspectives published by Morgan Stanley: The business fixed investment as a share of GNP has averaged close to 12% since 1980 as compared with 10.8% for the period from 1950 to 1987. The manufacturing share has declined from the average (for 1950 to 1969) of 45% of the total Plant and Equipment Spending to about 38% (for the period from 1970 through 1987). However, capacity expansion since 1983 has averaged only 5% of the total of manufacturing investment as compared with an average of close to 20% for the period from 1950 through 1980.

[30] This conclusion is confirmed by C. Jonscher, An Economic Study of the Information Technology Revolution, *Management of the 1990's Working Paper 88-053*, M.I.T., June 1988. Jonscher shows that the ratio of information technology to production technology equipment purchases has continued to increase from 1965 through 1983. All equipment purchases are stated in millions, 1985 dollars:

Year	Production Technology	Information Technology	Information/Production
1965	$60,355	$18,795	31%
1970	$63,449	$28,568	45%
1975	$68,613	$27.434	40%
1980	$96,725	$52,053	54%
1983	$77,221	$61,456	80%

[31] M.N. Baily and A.K. Chakrabarti, Innovation and U.S. Competitiveness, *Brookings Review*, Fall 1985.

[32] W. Bowen, The Puny Payoff from Office Computers, *Fortune*, May 26, 1986, p. 20.

[33] *Insight*, August 22, 1988, p. 46.

[34] The 1.5 billion hours from A.D. Little compare with only 796 million hours previously stated by the IRS. The $27 billion tax-filing cost estimate by A.D. Little is low insofar as it uses average labor costs, whereas tax filing is the work of premium-priced professionals. The cost of computer systems generating supporting data is also not included in either estimate.

[35] The estimate of the billions of hours spent in filling out tax forms comes from J.M. Rosen, Buyout Incentives of '86 Legislation, *New York Times*, January 2, 1989, p.L 30

[36] Legislators offered it as a simplification of the tax system. It is exactly the opposite from a paperwork standpoint.

[37] J. King, Section 89 Taxing Corporate M.I.S., *InformationWeek*, February 13, 1989, p.26. Six additional staff people were hired in the information systems department to design and test new computer applications.

[38] The volume of transactions and the estimated savings for the Social Security Administration were in a *Notice of Policy Guidance* of August 7, 1987 issued by the Office of Management and Budget (OMB), Executive Office of the President. OMB was soliciting comments on the development of a new policy concerning mandatory electronic collection of information by Federal agencies from business organizations.

[39] Assuming that a minimum of 10,000 firms must file Form W-2 electronically, at an annual cost of at least $40,000, it will cost industry a minimum of $400 million to save the Social Security Administration $35 million. The loss in tax revenues to the Federal government will exceed any administrative savings.

[40] S. Kerr, Information Systems: the Best Medicine for Drug Monitoring, *Datamation*, August 1, 1988, p.41, describing a case by Hoffman-La Roche, Inc.

[41] N. J. Perry, Who Runs Your Company Anyway? *Fortune*, September 12, 1988, p.146.

42 Environmentalists have been successful in imposing an "environmental impact statement" on major construction projects. Congress, in the Paperwork Reduction legislation, authorized the Office of Management and Budget (OMB) to approve new government forms only after checking on the amounts of work they create for the people who fill them out. Though this measure is a step in the right direction, it covers only the direct costs of filling out forms. It includes the full cost of compliance with the regulations but not the expense for the systems and procedures necessary to prepare for the submissions.

43 The Paperwork Grows Rapidly, *The New York Times*, February 28, 1990, p.A13. The same article mentions two small-town family doctors who now spend 40% of their time on paperwork. "...They recently bought a $75,000 computer system to handle their insurance forms. It does not eliminate the paperwork, it just makes it neater."

44 S. Marchasin, One Hospital Tells the Cost of Regulation, *Wall Street Journal*, June 26, 1990. Dr. Marchasin shows that from 1966 to 1990, the average number of patients did not change in the Sequoia Hospital in San Francisco. Meanwhile, the major staff increases were as follows: Business Office and Accounting, from 26 to 70, Medical Records, from 17 to 41, Nurses, from 374 to 533. Dr. Marchasin notes that government record-keeping consumes a major portion of the nurses' and physicians' time. Altogether, he estimates that it takes 140 out of 734 full time employees plus four computers to comply with regulations and government directives.

45 The amount of legislation, as measured by the pages per year, seems to grow independently of political persuasion according to *The Economist* (August 8, 1988, p.52). For instance, the Macmillan Conservative government in England (1959 to 1963) averaged 1,250 pages of legislation per year. The Labour government (1974 to 1979) kept the legislation under 2,000 pages per year. Mrs. Thatcher's Conservatives, elected on the platform of reduced role for the government, has averaged from 1979 through 1988 over 2,500 pages per year, with 1985 peaking at 3,200 pages.

46 The record-holder must be the Gosagroprom Agency for Agriculture Management in the USSR, which operates what must be the most ineffective large enterprise in the world. According to the November 21, 1989 *Wall Street Journal*, its instructions pass through thirty-two layers of administration before reaching the local farm organization where nobody pays attention.

47 Procurement regulations at the state level can be equally cumbersome. Early in 1986, I recommended to an institution within a state education department the purchase of a proven software package for on-line student support. There was no disagreement that introducing on-line teaching support in the State was long overdue. The Legislature had set aside money for improving its educational system. Unspent money had accumulated in a special account so there was no question of whether or not funding was available. The first step would be to purchase the software. Procurement paperwork was completed by the end of 1986. At this point, the State General Services Administration decided to solicit competitive bids. A year was spent in satisfying all of the regulations and replying to staff inquiries. The vendor confirmed that he spent more than a manweek in filling out forms and answering the identical questions for each approval level. The state purchased the software early in 1988 and installed it in 1989. By that time, all of the people involved in the 1986 decision had changed jobs and the software had become obsolete. I estimate that the cost of personnel time expended in the procurement exceeded the $18,000 purchase price. This does not include any loss from delaying educational improvements.

48 Department of Defense, Defense 89 Almanac, *American Forces Information Service*, Alexandria, VA, 1989, p.24.

49 N. R. Augustine, Defense: A Case of Too Many Cooks, *Fortune*, Dec. 5, 1988.

50 R. Davis, Convoluted U.S. Purchasing System is Blamed For Bad Habits of the $200 Billion-a-Year Buyer, *The Wall Street Journal*, September 2, 1988, p. 34.

51 The Congressional concerns about the excessive costs of toilet seats do not include accounting for internal Defense Department administrative expenses incurred in buying the $800 toilet seat and responding to Audit inquiries.

[52] The National Industrial Conference Board, New York, an industry organization concerned with management practices.

[53] The U.S. product liability system may aim at greater safety but imposes severe information handling costs, as noted by C. Lockhead, Liability's Creative Clamp Holds Firms to the Status Quo, *Insight,* August 29, 1988, p. 38.

[54] Rand Corporation data showing where money goes from lawsuits is quoted by R. B. Schmitt, Lawyers Face Major Push to Cap Fees, *Wall Street Journal*, August 26, 1988, p.18.

The U.S. has the highest concentration of lawyers among OECD countries, as noted in the *Economist* of August 22, 1987. The per population statistics are per 100,000 people. The U.S. legal profession overwhelms the judicial system, as indicated by the high ratio of lawyers to judges:

Country	Lawyers	Lawyers/Population	Lawyers/Judge
U.S.A.	655,000	279	23.3
Britain	64,100	114	2.3
West Germany	47,300	77	2.8
France	15,800	29	3.6
Japan	13,200	11	5.5

[55] The robotized National Bicycle Industrial Company of Japan, which once offered only 20 to 30 models of bicycles, now reportedly offers as many as 11,231,862 variations. That's variety, according to the article U.S. Brakes the Drive to Set Global Technology Standards, *Insight Magazine*, June 4, 1990, p.36

[56] Ashby's Law is the The Law of Requisite Variety named after Ross Ashby, an English cybernetician. The Law is one of the key principles governing systems design. It means that complexity can be governed only by complex systems of "requisite variety" which means sufficient flexibility to match all conceivable conditions. When management introduces complex organizational forms, produces additional new products or enters into new market segments, there is need for more complex systems. The growth of more elaborate computer programs is one of the manifestations of Ashby's law. The contrast between volume-driven costs and variety-driven costs comes from a discussion (G. Stalk, Time – The Next Source of Competitive Advantage, *Harvard Business Review*, July-August 1988, p.41) about the competitive disadvantages of the U.S. industry.

[57] IBM's manual on Executive Planning for Data Processing (A Business Case for DP Resources, *IBM Canada Publication G5092189*) specifies that companies estimate an increasing "complexity factor" with which to multiply their workload forecast. The "complexity factor" is obtained by asking the managers what they think about their future workload.

[58] Unconstrained decentralization of computing is an example of variety in information technology that is easy to start up but exceedingly costly to maintain. The greater the decentralization, the more important are the standards to guide the distribution of technology.

[59] J.W. Forrester, Industrial Dynamics, *The M.I.T. Press*, 1968 and M.R. Goodman, Study Notes in Systems Dynamics, *Wright-Allen Press*, 1974.

19

FINANCIAL GUIDELINES

Information technology permeates every aspect of a business and therefore only financial policies and methods provide the unifying measure of the dollar to cope with the diversity of its effects. Financial planning and budgeting are therefore the choice tools for dealing with questions that concern the costs and benefits of computers.

REALIZING BUSINESS VALUE

First determine benefits, then costs. Knowing benefits shapes your choices of information technology.

What distinguishes a company with a computer-supported strategic advantage from others without such an advantage who also have computers, access to the identical networks and use identical applications? The more productive companies do not spend more money on information technology than their competitors. Few companies have a decisive advantage because they possess unique information management technologies. "Productivity" and "strategic advantage" arises by adding other ingredients of success.

What do we know about success patterns in the use of information technologies? Why is it that after thirty years of intensive computerization, the productivity of the U.S. information workforce, using existing measures, has not shown much improvement? Why is it that polls of executives consistently show their strong belief in the powers of computers while they are not sure if they get a satisfactory return on their investments?

Conventional methods for justifying capital equipment purchases are not applicable to computers because they are unlike any other machine. When you buy a drill press, your industrial engineer can measure all costs, production volumes and direct profit contributions before and after installation. Management information systems rarely make a direct profit contribution. Computers, like blood vessels, are an essential part of the information flows[1] that affect every management function.

It is not possible to separate the contribution of computers from a company's marketing methods, the way it manages production and how it services its customers. To achieve superior productivity and a strategic advantage, computers need to support superior management processes. Spending more money and using the most sophisticated technology to do the wrong things faster won't generate any improvement.

To understand how information systems achieve their advantages, you must learn to identify opportunities, manage the benefits and measure patterns of success. Financial planning and evaluation techniques provide the key to managing the business value of computers.

How to Manage Computer Opportunities

*You do not know for sure who won or who lost unless
you also know how the score was kept.*

A useful way to view the benefits of computers relates to the time it takes to overcome difficulties. I use the following grid in my lectures to describe the relationship between difficulty and the time it takes to find out if you made the right decision:

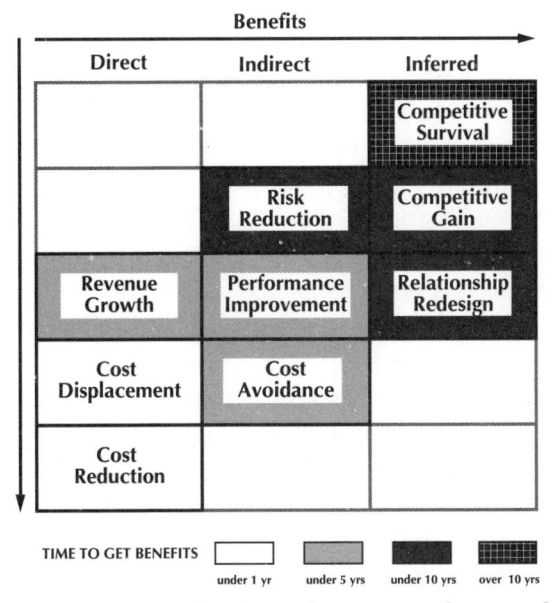

Figure 19.1: The Difficulty and Time to Realize Benefits

The easiest benefits are in direct cost-reductions which are immediate. The most difficult—and the largest—benefits apply to competitive survival. It may take decades before you can find out if information technology investments have secured this objective.

Direct Benefits

COST REDUCTION

Cost reduction is a short cut to increasing *Operating* productivity. It is easy to conceive and explain, and unambiguous to evaluate. For example, entering "on-line" orders from salespeople to central sales administration simplifies the materials ordering cycle. This eliminates re-entering data which should immediately show up as lower overhead expense.

The effects of cost reductions are measurable. These benefits are clear and their effects on the organization are easily seen. Using conventional techniques, you can find out what you are getting for the computer investment. Accounting reports will show if the administrative costs are down.

You should reduce the operating budget immediately by the amounts promised in a cost-reduction proposal. The next financial report will compare budget versus actual costs and will tell you if you are getting the expected results.

COST DISPLACEMENT

Cost displacement is the preferred method to simplify a business process through work-enlargement using computers. It is simple to do, especially if employees have the motivation to develop their talents. For example, in the traditional approach sales personnel transmit orders to central sales administration. The staff performs editing, checking credit, scheduling shipments and a variety of sales accounting tasks. Cost displacement makes it possible for the order to go directly to the plant. You eliminate administrative personnel but shift complex administrative tasks to the salesperson.

On balance, total costs should come down after allowing for a period of adjustment. I have difficulties with computer proposals that claim cost displacement benefits. I am never sure that I get a complete story that takes gains in one part of the company and offsetts them against expenses elsewhere.

Increasing some budget items and decreasing others to the net amount promised in the cost-displacement proposal is necessary to assure a sound business plan.

REVENUE GROWTH

Revenue growth is always an attractive approach because its benefits are direct, measurable and appealing to everyone.

For example, a salesperson can deliver additional products and services to a customer using computer-generated text for inclusion in a proposal. The computer helps the salesperson respond to customer requests for earlier and confirmed delivery dates. Company revenues will most likely increase and salesforce productivity will rise although it will take considerable time to upgrade the skills of the salesforce.

For success, revenue-enhancement projects depend on choosing the appropriate motivation for the people who use the computer-aided support tools. They also require superior training and avoidance of organizational conflict.

Whenever you see revenue-enhancement as the justification for further computer investments, you should examine the logic of such claims because they usually suffer from over-attribution of benefits.[2] For example, serving a new sales territory that generates $10 million of additional sales would give you only a small fraction of the $10 million as a net benefit. That would be the difference between the cost of supporting the added revenue with or without the funding of your proposal.

Make sure that computers offer the means for increasing gross profit margins as compared with other methods that can achieve the identical objective for less money. A revised departmental budget and a new sales plan that locks in the promised revenue gains will allow you to track the results.

Indirect Benefits

COST AVOIDANCE

It is not easy to identify and measure cost avoidance, because someone will always question why there are excess costs to begin with. For example, damaged goods and warranty claims decrease profits. Speeding up the ordering, manufacturing and delivery cycle lowers the risk of customer claims. Access to a comprehensive computer database by operating personnel diminishes the chance of disputes because it offers an opportunity to revise incorrect or inconsistent data about a customer order. However, these are only remedial measures that do not deal with the cause of the problems.

Cost avoidance is not a benefit unless every other conceivable improvement does not deliver the same or greater gains. A computer proposal that claims cost avoidance must show that an operation can not achieve comparable improvements by other means. There are many simple solutions which do not require the use of information technology. For example, I find the justification of video-conferencing a questionable solution to escalating travel expenses. You would have to demonstrate why you need big crowds of managers attending numerous meetings in the first place.

Steadily decreasing real costs over a period of several years will provide indirect evidence that an organization actively pursued cost avoidance.

PERFORMANCE IMPROVEMENT

The continuous evaluation of performance improvements will force a company to use its financial planning system to examine alternative options as to how to conduct its business.

For example, reducing delivery lead-time by means of computerized monitoring offers a way to serve customers who do not wish to stock all of your items at their plants. This is a powerful advantage when the customer's own schedules depend on your ability to react to changes.

I have witnessed many captivating presentations backing up multi-million computer projects to improve customer service. Colorful charts explain the new system and list dozens of reasons why the firm would realize inestimable performance improvements. After sober reflection I find that the only hard numbers given are the expenses. Benefits are usually unsupported promises which should never be a sufficient reason to spend money on information technology.

A plant manager should find it easy to prove approximate dollar benefits of a computer system that reduces his delivery lead-time. For financial justification he would have to demonstrate, on the basis of a statistically valid sample, what revenues were lost from dissatisfied customers.

Improving performance is always desirable. However, you should insist on justification of the additional expenses, because you may be taking funds away from more profitable investments. Performance improvements are measurable only indirectly as long term gains. You do not revert an essential operation to the old ways of doing things just to verify that performance would decline.

RISK REDUCTION

The toughest, most profitable and hotly argued computer investment proposals concern risk-reduction benefits that are inferred but never appear explicitly on any financial statements. Not losing customers, gaining on existing competitors and the ability to avoid damage are some of the risk-reduction results in which information systems play an increasingly important role. The real issue is the price you can afford to pay for reducing your risks. There is more to be gained from doing the job of serving the customer better than nibbling away at costs.

Unreliable performance characteristics, unpredictable quality and erratic deliveries cause losses. Information systems make it possible to produce and deliver goods and services with much closer conformity to the customer's expectations.

Risk reduction is an intangible benefit to the customer. It is usually present where customers are willing to pay additional premiums for a more reliable product or service. Risk reduction is also profitable when you cannot get insurance coverage for a reasonable policy premium to protect you. Risk reduction decisions are routine whenever managers must decide how many insurance policies they can afford to protect their business.

Unfortunately, the claimants for added risk-reduction investments do not apply the same logic to computers as to insurance coverage. The choices are similar because they require assigning probabilities and costs to unlikely events. When a manager proposes a $100,000 computer investment to protect against a $1 million error it will make a difference if the probability of the error is 1/100th, 1/1,000th or one chance in a million over a period of ten years.

To evaluate risk-reduction management must set up non-financial quality indicators, such as customer attrition rates, frequency of warranty claims, number of legal claims or any other measure that reflects the unique circumstances when risk affects profits.

Risk-reduction decisions are always *a priori* [3] estimates whereas penalties are always *a posteriori* [4] damage. Make sure that the justification of information technology investments does not mix up these fundamentally different forms of logic. I find that confusion arises frequently, especially if managers are looking for an easy proof that they applied with due diligence the most modern methods to protect against risks.

HOW TO MEASURE THE RESULTS OF INDIRECT BENEFITS

Cost avoidance, performance improvement and risk reduction can deliver large improvements in profit margins, revenue growth or better prices. The potential effects of such changes on profits can be very large though they are impossible to prove through conventional cost accounting methods in most instances. Executives can find out how much they might get for their computer investments by comparing plans that do or do not make use of computers.[5]

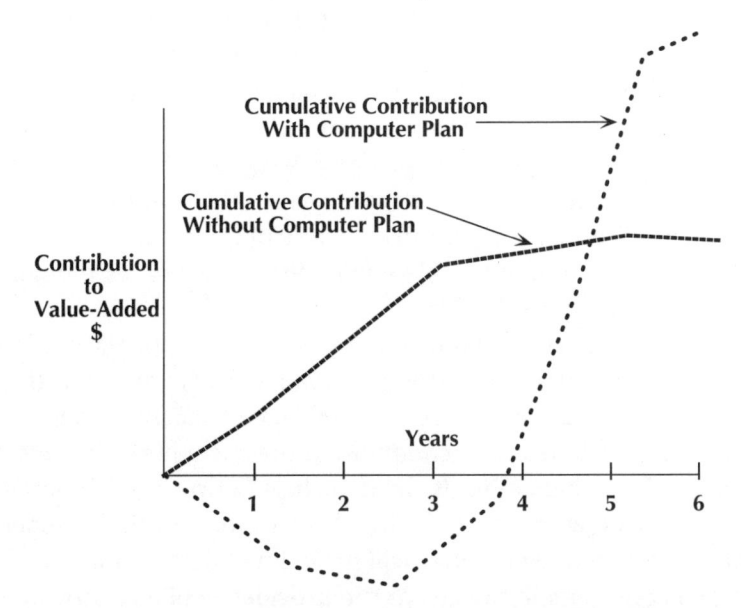

Figure 19.2: How to Evaluate Indirect Benefits of Computers

Such evaluations occur only while a plan is under examination and before plan execution begins. Once the plan is in effect, the best you can hope for is that actual results will track the planned solutions at every step.

There can be dozens of reasons why plans are either under-achieved or over-achieved. In case of a missing accomplishment, the cause should not be a failure in information systems. The measurement of indirect results from information technology is feasible only if the plan has well-articulated performance goals. The best way to evaluate the indirect contribution of information technology is to monitor those indicators that were defined in the plan such as completion of program milestones, cumulative expenses, delivery schedules, user satisfaction, error rates and unit operating costs. The plan should also state at what level a deterioration in indicators will cause either replanning or abortion of a project.

Inferred Benefits

> *"Intangibles" is a label for ignorance of causes.*

RELATIONSHIP REDESIGN

Relationship redesign calls for rethinking the traditional roles held by suppliers, producers, channels of distribution and customers.

For example, direct communication between suppliers and customers eliminates distribution and service intermediaries. On-line diagnostics, automatic reordering from the factory and tight cooperation in activities ranging from product design to equipment maintenance permit a new form of organization: the computer-coupled multi-firm alliance. This approach to organization can preserve entrepreneurial autonomy while linking firms together as though they were a part of the same organization.

Relationship redesign does not apply only to suppliers and distributors. It can reach into the customer's own habits. For example, the premium prices charged by food companies for convenience foods depend entirely on the laborsaving economics in the customer's kitchens. Very soon we will see changes in the relationships between professional services, such as law, finance, health, education, and their respective clients. Information technology will make it possible to offer these services at a considerable savings to the providers while improving their clients' convenience in access to these services.

The favorable effects of redesigning organizations for closer coupling through computer networks arise from a steady and long-term increase in the *Value-added* created by a firm. The successful firm will be able to deliver products and services which incorporate *Value-added* contributions that previously were in somebody else's costs. It may take more than a decade before this effect shows up as favorable financial results. Meanwhile, your firm should watch out not only for obsolescence of its products or services, but also for its possible displacement from the *Value-added* chain. The threats from relationship redesign are subtle and easily overlooked. It's not the threat that you know that is your challenge, but the threat you do not suspect that may displace you altogether.

Financial management should watch the economics of alternative delivery methods for current premium-priced services. For example, small banks earn substantial fees charging merchants for cashing credit-card transactions. This business is not profitable for most banks because of labor-intensive paper handling, credit risks and large investments in data processing. Recently, data processing companies entered into the specialized business of handling the merchants' credit-card transactions by connecting to cash registers in each store. The specialized data processing services enjoy a cost advantage over the bank's services.[6]

It is only a matter of time when small banks will not be able to compete in the business of processing merchants' credit cards unless they discover new ways to add value. Astute financial management will be alert to this situation and keep track of the gap between their own and the specialists' costs. They shall then know when either to quit or to change their relationships.

COMPETITIVE GAINS

Even the longest staircase is built one step at a time.

Improving a firm's market share is the consequence of balancing short-term profitability against long-term growth. Short-term profits come from direct and indirect benefits whereas long-term growth comes from competitive gains. You may attribute competitive gains to computers only after you have accounted for the direct and indirect benefits.

For example, every writer cites American Airlines' highly profitable SABRE reservation system as an example of competitive gains that arose from a clever strategic investment. I think such a conclusion is unfair to American Airlines as well as to its competitors. Others such as United,

Eastern and PanAm, made comparable long-term investments in reservation systems. However, American Airlines has an enviable and consistent record of vigorously pursuing simultaneous incremental improvements that deliver a steady stream of direct and indirect benefits.

Competitive gains are the result of a long sequence of well-conceived and competently implemented activities. There's no instance when a single computer application or technology has delivered a measurable increase in a firm's market share without other favorable factors also being present.

Grandiose designs are helpful to set the overall directions for gaining a competitive advantage. However, actual competitive gains arise from superb delivery of direct and indirect results, one at a time. Be distrustful of information technology proposals that claim to deliver competitive gains in the indefinite future, unless they also show how they will show tactical results at each milestone event.

To evaluate competitive gains requires meticulous research of the reasons why you lose existing customers, gain new customers from your competitors, and why the competitors' customers remain where they are. Such research must also show if your information technology makes a difference as you proceed. On the road to competitive gains, each of these measures should tell you whether you are losing or winning so that your overall design reflects reality instead of inspired hope. Information technology that does not create a measurable difference is indifferent and therefore has no value.

COMPETITIVE SURVIVAL

Competitive survival concerns defensive measures you must take when your competitors use information technology to innovate their products and services. Your best-conceived plans to achieve cost reduction, cost avoidance, performance improvement or risk reduction will lose their value if a competitor moves faster than you. In such a case you may carry all the burdens of computerization and receive few of the benefits. Much of the occasional frenzy to buy technology without a definite plan stems from a fear of falling behind others who may change the competitive rules.

To manage competitive survival requires investment in competitive intelligence so that you know what your competitors are doing with their computers and telecommunications.[7] You must also acquire a realistic understanding of the competitors' options and likely moves.

Good intelligence reduces the risk of spending scarce resources on poor and hasty projects. Good intelligence saves you from chasing improbable scenarios that frequently capture management attention.[8] The greatest advantage to competitive intelligence comes from learning about somebody else's mistakes. The benefit of learning what does not work is inestimable. You save money while the competitor expends scarce resources on projects that will produce no useful results.

Competitive intelligence allows you to invest only minimal funds in getting ready for rapid counter-action whenever that becomes necessary. You conserve cash while waiting for an opportunity to introduce new products and services faster and better than your competitor. The benefit of competing in a market where you can set the rules because of your early entry is inestimable.

Regrettably, corporate management does not spend sufficient time on obtaining information to form a realistic assessment of the competitors' capabilities to exploit innovative information technology. In the absence of an independent effort a corporation may fall prey to sources that have a vested interest in increasing spending on computers regardless of benefits.

Is it expensive to obtain competitive intelligence? I do not think so. Magazine articles, advertisements, employment interviews and trade conventions offer more information than you can possibly use. The problem with competitive intelligence is not acquiring it but storing it for easy retrieval. Do not accept an investment proposal claiming competitive survival as one of the "intangible" justifications for a new computer system unless it is supported by reliable data about your competitors' improved profitability. There is no point to investing in computer applications that will lower everybody's profits.

HOW TO EVALUATE THE RESULTS OF INFERRED BENEFITS

The greatest challenge to managing information technology is in solving problems posed by relationship redesign, competitive gains and competitive survival. The payoff from investments in these solutions will appear only after five to ten years. Organizational stability is another way to define the meaning of "inferred benefits." You will have to treat all commitments beyond two years as "inferred," in case your key operating executives change jobs every other year.

The contributory role of computers to success will be confounded with all other factors, because simultaneous changes will wipe out the financial traces that link original proposals to current operating results.[9]

How do you spend scarce funds today on benefits that may not show up for years to come, or not at all if conditions change? Computer investments are no different from other long-term business bets, such as new product development, a new plant, hiring promising talent or entering new markets. To invest intelligently you should remember the following rules:
- All large gains result from a bet with poor odds;
- All extraordinary predictions about the future are potentially wrong.

The evaluation of inferred benefits is largely a matter of risk assessment and risk minimizing before you commit large sums of money. There is no redesign, competitive gain or competitive survival application that cannot be subjected to small-scale testing prior to full implementation. At all times you should avoid an after-the-fact measurement dispute by documenting a before-the-fact assessment of your chances. Pilot installations, simulated environments, learning from the failures and phased installation are a few worthy practices.

Every top business executive must learn to make carefully hedged bets when investing in computer applications that have only inferred benefits. When in a fog, you had better drive slowly.

On Planning Methods

A microscope cannot do the job of a telescope.

The ability to judge the results of an investment in computers varies widely according to the project's difficulty, complexity and time span for implementation. If a cost-reduction project takes a few weeks to install and has a one-year break-even expectation it you can evaluate it by a simple cost/benefit comparison. The results from investments in computer technologies that assure long-term competitive survival may not be evident for decades to come. Challenges from existing or new competitors will largely shape the outcome. Scenario simulation methods offer one means to indicate potential investment payoffs and risks.[10]

Inbetween simple cost/benefit ratios and sophisticated scenario simulation models there is a wide range of planning methods available. They can be applied appropriately, according to the complexity of the project and preferences of management.[11] I have used the following descriptive grid in executive tutorials to explain the variety of choices available :

CHAPTER 19 — FINANCIAL GUIDELINES 479

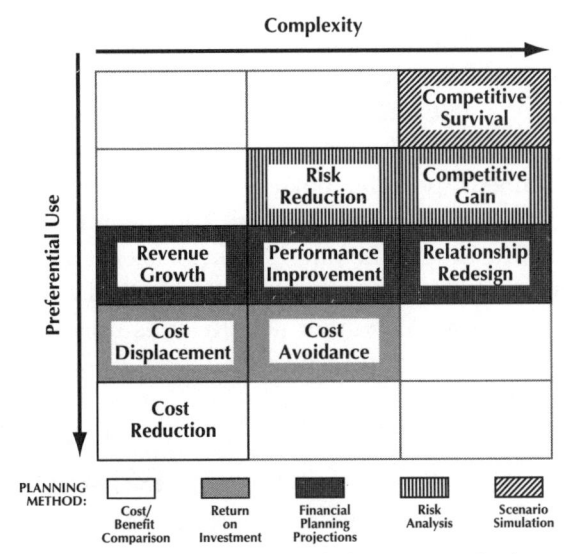

Figure 19.3: The Variety of Planning Methods

For example, conventional *Return-on-Investment* calculations work reasonably well in cost-displacement or cost-avoidance projects especially if industrial engineering techniques are used to prepare the cost and benefit estimates. The net present value (NPV) calculations of revenue-growth, performance improvement or relationship redesign opportunities may be evaluated by means of financial planning models.[12] Essentially, these are variations of ordinary spread-sheets, with special features to document planning assumptions and allow consolidation of detailed plans into a corporate aggregate. Advanced methods include elaborate tables with equations that relate revenues to volume, prices and costs. Changes due to any factor become reflected in a single measure of economic value such as discounted present value of future cash flows.

As was pointed out in Chapter 9, all major computer projects are uncertain and hard to evaluate, especially if their outcomes call for risk reduction and competitive gains. Formal techniques of risk analysis offer a planning methodology that can keep up with the lengthy computations necessary to explore the entire range of possible payoffs.

I usually recommend to clients to settle on a few planning methods and then use them in combination as conditions warrant. For example, in Chapter 10 I describe a case where *Value-added* analysis was used for strategic diagnosis, simulation analysis for an examination of alternatives, risk analysis for finding the easiest implementation and a proprietary financial planning model for calculating the shareholder value. It is the job of the chief financial officer to ensure that the organization has an adequate analytic tool-kit to cope with information technology investments. It is also his job to make sure that management has sufficient training to apply the tools.

Which financial planning and evaluation techniques are the most popular? Not surprisingly, the ones that are easiest to understand. That explains why cost reduction, cost displacement and cost avoidance are the benefits which management usually ends up getting from their investments in information technology. You can only expect to find what you are looking for.[13]

PLANNING AND BUDGETING FOR COMPUTER OPPORTUNITIES

It takes different time-horizons to realize different types of benefits from information technology investments. You need to know how much of it is in *Operating Expenses* (e.g., this year's expenditures for this year's results), *Development Expenses* (e.g., this year's expenditures for direct or indirect benefits beyond this year) and *Strategic Expenses* (e.g., this year's expenditures for inferred future benefits).[14]

OPERATING EXPENSE BUDGETING

The annual *Operating Expense Budget* should list detailed operating cost reduction objectives, unit cost indicators, productivity targets and revenue quotas that relate to any approved computer plans.[15]

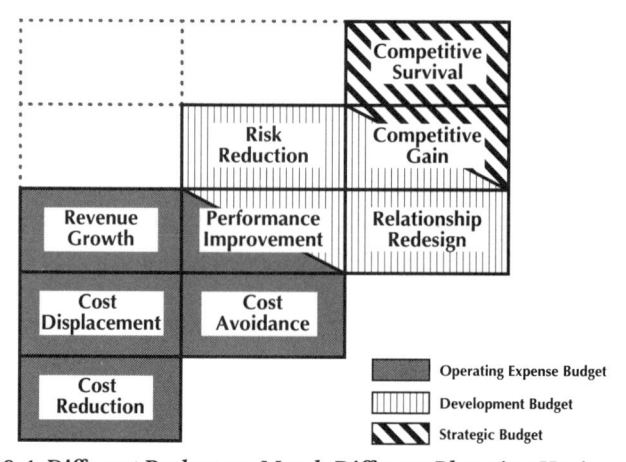

Figure 19.4: Different Budgets to Match Different Planning Horizons

Do not allocate the entire annual budget exclusively to operating, maintenance, cost reduction, cost displacement, cost avoidance and revenue enhancement projects. Companies that spend all information technology funds as operating expenses are liquidating their potential to make major improvements in information management practices.

DEVELOPMENT BUDGETING AND PLANNING

Revenue growth, cost avoidance and performance improvements should be an integral part of the business plan for an operating unit.[16] Usually, this calls for multi-year funding. Instead of using the annual operating budget the profit center's 3 to 5 year plan is the right vehicle for funding multi-year development programs. The General Manager of the profit center should request and manage the long-term development funds. The General Manager should be also accountable for delivering results that are as good as, or better than, the original promises.

STRATEGIC BUDGETING

The short- and medium-term focus of *Operating* and *Development* budgets has the disadvantage of creating enclaves of incompatible data formats and incompatible networks. All organizations eventually will make radical changes in how they organize their people and how they arrange information flows internally as well as externally.

My experiences suggest that large service companies currently go through major organizational upheavals every three to five years. Large manufacturing companies reorganize every five to seven years, and even government agencies and public utilities can expect major restructuring at least each decade. My colleagues tell me that the rate of organizational instability is increasing, which makes my estimates of reorganization frequency low.

Organizations will suffer from diminished flexibility and increasing expenses during each restructuring unless they share a commonality in data, program documentation, communication protocols and systems engineering. Therefore, every organization must set aside special funds for the protection of company-specific systems and data. It is necessary to subsidize the adoption of data-definition standards, operating systems compatibility and shared telecommunications links. These funds should be a part of the *Strategic* budget.

Operating and *Development* budgets should fund the implementation of standard databases and standard networks as the needs justify it. That may take as much as ten years to accomplish. However, during the transition, standardization efforts require strong central direction, supported by consistent and uninterrupted strategic funding. The strategic budget must cover the costs of developing and maintaining systems management methods such as data modeling, network directories and systems engineering tools that enforce the standards.

How to attain competitive gains should be the concern of those executives whose job is to have a planning horizon that extends well beyond the usual five-year plans. Unless a company is poor, a percentage of the total systems expenses in any year should be available for systems projects which do not have any readily apparent payoffs. Such investments should have the characteristics of acceptably large risks combined with a well articulated scenario of enormous potential gains in the long run.[17]

Every organization must also have long-term funding to support policy formulation, intelligence-gathering, competitive evaluation and auditing of systems during and after systems installation. This is why intelligence-gathering, executive training, the development of technical personnel and independent systems audits[18] must remain a strategically-funded activity.

Budgeting Methods		
Operating	Development	Strategic
		Data Base Standards
	Company-wide Applications	Operating Systems
Overhead Reduction	Multi-function Applications	Network Design
Lease Cancellation	Application Tasks	
Reducing Variable Cost		

PLANNING HORIZON: Under 1 yr — Under 5 yrs — Under 10 yrs — Over 10 yrs

Rise in Expenditures →

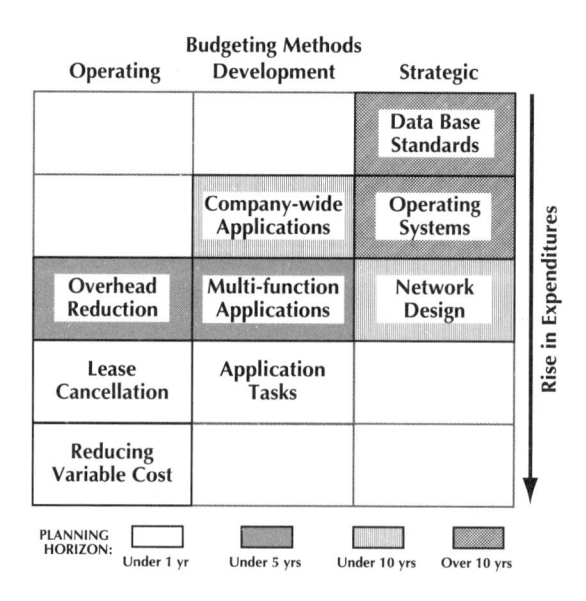

Figure 19.5: Budget Methods to Match Technological Lead Time

Matching of budgeting processes to the expected technological lead times clarifies how to fund computer technology. The funding of technology should remain in the *Operating* or *Development* budgets as long as computer applications meet a firm's policy and technical standards. Everything else should be in the *Strategic* budget, as outlined in the above figure which is a succinct way of explaining the scope of budget methods. The diagram also suggests that as you shift from *Strategic* to *Operating* budgets, the expenditures should rise.

MAKE VS. BUY DECISIONS

The use of packaged software has grown dramatically. Although in 1983 only 23% of major applications came from purchased software, that number was 44% in 1988.[19]

Rapid changes in technology and user needs will make it uneconomic to design and program custom-made systems for applications which are already available in the marketplace. The time period for the development and implementation of a totally customized major new application[20] is now in the three- to five-year range. The current rate of major corporate reorganizations is such that residual values of some applications programs after seven years are questionable for unstable companies. Therefore, the economics increasingly favors buying software, modifying it, and if necessary, changing unimportant company procedures to fit the available software features. The expanding software supply offers a sufficient variety of choices so that it can offer options that meet an enormous range of business needs.[21]

The advantage of purchased software is that it offers immediate results without the delay of long-term development, provided you do not get tangled up in elaborate modifications. By bringing in packaged solutions the internal system organizations may be able to reassert their credibility as the source that can deliver rapid results. When you buy packaged software from an experienced source, it is likely to be more cost-effective, timely and technically complete than that which you can expect to get from a custom-tailored solution.[22]

Software maintenance expenses over the life of a unique application can easily exceed the initial development expense by a multiple, which may be as high as ten. The software vendor will also incur large maintenance costs. However, because the vendor pools requests for improvements and features from all customers, the buyer of a software package should end up paying only a fair share of total maintenance and enhancement expenses.

The choice of designing your own unique applications or purchasing a standard software package is not an either/or proposition. Even if you decide to develop your own programs, there are many components (such as database software, report-generation utilities) that you should always buy ready-made. The real issue is how much of the code that will end up in your computer will be hand-crafted by your staff. A related issue is to what extent will you depend on software maintenance from suppliers.

You may find applications in your firm that have hundreds of thousands of lines of code (in addition to the manufacturer-supplied operating system), of which your own people wrote only 20,000 lines. The rest of the code came from several software vendors whose applications were stitched together by your systems integration staff. The integration of computer programs which originate from several sources, each pursuing different programming and operating standards, introduces a further risk.

Clearly, the decision to buy or build a system is not just a matter of initial cost and life-cycle maintenance expense. Uncertainty about your organization's ability to manage diverse software packages as an integrated whole should influence your cost projections. The lesson to remember is: never make the build versus buy decision on the sole basis of the initial project costs. For each software purchase, you should assess the long range costs of integrating it with all of the other software. Software errors in tightly integrated applications that consist of dozens of software packages are likely to cascade into system-wide failures. Complex systems that include even one unreliable software package will crash. If your staff cannot test the reliability of applications made up of programs from diverse sources, you should buy a complete system that offers performance warranties with penalties.

Future developments will favor the delivery of integrated computer services to replace company-made software as well as patched together purchased software. Your build versus buy financial criteria should therefore include the engagement of computer services as an alternative to do your work.

On Financial Justification

You can make only today's decisions.

A rigorous financial justification must support all requests to spend money for information technology. The decisive moment is when you sign an authorization for those expenditures. A project is headed for failure if the financial justification is incomplete, vague, misleading or erroneous. The quality of the financial justification therefore deserves greater attention than any other aspect of a proposal.[23]

The following checklist applies to all financial justification of information technology projects:

- The project makes superior use of company funds. The investment is at least as attractive as any alternative uses of funds, after an allowance for risk.
- The proposal includes a situation analysis which defines the specific conditions that it will measurably improve.
- The justification is credible. Prior comparable expenditures have delivered actual results that, on the average, met expectations.
- Financial evaluations project cash flow and do not necessarily follow accounting conventions. The financial payoff calculations show the risk-adjusted discounted present worth of cash flow for the expected life of the project plus any residual value.
- The financial outcome is measurable. The justification includes measurable success criteria which may include credible proxy indicators.
- The proposal describes the hierarchy of accountability for results. It specifies which individuals have accountability for the results.
- The proposal includes a contingency plan. The justification highlights events and circumstances that would invalidate the current proposal, and states what would require re-authorization. It also includes a scenario for the worst-case outcome.
- The financial justification ties into the financial plan. The

financial documentation shows how costs and benefits affect current financial projections. It also shows what would be the financial plan in case you decide not to proceed.
- The financial forecasts are subject to audit. There is an audit trail for independent auditors.
- The financial justification does not depend on unquantifiable benefits to make its case.

Use the above check-list to confirm that you have an acceptable proposal before investing in computers.

Controlling Systems Design

An executive cannot completely delegate systems design to the technical staff or a vendor. You must continually assert the dominance of operating financial results above technical considerations.[24] For example, you may want to specify that you need to reduce the order-to-delivery cycle by four weeks while reducing administrative expenses by 15%. Such a statement would make goals unambiguous to everyone and would allow for considerable freedom in the choice of technologies. If the results can be readily and efficiently accomplished with proven technologies then you should not allow the technical staff's enthusiasm for a new computer to sway their decisions.

Definitive Methods—Design First

One traditional approach to controlling systems design is "phased program" management, which usually consists of anywhere from four to seven distinct phases.[25] In the first two phases, your systems development team prepares detailed specifications using a variety of highly formalized techniques. In this process the system is defined in detail, often including report formats. At the end of the second phase of this planning effort the software, hardware and communications specifications are substantially complete.

The system now will have a well-defined design and be ready for implementation. However, your design team cannot assure you that you will meet your financial objectives. This is because what you have seems to be perfectly functional, but only on paper. The theoretical design is nothing but a claim that it will produce the expected results if everything works as planned. Nothing ever works as planned, even under ideal conditions.[26]

If your design team made an error by oversight or through insufficient understanding of the business dynamics, the design will suffer from fundamental faults that will guarantee that you miss your objectives. By committing to the overall design too soon, your systems designers can easily lock you into an unworkable situation. During implementation you will overrun the expected costs because you will be spending money to fix a faulty design. Your revised system design may indeed solve old problems but introduce new ones that nobody on the team can anticipate.

This is why technically-driven design teams should always have at least one "devil's advocate," whose sole purpose is to oppose the proposed system.[27] Design teams rely on consensus, and placate people who need assurance that proven practices will remain in place with minimum disturbance. This view is not conducive to finding problems that concern financial objectives. That is why you need an outsider to prod the designers to avoid compromises that may satisfy some people but at the same time sacrifice the financial results.

The failure to get the planned payoff from poor systems is rarely because of cost overruns or late schedules. If the system is economically sound, its benefits will exceed its costs by a wide margin. The payoff from successful systems easily absorbs moderate cost and schedule mistakes if the new system operates well.

Systems fail financially when expected benefits do not materialize. Displaced clerical personnel are swapped for expensive programmers and new experts to overcome problems that did not exist before. The automation of decisions requires additional auditors and security personnel. Procedural rigidity eliminates personal flexibility in dealing with customers and thereby loses market share. Complete mechanization of transactions increases the risk of business losses. No design team can anticipate all such contingencies, especially if they commit themselves to a tight schedule that focuses only on the delivery of technically functioning computer programs.

The traditional phased approach usually commits itself too early to the design of an application. In using this approach, you may incur some technical risks that are always manageable and repairable. However, technical risks become financial failures in situations where systems designers push too hard to include unproven technology or fixate unnecessarily on the lowest cost options. An independent technical audit should uncover unnecessary technical risks.[28]

The major problem with a prematurely defined design is that it does not safeguard the project's benefits. For instance, to cut the delivery cycle and to reduce administrative costs is an enormous human and organizational challenge. An independent audit will catch some of the most obvious mistakes. However, that will never be sufficient. Each new computer application has a practically unlimited potential for coming up with unprecedented mistakes. Though each defect may be small, their cumulative effects may wipe out the anticipated gains.

This is why master planning of large projects through excessively detailed program management, at the inception, is usually unsafe. Nobody can predict what unforeseen interactions will occur when the application is finally operating in the workplace and meets totally unanticipated conditions.

To better manage and control the realization of financial benefits, you have to resort to evolutionary design and incremental implementation.

Empirical Methods—Implement First

Always insist on the delivery of a working prototype if you are installing an innovative system which I define as one that alters existing workplace relationships. The goal of a prototype should be primarily to test for organizational viability and only secondarily for technical feasibility. Too often, prototypes are simply checkpoints in an implementation schedule after systems design and much programming are complete. With over half of project resources already spent, these tests are not true prototypes but the testing of decisions made in the distant past.

A true prototype is an open-ended and inefficient technical design using disposable computer code. A good prototype does not include all functions that are candidates for automation. It contains core essentials sufficient to give the operators a clear insight into what the new system can do. It is more like an architect's plywood and paper mockup of a room than a partially finished building. Making prototypes is an art. Traditionally-minded systems designers may resist it because it slows down their ability to complete the prescribed "systems design" phase. Making a prototype also removes much design control from the hands of the master planners and emphasizes the influence of the people who will ultimately have to use the system.

Such democratization of the design process can produce completely unexpected results, often defying the neat order of a master plan and substituting for it a variety of solutions. Financial executives especially contribute to the discord when they see expenses for assets that will end up as scrap. This comes from the mistaken notion that making computer programs is like making products. The control mentality, which aims at defect-free output, also militates against evolutionary design which is often disorderly and error-prone.

The executive in charge of systems planning must choose how much of a project's cost and time to devote to adaptive experimentation. The choice is between low-cost and controllable delays during early project development, and high-cost and uncontrollable chaos after implementation. Unless the new computer application is for a predicable environment, the economics will always favor extensive experimentation and evolutionary learning from actual experience.

Demand that your design team deliver an evolutionary system design if your computer application radically changes how people will work. Ideally, the evolutionary systems approach permits a gradual migration into the new method of operation using existing or proven technologies. While that takes place, insist that the systems design team include respected individuals who can articulate reasons for opposing design choices. The opinions of these individuals will need protection and recognition from top management.

After you learn more about the human and organizational dimensions of the new environment, you can verify if the anticipated benefits are likely to be real. Following this period of learning, you should be able to move up to more advanced and presumably less expensive technologies with lowered conversion costs and consequently much smaller risks of failure.

Your current planning and budgeting methods may inhibit evolutionary systems development because these mechanisms look for neat solutions that produce firm financial commitments early in the project.[29] Your technical team will also tend to oppose evolutionary systems development and point out that it will be either too costly or technically not feasible. You should resist accepting such arguments. It is best to do a new job with a proven tool before you start on a completely new job with a completely strange tool. The added expenses for sequential and progressive implementation cannot exceed the cost of failure, if the expected benefits are a large multiple of project costs.

Executive Responsibilities

"...Information Systems is the most difficult corporate staff to manage and to evaluate. It is also the most likely to increase in costs above average."[30]

It is a matter of wide ranging debate what tasks should be on the chief executives' agenda to manage information resources. Without exception, every function in the organization proclaims that it needs immediate and urgent attention at the highest levels of management. In the competition for access, dollars and influence, any time you can get from the top person is a privilege. The easiest way to secure this privilege is to institute procedures which will get information technology included in the normal business planning and budgeting approval cycle. Treating information technology as a unique activity that warrants special review and approval procedures sets in motion its eventual estrangement from the rest of the business.[31]

The systems consulting firm of Nolan, Norton and Company advanced the argument that top executives should assume additional responsibilities for managing the information function. In a 1987 internal publication they contrasted the practices of a past and present "era of executive neglect" with a recommended future "era of executive action."

During the era of executive neglect, the typical responsibilities for senior corporate management were:
   1. Approve the Information Systems budget;
   2. Monitor investments;
   3. Approve major projects.

In the new era of executive action, presumably since 1987, senior corporate management responsibilities ought to:
   1. Consider information technology as a business influence;
   2. Recognize the role of information technology as a business transformer;
   3. Focus on information technology investments;
   4. Set the tone for innovation;
   5. Fund major ventures;
   6. Link information technology to business planning;
   7. Support an information technology awareness program;

8. Support development of architectural policies through the Chief Information Officer;
9. Hold division management responsible for the health of information technology;
10. Monitor major information technology projects;
11. Review exceptional information technology situations.

There is merit in each of the recommended eleven actions. In a small organization, where top management is close to operating details, they may comprise an adequate check list. In a complex, multi-layered organization, the CEO must judge information technology as an integral part of the business plan. The task of monitoring major information technology projects is inseparable from monitoring the performance of all activities against the business plan.

How top executives presently influence the use of information technology is a matter of how they manage their business. There are companies that squeeze every penny of surplus out of their operations to provide corporate staffs with the discretionary funds to spend on information technology. This is how corporate staffs typically end up bankrolling their favorite projects. For example, one of the largest banks in the world ended up with a poorly utilized staff-inspired communications satellite for which operating units did not have much of a transmission load. In another case, one of the largest computer companies ended up with an unused corporate-wide manufacturing planning system that represented the corporate staff's view how all manufacturing should operate. Both cases illustrate the mismanagement of company assets when serving corporate staff agendas that are unsupported by the operating units.

It is untenable to hold operating management responsible for the health of their information technologies and at the same time sequester all application development funds so that decisions about operating methods are made centrally. What a CEO does to manage the information function depends on the planning horizon over which operating personnel can make choices.

In one scenario, the fiscal authority of operating people does not extend beyond delivery of annual results. Their budget does not allow for making investments in information technology with a payback longer than one year. In such a case, the list of top executive actions would be much longer than the eleven items mentioned above.

In another scenario, you have a business planning system that discriminates between *operating, development* and s*trategic* budgets. Operating management is accountable both for their short- as well as long-term profit contributions. The planning system allows the top executive to fold the recommended eleven actions concerning information technology into a single management planning and control process. Executive responsibilities for information systems planning then emerge as balancing resources among all business functions. A separate and distinct computer planning review would not appear on the CEO's agenda.

Among the CEOs I visit there is some ambivalence regarding choices about how to manage the information systems function. The CEOs always favor operating unit responsibility and accountability for information systems. Prior to a recent review of a large corporation, I received an elaborate charter from the CEO's staff, which said that operating units will manage the costs and benefits of their information systems activities. During my visit to the headquarters, the corporation had to put into effect immediate cost reductions. What did the CEO do? He ordered the Vice President of M.I.S. (who is responsible for central programming services and for the corporate data center) to scale back all projects with paybacks over three years, and to do that without further delay. This included the deferral of applications for several operating divisions. Although the cut-backs were necessary, the CEO's actions caused him to assume operating responsibilities for information technology because he suddenly became involved in the reallocation of divisional systems development budgets.

What should be a CEO's personal checklist of responsibilities for information technology? The CEO should not focus only on computer technology to answer this question. The CEO should examine the adequacy of the company's planning process to deal with 10- to 15-year decisions that create the technical infrastructure for long lead-time developments, such as databases and telecommunication. The CEO's objective should be to divest as many of the tough investment choices to operating units as possible, so long as that takes place within the limits of well understood policies. Operating executives should then have every opportunity to choose whatever information technology they need to support their commitments to deliver operating results. If the CEO delegates well, he will end up with a brief agenda for managing only information resources beyond the planning horizon of everyone who reports to him. This gives the CEO an opportunity to concentrate on setting new policies, which should be the CEO's job anyway.

Chapter Summary

The financial methods that are used to guide and control computer investments must meet executive needs for managing information resources. Information technology becomes inseparable from the way the organization operates. Because financial measures provide the metric for judging the effectiveness of all resources, they should be applied to dealing with the diversity and complexity of computer systems.

You can't control what you can't measure. You cannot tell whether you improve something if you cannot measure it. If you can't measure it you can't manage it. The purpose of financial comparisons is to sort out appearance from reality and to narrow expectations so that they can become commitments.

Financial management tools will transform information management into something that is not different from other business functions. This will call for refinements of how to plan and budget for computers as long-term commitments that have a longer planning horizon than organization structure, products, engineering or perhaps even markets. The financial policies and methods that guide information management decisions deserve the CEO's continued attention.

It is unnecessary for corporate staff to require mandatory reviews of all equipment acquisitions or project plans, provided that operating units make these decisions within prescribed policies and standards. The function of the corporate information management staff should be to review exceptions to policies and standards. The CEO should rely on information audits to protect corporate interests, including verification of compliance with policies and standards.

On the subject of policies and standards, I take the view that unless corporate rules specifically dictate what should be done, operating management should be encouraged to do whatever they think is necessary to deliver expected results. Corporate policies and standards for information management become the "constitutional" framework that replaces *ad hoc* interventions by corporate staff that leave everyone unsure of what to expect. The "constitutional" view also calls for setting up the framework for the separation of powers.[32] The CEO, supported by corporate policy staff assumes the functions of a "legislature." The operating units assume the power of the "executive branch," making sure that they further delegate the responsibility for information management wherever there is accountability for measurable results.[33] The information management audit organization assumes the powers of a "judiciary."

If consistent, comprehensive and well-articulated policies are in place, the CEO will be able to concentrate on creating new long-range goals for information management without abandoning controls over results.

CHAPTER 19 COMMENTS

[1] Information is like the bloodstream. It feeds the brain as well as the muscles. The circulatory system of the body offers useful analogies when thinking about the functions of information management. The heart of the enterprise would be its database.

[2] See Chapter 17 for more examples.

[3] From Latin legal usage, deductive reasoning that links causes to probable effects. It anticipates cost and risk before an event.

[4] From Latin legal usage, inductive reasoning that links actual effects to probable causes. It recognizes that actual costs are the result of known events.

[5] One of the reviewers of this book questioned my emphasis on the comparison of two plans. He said that comparing two plans may not be valid, because they involve comparing two different versions of wishful thinking from the same persons. Anyone who wants to promote the use of the computer can write a plan that will make it look better than any other alternative. I think that thoughtful executives can protect themselves against deliberate devaluation of non-computerized alternatives, because such cases are more transparent to an inquiry than the inflation of computerized benefits. If the proponent of the computerized alternative offers inflated benefits and under-stated costs, the prospect of locking both targets into revised operating budgets should discourage such habits.

[6] T.D. Stonier and D.B. Teixeira, Technology in Banking, *Dow Jones-Irwin*, 1990, Chapter 5. This book is perhaps the best discussion of the economics of computers. It contains comprehensive data collected by the firm of McKinsey & Company about the corrosive effects of computerization on banking. I highly recommend it to anyone who wishes to understand the competitive effects of information technology. The lessons from this book apply to other service industries as well.

[7] The craft of acquiring such intelligence covers a wide range of methods which are beyond the scope of this book. My favorite approach is to do computerized retrieval from a wide range of commercial databases, including DIALOG and Dow Jones. The quantity of text that is easily accessible through computer networks from any office computer is amazing. U.S. companies seem to have the tendency to talk about their intention of where to use information technology, which always produces publicity.

[8] I used to dread Tuesday mornings, because that's when I got clippings from the executives' weekend magazine perusal. In each case, the clipping was accompanied by a terse "How about this?" My colleagues in corporate research were recipients of similar notes. The shorthand for such notes was MBBW (Management-By-Business-Week) named after the most frequent source of the latest imaginative scenarios about the effects of technology.

[9] In case of failure, it won't matter how you measure results, since it will be too late to do anything about it anyway. The chances are that none of the of the original proponents will be in the same job. Victory has multiple fathers, defeat is always an unwanted foundling.

[10] Once computer simulations were prohibitively expensive and hard to implement. The new object-oriented programming languages are changing that. It is plausible

CHAPTER 19 — FINANCIAL GUIDELINES

and highly probable that by the end of this decade, all major organizations will include the capability to display the financial consequences of alternative business scenarios in their executive information systems. This approach already exists in defense agencies that can explore various strategies through war-gaming simulators. Some of these are extremely realistic since they can offer each commander second-by-second multiple views of identical battlefield actions.

11 Preferential use of planning methods reflects the sophistication and the experience of the management team. The choice of a planning method relates to the costs and the credibility of each technique based on prior experience. The planning methods, thanks to widespread availability of software, are inexpensive. The absence of training and not costs constrain the application of sophisticated techniques such as risk analysis and scenario simulation.

12 IFPS/Personal Business Modelling System and IFPS MindSight (*Execucom Systems Corporation*, Austin, Texas); ProForma—Planning the Business Venture *(The Company Company*, Alpine, Utah); Business Plan Toolkit *(Palo Alto Software*, Palo Alto, CA); Business Plan Builder, *(Lord Publishing*, Natick, MA).

13 This is another way of saying that a person who only has a wrench will end up tightening every nut or using it as a hammer.

14 Watch out for how organizations approach the definition of what are current expenses. Some companies capitalize equipment but not software. Some capitalize equipment and software but do not count depreciation as a current expense. In the Federal Government there is no depreciation and therefore all expenses are in the form of current appropriations, although there are as many exceptions to this rule as there are agencies. Next time you ask someone what he spends on information technology, better be ready with a spreadsheet to interpret the answer consistently with whatever definition you use.

15 Such as those detailed in Chapter 11.

16 For further detail see Chapter 17 on IBM's Systems Assessment Indicators.

17 What percentage of the total information technology expenses should fall into the "strategic" category is an interesting question. A study of the *R-O-M* database suggests that *over-achievers* need to spend more on risky strategic investments than *average* companies to maintain their hard-to-keep position of extraordinary profit gains. By the same reasoning, *under-achievers* should not spend anything on risky strategic investments because they may not survive long enough to reap the benefits.

Depending on the risks of an *over-achiever's* portfolio (see Chapter 9), this may require allocating up to 10% of the total computer expenses to "strategic" projects. In this respect the strategic systems budget would be equivalent to the money a company spends on basic research.

18 This includes an audit of compliance with security, privacy, software engineering, documentation, data administration, pre- and post-installation testing, competitive procurement, training, communication, cost-justification and cost-accountability standards. The independent audit staff is the ideal location for on-the-job training for potential senior systems executives.

19 C. Hartog and R. Klepper, Business Squeeze Pushes Software Sales up 184%, *Computerworld*, August 22, 1988, p.55.

20 I define a major new application as more than 100,000 lines of new code.

21 To quote a recent *InformationWeek* editorial: "Outsourcing is in and insourcing is out."

22 What about the frequent assertions that purchased software does not fit user requirements? Complying with user specifications does not guarantee the most economic results. The shopping list of desired features is often nothing more than archaic rules and habits accumulated over time. Frequently such rules do not apply to current business needs. They reflect relationships between people and groups that have ceased to exist. Avoid taking existing procedures and casting them into exacting user specifications, especially if everyone excludes the possibility of a purchased application. Make sure that on your application planning team there is always an influential champion favoring off-the-shelf procurement.

23 All risk assessments should include the verification that you have the appropriate personnel to do the job.

24 An astute observation on how to manage a successful systems function comes from Touche Ross International, The Impact of Technology on Banking, 1985: "The more successful banks have taken a market-driven approach to organizing their people and technological resources. Market-based organizations give direction to or have actual control over technological resources. This approach improves the alignment of costs and revenues with markets and establishes direct responsibility for results. Such an approach confronts historical industry wisdom—allocating resources and setting priorities around hardware. Many banks have been slow to react to changing conditions. They have maintained centralized functional organizations for technology management. The technology programs are developed by centralized organizations that are disconnected from the marketplace."

25 The work content for each phase is checked against an exhaustive list and the exit criterion for progressing from one phase to another is covered by elaborate checklists.

26 This reiterates the often quoted "Murphy's Law" which says that "if anything can go wrong, it will." Some people allege that "Murphy's Law," as applied to major application development, is the optimistic case. There is always a chance that a new computer application will never work at all, even after extensive repairs.

27 The best "devil's advocates" are wise old men or women generally acknowledged as sources of sound advice. Every organization has such experts who are mentally alert, innovative and have a deep loyalty to making their organization succeed in its missions. Their position should be sufficiently secure so that they need not fear offering unpopular advice. A knowledgeable CEO will treat these people as an irreplaceable resource.

28 This is an instance where a consultant can be of great value.

29 Government systems projects suffer from this unrealistic view, based on a misunderstanding that systems acquisition is primarily a matter of choosing technologies. Auditors and congressional committee haunt systems managers by comparing actual against premature cost estimates. The result is that public sector systems benefit neither from tough budgeting oversight, nor from the capacity to learn from evolutionary installations.

30 American Productivity Center and Cresap, McCormick & Paget, Positioning Corporate Staffs for the 1990's, *Cresap, McCormick & Paget*, Chicago, Ill, 1986

31 Such as the ubiquitous Corporate Systems Review Committees that try to ration money for information technology separately from business budgets.

32 Such a framework should make an allowance for setting up specialized institutions, such as review Boards concerned with functional methods, systems engineering tools, telecommunication protocols, data administration methods, data center costing, procurement contracts and personnel development. Groupware techniques (see Chapter 15) now make it possible to secure widespread participation by specialists regardless of organizational or geographic location.

33 Operating Divisions make much fuss about burdensome corporate reviews. Frequently they are extreme centralists in how they treat their Regions, Districts and Branches. A memorable comment encapsulating this attitude came from the Divisional General Manager of the Kraft Company in Atlanta, who said "The corporate decentralization policy stops in my office."

20

A POLICY CHECKLIST

Policy is what you actually do today.

A helpful management book should be a guide to action that a reader can apply immediately. I do not know of a better way for ending this book than giving you a checklist of policies for managing the business value of computers.

I use a similar checklist when I review the adequacy of an organization's methods for managing its *information resources*. Usually, a few dozen top executives will enter "Yes", "No" or "Partial" against each of the 137 policies that follow below.

You should not count the percentage of "Yes" replies as an indication that you are either an *over-achiever* or *under-achiever*. Only your *R-O-M* value can tell you that. However, organizations will more likely succeed in profitably exploiting their *information resources* if their policies clearly state what the CEO wishes to accomplish.

Each of the policies in this checklist leads to a result. Who will deliver that result and how to do it is something that only you can decide. *Information resources* management determines how your organization conducts its business and supports the management of *business resources* that account for its successes or failures. *Information resources* management is therefore unique, even for organizations with identical products and services. What your policies will state and how you will implement them will shape how your organization will operate in the decades ahead.

Every policy will not apply in your case. The checklist is not in order of importance. It represents one approach to portraying why the extraction of the business value from computers covers a broad range of topics. The long checklist should alert you to the need for comprehensive policies and better attention to issues that have not yet received adequate executive guidance.

POLICY FORMULATION

Role of Information Resources Management Policy

- Establish *information resources* policy as the definition, scope, organization and guidance for the management of *information resources*.

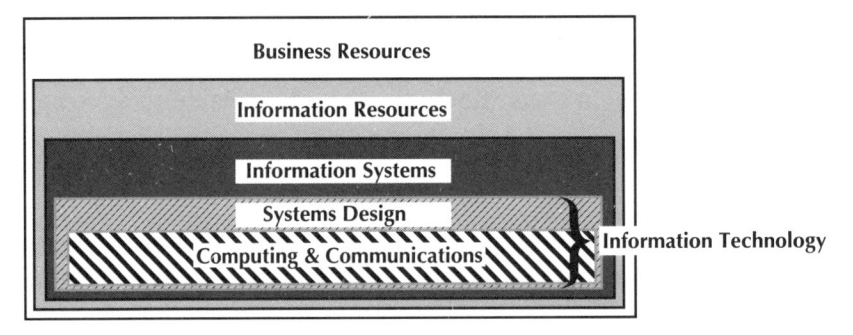

Figure 20.1: The Scope of Information Resources Management

Scope of Information Resources Management

- Define *information resources* as all expenses incurred in the creation, processing and distribution of information. This includes the fully allocated costs of personnel engaged in meeting, training, counseling, coordinating, recording, reporting, reading, calculating and writing, whether computerized or not. *Information resources* exclude product– or production-embedded *information*

technology, as well as all resources committed to physical delivery of products and non-information services.
- Define as *information systems* all formal and structured methods for dealing with management and mission critical systems, plus their interface to embedded *information technology* in products or services. *Information systems* include the fully allocated costs of systems specifications, project management, systems startup, operator training and procedural management for all computer and communications applications,
- Define *information technology* as the principal means for delivering improved *information systems*. The scope of *information technology* includes *information services* (e.g., computer operations, network operations, programming, telecommunications) and *systems design* (e.g., systems engineering, database design, information architecture).
- Make sure that the scope of telecommunications includes all voice, data, video and radio technologies.
- Take measures to prevent the management of *information technology* from becoming a substitute for the management of *information resources*

INFORMATION RESOURCES MANAGEMENT ORGANIZATION

Information Resources Policy and Execution

- Assign the responsibility for *information resources* management policy at an organization level consistent with key policy-making positions in finance, marketing and operations. Appoint a *chief information resources manager* to guide the *information resources* policy-formulation process and to see to it that these policies promote the delivery of improvements in business productivity. In fact, the CEO or the Agency Head is the *chief information resources manager* because information resources management is inseparable from the roles of managing. In a large organization this may be a staff position assisting operating management with policies and methods how to improve business processes.

- Assign the responsibility for the execution of *information resources* policies and management of *information resources* to operating managers with direct responsibility for operating results. Only operating managers can be accountable for the results of *productivity improvement* projects.
- Establish policies that specify which *information resources* management decisions take place at each level of functional or operating management. Unless explicitly retained at a higher level, all responsibility for *information resources* management should remain with the people applying the information.

Information Technology Policy and Execution

- Appoint a *chief information technology manager* to establish *information technology* policies and standards that link the objectives of *information resources management* to *information technology*.
- Concentrate on *information technology* standards that deal with databases, telecommunications and systems engineering.
- Assign the responsibility for execution to those who manage information technology as a service to operating personnel. Assign this responsibility, such as data center operations, programming services, systems design and integration, telecommunications, printing and technical support to one or more organizations that have an organizational structure that can emulate the best commercial practices.
- Assign the responsibility for evaluating the prices and costs for *information technology* services to the *chief information technology manager*.
- Place the responsibility for the computing and telecommunication networks under the same operating management.
- Separate the responsibility for *information technology* policy from *information technology* execution.

Information Management Audit

- Appoint a *performance and standards audit* organization that is independent of *information resources* and *information technology* management. The audit organization will be responsible for monitoring compliance with approved policies and standards.

STAFF & POLICY	OPERATING MANAGEMENT	SERVICES
Chief Information Resources Manager	Information Resources Manager	Computing and Communications Service Manager
Chief Information Technology Manager	Information Resources Manager	Computing and Communications Service Manager
Chief Information Technology Performance and Standards Audit	Information Resources Manager	Computing and Communications Service Manager

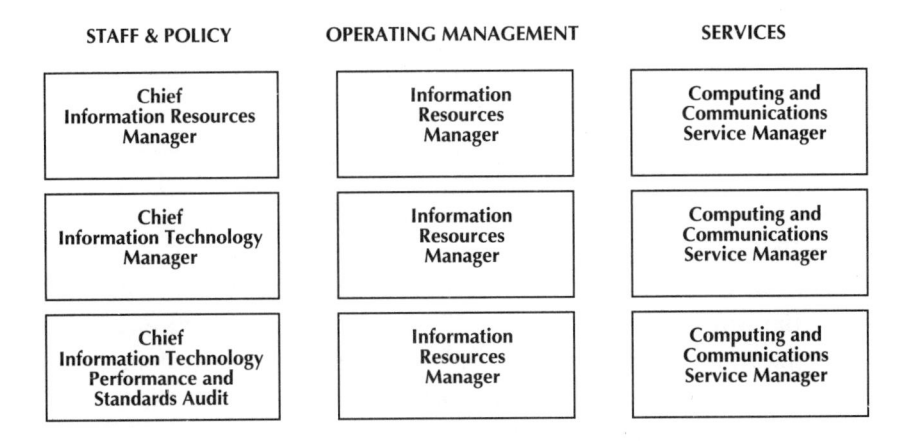

Figure 20.2: The Organizational Units of Information Management

- Promulgate policies to safeguard corporate information assets against unauthorized alteration, destruction and disclosure.
- Make the assignments for the organizational elements outlined in Figure 20.2, depending on the availability of scarce executive talent to fill the key jobs. Reporting relationships and reporting levels depend on local conditions, which may also dictate the merger of some of the functional units in Figure 20.2.

Business Strategy → Business Improvement Plan → Information Resources Policy → Information Technology Architecture → Information Technology Standards

CORPORATE RESPONSIBILITIES

Functional Improvement Plans → Information Improvement Project → Systems Requirements → Systems Design & Maintenance → Computing & Communication Services

OPERATING RESPONSIBILITIES

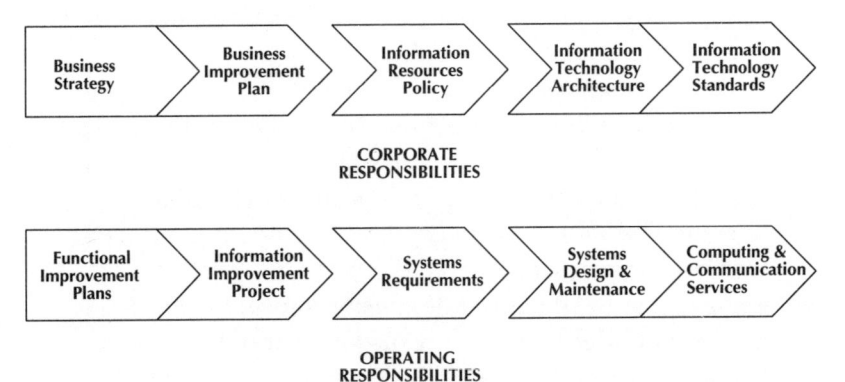

Figure 20.3: The Functions of Information Management

- Separate policy (e.g., corporate) responsibilities from execution.

Make sure that individual systems implementation projects are based on adequately articulated business strategies and on precisely specified business improvement plans.
- Base the technical implementation of every project on completely articulated information resources policies, which include an explicit information technology architecture and unambiguous information technology standards, especially especially those that concern data standards, communications and software engineering.
- Concentrate the efforts of *Information Resources Managers* on systems implementation issues, which include the specification of functional improvement plans, the definition of incremental implementation steps as information improvement projects and the articulation of systems requirements.
- Assure the availability of a low-cost and responsive *Computing and Communications Management Services* organization to deliver and operate systems that meet the requirements of *Information Resources Managers*. The relationships and tasks of these organizational functions are outlined in Figure 20.3.

Systems Design and Organization Structure

- Make every manager responsible for all *information resources* that affect his business. Make the management of *information resources* inseparable from the act of managing so that *information resources* management does not need to be a functional specialty.
- Decentralize *information systems* management by placing the responsibility for all economic choices and *systems requirement* specifications with operating management, provided that the choices follow policies and standards.
- Migrate *information technology* from a centrally controlled resource to workplace-managed *information systems*.
- Require that the technical designs of *information systems* are independent of current organizational structure. Information systems should be easier and faster to reconfigure than organization changes.

- Pursue policies that favor organization-independent processing of information. Organizational decentralization does not necessarily require a corresponding decentralization of *information technology* except where security may dictate it.
- Move the accountability for *information systems* costs and benefits into the hands of people who use it.
- Design *information systems* that make it possible for a customer to have a single contact for all routine communications with your organization.
- Increase the prescribed level of standardization as you proceed with decentralization of decisions about *information systems*. Increasing autonomy in a complex organization requires increased standardization of the infrastructure. Infinite variety is possible from standard components. Complexity that arises out of variety is manageable only with the narrowing of options about systems design elements.

[Comment: All life uses a limited set of standard components (DNA). Also, the delivery of low-cost electricity to an enormous variety of appliances is economically feasible only through standardization of power transmission.]

INFORMATION SYSTEMS POLICY GUIDANCE

Managing Planning

INFORMATION TECHNOLOGY AND BUSINESS PLANS

- Evaluate the business value of *information technology* as the risk-adjusted discounted present cash value of the *business plan* that results from the incremental contributions of *information improvement* projects. How to make such comparisons is suggested in Figure 20.4.
- Justify and monitor individual *information improvement* projects as elements of *productivity improvement* projects. Introduce or modify *information technology* only as a means for delivering *information improvement* projects.

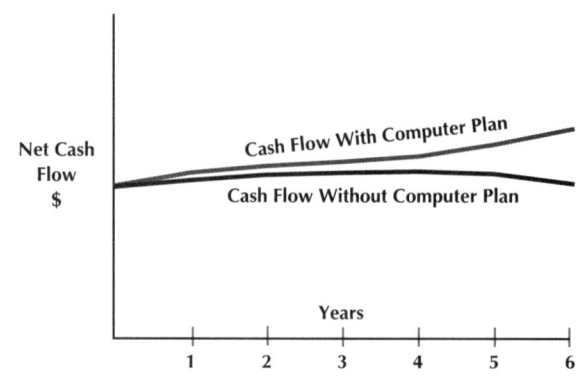

Figure 20.4: Comparing Cash Flows of Alternative Business Plans

- For planning and allocation of resources aggregate projects into *functional improvement* and *business improvement* plans:

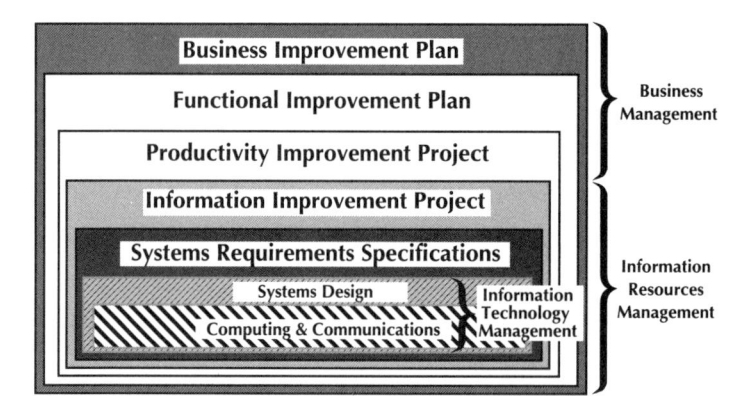

Figure 20.5: Relating Information Technology to Business Planning

- Include in your long-range plan for information technology a list of potential external threats and opportunities that will require monitoring.

PLANNING METHODS

- Make the assessment of *information improvement* projects an integral part of the business planning process.
- Use business planning models to evaluate the contribution of *information improvement* projects to increasing *Business Value-added*.

- Authorize the budgeting of individual phases of multi-year projects within the company's long-range plan.

STRATEGIC DIRECTIONS

- Emphasize the realization of project benefits instead of minimizing the costs of *information technology*.
- Assign to *information resources management* the role of reducing all administrative work that does not increase *Value-added*.
- Foster rapid and evolutionary implementation of applications to minimize investment costs and accelerate benefits. Keep track of the speed of installing systems modifications as a key performance indicator.
- Install pricing and budgeting procedures which make possible decentralized control of demand for information services. Encourage operating personnel to make tradeoffs between information and other resources.
- Compare the profitability of information technology investments with other uses of funds.

STRATEGIC DIAGNOSIS

- Diagnose the viability of your organization using external indicators to find out the opportunities for achieving major improvements.
- Use competitive comparisons to identify conditions which are below acceptable levels of performance.
- Compare the organization's internal measures of performance against external standards, not against prior achievements.
- Recognize that major threats and opportunities may come from outside your business. Systematically collect intelligence about your competitors' potential uses of computers.
- Listen to what executives in your industry, and especially your employees, say about applications of *information technology*. Do not allow parties that have a potential conflict of interest to become your primary sources of information about *information technology*.

PLANNING TARGETS

- Deliver a steady stream of cost reductions. The cost of information technology has shown, and will continue showing in the foreseeable future, the most dramatic cost reductions of any tool available in the global economy.
- Demonstrate continuous gains in the productivity of your development organization in delivering new applications and reducing maintenance expenses.
- Insist on including the option of purchasing computer services or commercially available software for all projects involving *information technology*.
- Refrain from supplying all internal *information technology* needs. Purchase from commercial sources all services beyond firmly predictable needs.

Managing Information Systems Development

INFORMATION SYSTEMS ARCHITECTURE

- Mandate inter-operability of all business systems with all computer applications which share a common corporate database:

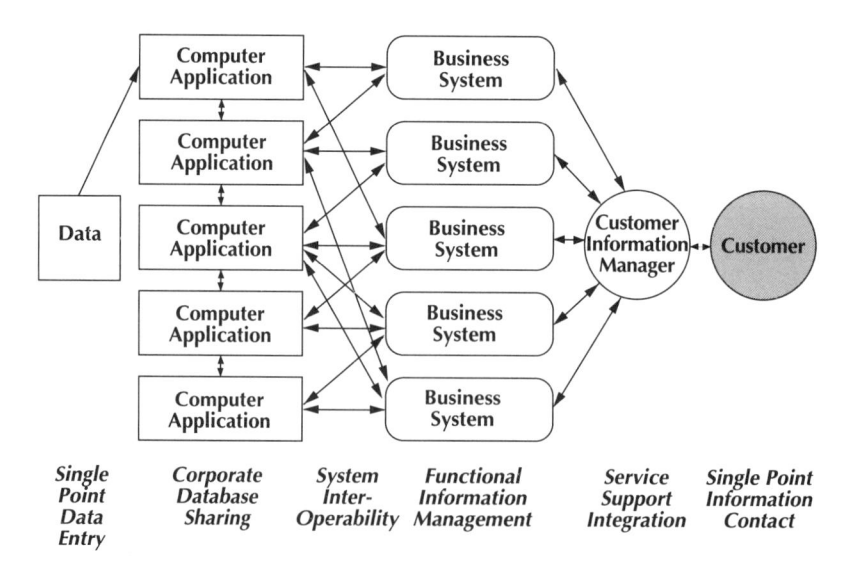

Figure 20.6: Information Management for Single Point Customer Support

- Embed *information technology* into products and services to fully automate information-handling.
- Make *information technology* a readily available service that does not require labor-intensive technical support.

COMMON INFORMATION SYSTEMS

- Develop common *information technology* to support *information systems* in diverse organizations for all applications where the *information resources* deliver comparable products or services.
- Design shared and common *information systems* to have an organization-independent core of business functions. In such designs, make allowances for adding variety that covers non-core business practices of organizationally independent *information resources*.
- Install common *information technology* for all applications that perform comparable business functions, unless unique conditions prevail. The burden of proof of what is unique lies with the organization that wishes to fund the singular solution.

COMMUNICATIONS ORIENTATION

- Improve group communications by taking advantage of the widespread availability of personal computers and networks.
- Attack the costly inefficiency of business conferences, committee meetings and group reviews by shifting routine interactions into electronic media.
- Assume that the rate of cost and performance improvement of computers will continue at present rates for the next 20 years. The most dramatic changes will occur in telecommunications, where wide-band circuits will become more affordable.
- Pursue a policy that calls for processing information independent of distance. Physical decentralization does not necessarily require physical decentralization of *information technology*, except in conditions where security or safety may dictate it.

DATA ENTRY

- Capture data from embedded computers as a by-product.
- Avoid using facsimile for transmission of reusable information.
- Specify that all data will enter into the computer network only once, at the point of origin. This rule extends beyond the scope of a corporation, and includes suppliers and customers by means of electronic data interchange.
- Achieve zero defects at all points of data entry.

Managing Results

INVESTMENT CONTROL PRACTICES

- Plan, budget and evaluate *information technology* costs as a direct cost for delivering products and services to customers. The justification of computer budgets should be the responsibility of the organizations that uses *information technology* products and services.
- Allocate a constant percentage of the total systems expenses for systems projects without readily apparent payoffs, such as small scale systems experiments. Readily provide limited exploratory funds without requiring any other financial justification than championship from an operating executive who may end up applying the new methods. Such investments should have the characteristics of an acceptable risk combined with a rational chance of enormous gains.
- Require full financial justification before a successful pilot project may proceed to full-scale implementation.
- Finance data center operations and programming services to meet investment criteria as if they were a commercial enterprise. Evaluate the financial performance of data center operations and programming services in a similar way as commercial ventures.
- Approve requests for additional equipment and resources of data center operations and programming services whenever revenues from paying customers will support it. If you funded *information systems* projects and approved *information resources* budgets, the providers of *information*

technology services should not require further approvals as long as they are meeting cost reduction targets.
- Take advantage of decreasing prices of computer hardware. Let computer leasing companies assume the risks of residual values of used computer equipment.
- Acquire hardware and software technologies through competitive procurement, unless sole source procurement offers demonstrable financial advantages.

OPERATING CONTROL METHODS

- Avoid revenue ratios for comparing expenses. Changes in the financial structure may yield misleading indicators. Reject composite ratios made up of arbitrary weighting factors for all investment decisions, because they will not reflect a project's contributions to cash flow.
- Refrain from applying asset-based ratios to evaluate *information technology* investments. Measure and evaluate the productivity of people, not the productivity of invested assets, by adopting *Value-added* measures. Measure the productivity of management whenever information technology supports managerial functions.
- Identify individuals or management positions that are accountable for delivering measurable results for each *project*.
- Count only net cash gains as savings, not cost avoidance of expenses you need not incur.
- Evaluate staff in terms of their contribution to improving *Business value-added*.
- Keep track of cumulative operating and maintenance expenses for all applications.

PRICING OF INFORMATION TECHNOLOGY SERVICES

- Bill computer services to customers using standard transaction prices. The standard prices must itemize the resources consumed in the delivery of the transaction. The cost sheets should be open for examination to identify cost reduction opportunities.
- Allow the customer to invest in software and hardware improvements so that they will realize immediate reductions in standard prices for computer services.

- Bill for access privileges, equipment rentals and technical support on the basis of periodic fixed charges from a standard price list.
- Benchmark intra-company prices for computer services against competitive commercial service offerings. Reduce intra-company prices to allow for profit, marketing expenses, volume discounts and cost of capital to make comparisons with commercial prices valid.
- Display on each individual workstation the total cost for a transaction, so that operators can make informed choices about their consumption of information services. Individual operators should receive a periodic invoice itemizing charges for database, central computing and network services.
- Offer alternative pricing options for executing individual transactions, and display the costs of alternative processing methods on demand.
- Set the prices for information technology resources on the basis of anticipated productivity gains.
- Bill for systems design services on a similar basis as commercial firms competing for the same business.

SECURITY AND SAFETY

- Provide controls and security for all applications that have a potential exposure to incur financial losses.
- Engage independent agents to randomly test the protective measures.

Managing People

WORK DESIGN

- Prior to automating:
  Eliminate all non-essential work;
  Simplify work-flow;
  Enlarge an individual's work roles;
  Restructure how organizations cooperate to complete a transaction.
- Do not start a new systems development unless work elimination, simplification, enlargement and re-structuring precede systems design.

- Involve the operators in major project decisions that affect them in order to ensure responsiveness to business needs.
- Test if new operating methods are acceptable to operators prior to installing a new system.
- Find out how operators actually use a computer application and compare the results with the original intent.
- Install only systems that meet standards of ergonomically acceptable design.
- Design systems that have the potential of making individuals or small groups autonomous profit or *Value-added* centers.

APPLICATIONS DESIGN

- To reduce the burden of technical details, automate access procedures to databases, computers, telecommunications and applications.
- Specify standard graphic interfaces for displays and commands to minimize operator training and use costs.

EXECUTIVES' TECHNICAL KNOW-HOW

- Acquire only the specific technical computer skills needed to do your own work.
- Do not dabble or tinker with computer technology in complex computer applications, because you will always be an amateur. Managers should concentrate on *information resources management* of their functions, and not on managing *information technology*.
- Decentralization of *information resources management* does not mandate decentralization of *information technology*. Some of the most decentralized examples of *information resources* management reside in centralized environments.

MANAGEMENT TRAINING

- Concentrate management training on case studies of excellent and poor management practices, and on analyzing the life-cycle economics of *information resources management* solutions. Be an expert on causes of computer systems foul-ups.
- Learn how to obtain workable solutions to your information systems needs from vendors and experts.

- Provide thorough training on *information resources management* policies and practices prior to allowing a manager to assume responsibility for this function.
- Show managers how to improve management methods through information systems.
- Teach all personnel how to apply computers to improve business effectiveness.
- Institute systematic management reviews of errors and system malfunctions as a preferred training method.

EMPLOYEE TRAINING

- Specify required computer skills for all jobs. Make the specified minimum skills a job prerequisite.
- Include a test of the adequacy of an operator's skills whenever he or she will use information technology.
- Provide or require employee training to meet minimum skills necessary prior to proceeding with any systems implementation.

PRESERVATION OF TECHNICAL SKILLS

- Place high priority on attracting and keeping technical staff that can plan, evaluate, design and manage the integration of diverse sources of information technologies.
- Provide career diversification for your technical personnel that will allow them to acquire company-specific experiences through cross-functional assignments.

MANAGING RELATIONSHIPS

- Institute procedures which will allow managers responsible for *information resources* management to deal with those responsible for *information technology* services as customers deal with their closely cooperating suppliers.
- Beware of a vendor's assistance in planning and managing *information resources*. The vendor's economic interests are not always identical to those of the purchasers.
- Establish long-term relationships with hardware and software vendors, as well as with consultants who specialize in technical fields in which you cannot afford to be self-sufficient.

- Create a corporate-wide electronic network connecting everyone involved in specifying, designing and implementing information improvement projects. The network should include contractors, consultants and suppliers.
- Encourage intensive use of electronic conferencing and computer-supported work groups. Use this means to share expertise irrespective of geographic boundaries.

Managing Projects

PROPOSAL JUSTIFICATION

- Include in each proposal the projected life cycle costs and benefits, including residual value, using the cash method of accounting.
- Insist on systems that have a built-in capacity for rapidly adapting to volatile business conditions.
- Disclose, when making an investment proposal, the full range of possible gains and losses.
- Count a benefit only if your competitors will let you keep it.
- Reject cash-less cost avoidance as the principal justification for projects.
- Disregard the over-attribution of benefits to computers if the productivity improvements derive from new work methods or new skills of the employees. Computers rarely save money—mostly people do that.
- Dismiss benefit estimates based on an analogy. The benefits of computers are unique to each organization.
- Require that each application proposal includes initial and ongoing training time in the estimates of life-cycle costs.

MANAGING QUALITY

- Place a cash value on the effects of computers to improve the quality of products and services. Unless you can quantify "intangible" savings, you cannot include them in calculating investment payoffs.
- Recognize that the improvement in the quality of goods and services is potentially the most important contribution of *information systems*.

- Pursue evolutionary design and implementation of projects that emphasize incremental quality enhancement and organizational learning.
- Keep error statistics for all applications. Apply sampling techniques to extreme situations as a way to reduce the costs of tracking performance.
- Use the resolution of quality problems to determine how to improve information systems.

Rapid Implementation

- Avoid the implementation of large a multi-year projects except in cases which require unique innovations or simultaneous implementation of a full set of complex features.
- Remove the planning for changes in business methods or for the acquisition of information technology from individual project plans. The inclusion of these planning tasks within the scope of an invidual project elongates its completion schedule, increases acquisition costs and prematurely forces the commencement of the maintenance phase:

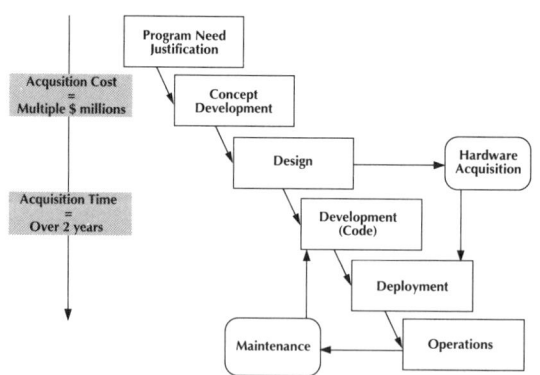

Figure 20.7: Current Approach to Project Management

- Emphasize speed of coordinated project implementation as the primary strategy for cost and risk containment. To realize this goal shift to incremental delivery of small projects within the framework of an overall business and information technology program:

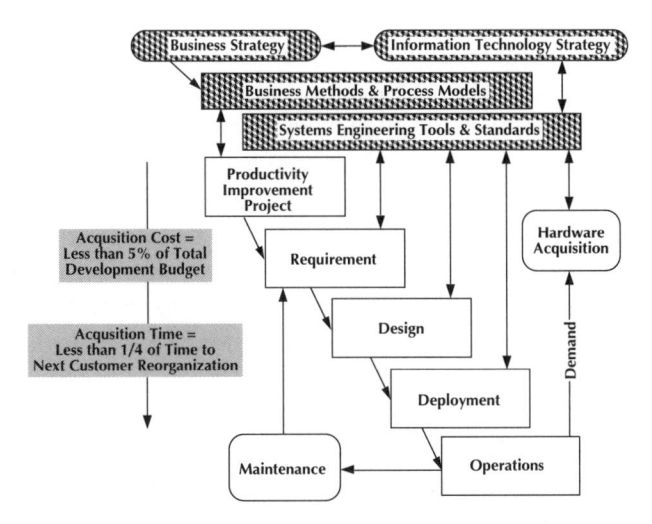

Figure 20.8: Recommended Approach to Program Management

- Allow individual projects to proceed only if they follow an explicit and approved business strategy, if they fit within improved business method and process models, if they comply with the information technology strategy and if they apply standard systems engineering tools and methods, unless an exception is approved at the policy level.

Information Technology Policy Guidance

Adherence to Standards

- Use only vendor-independent commercial hardware and software technologies that have widespread commercial acceptance, unless vendor-unique or company-developed technologies prove demonstrably less costly.
- Adopt open systems interconnection standards that will assure the portability of applications across different types and brands of computers.
- Define standards for controlling the definitions of all "corporate" data to be placed in a corporate data dictionary. This includes the management process for including a data element as a "corporate data element."
- Pick a computer-aided system engineering methodology for specifying and maintaining all software. Include in this

choice data modeling tools to allow corporate-wide sharing of design information about corporate data elements.
- Select computer languages as a way to share technical information. This would include a standard language for specifying information from applications such as executive information systems, computer-aided engineering, and function-specific applications. Promote linguistic standards within computer applications to reduce the ambiguity in business communications, especially if this involves cross-cultural cooperation.
- Specify standard commercial software for: database management, word processing, graphics, spreadsheet, publishing, backup, encryption, file management, programming language, sorting, back-up, communications access, data dictionary, etc. This will minimize training expenses and provide for easier systems integration.
- Provide rapid turnaround to requests for exceptions from standards. Approve such requests if they support experimental use, or if they could lead to new standards.

Design Principles
- Make sure that authorized workstations can have access to databases that store corporate data. Assure the inter-operability of applications that require access to multiple databases.
- Design computer applications so that their functions are independent of the specific hardware or software choices for database management methods and telecommunication protocols.
- Prefer reverse engineering of existing applications instead of initiating new software development, to the greatest extent possible.
- Maintain software through reengineering methods to make it independent of specific technology choices and to extend its residual value.
- Migrate applications into the operators' workstations as soon as this becomes economically feasible. View databases, central computing resources and networks as servers that support personal workstations.
- Apply "rule-based (expert) systems" to all operator-

machine interactions to reduce training costs, eliminate errors and simplify the display of complex information.
- Include "decision-support" routines in applications that generate complex or voluminous outputs from calculations. The purpose of "decision-support" software is to pre-digest the computer-generated results and present them in a format that is easy to use.

Containing Technology Risks
- Favor applications that have demonstrated successful pilot program results.
- Proceed with rapid and small scale implementation of applications using proven technology and only absolutely essential features. Your design should allow for the easy addition of rarely used features and scaling up transaction volumes, after scoring success with the initial installation.
- Avoid projects that simultaneously attempt implementation of major organizational, technological and work-design changes. Attempt dealing with only one major risk at a time, if possible.
- Recognize the vulnerability of computer networks to disruption and damage. Maintain expertise to identify potential failures and supervise the installation of safeguards.
- Protect the access to all databases and networks by specifying security and access methods for all corporate information resources. Safeguard against unintentional and unauthorized alteration, fraud, destruction and disclosure of all computerized data.

CONCLUDING REMARKS

A computer is worth only what it can fetch in an auction. Its business value is its most economic alternative solution. Anything not worth doing is not worth doing well on a computer.

Computers add value only if surrounded by appropriate policy, strategy, methods for monitoring results, talented and committed people, sound relationships and well designed information systems.

The business value of a computer is its *Management.* The productivity of management is the decisive element that makes the difference of whether a computer hurts or helps.

You may question whether organizations require policies and analyses to govern their information resources. Do rules restrict the freedom of managers to act according to their best judgment? Effective information management enhances individual freedoms, personal creativity and the capacity to add value to society. Policies that do not meet these criteria must be discarded.

Learning from the accomplishments and mistakes of others makes possible the freedom to innovate. Progress takes place only if you can build on what others have tried before so that you can benefit from their experience. Organizations prosper if they can rely on methods that do not require re-invention. I trust that this *Executive Guide* will serve that purpose.

INDEX

3M 10
A.D. Little 464
A.E.Staley 70
Abdominal Pain 400
Action Technologies 406
ADAPSO 277
Air Force RF-4c 278
Akamatsu 191
Akzo Coatings 173
All-in-One 379
Allen-Bradley 71
Allied Stores 434
Allstate Insurance 323
Alper 318
Alter 320
American Airlines 27, 158, 165, 179, 190, 192, 303, 319, 336
American Hospital Supply 158, 165, 432
American Productivity Center 461, 496
American Ultramar 275
Ames Stores 13
Amstar, 70
Analog Devices 372
Andersen Consulting 275
Andrews 354
Angus 354
Annex Research 275
Apian Software 380
Apollo 179
Apple Computer Company 191, 431
ArchiText 382
Arthur Andersen 126
Arthur D. Little 452
Arthur Young 323
Ashby 466
Ashby's Law 457, 466
AT&T 8, 95, 108, 398, 436
AT&T Long Lines 341
Athanasopoulos 55, 70

Atlas Door Company 168, 312
ATM 19, 26, 105
Augustine 465
Automatic Data Processing 277
Automatic Teller Machines 19, 327
Baily 464
BANC One 165
Bank of America 325, 331, 340
Bank of Japan 444
Banker 462
Bankers Trust 50
Banking automation 49
Base period 437
Baxter 274
Baxter Travenol Laboratories 432
Belitsos 398
Bell Atlantic 264, 277
Bell Canada 409
Bennett 252, 293, 398
Benson 56, 422, 427
Berkshire Hathaway 13
Best Products 13
Beta coefficient 96
Betts 355
Betty 293
Bible, I Kings 11
Birch 321, 462
Black Death 60
Blockbuster 407
Blue Cross 324
Blue Shield of Wisconsin 324
Bobrow 381
Boeing Computer Services 303
Bond 327
Booker 56, 353
Boone 410, 432
Booz, Allen & Hamilton 432
Borden 70
Borg Warner 160
Boston Consulting Group 419

Bosworth 432
Bowen 464
BrainPower, Inc. 382
Branco 129
Bridgestone Corporation 161
Brimelow 71
British Airways 319
Britt 11
Brody 432
Brookings Institute 451
Brooks bill 30
Brown 71
Browser 373
Brumm 12, 54, 319
Bureau of Labor Statistics 432
Burlington 160
Burr 188, 194
Business Modeling System 495
Business Systems Planning 56
Business Value-added 61, 62, 67, 154
Butler Cox Foundation 12
Buzzell 72, 126, 161
Caldwell 277, 318, 320
Calma 406
Campbell Soup 70, 174
Capital Value-added 68
Capture Laboratory 381
Carlson 430
Carlyle 12, 131, 274, 278
Carnation 70
Carnegie-Mellon 399
Carter Hawley 434
Caudle 159
CBEMA, 318
CCITT 380
Chakrabarti 464
Charter Medical 13
Chase Manhattan Bank 327
Chief Information Officer 55

Chrysler 319, 409
Cinelli 28
Citibank 55, 158, 327
Citicorp 72, 165, 303
City of New York 452
City of Richmond 323
Claremont Business School 393
Clemons 191, 352, 409
Clerical Support Ratio 147
COBOL 332
COBOL Lines-to-Revenue 8
Coca-Cola 72
Collaboration Technology Center 381
Collaborative Management Workshop 381
Comdisco 13
Commerce Department 337
Committee on White Collar Productivity 70
Compuserve 379
Computer and Business Equipment Manufacturers Association 463
Computer Economics 275
Computer Personnel-to-Total Employment 8
Computer Sciences 275
Computer-Aided Design 247
Computer-Aided Manufacturing 247
Computerworld 39, 48, 49
Computerworld Premier 100 39
Concensor 379
Conference Board 455
Congressional hearings 455
Connect, Inc. 380
Connell 398
Connolly 192
CPC International, 70

Crandall 303
Credit Suisse 336
Cresap, McCormick & Paget 496
Critical Success Factors 166, 416
CSX 160
Curtin 398
Dana 160
Dart & Kraft 70
Data General' 379
DataDesk 56
Datar 462
Datas 192
Davis 96, 465
Davis & Associates 320
DCNY 13
De Long 398
Decision Analysis 381
Decision Pad 380
DeDombal 400
Defense Department 455, 465
DeKoven 382
Deloitte Touche 387
Delphi 433
Delphi Research Center 55
Delta Airlines 192
Department of Commerce 438
Department of Defense 465
Department of Labor 438
Departmental Computing 21
Deutsch 319
Dialcom 379
DIALOG 494
Dickson 400
Diebold Associates 6, 408
Diebold Group 28, 33, 39
Digital Equipment Corporation 193, 275, 320
Discounted Cash Flow 94
Doe 463
Donovan 278

Dorsey 278
Dow Jones 100, 494
Driscoll, 320
Dryden 303
Du Pont 174
Dun & Bradstreet 165, 408
Durand 293
EasyLink 379
Eatman 318
EDI 19
Educorp Corporation 382
Effectiveness Score 39
Ein-Dor 320
Electronic Data Interchange 19, 71
Electronic Data Systems 267, 275, 278, 323, 324
Emery Freight 13
Employee Retirement Income Security 453
Enron Corporation 268
Envos Corporation 382
Epistemology 94
Execucom Systems Corporation 495
Executive Committee 1
Executive Information Systems 23, 24
Executive Planning of Data Processing 56
Factory automation 151
Federal Express 165, 432
Federal purchasing rules 455
Federal Reserve Bank 333
Federal tax filing 452
Feeny 193
Ferreira 192
Fidelity Union Life 176
Firestone Tire & Rubber 161
First Interstate Services 276
Flamholtz 95
FMC Corporation 276

Food and Drug Administration 453
Food Industry 33
Forbes 6, 12
Form 1040 451
Form W-2 464
Forrester 191, 466
Forsythe 273
Foster 381
Frameworks 418
Framingham Experiment 96
Frand 11
Frank B. Hall 13
Freedman 432
Freiser 408
Frito-Lay 179
Frost 273
Frozen cottage fries 461
Fuji-Xerox 9
Fujitsu 8, 124
Galbraith 433
Gale 72, 125, 126, 161
Garrett 398
Gartner Group 29, 100, 319
Genentech 177
General Accounting Office 206, 354, 398
General Electric 72, 103, 177, 296, 406
General Foods 70, 332, 354
General Mills 70
General Motors 267, 296
General Motors Center for Machine Intelligence 381
General Services Administration 465
Gerber Company 35
Gerber Products, 70
Gibson 433
Global financial networks 461
Gochenouer, 293

Goodman 466
Gordian knot 299
Gordon 462
Gorla 11
Gosagroprom Agency 465
Graham 252
Grant 321
Gray 433
Greenberg 28
Griffiths 398
Grosch 400
Grover 11, 190, 400
Guide International, 274
Gutenberg 377
H.J.Heinz 70
Haliburton 13
Hammer 319, 327, 352, 353
Hanson 160
Harris 393, 400
Hartog 495
Hatsopoulos 463
Hawthorne Effect 252, 397
Hayes 71
HBO & Co 274
Heany 125
Hector 352, 355
Heidrick & Struggles 320
Heinz 160
Heizer Software 382
Henderson 190
Hendricks 252, 398
Herbert 433
Hershey 318
Hershey Foods 70
Hewitt 318
Hewitt Associates 55
Hewlett-Packard 30
Higgins 321
Hippe 277
Hitachi 124

Hochstrasser 398
Hoffman-La Roche 464
Hogg 278
Holland 356
Hood 58
Hopper 190, 319, 340
Horrocks 400
Horwitt 192
Hospital Corporation of America 274
Houdaille Industries 347
Howarth 320
Howell 71
Huberman 278
Hufnagel 190, 400
Hunter 354
Hypercard 381
Hypertext 370, 371
IBM 8, 10, 38, 71, 95, 127, 172, 191, 246, 260, 275, 379, 383, 390, 400, 401, 422, 426, 428, 430, 466
IBM 4381 257, 275
IBM 7090 354
IBM 9377 275
ImagineThat 278
Imperial College 387, 398
Index Group 253, 396, 398, 400
Industrial Dynamics 466
Industrial Era 78
InfoPlex 379
Information 6
Information Centers 20
Information Management Audit 500
Information Resources 498
Information Resources Management 125
Information Resources Policy 499
Information Systems Architecture 506

Information Systems-to-Revenue 37
Information Technology Policy 500
Information Technology-per-Business Value-added ratio 153
Information Technology-per-Revenue 153
InformationWeek 50
Inside Information 381
Institute for Better Meetings 379
Interactive Terminals 22
internal rate of return 94
Internal Revenue Service 339, 451
International Communications Association 13
International Data Corporation 39, 100
International School of Information Management 380
Irving 321
ISIS 38, 55, 199, 426, 427, 428, 434
Jackson 433
Jaikumar 71
Japanese electronic companies 444
Japanese productivity 444
Johnson Wax 318
Johnston 191
Jonscher 462, 464
Kahn 381
Kao Corporation 172
Kaplan 462
Kass 30, 275
Katz 393, 400
Kay 96
Kearney 12, 398
Kelleher 353
Keller 355
Kellogg 70
Kennestone Oncology Center 335
Kephart 278
Kerr 321, 464
Keys 252, 398
King 190, 400, 464
Klepper 495
Knowledge workers 462
Knowledge-gaining web 369, 370
Kobler Unit 398
Kodak Corporation 10, 276
Kornel 354
Kraft Foods 496
Krass 276
Kriebel 125, 399
Kumar 356
Labor Value-added 68
Lanning 381
LaPlante 191
Lawrence 191
Layne 277
Lederer 390, 399
Leibowitz 275
Lincoln Continental 30
Litton Computer Services 278
Lockheed 466
Lockheed Aircraft 179
Lotus Development Corporation 380
Loveman 125, 391, 399
Ludlum 56, 399
M.D.C. Holdings 13
M.I.T. 329, 391
M.I.T.Media Laboratory 382
Macintosh 191, 381, 404, 405, 431
Macmillan 465
Management Costs 134
Management productivity 84, 158, 161
Management Productivity and Information Technology 133
Management Value-added 134
MANTIS 72, 129

Manufacturers Hannover 274
Marchand 159, 194
Marchasin 465
Marx 95
Marxist economies 78
Materials requirements planning 347
Mattel 178, 192
Mattson 253
Mayfield 398
McDonnell Douglas 274, 278
McFarlan 433
MCI Mail 379
McKenna 192
McKesson 165, 170, 191
McKinsey & Company 494
McLean 58
McNurlin 430
McWilliams 434
Measures of Effectiveness 46
Melloan 192
Melymuka 319
Mendelow 390, 399
Mercer 356
Merrill Lynch 165, 260, 431
Messer 433
Metaphor Computer Systems Corporation 432
Metatext 373
Meyer 410, 432
Microlytics 381
Microsoft 173, 191
Microvax 3500 261
Midland Bank 57, 273
MindSight 495
Minsky 368, 381
Mintzberg 433
MIPS-per-Employee 8
Miromoto 463
Mischel 462

Moore 160
Moran 294
Morgan Stanley 127, 131, 399, 447, 450, 462, 463, 464
Motor Vehicle Department 338
MPIT 96, 104, 113, 123, 133, 140, 161, 379, 391, 399
Mrs. Field's Cookies 178
Multiple regression 67
Murphy 125
Murphy's Law 496
MVS-XA 257
Nabisco Brands 70
Nath 253
National Association of Accountants 389
National Bicycle Industrial Company 466
National Industrial Conference Board 466
National Intergroup 13
National Productivity 82
National Science Foundation 97, 277
NCR Tower 274
NEC 124
New Jersey Turnpike 191
New Products Percentage 156
New York City 91
New York Life Insurance 409
New York University 392
Nolan 55
Nolan, Norton & Co. 28, 55, 399
Normani 278
Notes 380
O'Leary 275
Odesta Corporation 56
OECD 32, 83
Office of Management and Budget 355, 414, 464, 465

Oldsmobile 25
Olivetti 8
Olson 398
Orwell 321
Over-achievers 133
Overhead Costs 64
Oxford English Dictionary 29
Oxford Institute of Information Management 398
P.B.T. method 425
Palo Alto Research Center 381, 382
Pan American 190
PanAm 13
Pantages 318
Paperwork Reduction legislation 465
Pareto 404
Parke-Davis 177
Parker 56, 422, 427
Parkinson 144
Pars 179
Peat, Marwick 126, 191, 275, 324, 389, 404, 431
Pelton 353
PeopleExpress 188, 190
Perkin-Elmer 10
Perry 464
Pettibone 409
Phillips 192
Pillsbury 432
PIMS 68, 72, 81, 101, 104, 125, 128, 161
Pitney-Bowes 8
Pittston 13
Pope Clement VII 433
Porat 462, 463
Price Waterhouse 12, 164, 293, 398
Procrustes 57
Procurement regulations 465

Productivity 75
PROFS 379
Pryor 71
Quaker Oats, 70
Quality Award 130
R-O-M 84, 109, 129, 158, 187, 230, 294, 495, 497
Rada 193, 443, 463
Ralston Purina 278
Rand Corporation 466
Rappaport 72
Reed 303
Relative Market Growth 156
Relative Market Share 155, 156
Relative Quality 155, 156
Rentals-to-Revenue 8
Research Board 320
Residual value 203
Return-on-Assets 65
Return-on-Equity 65
Return-on-Investment 65, 104
Return-on-Management 84, 133, 134, 157
Return-on-Sales 65
Revenue-per-Employee 6
Reynolds 277
Rhone-Poulenc 175
Richard III 432
Ricketts 354
Roach 126, 447, 448, 449, 463
Roethlisberger 400
Rogow 319
Rosen 464
Rosenbaum 161
Rothfeder 320, 352
Rudnicki 252, 398
Russian steel industry 461
Sabherwal 11
SABRE 127, 179, 336

Saltarelli 347
Samuel 277, 399
Sassone 252
Schendel 433
Schlender 30
Schmitt 466
Schneiderman 382
Schoeffler 72, 103, 125, 129
Schwartz 398
Scott Paper 432
Scott-Morton 277, 329, 399
Seed 71
Segev 320, 433
Seligman 320
Sequoia Hospital 465
Seven-Eleven 193
Shakespeare 432
Shared Medical Systems 274
Shareholder Returns 42
Shareholder Value-added 136, 154
Sierra Group 273
Sifonis 190
Simmons 379
Sing Yap 395
Singapore 37
Singer, 433
Sloan School 329, 391, 399
Social Security Administration 90, 331, 452, 464
Society for Information Management 396
Socratic tradition 184
Solomon 130, 462
Sony 124
Soucy 71
Soviet Union 29
SRI International 274
Staley Company 35
Stalk 191, 466

Stamps 319
Standard & Poor 100
Standard Industrial Classification 440
Standard Industrial Code 443
Stata 372
State of California 326
State of Oklahoma 323
Statland 190
Stefik 381
Steiner 398, 494
STK Company 242
Stokely-Van Camp 70
Strassmann 57, 70, 129, 379
Strassmann Dolan 72
Strategic Business Unit 126
Strategic Planning Institute 104, 391
Strom 461
Subaru of America 13
Suchman 381
Sullivan-Trainor 276, 434
SWAG 433
Swire 125
Synnott 319
Syntex 453
SystemOne 180
Systems Review Boards 2
Tax Reform Act of 1986 452
Taxes 87, 153
Taylor 76, 276
Technology-to-Revenue 38
Teece 327
Teixeira 352, 398, 494
Telemail 379
Telenet 379
Terminals-per-Employee 8
Tesoro 13
Texas Air 180

Thatcher 465
The Limited 13
Thomas 192
Thompson 8
Thomson Travel 192
Tiger International 13
Todd 274
Toshiba 124
Touche Ross 320
Touche Ross International 388, 399, 496
Toyota 169, 191
Trainor 422, 427
Transaction Processing Facility 340
Transamerica 160
Transcon 13
Treacy 192, 329
Tree Age 381
Tucker 276
TWA 179
U.S. Air, 27
U.S. competitiveness 449
U.S. electronic companies 445
U.S. legal profession 466
U.S. Patent Office 337, 344
U.S. Sprint 379
Under-achievers 133
Union Bank 335
United Airlines 165, 179, 190
United Education & Software 326
United Research Corporation 398
United Services Auto 165
Universal Product Code 434
University of Arizona 381
University of Michigan 381
University of Pittsburgh 396
UNIX workstations 275
Value-added 60, 68
Van Nievelt 125

Vertical Integration 62, 71
Vincent 55, 70, 127
Wal-Mart 13, 42, 56
Wang 379
Warner Amendment 30
Warner-Lambert 277
Waste Management 13
Waters 433
Watson 319
Webber 192
Wechsler 96
Weill 392, 393, 398, 400
Wells Fargo 55
Western Electric 252
Western Union 379
Wharton School 409
White House Conference on Productivity 70, 77
Wilder 253, 398
Wisseman 433
X.400 standards 380
Xerox 1, 95, 264, 332, 378
Xerox 5090 30
Xerox Computer Services 127
Xerox Executive Committee 3
Yap 400
Zaharoff, 352
Zenith 95